ol 1st April 15. 1837.

Works O LORD GOD ALMIGHTY

day of July AD 1834 in fulfillment of Revelation

or the consolation of Israel Anna long had look'd and rejoiced
hat she could now the ancient path pursue, upon the scene her
aughters saved as if to say Great God prepare us likewise thy
ill to do. Seth in his early youth was not too young his God to se
ve, he desired to follow the example of his father, mother, and brother
as they might be one. Ozem, Hannah, and John, the parents & brother
f Seth were baptized on the 12 of July 1839 as my Journal declares
Dwight though not of consanguine blood to me desired baptism
t my hands for by the blood of christ we were united,
hrice the cross he strove to pass & as oft the spirit pressed this

onest soul & he submitted to obey. Thus ended this scene of
yonder shall I say I yes and of mercy to, for heaven counten
need the deed for it was Gods command an ordinance of the
ospel.   To be permitted to stand in ones own native land the gosp
l of JESUS CHRIST to declare in the last dispensation & while
ividing the word through the power of the priesthood to his kindr
is townsman to behold the pride of the great, the rich, the lea
ned, by the spirit of God humbled at his feet then to exper
ence the living reality of a Father, a Mother an only Sister
meekly with other kindred receiving the ordinances of the
house of God at the hand of their Son and Brother is to me
at least a scene of interest. As we retired from the rolling
stream to a Father's roof my spirit was ready to say forget this
not O my soul regard it as the mercy of thy God while thou dost
ay thy vows thy covenants fulfill. While upon the head of these
Saints my hands were laid I implored the mercy of God for the
Holy Ghost upon them to rest & guide them right. The bread and wi
e was bles'd & we partook to remember him who died for us. O Eternal
od these Saints inspire, protect, support, & defend untill in Zion they stand
and with celestial glory crowned an heir with GOD AND CHRIST

A House Full
of Females

PHEBE W. WOODRUFF

Scarborough Maine July 14ᵗʰ 1834

A House Full of Females

Plural Marriage
and Women's Rights
in Early Mormonism,
1835–1870

LAUREL THATCHER ULRICH

ALFRED A. KNOPF   New York
2017

Library of Congress Cataloging-in-Publication Data
Names: Ulrich, Laurel Thatcher, date.
Title: A house full of females : plural marriage and women's rights in
early Mormonism, 1835–1870 / Laurel Thatcher Ulrich.
Description: First Edition. | New York City : Alfred A. Knopf, 2017. |
Includes bibliographical references.
Identifiers: LCCN 2016008859 | ISBN 9780307594907 (hardcover) |
ISBN 9781101947975 (ebook)
Subjects: LCSH: Mormons—Diaries. | Families—Religious life. |
Families—Religious aspects—Church of Jesus Christ of Latter-day Saints. |
Families—Religious aspects—Mormon Church. | Church of Jesus Christ of
Latter-day Saints—History—Sources. | Mormon Church—History—Sources.
Classification: LCC BX8693 .U47 2017 | DDC 289.309/034—dc23
LC record available at https://lccn.loc.gov/2016008859

Book design by Cassandra J. Pappas
Front-of-jacket image: *Weighing the Body* by Carl Anton Christensen (1872),
oil on canvas, 8 × 10 in., Springville Museum of Art
Jacket design by Stephanie Ross

In memory of

Hezekiah Thatcher
Alena Kitchen
Nathan Davis
Sarah Woolley
John Bethuel Thatcher
Rachel Davis
Jeppe Folkman
Anna Serena Anderson
Robert Siddoway
Emma Jackson
Henry Hugh Harries
Mary Rees
Daniel Robison
Rachel Smith
Charles Turner
Elizabeth Wilkins
Hannah Ringrose

Organize yourselves; prepare every needful thing; and establish a house, even a house of prayer, a house of fasting, a house of faith, a house of learning, a house of glory, a house of order, a house of God.

—*Doctrine and Covenants of the Church of The Latter Day Saints,* Kirtland, Ohio, 1835

The house was full of females quilting sewing etc.

—Wilford Woodruff Diary, Salt Lake City, Territory of Utah, 1857

The records of this House shall prove
We're neither slack nor slow.

—Eliza Roxcy Snow, "Hymn for the Dedication of the Fifteenth Ward Relief Society Hall," 1869

Contents

An Indignation Meeting

Salt Lake City, Utah Territory, 1870

Light snow obscured the view of the mountains on January 13, 1870, as masses of Mormon women crowded into the old peaked-roof Tabernacle in Salt Lake City. The pine benches were hard, the potbellied stoves inadequate against the cold. No matter. They would warm themselves with indignation. The news had come by telegraph a week before. The much-feared Cullom Bill had passed the United States House of Representatives. If the Senate concurred, the government would soon have the power to confiscate Mormon property, deprive wives of immunity as witnesses, and imprison their husbands.[1]

This wasn't the first time Congress had attempted to outlaw the Mormon marriage system. Calls for federal action had begun fourteen years before with the Republican Party platform of 1856, which linked polygamy in Utah and slavery in the South as "twin relics of barbarism." Representative Justin S. Morrill of Vermont enunciated the essential argument: "Under the guise of religion this people has established and seek to maintain and perpetuate, a Mohammedan barbarism revolting to the civilized world."[2] Novelists and the new illustrated weeklies took up the chorus, linking Utahns not only with Southern slaveholders but with Turks, Africans, and Indians on both sides of the world. Although Congress responded by passing an anti-polygamy statute in 1861, there was little hope of enforcement in the midst of the Civil War. Now, with Reconstruction under way in the South, reformers decided to try again. Arguing that Utah women were "slaves to a system worse than death," they scoffed at the "sickly sentimentality which proposes to punish nobody, which proposes to hang nobody, which proposes to let all the unchained passions of the human heart become free to prey upon mankind."[3]

"What nonsense!" Eliza Snow exclaimed from the platform of the Old Tabernacle. She and other leaders among Salt Lake City women had acted quickly to organize an "indignation meeting," a well-recognized form of protest in the nineteenth-century United States. Indignation was more than anger. It was "sympathetic outrage" directed at an injustice. The goal was *publicity* in its broadest sense.[4] Cleverly banning all males except the press, they showcased their most effective speakers. Amanda Smith, widowed years before by anti-Mormon mobs in Missouri, brought tears to her listeners' eyes as she repeated the story of her suffering. Hannah King, an English immigrant, asked, "Are we really in America, the world-renowned land of liberty, of freedom, of equal rights? The land of which I dreamed in my youth . . . where freedom of thought and religious liberty were enjoyed by all?" Eleanor Pratt said she had been turned out of doors for her faith and would willingly give her life for it. Phebe Woodruff warned that if Congress chose to imprison Mormon men they would have to "make their prisons large enough to hold their wives, for where they go we will go also."[5]

The reporter for *The New York Herald,* disgusted at the sight of "infatuated females" speaking in favor of a system repugnant to "women of finer feelings," nevertheless produced a full-page account of the speeches. The San Francisco *Evening Bulletin* pronounced the meeting "one of the most remarkable, perhaps, that has ever congregated on the Continent. To see a mass of between 3,000 and 4,000 women, nearly all Anglo Saxon, many of them American born and raised, meeting together to advocate the claims of polygamy and defend the men who practice it, is food for reflection and moralizing." For *The Daily Cleveland Herald,* the explanation was obvious—"the women were as strongly attached to their peculiar and unpopular faith as the men can be."[6]

The Mormon-dominated legislature in Utah soon demonstrated their confidence in their wives and sisters by passing a bill granting women the vote. Although the question of woman suffrage had been raised in Washington during debates over granting rights of citizenship to freed slaves, only the most radical among Eastern reformers were prepared to embrace it. When the tiny Wyoming legislature passed a woman suffrage bill in December 1869, most people considered it a stunt, since there were so few white inhabitants in Wyoming Territory and six times as many males as females. The situation in Utah was different. Females composed a slight majority of the territory's eighty-six thousand nonnative residents.[7] Ironically, the idea of enfranchising Utah women first appeared in a *New York Times* editorial, the writer surmising that if women were empowered they would eliminate polygamy. No one imagined they would stand up and defend it. "And what is the use of woman suffrage if it is to be used to bolster up an institution so degrading to the sex and demoralizing to society?" concluded a reporter from New Jersey.[8]

The spectacle in Utah soon attracted the attention of Elizabeth Cady Stanton and Susan B. Anthony, two of the most powerful advocates for woman suffrage. Still smarting over the refusal of Congress to embrace their cause, they added Utah to the itinerary for a journey west in 1871. After several days in Salt Lake City, Stanton told the press that antagonists on the Mormon question had missed the point. Polygamy and monogamy were *both* oppressive systems. She argued that those who opposed the Latter-day Saints were every bit as befuddled as the Saints themselves: "The condition of women is slavery to-day and must be so long as they are shut out of the world of work—helpless dependents on man for bread." She was nevertheless pleased that Utah women had the vote. Eventually, she accepted polygamous wives as allies.[9] Mormon women responded by becoming ardent members of Stanton's movement. For forty years, the *Woman's Exponent,* founded in 1872, advocated for "The Rights of the Women of Zion, and the Rights of the Women of all Nations."[10]

The emergence of Utah women as political actors was so remarkable, so unexpected, that even today it is often dismissed as an anomaly, one of those strange events so out of the mainstream as to defy explanation. The word "paradox" appears again and again in books and articles dealing with the topic.[11] How could women simultaneously support a national campaign for political and economic rights while defending marital practices that to most people seemed relentlessly patriarchal?

At one level, the answer is obvious. Their own community was threatened. By standing up as women, they defended their homes and their religious identity. But that explanation is too simple. If an Eastern newspaper dropped a match that ignited a woman's rights movement in Utah in 1870, the fuel for that blaze had been accumulating for years. Utah may have looked like an Old World patriarchy, with its Biblical terminology, theocratic government, and retreat into a valley with a dead sea and a River Jordan, but those who migrated there had been touched by the radical energies of the 1830s and 1840s. By the time the Mormons arrived in Utah, female as well as male leaders knew how to circulate petitions, sign affidavits, lobby public officials, and employ the power of the press.[12]

By embracing Mormonism, the leaders of the indignation meeting had already shown a willingness to push against the grain. Some had abandoned homes, families, and legal husbands in order to do so. They were religious seekers who before becoming Latter-day Saints had been Methodists, Quakers, Anglicans, Campbellites, and everything in between. As Latter-day Saints, they had experimented with health reform, dress reform, and communitarianism. Some practiced, even if they did not yet preach, forms of "sex radicalism," the idea that a woman should choose when and with whom she would bear children. Their indignation emerged from religious passion, from a yearning for millennial justice, from the experience of being hounded and driven from place to place, and from the frustration of vainly petitioning judges, governors, and presidents for redress.

As Latter-day Saints, they were victims of ignorant and sometimes willful misrepresentation by outsiders, but they were surely exaggerating when they claimed they had experienced nothing but liberty in Utah. As their own writings attest, they had endured both condescension and open opposition from church leaders. By 1870, they had demonstrated their facility as organizers by banding together to solve problems in Utah and by rebuilding the Female Relief Society, a women's voluntary society founded in Nauvoo, Illinois, in 1842 and dissolved by Brigham Young in 1845. They planned their indignation meeting in a newly dedicated Relief Society Hall that had an upper floor for meetings and a lower one for selling goods created through cooperative labor.

Without question, Congress's attempt to outlaw polygamy outraged them, but it also strengthened their position within their own community as they rose in its defense. Their support for their brethren was sincere, but it was also strategic. They knew when and how to ask for the things that they wanted, and they wanted the right to vote. When the woman suffrage bill passed, they quickly appointed a committee to thank the territory's acting governor, a non-Mormon, for signing it, then went about teaching citizenship to women in outlying parts of the territory.[13]

The history of the Church of Jesus Christ of Latter-day Saints typically focuses on its founding prophets—Joseph Smith, who in 1830 published the *Book of Mormon* and then, over the next decade, established communities in Ohio, Missouri, and Illinois; and Brigham Young, who, after Smith's murder in 1844, led the largest faction of Latter-day Saints to the

Rocky Mountains. Smith and Young were powerful and charismatic leaders. But Mormonism, like other religious movements, flourished because it attracted strong women.

Collectively, the twenty-nine leaders of the indignation meeting had experienced the entire history of the Church, from its founding in upstate New York in 1830 through the epic migration to Utah. Two-thirds of them had become Latter-day Saints before Smith's death. All but two had arrived in Utah by 1855. If there was a Mormon culture in the territory in 1870, they had helped create it. They came from Cambridgeshire, Wilshire, Kent, Devon, and Oxfordshire in England; from Wales, Scotland, and "Upper Canada"; and from the states of Georgia, South Carolina, Virginia, Pennsylvania, New Jersey, Massachusetts, New York, Maine, and Vermont. Few had stayed long in one place. Eliza Snow, though born in western Massachusetts, grew up in Ohio. Eleanor Pratt, a Virginian, met Mormon missionaries in San Francisco, Mary McMinn in Philadelphia, and Harriet Cook in Boston. Mary Isabella Horne started life in England, migrated to Canada, and then, as an early convert, joined the Saints in Ohio. Phebe Woodruff worked as a teacher and dressmaker in coastal Maine before migrating to Ohio. Later, she lived with her missionary husband in Lancashire, England, and in Boston.[14]

Well before plural marriage became a recognized practice in the Church, these women had learned to value bonds of faith over biological or regional connections. "I am proud to say to you that I am not only a citizen of the United States of America but a citizen of the kingdom of God," Willmirth East exclaimed from the pulpit of the Old Tabernacle. Jealous of their rights as Americans even if born outside the United States, they did not want to be rescued by those who neither understood nor valued their faith. When Harriet Cook claimed both the rights of American citizenship and the privilege of marrying a "husband of her choice," she was defending polygamy. All of the speakers stood up for the practice, even if they had not lived it. Sarah Kimball, who presided over the meeting, had never been a plural wife, nor had Amanda Smith or Hannah Tapfield King. Yet all three embraced plurality as a theological concept.[15]

The reporter from San Francisco found the sight of several thousand women becoming advocates for polygamy "food for reflection and moralizing." Today, the same phenomenon offers food for historical investigation. Others have written and will continue to write about what happened after Utah women won the vote. This book focuses on the decades-long struggle that brought them to that point. It explores the pathways they

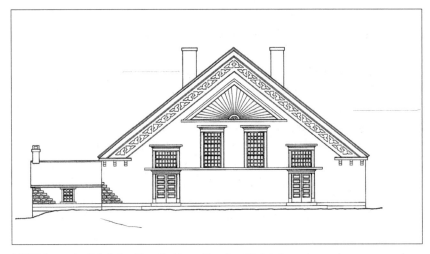

Old Tabernacle, Salt Lake City. Dedicated in 1852, Utah's first tabernacle was set partly underground to conserve heat. The carved sunburst in the triangle over the south entrance was painted bright yellow and orange. See color insert 2, page 8. *(Drawing by Cory Jensen and James Gosney, Western Regional Architecture Program, University of Utah.)*

traveled from monogamy to polygamy, and from urban boarding houses, Midwestern farms, and English cottages to the slant-roofed Old Tabernacle in Salt Lake City. It asks why so many women "nearly all Anglo Saxon" were willing to defend a system others considered degrading.

"Plural marriage," as the Saints called it, emerged gradually and in secret in Nauvoo, Illinois, the utopian city the Saints built on the banks of the Mississippi River after being driven from Missouri. Joseph Smith took his first "plural wife" in the spring of 1841 and over the next three years was "sealed" to more than two dozen women (the exact number is uncertain). One historian refers to these early sealings as "protopolygamy" (*proto* meaning giving rise to or being ancestral to), to distinguish it from the later, more developed practice.[16]

The Female Relief Society also developed in Nauvoo. In a meeting above his redbrick store, Smith promised he would make of the society "a kingdom of priests as in Enoch's day—as in Pauls day." Within two years it had more than thirteen hundred members devoted to poor relief and support for construction of a massive temple. Shortly before his death, Joseph and his legal wife, Emma Hale Smith, prepared a select group of women and men to officiate in temple ceremonies, even though the temple itself was not yet complete.[17]

Polygamy and temple rituals flourished in the months after Smith's death. The Relief Society did not. When Emma Smith, who was its president, rejected Brigham Young as her husband's successor, he disbanded it. Although most of its members followed Young to Utah, roughly 15 percent stayed behind, among them Emma Smith, who raised her children to believe that their father had never had other wives.[18] Thus, at the heart of the succession from Smith to Young was a division in the female community. Eliza Snow, who had been one of Smith's plural wives, carried the Relief Society minute book with her to Utah. In the years to come, she used it to remind her closest associates of the promises they had received in Nauvoo.

For Latter-day Saints, plurality was not just a social system. It was a means of salvation. Joseph Smith shocked his contemporaries by teaching that human intelligences (he used the plural form) were co-eternal with God. "Moreover, all the spirits that God ever *sent* into the world are susceptible to enlargement." Enlargement included but was by no means limited to biological reproduction. In a poem written to a female friend, Eliza Snow portrayed individual affinities as nodes in an interlocking web that connected "noble spirits" across the earth and "from earth to heav'n, / And still extending on from world to world / Unto creation's undefin'd extent." To her it did not matter whether a woman was the only wife or one among many, since all the righteous would eventually be bound together. She insisted that spiritual bonds produced "a holier feeling" than friendship, witnessing the possibility of an eternal network of souls "twin'd / And intertwin'd, combining and combin'd."[19]

After Joseph Smith's death, Eliza Snow joined Brigham Young's household. In 1870, she was living with a dozen of his other wives in the Lion House, a gabled structure on South Temple Street that took its name from a stone lion that stood over the door. Although outsiders referred to it as Brigham's harem, it could also have been described as an experiment in cooperative housekeeping and an incubator of female activism. For years, Zina D. H. Young, who gave the prayer at the indignation meeting, lived across the hall from Eliza. Harriet Cook Young, one of the more flamboyant speakers at the meeting, lived two doors down. As an architectural structure, the Lion House was unique. Most polygamous wives lived in houses that, whether large or small, looked like vernacular

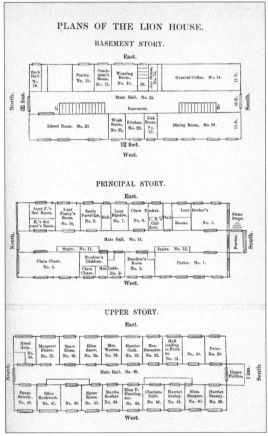

"The Prophet's Block" and "Plan of the Lion House Interior" from C. V. Waite, *The Mormon Prophet and His Harem*, 1866. The Lion House was one of a very few Utah dwellings explicitly designed to accommodate plural wives. *(Photograph courtesy of Harvard University Library.)*

dwellings found elsewhere in the United States. Yet the concept of female cooperation was widespread.[20]

Mormonism reinforced and at the same time transformed patterns of association common to rural societies everywhere. Women banded together to spin, weave, and care for the sick, but also to participate in sacred rituals. The defining concept was not plural marriage but *gathering,* a belief that those who accepted the faith had a duty to join their fellow believers in building a new Zion. Plural marriage was pervasive but far from universal. Although by 1860 more than 40 percent of the territory's inhabitants—men, women, and children—lived in plural households, the composition of those households varied widely. Two-thirds of polygamist husbands had only two wives. Another 20 percent had three. Those who had four or more were often members of high church councils or bishops of local congregations, and, as in any society, birth, death, and migration reshaped families. Over time, a monogamist might embrace polygamy or a polygamist, through death or divorce, find himself with one wife or none.[21]

A small oil painting completed in central Utah in 1872 portrays the interior of an ordinary Utah house shortly after the birth of a baby. The midwife and several female attendants have tucked the new mother into bed and are now weighing the infant. This is a classic gathering of women performing classic female work. There is nothing in the painting to tell us that the woman in the bed is twenty-nine-year-old Gunhild Torgerson Dorius, who has just given birth to a son named Hyrum. Nor, without family records, could we know that she and Kaia Frandzen Dorius, the tall woman in the center of the picture, were both married to the man at the door, Frederick Ferdinand Dorius, a Danish immigrant who was a friend of the painter C. C. A. Christensen.[22] (See color insert 2, page 5.)

Gunhild and Kaia were plural wives who belonged to a more expansive sisterhood built through spiritual, social, and economic associations. In all likelihood, the midwife who was weighing the baby was empowered to bless and anoint the mother as well as to officiate at the birth. Years later, a granddaughter remembered Gunhild as "a quiet, gentle, little lady" who "carded and spun her own wool for cloth" and "believed polygamy to be a sacred principle." When visitors came, she pointed with pride to a picture of her husband dressed in prison stripes with other Mormon men incarcerated during the anti-polygamy raids of the late nineteenth century. She said his imprisonment proved that he loved her because he could have avoided prosecution by renouncing their marriage.[23]

To outsiders, the Lion House represented the gothic strangeness of Mormonism. To an insider like C. C. A. Christensen, the Dorius house represented its comforting familiarity. Both kinds of houses were part of the Mormon story, as were the public buildings where Latter-day Saint women engaged in collaborative work and eventually in political protest.

On a winter day in 1857, a fifty-year-old Mormon Apostle named Wilford Woodruff visited the Fourteenth Ward Meeting House in Salt Lake City. In his diary, he noted, "the house was full of females quilting sewing etc." Wilford had three wives and was about to acquire a fourth; his own house was full of females. But this gathering was different. Sometimes as many as fifty women assembled for meetings of the Ward Relief Society. His first wife, Phebe, was its president. Remarkably, one of the quilts its members were making has recently been found. Completed in the autumn of 1857, it was later sold at a raffle. The man who won it cut it down the middle years later and gave one half to each of his two grown daughters. They and their heirs passed it on, until no one was quite sure where their own piece came from and what had happened to the other. Brought together in 2004, the two halves, only slightly damaged by time, reveal the signatures, in ink and in thread, of the sixty-seven women who made it. Phebe's autograph appears on one half, her appliquéd fruit and flowers on the other.[24] (See color insert 2, page 2, Fourteenth Ward Album Quilt.)

The sundering and reuniting of the quilt offers a metaphor for the losses and recoveries that characterize women's history. This book is a kind of quilt, an attempt to find an underlying unity in a collection of fragments. Because I want to understand early Mormonism from the perspective of those who embraced it, I have chosen to focus on diaries and other day-by-day records, such as letters, occasional poetry, and minutes of meetings. Some historians silently merge documents like these with autobiographies and memoirs written decades later. I have not done that. Retrospective accounts are valuable, but they have to be understood in relation to the conflicts and commemorations that produced them. Since every word written about early Mormonism was, and is, controversial, it is important to know when as well as what people wrote. This is not to say that diaries are more truthful than memoirs, just better at conveying the instability of events as they unfolded. Diarists did not know how things would turn out.

When Wilford Woodruff began keeping a diary, in 1835, not only were there few Mormon diarists, there were few Mormons. Over his lifetime, he did his best to change both of those things. Remembered as a prodigious missionary, he also preached the gospel of diary keeping. In March 1857, he told a gathering of Mormon leaders, "I have kept a Journal of almost evry day of my life for the last 24 years. I could tell each day what I had done, what Company I was in & what was transpiring around me." He admitted that this had been a lot of work. "But what of it?" he continued. "I have never spent any of my time more profitably for the benefit of mankind than in my Journal writing."[25]

It would be hard for a modern-day historian to disagree. Woodruff's meticulous record (over five thousand pages in typescript) is a powerful account of nineteenth-century Mormonism. It is also a great American diary. He once told a group of Mormon missionaries that he did not care whether they wrote down what they ate or drank unless they were fed in a desert by ravens, like the Prophet Elijah. If that happened, they should record it. Otherwise, they could ignore mundane things. Fortunately, he did not follow his own advice. While visiting with Phebe's relatives on the coast of Maine, he even jotted down directions for making a chowder. Perhaps he realized that it wasn't always possible to distinguish ephemeral from enduring things. As he told the missionaries, "We are not apt to think of the importance of Events as they transpire with us but we feel the importance of them afterwards."[26] That may be why his diaries are so much more interesting than his memoirs, especially for understanding women's history, which often depends on recovering things later deemed unimportant, like a gathering of women quilting and sewing.

The steady dailiness of Woodruff's diaries helps link smaller and more intermittent pieces left by others. One scholar has estimated that, in Mormon archives, men's diaries and memoirs outnumber those of women by ten to one.[27] That may actually underestimate the problem. Although limited education may have contributed to the scarcity of women's writing, a more important factor was the cultural assumption that their words—like their duties—were essentially private and therefore beyond the reach of history. Men, not women, routinely served missions, and diary keeping was a missionary duty.[28] Missionaries commonly wrote in bound journals. In contrast, female diarists often used the blank pages of other people's diaries, homemade packets stitched together from folded paper, children's schoolbooks, and in one case the back of old maps.[29] In archives, their words often fade into the page as though they had been

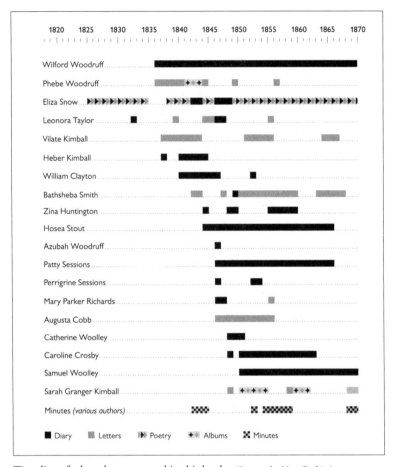

Time line of selected sources used in this book. *(Samantha Van Gerbig.)*

exposed to rain, sun, and sleet, if not a laundry tub. Some pages are over-laid with the scribblings of children.

Eliza R. Snow, Zina D. H. Young, and Bathsheba Smith were promi-nent leaders in nineteenth-century Utah, yet their personal journals, like the Fourteenth Ward quilt, almost disappeared.

In the 1940s, the diary Eliza began in Nauvoo narrowly escaped a bonfire when the collateral relative who inherited it died without heirs. Fortunately, a neighbor helping to clean out her house looked inside the corrugated cardbord box where the diary had been stashed, thought it looked interesting, kept it for a while, and then passed it along to a friend who had an interest in history. Almost by accident, it found a place in Latter-day Saint archives. Another of Eliza's diaries found its way to

Zina Huntington Young, Bathsheba Smith, Emily Partridge Young, Eliza Snow. All but Bathsheba were inhabitants of the Lion House; Bathsheba lived two blocks away on South Temple Street. Zina, Eliza, and Bathsheba kept early diaries; Emily's daily diary and memoir were written many years later. *Photograph by Edward Martin, taken July 16, 1867. (Church History Library, Salt Lake City. © Intellectual Reserve.)*

California, where it became part of the collections of the Huntington Library.[30]

One cache of Zina Young's papers rested for years in a red tin bread box she had brought from Nauvoo. In the late twentieth century, a great-granddaughter rediscovered it in the basement of her mother's house while looking for Christmas decorations. Other relatives found documents hidden behind the log walls of a pioneer house in Canada. Later, a great-great-granddaughter found more materials in a locked trunk she had been using as a sofa table but had not been able to open. These documents eventually found a home in the Church History Library in Salt Lake City. In their acid-free folders, the more fragile among them look like the tattered remnants of old lace.[31]

Bathsheba Smith kept her overland-trail diary in a hand-me-down journal. She or someone else cut out the earlier pages, leaving a ragged residue along the spine. Years later, a granddaughter dropped this mutilated document into a protective bag stitched out of cotton drapery fabric. Another descendant added a scrap of paper explaining the origin of the bag but not the diary. Eventually, a third person deposited the whole package in Special Collections at the University of Utah under the name of Bathsheba's husband, George Smith, noting that it had been passed from Bathsheba to a granddaughter named Merrill and then Fisher to a great-granddaughter named Affleck. At any stage in this complex journey, the diary itself or its association with its creator could have been lost.[32]

Records can of course survive without being read or understood. The ledger in which Eliza kept the minutes of the Nauvoo Relief Society is arguably one of the most important documents in Latter-day Saint history. She carried it with her when she left Nauvoo, consulted it, discussed it with others, and after 1867 used it to establish the pattern for Relief Society minute books kept throughout Utah. When Bathsheba Smith became general president of the Relief Society in 1901, she cared for the ledger. In 1911, after her death, her daughter presented it to the Church Archives, where it was seldom consulted by scholars until the feminist revival in the 1970s. Because some of the passages appeared to contradict well-established ideas about female access to priesthood, church leaders carefully controlled its use. The full minutes have only recently been published in a scholarly edition.[33]

In any field, the writings of ordinary people alter descriptions of the past. In the nineteenth century, as today, Mormon theology celebrated the eternity of the marriage covenant and the sacred meaning of families. But Mormon ideas about marriage and families have changed remarkably over time. If plural wives stood up for their Church in the 1870s, it was not just because pioneering had made them strong but because the concept of gathering that was at the heart of Mormon theology taught them that retreating into a private haven was neither possible nor righteous. They wanted to change the world, and they believed God had shown them a way to do it. In that, they were much like other Americans who had their boots in prairie mud and their heads in the stars. They remind us that common men and women, like the prophets they revered, dreamed dreams and saw visions.

Mormon diarists loved God and their fellow Saints. They also embraced sentimental poetry, phrenology, and the herb lobelia; brass bands, mechanical gadgets, and speaking in tongues. While waiting for the second coming of Jesus, they filed claims to frontier land and laid out street plans. Their newspapers published advertisements for daguerreotypists and itinerant painters as well as sermons, and on the overland trail as well as in every settlement they established, they struck up the fiddle and danced.

In an 1853 sermon, Wilford Woodruff told a group of male leaders: "Should we ever have the privilege in our resurrected bodies of visiting other planits & the inhabitants of the same we should want to learn the history of that people. If they had kept no records of their lives & the dealings of God with them so we could get their History we should feel much disappointed. So would they should they visit us."[34] For those who find the past not just a foreign country but a different planet, records matter. The writings of early Latter-day Saints expose their peculiar values. They also reveal the many things they shared with those who considered them aliens.

A House Full
of Females

I

"Wonder on wonder strikes my sense"

Ohio, Connecticut, and Maine, 1836–1838

Walking toward Kirtland, Ohio, in late November 1836, Wilford Woodruff caught sight of the temple standing on a bluff above the flats. When he left Kirtland two years before, the temple had been only a dream. Now it rose before him, more magnificent, he thought, "than Kings ever saw or Princes ever Knew." His excitement grew as he entered the village. In 1834, the little band of Latter-day Saints in Ohio had been poor and despised by their neighbors. Now there were signs of progress everywhere. He and his companion, a Kentuckian named Abraham Smoot, lost no time in touring the temple, from the light-filled assembly rooms on the lower levels to the offices in the attic, where Joseph Smith kept the Egyptian mummies and fragments of papyri that he said contained the writings of the Biblical Abraham. "Wonder on wonder strikes my sense to look into the Casket of the great work of Israels God in these last Days," Wilford wrote.[1]

For a newly settled town in Ohio's Western Reserve, the building was indeed impressive. Sited on the highest point of land in the region, it had a soaring sanctuary on each of its main floors and a polychrome tower reaching to the sky. Some said that on a clear day visitors to the tower could see across Lake Erie to Canada. Color added to the building's glory. The roof was a deep brick red, the exterior walls a glistening gray-blue created by grinding broken glass and cobalt-glazed ceramics into the stucco, then painting lines to simulate stonework. Two olive-green doors opened into the interior. A model of Yankee ingenuity and rural pretension, the temple had Greek pilasters and Gothic windows, ascending pulpits on both ends of the major rooms, movable seats in the pews, and adjustable

Kirtland Temple. Dedicated 1836. Now owned by the Community of Christ, the restored temple is open to visitors. *(Historic American Buildings Survey, Library of Congress Prints and Photographs Division.)*

Lower auditorium, Kirtland Temple. This photograph from the early twentieth century shows the ascending pulpits in one end of the main sanctuary. *(Historic American Buildings Survey, Library of Congress Prints and Photographs Division.)*

curtains operated by pulleys to subdivide the spaces. Red velvet drapery ornamented the pulpits.[2]

Latter-day Saints believed God, speaking through Joseph Smith, had commanded them to build the temple. Smith's revelation called it a "house"—"a house of prayer, a house of fasting, a house of faith, a house of learning, a house of glory, a house of order, a house of God."[3] At its dedication in March 1836, some heard the sound of a mighty wind as a pillar of light descended. Others saw angels soaring through the windows to settle on the high pulpits.[4] It was a house of glory built by ordinary folk. Bolstered by contributions gathered by missionaries like Wilford, its construction provided work for common laborers as well as for skilled carpenters like Brigham Young.[5] God may have prescribed the dimensions of the building, but human beings quarried the stone, planed the planks, stitched the draperies, and constructed the window mullions and sashes, using carpenters' manuals and Smith's visions for their guide.

On his first Sunday back in the town, Wilford stood in one of the pulpits and reported on his mission. He took as his text a passage in Isaiah about God's power to graft into the House of Israel even "the son of the stranger." Wilford was talking about the men and women he had baptized in Kentucky and Tennessee. He was also talking about himself. The scripture promised, "Even unto them will I give in mine house and within my walls a place and a name better than of sons and of daughters: I will give them an everlasting name, that shall not be cut off."[6]

Like many New Englanders of his generation, Wilford had migrated west in search of new opportunities. Now, nearly thirty, he had neither a wife nor a home of his own, but in Kirtland he had a place of honor in God's house. Soon, though he did not yet know it, he would find a wife—a resolute New Englander named Phebe Carter. Together they would begin a journey that would take them to their old homes in Connecticut and Maine and then to the Fox Islands, off the Atlantic coast, to gather others—relatives and strangers—into a faith that promised wonders on wonders.

"The First Book of Willford"

Born in Connecticut in 1807, Wilford was the youngest of Aphek and Beulah Woodruff's three children, all boys. When he was just a year old, his mother died in the midst of a spotted-fever epidemic that also claimed his grandfather. When Wilford was not yet three, his father married Azubah

Hart, who gave birth to six more children, five boys and a girl. Azubah's boys were haunted by death. Julius died shortly after birth, Franklin at three months; Newton drowned at two. Sixteen-year-old Philo fell ill after dreaming that there would soon be a funeral in the family. His death provoked Wilford, who was then twenty, to consider his own spiritual state. He asked a local Baptist preacher to baptize him by immersion, but he did not join any church.[7]

After a short stint at the Farmington Academy (his family could not afford more), he moved with his older brother Azmon to a farm in upstate New York. When Mormon missionaries came through in 1833, both accepted baptism.[8] In 1834, Wilford, the more zealous convert, headed to Ohio to meet Joseph Smith. There he joined "Zion's Camp," a quasi-military expedition sent to relieve Mormon settlers who had been driven from their homes in Jackson County, Missouri. From there, he accepted a call to serve as a missionary in Tennesee and Kentucky. During his two years in the backcountry, he supported himself by selling subscriptions to the *Latter Day Saints' Messenger and Advocate*, performing day labor, and accepting food, lodging, and cash donations from church members and strangers.[9]

One of Joseph Smith's revelations assured newly called missionaries that "whatsoever they shall speak when moved upon by the Holy Ghost shall be scripture."[10] Wilford took those words seriously. He learned to preach, and he learned to keep a diary, labeling his four-by-six leather-bound journal "The First Book of Willford." At first, he wrote in a loose, almost unformed scrawl, taking rough notes that he later transcribed, first in cursive, then in a kind of Roman print that appeared to imitate type. To make it easier to find things, he began setting off certain entries with special symbols or borders, using the calligraphy skills he had acquired during his short time at school.[11] Thanks to his end-of-year summaries, we know that during his two-year mission he traveled 6,557 miles, held 153 meetings, participated in four debates, baptized twenty-seven persons, blessed nineteen children, healed four persons, and escaped from three mobs.[12] The mobs were an affirmation of his calling. Hadn't the ancient apostles also suffered opposition?

At a place he called "Bloody [Creek?], Kentucky," he gave a full page to a dream or vision of the sun going dark and the moon turned to blood and "the horizon covered with burning cities," as prophesied in scripture. He then saw the resurrection of Jesus and witnessed the joy of members of the Church of the First Born clothed in white. Words were not enough to describe such an experience. He ornamented his page with tiny sketches of the things he had seen.[13]

When he returned to Kirtland late in 1836, he expected even more powerful manifestations of God's presence. He enrolled in something called the "School of the Prophets," an adult-education program for Mormon preachers, where he learned a smattering of Latin, Greek, and Hebrew. Between January and May 1837, he attended evening meetings of the Quorum of Seventies, a group of men with special callings to preach. He participated in private "feasts," during which food was distributed to the poor, and in "blessing meetings," where Joseph Smith's father, who had been called as church patriarch, laid his hands on the heads of members to offer consolation, affirmation of lineage in the House of Israel, and the promise of future redemption. When Father Smith blessed Abraham Smoot, Wilford served as scribe, taking down the blessing in his neat Roman hand.[14]

For Wilford, the most important gatherings occurred within the temple. Here he could listen to Joseph Smith and the Apostles speak and participate in holy rituals. The Prophet had already adopted the Christian practice of washing feet, but in 1836 he reached backward to the book of Exodus, building on a passage that described Moses bringing Aaron and his sons "to the door of the tabernacle of the congregation" for a special washing and anointing that allowed them to minister as priests. On April 4, 1837, Wilford and twenty-two other men gathered at a private home and washed themselves "with clean watter & perfumes" before repairing to the temple for an anointing. Although the Old Testament recipe called for myrrh, sweet cinnamon, calamus, and cassia, the Saints made do with cinnamon.[15]

After the anointing, Wilford joined two other men in a veiled space in the temple. They knelt in prayer and, in Wilford's words, vowed "that we would not give sleep to our eyes neither take food until we receieved a blessing from God by the outpourings of his spirit upon us if it was until the end of three days." Alternately praying and contending with a fatigue they associated with Satan, they continued through the night. Then, having "gained a good degree of victory over the Devil," they left the temple, to return that evening for another round. In contrast to the elaborate vision he had recorded in Kentucky, Wilford measured the success of this experience not by a visual manifestation, but by the peace he felt: "The spirit of God sat upon us & we were satisfied with our blessing."[16]

Years later, a church leader who had been in Kirtland said that, when

Joseph Smith introduced the ritual of washing and anointing to male leaders, some women got "right huffy about it," feeling that they had been left out.[17] If so, they neglected to record their complaints. Their memoirs recall spiritual manifestations, such as an outpouring of glossolalia or "speaking in tongues." Some heard an invisible choir during services in the temple. One young mother claimed that her six-month-old baby slept quietly through the seven-hour dedication ceremony, then joined the crowd in shouting "Hosanna!"[18]

The completion of the temple nevertheless marked a subtle transition in Latter-day Saint worship, which had previously focused on small gatherings in homes.[19] In Kirtland, Elizabeth Ann and Newel Whitney often hosted "Feasts for the Poor," like the ones Wilford attended, occasions when guests fasted for two meals, then brought butter, bread, or other foods to share with the needy.[20] When held in the temple, fast days like these took on a more formal quality. On March 23, 1837, Wilford arrived early and retired to a veiled area with several other elders for prayer. As the crowd gathered, he emerged into the main space, where, at the invitation of the Prophet's father, he read a passage from the Book of Mormon while the congregation stood. Then the curtains dropped, dividing the room into four parts—"the females occupied two parts & the males the others." Male leaders presided in each of the divisions as people engaged "in singing, exhortation, & prayer. Some had a tongue, others an interpretation, & all was in order."[21]

The reference to "order" is significant. Joseph Smith had been shocked when he first arrived in Kirtland by the extremes of "enthusiasm" that greeted him. The temple became a setting for encouraging and at the same time containing ecstatic expression.[22] With the room divided, four times as many people had an opportunity to participate, but the presence of a member of the presidency in each group prevented things from getting out of hand. Wilford explained that, after the separate meetings, "the Veils were all rolled up together which brought the whole Congregation in full view of each other and while the presence of the LORD filled the house the congregation of the Saints fell upon their knees & all as one man vocally poured forth rejoicing, supplication & Prayer, before the God of Israel."[23] Presumably, the phrase "one man" included women, though we cannot be sure.

Movable seats in the pews allowed people to face pulpits on either the east or the west side, as required. The pulpits themselves ascended in four levels, with three stations in each. Those on the west held the presidencies of the Melchizedek or the "higher" priesthood; those on the east, the Aaronic, or "lesser." With eight presidencies and twenty-four men involved, authority was both widely distributed and hierarchically ordered. Joseph Smith and his two counselors commanded the top tier in the Melchizedek pulpit.[24]

While Wilford filled his diary with details about temple worship, something else was happening unnoticed. In early April, he set off a blank space with a distinct border and reported dryly, "My first acquaintance with miss Phebe W. Carter was on the evening of the 28th of Jan. 1837 at which time I was introduc'd to her at Elder Milliken's by the politeness of Elder M. Holmes. After two & half months acquaintance we were joined in matrimony."[25] In the midst of religious ecstasy, he had found a wife.

"to leave my paternal roof"

Phebe Carter was born on March 8, 1807, in Scarborough, Maine, a coastal town south of Portland. She was just seven days younger than Wilford and, at the age of thirty, a true peer, having embraced the Latter-day Saint gospel wholeheartedly and on her own. Unlike him, she had grown up in a house full of females. When Mormon missionaries came through Scarborough in 1834, Phebe's younger sisters Rhoda, Shuah, and Mary, all in their twenties, were still at home, and the one married sister, Sarah Foss, lived nearby. In the minority were the three brothers, Ezra, Fabyan, and Ilus.[26] Like many young women of her generation, Phebe had worked off and on as a teacher and a dressmaker. In a period when an increasing number of women remained single, she must have wondered whether it would be her lot to live and die in the big house where she had been born.

Almost as soon as she was baptized, she contemplated moving, or "gathering," to Kirtland. Believing that the second coming of Jesus was imminent, missionaries taught that newly baptized members had a duty to migrate to the Mormon Zion to become "the first laborers in this last kingdom."[27] Although hundreds of New England women left home to work in nearby textile mills or teach in a rural school, very few set off alone to join a religious community seven hundred miles away. Phebe's family opposed her plan, and when it came time to leave, she was too overcome with emotion to say goodbye in person. Instead, she composed a letter for them to read once she was out of sight.[28]

That the letter survived suggests that her family cherished it. Written in a neat and legible hand on two long sheets of cream-colored paper, it

Phebe Carter to "Beloved Parents," c. 1836. The succession of postscripts on the second page of Phebe's farewell letter to her family shows her reluctance to part with her siblings. *(Church History Library, Salt Lake City. © Intellectual Reserve.)*

displayed a better-than-average education, a mastery of religious rhetoric, and significantly less sentimentality than Wilford's writing. "Beloved Parents," she began, "I am now about to leave my ~~parent~~ paternal roof for a while but I know not how long—but not without grateful feelings for the kindness which I have receivd from my infancy until the present time." There are no protestations of love in this opening, just a straightforward statement of the situation. She appreciated all her parents had done for her, but wanted them to know that it was time for them to part.

Providence had willed it thus. That she began to write *"parent[al],"* then shifted to *"paternal* roof" may reflect an inbred sense that houses belonged to fathers. The change also hints at her bookishness. Although the phrase "paternal roof" was common in both fiction and poetry between 1800 and 1840, the term "parental roof" was seldom used before the twentieth century. To Phebe it probably didn't have quite the right ring.[29]

Shifting in the next sentence from "I" to the collective pronouns "us" and "we" allowed her to transform a personal dilemma into a generic struggle between doubt and faith: "Let us commit all these things into the hands of Providence and be thankful that we have been permitted to live together so long under so favourable circumstances as we have, believing that all things will work for our good if we love God supremely."

And what did it mean to love God supremely? Almost despite herself, Phebe shifted from a classic invocation of Providence to an assertion of her own right to revelation, though she muted her argument by maintaining that distancing "we":

Let us realize that we can pray to one God ~~which~~ who will hear the sincere prayers of all his creatures and give us that which is best for us.

Phebe had listened to the missionaries when they pointed to the passage in the Book of Mormon that enjoined all those who received the book to pray sincerely and ask God if it was true. She knew she should gather with the Saints. She also recognized that it was time to prepare for Christ's second coming and for the great millennium to come.

May we strive to have that spirit in us that raised Christ from the dead that our mortal bodies may be quickened and come forth in the morn of the first resurrection to reign with Christ a thousand years where parting will be no more—Glorious thought (may it ever stimulate us to be diligent in keeping all the commands of God and not count our trials here too much to gain such a prize).

Her preaching was measured but clear. Her pain was also palpable. At the end of her letter, she stepped down from her literary pulpit to address directly the parent who had obviously been the chief opponent of her leaving, the person who, as she explained years later in a short autobiography, had wished her dead rather than among the Mormons.

Mother, I believe it is the will of God for me to go to the west and I have been convinced that it has been for a long time—now the way has opened and you seem to be reconciled to it which is the greatest consolation to me of any thing earthly; I believe that it is the Spirit of the Lord that has done it which is sufficient for all things—O be not anxious for your child the Lord will comfort me, I believe that the Lord will take care of me and give me that which is for the best.

She reassured her mother that, in accepting Mormonism, she had not rejected her family. "Believe not that all these things are against you for they are not." Then she added a promise: "although the ways of Providence seem dark; I shall come home to see you the first suitable opportunity whether I like or not." Finally, she offered an explanation for the strange method she had chosen of saying goodbye: "I have taken this method of speaking my mind because it seems easier than verbal conversation—I have written already much more than I expected, so I must bid you good bye Father & Mother for the present."

Phebe's letter should have ended here, but since there was still space left on the second page, she addressed postscripts to her sisters Rhoda, Shuah, and Mary and her brother Fabyan, underlining each with a scalloped line. She urged them to obey God, to embrace the light they had been given, and—the implication was clear—to join her in gathering with the Saints. The postscripts extended the letter into a long farewell she wasn't able to manage in person, as though she were waving at them from the carriage window as it disappeared around a bend in the road.

> Brother Fabyan and Sister Rhoda. . . . I do know that there is peace in obeying the commands of God. . . . <u>Why tarriest thou</u> Good bye
>
> Sister Shuah. . . . Never deny what God has done for you, but ever believe that the kingdom of God has come nigh to you—So I must bid you good bye untill I See you again
>
> Sister Mary I must say to you be not discouraged but be diligent in keeping all the commands of God and it will be well with you—and you shall receive a great reward. Good by P.[30]

If the letter overreached in its preaching, that was surely because the decision to leave had been so difficult. Only by enlisting God as her ally could Phebe muster the courage to break with all that she knew. As she later recalled, "In the year 1834, I embraced the Gospel . . . and, about a year after, I left my parents and kindred, and journeyed to Kirtland, Ohio, a distance of one thousand miles, a lone maid."[31]

A lone maid. In Kirtland, Phebe, like Wilford, understood herself as a sojourner among strangers. She wasn't the only unmarried woman to join the Saints. Nor was she the only female to travel from the far Northeast. But, taken together, her single status and the distance she had come set her apart. Eliza Snow, who was already establishing a reputation among the Saints as a poet, was single, but she had only moved twenty or thirty miles from her home in Mantua, Ohio. Caroline Crosby, a convert exactly the same age as Phebe, had traveled more than eight hundred miles from a village near Montreal, Canada, but, like most of Kirtland's adult women, she came with a husband.[32] Zina Huntington, who was almost fourteen years younger than Phebe, arrived with both parents, two younger siblings, and a married brother and sister.[33] A few years later, Eliza, Caroline, and Zina would each begin a diary. Phebe never did. Her life has to be reconstructed from the one kept by her husband and from scattered letters between them.

A broader sense of what it meant for the early Saints to gather to Kirtland can be gleaned fom the blessings that Joseph Smith, Sr., the Prophet's father, gave them. In an era of massive migration, converts sought not only spiritual sustenance but ways of healing ruptures in human relationships. Technically, a "patriarchal blessing" should have come from the recipient's own father, but many had no fathers. Through his calling as patriarch, "Father Smith" replaced the literal fathers who had died or resisted conversion. More than half of the 341 blessings he gave in Kirtland between 1835 and 1837 went to men destined to take up priesthood callings, but 130 (38 percent) went to women. Some women received their blessings alongside their husbands, but about a quarter appear to have been, like Phebe, alone.[34]

The patriarch consistently promised single women, especially those in their teens or twenties, that they would find "companions." Sometimes his prophecies took only a few months to fulfill; twenty-three-year-old Eliza Brown received her blessing in May 1835 and was married to William Perry in October.[35] Perhaps blessing meetings, like the one Wilford attended with Abraham Smoot, helped to facilitate such an outcome. But for some Kirtland women, the problem was not being single but being legally bound to a man who had deserted them—or the Church. Father Smith told Susan Wells, age twenty-eight, "Thou art in affliction for thy husband for he is in the world, his faith is shaken, thy heart aches and is concerned for him." He promised her that, through her prayers, her husband might yet become a man of God.[36]

More difficult was the situation of women who had themselves fled alcoholic or abusive spouses. Lydia Goldthwaite was only twenty-four when she ran away to her parents' house, then, fearful that her husband would seek revenge, fled to Canada, where she met Mormon missionaries and, with Joseph Smith's blessing, married Newel K. Knight. Although in the eyes of the law this was a bigamous marriage, the Prophet's father assured her that God understood her sorrow and had blessed this union. "Thou hast been afflicted much in thy past days and thy heart has been pained many tears have fallen from thine eyes, and thou hast wept much," he began. He promised her in the name of God that this marriage would last. "The Lord loves thee and has given thee a kind and loving companion for thy comfort and your souls shall be knit together and nothing shall be able to dissolve them neither distress nor death shall separate you." Since there had been no divorce, her marriage to Knight was illegal, but in this community obeying God sometimes meant disobeying the laws of man. In situations like this, religious affirmation helped to ease anxiety and guilt.[37] In a later memoir, Eliza Snow euphemistically described her sister Leonora Leavitt as a "young widow" when she came to Kirtland. Actually, she, too, had left her husband, abandoning her son and bringing her two daughters with her to her parents' home. In June 1836, Father Smith blessed one of these daughters, ten-year-old Lucia Louisa Leavitt, telling her that, though she was "as it were an orphan in the world," the Lord had looked upon her mother and blessed her.[38]

Evidence of a more startling incident of family disruption emerges from the blessing Father Smith gave to Nancy Richardson in 1837. "Because you have obeyed the commands of your heavenly father, come out of Babylon and brought these little children with you to this place that you might have a better opportunity of knowing the minds and will of God . . . thou shalt be blessed and these children shall grow up and be a comfort and a blessing to you, and thou shalt have thy sister the mother of these children to help you take care of them." Apparently, Richardson had brought two of her younger sister's children with her from Connecticut, intending to raise them as her own. Family tradition says that one of those children, when grown, tried to reconnect with his parents, unsuccessfully. Was this an adoption or an abduction? It is not clear. What is certain is that Richardson herself was single, a mother but not a wife. Yet, in the patriarch's view, her faith qualified her for the blessings of salvation.[39]

Father Smith showed compassion for women who felt bound by the patriarchal authority of husbands or fathers. He told Sophronia Hinkly, "Thou
art an orphan thy father was opposed to the truth and did not come into
the Kingdom, and is now gone from the earth, and thou art at liberty to
follow the Lord."[40]

His promises of future blessings were often stunning in their speci-
ficity. He promised Mariah Crandall that she not only would see Jesus
return in a cloud, but would receive forty days' notice of his arrival.[41] He
told twenty-year-old Mary Baldwin that she, like the Biblical Mary, would
experience the ministry of angels, and that she would someday teach the
"Daughters of the Lamanites," an apparent reference to the Native Americans, whose lineage Mormons traced to the Book of Mormon.[42] He told
Esther Loraine Brown that, though she may have sinned in her heart, she
was innocent. As a daughter of Abraham, she would bear children who
would become "prophets and prophetesses."[43]

At a blessing meeting held in the temple on November 10, 1836, Father
Smith put his hands on Phebe Carter's head and said things she probably wasn't even able to say to herself: "Thou hast suffered . . . by being
deprived of friends unto whom thou couldst unbosom thy mind; thou
hast sorrowed in the night season and in solitary places. No one knew
thy sorrow or saw thy tears but God thy Father." Phebe had apparently
been less confident when she arrived in Kirtland than when she wrote her
farewell letter to her family. The patriarch assured her that even the most
devout Christian might find it difficult to part with those they loved. "Be
Comforted," he said, "for thy troubles are over and God will pour out his
blessings to thee." He prophesied that her future husband would be "a man
of Wisdom, Knowledge, and understanding" and that her children would
be ornaments to the Church. (Since Wilford had not yet arrived in Kirtland, Father Smith cannot have had him in mind. Wilford later recorded
the date of Phebe's blessing in his diary.) Father Smith also prophesied
that Phebe would "sew the vail of the Temple" and, if she remained faithful, see all her relatives become "members of the Covenant."[44]

Phebe never said what it was that filled her soul with such great cer-
tainty that she was willing to leave her home and family. Conversion surely
involved what Latter-day Saints called "personal revelation."[45] But it was
also a social process. Wilford's oddly formal announcement that he had
met Phebe "at Elder Milliken's by the politeness of Elder M. Holmes" suggests that, even in a town of fewer than two thousand inhabitants, social
networks mattered. Milton Holmes had marched with Wilford in Zion's

Camp and, like him, had returned from a mission to become a member of the Quorum of Seventy.[46] Nathaniel Milliken was also a Seventy, and he and his wife, Mary, were from the same part of Maine as Phebe. Perhaps they had traveled together to Kirtland.[47] However it happened, the little Mormon community in Ohio brought together a thirty-year-old man from Connecticut and a thirty-year-old woman from Maine, a couple who would have been unlikely to meet had they remained in their home states.

In 1837, there was as yet no hint that Joseph Smith would within a few years radically revise the meaning of marriage among the Latter-day Saints, not only by declaring it essential for salvation but by proclaiming "plural marriage," or polygyny, as the divine order.[48] In the year when Phebe and Wilford were married, Mormon ceremonies looked pretty much like other marriage ceremonies elsewhere in the rural United States, except that they seemed more egalitarian. Husband and wife took identical vows. He stood on the right, she on the left, and, as "directed by the holy spirit," the officiator called each by name and asked if "both mutually agree to be each others companion, husband and wife, observing the legal rights belonging to this condition, that is keeping yourselves wholly for each other and from all others during your lives." If they answered yes, the officiator pronounced them husband and wife "in the name of the lord jesus christ and by virtue of the laws of the country." That was all.[49] The congregation might sing a hymn, family and friends might serve wine and cake, but there was no giving the bride away, no ring, no veil, and apparently no promise to obey.

After performing such a wedding, Joseph Smith wrote in his own diary, "I doubt whether the pages of history can boast of a more splendid and inocent wedding and feast than this for it was conducted after the order of heaven."[50] For Latter-day Saints, the order of heaven came not from the ceremony itself but from the authority of the man who performed it. Even though he acted under the laws of Ohio, he held a holy priesthood that gave him the right to speak in the name of God.

Wilford and Phebe were married at the Prophet's house on April 13, 1837, at two in the afternoon. Another couple was married at four, and then "the whole company consisting of about 16 Couple" walked to a nearby home to witness a third wedding. "No day more pleasing than April thirteenth 1837," Wilford wrote, straining for imagery worthy of the occasion. "The sun in the east arose to gladden earth & shed oe'r nature his pleasing beams to welcome the return of delighted spring that dreary winter might be forgotten." The allusion was odd. According to his diary, the winter had not been dreary at all. From all appearances, he had experienced one long succession of religious rapture. Still, the contrast between spring and winter was a ready-made metaphor, so he used it. "While all nature smiled without friendships purest joys were felt beneath a prophets roof."[51] Yes, friendship. That was the right word to describe not only the sort of companionship he and Phebe would have, but the joy they felt in being married in a room surrounded by other Latter-day Saints.

Then his tone shifted. Was there perhaps a dark spot in this otherwise perfect day? The wedding had taken place in the Prophet's home, but the Prophet was not there. Wilford could not ignore that fact, or the hints of future trouble it foreshadowed. "The prophet Joseph from his wife, children, & house for a moment had fled. Had torn himself from their embrace in some lonely place to seek a shelter to escape the blood thirsty gentiles hands against him raised for bearing the testimony of Jesus Christ." The Prophet's father, who performed the ceremony, assured the brides that their prayers would protect their mates if they, too, were "bound in chains & vaults [or] in prisons cast for the word of God & the testimony of Jesus," suggesting that the fate that befell the Prophet on that April day might also fall upon them. "O heaven protect the four," Wilford wrote, closing his meditation with a Latin flourish: *Vera Amicitia est sempiterna*" ("True friendship is eternal").[52]

Wilford knew that he was about to leave Kirtland to serve for the second time as a missionary. On May 31, 1837, he took "the parting hand with the saints in Kirtland," prepared to go again "into the vineyard to proclaim the word of God." Phebe was going, too, though the two of them would travel separately, she by coach and canal boat, he mostly walking, preaching along the way.[53] In Connecticut, Wilford would try to reconnect with his family. In Maine, Phebe would for a time sleep under a "paternal roof" with her husband beside her.

A Mission to New England

Wilford's return to Connecticut became a sentimental journey that led him backward, to scenes of youth and early childhood. On June 4, a Sunday, he and two companions walked to his brother Azmon Woodruff's farm in Oswego County, New York, where he sensed "sumthing of a Coldness manifest towards me," especially from Azmon's wife, Elizabeth. She gave the missionaries supper but refused them a place to sleep. Perhaps she was angry that Wilford had abandoned the farm. "O, scenes of life how variant, how transcient, how painful thou art," Wilford wrote. He prayed that Azmon might regain his faith but he could not bring himself to leave a blessing either in English or in his newly acquired Hebrew. "Kin after the flesh were not always kindred in spirit," he wrote.[54]

Things went a bit better in Connecticut. On June 22, he found his half sister, Eunice, teaching school near the mill their father had once managed. "We saluted each other with a harty Shake of the hand," he wrote, adding in shorthand, "and a kiss." Eunice was only twelve when her brothers left

Map showing Woodruff journey from Albany, New York, to the Fox Islands, Maine. (*Samantha Van Gerbig.*)

for New York. She was now a young woman in her teens. He spent a day in her light-filled school, struggling with his emotions. While she taught, he read a packet of letters she had received from their twenty-three-year-old brother Asahel, the last of Azubah's surviving sons, who was seeking his fortune in Indiana. Reading the letters, Wilford smiled and wept, thinking of their brother Philo, who had died at about the age Eunice was now. "I beheld my sister my ownly Sister seventeen years of age, adorned with youth, modesty, and lovliness, her face veiled with the true picture of PHILO." His melancholy deepened as he and Eunice walked through the town of Colebrook. They visited their parents' former dwelling at Sage's Mills. The house was now "silent as death." While Eunice plucked a rose, Wilford "drop'd a tear."[55] Wilford's romantic longing had multiple sources. Reading Asahel's letters had awakened his desire to see a brother who for a time had shared his own religious quest. Seeing the empty house reminded him of his father's struggle to launch his sons. After mortaging his property to purchase more land, he had lost possession of the mill he had once owned in Avon, sliding downward from owner to hired operative. Of Aphek's living children, only Eunice remained in Connecticut.[56]

From Colebrook, Wilford moved on to Avon. Here were more scenes to remind him of time's passing. He took the path along the Farmington Canal to "mills built and formerly owned by my father." Then he walked by the house where he was born, and the schoolhouse where he had spent so many "youthful days," to "the grave yard in which lay the bones of many of my progenitors & friends." He copied the inscription on his mother's stone:

A pleasing form a generous gentle heart
A good companion Just without art
Just in her dealings faithful to her friend
Beloved through life lamented in the end.

Beulah Woodruff was twenty-six years old when she died, four years younger than Wilford and Phebe were now.[57]

At Farmington, Wilford's father and stepmother, Azubah, made him "heartily welcome." He spent the next week going back and forth to nearby towns, preaching in private homes, schoolhouses, and occasionally a church. In Collinsville, a crowd tried to drum him out of the city hall, but in Avon his old friends and some of his extended kin were kind enough—or perhaps simply curious enough—to listen respectfully. On

July 11, he preached at the Lovely Street School House in Avon. He and his uncle Ozem and aunt Hannah Woodruff and their son John stayed up late talking religion. At 2:00 a.m., they told Wilford they "believed the fullness of the everlasting gospel" and he "led them fourth at the Same hour of the night and baptized them for the remission of their sins." Wilford felt certain this was a fulfillment of a vision he had received when still a child.[58]

When he got back to his parents' home in Farmington, he found a letter from Phebe. After ten days' journey, she had at last arrived at Canaan, in the far corner of Connecticut, where she had expected to meet him. Since she was fatigued from her journey and no one could predict whether Wilford was coming back, she thought she would stay a few days. She added in a postscript: "Don't let any one see this sad looking letter for I am in great haste and have a bad pen and no Willford to mend it."[59] In truth, both her penmanship and her spelling were better than her husband's, though he usually had more to say.[60]

Phebe arrived in Farmington in time to hear him preach at the schoolhouse on July 16. On July 21, they "took the parting hand" with his parents and began the next leg of their journey. They took a stage together to Hartford, then Phebe continued toward Maine while Wilford walked through central Massachusetts toward the New Hampshire coast, preaching and holding meetings along the way. On August 8, they met in Scarborough, Maine.[61]

Unlike the Woodruffs, the Carters had retained their ancestral perch. Their house, built in 1815, stood on land inherited from Phebe's maternal grandfather, Joshua Fabyan, a man remembered in Scarborough as "Squire Fabyan" because of his service as justice of the Court of Common Sessions in York County. The house was an imposing though somewhat conservative building for its time, with chimneys on both ends, a Georgian façade, and wide floorboards and wainscoting made from old-growth pine. Mature apple trees and elms surrounded it.[62]

The names the Carters gave their children show the importance they attached to both sides of the family. All the sons received their mother's maiden name as a middle name, although only Joseph Fabyan was routinely called "Fabyan."[63] Phebe was named "Phebe *Whittemore* Carter" for her paternal grandmother; Sarah was "Sarah *Brackett* Carter" for her mother's mother.[64] After the quiet house in Farmington, the Carter home must have seemed full indeed. Phebe's widowed sister, Sarah Foss, and her seven children were there when Phebe and Wilford arrived, as were

Fabyan with his wife and daughter and the three sisters still at home—Rhoda, Shuah, and Mary. "It was an affecting meeting," Wilford wrote. Two days later, Phebe's brother Ezra and his wife arrived from Portland. The only one missing was Ilus, who at age twenty may have been at sea.[65] Unlike Wilford, Phebe had grown up in a region that was gaining rather than losing population. While Connecticut had stagnated, Maine had more than doubled in size since 1810, though by 1840 Ohio far outstripped all the New England states.[66]

Wilford, who was an avid trout fisherman, took an excursion with Phebe's brothers and for the first time "saw a fish belonging to that kind that swallowed Jonah." Since Father Smith had promised him he would preach on the "islands of the sea," he was determined to love the ocean, but in a shorthand addendum, he admitted to being "somewhat sea sick."[67] In mid-August 1837, he headed for the Fox Islands in Penobscot Bay. Although he pronounced the South Island "as near being without any form or void as any land I ever saw," he found the inhabitants "generally wealthy, healthy, intelligent, industrious, generous, and hospitable to strangers."[68] He wrote of sailing through what seemed to him acres of leaping fish and later bathing in salt water surrounded by seals. The harvest of souls was just as impressive. He and his companion held meetings in schoolhouses, in fields, and even in the Baptist meetinghouse, boasting a full house on a Sabbath when the regular pastor "had not one soul beside himself." Wilford believed he knew the reason: "The spirit of God is like leaven through the Island."[69]

In October, he went back to Scarborough and collected Phebe, thrilled to have "a bosom friend & a helpmeet" to share his work. She remained with him through the autumn and winter of 1837–1838. When he was discouraged, she cheered him. When he was ill, she healed him by the laying on of hands. His reference to the healing, written in shorthand, is important evidence that in the 1830s Latter-day Saint women were already engaged in a spiritual practice that, though challenged, would be affirmed by Joseph Smith in Nauvoo.[70]

Phebe was still with him when a new male companion arrived. Joseph Ball was a Bostonian, the son of a Jamaican immigrant of mixed racial descent who had in 1796 helped found the African Society, a voluntary association and mutual-aid society. Although Ball's father was deceased by the time he accepted Mormonism, his mother, who was white, was still living. His sisters, Lucy and Martha Ball, were active in the Boston Female Anti-Slavery Society.[71] If Woodruff was at all concerned about

Ball's racial heritage, he did not show it. Nor did it have any effect on the success of their mission. When the two men left to preach in another part of the island, Phebe kept them informed about events in her area, sometimes with a bit of humor, as on March 1, 1838, when she told Wilford that the Saints in Vinalhaven had had a good meeting and that "brother Crocket was wide awake."[72]

As the crowds grew, Wilford saw signs in the heavens telling him that the second coming was at hand. Small miracles testified that God was gathering the blood of Israel from all nations. One prospective convert accepted baptism when a very large fish, seldom seen near shore, unaccountably swam straight toward him as if to summon him to baptism. By March, Wilford and Joseph Ball had gathered as many as a hundred converts on an island with fewer than two thousand inhabitants.[73]

This success did not come without opposition. On January 13, somebody shot off a cannon outside their meeting. Three days later, they heard gunshots. During a sermon in a schoolhouse, people "of the baser sort" deliberately disrupted "by walking across the house & talking, whistleing, Singing, dancing, &c." The missionaries also experienced an indignity suffered by the Prophet Elisha, who was mocked by little children. Unlike their Biblical predecessor, they did not call on bears to devour their tormentors. Instead, they washed their own feet in pure water as a testament against all those who rejected their message, including the Methodist and Baptist preachers on the islands.[74]

It wasn't local opposition, however, but trouble in Kirtland that ended the mission. In the year after the Woodruffs left Kirtland, the bank failed, debts came due, and once-loyal members left the Church. As the community crumbled, Joseph Smith and his family fled Ohio for Missouri.[75] Opening a letter from Kirtland rimmed in black, Phebe was astonished to learn that many of their old friends were among the dissenters—"but I hope not Willford and Phebe," she wrote in a hasty letter to her husband. The disaffections were worse than she imagined. Although Kirtland had almost two thousand inhabitants by 1837, the Church lost between 10 and 15 percent of its membership and as many as a third of its general officers, including four of the twelve Apostles. In Phebe's words, "I think that these times will try the faith of the saints."[76]

Phebe, who was six months pregnant, realized that her days as a missionary were limited. On April 17, she boarded a ship for Scarborough.[77] Over the next few days, Wilford and Joseph Ball visited church members to tell them that the time had come to gather to Zion. Then they, too, headed south. Walking most of the way to save money, they arrived at the Carter house on April 30 with painfully blistered feet.[78] They rested briefly, then set out on a different kind of mission, hoping to encourage Latter-day Saints scattered along the Atlantic coast, from Massachusetts to New Jersey, to join the Prophet in Missouri.

On May 11, 1838, after a three-day journey by foot from Portsmouth, New Hampshire, the two men arrived in Boston. "No day of my life was ever attended with more of a change of circumstances & places which my eyes beheld & ears heard & heart felt than on this day," Wilford wrote. This Connecticut native had never seen Boston. He walked on the Revolutionary War entrenchment on Bunker Hill, then visited the navy yard in Charlestown, perused the new market built by Mayor Josiah Quincy, and climbed to the cupola of the State House on Beacon Hill. After satisfying his curiosity as a tourist, he walked over the bridge from Boston to Cambridge to visit Albert Rockwood, a fellow Mormon, who was imprisoned for debt in the Middlesex County jail. Like common people everywhere, Rockwood was suffering the consequences of a widespread economic depression triggered by the Panic of 1837. Wilford did his best to comfort him.[79]

After leaving the jail, Wilford had an experience common to Boston visitors: "Crossed into the City & being alone & a stranger & in the darkness of the night I lost my way." He eventually found Myrtle Street, where a small gathering of Latter-day Saints was waiting at the home of an upholsterer named Polly Vose. This was his first experience with a primarily female branch of the Church. He did not list names, but his diary entries over the next few days refer to several meetings with "the Sisters of the Church." Indeed it was women, some of whom ran boardinghouses in Boston in the 1830s, who spread the "good news" of Mormonism among their friends and associates, laying the foundation for a lively branch of the Church that sent zealous converts west, including Augusta Adams Cobb and Vienna Jacques, who will appear later in our story.[80]

On June 8, Wilford parted with Joseph Ball at Fishkill, New York, and began a three-day journey on foot through a "rough and mountainous" part of Connecticut to his father's house in Farmington. On July 1, he baptized his father, his mother, his sister Eunice, his cousin Seth Woodruff, his aunt Anna Cossett, and a hired hand named Dwight Webster. Then he organized the whole group, along with Uncle Ozem, Aunt Hannah, and Cousin John Woodruff, whom he had baptized the year before, into the Farmington Branch of the Church. For him, this was the crowning achievement of his year in New England. On July 3, he said goodbye to his parents, walked through ninety-degree heat to Worcester, Massachusetts, and boarded a train to Boston and a ship to Portland, Maine. After stopping at Phebe's brother Ezra Carter's store in Portland to buy an autograph album for Phebe, he arrived in Scarborough on July 6, relieved to know that he had not missed the delivery of his first child. While waiting for the birth, he worked on transforming the rough notes he had taken on his journey into his diary.[81]

"by the blood of Christ united"

Wilford's retrospective account of the events of July 1, 1838, began as in an ordinary diary entry with the month, day, and year. Then he fell into a kind of rhapsody.

> On this seventh month the first day of the month and the first day of the week which is called Sunday some of the most important events transpired with me that I ever witnessed since I had a being, events worthy to be recorded upon the ARCHIEVES OF HEAVEN. Or to be engraven with an iron pen & laid in a rock forever upon the EARTH.[82]

The distinction he drew between heavenly archives and earthly records captured the paradoxical nature of Mormon revelation. Joseph Smith claimed to have translated the Book of Mormon from metal plates excavated from an actual hill in upstate New York, but he also said that an angel led him to the plates, then took them away when the translation was complete. To Latter-day Saints, revelation from heaven was recorded on earth, and events recorded on earth were marked in heaven.

In the two pages that followed, Wilford used his own pen to give material shape to sacred things. On the left-hand page, inside an arched frame, he described the baptism of his parents, packing more than eight hundred words into a framed space about the size of a three-by-five card. It is almost impossible to read it without a magnifying glass—perhaps he used one to create it. Although he prayed that God would direct his pen, he also relied on a straightedge and compass, using techniques taught in academies like the one he had attended in Connecticut.[83]

On the right-hand page, inside a ruffled circle, he wrote the names of the new members of the Farmington Branch of the Church, adding an ornamental swirl typical of those used by village calligraphers. The result

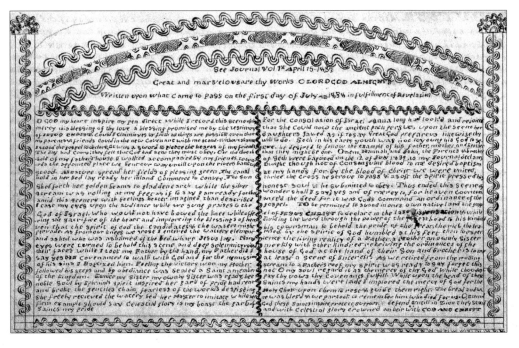

Ornamented two-page spread from Wilford's journal, 1838. While waiting for the birth of his first child, Wilford occupied his time creating ornamental pages in his diary, such as this double-page spread (above) detailing the baptism of his parents, and (below) an account of the creation of a branch of the Church in Farmington, Connecticut, listing the names of those baptized (July 1838). *(Church History Library, Salt Lake City. © Intellectual Reserve.)*

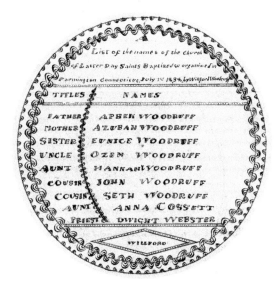

was a family record that acknowledged kinship both by blood and by faith. Wilford had administered the ordinance of baptism to "a Father, a Mother, an ownly Sister," and to Dwight Webster, who was "not of consanguine blood to me." The members of the newly created circle were "by the blood of Christ united."[84]

Wilford believed that the baptisms of his relatives fulfilled a promise made in the House of the Lord in Kirtland on April 15, 1837. On that day, the Prophet's father and patriarch of the Church told him that if he lived by faith he might bring all of his friends (that is, his relatives) into the Kingdom of God. That promise extended beyond present and past generations into the future. "Thy sons shall receive the priesthood and be an ornament to the church of Christ," the patriarch said.[85] As he laid out the pages describing the baptisms in Connecticut, Wilford was surely thinking of these words. He may also have remembered the papyrus he had seen in the attic of the temple, writings he believed had been left by Abraham himself. In one of them, a particularly compelling set of hieroglyphics sat within a tightly drawn circle. Wilford struggled to express with his pen a union of heaven and earth, of spiritual and biological kinship, and, beyond that, a new relationship between priesthood and progeny.

On July 14, 1838, at half past five in the morning, Phebe passed through "that scene of Sickness which is common among women in every age of the world," and delivered a healthy baby girl. Wilford celebrated the occasion by creating another ornamented circle, this one on the first page of the album he had bought Phebe in Portland. Inside, he wrote her name and the date. (See frontispiece.) In a separate diary entry, he prophesied: "Our daughter Sarah Emma in half an hour after she was born performed a journey in the arms of Sister Sarah Foss through the garret, Chambers, & lower room, & principly through the whole house. Is not this an omen of her being an extensive traveler in her day?"[86] For Wilford, the baby's introduction to her grandparents' house was a prophecy that she would soon abandon it.

As soon as Phebe and the baby were ready to travel, the Woodruffs planned to leave for Missouri with as many of the Fox Island Saints as they could gather. Over the next few days, Wilford helped Phebe's sister Sarah Foss with haying, then headed back to the islands to make sure that his little flock were prepared to join the migration. While there, he received a letter that increased his sense of urgency. He had been called to the Quorum of the Twelve Apostles and was expected to gather at the temple site in Far West, Missouri, on April 26, 1839, and from there "depart for other climes across the mighty deep!"[87] The date set by revelation was less than eight months away, and the journey to Far West was more than a thousand miles. He and Phebe had no time to lose.

Back in Scarborough, he found a letter from his brother Asahel that filled his soul with rapture. "I now find my brother earnestly enquiring what he shall do to be saved, & searching deep for light & truth with a desire to embrace it." Surely, this was an additional omen that it was right for them to begin the journey without delay. If all went well, he and Phebe would be able to visit Asahel in Indiana on their way. Wilford went to work to prepare for the journey. He built a two-and-a-half-by-three-foot box, which he filled with three hundred pounds of goods, perhaps things considered part of Phebe's marriage portion. In addition, Father Carter gave the young couple a hundred dollars, for which they "signed an article or writing that we were satisfied & would hold no further Claim" against the estate.[88]

Meanwhile, Wilford used his calligraphy skills to make family records for Phebe's brother Fabyan and her sister Sarah Foss and an acrostic for her sister Shuah. He went fishing with Father Carter and Fabyan, landing the boat on a rocky outcropping, where they fried out pork in an iron pot, then added some of the fish they had caught, along with potatoes, crackers, and seasoning. Explaining that it was "what Seaman or fisherman call a chouder," Wilford proclaimed it "as rich a dish as would be necessary to set before a king," adding that they "all sat down & ate uncommonly hearty, using clam shells for knives, forks, & spoons." Back on shore on the last day of summer, he and Phebe gathered seashells and barbary berries "to carry to the land of Zion for domestic use, & in memory of the place."[89]

The family idyll was disrupted when two-month-old Sarah Emma came down with "a severe attack of the Hooping Cough." Given the baby's illness, Phebe's family questioned "the propriety of our gathering with the Saints to Zion." The arguments grew more intense when local newspapers reported that Mormons had clashed with non-Mormons on election day in Daviess County, Missouri, and that mobs had arisen to drive them out of the state. "My trials are as great about these days as at any time since I have been a member of the Church of Jesus Christ of Latter Day Saints," Wilford admitted, engaging in a kind of dialogue with himself. Had his faith failed him? "No, God forbid." What was the matter, then? "I'll tell you: The Lord has Commanded me to go to Zion spedily & while I am setting myself about it the devel with all his agents are using their combined exertions & power to hinder me." Would he give up? Of course not. Packing seeds from Father Carter's apples into a box, he vowed that he would plant them in Zion.[90]

On October 3, eight families and one single male from the Fox Islands "hove in sight." The next day, Phebe, Wilford, and the Maine pilgrims packed themselves into ten wagons pulled by nineteen horses and began their journey.[91] The first night, they camped thirteen miles down the Maine coast, near a sawmill. "It was for a moment a trial to my feelings to take my tender wife with an infant at her breast into a cold tent to sleep upon the ground," Wilford wrote. A nearby family came to their rescue, offering Phebe and her infant a place in their house. Wilford lay down in the tent, but he couldn't sleep. After taking his turn standing watch, he opened his diary: "I sat up the remainder of the night built up a fire & wrote these lines by it."[92]

One by one, as they moved farther west, the converts they had brought with them dropped out, hoping to find temporary work and shelter for the winter, each promising to catch up with the others in the spring. In Indiana, Phebe succumbed to what Wilford called "brain fever," a headache so severe that she could not endure the jostling of the wagon. Terrified that she would die, he found a place for them to stay, then anointed her with oil and, with all the power of his priesthood, rebuked the Destroyer. Phebe revived, telling him that at the height of her illness her spirit seemed to leave her body, and she saw herself lying in bed, with her sisters weeping around her, as two messengers came into the room carrying a coffin. They told her she had a choice. She could "go to rest in the spirit world" or she could continue upon the earth, but only on the condition that she agree to stand by her husband "through all the cares, trials, tribulations, and afflictions" he would be called upon to endure "for the gospel's sake." She chose to stay with him.[93]

Renewed in faith, they pushed on, hoping to reach Terre Haute, Indiana, where Wilford's brother Asahel ran a bookstore. Less than a day's travel from their destination, they spotted a newspaper story reporting Asahel's death.[94] Wilford drew a coffin across a page of his diary, then penned a lamentation. "O Asahel among strangers thy lot was cast. Among them thou hast fallen & found a grave." His only comfort was in securing his brother's journals and letters, objects he considered of more value "than the gold of Opher or the rubies of Peru."[95]

As the Woodruffs moved into Illinois, they learned that even if they wanted to join the besieged Saints in Missouri, they could not. The ice over the Mississippi River was frozen fast, and no ferries were running. During the last week of December, they settled into a rented house near Rochester, Illinois, "in a grove of woods on the borders of a prairie." Still determined to reach Missouri by spring, Wilford went to work to support them, pronouncing their short stay in Illinois "the first of my housekeeping."[96]

⁂

2

"There was many Sick among the Saints"

From the Half-Breed Tract to the British Mission, 1839–1841

The Mormon troubles in Missouri in 1838 and 1839 were the culmination of a conflict reaching back to July 1833, when Jackson County vigilantes destroyed the Church printing press at Independence, tarred and feathered their bishop, and demanded that Mormon settlers leave the county. Taking refuge across the river in neighboring Clay County, the Saints sought redress for their loss of land.[1] When that failed, they accepted an offer from the state to take up new land in northwestern Missouri. This solution might have worked if the call to gather had not been so successful. In 1838, families from Kirtland joined new converts in Missouri, eager to make a fresh start. The first clash in the new counties occurred on election day on August 8, 1838. Armed conflict followed, leading to a battle at Crooked River in October in which one Missourian and three Mormons, including Apostle David Patten, were killed. A few days later, Governor Lilburn Boggs issued his infamous executive order demanding that the Mormons be "exterminated or driven from the state." Missourians, many of whom were new settlers themselves, had no desire to see a "New Jerusalem" rise in their midst, especially one inhabited by people they perceived to be Northern fanatics.[2]

During the winter of 1839, between eight and ten thousand Saints fled Missouri, traveling eastward 150 miles across frozen prairie to find refuge in nearby states.[3] Many found temporary quarters in Quincy, Illinois, where the Woodruffs joined them in the spring. By summer, the Church had a new gathering place fifty miles upriver from Quincy at a town called Commerce. Despite its hopeful name, Commerce had few habitable buildings. People took shelter in wagon boxes, tents, or crude wikiups made from oak, hazel, and blackberry brush. Some, including the Woodruffs, moved into an abandoned army barracks across the Mississippi in Montrose, Iowa, a place known in a government treaty with the Sauk-Fox Indians as the "half-breed tract." Malaria was endemic on both sides of the river.

In Mormon literature, two sets of "faith-promoting" stories emerge from this period. The first, which originated in Wilford's diary, tells how, on July 22, 1839 (he called it a "day of God's power"), the Prophet Joseph rose from his sickbed in Commerce to heal those who were suffering: "There was many Sick among the Saints on both sides of the river & Joseph went through the midst of them taking them by the hand & in a loud voice Commanding them in the name of Jesus Christ to arise from their beds & be made whole & they leaped from their beds made whole by the power of God." Later versions added Wilford himself to the story, explaining that, when a non-Mormon settler begged the Prophet to ride two miles back onto the prairie to bless his infant twins, who were dying, Joseph gave Wilford his red silk handkerchief and told him to go with the man, promising that if he stroked the babies' faces with the handkerchief they, too, would be healed. And, according to these long-cherished tales, they were. Today, a silk handkerchief said to have belonged to Joseph Smith is in the Woodruff collection in the church museum.[4]

These narratives show what God might do for his Saints. A second set of stories explains what the Saints might do for God. Members of the Quorum of the Twelve Apostles had risked their lives by going back into Missouri in secret to meet on April 26, 1839, at the site of the unbuilt temple at Far West. During this secret meeting, Wilford was ordained an Apostle. With the others, he promised "to go over the great waters" to England to promulgate the gospel.[5] When the time came to leave, he and most of the others were prostrate with malaria. Yet, one by one, they dragged themselves out of bed and began the journey.[6] Somehow, they made it across the Atlantic, reaping a harvest of souls that within a few years revived the weakened Church. The forty-six hundred English converts who migrated to America helped transform swamp-ridden Commerce into the thriving city of Nauvoo, a name derived from a Hebrew word for "beautiful."[7]

For believers, the account of how Joseph Smith sent his most talented and reliable leaders to England at a time when he needed them at home is every bit as powerful as the story about the miraculous healings at Commerce and Montrose. In both narratives, men endowed with priesthood power accomplished impossible things.

The few women who appear in these stories are shadowy figures, languishing in bed with their newborn babies or standing, nameless and meek, in the crowds surrounding earnest preachers. Their absence is not just a consequence of limited evidence. Stories about them are there for the taking in petitions for redress, in the missionaries' own diaries, and in the letters women wrote. But the hunger for miracles makes it almost impossible to see them. If a woman wrote her missionary husband that she lacked food or flannel for her children, she risked sounding like Sariah in the Book of Mormon, a "murmuring" wife who complained about her visionary husband. If, on the other hand, she remained resolute in the faith, she disappeared like the "tender wives" in another famous passage from the Book of Mormon, godly women whose sobbings ascended to heaven but who otherwise remained nameless.[8]

Bringing women fully into such narratives helps us to see the often haphazard voluntarism as well as the idealism that sustained Mormon expansion. It also helps us understand how Mormon faith pushed against conventional notions of marriage even before the introduction of polygamy. Men called to preach no longer had the ability, or even the obligation, to provide for their families. The overall consequence was a curious reversal of roles. Missionaries relied on female converts in England for spiritual as well as material sustenance, their wives on the kindness of strangers or their own non-Mormon relatives. Adding women to the narrative allows us to see the courage, the piety, the generosity, and the foolhardiness of a people hungry for a witness of God's power. Women's voices trouble the old stories.

"a distressing disease"

Malaria was the unseen protagonist in the Mormon miracle stories of 1839. Nineteenth-century Americans had only an experiential understanding of a disease they described variously as "the ague," "chills & fever," or simply "the shakes." They knew it had something to do with environment, but until 1900 no one fully understood its actual etiology. We now know that malaria depends on the complex interaction of a parasite (genus *Plasmodium*) with a mosquito and a vertebrate host.[9] Although diagnosing disease from historical documents is notoriously difficult, medical historians suspect malaria if there is evidence of fevers and chills occuring every two or three days in populations living near stagnant water or marshy areas, and if the fevers seem to subside with the use of some form of quinine.

The time of year also matters. In temperate climates, the usual period of infection is summer and fall.[10]

Wilford Woodruff's case fits these criteria. In August 1839, three days after he assisted Joseph Smith in healing the sick in Montrose, he became ill. "On this day for the first time in my life I have an attack'd of the chills & fever & I find it a distressing disease," he wrote. The next day he took a course of medicine patented by a lay healer named Samuel Thomson, a system of healing wildly popular on the Western frontier at the time. When Thomsonian remedies failed, he concluded that the Church's old enemy, the Devil, was "striving to bind us down that we shall not go into the vineyard."[11]

He shivered and burned through the next few days, then worked up the courage to leave Phebe and Sarah Emma in the old fort and cross over the river to Commerce. He was so exhausted by the time he reached the dock that he collapsed on a pile of hides. With John Taylor, a feverish fellow Apostle, by his side, he eventually pushed on. A few days into his journey, he somehow acquired a box of "Sappington's Anti-fever pills." He swallowed an entire box and began to feel better. The pills, manufactured by a Missouri physician named John Sappington, contained small doses of Peruvian bark or quinine. Pleased with the results, Wilford wolfed down

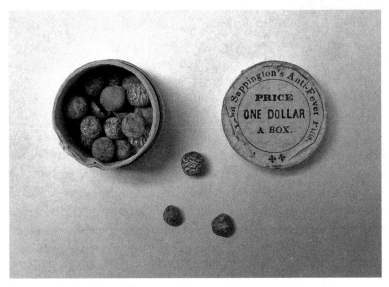

Sappington's Anti-Fever Pills, 1840s. This box of an anti-malaria remedy developed by Dr. John Sappington survives in a Missouri museum.
(*Courtesy Friends of Arrow Rock.*)

fourteen more pills the next day, and reported to his diary that they had "entirely broaken the ague . . . to all appearance."[12] He was fortunate in having left malaria behind, and he knew it. After arriving in England, he again fell ill. "My friends held a council upon the Subject & pronounced my Disese the Small pocks as I had been much exposed to it I told them I had rather it would be that than the Ague So I went to bed & prepared for it." Fortunately, he had neither the ague nor smallpox and was better in a few days.[13]

The wives and children of the missionaries were not so fortunate. In her first letter to Wilford after he left for England, Phebe reported that, though no one had yet died in Montrose, there had been deaths in Commerce and Quincy. She added, "There are not enough well people in Montrose to take care of the sick and therefore they suffer for want of attention."[14] The letters of other women fill in the details. Taylor's wife, Leonora, who was also living in the fort, reported the death of a neighbor's baby and worried that her own would die, too. Her letter, written in both directions, filled every available inch of the folded sheet as she added updates over the course of several days. When she was hit with chills and fever, she felt obligated to wean fifteen-month-old Joseph, lest he take the disease from her. "The first Night he cryd all night; afterwards he lay about the flore as if his heart was broken." Despite her best efforts, he, too, began shaking. Six-year-old George's fever was so intense "he fell back on the floor in a Fit and had Chile and Feaver." In the midst of the chaos, poor little Mary Ann, who was almost four, cried and cried for her father.[15]

Today, epidemiologists remind us that an outbreak of malaria is never simply a matter of biology. Malaria is more likely to assume epidemic proportions where there is poor housing and nutrition, where people are crowded together in small spaces, and where there are few farm animals to serve as alternative hosts for invading insects. A high proportion of pregnant women, infants, and children also accelerates the danger, as do social disruption and despair. The Mormon refugee camps along the Mississippi were a perfect target for a pandemic.[16] The majority of the inhabitants had been through at least one traumatic dislocation, most of them in the expulsion from Missouri. Some had lost loved ones, virtually all had lost property, and most had been forced to abandon or reinterpret their dream of living in a Latter-day Zion.

"My very Dear Husband, With a weak and trembleing hand I attempt to write a few lines," Apostle Heber C. Kimball's wife, Vilate, began.

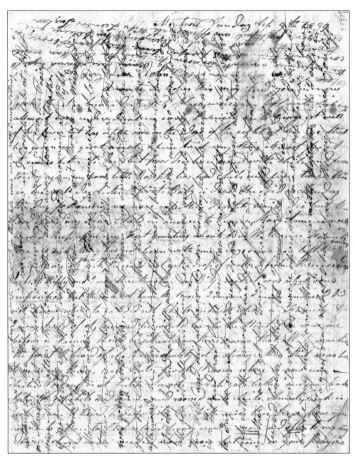

Leonora Taylor to John Taylor, September 9, 1839. To save both paper and postage, nineteenth-century writers often filled a page in one direction, then rotated it and continued writing in the other. *(Church History Library, Salt Lake City. © Intellectual Reserve.)*

She assured her husband that she was reconciled to his leaving her, even though she had been suffering almost from the time he left. She had been struck early that morning "with a shake, and shook about an hour and a half so hard as I ever saw any body in my life, and then weltered under a fever and extream pain until about night." Although she, like the others, assured her missionary husband that she was prepared to endure whatever trials lay ahead, she made sure that he knew she was suffering. Heber responded in the only way he could—with sympathy, assuring Vilate that he could cry like a child at the thought that he had for one moment been the cause of her distress.[17]

The Apostles left for England confident that the Church, meaning local bishops and their assistants, would care for their wives and families. No one counted on the difficulties of organizing relief in a population where nearly everybody was poor and most were weakened by illness. There was also the perennial problem of deciding whose needs came first. In a September letter to Wilford, Phebe described a kind of musical chairs taking place in the old fort just before the last of the Apostles set out on their journey: "Sister Tailor's going in with me as she had to move out of brother Youngs house she went into my room with sister Pratt," a description that makes it difficult to know where anyone actually was."[18]

Phebe's cryptic summary expanded into a full-scale drama in Leonora Taylor's letters to her husband. Apparently Brigham Young, who had helped organize the exodus from Missouri, believed that distributing resources was a matter of math, that women with fewer children ought to make way for those with many. He was determined to find a place for his pregnant wife, Mary Ann, and their five children.[19] According to Leonora, he said "it was a Greivous imposition that they could not have the Room I was in. I made answer I did not know where to go. . . . He said he would lie in the Street if he was me before a Family should be situated as theres was." Leonora quickly got someone to move her things into a room where Orson Pratt's wife, Sarah, and her two-year-old son were living, but Brigham's words obviously rankled, and Leonora confided in a male friend. He told her that, although he dreaded Young's anger more than death, he thought that in this case she ought to overlook his harsh words, because he, too, "was sick and fretful." Even if Leonora was humiliated at being ordered out of her apartment, she swallowed her pride. She told her husband she planned to tell everyone she had left voluntarily "on account of Sister Young's confinement." Then, perhaps worried about what she had already said, she told him to burn her letter after reading it.[20]

That the Saints had found refuge in an area once designed as a boundary between Anglo-Americans and Indians added an ironic twist to their situation. Mormon missionaries had first entered Missouri to preach to Indians living on government reserves west of Independence. Now they, too, were perched on a kind of reserve. An 1824 treaty between the U.S. government and the Sauk leader Keokuk had designated the site that became Montrose as a "Half-Breed Tract" for the mixed-race descendants of European traders and their Indian partners. Alliances between French traders and native women had once been the foundation of an expansive fur trade. When the Americans displaced the French in the Mississippi Valley, persons who had once been essential to commerce were now considered marginal. The Sauk and their close relatives, the Meskwaki (referred to by the French as *renards,* or Fox), had originally ranged from the St. Lawrence River Valley through the present states of Michigan, Wisconsin, Illinois, Iowa, and Missouri. After their defeat in the Black Hawk War of 1832, the Sauk lost all claim to Illinois lands.[21]

The Saints purchased an old fort and remnants of what had been the "Half-Breed Tract" from speculators who hoped to recover what they had spent on uncertain claims.[22] Only a few crumbling adobe chimneys remained of mixed-race occupation, but a series of earthen mounds offered tantalizing evidence of an earlier native presence. Wilford was convinced that the Indians he saw "wandering about among the gentiles cast down & dejected with nothing more than a blanket upon their naked bodies" would soon be converted to Mormonism. Phebe nourished this dream when she wrote him that an Indian and his wife and daughter had been baptized in Commerce.[23] In truth, the Mormons made few converts among nearby Indians, although those still in the neighborhood were friendly. On New Year's Day 1840, Leonora Taylor invited "three Indian women, a papoose and an elderly Man, all very clean," to have supper with her. "They sat around the fire and talked away quite comfortably. Little Joseph liked the little papoose and was delighted with it." On another day, Leonora and two of her neighbors took a long walk along the river. "There were a great number of our brethren Lamanites going before us," she wrote. "Amongst them was Black Hawk's son and two sons-in-law. His son can speak English. If I had not been alone I would [have] liked them to come in." On another day, they came to her door "dressed very fine, bells on their legs and feathers on their heads."[24]

There were no such stories in Phebe's letters. Perhaps she was less interested. More likely, she had moved away from the area where remnants of Black Hawk's band occasionally visited. Believing that a site so close to the river was bad for her daughter, she let Abraham and Margaret Smoot keep Sarah Emma for more than a week after Wilford left, and then, when she and her daughter both became ill, moved in with them herself. Although the Smoots' house was unfinished, it was more comfortable than the makeshift apartment in the fort. "Morn has come and found me for the first time without a chill or shake," she reported in a letter to Wilford, adding that some brethren had come to raise a new house for her. She hoped they would finish it by the time she was well enough to move in.[25]

Leonora Taylor told John that, if the house materialized, Phebe had promised to share it with her, and the two of them would "croak together." She was in fact worried about Phebe, who had been suffering for weeks from the ague. "A Doctor who is here to day says it will go hard with her," she wrote. She was obviously alluding to the fact that Phebe was once again pregnant. Then, worried that she had been indiscreet, Leonora cautioned John not to tell Wilford that Phebe was failing.[26] In her own letters, Phebe tried not to complain. She considered Wilford's mission hers as well. "I have not for the first moment wished you at home since you left but desired and prayed for your spead and success on your mission," she assured him. But, lest he doubt that he was wanted at home, she quickly added, "Sarah sends a lock of her hair to you with a kiss by kissing the letter. She often calls pa-pa-pa very loud don't you hear her?"[27]

Communicating by letter was frustrating, since the men constantly changed their location. John Taylor cautioned Leonora about sending letters to Preston, in Lancashire, because after eight days the post office there sent unretrieved letters to the dead-letter office in London. Fortunately, Liverpool had a "strangers letter office" similar to that in New York, which made it a bit easier to receive mail there.[28] Knowing how difficult communication was going to be, Wilford and Phebe devised a plan to help maintain their closeness. Each day, at sunset, they would pray for each other, imagining that the revolving sun connected them. As a physical token of his care, Wilford had left his most recent diary where Phebe would find it: "Phebe farewell Be of good cheer. . . . I leave these pages for your careful perusal while I am gone. I shall see thy face again in the flesh. I am gone to obey the command of JESUS CHRIST."[29]

As a surprise, Phebe had tucked a lock of her hair, perhaps fashioned into a wristband or an ornament, into Wilford's luggage, along with a poem. The poem, which she had written in rhymned couplets with four feet to a line, asked God to bless him with the wisdom of Solomon and the meekness of Moses. Then, in a more practical vein, it begged that he be supplied "with raiments, and with food," adding:

> While onward he his footsteps bend
> May he find Mothers, and kind friends.[30]

Phebe knew that in England other women would wash her husband's shirts, cook his meals, and perhaps lift his spirits at the end of a day.

"like the holy women in the days of Paul"

By the end of 1840, Wilford had traveled 4,469 miles in England and Wales, held 230 meetings, planted Latter-day Saint congregations in forty-seven places, and baptized 336 persons, fifty-seven of whom had been preachers in other sects.[31] He had his greatest success at a place called Froom's Hill, in Herefordshire, where he baptized a prosperous farmer named John Benbow and his wife, Jane. There men and women sifted out of other churches into a group called the United Brethren listened to his message as though he had been sent directly from heaven. Their zeal almost frightened him. "It seemed as though some would worship me while they cried out here is a man of Zion the man of God that we have so long looked for. . . . I told them to worship God for I was ownly a servant."[32]

Wilford was constantly in motion, preaching in one village after another and then moving on. He found much to admire in England. Touring the potteries at Stoke-on-Trent, he was delighted when a church member purchased a china box and some small bottles and pitchers as gifts for his family. In London, he was so intrigued by the Egyptian displays in the British Museum that he made an appointment to take a second look. He was deeply moved by the view from the summit of Malvern Hill, where he could see the cities of Worcester to the north and Gloucester to the south and the surrounding countryside for many miles.[33]

But parts of England seemed to him the closest thing he had ever seen to "the Lake of fire & Brimstone Spoken of by the Revelator John." The earth, the air, the buildings, and the people themselves all seemed covered with "fire, cinders, Gas, soot, & smoke," as though the Devil was churning out human misery from the furnaces and pits below. He was horrified by the sight of little children freezing on the streets of London, and astonished when he saw a boy running barefoot alongside a fast-moving coach to catch coins thrown by the passengers.[34] At Preston, the rattling of wooden clogs on the pavement as workers—women as well as men—went into the factories made him think of the children of Israel in bondage in Egypt. One night he dreamed that people were being killed for food "because of the soreness of a famine."[35]

Men like John Benbow helped finance church publications and pay for the gathering to America, but the missionary effort in England, as in the United States, was financed by thousands of small contributions, gifts of oranges and raisins, or the making of a pair of shoes, by people with little else to give. Sometimes the thing that they gave was affirmation of the men's calling. One day, a sister told Wilford she had seen an angel dressed in white standing behind him as he was preaching. A few days later, he gave her five pounds to help her take her husband and children to America, lamenting that he had so little to give when the need was so great.[36] Wilford's diary became an unintentional witness to the influence of women on the success of his mission. "We spent a pleasant evening together at Sister Dawson's," he wrote shortly after arriving in Preston. "Their was 6 Elders of us together . . . & a number of warm harted Sisters." At Gadfield Elm Chapel, in Worcestershire, he baptized eleven women in one session, among whom were "three generations a Daughter, Mother & Grandmother." Sixty-two percent of the names in the little baptismal record he kept in Herefordshire were female.[37]

In April, eight of the Apostles met in Preston for "The first Council of the Twelve among the Nations." There were by then twenty-two Latter-day Saint congregations in England, with a total membership of 1,671. Determined to push forward in a work they believed unstoppable, the men approved the establishment of a Latter-day Saint newspaper to be published monthly in Manchester, with Parley Pratt as editor.[38] In the August issue of the *Latter-day Saints Millennial Star,* Pratt took up a burning social question of the time. An unnamed church leader had asked him to "set forth the duty and standing of women in the church . . . as some of our sisters feel a little disposed to get out of order." With characteristic wit, Pratt suggested that the good brother read the scriptures and, while noting instructions to the sisters, pay even more attention to admonitions directed at himself.[39]

Then he proceeded to answer the query, summarizing New Testament prescriptions familiar to Christians everywhere. Women should adorn themselves with "a meek and quiet spirit." They should "marry, bear children, guide the house," "teach the young women to be sober, to love their husbands, to love their children," and so on. He did not forget the escape clause embedded in Christian teaching. If God required wives to submit to their husbands, he also expected husbands to love and care for their wives, as Christ did the Church.[40] This was patriarchy with a soft voice, male dominance with a caress. There was nothing here to distinguish Latter-day Saints from other Christians.

The emphasis on revelation, however, joined Latter-day Saints with other charismatic groups, like the primitive Methodists, who invited ordinary women to prophesy. Although women had no right to "control the Elders and Officers in any manner," it was "their privilege and duty to warn all, both men and women, of what God is doing in these last days, so far as they have opportunity,—and invite all to come and submit themselves to the gospel of Christ." With permission of the elders, they could "pray, testify, speak in tongues, and prophesy." Not surprisingly, it was also "their privilege to make and mend, and wash, and cook for the Saints; and lodge strangers." They also had the honor of washing feet, Pratt explaining that it was "a most acceptable treat to the servants of God when they are weary, and their feet are sore with long travels: and we rejoice that the sisters esteem it a privilege thus to minister to our necessities; and it is their privilege, in all such things, to labour with us in the gospel, like the holy women in the days of Paul."[41]

Wilford's diary shows that female converts fully embraced their "privileges." Week after week, the sisters provided food, shelter, and clothing for the elders, opened their houses or rooms for meetings, served as couriers and guides, and prepared copies of the *Millennial Star* for shipping.[42] Some of them were also adept at prophecy. Through experience, missionaries learned to pay close attention to Eliza Bromley, a twenty-four-year-old woman who lived near Stoke-on-Trent. During a period of discouragement over his lack of success in London, Wilford received a letter from her reporting that she had had "a dream that we Should soon Baptize a man that would do much good." That very day, a London watchmaker "went forward with us to a public Bath & was Baptized."[43] When another missionary stopped at Eliza's house on his way to Birmingham, she told him he should delay his journey because Elder Woodruff wanted to see him. Just as predicted, Wilford soon arrived at her house.[44]

The next day, Wilford had a long talk with Eliza, who shared a "remarkable vision" she had received less than a week before. She told him she had awakened from sleep to find a person clothed in white linen beside her. The divine messenger told her that, because she had fed and clothed God's servants, God would take care of her. "Some have desired their office & some will fall by their desires," he continued, cautioning her that she should desire "no one thing but that which is given thee from the father." She asked him if she should keep the things he had said to her from the world. "He said thou wilt know by the spirit of God that is within thee who to tell." Clearly, Wilford believed he had been chosen to receive Eliza's story. He recorded it in his diary in her own words, carefully dating it: "Lane End Statfordshire Oct 8th 1840."[45]

Theodore Turley, a native of England who had immigrated to the

United States and then returned as a missionary, also left stories about Bromley. When he was imprisoned for an old debt or for preaching without a license, she fed and clothed him and visited him in prison. "I Pray God to reward her an hundred fold in the Kingdom of our father and that this her kindness should be handed down to future generations as a memorial of her," he wrote.[46] Yet she, like so many others, has disappeared from history. Scattered records tell us that she married Richard Rushton, the son of a silkmaker from Leeds, and that twelve days later they set sail for New Orleans, presumably planning to continue up the Mississippi River to Nauvoo. At that point, her story fades.[47]

Visiting in Manchester, Wilford noted in a matter-of-fact way, "We took tea with Sister Katherine Bates the Prophetess." A few days later, he had a long conversation with Bates about the persecutions and trials that might face the Saints. "She spoke of many things past & to come, & among the many things she says Br J. Smith Jr with his Councillors are on their way to England & will be here soon." A more likely vision, painful for Wilford to hear, concerned Phebe and Sarah Emma: "She says my family suffer the most for clothing of any thing at present She says my wife has many sorrowful hours & sighs much in my absens."[48] Bates may have had a gift for dire prophecies. A young English convert named William Clayton, who was serving as president of the Manchester Branch, was eating dinner at Bates's house when she prophesied an early death for one of the Apostles. His later comment about her "prophecies bad" may explain why he, or a later custodian of his diary, blacked out sixteen lines reporting a conversation with her.[49]

The only other excised section in Clayton's diary sits in the middle of a story about a woman named Sarah Crooks, who had given him oranges and raisins, sent gifts to his family, and eventually found lodging in the boarding house where he lived. She was the only woman mentioned in his diary who consistently washed his feet. When she told him she was thinking of marrying, he was distraught. "I was much troubled and tempted on her account," he admitted, "and felt to pray that the Lord would preserve me from impure affections. . . . I certainly feel my love towards her to increase but shall strive against it." Yet his diary showed no sign of diminishing his contact.[50]

When called as missionary, Clayton had left his wife, Ruth Moon, and two young daughters with her parents. Although ardent members of the Church, the Moons felt the strain financially. Clayton's own mother warned him that Ruth was dissatisfied with the situation.[51] In January

1840, he reported that there had been "several dreams in the church concerning my wife the last 10 days." One sister dreamed that Ruth was "either dead or dying" and his children crying for bread. In one of his own dreams, Ruth disappeared while they were picking fruit together; in another, he dreamed he was "a single or unmarried person." Clearly, his absence from his wife was a subject of concern to him and to those around him, perhaps because, unlike the American missionaries, he could easily have returned home for a visit or worked to support his family.[52]

Because the American Apostles were constantly on the move, they had less opportunity to develop the kind of intimacy that tempted Clayton. Wilford's single account of foot washing is dutifully formal: "A worthy Sister wished to wash my feet. I gave her an opportunity & she did so. I had the spirit of prophecy concerning her & delivered it unto her." The prophecy, which he recorded in shorthand, promised among other things that the woman's sons "should be the priests of God and live in the millennium," and that she was herself "of the blood of Ephraim and will remain until the coming of Christ." He did not record her name.[53]

His descriptions of his own dreams were filled with wonder. Given his own love of angling, it is hardly surprising that they often involved fishing. One night, he dreamed he was standing by a river much like the one in Farmington, Connecticut, where his father ran a mill. A ship was sailing from the other side of the river toward the place where he stood reeling in a fish that was so big they had to call a bellman to divide it. Wilford pondered the meaning of this dream. Perhaps he was about to baptize some noted person. Maybe it meant that elders were coming from New York to divide the work. "What this Dream means time will soon Determine," he concluded.[54]

He had always been a fisherman, but now, like the New Testament apostles, he had become a fisher of men. After an exhausting day at a church conference, "healing many that were Sick, Shaking hands with about 400 Saints, walking 2 miles, & Preaching 4 hours in the Chimney Corner," he went to bed and once again "dreamed of Ketching fish." In these nocturnal fishing expeditions, he sometimes fished with a pole, other times with his bare hands. Once, after eating a supper of two-inch-long sprats, he dreamed of catching "fowl, geese, and turkeys" in a net.[55] Dreams of fishing were usually reassuring. But in times of stress, serpents invaded his sleep. Some were dead ones, like antiques made of stone. The live ones "Pitched at me like Draggons," he wrote, "& I fled from them & arose into the air & sailed a great distance with the greatest ease & delight singing Victory." Later that night, he dreamed of seeing Phebe and his daughter, Sarah Emma.[56]

Missionaries and members alike pondered the religious significance of dreams. Wilford and Brigham Young were both impressed with a dream or vision reported by a woman named Ann Booth. Wilford set it apart with a special border in his diary; Brigham sent a version to Mary Ann in Nauvoo.[57] Booth said she had entered "the place of departed spirits," where she saw twelve prisons built of stone with a large, thickset man, with dark eyes and eyebrows and a smiling countenance, holding the keys. Although she had never seen this man before, she somehow knew he was "one of the 12 Apostles of the Lamb who had been martered in America." He wore a crown of gold "or sumthing brighter," and had four stars on the breast of his white robe and a "golden girdle about his loins. His feet were bear from above the ancles downwards, and his hands also bear," and as he entered the prison he seemed to stand three feet above the floor. Light surrounded him as he began preaching to the inhabitants of the prison. Then the marble floor fell away to reveal "a river of water Clear as Cristle," and he began to call people by name, first John Wesley, then others whom Booth knew as leaders of "the New Connection of Methodists." He baptized and confirmed them. Next, Booth's own grandfather came forward, and her mother, a sister, and an uncle, relatives who "had lived & died Methodist." The man Booth believed to be a Mormon apostle continued his work until he had baptized hundreds of those she knew to be dead.

She awoke from her vision "so happy & overjoyed" that she could not remain in bed. She awakened her husband and together they opened the Bible. Three times it fell open. First to Isaiah 24:22 ("And they shall be gathered together, as prisoners are gathered in the pit, and shall be shut up in the prison, and after many days shall they be visited"), then to John 1:5 ("And the light shineth in darkness, and the darkness comprehended it not"), and finally 1 Peter 3:18–20 ("For Christ also hath once suffered for sins. . . . By which also he went and preached unto the spirits in prison; Which sometime were disobedient"). By the time Booth shared her story with Wilford, she had obviously discussed it with others and perfected it, building into her narrative answers to skeptics who might question her interpretation. "Being before ignorant of these texts & opening upon each Providentially I was astonished beyound measure," she explained. "I would further state that at the time I had this vision I had never herd of the Death of David W. Patten whom I have since learned was one of the Twelve Apostles of the Latter Day Saints in America & was slain in the late persecution in the fall of 1838 But in the Vission I knew it was an Apostle who had been slain in America." She then gave her name and "set my seal in witness to the Same well knowing that I shall stand before the Judgment Seat of Christ."[58]

By connecting her dream with scripture, Booth solved a puzzle that had troubled many before her and that, with the arrival of Mormon missionaries, had become urgent. If baptism was necessary for salvation, and if Mormon preachers were at present the only ones with authority to baptize, what happened to those who died before they had a chance to hear this message and act upon it? The answer was clear. Preaching continued after death—and baptism, too, or so it seemed. For Booth, this concept came as an immense relief. Her mother, sister, and uncle, and John Wesley himself, would yet have a chance to hear Mormon preaching. They were good people. She knew that they would listen.

Booth's vision took on additional power when word reached missionaries that Joseph Smith had begun teaching a new doctrine about baptism for the dead. Brigham had written about Booth's vision in a letter to Mary Ann on May 20, 1840. His letter may or may not have reached Nauvoo by the time Joseph gave his first sermon on the subject on August 15.[59] Joseph taught that missionary work would indeed continue after death, but because baptism was a physical act, it had to be done in an earthly body. Baptism for the dead meant vicarious baptism. With proper authority, a living person could be baptized by immersion "for and in behalf" of someone who had died. Like Booth, people in Nauvoo had also been worrying about the fate of their dead friends and family. By October, Phebe could report them "going forward in multitudes." Some, she said, were "going to be baptized as many as 16 times."[60] Vilate Kimball wrote Heber that she hoped to be baptized for her mother. "I calculated to wate until you come home but the last time Joseph spoke upon the subject he advised every one to be up and a doing and liberate their friends from bondage as quick as posable." The ceremony took place in the Mississippi River, with Joseph himself officiating.[61]

In light of the possibility that missionary work and even baptism might continue after death, Wilford's dreams of fishing took on deeper meaning. He pondered for some time a dream he had had in October, long before he learned about Smith's new teachings. He finally recorded it in his diary, in the section where he had copied Booth's vision. He dreamed that he was home, in Farmington. Seeing that the trench under the saw-mill was full of pickerel, his father opened the gates, and the fish started to run downstream. Wilford jumped into the trench, & caught a great many large fish with his hands as they came down. The story continued:

> I then went to the mill & Brother Asahel Woodruff who has been dead two years came & brought many fish & showed me which he caught in the trench. We then commenced eating peaches with other friends & talked about & rejoiced in the glories of IMMORTALITY.[62]

This was a dream about family and fish and life after death, about working side by side with his father and sharing the sweetness of faith with a beloved and now dead brother. It was a dream about discovering life beneath the rasping machinery of his father's mill. The peaches perhaps alluded to a passage in the Book of Mormon that described the Prophet Lehi's dream about following an "iron rod" along a river to a tree laden with fruit sweeter than anyone had ever tasted. After eating the fruit, Lehi had only one desire: that his family might feast on it too.[63]

"I had been living by the wayside"

"I told you in my other letter that I had been living by the wayside as it were," Phebe wrote her husband in April 1840, explaining that she had moved four times since he left her, first "from Montrose to brother Smoots, then to my new home, then to father Clarks, then into a small house of his in the same door yard." In three letters penned over that spring and summer, she told the story of her perambulations, adding new and potentially more disturbing details each time she wrote. She repeated herself because she feared Wilford had not received her earlier letters, but also because she wanted to be sure he understood what might have seemed at a distance merely fickle behavior.[64]

She was an intelligent and resourceful woman, but in letters sent from Montrose, she fell back on a sentimental portrait of herself as a lone woman dependent on the kindness of strangers. Her first rescuer, Abraham Owen Smoot, had been Wilford's missionary companion in the Southern states. Although it was surely his wife, Margaret, who nursed her and Sarah Emma through the ague, it was in "brother Smoot's" house that she found shelter. When she found herself in difficulty later because the "new home" built for her by the Church had neither a door nor a window and was so open to the weather that in December she had to cope with snow on the floor, sixty-two-year-old Timothy Baldwin Clark came to her aid.[65] In the midst of the Missouri persecutions, he had lost his wife. Although Phebe acknowledged that she did sewing for his family during the time she lived with them, it was his role in providing for her needs rather than hers in providing for his that dominated her letters: "Father Clark says that you need not be concerned about me untill you get back, only pray for me, he is verry kind," she wrote.[66] If Smoot was a substitute brother, Clark was a surrogate father.

Advancing pregnancy added to her vulnerability. On March 22, 1840, almost eight months after Wilford's departure, she gave birth to a healthy eight-and-a-half-pound boy. She was then living in the little house standing in the Clarks' dooryard. She named the baby Wilford Owen—Wilford for her husband, and Owen for Abraham Owen Smoot. She assured Wilford that, though she had had "everything at that time that was necessary to make me comfortable," she missed him more than ever. "Oh! Thought I if I could but have my Willford to call on instead of strangers what a comfort it would be to me."[67] Phebe wasn't talking about the management of the delivery—that was women's work—but about such necessities as a good fire, a sound roof, a horse to transport her attendants, and whatever food, drink, or medicine she required. She was grateful that other men were willing to provide what Wilford could not, but she wanted more than material support. She wanted spiritual and emotional comfort. She wanted Wilford to witness her triumph over pain and share her joy in welcoming a little "black-eyed boy" everyone thought looked like his mother.

Phebe had mastered the language of sensibility. She wondered if Wilford remembered a ride they had taken out onto the prairie just before he left for England. "The prairies were most delightfuly clothed with flowers and verdure and I thought it the most pleasant ride we ever had together," she recalled. The Sabbath after he left, she had taken the same ride with a group of Saints going to meeting. Although "the flowers were there . . . they with every thing else were dressed in gloom and looked [as] lonely as I felt." She admitted that, though such reflections passed and repassed through her mind, "in the midst of them something whispers Phebe do you want your companion to come home to you before he has filled his present mission my heart answers <u>no</u> but Lord give me <u>patience</u> and a <u>willingness</u> to wait his <u>return</u> and hasten the time that he shall be returned to the bosom of his family."[68] It was the old tug between family, as she understood it, and faith.

After her son's birth, her writing became more upbeat. She reported on the state of her cow and the two hens and twelve chickens that, as she said, "compose my stock at present."[69] She enclosed a little jingle she had made up while nursing baby Willie. In her search for a rhyme, she expanded the number of Moses's commandments:

> Sleep sweet babe and take thy rest,
> For God looks down and will thee bless,
> With all that's good, in earth, or heaven,
> If thou wilt keep the commandments eleven.[70]

She invited Wilford to imagine what he might see if he were able to "look over here on a rolling prairie near timber into a little small house with one door in it." She assured him she would be there in her rocking chair with her baby boy in her arms and little Sarah Emma clinging to her side singing "pa-pa ma-ma and bilo." Although she didn't need to say it, she added, "I find my little ones are much company."[71]

In May, she wrote that Willie had been taken with the whooping cough but was now well. "I and one of the sisters took hold in faith and all the powers of mind that we could muster and the Lord heard and answered us," she reported, then added that she could not write more because she was so busy. Happy to hear news of Wilford's progress in England, she appeared to have settled into her life in Montrose.[72] Surprisingly, she seldom referred to her nearest female neighbors in her letters, though she sometimes inserted a bit of news about the wives of the other missionaries. Their husbands, she knew, would want to hear about them. Mostly, though, she focused on her own lonely state. We don't know who was with her during her delivery or, more significant, which sister was able to join her in praying for her baby's recovery. Perhaps Father Clark's married daughter, Laura Phelps, who was a midwife, assisted her. A woman renowned for both courage and faith, Laura had helped her husband, Morris, escape from prison in Missouri by following a plan she had received in a dream or vision. She must have been an impressive person, but Phebe never mentioned her name.[73]

By July, Phebe had grown anxious about Wilford. He had been gone almost a year. In the past five months she had heard nothing from him. Was he in prison or ill? In one of her unanswered letters, she warned, half in jest, that the next time he was called on a mission "we will put on the big pot and all go for I am quite tired of living alone." Then she reverted to her faithful stance. No, not once had she ever wished him to return before his mission was complete. She wanted him to do the Lord's will.[74]

Two weeks later, her world fell apart. Sarah Emma had eaten her dinner as usual, then, about four in the afternoon, "was taken with a prestness for breath." Phebe called her neighbors and then the elders, who anointed and blessed the child, but with no effect. On July 18, she wrote:

> My dear Willford what will be your feelings when I say that yesterday I was called to witness the departure of our little Sarah Emma from this world—yes she is gone—

Still in shock, she packaged her despair in conventional pieties.

> [T]he relentless hand of death has snatched her from my embrace— but Ah! she was to lovely to kind to affectionate to live in this wicked world—when looking on her I have often thought how I should feel to part with her I thought I would not live without her especially in the absence of my companion—but she is gone—the Lord has taken her to himself for some wise purpose.

She added that Sarah Emma "left a kiss for her pa-pa with me just before she died."[75]

Phebe added to her letter a few days later. She, explained that she and her neighbors had carried the body to Nauvoo for burial, that Father Clark's son-in-law, Morris Phelps, had officiated at the grave and promised to preach a funeral sermon the following Sunday, and that Stephen Luce, a friend from Maine, had agreed to make a little fence around the grave. She lamented that Sarah Emma "had no relatives to follow her to her grave or to shed a tear for her but her Ma and little Willford." Margaret Smoot added a tearful note of her own, calling Sarah Emma "one of the loveliest flowers that ever blossomed," informing Wilford that his daughter "expired in my arms" and that "I done the last honor to her that was in my power I closed her precious little eyes washed her kissed her again and again and today with her weeping mother consigned her to the grave to wait until Gabriel trump sound." Margaret signed herself "your sister in Christ."[76]

Phebe folded the letter with its sorrowful news and handed it to Eliza Snow's brother, Lorenzo, who was about to leave for England. It took three months for Wilford to receive it.[77]

With no acknowledgment that her husband knew of her sorrow, Phebe continued to mourn. On September 1, she began another letter, summarizing all that had happened to her since he left. This time she added details that had not been there before. She told him that, during her illness the year before, she had had a young girl live with her, but "got much slandered for having the girl so long." Worse than that, when she called on the bishop for help, he was cross and complained. And when she moved into her own house, "the people in Lovely Street" (apparently, her nickname for the fort at Montrose) were upset with her for not selling her calf or her clothes to provide for herself. She hoped such days were over. Father Clark and his family were kind. But she was worried. She had had almost continuous trouble since Wilford left her, and since Sarah Emma's death, she found it hard to be reconciled to her situation, especially when her surviving baby was also ill.

> I have to bear my trouble alone no Willford or relative to sympathize with me and can you tell me my dear companion who has a better right to share a part of your attention and kindness than your best friend.

There it was. She had finally said it. "Had you been home I think our dear child might have been living." If Wilford was absolutely certain that the Lord wanted him in England, she supposed she would have to submit, "and if I live, live through another cold lonely winter. Yea my heart sinks within me when I think of spending my life mostly alone."[78]

She knew she had said too much: she did not send the letter. But she and her descendants kept it—a significant fact, since so many of the letters she wrote over the years have disappeared. It not only provided evidence of how much she had suffered during this painful separation from her husband. It revealed how close she had come to asking whether God, if it was indeed God, had asked too much.

On September 8, she began a more restrained, pious, and artful letter. Although she again revisited Sarah Emma's death, reminding Wilford that their daughter had been torn from her embrace and laid in the silent grave, she managed to find positive news as well. She had met some of the new emigrants from England, including a family with whom Wilford— "the man of God as they called you"—had spent two months. She liked them, "perhaps more for their having been acquainted with you." She ended by planting kisses on the page from little Willie, leaving room on the other side for a note from Father Clark's son William, who assured Wilford that he should have no uneasiness about his family, for they

"Shall Not Suffer for anny thing that we Can bestow & may God hold it as an everlasting Covinent between me & thee (for I have found her Worthy)." True, he was about to leave on a "mishon" himself, but that was no matter. Her needs would be met. Significantly, his covenant, or promise, was with Wilford, not with his wife. He pledged himself as a surrogate for the husband who was now unable to fulfill his own covenant with Phebe as her protector and provider.[79]

A month later, Phebe wrote again, clearly upset that in the only letter she had gotten from Wilford he was still unaware of his daughter's death. She told him that his comment about sending kisses to their daughter was like a dagger to her heart. Still she was determined to overcome grief. As much to assure herself as him, she copied into her letter a long poem of assurance. Surely, her "lovely child" was now at home, free from pain, and looking down on the "simple things of time."

> Or if permitted, to the earth descends,
> And gladly mingles with her earthly friends;
> Although unseen her happy spirit near,
> May hear the sigh, and see the falling tear,
> May with concern behold maternal grief,
> And fondly wish to sooth and give relief.

If there was no living friend nearby, Phebe could at least imagine that Sarah Emma understood her sorrow.[80]

She copied the poem on one side of the page, then, on the other, offered a lively description of baby Willie: "He is now in my lap pulling & scratching round so that I can hardly write he has just torn up the almanack before I saw what he was doing, he grows finely considering the sickness he has had. . . . He is now reaching and trying to get my pen I will give it him and see what he will write." Holding the baby's hand, she added a rough note: "Dear pa pa do come home and see me W.O. Woodruff." Then she once again gave vent to grief: "You cannot think how much I miss little Sarah Emma her death has disarmed me of all courage faith & fortitude I have had almost one scene of trouble since you left by sickness etc but I thought they were all light afflictions when compared with that O pray for me Willford!"[81]

Struggling to overcome her despair, she wrote again within the week, vowing to keep a little journal for Wilford with a bit about her activities each day. What followed was as close to a daily diary as Phebe ever wrote.

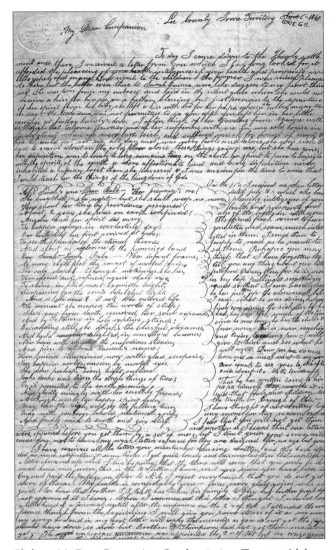

Phebe to My Dear Companion, October 6, 1840. To cope with her daughter's death, Phebe turned to poetry, using a squiggly line to separate her homemade verses from the more conventional part of her letter. (*Church History Library, Salt Lake City. © Intellectual Reserve.*)

On October 27, she reported that Willie had again been ill, but that she had broken his fever with Sappington's Pills. By October 31, she was busy making a cap for someone else. On Sunday, her name and those of Sarah Emma and Wilford were added to the records of the branch. "Wm Clark is the president of the branch has gone to nauvoo or Commerce today and says that I must preside over the meeting," she wrote, adding that there were a number of elders there and she would be happy if one of them took her place. Then, despite all her efforts, the tears resumed. "O poor little Sarah is gone how can I bear it. . . . O tell me Willford why she was taken from me when you was gone it seames sometimes that I can hardly help murmering at it." When she posted the letter, her would-be journal ended.[82]

Phebe dealt with her personal grief in the midst of a collective effort among her neighbors to secure redress for their losses in Missouri. Most had taken out land under the federal Pre-emption Act of 1830 and had made improvements in order to secure their claims. Encouraged by meetings in Washington, D.C., church leaders had appointed a committee "to go round among the brethren and get their affidavits and bills of damage." Among the more than six hundred petitioners were seventy women who had been widowed in Missouri. Their words place Phebe's private anguish in a larger context. Those who lived through the assault on a place called Haun's Mill had witnessed unspeakable violence. Catharine McBride saw the mob murder her husband, then cut him "to peases with a syth blaid." Mariah Bennor testified that they stripped the clothes off the backs and the boots and shoes from the feet of the dead and wounded.[83]

Those who had begn to improve their property not only lost loved ones but a livelihood and the "rights of citizenship." Hannah York did not know how to sign her own name, but the testimony she dictated took on a Biblical cadence: "Alas our corn is gone whet is gone our hay is gone our Cow is gone yea and my Companion . . . was kild and I the wife of John york . . . with my two helpless Children have a Blige to leave the state of missoury."[84] Old Truman Brace echoed her lament: "My children are gone & scatred from me by reson of the mobers of misoughry." Even worse was his loss of hope in his fellow Americans. "I could relate many potickelars which are of seris consideration but am about to leve the subject lest it shold be in vain because of the hardness of the harte of this generation."[85]

Phebe's rescuer Abraham Smoot was not alone in demanding redress from the government for being forced "to leave the State of Missouri with all of my flattering prospects of futer welth & Ease." He had lost not only the value of his own labor but his hopes for a better future.[86] Phebe's friends the Clarks suffered a similar decline. With six sons to assist him, Father Clark had laid claim to 480 acres, of which he had about a hundred in cultivation, "with a small orchard and Nursery" and the "necessary buildings of a farm." But, as he explained in his deposition, an armed company "came and took myself and my three Sons prisoners, and threw down my fences and opened my gates and left them open and left my Crops to be destroyed and while I was a prisoner they . . . took from me two yoke of Oxen and three Horses and two Wagons and compelled me and my Sons to drive them loaded with produce of my own farm, to supply their Army." Struggling to comprehend their own losses, both men and their families had reached out to Phebe. In the face of her neighbors' struggles, she may have found it difficult to express her own anguish except in letters to Wilford.[87]

For the Clarks, collective loss and private misery came together. Fragmentary writing in their family papers shows that in the midst of the Missouri conflict Father Clark's wife, Polly, had died from some unknown illness. Their son William, returning from a mission in the Southern states, heard the news only a few miles from home. The shock provoked him to write something like a poem:

> It was at Supper time a Strong young man
> Observed your mother Dead your
> Mother Dead Ah Lord thought I
> It Can Not be it Can not be Night
> Passed but Sleep had fled & left me still
> Orwhelmed in Tears & Sorrow Deep[88]

As Phebe Woodruff knew, sentimental poetry, even poetry with an uncertain meter and random rhymes, gave form to feelings too chaotic to bear.

The Missouri experience offered something that the quiet passing of a child did not. It gave people someone to blame. Mormons knew that it wasn't an invisible Destroyer who brought death and destruction to their houses, but men with names and faces.[89] Joseph Kingsbury could identify a militia officer named Bradford as the one who forced his sick family to leave their house, and Perry Keyes could blame a man "by the name of Yocum" for holding him while John Youngs whipped him with twenty-three lashes.[90] But though Nancy Cary knew that a militiaman named Donihue struck her husband "with the britch of his gun and broke his Skull," she also knew that for "the loss of my companion [and] Deprivation of CitizenShip there is no Earthly Concideraton will Satisfy me."[91] Lydia B. English expressed the same sentiment in different words: "No money can amply atone for such losses & crosses."[92]

The redress petitions failed. For Latter-day Saints who survived the horrors of Missouri, the only recompense was in the power to tell their own stories. By narrating their suffering, they forged a collective identity as God's people.

In contrast, Phebe's sorrows—and her rescue—remained personal. On December 6, she began another letter to Wilford. "I presume you will be somewhat surprised when you learn where this letter was written but perhaps not more surprised than I was when I went to my door in Iowa and saw brother I. F. Carter and L. Scammans ride up to the door. I could hardly think that they could be there but truly strange things happen in these last days." Her brother Ilus Carter and her brother-in-law Luther Scammon had ostensibly come "to see the country," but that cannot have been their only motive. They could read the newspapers. They knew that the Mormons had been exiled. They also knew that Wilford was in England. They insisted that Phebe return with them to the East. Writing from Ilus's home in New York City, she told Wilford that within a few days, she would be in Maine. She wanted him to know she had left her household goods with Father Clark and had loaned a widow woman her cow.[93]

A month later, she wrote from Scarborough, happy and rested from her journey and pleased that she had already heard from Vilate Kimball, who was caring for the things Wilford had sent from England. Yes, being deprived of his company had been a great sacrifice. Had it not been for Christ's sake she did not think she could have done it. But after all she had been through, she felt she could say with the poet:

> In hopes of that immortal crown
> I now the cross sustain
> And gladly wander up and down,
> And smile at toil and pain.

No, never had she wished him home before his mission was complete.[94]

Six months later Wilford, too, arrived in Scarborough. He was overjoyed to once more "embrace my Wife & also a son which I had not before seen." The Woodruffs left Maine together on July 6, 1841. They spent more than a month in Connecticut, where Wilford officiated at the wedding of his sister, Eunice, and Dwight Webster, and "visited the African School" where Cinque and the other slaves taken from the ship *Amistad* were in residence. "They make good proficiency in learning," he wrote.[95] By the end of August, they were in New York City, where he conducted church business and perused newspapers from Nauvoo and Liverpool while Phebe and her baby visited with her brother Ilus and his wife. The stress and the travel had nevertheless taken a toll. On August 24, Wilford returned home to the Carter house to find Phebe "upon her bed almost speechless & sensless with pain in the head and Jaw. Her Jaws were stiff & almost set." After a blessing, the pain subsided and she had a good night's rest. Wilford noted that she was "still unwell" for several days afterward, but he offered no details.[96]

Soon they were packing their trunks and heading west. On September 28, after a thousand-mile journey by rail and steamship, during which they survived a storm on the Great Lakes alongside three hundred other passengers and "a large quantity of luggage & Jack Asses," they arrived in Chicago, where Wilford hired a teamster to carry them to Nauvoo. After more than two years away, Wilford was impressed with the progress of the town. Phebe was perhaps more wary. She and Willie stayed with the Clarks while Wilford searched for housing. On October 19, they crossed the river with a load of goods and carried them to the unfinished house he had secured in Nauvoo. "I was sick," Wilford wrote. "But I felt to rejoice to spend a night with my family under a roof of my own it being the first time that I have ever injoyed such a privilege since we were married."[97]

3

"I now turn the key to you"

Nauvoo, Illinois, 1842

After returning to Nauvoo, Wilford worked hard to transform himself from an itinerant preacher into a dutiful husband. He began by working on his unfinished house. To earn money for bricks and lime to build a chimney, he mowed and stacked hay for other men, then walked fifteen miles to find a mason, paying the man with some of his own clothing. Once the chimney was up, he went to the kiln for more lime and began lathing and plastering the house's interior. When the plastering was finished and a floor in the bedroom installed, he turned to outdoor work, cutting and stacking firewood in the dooryard.[1] He was determined that Phebe and little Wilford would not suffer as they had done while he was in England. He had reason to hurry. On March 4, 1842, exactly nine months after his return, Phebe gave birth to a daughter, Phoebe Amelia. Wilford spent the day of his daughter's birth at the church printing office, where he was now employed as business manager. "Mother & babe doing well," he reported.[2]

From all appearances, Nauvoo was thriving. As new converts poured in from other parts of the United States and Britain, the population grew. Stores and shops multiplied. Men organized a Masonic society and paraded in a militia they called the Nauvoo Legion. (Although Mormons had special reason to arm themselves after their experiences in Missouri, militia duty was a routine civic duty in American towns in this era.) Nauvoo women flocked to meetings of a newly established Female Relief Society. Baptisms for the dead moved from the river to a font installed in the roofed-over basement of the unfinished temple. The printing press attracted national attention by publishing installments of Joseph Smith's life story and passages from his translations of Egyptian papyri.

Residence in Nauvoo gave Wilford a stability he had never had before. It also changed his diary. Since he was no longer traveling, he had fewer adventures to report, and since he and Phebe were together, there was no need to write things down so he could share them with her later. Sometimes he collapsed an entire week's work into a single sentence, as in: "February 7, 8, 9, 10, & 11, I spent in the printing office & was busy in setting in order many things about the office."[3] He filled only a third as many pages in his diary in 1842 as in any of the years immediately before and after. The routine nature of his work only partially explains the change. He may have written less because he knew more. In a meeting with members of the Quorum of the Twelve late in 1841, Joseph Smith warned that God would not reveal his secrets to his servants unless they were willing to keep them.[4]

Small drawing of phoenix from Wilford Woodruff's diary, March 15, 1842. Wilford used tiny drawings to highlight the spiritual significance of events only briefly described in his daily entries. (Church History Library, Salt Lake City. © Intellectual Reserve.)

Facsimile 2 as published in *Times and Seasons,* Nauvoo, March 15, 1842, and a related drawing from Wilford Woodruff's diary, October 5, 1844. Notice Wilford's effort to replicate one of the elements in the papyrus fragment, the birdlike figure in the upper left corner that appears to be in a boat. *(Church History Library, Salt Lake City. © Intellectual Reserve.)*

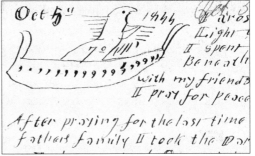

Wilford wanted to be worthy to receive God's secrets. As a substitute for words, he added new doodles and borders to his pages. Above a reference to the Masonic lodge, he sketched a tiny bird emerging from fire like a phoenix.[5] To mark a day spent performing baptisms for the dead, he drew a crowned figure, much like the "soul effigies" on early Connecticut gravestones, floating with its arms outstretched above a stylized stream.[6] In late April, he experimented with Masonic symbols, filling part of a page with variations on the twenty-four-inch gauge and gavel related to the First Degree.[7] After setting type and arranging illustrations for the first printing of the Book of Abraham, a text Smith claimed to have translated from the Egyptian papryi once displayed in the Kirtland Temple, Wilford began to compose his own hieroglyphics.[8] Above a diary entry reporting a militia muster and baptisms, he added a row of diagonal strokes much like those translated from the papryi as "to be high, or in the

Drawing of house with keys, May 5, 1844. There are many representations
of keys in Wilford's diary. Most acknowledge the restoration of priesthood
authority to give temple blessings. *(Church History Library, Salt Lake City.*
© *Intellectual Reserve.)*

heavens." Above an entry reporting his own work in performing baptisms,
he inserted a tiny key.[9]

All these things—Masonry, a rising phoenix, baptisms for the dead, a
soul effigy, drawings on Egyptian papyri, and a key—signified emerging
revelations. But keys were especially important. They were crucial elements in Mormon thought and central to Wilford's evolving understanding of Joseph's teachings. In Masonic iconography, a key represented the
ability to keep a secret.[10] In Latter-day Saint scriptures, keys represented
access to divine authority, as in the promise Jesus gave his apostles "that
whatsoever thou shalt bind on earth shall be bound in heaven." Sixty
verses in the canonized revelations of Smith elaborate this theme. The
Mormon prophet claimed to have restored keys to the gathering of Israel,
the translation and interpretation of scriptures, the performance of rituals
such as baptism, washing and anointing, and the laying on of hands, and
for determining when a supernatural manifestation was of God or of the
Devil. Keys opened the promised "dispensation of the fullness of times,"
a period in which all the things God had ever revealed would be restored
to the earth. Above all, keys offered assurance of salvation, the power to
unlock the gates of hell and death.[11]

In a string of poems published in the Church's newspaper, *Times and
Seasons,* Eliza Snow employed many of the same symbols. She assured her
fellow Saints that "a glorious scene was drawing nigh" and that the Messiah would soon reappear. Like Wilford, she imagined the Nauvoo Legion
as a phoenix emerging from the charred ruins of Missouri. For her as for
him, keys were central. When Joseph told the women of the Female Relief

Society, "I now turn the key to you," she wrote it down in the minutes she was keeping as secretary.[12] Eliza was also learning to keep secrets. In an affidavit signed in Utah many years later, she testified that on June 29, 1842, the day she began a personal diary, she was "married or sealed" to Joseph Smith. Although her first entry suggested that something momentous had happened that day, she did not mention Joseph or a marriage.[13] In truth, there were so many secrets in Nauvoo in 1842, and so many rumors, contradictions, and denials, that it is impossible to know precisely what happened and when. There is no question, however, that Joseph had begun experimenting with what people later came to understand as celestial marriage and that these new relationships were creating ripples not just among Joseph's closest associates but in the councils of church leaders and meetings of the Female Relief Society.

In March, Joseph asked the Relief Society to investigate gossip about his supposed involvement with his widowed sister-in-law, Agnes Coolbrith Smith. In April, his brother Hyrum ridiculed stories about church leaders allegedly locking an English immigrant in a room to persuade her to become a plural wife. In June Wilford reported that in a public meeting Joseph spoke "in great plainness concerning the iniquity & wickedness of Gen John Cook Bennett," claiming that his former friend had been preaching false doctrine and making illicit proposals to Nauvoo women.[14]

Bennett, a physician who had risen rapidly in Nauvoo to become mayor of the city and assistant church president, retaliated by painting Joseph as a seducer and a libertine and by implicating him in an assassination attempt against Governor Lilburn Boggs of Missouri. By the fall, Bennett was touring the nation with a lurid, book-length exposé, charging Mormon leaders with "infidelity, deism, atheism; lying, deception, blasphemy; debauchery, lasciviousness, bestiality; madness, fraud, plunder; larceny, burglary, robbery, perjury; fornication, adultery, rape, incest; arson, treason, and murder." He said Smith and his followers "out-heroded Herod, and out-deviled the devil, slandered God Almighty, Jesus Christ, and the holy angels, and even the devil himself."[15] The charge of complicity in the attack on Boggs had the greatest impact in Nauvoo, because it revived efforts to return Smith to Missouri. In the short run, however, Bennett's tales fell flat, in part because church leaders, with the cooperation of the Female Relief Society, mounted a successful defense.

Although the fight between Smith and Bennett continues to attract attention from scholars interested in this period, few have fully recognized the emergence of the Female Relief Society as a force in Nauvoo or the significance of Eliza R. Snow as a contemporary witness. As Wilford's voice faded, Eliza's emerged. Neither her poems, her Relief Society minutes, nor her personal diary explicitly mention plural marriage, but when read alongside other sources, they provide rich insights into the place of women in Nauvoo.

"We are going to do something extraordinary"

The Relief Society was the brainchild of Sarah Granger Kimball, the twenty-three-year-old wife of a Nauvoo merchant and land developer. Sarah's parents had been stalwarts in the Church since Kirtland.[16] Although Hiram, her husband, was not yet a Latter-day Saint, he knew how to cultivate the good will of the town's leaders. On Christmas Day 1841, he and Sarah hosted a dinner for the newly returned Apostles. "It was excellent Slaying & I got a horse & slay & carried the wives of the Twelve to Mr Kimballs & home again," Wilford wrote, adding that after "an excellent feast," Hiram gave each of the Apostles a plot of land in the section of the city he was developing.[17]

Sarah was more religious than her husband, but just as clever. In a memoir written in Utah many years later, she explained that when their first child was born she asked Hiram if he thought their son was worth a thousand dollars. When he assured her that the boy was worth that and more, she asked if he agreed that she owned half of him. When he acknowledged that she did, she said she intended to contribute her half to the construction fund for the Nauvoo Temple. Amused rather than annoyed, Hiram shared the joke with Joseph Smith, who responded in kind, telling him he could redeem his baby for five hundred dollars. Hiram paid.[18]

Legally, married women in the United States during this period had little control over the property they brought into marriage or helped to acquire afterward. Sarah's joke notwithstanding, it was not even clear they had a full claim to their children. In marital disputes, judges still routinely awarded custody to fathers.[19] But women blessed with harmonious marriages obviously had informal access to resources, especially when directed toward charitable associations. Prosperous women, like Sarah Kimball, could contribute money or materials. Those who had little access to cash could offer their labor. Although Latter-day Saint women had always contributed informally to the Church, as Phebe Woodruff did when she sewed curtains for the Kirtland Temple, they had never been called upon to raise money independently. In Kirtland and Missouri, the Church promoted a "law of consecration," a communal economic system in which families symbolically deeded their property to the Church, contributing whatever surplus they had for redistribution to the poor. The system never worked very well, in part because there was always more need than surplus, and it completely broke down after the devastating loss of property in Missouri.[20]

In Nauvoo, massive immigration from England and a new temple-building project increased the need for voluntary fund-raising. When Sarah Kimball's friend Margaret Cooke lamented that she did not have any money to contribute to the temple, Sarah offered to furnish fabric that Margaret might use to make shirts for workers. Then she invited a few neighbors to her house to form a "Ladies Society." She asked Eliza Snow to compose a constitution and bylaws. When Eliza showed her draft to the Prophet, he praised her efforts but said he had "something better for them than a written Constitution" and invited the sisters to meet with him the following week.[21]

On March 17, 1842, twenty women, including the Prophet's wife, Emma, gathered with Joseph and the Apostles John Taylor and Willard Richards in the large room above the Prophet's store, where, two days before, Nauvoo's male leaders had organized the Masonic lodge. Although Joseph opened the meeting, he quickly gave the sisters responsibility for choosing their own officers. Not surprisingly, they chose Emma as president. As Joseph's wife, she would add stature to the organization. She was also the only one among them who had been the subject of a published revelation. Given only a few months after the organization of the Church in 1830, the text now known as *Doctrine and Covenants* 25 honored her as "an elect lady," an allusion to a passage in the New Testament. In the voice of God, it continued, "And thou shalt be ordained under his hand to expound scriptures, and to exhort the church, according as it shall be given thee by my Spirit." It invited her to give her time to "writing, and to learning much," and to selecting hymns for worship.[22]

Although Emma had edited the Church's first hymnbook, she had found little time in the intervening years for either study or exhortation. Between 1828 and 1842, she gave birth to eight children, five of whom died in infancy, the latest just five weeks before the Relief Society was founded. She had also lost one of the twins she adopted after her own child died, all of this while enduring migration, legal threats against her husband, the horrors of Missouri, and the difficulties of living with malaria in Nauvoo. Despite her trials, she remained a handsome and resilient woman, admired and loved by her fellow Saints.[23] It would have been foolish for Joseph to encourage any sort of organization among the Church's women without consulting her. Emma selected as her counselors forty-one-year-old Elizabeth Ann Whitney, who had been a mainstay of the Church since Kirtland, and fifty-three-year-old Sarah Cleveland, a recent convert who had opened her Nauvoo home to the Smith family when they fled Missouri. The brethren set Whitney and Cleveland apart by the laying on of hands, but Emma, who had already been ordained, required only a blessing. She was both elected and Elect.[24]

When the sisters chose Eliza Snow as their secretary, Richards, who was then serving as the Prophet's clerk, gave her an impressive record book, bound in leather and stamped on the spine with the word "Ledger." Since Eliza had served as a clerk for her father when he was a justice of the peace in Ohio, she knew how to handle such a volume. It was too heavy to carry back and forth to meetings, so she took notes on loose paper and then copied them into the book, occasionally correcting an error in transcription or composition by scraping away the original ink and neatly writing over it.[25] Until attendance at meetings grew too large for much discussion, she recorded the comments of individual members as well as speeches by the Prophet, who visited often.[26]

The minutes of the first meeting show that, even when the men were present, the sisters could think for themselves. When Cleveland moved that the new organization be called the Nauvoo Female Relief Society, Whitney seconded her motion. Taylor, who seemed to have forgotten that this was a women's meeting, offered an amendment, suggesting "that it be called The Nauvoo Female Benevolent Society, which would give a more definite and extended idea of the Institution." Emma objected. She did "not wish to have it call'd after other Societies in the world."

Eliza agreed with Emma, arguing that, "as daughters of Zion, we should set an example for all the world, rather than confine ourselves to the course which had been heretofore pursued." Then, in what was perhaps a diplomatic nod to Taylor, she admitted that "one objection to the word Relief is that the idea associated with it is that of some great calamity—that we intend appropriating on some extraordinary occasions instead of meeting the common occurrences." Emma countered, "We are going to do something extraordinary—when a boat is struck on the rapids, with a multitude of Mormons on board we shall consider that a call for <u>relief</u>—we expect extraordinary occasions and pressing calls." Taylor withdrew his amendment; Eliza offered a slight transposition of words; and the sisters voted to call themselves "The Female Relief Society of Nauvoo."[27]

In a brief speech at the beginning of the meeting, Joseph suggested a dual role for the society in "looking to the wants of the poor" and in "correcting the morals and strengthening the virtues of the female community." The part about caring for the poor reflected Sarah Kimball's original plan. The goal of correcting morals may have taken some of the women by surprise. They had imagined a charitable society, not a moral-reform society. But Emma fully embraced her husband's agenda. At the second meeting, she presented a report about a young woman named Clarissa Marvel, who had supposedly been spreading "scandalous falsehoods on the character of Prest. Joseph Smith, without the least provocation."[28] Although Emma may or may not have known about plural marriage at this point, she surely knew that Joseph was the one who had asked the society to investigate.[29] She probably also knew that the rumors had something to do with Joseph's relationship with Agnes Coolbrith Smith, the widow of Joseph's younger brother Don Carlos. Agnes may by this time have become Joseph's plural wife.[30]

Emma urged the sisters to devise a plan to bring Marvel to repentance, adding that she supposed some of the women in the room knew more than she did about the young woman's behavior. Agnes quickly responded, saying that Marvel had lived with her "nearly a year" and that "she had seen nothing amiss of her."[31] At the third meeting of the society, two sisters assigned to investigate reported that the girl's other employers had never heard her speak of Joseph Smith and his family except in a respectful manner. When someone suggested that two other young women might have contrary evidence, Sarah Cleveland asked Elizabeth Durfee, a woman who had frequently nursed the Smith family in illness, to look into the case. When Durfee demurred, Emma insisted she either do it or find somebody to take her place.[32] Emma was not going to let the matter drop. She was clearly distressed by the rumors, and perhaps as well by anxiety over Joseph's relationship with his brother's widow.

At the fourth meeting, Cleveland reported "that the case of Clarissa M. had been satisfactory settled, she having testified in her own handwriting that she had said no wrong." (Cleveland had apparently not seen the affidavit, which Marvel signed with an "X.") In oral testimony, Marvel claimed never to have "seen or heard any thing improper or unvirtuous in the conduct or conversation of either <u>President</u> Smith or Mrs. Agnes Smith."[33]

By then, rumors about sexual indiscretions had apparently spread more broadly. At the same meeting in which the society cleared Marvel, Emma read an article sent by the Nauvoo City Council warning the sisters against "unprincipled men" who might try to deceive them. "We do not mention their names, not knowing but what there may be some among you who are not sufficiently skill'd in Masonry as to keep a secret." The allusion to Masonry was patronizing. Masonic societies in this era did not admit women, supposedly because they had difficulty keeping secrets. The target of the warning about "unprincipled men" was surely John C. Bennett, who still held the position of assistant church president, but it also served to squelch rumors about Smith himself by honoring women with the authority to judge for themselves. If men attempted to teach them things "contrary to the old established morals & virtues & scriptural laws," they should dismiss them as "liars & base impostors . . . whether they are prophets, Seers, or revelators; <u>Patriarchs</u>, <u>twelve Apostles</u>, <u>Elders</u>, <u>Priests</u>, Mayors, Generals, City Councillors, Aldermen, Marshalls, Police, Lord Mayors or the Devil."[34]

Most of the men who signed the letter, as well as the great majority of the women who heard it read, were surely unaware of the Prophet's heterodox sealings. Those who knew of or had participated in plural sealings no doubt believed that they conformed to "scriptural laws." As readers of the Bible, they knew that the ancient patriarchs had plural wives. They also believed that Joseph Smith was a prophet. By the time the Relief Society was organized, he had likely been sealed to five Nauvoo women. Emma may or may not have known about these sealings. Her insistence on tracking down rumors can be interpreted as anxiety over her husband's behavior or concern for his (and her own) reputation.

Some biographers assume that Joseph invented the doctrine of plural marriage in order to justify illicit relations with vulnerable young women. There is some evidence to support that assumption. After the breakup in Kirtland, one former friend spread rumors that Joseph had been involved with a household servant. Later, in Nauvoo, he had himself sealed to young women who lived with his family. But the early Nauvoo sealings do not fit this profile. His first Nauvoo wife was twenty-seven-year-old Louisa Beaman, a longtime family friend. His next sealings were to two sisters who were already married to other men. Zina Jacobs was twenty-one; Presendia Buell was thirty-two. His sealing to Agnes Coolbrith Smith in January 1842 may have been an attempt to replicate the Old Testament practice of a man marrying his brother's widow. She was thirty-one. Patty Sessions, who was sealed to Joseph a week before the organization of the Female Relief Society, was a forty-seven-year-old midwife. The one thing all these women had in common was intense religiosity. Louisa died young. Agnes eventually left, but Zina, Presendia, and Patty became powerful leaders among women after Joseph's death.[35]

To understand the emergence of plural marriage in Nauvoo, we must attend to what these women and others like them cared about. The letter from the city council ended with allusions to a developing theology of eternal marriage. Without any reference to plurality, it assured the sisters that they had the power to bestow glory not only upon their husbands but ultimately upon themselves, that they might become "an ornament unto those to whom you belong, and rise up and crown them with honors, & by so doing . . . be crown'd with honor in heav'n and . . . sit upon thrones."[36]

Eliza Snow valued such teachings. Although she dutifully kept minutes of the routine business of the society, she was even more interested in the Prophet's theological notions. In her mind, these were the "something better" he had promised when he rejected her written Constitution. According to her minutes, his sermons frequently drew parallels between the new female society and existing male quorums. He said that the Relief Society president and her counselors should preside over their society "just as the Presidency preside over the Church," and that if they needed additional officers, these should "be appointed and set apart, as Deacons, Teachers &c. are among us."[37] At the third meeting, he promised "to make of this Society a kingdom of priests as in Enoch's day—as in Pauls day."[38]

On April 28, responding to complaints that the sisters were overstepping their authority by laying on hands to heal the sick, Smith alluded to the promise given in the New Testament that spiritual gifts would follow all those who believed, assuring them that these signs of faith would be given to all believers "whether male or female." He asked the sisters "if they could not see by this sweeping stroke, that wherein they are ordained," concluding, "If the sisters should have faith to heal the sick, let all hold their tongues, and let every thing roll on." He urged members to place confidence in their society's leaders and arm them with their prayers, adding that "the keys of the kingdom are about to be given to them, that they may be able to detect every thing false—as well as to the Elders."[39] For sisters to be armed with keys was no small thing.

Smith predicted that within ten years the queens of the earth would bring their millions to the society for the relief of the poor. He encouraged the members to be charitable, but he also emphasized the authority of female leaders.

> This Society is to get instruction thro' the order which God has established—thro' the medium of those appointed to lead—and I now turn the key to you in the name of God and this Society shall rejoice and knowledge and intelligence shall flow down from this time.[40]

In a rare editorial comment, Eliza added, "The spirit of the Lord was pour'd out in a very powerful manner, never to be forgotten by those present on that interesting occasion."[41]

The concept of a formal ecclesiastical organization for women may have been new to the sisters, but they had no difficulty with the idea that females as well as males were endowed with the gifts of the spirit. Since the earliest days of the Church, they had exercised the gifts of healing, prophecy, and speaking in tongues, and they intended to develop those gifts as they cared for the poor and uplifted the morals of their community. On April 19, the Relief Society gathered in the Lodge Room for a special meeting to admit new members. Neither Emma nor Joseph was present. After admitting the new members, Sarah Cleveland, who was conducting in Emma's absence, said that because there was not much additional business to attend to, she thought the sisters might "spend the time in religious exercises before the Lord." She established the theme of the meeting by acknowledging "the happiness she felt in the present association of females."[42]

Elizabeth Durfee built on that comment by testifying that the blessing she had received from the sisters after the last meeting had done her as much good as any she had ever had, affirming that she had been healed, and observing that she "thought the sisters had more faith than the brethren." Presendia Buell rose to say that, even though she lived too far away from Nauvoo to attend many meetings, she rejoiced in having been admitted to membership. Then, as Eliza's minutes described it, "Miss Snow . . . said she had a blessing for Mrs. Buel." Alluding to the scripture in which the Apostle Paul spoke of the Church as the body of Christ, Eliza told

Presendia that, just "as the spirit of a person pervades every member of the body, so shall the Spirit of the Lord which pervades this Society be with her," adding that she would be able to contribute a great deal to the Society and "warm up the hearts of those who are cold and adamant."[43]

One of the hearts Presendia had been unable to "warm up" belonged to her own husband. Although Norman Buell had joined the Church at the same time as his wife, he had become an unbeliever and bitter opponent of the work. He may not have known that his wife and her sister Zina had already been sealed to Joseph Smith.[44] Sarah Cleveland ended the meeting by speaking in tongues. The midwife Patty Sessions interpreted her offering, reassuring the sisters that "God was well pleas'd with this Society and . . . would pour out upon the members generally the gift of prophecy." Eliza noted that nearly every woman present had spoken during the meeting and that "the spirit of the Lord like a purifying stream, refreshed every heart."[45]

Although members of the new society sought spiritual refreshment, they were also deeply concerned about the material needs of their fellow Saints, especially the plight of widows, poor laborers, and newly arrived immigrants. As they became better organized, they exerted social pressure by "discountenancing" those who refused to pay just debts to widows. They accepted offerings in kind as well as in cash, accepting old and new clothing, household provisions, and exchanges of labor in palm-leaf braiding, knitting, and sewing.[46] Joseph Smith had introduced them to doctrinal mysteries, but without his instruction, they showed themselves well versed in the kind of "mysteries" Apostle Heber Kimball liked to talk about when he told congregations, "It is a great mystery that an Elder in this church should want a pair of briches" and the Saints not supply it.[47]

Eliza's minutes show how the sisters provided "briches" to a man in need. When one woman said she had coarse linen, or tow, to spare, another offered to spin it, two others donated cotton thread for weft, and a fifth proposed doing the weaving.[48] This was the sort of household industry Eliza and other nineteenth-century poets liked to celebrate. In a poem published in *Times and Seasons* shortly before the founding of the Relief Society, she asked, "Now who, beneath proud Fashions' peal, / Will *dare* draw music from the wheel, / Or regulate the kitchen, when / Eliza stops, to wield the pen?"[49] Her minutes show that at least some women in this burgeoning river town still knew how to spin and weave. In a typical gesture, Mary Woolley, whose husband, Edwin, was a leading merchant, said she had red yarn that she had planned to use for a carpet, but had decided it would "do more good in mittens & will contribute it for the sisters to knit." Over the months of the society's operation, the minutes show the intertwining of household production with commerce, as in Sarah Kimball's original scheme of providing cloth for other women to sew. Many contributions were in cash. Woolley was generous in offering goods from her husband's store.[50]

In her poetry, Eliza expressed some frustration that so much of the society's energy had been devoted to putting down scandal. In a witty poem published in *The Wasp,* a Nauvoo newspaper edited by Joseph Smith's brother William, she disdained the "Poor brainless skull!" that admitted every idle tale, then spread it abroad with a flapping tongue. In a tribute to the Relief Society published a few days later, she honored its responsibility "To put the tattler's coinage, scandal, down, / And make corruption feel its with'ring frown." For her, the primary purpose of the society was not moral reform but charity. The Relief Society, she wrote, was "an Institution form'd to bless / The poor, the widow, and the fatherless," and to extend with open heart "the friendly hand / To hail the stranger, from a distant land."[51]

The organization of the Female Relief Society of Nauvoo gave new visibility to female enterprise in Nauvoo and to spiritual gifts long practiced among Latter-day Saint sisters. Without question, it expanded the place of women in the organizational life of the Church. In perhaps predictable ways, it also exposed the limits of their authority. Like the broader church government on which it was modeled, it was dependent on both the will of its members and the voice of its leaders. That Emma Smith was simultaneously president of the Relief Society and the legal wife of the Prophet gave her immense power, and at the same time a troubling new vulnerability, as she and her sisters coped with the dimly glimpsed and still inchoate implications of plurality.

By late June, Eliza was confronting the contradictory promises in the strange new teachings emerging in Nauvoo.

"a day of peculiar interest to my feelings"

Inside the ledger in which she kept the Relief Society minutes, Eliza wrote: "This Book, was politely presented to the Society by Elder W. Richards: on the 17th of March, AD. 1842."[52] In the more ladylike journal in which she began her personal diary, she acknowledged, "This Album

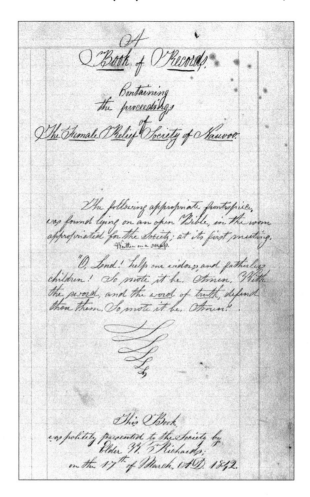

Title page of Nauvoo
Relief Society minutes,
1842. Willard Richards,
who was then serving
as Joseph Smith's
scribe, provided the
ledger. *(Church History
Library, Salt Lake City.
© Intellectual Reserve.)*

was politely presented to Eliza R. Snow by Mrs. Sarah M. Kimball City
of Nauvoo March, 1842."[53] That the two books were "politely" presented
in the same city in the same month suggests that Kimball, like Richards,
offered Eliza a volume in which to keep minutes. When Kimball's sewing
society became the church-sponsored Relief Society, Eliza set Sarah's gift
aside for later use.

Three months after the organization of the Relief Society, she picked it
up, inscribed the date, June 29, 1842, and wrote, "This is a day of peculiar
interest to my feelings." Then she stopped, unable to describe either the
day or her feelings. "Reflecting on past occurrences, a variety of thoughts
have presented themselves to my mind in regard to events which have
chas'd each other in rapid succession in the scenery of human life."[54]
What events? Whose thoughts? Which scenery? She could not say. She

had a secret so startling and, to her mind, sacred that she could neither reveal it nor totally keep it to herself.

Twenty-five years later, she acknowledged that on the day she began her diary she had been "married or sealed" to Joseph Smith. Depending on how one counts, she was somewhere between the sixth and the thirteenth woman to accept that honor.[55] By the time of his death two years later, Smith was purportedly allied to thirty or forty women, this during a period when he was managing an increasingly complex ecclesiastical organization, overseeing land distribution in a rapidly growing city, directing the construction of a massive temple, preaching and teaching in public and in private, and outrunning enemies determined to serve warrants or kidnap him and return him to Missouri to face trial for supposedly plotting Boggs's assassination. In such a setting, it is hard to imagine what Eliza's "marriage" actually meant. None of the traditional criteria applied. The ceremony was performed by Brigham Young and witnessed by Eliza's friend and landlord Sarah Cleveland, but there was no public acknowledgment of the vows, no cohabitation, and apparently no promise of material support. No one knows whether Joseph Smith's relationship with Eliza involved sex.[56]

Nevertheless, the events of that June day provoked her first attempt to keep a prose record of her own life. "As an individual, I have not passed altogether unnoticed by Change," she began. The changes she noted in the next few lines seem both innocuous and oddly specific.

> Two weeks and two days have pass'd since an intimation was presented of my duty and privilege of remaining in the city of the saints in case of the removal of my father's family: one week and two days have transpired since the family left, and though I rejoice in the blessing of the society of the saints, and the approbation of God; a lonely feeling will steal over me before I am aware. [57]

Somehow, the departure of her parents from Nauvoo had become mixed up with a whole lot of other things that had happened in the previous sixteen days.

Was that unspoken "duty and privilege" a promise of employment, a place to stay when her parents departed, or a proposal that she violate every rule of female behavior she had been taught by acquiescing to an alliance with a married man, a person she revered as a prophet of God? She could not say. Eliza's situation was indeed fraught with peril. Single and seemingly beyond the normal age of marriage, she was responsible for her own support. Like other women in her situation, she alternately taught school and worked with her needle.

As she bent over her diary, the sky darkened outside her window and a torrent of rain and hail descended. "O God," she wrote, "is it not enough that we have the pre-possessions of mankind—their prejudices and their hatred to contend with but must we also stand amid the rage of elements?" Then, as if frightened by her own fears, she quickly added, "I will put my trust in Him who is mighty to save."[58] She did not make another entry in her diary for a month.

Eliza had reason to worry. By June, the rumors that had roiled the early meetings of the Relief Society had erupted into open conflict. On June 18, in a huge outdoor meeting near the temple, Smith charged Dr. John C. Bennett with seducing women by falsely claiming priesthood authority. Once, Bennett had seemed invincible. Now he was in disgrace, banished from the Masonic lodge and excommunicated from the Church.[59] After he left Nauvoo for Springfield, he turned the charge of sexual misconduct on Smith himself. Adding stories about secret rituals and avenging warriors, he carried his crusade to St. Louis and beyond. By late summer, he was lecturing on the East Coast to promote a book-length exposé.[60]

Forced to explain why he had spent so much time with a people he

Portrait of John Cook Bennett from his book, *A History of the Saints: Or, An Expose of Joe Smith and Mormonism,* 1842. Like Joseph Smith and many other frontier Americans, Bennett took pride in his militia rank. *(Photograph Courtesy Harvard University Library.)*

considered despicable, he insisted that he had only joined the Saints in order to expose them. Surely, any patriotic man would have done the same had he discovered an insidious plot to lick up the nation like salt and drop its citizens "into the immense labyrinth of glorious prophetic dominion!"[61] Not all the accusations were original with him. He revived the story that had circulated in April, about a sister shut in a room for several days while church leaders tried to induce her to believe in the validity of having two wives.[62]

There may have been some truth to that story. In July an affidavit signed by an English convert named Martha Brotherton not only showed up in a St. Louis newspaper but was reprinted in the generally sympathetic *New York Herald.* Brotherton charged that when she arrived in Nauvoo, in January 1842, Brigham Young and Heber C. Kimball attempted to convince her to become Young's plural wife. Something like this may have happened, since Young and Kimball were both among the earliest Nauvoo men to accept plural marriage, but Bennett probably had a hand in transforming the story into a semi-comic narrative in which Brotherton appears as a young innocent and Kimball and Young as buffoons.[63]

Through the summer and fall, church leaders were kept busy gathering affidavits and printing newspapers and broadsides in an effort to refute Bennett's charges. Competing narratives offered a bald choice. Smith was either a duplicitous lecher or a maligned prophet of God. Bennett was either a lying reprobate or a courageous whistle-blower. The portraits of women were equally polarized. In Bennett's exposé, Brotherton was "a very good-looking, amiable, and accomplished English lady, of highly respectable parentage." In the testimony of her brother-in-law John McIlwrick, she was a young woman who had earlier "stooped to many actions which would be degrading to persons of common decency, such as lying on the top of a young man when he was in bed, and seeking Aristotle's work from a young seaman's box." (The reference is to *Aristotle's Masterpiece,* a popular manual used in this period both by folk healers and midwives and by men seeking titillating pictures of women's bodies.)[64]

On July 23, Emma proposed that Relief Society sisters take up their pens to express their feelings "in reference to Dr. Bennett's character." She said Bennett had warned her that any response by the society "would be the means of a mob forth coming," but she said that she wasn't afraid of mobs, that the sisters had "nothing to do but to fear God and keep the commandments."[65] By the end of July, the Relief Society had gathered more than a thousand names attesting to Joseph Smith's virtue, honesty, and integrity.[66] Eliza helped deliver the petition, noting, in what was only the second entry in her diary, that she had "just returned from Quincy, where I visited the Governor in company with Mrs. Emma Smith." Although the governor had received them with "affability and politeness" and assured them of his protection, Eliza was wary about relying on his promises: "it remains for time and circumstance to prove the sincerity of his professions."[67]

On August 31, Joseph met with the Relief Society. "All the fuss and all the stir against me, is like the jack in the lantern, it cannot be found," he assured them. "Altho' I do wrong, I do not the wrongs that I am charg'd with doing—the wrong that I do is thro' the frailty of human nature like other men. No man lives without fault." He praised the Relief Society for having taken "the most active part in my welfare against my enemies."[68] He also rallied the brethren, calling a special conference in which, according to Wilford Woodruff, "three or four hundred Elders were called upon to go into the vineyard."[69]

When Sarah Cleveland, whom Eliza referred to in her diary as "my excellent friend Mrs. C.," moved to a farm outside the city in August, Eliza was left without a home. Emma came to her rescue in what appears to have been a gesture of friendship rather than an invitation to polygamous cohabitation. Living in the Smith house gave Eliza a perch from which to observe an unfolding drama. Between August 3 and October 12, she made only thirteen entries in her diary. All but three referred to attempts by Missouri officials to extradite the Prophet to answer the charge that he had plotted the attempted assassination of Boggs.[70]

On August 18, she reported that men in disguise had been sighted at a local tavern. A week later, news came that the Missourians had secured a new writ and would soon attempt to serve it. Everything remained ominously quiet for several days. On Saturday evening, Joseph "met in the large drawing room with a respectable number of those considered trustworthy." He counseled them to proceed on their autumn missions as planned. Eliza busied herself with needlework to help them prepare.[71] On September 4, she wrote:

> The little season of quietude with which we have been bless'd for a few days, has gone by, and our City is again infested with some eighteen or twenty men, who are lying in wait, for the blood of the innocent!

Yesterday, Pitman from Quincy and Ford from Mo. with another stranger arrived about one o'clock at the house of Prst. Smith, who having a moment's notice, left the dinner table, where he was seated and made his escape. Pitman enquired for him and ask'd permission to search the house. Mrs. S. said she had no objection if he had the proper authority. Pitman said he had <u>no authority</u> but with her consent he proceeded to search, preceded by John Boynton and D. Huntington, who Mrs. S. requested to show them into the rooms.[72]

Dimick Huntington was a solid supporter, a man who had fought in Missouri and who in the autumn of 1841 had purportedly officiated at ceremonies sealing his sisters Zina Jacobs and Presendia Buell to Smith. John Boynton had been an "on-again, off-again" church member for years, but at this point he, too, seems to have been on the Prophet's side. The two men succeeded in diverting the writ servers while Joseph slipped out the back door, through a corn patch, to the redbrick store, where Elizabeth and Newel Whitney hid him until he could get to another refuge under cover of night.[73]

By this point, the Whitneys' seventeen-year-old daughter, Sarah Ann, may also have become one of Joseph's plural wives. Two documents relating to this marriage survive in Church archives. The first, dated July 18, 1842, and given in the language of revelation, instructed Sarah's father to officiate at the ceremony by asking the couple to join hands and mutually covenant to be each other's companions so long as they both should live. He was to do so in his own name and in the name of his wife, and by virtue of the Holy Melchizedek priesthood. The second document is a letter in Joseph Smith's handwriting, dated August 27, 1842, in which the exiled prophet begged the Whitneys and their daughter to visit him in his "lonely retreat." He was determined "to git the fullness of my blessings sealed upon our heads." The language is curious. It may allude to a promise in the revelation that by giving their daughter to Joseph, the Whitneys were forging an eternal bond between Joseph, themselves, their progenitors, and their descendants.[74]

Joseph warned the Whitneys against coming on a day when Emma was planning a visit, for "then you cannot be safe, but when she is not here, there is the most perfect safty; only be careful to escape observation, as much as possible." Some have interpreted this passage as evidence that Emma did not know about her husband's secret marriage to Sarah, others that Joseph was worried about his friends' safety if his enemies followed Emma to his hiding place. Either of these assumptions is plausible. No one knows what Emma knew at this point.[75]

Smith was in and out of hiding for much of the autumn. In a poem written during one of his episodes away from home, Eliza mused on a portrait displayed in the house. She found the image unsatisfying.

> It is only a picture! for where is the speech,
> That most noble conductor of thought
> With which thou art gifted the nations to teach,
> And by which we desire to be taught?

To Eliza, the frame around the portrait held her beloved Prophet "like a prisoner bound," offering little sense of the living man.[76]

Eliza's personal diary has some of the stiffness of that portrait. It documents Joseph's presence but little of his speech, and it offers nothing that directly alludes to an intimate relationship with him. Eliza noted when Smith "left" or "was taken," but only once did she offer a glimpse of his teachings. In this regard, the diary diverged dramatically from the Relief Society minutes, which are filled with his words. Ironically, the formality of verse gave her more scope for self-expression. The poems she copied into her diary (and sometimes published) show how she used her facility with words to create a place for herself in his life. In October, Emma was confined to bed for almost two weeks with an extended bout of chills and fever. Since "Prest Smith" was once again in hiding, Eliza sent him an animated little missive that not only reassured him of Emma's condition but of her own role as witness:

> So, for your consolation permit me to tell
> That your Emma is <u>better</u>—she soon will be <u>well</u>;
> Mrs. Durfee stands by her, night & day like a friend
> And is prompt every call—every wish to attend;
> Then pray for your Emma, but indulge not a fear,
> For the God of our forefathers smiles on us here.[77]

The pronoun "us" in the last line brought Eliza into the circle with Emma and her nurse, "Mrs. Durfee."

Although Eliza never explicitly addressed her own feelings for the

Prophet, a poem she inscribed to an unidentified "Miss L. for the Bridal Morning" may reflect her own idealized view of the man she later dared call her husband:

> My bosom's best affections
> I never could resign,
> Until thy goodness drew them forth,
> And now my heart is thine. . . .
> The world has smil'd upon me—
> I scorn its flattery,
> For nought but thy approving look,
> Is happiness to me.[78]

If so, it was Smith's "goodness," not just his person, that attracted her. She was in love with an ideal as much as with a person.

Bennett's exposé placed her and the other women who had been secretly "sealed or married" to the Prophet in an extraordinarily difficult position. Defending him, they were forced to hide their own relationships from their fellow Saints as well as from the world, and perhaps even from one another. In the opening stanza of an unpublished and perhaps unfinished poem that she copied into her diary in September, Eliza lamented:

> O, how shall I compose a thought
> Where nothing is compos'd?
> How form ideas, as I ought
> On subjects not disclos'd?[79]

What did it mean to be "sealed" to a man who was already married to another? If her relationship with Joseph wasn't adultery or polygamy, what was it?

"Adulterors fornicators & evil persons"

On May 27, Wilford for the first time hinted at the scandals engulfing Nauvoo, writing that church leaders, in alliance with the "virtuous part" of the community, were "making an exhertion . . . to clense the Church from Adulterors fornicators & evil persons for their are such persons crept into our midst."[80] The minutes of the Nauvoo High Council fill in this bald statement with names and places and the sort of detail that social historians love. Obviously, rumors like those that animated the meetings of the Female Relief Society were also disrupting the lives of persons who normally lived their lives outside the purview of official documents. The scandals fell especially hard on unattached women and on newcomers trying to find their places in a still-forming community. Claiming that the Prophet saw no sin in illicit alliances, aggressive lovers propositioned vulnerable girls, and people once married pursued new relationships without the benefit of divorce or permission of church officials. Rumors about Smith's teachings, counterfeit or not, appeared to have reinforced behaviors common in other communities at the time.[81]

On May 23, Catherine Fuller Warren (referred to alternately by her neighbors as "Mrs. Warren" and "Widow Fuller") testified that Bennett had "proposed unlawful intercourse" about a week after their first acquaintance. "I told him I was not guilty of such conduct and thought it would bring disgrace on the church if I should become pregnant. He said he would attend to that." Since Bennett was a physician, that charge may have seemed credible. Warren testified to having had relations five or six times over the past year with Chauncy Higbee, and once or twice each with three other men, but insisted, "John D. Bennett was the first man that seduced me—no man ever made the attempt before him."[82] Despite her self-confessed transgression, her willingness to incriminate Bennett saved her from church sanction. The Council unaminously forgave her and restored her to fellowship, since she "covenanted that she would hence forth do so no more."[83]

Judging from the depositions, the "virtuous part of the community" was composed of upright matrons who kept watch on suspect houses, noting who went in and out or had extended conversations across fences. These women kept track of young women who rode out with men, two on a horse, and came back late. Melinda Lewis testified that she frequently saw Darwin Chase go into Widow Fuller's house after dark and "thought he had no right to be there." One night, she and another neighbor rapped on the door. When there was no answer, they "pulled a curtain sideways that was hanging over a crack in the door" and soon after saw a man go inside. "We felt grieved because we knew our husbands were supplying her with fuel and we talked to her somewhat aggravating but for her own good." Although their rapping resulted in a conviction for breaking the peace, they were glad they had done it and happily testified before the

Council. Another woman admitted that the reason she had objected to admitting a "Sister Barriss" to the Female Relief Society was that this woman was too friendly with Fuller.[84]

Besides reflecting some of the same concern over reputation apparent in the Relief Society minutes, the women's statements also expose tensions over methods for providing relief to the poor. The men who were chopping wood for Widow Fuller were fulfilling a male responsibility to care for widows and the fatherless. They were probably acting under the direction of the local bishop or their own priesthood quorum. Their wives wanted to know that the recipient of their husband's labor was truly worthy. One can only imagine how they might feel if church leaders had instructed the men not only to provide wood for the unattached women but to marry them. There was already conflict in these neighborhoods over the sexual behavior of single women, especially those who were poor. Sarah Miller, another widow targeted by the Council, said Chauncy Higbee and the prophet's brother William both told her Joseph taught that "there was no harm to have sexual intercourse with women if they would keep it to themselves." When she heard the Prophet speak against such behavior in a lecture to the singing school, she decided she had been deceived, but Higbee assured her the Prophet spoke in such a manner "of necessity, on account of the prejudices of the people."[85]

The astonishing thing about these records is not that people were gossiping about the sex lives of important men, or that some women and men took advantage of salacious rumors to justify their own behavior, but that, in the midst of public turmoil, Smith continued to expand the practice of plural marriage. If retrospective dates are correct, he was sealed to Sarah Ann Whitney and perhaps one other woman in the midst of his conflict with Bennett. Brigham Young, a man well known for his prudence, may also have taken his first plural wife while the High Council was still trying to untangle accusations of extramarital sex.[86] Perhaps the dates are wrong. If not, Young must have been confident of his ability to distinguish between "plurality" as the Prophet taught it and the plebeian deviance described in court documents. That would, of course, have been much easier if plural "marriages" were purely spiritual. But if that was so, why the obsession with secrecy?

On the evening of July 14, Apostle Orson Pratt was seen drafting some sort of document in the printing office. The next day, a Nauvoo carpenter found a composition signed by Pratt lying in the road. It seemed to be a suicide note. Pratt had apparently heard rumors that his wife had been unfaithful to him while he was in England on a mission. Sarah Pratt claimed that Smith had attempted to seduce her. Smith insisted that Bennett, not he, was the culprit. Pratt did not know whom to believe. "I am a ruined man," he wrote. "My future prospects are blasted! The testimony upon both sides seems to be equal!" If Smith was lying, Pratt had been deceived by the man he had served for more than a decade. If Sarah was lying, his family was ruined. "Where then is my hope in this world?" he asked. "It is gone—gone not to be recovered!!"[87] The note, which survives in the Church Archives, shows that, even in despair, Pratt took time to proofread and correct his sentences. But his tone was alarming. Smith ordered a search party, fearing that the distraught Apostle was about to take his own life. Pratt eventually returned home, but refused to sign a petition attesting to Smith's good character, and was for a time dropped from the Quorum of the Twelve.[88]

Had Bennett been a more credible character, his assault on Smith might have been more effective. His exposés were so exaggerated and laced with fantasy that even today it is almost impossible to sort out what he actually knew from what he imagined or simply made up. The book he published in the fall was filled with long passages culled from other anti-Mormon writers and padded with quotations from English poetry. When he wanted to portray Smith as a blood-soaked tyrant, he pasted in patches from Shakespeare's history plays or *Hamlet*.[89] To enhance his descriptions of sexual perfidy, he lifted long passages from Lord Byron and other Orientalist poets, employing stereotypes common in European and American portrayals of Muslims and Jews.[90] His biggest mistake may have been slandering the members of the Female Relief Society by portraying their organization as a seraglio or harem set up to provide sexual services to "Holy Joe." "Was there ever known, in the history of the world, a more diabolical system than this?" he charged.[91]

A New York editor sympathetic to the Mormons dismissed Bennett's book as a collection of "newspaper trash." A Boston reviewer with little sympathy for the Saints was equally disdainful. He questioned whether it was right even to acknowledge such a "catchpenny" publication, arguing that, though Mormonism was a humbug, Bennett's diatribe was worse.[92] The Church fought back by printing affidavits attesting to Bennett's perfidy, by engaging in a newspaper war with hostile editors, and by calling missionaries to "deluge the States with a flood of truth."[93] At some point, Smith and his allies decided that trying to differentiate his teachings on plural marriage from Bennett's "iniquity" was not worth the risk. Outright denials that anything unusual was happening in Nauvoo seemed safer, and also more likely to restore public sympathy and internal cohesion. In the short run, that strategy worked. Called upon to defend the Prophet, the community rallied. Without question, the support of female leaders was essential. Most women, of course, knew nothing at all about plural marriage. At this point, those who did, remained loyal.

During all this excitement, Wilford's job was to keep the printing press going. At the end of July, he took a nightmarish journey to St. Louis to buy paper, an adventure that re-energized his passions as a diarist. He wrote that, after four days and nights waiting at the landing for a steamboat, he finally boarded a vessel loaded with seven thousand pigs. The water was low, and the smelly pigs were so heavy that the boat kept getting stuck on sandbars. As if that weren't enough, he was ill. "A severe cold has settelled through my body. I have the Rheumatism, teeth ake, head ake, bones ake, have got the musketoe fever, Bilious fever, & sick Stomack, & am fearful that if we run on to many more Sand bars & am many more weeks getting to St Louis & if the Musketoes do not favor me more than they have done, that it will be a question whether I ever reach home or not." He reached St. Louis and he did buy paper, but on the return trip, he coughed so hard he got a nosebleed. When the boat drew closer to Nauvoo, he went ashore and took the stage home; he arrived in Montrose on August 6, "in the midst of a Masonic possession." Finding the printing press stopped for want of paper, he went back down the river in a skiff to retrieve what he could, "rowing over the rapids back again." After the steamboat docked, he secured the rest of his cargo, then took to his bed for the next forty days. He attempted to attend a meeting to try the case of Orson Pratt, who was still refusing to support Smith, but he collapsed and had to be carried home. He may have been relieved to escape such a fractious hearing.[94]

By the end of the year, a new governor and assiduous work by the Church's lawyers resulted in a denial of Missouri's appeals for extradition. Joseph and Emma celebrated the occasion by hosting a lavish dinner on January 18, the sixteenth anniversary of their marriage. Wilford and Phebe Woodruff were there, with most of the other Apostles and their wives, as well as those who had accompanied Smith to Springfield for extradition hearings. Woodruff thought there were about seventy-five persons in attendance, so many that dinner had to be served in shifts. Joseph and

Emma waited on tables. Their guests told stories, sang songs, and shared jokes.[95] Adding to the joy of the season was Orson Pratt's return to full fellowship. He had "repented in dust & ashes as it were of opposing Joseph & the Twelve," Wilford wrote.[96]

Eliza composed a song for the occasion that ended with a gracious tribute to the party's host and hostess:

> Now let the Prophet's soul rejoice—
> His noble Lady's too;
> While praise to God with heart and voice
> Is heard throughout Nauvoo.[97]

Read silently, these lines acknowledged the magnanimous (and monogamous) unity of Nauvoo's first couple. But when recited aloud or sung, "Lady's" might well have been "Ladies'." Perhaps no one noticed that beneath the harmonious sounds of jubilee lay the impending discord of plurality.

4

"a favor which I have long desired"

Nauvoo, Illinois, and a Journey East, 1843

When the Relief Society rallied against the accusations of John C. Bennett in July 1842, there may have been only two male polygamists in Nauvoo—Joseph Smith, who had been sealed to perhaps a dozen women, and Brigham Young, who had only recently acquired his first plural wife. Eighteen months later, twenty men and as many as seventy-six women, including first wives, were involved in some way.[1] In a city with a population of over ten thousand, that may seem like a small number, but it included Hyrum Smith, the Prophet's brother, plus six members of the Quorum of the Twelve Apostles, including Heber Kimball, Willard Richards, Orson Hyde, Parley Pratt, and John Taylor. Wilford Woodruff had not yet taken a plural wife, although he surely must have been aware of what was happening. Relatives of Joseph Smith's own wives were among the new polygamists. Eliza Snow's sister, Leonora, married old Isaac Morley by December 1843.[2]

Years later, many of those who accepted plural marriage in Nauvoo claimed they were horrified by the idea when it was first introduced. John Taylor said it made his flesh crawl. Lucy Walker compared it to "a thunderbolt" and said every feeling of her soul "revolted against it." Brigham Young claimed it was the first time in his life he had ever desired the grave.[3] Lorenzo Snow testified that Joseph, too, resisted the revelation until an angel "appeared before him with a drawn sword threatening him with destruction unless he went forward and obeyed the commandment."[4] Joseph apparently shared the story about the angel with Dimick Huntington, who passed it on to his sister Zina. She had earlier rejected the Prophet's proposal, but when she heard about the angel, she prayed and received "a testimony for my self that God had required that order to be established in this church."[5]

In these stories, resistance prepared the way for revelation. Heber C. Kimball's oldest daughter said her father shed "bushels of tears" when Smith told him he must take another wife. Unable to eat or sleep, he paced the floor, wringing his hands and weeping. When his wife, Vilate, asked him what was the matter, he could not bring himself to tell her. In desperation, she knelt in prayer and begged God to let her know why her husband was in such misery. A vision opened, and she saw "the principle of celestial marriage illustrated in all its beauty and glory." When she shared her epiphany with Heber, they rejoiced together.[6]

There is no reason to doubt that these earnestly religious people were shocked by the new teachings, or that they accepted plural marriage for the same reason they accepted Mormonism itself, because a vision, a feeling, or even an angel told them it was right. Yet autobiographies composed many years after the fact may exaggerate these sudden reversals. Although Eliza Snow declared in 1877 that plural marriage was "very repugnant" to her feelings, she did not use the word "repugnant" in the diary she began on the day she married Smith. She said the events of that day had been of "peculiar interest" to her feelings.[7] Nor is it apparent that she or any of the others fully understood what precisely they were being asked to do. Were these marriages as the world understood them? Or alliances being formed for millennial glory? Vilate Kimball may well have had a vision in 1842, but a few months later, she admitted she really didn't know much about the strange practice she had embraced.

Plural marriage did not drop out of the heavens fully formed. Nor was there a single path to its acceptance. Repugnance there was, but also curiosity and ambition to be part of an elite inner circle. Eliza Snow's diary suggests that, as early as 1843, a subset of Joseph's wives had bonded with one another through him. In the secrecy of Nauvoo, they forged a religious vocation. For some women, plural marriage offered spiritual and economic security. For a few, it was a way of defying convention, and for others a religiously sanctioned way of leaving a troubled marriage. After visiting Nauvoo, a Boston convert named Augusta Cobb whispered to a friend, "I have something to tell you that is *glorious*." One of several women who left legal husbands to embrace plurality, she became Brigham Young's second plural wife, in 1843.[8]

For some men, plurality was an answer to troubling sexual feelings. That was surely the case for William Clayton, an English immigrant who became Joseph's clerk. As we have seen, he agonized over his growing love for a woman named Sarah Crooks while serving as a missionary in Manchester, England. Joseph's teaching on plural marriage comforted him. When offered the privilege of taking another wife, he admitted it was "a favor which I have long desired."[9] His astonishingly candid diary is the only detailed contemporary account of plural relationships in Nauvoo. It not only recounts his own adventures with plurality but provides glimpses of Emma Smith's growing resistance to the practice. According to Clayton, her opposition led to the first written revelation on plural marriage, a document Clayton wrote down as Joseph dictated.

Clayton fancied himself a trusted confidant of the Prophet, and in some ways he was. Perhaps Joseph, who was under acute stress, found relief in unburdening himself to his bumbling but trusting junior clerk. He may not have known how much of what he said got into Clayton's diary. Because it did, we are able to document day-to-day struggles in the Smith household, at least as Clayton understood them. Clayton's writings enlarge fragmentary and veiled allusions to plurality in the writings of Heber and Vilate Kimball, Wilford Woodruff, and Eliza Snow. Beyond that, Clayton's anguished responses to his own domestic troubles provide entry points into the broader cultural context of Mormon plurality, including its relationship to nineteenth-century ideas about sex.

Although Mormon apologists and dissenters will continue to debate the character of Joseph Smith, it is impossible to understand his teachings without considering the complex lives of those who attempted to translate his precepts—including his advocacy of plurality—into practice.

"some instructions on the priesthood"

William Clayton grew up in Penwortham, England, a village southwest of the major industrial city of Preston. Educated by his schoolmaster father, he had secured work as a clerk by the time he and Ruth Moon married in 1836. She was nineteen and he twenty-two. In October 1838, he left Ruth and their year-old daughter with her parents, while he presided over the LDS Manchester Branch. In the fall of 1840, they, their two daughters, and their extended families sailed for America.[10] They settled briefly on the Iowa side of the Mississippi, where Ruth gave birth to a third daughter on May 6, 1841. In August, both the new baby and Ruth's father died.

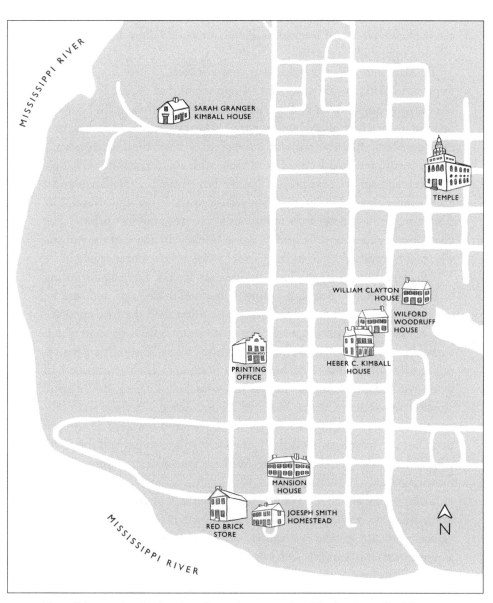

Map of Nauvoo showing location of some important sites. The drawings of buildings are not to scale. Although the lowest level of the temple was used for baptisms, the building was not completed until 1845. Wilford Woodruff's house was also under construction. *(Samantha Van Gerbig.)*

Soon William was bedridden with malaria. In September, he managed to harvest some of the family's half-frozen potatoes by working between fever fits. Ruth and her younger sister Lydia finished the work. In February 1842, Joseph Smith rescued William from sure failure as a farmer by offering him a job as a clerk.[11]

Residence in Nauvoo brought a secure income, better housing, and improved health. It also gave him an opportunity to pursue his musical interests. In England, he had mastered the violin and piano. In Nauvoo, he sang in the choir, played in the band, helped draft bylaws for the new Nauvoo Music Association, and attempted to learn the French horn.[12] When Ruth presented him, early in 1843, with their first son, his happiness seemed complete. He prayed that the boy would be "intelligent and a great genius," would live to see Jesus return to the earth, and would, like Abraham, produce progeny as numerous as the sands on the seashore. The Claytons gave their boy the middle name "Heber" in honor of the Apostle who had introduced them to the Gospel and was now a near neighbor.[13]

On March 7, 1843, William wrote that after a meeting regarding Church real estate, "Brigham Young called me on one side and said he wants to give me some instructions on the priesthood the first opportunity. He said the prophet had told him to do so and give me a favor which I have long desired."[14] There were, of course, many "favors" that Joseph might have offered his clerk, but it soon became clear that this one had to do with plural marriage. Joseph had somehow learned of William's attachment to Sarah Crooks. When William assured him there was nothing more between them than what was proper for "a brother and sister in the Church," Joseph responded, "It is your privilege to have all the wives you want." He even offered to loan William the money to bring Crooks from England.[15]

Long before she arrived in Nauvoo, William's attention had turned to his wife's twenty-three-year-old sister, Margaret. On April 22, he "conversed" with her "on the priesthood," a term that for him was becoming a euphemism for plurality. On April 24, she accompanied him on a trip to the county seat at Carthage to pay taxes. "She is a lovely woman," he wrote, "and desires to do right in all things and will submit to council with all her heart." Three days later, she was, in his words, "sealed up by the priesthood by the president and m. [married] to me." The "president" was of course Joseph Smith. That evening, he "told Mother in law concerning the priesthood," apparently breaking the news to Mother Moon that two of her daughters were now his wives.[16]

Marriage to Margaret did not alter William's feelings for Sarah Crooks, who arrived in Nauvoo on May 31. Delighted that she seemed "willing to comply with her privilege," he anticipated adding her to his kingdom.[17] Unfortunately, his relationship with Margaret had hit a bump. Less than six weeks after the wedding, she received a letter from Aaron Farr, a near neighbor who was about to return from a mission.[18] Alarmed by her reaction, William made her promise "she would not marry A if she can possibly avoid it. And if she ever feels disposed to marry she will tell me as soon as she thinks of it." A promise not to marry seems like a strange vow for a woman who had recently been "sealed up" by the priesthood. It took William a month to persuade Margaret to send a letter, which he dictated, telling Aaron she did not intend to marry him.[19]

Meanwhile, Joseph was facing obstacles of his own. One day, he was conferring in an upstairs room with Eliza Partridge, the daughter of close friends, who was living with his family as a household helper. When Emma banged on the door and tried to force the lock, Joseph calmly opened it and told her he had been talking to the girl about a matter concerning a hired hand and did not want to be disturbed. She was "much irritated." Years later, Eliza and her sister Emily testified that they were both sealed to Smith in 1843, first in secret, later with Emma present. They said that after the second sealing, Emma insisted that they leave the house.[20] Most biographers believe Emma vacillated in her support for plural marriage, sometimes acquiescing to Joseph's sealings, sometimes resisting. Even if she had agreed to some sort of bond with the Partridge sisters, she was understandably disturbed by this incident. She did not want her children to see their father meeting with a maidservant behind locked doors.[21]

Since Clayton was responsible for recording Relief Society contributions to the temple fund, he wanted to remain on good terms with Emma, who was still president of the society. She seemed friendly, perhaps too friendly. When she spontaneously presented him with fabric and trimmings for a waistcoat, Joseph was disturbed.[22] He asked William point-blank if he had "used any familiarity with E." William assured him that he had not. Joseph warned his young clerk that Emma might try to make a play for him. "She thought that if he would indulge himself she would too," William confided to his diary, adding that the Prophet "cautioned me very kindly for which I felt thankful." He did not seem alarmed by the notion that Joseph might "indulge himself." Joseph was his hero, and he was determined to follow his lead. "I would rather die than lose my interest in the celestial kingdom," he wrote.[23]

The turmoil from within the Smith household was soon matched by trouble from without. On June 13, Joseph and Emma left Nauvoo to visit her sister near Inlet Grove, Illinois. They were sitting at dinner when two officers with loaded pistols presented Joseph with writs signed by the governors of Missouri and Illinois. Unable to extradite him on the attempted assassination of Boggs, the Missourians had pulled up an old charge of treason. After learning of the writ, William rode 190 miles on the Prophet's best horse to warn him. When he arrived too late, he sped back to Nauvoo by carriage and steamboat to alert church leaders that Joseph had been captured. Hyrum quickly assembled volunteers, who succeeded in intercepting the sheriff's party before it could cross over to Missouri. They demanded a writ of habeas corpus and insisted on returning the Prophet to Nauvoo.[24]

Joseph rode into the city in triumph, welcomed by a band, a number of ladies on horseback, and a parade of loyal citizens in carriages.[25] William described him greeting his mother with "tears rolling down his cheek" as his seven-year-old son implored, "The Missourians won't take you away again, will they?" While waiting for action on the writ submitted to a friendly Nauvoo court, Joseph treated the Missourians to dinner.[26] Wilford Woodruff thought he heaped coals of fire upon the heads of his enemies by "setting them to the head of his table & giving them the best he had served unto them by his own wife the vary woman they had refused to [let] see her husband as he was taken from her by the force of Arms unlawfully."[27]

Emma gave Eliza Snow all the "particulars" of the capture. Eliza worked the story into a ballad. In her version, the sheriff had not just served the writ. He had thrust a cocked pistol to Joseph's head and snarled, "God damn you I will shoot you." When he repeated the threat, Joseph supposedly turned to him, opened his shirt, and said "shoot away."[28]

> He bared his breast before them
> But as they hurried near
> A fearfulness came o'er them—
> It was the coward's fear. . . .
>
> "What means your savage conduct?
> Have you a lawful Writ?
> To any LEGAL process
> I cheerfully submit."

"Here," said the lawless ruffians
"Is our authority;"
And drew their pistols nearer
In rude ferocity.[29]

To Eliza, the Missourians were "kidnappers," even though they had an extradition order signed by two governors. When the Nauvoo court ruled the charges insufficient, the governor of Illinois, fearing a border war, denied the Missourians another attempt. Once again, Joseph had been rescued.

"a Revelation consisting of 10 pages"

Joseph's jubilant return did nothing to solve the conflict with Emma. Hyrum, who had only recently become converted to polygamy himself, felt that if she could read a revelation on the subject, she would be convinced. He urged Joseph to write out the ideas he had so far shared only in bits and pieces. Doubtful that this would make a difference, Joseph complied. On July 12, 1843, William "wrote a Revelation consisting of 10 pages on the order of the priesthood." The Prophet dictated it line by line, and then had him read it back to make sure every word was correct. It took him three hours to get it onto the page.[30]

It began with a question: How could God justify ancient prophets' having many wives and concubines? Rather than going straight to the answer, it laid out the conditions under which any earthly association might be approved by God. The language was legalistic: "All covenants, contracts, bonds, obligations, oaths, vows, performances, connections, associations, or expectations, that are not made and entered into and sealed by the Holy Spirit of promise, of him who is anointed . . . are of no efficacy, virtue, or force in and after the resurrection from the dead." For Latter-day Saints, this was familiar doctrine: agreements made on earth were only binding in heaven if performed by one with authority.[31] The more explosive point came next. Marriages contracted through this "Holy Spirit of promise" not only endured in the heavens, but allowed men and women to achieve unimagined heights of exaltation: "Then shall they be gods, because they have no end; therefore shall they be from everlasting to everlasting, because they continue."

Today, a biologist might express the concept of continuance as the ability to pass on one's genes, or a philosopher as the capacity to extend some essential part of the self beyond death. In Smith's cosmos, biology and philosophy merged. Reproduction was the great work of heaven. Only by multiplying could a person achieve ultimate glory. Those who failed to marry might be saved, but would remain single in the eternities, serving others as ministering angels.[32] There was no reference to polygamy in this part of the revelation. It spoke of "a man" and "a wife." Not until verse 30 did it return to the original question, explaining that Abraham received his wives from God. "This promise is yours also," it continued. "Go ye, therefore, and do the works of Abraham; enter ye into my law and ye shall be saved."[33]

In less exalted language, the last section dealt with Joseph's conflict with Emma. It urged both of them to repent of their transgressions and forgive each other. Although it told Emma that God had seen her sacrifices and her obedience to his commands, it insisted that she "receive all those that have been given unto my servant Joseph, and who are virtuous and pure before me," and it enjoined her "to abide and cleave unto my servant Joseph, and to none else." If she did this, she would receive great blessings. If she did not, she would be destroyed.[34] Alluding to the Biblical story of Sarah's offering Hagar to Abraham, the revelation explained that if a man taught his wife "the law of my priesthood" and she refused to concur with his decision to take another wife, he was "exempt from the law of Sarah" and could move forward without her consent.[35]

As Joseph predicted, Emma was incensed. When Hyrum read her the revelation, she "said she did not believe a word of it." How could she? For sixteen years, she had been Joseph's partner in triumph and in poverty. She had borne his children, kept his household through adversity, generously shared what few resources and what little space she had with strangers as well as with his many relatives and friends. She had endured rumors of his infidelity, had petitioned public officials and her own relatives for help. Was she now to be cast out if she could not accept a revelation that, while offering her sympathy and forgiveness of her sins, also consigned her to darkness if she did not acquiesce in his obsessive acquisition of wives?

Some historians assume she was primarily opposed to Joseph's involvement with other women. William Clayton's account suggests that she was also concerned about the well-being of her family. If Joseph's disdain for community norms once again led to his arrest, or worse, she would be left alone and penniless with four children to raise.

The day after recording the revelation, William witnessed an agreement between Joseph and Emma, giving her deeds to a steamboat he had purchased for the Church, the *Maid of Iowa,* and to more than sixty city lots in Nauvoo. "They both stated their feelings on many subjects and wept considerable," he wrote. "O may the Lord soften her heart that she may be willing to keep and abide by his Holy Law."[36] Under Illinois law Emma probably could have divorced Joseph. Instead, she appears to have used the threat of divorce to get a financial settlement she believed would give her some security.

On July 20, Eliza Snow received a mysterious visitor. "Sister [blank] called to see me," she wrote. There is little mystery about who this was. In her diary, Eliza without exception referred to other women, even her closest friends, with a polite "Mrs" or "Miss." She called only two persons "Sister," her own biological sister and "Sister Emma." "Her appearance very plainly manifested the perturbation of her mind," Eliza wrote. "How strangely is the human countenance changed when the powers of darkness reign over the empire of the heart!" There is no way of knowing what Emma said to Eliza, but it is obvious she expected her to feel guilty. Eliza's heart must have been pounding, but she claimed, "I felt as calm as the summer eve, and received her as smilingly as the playful infant, and my heart as sweetly reposed upon the bosom of conscious innocence, as infancy reposes in the arms of paternal tenderness & love."[37] Having reduced herself to a state of infancy, Eliza denied any moral responsibility for Emma's distress. Emma may have expected contrition or sympathy. Instead, her once-close friend consigned her to darkness.

A few weeks later, Emma confronted William Clayton about two letters she had found in Joseph's pocket. "They appeared to be from E R Snow," he noted, adding that Emma seemed "vexed and angry."[38] Emma probably would not have been pleased had she read the poem Eliza inscribed in her journal shortly after this encounter.

Tis good—'tis soothing to the mind
If friends we cherish, prove unkind
And meet us in an angry mood;
To know we've always done them good.[39]

"My soul loves M"

On July 16, Smith preached at the grove near the temple on the "law of the priesthood." Although he said nothing about the revelation on plural marriage he had recently dictated, he did capture one essential aspect of it—"that a man must enter into an everlasting covenant with his wife in this world in order to have her in the next." A few days later, he came to the Clayton house and "pronounced a sealing blessing" upon William and Ruth, who "mutually entered into an everlasting covenant with each other." Alas, affirming his commitment to his first wife did nothing to repair the growing rift with his second. Aaron Farr had come home from his mission, and Margaret was miserable. "She appears almost to hate me and cannot bear to come near me," William lamented.[40]

In desperation, he asked Margaret if she wanted their covenant revoked. All she would say was, "If it had not been done it should not be." William pressed her. Would it make a difference if she knew that Aaron would still take her "under all circumstances"? Again, she refused to give a clear answer. He was beside himself. He wanted her, but he wanted her willingly. He prayed that she would learn to "love those who she ought."[41]

By late July, his mother-in-law, Mother Moon, had become concerned about their relationship. Although he had talked with her "about the Priesthood" on the day he and Margaret were sealed, she seems to have had only a rudimentary idea of what it meant. Mother Moon began to monitor the house she shared with the Claytons, threatening suicide when William spent most of a morning upstairs with Margaret.[42] On August 13, she went into the garden at evening to pray. When she didn't return, Margaret and her sister Lydia went outside and found their mother on her knees in a state of hysteria. As Clayton described it:

> She came into the bed room trembling and seemed as though she had been frightened but was altogether delirious Her feet and legs were cold and I feared she was going to die. She got into bed and we got some hot water to her feet and rubbed her legs and feet with flannel and went to bed. She soon seemed some better. From her conversation with Lydia this afternoon it seems she took President Joseph's remarks very deeply to heart and that with her fears for Margaret overwhelmed her.[43]

Smith had preached that day on sealing power, skirting the subject of plurality by emphasizing the broader mission of Elijah to turn the hearts of children to their fathers. "When a seal is put upon the father and mother, it secures their posterity, so that they cannot be lost," he proclaimed.[44]

Something about that sermon seems to have upset Mother Moon. Perhaps she feared that Margaret was about to offend God by rejecting the seal that the Prophet had placed upon her. Or was she herself at fault for questioning God's will? Spiritual issues were entangled with a more practical question: What if Margaret became pregnant? Smith may have sealed up her daughter by the power of the priesthood, but could he seal up the wagging tongues around them if such a thing should happen?

William had similar worries. Aaron Farr's family lived only a block away. When a friend hinted that the Farrs were conspiring against him, William pressed Margaret for information. She admitted she had told Aaron they had slept together. Once again she uttered that cryptic reminder: "If it never had been done, it should not be." The repetition suggests a proverb of some sort, an idiomatic response to a person in trouble. "If it never had been done" implied that if a person had not taken the first step, he wouldn't be suffering the consequences now. For William, that was small comfort. He now knew that Aaron had "a plea and a weapon" against him.[45]

The next day, Aaron's sister Diantha came to the Clayton house, distressed at the division between their families. She said "she almost felt disposed to go to every house in the city and tell all she knew and then come home and kill herself." Somehow, the Claytons and their friends had become trapped in a web of feelings so complex and intertwined that one woman's despair became another's vexation or delirium. What was a man to do? "My soul loves M," William lamented.[46]

Margaret was indeed pregnant. Judging from her delivery date, she conceived sometime between May 24 and June 1, roughly a month after their sealing.[47] Had this been an ordinary marriage, that would have been normal. Among plural wives, it was unprecedented. Scholars have long puzzled over the absence of documented births to women sealed to Joseph Smith.[48] Almost as startling is the scarcity of babies born to other plural wives in this period.[49]

Either sexual intercourse was a less essential part of these marriages, or couples were practicing some form of contraception. Some may have been aware of *coitus interruptus* (withdrawal before ejaculation), a practice advocated by Robert Dale Owen, the founder of socialist utopias in Ohio, but Mormons seem unlikely to have approved such a remedy.[50] The low conception rate in Nauvoo was probably a consequence of multiple factors—personal restraint, uncertainty about the meaning of sealing, fear of exposure, and limited opportunity. Couples had reason to feel anxious. Whatever their motivation, they were attempting to create a holy society while violating the most cherished norms of middle-class respectability.

Standards of male sexuality promoted by reform literature in this period urged restraint. Some experts argued that, even within marriage, too frequent indulgence in "venery" might drain a man's body of vital fluids. Others accepted the notion that respectable women were essentially passionless. Even those who challenged that idea believed that sexual arousal during pregnancy and lactation might affect the character as well as the health of the child.[51] It may not be accidental that so many Latter-day Saint men left on missions just before or after the birth of a child, or that William Clayton contracted his first plural marriage while Ruth had a young infant.

Although he desired to "do right," he couldn't always tell whether that meant denying or fulfilling his own impulses. In his confusion, he turned to others for affirmation—to Smith, who was simultaneously his employer, his mentor, his guide, his spiritual counselor, and his hero; and to Heber Kimball, who stood just below Smith in his estimation. By the summer of 1843, Smith had troubles of his own, and Kimball had left Nauvoo for an Eastern mission. Perhaps William turned to Ruth for affirmation. It is impossible to tell whether her invisibility in his diary indicates her support for his attempts at plurality or his indifference to her opinions. That she accepted the covenant offered them in June is one indication of the continuing vitality of their marriage. That she continued to bear a child every two years is another.

In mid-August, Joseph confided that Emma had "resisted the P[riesthood] in toto and he had to tell her he would relinquish all for her sake." He was afraid that if he acknowledged his secret sealings she would "pitch on him and obtain a divorce and leave him."[52] When Joseph reported that Emma was also "considerably displeased" over Margaret's situation, William's anxiety increased. He wrote:

> In the agony of mind which I have endured on this subject I said I was sorry I had done it at which Joseph told me not to say so. I finally asked him if I had done wrong in what I had done. He answered no you have a right to get all you can.[53]

It is not entirely clear what William thought he had done wrong. Since Smith had himself performed the ceremony, the sealing can't have been at issue. Was it the pregnancy? Had William been too quick to turn a spiritual bond into physical intimacy? More likely, the issue was whether he had violated a code of honor among men by marrying Margaret when he knew she had been claimed by Aaron Farr. Nauvoo men had internalized the modern notion that women had the right to accept or reject proposals of marriage, but, like other nineteenth-century Americans, they had not abandoned the idea that women were the wards if not the property of men. If a woman was sexually violated, it was her male protector—her brother, her father, or her spouse—who sued for damages. Margaret had no father or brother.[54] As her brother-in-law, Clayton was her closest legal protector—unless, of course, Aaron Farr came forth as her intended spouse. Even Smith's revelation appeared to acknowledge such a code, saying that a man might espouse a virgin without committing adultery as long as she had been "vowed to no other man."[55]

Joseph's strange comment that William had the right to "get all you can" disoriented him. Over and over again, he reassured himself, "My desire is to do right." In late August, he asked Mother Moon if she would allow Margaret to move upstairs with him and Ruth. "She appeared very rebellious and would not consent but said we might do as we had a mind." Given that he was the one who had asked for her permission, his comment is curious. Apparently, as in Joseph's revelation, a woman might "rebel" by not offering her consent when asked. William's goal was obviously not to solicit Mother Moon's permission but to get her to affirm his decision to sleep with her daughter. When she turned the query back to him, telling him they "might do as we had a mind," she made him responsible for his own behavior.[56]

He diverted himself by thinking about other potential wives. The arrangement with Sarah Crooks had not worked out. "She has got a wicked spirit in her and will be cursed if she do not repent," he concluded. He remained on good terms with Ann Booth, the visionary Manchester woman who had so impressed Wilford Woodruff with her vision of vicarious baptism. For a time, he hoped that Booth's daughter, Sarah Ann, might join his experiment in plurality. That, too, came to nothing, as did his brief flirtation with Jane Charnock, an English immigrant, who told him, in jest or not, that she would sooner "unite" with him than with her current suitor.[57]

In September 1843, his main hope lay with Ruth's and Margaret's seventeen-year-old sister, Lydia. That prospect was dashed when he discovered that he had a rival.

President Joseph told me he had lately had a new item of law revealed to him in relation to myself. He said the Lord had revealed to him that a man could only take 2 of a family except by express revelation and as I had said I intended to take Lydia he made this known for my benefit. To have more than two in a family was apt to cause wrangles and trouble. He finally asked if I would not give L to him. I said I would so far as I had anything to do in it. He requested me to talk to her.

On the face of it, Joseph wanted Lydia for himself and concocted a revelation to support his claim. But Joseph was notorious for testing his friends by asking them to give up something they wanted. If this was a test of loyalty, William passed by docilely accepting the new revelation, even agreeing to propose to Lydia on Joseph's behalf. Lydia rejected both men, explaining that she had promised not to marry while her mother lived. She told Joseph she wanted "to tarry with her sisters."[58] At least one woman in the Moon family knew how to say no.

In October, Joseph told William that Emma had "turned quite friendly and kind." He attributed the change to her participation in new rituals he was preparing for the temple. "She said that it was her advice that I should keep M at home." Joseph agreed. "Says he, just keep her at home and brook it and if they raise trouble about it and bring you before me I will give you an awful scourging and probably cut you off from the church and then I will baptize you and set you ahead as good as ever."[59] Having survived another threat from Missouri, the Prophet was surprisingly cavalier. Fortunately, Margaret seemed reconciled to her situation. Returning home from a journey outside Nauvoo, William found her alone. "We had a joyful meeting, and she gave me a warm evidence of her love, and never did my affections glow more warmly than during our meeting embrace and until 3 o'clock when the rest of my dear family returned home."[60] To this earnest polygamist, there was no contradiction between his love for Ruth and her children and his devotion to Margaret.

"Take from us all traditions that shall stand in our way"

During the months that William Clayton was agonizing over his relationship with Margaret, Wilford Woodruff was dealing with more practical problems. On April 19, he learned that he and several other members of the Quorum of the Twelve were "to take a mission in the East" to raise money for the temple and other projects. Worried about what that would mean for Phebe, who was once again pregnant, he decided it was time to build a better house. When "several of the Brethren" offered to help him pay for materials, he staked out the ground and began laying the foundation for a two-story brick dwelling. It would be in the same block as Heber Kimball's house and immediately across the street from the one Clayton was about to finish.[61]

On May 24, a dozen neighbors turned out to help dig a cellar. "I worked myself more so than was for my good," he complained. He must have looked with envy as the carpenters finished their work on the Clayton house a few days later. While helping a mason curb a well, he injured himself by "drinking water while vary warm." Things got worse when he went out onto the prairie to fence and plant his five-acre lot. His wagon broke down and, in trying to fix it, he bruised his arm. He nevertheless managed to complete eighty-two rods of worm fence by the end of the day, but when he went to a neighbor's house for a drink of water, the man's dog bit him through the calf. He had to take time off to recover.[62] On June 27, he nevertheless hauled eleven bushels of lime to the house site. Two days later, he "went into a Brick kiln & flung out about 7 thousand Brick," nearly melting himself in the process. But when the carpenters were unable to finish his window frames in time for the masons to begin laying brick, he decided the house would have to wait until he returned. On July 7, he blessed Phebe, then boarded a steamboat for St. Louis. He was at Ilus Carter's house in New York City on August 24 when he opened a letter reporting the birth of his daughter, Susan Cornelia, a month before.[63]

Although Phebe's letters from this period have not survived, other sources produced during the summer missions confirm patterns glimpsed in William Clayton's diary. Plural marriage generated conflict and gossip. Some men competed for women. Wives as well as husbands negotiated alliances and dispensed advice. Emotions pivoted from rage to melancholy and from joy to despondency.

In Boston on September 8, Wilford shared a room with Heber Kimball, who read him one of Vilate's letters.[64] She reported that Joseph had taught Apostle Parley Pratt "some principles and told him his privilege and even appointed one for him." She said Parley's wife, Mary Ann, had been "rageing against these things. She told me her self that the devel had ben in her until within a few days past. She said the Lord had shown her it was all right. She wants Parley to go ahead, says she will do all in her power to help him." Vilate was concerned. "They are so ingagued [engaged], I fear they will run to[o] fast." She said she told them that these were "sacred things" and that she didn't feel comfortable offering advice, especially since she knew so little herself. Mary Ann Pratt was indeed engaged. According to William Clayton's diary, she made proposals on Parley's behalf to a Lancashire immigrant named Mary Aspen. When the girl declined Parley, Mary Ann cautioned her against getting involved with Clayton, saying "the Twelve would have more glory" than he.[65]

In the same letter, Vilate hinted that the plural wife of another friend, Joseph Noble, was pregnant. "They are tickled about it," she wrote. "How they will carry it out, is more than I know. I hope they have got more faith than I have."[66] Vilate's comment that it would take more faith than she had to manage such a pregnancy, casts doubt on an oft-repeated Kimball tradition that Heber fathered a child born in 1842 to Sarah Noon.[67] Heber did at some point marry Noon, but the date of their sealing is unknown. Sarah migrated from England with her husband, who was still in Nauvoo when the child was born. Though he left a few months later, Vilate's letter reported that Sarah had recently received a parcel and letter from him.[68] That Sarah Noon sent Heber her "best love" may be significant, but in the same paragraph in which she sent Noon's love, Vilate conveyed love and best wishes from "Sisters Winchester, Whitney, Billings, Adams, Juman, and I don't know how many more," joking that she had love enough to fill a page.[69] Taken together, Vilate's comments about "not knowing much," her assertion that a plural pregnancy required "more faith" than she had, and her warm but matter-of-fact report on Noon suggest that the Kimball family tradition needs revising.

Vilate's casual allusions to plural marriage understate the anxiety both she and Heber experienced as they contemplated the effect of the new practice on their own close relationship. Heber's diary and letters drip with affection for Vilate. He prayed that he and "the Love of my Youth" might "dwell together through out all Eternity, and there be in thrond [enthroned] on worlds, to propagate that thare may be no end to us or our Seeds."[70] He was open about his own quite earthly feelings for his "dear bosom friend."

> You was speaking about if I had sent a kiss to you. I will send you sevrel on the top of this page whare those round marks are, no less then one dosen, I had the pleasure of reseving those that you sent. I can tell you

it [is] a pleasure in some degree but when I come home I will try the Lump it self.[71]

Perhaps he had concerns over plural marriage in mind when he assured Vilate that he could weep like a baby at the thought of doing anything to hurt her, swearing, "Thare is no Soul that can fill your place in my heart."[72] Then embarrassed at his own effusions, he begged her not to expose him to anyone.[73] Although Vilate could also be effusive, her letters were in general more measured.[74]

Wilford was even more reserved. When he got a phrenological reading in Boston, no one was surprised to learn that the bumps on his head showed him to be a man of great resolution who loved plain, unvarnished facts and met difficulties with an increase in action.[75] But his account of a side trip to see Phebe's family in Maine showed that he, too, had a softer side. He was overcome with melancholy when Mother Carter lighted him to bed in the front chamber, where he spent the night "lonely like a dove without its mate." Mother Carter gave him a tour of the house the next day, pointing out all the new appointments, but when they reached the back chamber, where he and Phebe had spent so many days, he turned away: "It was vacant. She want there. It was gloomy."[76]

Over the next five days, Wilford filled his diary with miniatures of domestic life, describing how his mother-in-law had "done me up Babary & dandalions to take to Phebe." He gathered kisses to carry home and penned a detailed chronicle of each day, "So when <u>Phebe</u> reads this journal she can partake in part of this visit with me & put me in mind of these things for which Purpose I have written them."[77] Diverting his pen from church business was his way of expressing his love.

On October 8, he wrote from Lancaster County, Pennsylvania, where he was waiting for money to buy printing supplies. In a previous letter, Phebe had asked if he thought their "affections or hearts should ever be divided in eternity." He responded with a very long poem written in his own tiny printing. It attested to his love while demonstrating his limited capacity as a poet. In one stanza, he admitted that living with him may not have been easy: "Thus far with my follies she has patiently bourn / May I comfort her heart and not cause her to mourn." Although he lacked Heber's talent for treacle, he, too, feared causing his wife any pain. The one possible allusion to plural marriage is in the eleventh stanza: "Take from us all traditions that shall stand in our way / Of arriving at glories and diminions in eternal day."[78] Like Heber, he wanted to reign in heaven with his beloved wife.

Having succeeded in raising money for printing supplies, Wilford packed up five thousand pounds of freight and headed home, traveling by railroad and canal boat from Philadelphia to Hollidaysburg, where he began the most "awful, fearful, dangerous, exciting, affecting, grand, sublime and interesting days Journey" of his life. The Allegheny Portage Railroad linked water travel between the Susquehanna and Ohio Rivers by loading specially constructed canal boats onto railway cars, which were then lifted across the mountains by means of cables attached to stationary engines. The incline rose 1,171 feet in one direction and 1,399 in the other. Wilford was terrified "to be thus suspended almost in the air with . . . lives and freight depending upon a knot, a twine, a rope, a pin, an engine." If something snapped, the whole contraption would plunge down the precipice, destroying "all flesh that was on board." The workman he talked to later may or may not have been exaggerating when he said that the passengers "were not sensible of one half of the danger that were in during the proceedings of that day." In actuality, the railway operated for twenty years without a serious accident. In its time, it was considered a marvel of engineering.[79]

After his harrowing passage over the mountains, Wilford could hardly object to the discomforts of an ordinary riverboat. But he did. The boat was "stoved so thick with Black & white male & female that they could scarsly stand." Complaining was his way of coping. When he got home, he lamented the lack of progress on his house: "I have found by experience that a mans business will not prosper as well when he is absent as present." He was nevertheless happy to see his family. "Once more I took pleasure in presenting to my wife & Children some articles of clothing & necessaries which I had brought home. Distance from Pittsburg to Nauvoo 1500 miles."[80] The idea of living forever with those he loved was appealing. The problem was how to translate that vision on earth.

"she had something to tell me which was glorious"

Udney Hay Jacob knew exactly why the nation needed polygamy. Women had grown too powerful. He made his case in a thirty-six-page pamphlet called *The Peacemaker,* published in Nauvoo late in 1842.[81] He was not then a Mormon. In fact, when his eldest son joined the Church, he told him he would rather have heard he was dead than that he had become a Latter-day Saint. Udney was, however, a religious man. In 1840, he offered President Martin Van Buren a Biblical treatise he claimed would not only save the

nation but ensure the president's re-election. This was apparently a longer document, from which *The Peacemaker* was taken.[82] Although Joseph
Smith was listed on the title page as the printer, he quickly dismissed the
pamphlet as "an unmeaning rigamarole of nonsense, folly, and trash," saying he had not authorized its publication. A few years later, John Taylor, who
had been managing the press at the time, also dismissed the work, blaming
Joseph's younger brother William for its continuing dissemination.[83]

The Peacemaker is an odd book. But sometimes an off-center document has things to teach.[84] Like Joseph Smith, Jacob believed the Bible
offered grounds for polygamy, but he made no attempt to disguise his
real object, which was to check what he perceived to be the dangerous
and growing power of women. At first glance, his notion that nineteenth-
century women were all powerful seems ridiculous. A vow to obey was
still an essential part of most marriage ceremonies, and economically and
politically wives were subordinate.[85] Yet, for all his eccentricity, Jacob recognized that something was changing. "Gentlemen, the ladies laugh at
your pretended authority. They, many of them hiss, at the idea of your
being the lords of creation. Even in the public prints they have styled you,
the would be lords, etc." The phrase "lords of creation" alluded to the Biblical notion that when God created Adam on the sixth day, he gave him
dominion over the earth.[86]

By the mid-nineteenth century, advocates for women's rights had
begun to use the phrase sardonically. A rollicking satire by the Boston
anti-slavery activist Maria Chapman begins:

> Confusion has seized us, and all things go wrong;
> The women have leaped from "their spheres,"
> And, instead of fixed stars, shoot as comets along,
> And are setting the world by the ears! . . .
> So freely they move in their chosen elipse,
> The "Lords of Creation" do fear an eclipse.[87]

Chapman was responding to clerical attacks on her friend Angelina
Grimké, who in 1837 astonished the world by taking a speaking tour
throughout the Northeast, during which she addressed forty thousand
people in sixty-seven towns and generated as many as twenty thousand
female signatures on anti-slavery petitions.[88] Could Jacob have been
thinking of women like her? There is no question about his dislike of
abolitionists.[89]

A close reading of his pamphlet suggests that he was after something bigger, more mainstream, more insidious—a cultural transformation that historians have tried to capture with phrases like "companionate marriage," "legal paternalism," or "Republican womanhood," subtle changes that over the course of the eighteenth century began to soften hierarchical conceptions of the family. As Jacob understood, these shifts were exemplified in the way certain people began to use the term "lords of creation." In the eighteenth century, "lords of creation" became a mock-serious synonym for "white males," appearing first in English novels of the 1740s, then spreading to poetry, songs, and early feminist writings, as in Judith Sargent Murray's saucy assertion, "Yes, you lordly, you haughty sex, our souls are by nature equal to yours."[90] A music-hall song from the 1770s claimed that when "fair liberty" ruled over wedlock, "the lords of creation must pull in their horns."[91]

By 1838, a more refined version of the same argument located female power in smiles, tears, and a strategic ability to let men think they really were in charge: "For did not Adam, the very first man, / The very first woman obey?"[92] Jacob was horrified at such claims. He wanted people to remember who brought sin into the world—"Adam was enslaved by the woman, and so are we." In Jacob's view, the secular law of marriage undermined male authority. He disdained mutual covenants between husband and wife. "*What an absurdity! What an attempt to an impossibility!! what a confusion!* There is no head here, or there is a doubleheaded monster, with two different sets of brains that pull different ways!"[93]

The solution was simple. Reinstitute polygamy so a wife could no longer use her sexual power to rule her husband, and give the sole power of divorce to men. Jacob defended his arguments with complicated interpretations of scripture, but his fundamental premise was transparent: female power was dangerous.[94] Although Jacob's defense of polygamy was vigorous, the most detailed part of his argument dealt with divorce. Here he may well have been responding to local circumstances (if not to his own family situation). Although most states gradually liberalized divorce law after the American Revolution, Illinois was among the vanguard. Abraham Lincoln and his partners had a lively divorce practice, as did Stephen A. Douglas. Although, by modern standards, grounds were still limited, almost two-thirds of plaintiffs were women.[95] Jacob found this outrageous. Men married, but women were *given* in marriage. "*A divorced man is a creature no where recognized in the scriptures, or in the law of God. . . .* How can property put away its owner?"[96] The sole ground for divorce should be a wife's refusal to reverence her husband and submit to his authority in all things.[97]

That was not a principle that Joseph Smith embraced. At Kirtland, he officiated at the wedding of Lydia Bailey and Newel Knight, even though she was still legally married, having abandoned a drunken husband in another state. In Missouri, he married Abraham Smoot to Margaret McMeans, even though he knew she had left an unfaithful spouse in South Carolina and taken her only child with her. He told Smoot that Margaret's son would become bone of his bone and flesh of his flesh. To Margaret, those words seemed "like apples of gold in baskets of silver." In Nauvoo, such practices continued. Although Sarah Noon's husband technically abandoned her, she became Heber Kimball's plural wife long before any legal process for terminating her marriage could have occurred. She was not alone. As many as 20 percent of women who became plural wives before Joseph Smith's death had at some point been married to other men. Some husbands conveniently disappeared. Others hung around. A few fought back.[98]

Augusta Cobb was precisely the sort of wife Udney Hay Jacob despised. Joseph Smith welcomed her to Nauvoo. Her husband, Henry Cobb, a Boston shoe-and-leather dealer, was not pleased when she joined the Church in 1832. Yet she persisted in associating with the Saints, even after moving to Lynn, Massachusetts, a shoe-manufacturing town a few miles to the north of the city.[99] She may have been among "the sisters" Wilford Woodruff met during his first visit to Boston in 1838. He and Phebe encountered her again in 1841, when they were on their way back to Nauvoo after his mission to England.[100]

In 1843, she joined the Apostles on the return journey to Nauvoo. At the time, she had seven living children, ranging from eighteen-year-old Henry, who was about to enter Harvard College, to an infant whom some people called "George" but she had renamed "Brigham."[101] On September 30, Wilford found her with Brigham Young at a member's house in New York City on their way west. She had brought seven-year-old Charlotte and baby Brigham with her.[102] When the baby died near Cincinnati, she insisted on placing his body in a tin box and carrying it with her to Nauvoo for burial.[103] On November 2, 1843, Joseph Smith sealed her to Young in the presence of his legal wife Mary Ann, his sister Fanny Murray, and Harriet Cook, another former member of the Boston Branch. Smith then sealed Harriet to Brigham, with Augusta, Mary Ann, and Fanny as witnesses.[104] Augusta stayed in Nauvoo until Henry came after her and threatened to take Charlotte unless she returned to Boston with him.

"I suppose my dear children are in much trouble about their mother," he wrote a grown daughter. "But I have done right." To outsiders, Henry and Augusta seemed engaged in a classic conflict over religion. Like Udney Jacob, Henry believed the cause went deeper: "The main cause of all our trouble was her constant rebellion against my wish & will, and . . . speaking of me as an enemy."[105]

Although Henry Cobb forced Augusta to return to Massachusetts, he did not subdue her will. Her friend Catherine Lewis never forgot a visit Augusta made her shortly after she arrived:

> [S]he sent for me—said she had something to tell me which was *glorious.* She said she would tell me under the injunction of secrecy. I replied, "I could not promise, before knowing." After a little pause, she said, "The plurality of wives is true, etc. I have brought an invitation to you from *one* of the Twelve, and do not refuse; for you know not what you will lose if you do. It you are not satisfied with *him,* there are *two* others, and you can have your choice of either; they stand higher than he does; and if you take either of these you will be highly exalted, and all your friends, both dead and living, will be benefitted thereby. . . ."[106]

Lewis, who later left the Church, claimed that she disdained such an offer, but she could not deny that she was interested enough in what Augusta had to say to travel to Nauvoo to investigate.

Augusta Cobb was attracted by Latter-day Saint concepts of a life hereafter, but her rebellion had also been nourished by the world around her. Lynn, Massachusetts, in this period was a hotbed of rebellion, a place where residents might not only meet Mormon missionaries but listen to labor, temperance, and health reformers, or to the flamboyant abolitionist Angelina Grimké. While living there, Augusta became friends with a controversial health lecturer named Mary Gove, whose later writings portrayed her own suffering in a loveless and abusive marriage. Like Cobb, Gove eventually left her first husband and married a charismatic reformer in a utopian community.[107]

The expansion of plural marriage in Nauvoo in 1843 provoked wildly divergent emotions. Augusta Cobb rejoiced. Emma Smith raged. Vilate

Kimball urged caution. Mother Moon collapsed in despair. The portraits of Joseph Smith that emerged from this moment were also contradictory. In Eliza Snow's ballad, he was righteously defiant. In William Clayton's diary, he was crafty and insecure.

Running through all these stories is an unresolved concern over consent. Although Clayton fits the model of a man on the prowl for women, the lamentations in his diary suggest that he craved approval as well as sex. He wanted to be accepted not only by the women he loved but by his hero, Joseph Smith, and by God. In his own way, Joseph also sought affirmation. He apparently got it in the revelation he dictated at Hyrum's request, but when Emma threatened to divorce him, he wept. Heber Kimball wept, too, at the thought that he might do anything to injure Vilate. Despite their patriarchal posturings, these men wanted to attract, not command, female loyalty. Even Wilford for a time grew sentimental. When he returned from his mission, however, he went back to the language he knew best, constructing a better house for Phebe, one agonizing brick at a time. If he could not be a prophet or a poet, he was determined to be a provider.

5

"Menny feemales was recieved in to the Holy Order"

Nauvoo and Beyond, 1844–1845

In the months after returning from the East, Wilford worked hard on his unfinished house. He hauled brick and lumber, installed window frames, and built gangway doors into the cellar. By mid-January, he had a man laying shingles and installing a tin gutter on the roof. As usual, he documented the obstacles he faced, including "cold blistering rain," a painful boil on his neck, and a deranged animal. "I had a pig in the sullar & I believe the devil got into him. He leaped out of the pen destroyed one Jar of Butter one Jar of lard scattered ashes all over the sullar & kapered about over the Corn." Wilford sent the pig away.[1]

On January 28, a Sunday, he was astonished to see the thermometer at fifteen degrees below zero. When he went into his unheated bedroom to shave and wash, he took a pot of coals with him. Soon he and Phebe were both feeling faint, from "the effects of the Charcoal." Although he opened the windows and disposed of the coals, they both collapsed on the bed. They had not rested long when two-year-old Phoebe Amelia tipped over in her chair and "nearly smashed her nose," spurting blood all over. Carbon monoxide from the unvented combustion could have killed them all.[2] Ordinarily, Wilford would have marked such a day with an ominous arrow signifying peril. But this day was not yet over, and by the time he sat down to write in his diary, he had better things to report.

In the evening, he and Phebe attended a meeting of the "Quorum of the Anointed." Established only a few months before, it was the first priesthood unit in the Church to include women as well as men. As Heber Kimball observed, "Menny feemales was recieved in to the Holy Order."[3]

The new order had two purposes—to introduce ceremonies to be used in the temple, and to engage in intercessory prayer.[4]

The Woodruffs' induction began at a gathering two months before at Leonora and John Taylor's house, where Hyrum Smith offered instructions on "the New & everlasting covenant" of marriage.[5] Later, at Joseph and Emma Smith's house, they received "the endowment," a complex ritual that over several hours engaged participants in a symbolic re-enactment of God's dealings with his children, from the creation of the earth, through the fall of Adam and Eve and the trials of mortality, into eternal life. Because the endowment began with an anointing, those who received it became members of the "Quorum of the Anointed."[6] As the first female initiate, Emma Smith played an important role in blessing and anointing other women. That only legal wives participated during Joseph's lifetime may have been a condition of her participation. Years later, Bathsheba Smith remembered Emma warning newly anointed sisters, "Your husbands are going to take more wives, and unless you consent to it, you must put your foot down and keep it there."[7]

Some people believe Joseph was alluding to these new rituals when he told the members of the Female Relief Society that he would make of them "a kingdom of <u>priests</u> as in Enoch's day—as in Paul's day."[8] In the endowment, both sexes were clothed in priestly robes and both received sacred garments marked with symbolic reminders of the covenants they had made to obey God, remain true to each other, and devote themselves to building Christ's kingdom on earth.[9] Wives as well as husbands learned that if they were faithful to the first anointing, they might receive a second that promised "thrones, kingdoms, principalities, and powers" in the life to come.[10]

Considering the events of January 28 too sacred to document fully in words, Wilford wrote only that he and Phebe had met with others "for instruction" and "had an interesting time." Then he drew two little frames marked "WW" and "PWW."[11] (Phebe always used her middle initial.) On the opposite page, he drew an immense heart embellished with smaller hearts containing keys.

Hand-sketched hearts were ubiquitous in popular culture during this period. They appeared in valentines, friendship tokens, quilts, embroideries, and in the "spirit drawings" of the Shakers. In New England, they also showed up in family registers. A pair of hearts usually symbolized a married couple, with smaller hearts representing their progeny grouped around them.[12]

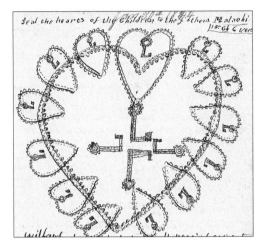

Drawing from Wilford Woodruff's diary, January 28, 1844. Although less polished than his earlier drawings, this hastily sketched heart symbolized the scriptural passage printed above it, that the Prophet Elijah would restore the keys (or authority) to turn the hearts of children to their fathers. *(Church History Library, Salt Lake City. © Intellectual Reserve.)*

Wilford's wreath of hearts had a more expansive meaning. It alluded to the Old Testament promise that the Prophet Elijah would appear in the latter days and turn the hearts of the fathers to their children and the hearts of the children to their fathers. Latter-day Saints believed that this prophecy was fulfilled when Elijah appeared to Joseph Smith in the Kirtland Temple and gave him the keys to the gathering of Israel.[13] In Mormon theology, as we have seen, keys symbolized priesthood authority. In the big heart, Wilford placed four keys at the cardinal points of the compass. To him, these may have symbolized different stages in the ceremonies performed in the Quorum of the Anointed. The wreath of hearts represented the binding together of Israel's tribes with Jesus Christ at the head.

The culminating ritual in the second anointing built upon a beloved Christian story. It took place in the privacy of a couple's home and at a time of their choosing. Heber and Vilate Kimball left the only explicit description. On a page in his journal headed "Strange Events," Heber wrote, "I Heber C. Kimball received the washing of my feet, and was anointed by my wife Vilate fore my burial. . . . Even as Mary did Jesus, that she mite have a claim on Him in the Resurrection." The Biblical reference was to the story of Mary, the sister of Lazarus, who took a pound of ointment and anointed Jesus's feet just before the crucifixion.[14] The gender symbolism can be read in more than one way. In the role of Mary, the wife acknowledged her husband as lord. In the role of priestess, she blessed him.

Phebe and Wilford waited until May 4, the day after they moved into their new house, to complete this part of the ritual. "Phebe washed my feet that I might be clean every whit," he wrote. Then he drew a tiny house with a pair of keys suspended from the top. The next day, he left for another summer's preaching.[15] When he returned, everything in Nauvoo had changed.

"A number of Apostates met together"

By 1844, an expanding Mormon population threatened the economic and political power of non-Mormons in Hancock County. When Joseph Smith suddenly switched his vote from a Whig to a Democratic candidate for the state legislature, local Whigs, supported by a firebrand editor in the town of Warsaw, began to whip up opposition to him and his church. Joseph made the switch in part to prevent Governor Thomas Ford, a Democrat, from accepting another extradition order from Missouri. Courting Ford made his opponents angry without fully winning the governor's support.[16]

Threatened by animosity around them, the Church appealed to the nation. In the fall of 1843, they had sent Congress a fifty-foot-long petition filled with 3,419 signatures begging for reparations for what they believed was their unlawful expulsion from Missouri. Then they sent printed appeals to members of Congress from Massachusetts, Maine, New York, Tennessee, Pennsylvania, and Vermont, places where leaders might remember some of their converts. Joseph capped this public-relations campaign in February 1844 by declaring himself a candidate for president of the United States. He knew he had no chance of winning, but, like many minority candidates since, he believed that the publicity would allow him to present to the nation his own story and the plight of his people. At home, it would allow the Saints to avoid taking sides in the contest between Whigs and Democrats.[17] Recognizing that all these efforts might fail, and that the Saints might ultimately have to leave the United States, he explored opportunities for settlement in Oregon, Texas, and California. By March, he had established another secret conclave, a so-called Council of Fifty, to plan the government of a new Mormon empire, a place to prepare in peace for Christ's second coming.[18]

Meanwhile, affairs in Nauvoo began to slip from his grasp. He seems to have lost some of his ability to charm or appease his antagonists. On January 30, while "conversing with a gentleman from Quincy who tantalized him some about his religion," he prophesied the man's death. With his own flock, he ordered disciplinary councils. Outraged at Joseph's attempt to call him to account for some offense, a former ally threatened to sue him in county court. At a public meeting in early March, Joseph lashed out at his old friend Hiram Kimball in an argument over taxes. Warning Kimball against going to court in Carthage, the increasingly anti-Mormon county seat, he said he would not appeal to such a court "if I died a thousand deaths," an eerie foreshadowing of his fate.[19]

Although economic and political issues drove opposition from outside the city, Joseph's still secret teachings on plural marriage created the most lasting damage within. In March, concerned about rumors that charged him with making propositions to Sarah Foster, the wife of a respected Nauvoo merchant, Joseph visited her, taking Clayton with him. "President Joseph asked Sister Foster if she ever in her life knew him guilty of an immoral or indecent act. She answered no." Had she ever heard him preach the spiritual-wife doctrine? Had he ever proposed to have illicit relations with her? Each time she answered no.[20] The more Joseph insisted on his innocence, the less credible he seemed to those who had heard of his still-secret revelation or who knew of his puzzling assignations.

Nauvoo's stake president William Marks later claimed that Joseph had by this time vowed to abandon plural marriage. His own sealings did indeed appear to stop in July 1843, not long after the confrontations with Emma that Clayton recorded, but there was one last marriage in September, leaving aside a seemingly ceremonial sealing to Brigham Young's fifty-six-year-old sister, Fanny, who as a widow was initiated into the Anointed Quorum.[21] But the rift with Emma that had seemed to be closing now widened. In early March, Emma found a way to engage the Relief Society in a campaign for reform. Here her main target may not have been Joseph but Hyrum, who had been converted to plurality by the very revelation that she found so outrageous. When Hyrum initiated a slander suit in Nauvoo's municipal court against a man named Orsemus Bostwick for claiming that women in Nauvoo were promiscuous, Emma edited a turgid and sentimental defense of women written by William W. Phelps that compared accusations of sexual misbehavior to the hellish mobbings in Missouri.[22]

For two successive weeks in March, she held morning and afternoon sessions of the Relief Society, so that every sister who wished could hear Phelps's essay read aloud. Fully living up to her calling to "exhort the church," she reminded them that one of the responsibilities of the Relief Society was to correct morals and strengthen the virtues of the community, claiming, "If their ever was any Authourity on the Earth she had it."

She urged the sisters to heed Brother Joseph when he preached against vice, and she reread the letter he had sent to the society two years before about upholding moral law. She asked for reformation "in both Men & Women," inviting them to affirm their support by raising their hands.[23] At this point, only a few of the thirteen hundred members of the Relief Society knew anything about plural marriage, though some had surely heard rumors. Those who were ignorant about the practice were no doubt reassured by Emma's campaign. Those who were themselves plural wives probably considered their sealings sanctioned by God and therefore moral.

Hyrum Smith was not pleased with Emma's campaign. By this time, he had added two plural wives, including Mercy Fielding, his legal wife's sister, to his family. In the April general conference, he deliberately side-stepped the Relief Society by proposing that the sisters contribute a penny a week to help buy window glass and nails for the temple. He emphasized that the widow's two mites were worth more in the eyes of the Lord than a rich man's bounty, and added, "No member of the Female Relief Society got it up; I am the man that did it; they ought not to infringe upon it; I am not a member of the Female Relief Society; I am one of the committee of the Lord's House."[24]

Other prominent male leaders were alarmed by what they saw as increasingly erratic behavior by Joseph. His former counselor William Law, who had been inducted into the Anointed Quorum with his wife, Jane, rejected the new teachings on plurality. According to his own account, he had tried to counsel with Joseph in private. When the Prophet rejected his entreaties, he joined other disaffected men in Nauvoo in a public challenge.[25] On May 6, Wilford noted, "A number of Apostates met together & organized a new Church or pretended to & took a strong stand against the Prophet Joseph & the Twelve & against the Church."[26] Joseph was certainly exaggerating when he claimed, "I never had any fuss with these men until that Female Relief Society brought out the paper against adulterers and adulteresses."[27] Yet, by holding her husband accountable for his public statements, Emma had made him even more vulnerable to charges of hypocrisy.

A month later, the dissenters published the first and only issue of the *Nauvoo Expositor,* a newspaper that claimed adherence to Latter-day Saint doctrines "as originally taught" but denounced new concepts and practices "taught secretly, and denied openly." In a signed affidavit, William Law affirmed that Hyrum Smith had read to him a revelation "so called" that authorized certain men to have more than one wife. Jane Law added

her own statement, explaining that the purported revelation "set forth
that those women who would not allow their husbands to have more
wives than one should be under condemnation before God." Their statements were powerful because they were simple, straightforward, and true.
Yet, linked on the pages of the *Expositor* with reprints from other papers
calling "Joe Smith" a "rough customer" and a "self-constituted Monarch,"
and calling for "the UNCONDITINAL REPEAL OF THE NAUVOO CITY CHAR-
TER," they fanned a fury that soon exploded in violence.[28]

When the Nauvoo City Council declared the *Expositor* a public nui-
sance and destroyed its press, Warsaw's combustive editor aroused the
countryside. "War and extermination is inevitable!" he screamed. "Can
you *stand* by, and suffer such INFERNAL DEVILS! To ROB men of their
property and RIGHTS, without avenging them. We have no time for comment, every man will make his own. LET IT BE MADE with POWDER AND
BALL!!!"[29] Responding to promises of protection from Illinois governor
Thomas Ford, Joseph and Hyrum submitted to arrest on charges of riot
and destruction of public property and were taken to the county seat at
Carthage. When the judge granted bail, a dissenter quickly entered a
new charge of treason, claiming that the Church had attempted to use
the Nauvoo Legion against the state militia. The judge sent Joseph and
Hyrum Smith, Willard Richards, and John Taylor back to jail, ostensibly
"for their protection."[30]

By then, Wilford and other members of the Quorum of the Twelve
were on their way east, prepared to launch Joseph's campaign for the
presidency.

"My heart said Lord bless those Dear men"

The men's absence gave rise to a remarkable set of writings that allow us
to trace events as they unfolded from the vantage point of women. Two of
Phebe Woodruff's letters and one from Mary Ann Young have survived.
Vilate Kimball's and Bathsheba Smith's letters became journals, as they
added entries day by day until they were able to send their letters east. The
earliest surviving diary of the woman later known as Zina D. H. Young
also dates from this period. In 1844, she was the twenty-three-year-old
wife of Henry Jacobs, who had apparently not objected when his wife's
brother Dimick Huntington sealed her to Joseph Smith. Zina's bond with
Joseph was secret and perhaps in her eyes purely spiritual, though it was
intense.[31] Taken together, the writings of the five women show how faith

competed with fear as the mounting tumult intersected with the mundane activities of their lives.

When Vilate Kimball started a letter to Heber on June 9, things actually seemed to her a bit dull. She had gone to meeting on Sunday, but a man named Noah Packard had done the preaching, "and you may be sure I was glad when he got through." She told Heber she had paid too much for the three pints of cherries she brought home after a picking party at a neighbor's house, but had compensated by eating as many as she could while there. "I do not begrudge myself any thing that I can eat now days, and I know that you don't nor never did. I am so sick and faint that I cannot set up a good deal of the time." Having announced her eighth pregnancy via the cherries, she turned to the weather. It was terrible. One of the brethren told her, "The quorum had better get togather and pray for the rain to be stayed, or we should all be sick."[32]

It was still raining on June 11, when she added her next installment. Her son William had gone to Ramus for a cow and found the bridges washed away in every direction. "But I do not know as we shall want cows or anything els here much longer. Nauvoo was a scene of confusion last night, some hundred of the Brethren turned out and burned the printing press, and all the aparatus pertaining to the office of the opposite party. This was done by order of the City Councel They had only published one Paper, which is considered a public nucence. But I do not know whether it will be considered so in the eyes of the Law or not. They have sworn revenge, and no doubt they will have it."[33] Although Vilate's letters sometimes meandered, she knew there would be consequences for the Council's action.

Phebe claimed not to be worried. On her way to milk her cow, she had stopped in to see her friend Bathsheba Smith, who invited her to write to Wilford in the letter she was sending George. Phebe quickly reported on the state of her garden (it was doing well) and the house (it still lacked flooring). She was pleased to report that Wilford's sister Eunice and her husband, Dwight Webster, were there and helping. She had heard from Maine that she was unlikely to have any visits from her relatives this summer. If Wilford was able to visit Scarborough, she asked him to buy two yards of dark-brown ribbon for her mother and tell her "she has not got a child in the world that loves her better or will do more for her than her wandering Phebe."[34]

Phebe acknowledged that there had been "much talk of a mob here but I have not had the first anxious thought about it." She said that the dissenters had fled, and that when they tried to stop at a town down-river, the inhabitants wouldn't let them. She had also heard that Joseph had dreamed about the two brothers Wilson and William Law, who were among the leaders of the opposition.

> he thought they bound him and cast him into a pit or well like Joseph of old but he made a struggle and got to the top of the well so to look out and he saw a little distance from him one of them in the grasp of a tiger the other a snake and they were calling to him to help them he told them they had tied him and he could not help them a brother soon came along and took brother Joseph out.[35]

Phebe believed in dreams. She knew Joseph had been in tight places before and had always prevailed.

In her part of the letter, Bathsheba told George that she had been mopping and cleaning the house and that her hired girl had fixed three flower pots. Unfortunately, the cellar was full of water. It had been rain-ing, sometimes hard, for seven weeks straight. Why hadn't she heard from him? Was he ill? Were the roads also bad where he was? She assured him that young George "begins to look helthy eats harty laughs a good deal is not half so much trouble stands on his stool to eat has a plate to himself." He missed his father, often talked about him. "I think he will not forget you."[36]

The roads were still bad on June 24, when Vilate added another page to her letter. The mail had stopped, whether because of the flooding or the mob she did not know. Her courage almost left her on Sunday, when she learned there was a warrant out for the men who had destroyed the printing press. Word had spread through the town that "Joseph had fled and left word for the brethren to hang on to their arms and take care of themselves the best way they could." Her fear increased when she heard that the Whitney family were packing up. "Some were tried almost to death to think Joseph should leve them in the hour of danger." To her great relief, he "went over the river out of the United States, and there stoped and composed his mind, and got the will of the Lord concerning him, and that was, that he should return and give himself up for trial." She was convinced that, by voluntarily submitting to arrest, the Prophet and the others who were with him had saved the city from sure destruc-tion. "My heart said Lord bless those Dear men, and presurve them from those that thirst for their blood."[37]

In her diary, Zina penned a similar prayer: "O God save thy servents save them for Jesus Sake." She added that the governor's men had confiscated the cannons and other arms belonging to the Nauvoo Legion. More trouble seemed imminent. "This night after the brethren left here for Carthage the Hevens gathered Blackness, the thunder and lightning was dreadful, the storm arose in the west." On June 25, she heard that the governor had paraded the prisoners before the mob in Carthage, but was reassured by reports that their lawyers had done all they could to ensure the prisoners' safety. Then, on "the ever to be rem[em]bered awful day of the 27 of June 1844," she received the terrible news. A hundred men with painted faces had rushed the jail. Hyrum fell first. Joseph discharged three of the barrels of a six-shooter, then leaped from the upper window, as "the bullets flew like hail in A violent storm." "Thus in one day about 3 or 4 oclock fell the Prophet and Patrarch of the Church of the Laterday Saints, the kind husbands, the affectionate Father, the venerable statesman, the Friends of mankind." Willard Richards miraculously escaped injury. John Taylor was wounded.[38]

The next afternoon, with hundreds of others, Zina filed through the Smith house "and there saw the lifeless speechless Bodes of the two Marters." Perhaps thinking of the women who came to the tomb after the crucifixion, she offered to wash Joseph's and Hyrum's clothes. A few days later, she and two of Joseph's other secret wives, Agnes Coolbrith and Louisa Beaman, with several others spent the day together. The weather was pleasant "but ah what dreariness and sorrow pervades evry bosom. The once noble banner of liberty is fallen, the bo[a]sted land of freedom is now sta[i]ned with innocent blood. O God wilt thou save us." On July 15, Zina noted quietly, "The brethren are a going afishing like unto the days of old when Jesus was slain."[39]

Mary Ann Young's June 30 message to Brigham was blunt: "Our Dear Br Joseph Smith and Hiram has fell victims to a verocious mob." She urged Brigham to be careful on his way home and not expose himself to danger.[40] Vilate Kimball was almost overcome with grief. "I shall not attempt to describe the scene that we have passed through. God forbid that I should ever witness another like unto it." She had seen the lifeless corpses brought into Nauvoo, and had witnessed the tears and groans of the dead men's loved ones; "yea, every heart is filled with sorrow, and the very streets of Nauvoo seam to morn." She did not know what else might lie in store. "We are kept awake night after night by the alarm of mobs." Worse that that, blood had mysteriously appeared on drums used by the

Nauvoo Legion. Her son William had seen it himself. "But I try to submit all things into the hands of God," she affirmed.[41]

Bathsheba was relieved when, on July 6, she finally got several letters from George, after waiting so long to hear from him. "I did not think it was your falt, but I thought on account of the rain or the mob for the mail did not come in regular." It pained her to write about the things the city had been through, but she thought the governor had begun to open his eyes. "He says we are a law abiding People and he has pledged himself and the faith of the States that he will protect us." Like Mary Ann Young, she urged her husband to take care of himself and not let the mobbers get him. She assured him that her faith remained firm. "A great many ould women expected our City to have been in ashes before the time but I have not been bad enough scared to make me trimble, though I have had some bad feelings."

By the time Phebe wrote to her parents at the end of July, the meaning of the murders had begun to take shape. Phebe was convinced that Joseph knowingly went to his death. She told her parents that after he left he had come back three times to bid his family farewell. "The last time he says farewell Mother, farewell Mother, farewell mother, she says to him Joseph what does this mean are you not comeing back again he answered her not a word but went out." Unlike Bathsheba, she had little use for Governor Ford's promises of protection: "Some think he was acquainted with the whole affair before it took place—but time will bring all things forth." Phebe's trust was in God. "Yes I believe Joseph & Hiram are where they can do the Church much more good now than when with us." As for herself, she was willing to face whatever came. "I say stand still and watch the signs of the time. If the word of the Lord to us is to leave here and go into caves of the earth or dens or among the Lamanites or to the Rocky mountains, I am willing to go." She wanted her parents to know that on the morning of the resurrection they would know how much she loved them and why she had embraced this gospel. She promised to write them at least once a month "until this disturbance with us is settled."[42]

Far away from Nauvoo, the missionaries pushed ahead with their summer's journey, unaware of what was happening at home. Touched to see "men and thare wives walking out two by two" near the U.S. Capitol, Heber lamented, "O that I had my dear Vilate with me." That night he consulted the divining rod he carried with him to see if he could discern her situation.[43] By the time the Apostles reached Boston on June 27, the newspapers were reporting unrest in Nauvoo, but to Wilford the situation in the East seemed much worse. There were anti-Catholic riots in Philadelphia, with more than a dozen deaths, as armed militiamen confronted rock-throwing Protestants.[44] Somehow, this all seemed predictable, a portent of the wars and rumors of wars that would precede Christ's second coming. He wasn't surprised that violence broke out in the Mormon convention in Boston when the anti-slavery activist Abby Folsom interrupted the meeting and ruffians in the gallery shouted back. Apostle Lyman Wight "thought it best to send some sax & fox Indians to Boston to civelize the city."[45]

Wilford heard about the murders at Carthage on July 9, when he was in Portland, Maine. A few days later, he and Brigham went to the home of Polly Vose in Boston. Brigham took the bed. Wilford sat in the big chair, covered his face, and wept.[46] While waiting for the other Apostles to gather for the journey home, Wilford impulsively borrowed ten dollars from a local Mormon and took a quick trip to Connecticut. He had been thinking for weeks that he had something to do for his parents before they died, and he decided this was the time. When he had worked up the courage, he invited them to receive a special blessing, then ordained his father to the high priesthood and "sealed him up unto eternal life." Beside his description he drew three interlocking hearts, representing his father, his long-dead mother, and his stepmother, praying that when his mother emerged from the grave their union would be "like a three fold cord not easily broken." Beneath the entry, he drew a miniature version of the wreath of hearts that had marked his and Phebe's second anointing.[47]

The Apostles were back in Nauvoo by August 6. On August 8, the Church accepted Brigham Young, president of the Quorum of the Twelve, as its new leader. "Thanks be to Him who reigns on high," Zina wrote.[48] Brigham accepted the Keys of the Kingdom with enthusiasm, determined to complete the temple and continue Joseph's mission on earth. On August 12, the Quorum proposed sending Wilford and Phebe to England, where he would preside over the British Mission.[49] Before leaving, they asked an English convert to copy several pages from Eliza Snow's minutes of the Female Relief Society into a blank section of Wilford's 1842 diary. They included the speech where Joseph defended the right of women to pray and heal the sick, the one that concluded, "I now turn the key to you in the name of God."[50]

At midnight on their last day in Nauvoo, Wilford and Phebe and a few friends walked up the hill to the temple. "After gazing a few moments . . . they ascended the ladders unto the top of the walls," kneeling on the southwest corner to pray. They returned to their houses "with joy and peace" in their hearts. While they were in England, little Willie would stay with the Benbows, across the river, in Iowa. Phoebe Amelia would remain with her grandparents in Maine. Baby Susan Cornelia would accompany them.[51] They did not know that, by the time they returned, most of their fellow Saints would have fled Nauvoo.

"*The thoughts of my heart or the emotions of my minde*"

The most striking thing about Nauvoo in the last two years of Mormon occupation was the intensity with which the Saints who remained dreamed of a reality beyond mudflats, riverboats, and half-finished houses. Knowing they would soon be cast into the wilderness, they continued to work on the temple, seeking the assurance it offered of eternal salvation. No source gets us closer to this yearning than the diary kept by Zina Jacobs.

Zina moved through her days softly, as though she were already halfway to heaven. Certain only of God, she sought comfort in prayer as she braided palm-leaf hats, nursed the sick, and gently eased the dying into a world she would enter if she could. Over the fifteen months she kept her diary, she systematically noted Sunday meetings, often summarizing the content. She also mentioned less formal gatherings. When her father spoke in tongues at a neighbor's house, she "interpreted the talk by the help of the speret of God." When her husband responded by singing in tongues, she pronounced it "very good."[52] She was thrilled when Heber Kimball preached that, if the Saints would all adhere to counsel, "we should grow right into the Mellenium." At the funeral of a friend, she imagined "shaking hands with her after the resurrection."[53]

Zina grieved over the trials of mortality. Nursing her three-year-old son, Zebulon, who was ill, she asked, "O Lord how long shall we labor under these things, even children suffering so sore?" Her answer was to pray for Christ's coming, believing that the Saints would then "have power over the destroyer."[54] When an abscess between her chin and ear broke and "discharged wonderfully," she contemplated her own death. "O living mortality, how soon thou canst decay. O may I be prepared at the Great and last change."[55] Learning that Eliza Snow had been confined to her bed for weeks, she paid a visit, marveling at Snow's patience—"She is worthy of imitation," she wrote. Later that week, she felt inspired by a Brigham Young sermon that mixed millennial hope with cosmic speculation. "He spake of the power the Saints would have over disease, The fall of the Earth, its redemption, also all those that ware destined to this planet or world."[56]

She was entranced by Sylvia Lyon's report of a conversation she had with Heber Kimball concerning "ordinations before we came here." She wanted to know every detail of what Latter-day Saints came to call "the plan of salvation," a drama that in Mormon theology extended from a preexistence as spirit children to the life hereafter.[57] Unlike Wilford Woodruff, she provided the topics of these conversations but not the details. It would be interesting to know more about the Brigham Young sermon she pronounced "the greatest that has ever ben Given to the Church, uppon Priesthood, the Godhed, the dutes of Male & Female, there exaltations &c." "O Father wilt thou enlarge my minde," she prayed.[58]

Although her diary is a spiritual chronicle more than an accounting of daily life, she gradually added more detail about whom she had seen and what she had done. Like other nineteenth-century diarists, she used the term "friend" broadly. "What a blessed privilege to have the Society of one[e]s friends," she wrote on a day when she had received visits from both family members and strangers who had been kind to Henry or her brothers on their missions.[59] When someone brought her flour or eggs, she used an old proverb, "A friend in need is a friend in deed."[60] When her stepmother paid a visit, she expressed herself in Biblical terms: "Behold how lovely it is for Friends to dwell together in unity." For her, friendship involved reciprocity, but because God was responsible for rewarding good deeds, she repaid kindnesses from one person by doing the same for others.[61]

If relatives were friends, then nonrelatives could be kin. She routinely referred to older women as "mother," twice noting that a woman she called "Mother Brower" was "a Fine old lady aged 61 years."[62] Because she was interested in nursing, she loved to visit "Mother Sessions," who amazed her with her equanimity in the face of death.[63] She felt especially comfortable with "Old Sister Lyman," a woman who had known Zina's parents when they were children in New Hampshire.[64] Her circle of friends included several women who, like her, had been secretly sealed to Joseph Smith. It also included persons otherwise invisible in Nauvoo records. In September 1845, she wrote:

> Lewes Damp, a Lamanite, gave me a money purse that his step Daughter Nancy sent to me from the Mo Territory. She has ben here and was baptized some years ago. When she left me or this plac[e] for the far west, I took a ring from my finger and gave it to her. She was a

fine apperended [appearing?] girl. The purse is velvet, beautifully ornamented with beads or her own hands work.[65]

Although Zina imagined American Indians as descendants of the Lamanites written about in the Book of Mormon, her friendship with Nancy
went beyond ethnicity. Zina admired people who could make beautiful
things.

She recorded none of the wrangling so apparent in William Clayton's
diary. Conflicts and jealousies surely existed, but Zina was not the sort of
person to memorialize trouble. Many years later, others claimed that her
marriage to Henry Jacobs had not been happy, but there is no indication
of that in her Nauvoo diary.[66]

On March 7, 1845, she wrote, "4 years ago today since we ware Married. O God let thy hand be over us still to prosper us."[67] Henry appears
to have shared her commitment to the faith. On one occasion, he sold his
coat, vest, and hat "to answer up on his tithing." Whether he needed to
sell his clothes because he was a poor manager or simply because he was
poor, Zina prayed, "O may he be enabled to pay his tithing that he or we
may receive the promised blessings of the Lord."[68] When he was called
to a short-term mission, Zina worked hard to prepare him. "Wilt thou
Preserve me in his absence, O Lord, and my little son," she prayed. When
he returned, he, like other men, set to work "drawing frame and stone for
his house."[69]

Clearly, however, something unsaid was rippling beneath the surface.
On May 3, 1845, Zina began the day's entry with a curious statement, "I am
writing," as though she had to remind herself. "God only knows my heart
this day," she continued. "The thoughts of my heart or the emotions of
my minde causes my very head to acke."[70] Although the phrase "thoughts
of my heart" appears in the book of Job, Zina reinforced the strange construction by adding a second oxymoron: "emotions of my minde." In a
world where boundaries between heaven and earth had begun to bend,
she could no longer distinguish between thought and feeling.[71]

Around 11:00 p.m. on May 9, something happened that kept her
awake. Perhaps she or her husband or both of them had finally come to
terms with what it meant for a woman to be bound eternally to a man
who was dead. If Zina belonged to Joseph in the hereafter, where did that
leave Henry? Was he to be a lone man, a ministering angel, in heaven, or
was he supposed somehow to acquire another wife, a woman willing to

be sealed to him for eternity while he remained bound body and soul to Zina?

Whatever happened provoked one of the most intense—and opaque—entries in Zina's otherwise placid diary:

> I am very tired at night. Never to be forgotten at 11 oclock, O then what shall I say. At or after 4 I went to sleep. O Lord have mercy uppon my Sole. Teach me the ways of eternal life. Give me that gift above all others. Behold this is the desire of my hart. Comfort us, yes, Henry in his trouble, for he has not repined a word. Accept of our thanks for life, forgive the weakness of my heart, and let me do nothing but what shall be to thy honour and Glory and my soles salvation.[72]

Zina's statement that Henry had "not repined a word" suggests that he might have had a reason to complain about something. But *what*? Like Eliza, Zina simply could not bring herself to express in words all that she was experiencing. A month later, she noted that Henry had gone to seek counsel from Brigham Young "upon his and families situation." She added, "O God be merciful unto us."[73]

If Henry's love for Zina was anything like Heber Kimball's love for Vilate, he wanted to be with her forever. Her sealing to Joseph Smith precluded that. This issue would have taken on a more intense reality if Zina, like other women sealed to Joseph Smith, had been offered the chance to receive her endowments and join the Anointed Quorum. In late January, Eliza Snow, Louisa Beaman, and four of Joseph's other plural wives had done so.[74] If Zina were to accept admission, she would need to make a choice. Did she belong to Joseph or to Henry? Although Brigham had relaxed the earlier restriction on plural wives, a woman could not have two husbands.[75]

Church leaders had also begun to assume temporal responsibility for Joseph's many widows. Brigham Young eventually married seven of them, including Eliza Snow and her friend Louisa Beaman. Amasa Lyman was sealed to Eliza Partridge.[76] Heber Kimball married Zina's sister, Presendia, even though she was still living with her legal husband, Norman Buell. Kimball's young daughter Helen Mar chose to be sealed "for time" to a young and then monogamous suitor, Horace Whitney.[77] All these marriages would be "for time," with any children born belonging to Joseph in the hereafter. Clearly, Zina and Henry faced momentous decisions.

Zina said no more about Henry's visit with Brigham. On June 14, she spent the day braiding him a straw hat and sewing on his vest. As she recounted the day's labors, her words fell into a rough kind of verse. She asked God for "Grace divine. A minde sublime a Pure Heart that's ever clean that all my dreams may be serene that the truth may stand at my right hand that come from above that's filled with Love to Give this to me that I may be free from sin and from strife that at the end of my life I may be Clear as the sun pure as Gold that my Saviours fase I then may behold."[78] Zina was no poet, but she had her own kind of eloquence.

On May 24, 1845, almost a year after Joseph's death, she rose at 6:00 a.m. and walked to Temple Hill. "The morning was serene and silent. The Sun and Moon ware at about equel hith [height] in the horizon, as if to rejoice wit[h] the Saints in Praises to the most high." William Clayton and the band were there; "the banner of liberty was floating in the gentle breeze"; and as workmen lifted the last stone onto the body of the temple, the crowd shouted as if with one voice, "Hosanah to God and the Lamb."[79] On June 27, the first anniversary of the Smiths' murders, the roof of the temple was ready for shingles. Two weeks later, the "Last shingle was lade."[80] The work of the stonecutters and masons had ended. Zina's father "locked up his chest of tools," having labored 818 days on the stonework. It was now time to raise the three-tiered tower.[81]

In the midst of progress, violence threatened. For the first time in her life, Zina saw two men she knew come to blows in the street outside their house. To her, this was sure evidence that the great winding-up scene was near.[82] By mid-September, there was trouble everywhere:

> When I cast mine eyes out, what do I behold, evry brother armed, his gun upon his shoulder to protect his family and Bretheren from the violence of the furious Mob, who are now burning all that falls into their way round about the Country.

At sunrise, the first thing she saw when she looked toward the temple was a white flag signaling men to gather to defend the city.[83]

Antagonists who had hoped the Church would disintegrate after the death of Joseph Smith were disturbed by continuing signs of vitality in Nauvoo. The rising temple reinforced their fear that the Saints would remain in the county to dominate politics and land sales. Men from neighboring towns began to organize "wolf-hunts" to drive those living in outlying settlements from their farms. "The mob are raging, burning buildings, grain, driving all before," Zina wrote on September 13, and, two days later, "The enmy still continues to burn and drive in the Bretheren, not even giving time to save all there furniture. O God, all flesh is in thy hands." Even moderate leaders in the county began to demand that the Mormons go. Brigham surprised many by saying that they would. He asked only that they be allowed to remain in the city through the winter, to prepare for an orderly departure. His goal now was to complete the temple so that the exiled Saints could receive sacred ordinances before once again beginning their quest for a new Zion.[84]

"up in the tower of this Temple"

Given the fractious atmosphere in the county, William Clayton was surprised by how many strangers came into Nauvoo to view the temple as it neared completion. "They seem filled with astonishment," he wrote. He considered the temple "the most beautifull piece of architecture I ever witnessed."[85] From ground level to the top of the tower, it rose 165 feet. Blazing sunstones with mysteriously carved faces surmounted its massive pilasters. The temple was both an expansive public-works project and a portal to eternal life, a place where, as Eliza Snow put it, "those ordinances may be administered which are necessary preparations for the world to come."[86]

Saints from as far away as Manchester, England, had contributed to its construction. By 1845, there were notices that funds were being gathered in Hansley, Burslem, and Lane's End, with promises that Wilford Woodruff would transfer them to Nauvoo to be recorded in "The Book of the Law of the Lord."[87] From Massachusetts, Catherine Lewis wrote Brigham Young to make sure that her own contribution—fifty yards of fringe valued at fifty cents per yard—had been recorded. She hoped to come to Nauvoo soon, would bring her small fringe-making "meshene," and, if still needed, would make more trimming there. Although her contribution was small, she knew that "jesus notised the widos might."[88]

William Clayton knew exactly how much had gone into the temple's construction. As temple recorder, he had the job of keeping track of donations and disbursements. Much had happened in the Clayton household since Joseph's death. In the summer of 1844, Margaret's six-month-old baby, Daniel Adelbert, died. "Thus has ended the earthly career of an innocent sufferer who has known no comfort in this life but has suffered since his birth," William wrote, observing that the "tongue of slander has swung freely against him." Margaret continued to grieve, not only for her baby but perhaps for Aaron Farr. It didn't help that William was courting Farr's sixteen-year-old sister, Diantha.[89]

In December 1844, he had recorded a long and earnest prayer focusing on the women in his life. He asked that Ruth continue to be "a help to thy servant," that Margaret place "her entire affections" upon him, and that Diantha "no longer delight in the society of the gay and trifling." He married Diantha in January 1845, with her parents' and Heber Kimball's blessing. She continued to live at home and attend school.[90] By summer, there were signs of trouble. On July 1, 1845, after attending a party at the Masonic Hall, she fell ill and for a time "lost her reason." Two weeks later, Clayton feared she was "likely to have another fit of mental derangement." After they took an evening walk together, she seemed upset about something and refused to go to her room. Mother Farr made a bed downstairs, and together they "put her to bed by force."

Scene of Nauvoo with temple, 1846. This famous view of the Nauvoo Temple shows unfinished buildings in a town that grew rapidly during the seven years it was occupied by Latter-day Saints. *(Church History Library, Salt Lake City. © Intellectual Reserve.)*

Soon as she got laid down she began to toss about and rave as if in great pain which seemed to increase until she was perfectly out of her mind and raging

She tore her hair and I then held her which required all the force I had got to hold her hands.

When the paroxysm passed, she began conversing with someone as though she had entered the world of spirits. For two hours, she spoke with Joseph and deceased relatives and friends. Then she blithely bade them farewell, saying "she would like to tarry but she could not leave father and mother and another, but she would soon return and bring them with her and then she would tarry with them." She gave each of her unseen friends a cordial "good-bye," until she came to Joseph. "I am not in the habit of kissing men but I want to kiss you," she said.[91] The next day, she could not remember anything that had happened.

On Sunday, August 24, 1845, Clayton walked up Temple Hill with Mother Moon, his three wives, and Ruth's four children, aged eight months to eight years. He wanted them all to see how much progress had been made. As they toured the building, he was astounded by their courage: "Margaret, her mother and Diantha ascended up the ladders to see the top of the Temple." Diantha happily paraded on the roof while Margaret and her mother scrambled up the remaining ladders. "They are the first females who have ever been up in the tower of this Temple," he continued. "Diantha only went to the Bell section, Margaret & her Mother seemed to have no fear about them Although the latter is over 60 years old."[92]

The temple had risen without the help of the Relief Society. On March 9, 1845, a week shy of its third anniversary, Brigham Young formally disbanded it. In a discourse delivered to male leaders, he said, "When I want Sisters or the Wives of the members of this church to get up Relief Society I will summon them to my aid but until that time let them stay at home & if you see Females huddling together veto the concern and if they say Joseph started it tell them it is a damned lie for I know he never encouraged it." In a meeting of High Priests that same day, he pronounced a curse on any man who "lets his wife or daughters meet again." Clearly, he was still angry with Emma Smith, whose opposition to plural marriage he believed had encouraged dissension in the Church and ultimately led to the deaths of Joseph and Hyrum. "What are relief societies for?" he asked. "To relieve us of our best men—They relieved us of Joseph and Hyrum—

that is what they will lead too—I don't [want] the advice or counsel of any woman—they would lead us down to hell." Then, perhaps concerned that he had gone too far, he urged men to treat their wives well, to make of them queens rather than lackeys.[93] In his view, a woman became a "queen" as she accepted the new order of marriage and lived in a way worthy of celestial glory. The temple symbolized that glory.

Completion of the temple added urgency to decisions that may once have seemed tentative and experimental. With the dissenters gone, embracing plural marriage became a mark of loyalty to the now dead Prophet. The rituals that had earlier been available to a select few would soon be available to all. People had to decide whether they were willing to embrace them. As finish carpenters worked on the assembly rooms below, men hung curtains in the attic to set off the various stages in the endowment. Without time or resources to produce the colorful murals used in later temples, they made do with what they had. In the area designated as the Garden of Eden, a grapevine with a cluster of raisins on it signified the forbidden fruit. An improvised "celestial room" offered a strikingly domestic view of heaven, with family portraits, sofas, and a "fine rocken chare." On December 3, Brigham appointed Christian Hansen, "a Dane," as doorkeeper and fire maker. As they prepared to administer the rituals they had earlier received, members of the Anointed Quorum met for prayer and instruction.[94]

On December 10, Kimball handed his diary over to William Clayton, who became responsible for documenting temple ordinances.[95] In the next two months, an expanding cadre of men and women belonging to the Anointed Quorum initiated others. In a few short weeks they performed more than five thousand endowments. Among women, Vilate Kimball, Mary Ann Young, Leonora Taylor, and Elizabeth Ann Whitney took the lead; at least forty other female officiators joined them. Eliza Snow served as a clerk, helped make cushions for an altar, and, with Margaret Moon and others, stayed late to wash temple clothing. On at least one occasion, Eliza slept in the temple overnight in order to prepare for the morning. Although leaders weren't ready to announce plural marriage to the world, they openly acknowledged it within the temple, sealing plural wives to their husbands and performing vicarious ordinances for Joseph, Hyrum, and others.[96]

Plural marriage and the temple came together in 1845 to bind women and men in interlocking chains that gave them hope of eternal glory and ensured more trials on earth. For women like Leonora Taylor, that meant more self-sacrifice and greater reliance on God. She had begun a diary twenty years before in a hand-me-down journal. She or someone else cut out the first seventeen or eighteen sheets, the pages that had been written on by its first owner. She wrote about her journey from England to Canada in 1834, her homesickness and concern about the state of her soul, the kindness of her new employers. Then she stopped.[97]

She did not pick up her little book again until after Joseph's and Hyrum's murders. Then, on four tiny pages, she composed a concise summary of her life between 1834 and 1844, giving the dates of her marriage, the births of her children, her baptism into the Church, her family's removal to Missouri, then a somewhat longer account of her sufferings in Montrose, Iowa, after her husband was called to the British Mission. She noted the birth of her last child in June 1840, then summarized the next four years with a jumbled list of undated events, the chaos of the telling suggesting that she wrote in both haste and despair:

Mr T had a bad feavor nigh to death I cut my finger with glass it got very bad my dear Child took sick my sweet baby died on the 9th of Sept buried the 10th on the 14th I had the middle finger of my left hand taken off and buried with my Baby, I had many trials about this time but I am yet alive, The Brethren were taken to Carthage Brother Joseph & Hyrum killed, Mr Taylor was Wounded very badly but the Lord mercifully spared his life. Docter Richards was in the Prison at the time.[98]

In this account, the cut finger has received the most attention. In the late nineteenth century, an anti-Mormon writer imagined that, in an outrage over polygamy, Leonora thrust her clenched fist through a window and cut her hand. Aside from the fact that this is an awkward way of explaining a cut finger, it is not what her diary says.[99]

She wrote that her husband nearly died from a fever and then was wounded badly while in prison with the Prophet. She said that her cut finger became infected and was amputated at about the time that her dear child died. That she buried her finger with her daughter may seem bizarre to modern readers, but to her it was a powerful symbol of the loss of some part of herself when her youngest child died and an acknowledgment that in the resurrection they would rise together and that every part of her body would be restored. The deaths of Joseph and Hyrum matter in this account, but they are set alongside her own gratitude for surviving such adversity and her thankfulness for God's mercy in sparing her husband's life. This is a ragged memoir, a spilling forth of events without regard to chronology, a mixture of minor incidents, like the appearance of skunks, with major trauma. She didn't pause to mourn any of it. She just wanted to get it down, before she turned a corner, which she did.

On the back page of her diary, past scrawled remedies for whooping cough, worms, and the "salt rhum," she concluded: "The Lord has often led me by a way that I knew not and in a path that I naturally did not wish to go, evry sweet has its bitter, the way seems to be narrower evry day without his Almighty power to help me I cannot walk in it to whome shall I go or look for succor but unto thee my Father & my Friend." She dated her meditation, "Nauvoo Jan 28th 1845 12 aniversary of my Marriage." By then John Taylor had been sealed to five plural wives.[100] Whatever her feelings, Leonora worked alongside Vilate Kimball in the temple, joined John and others in ritual prayer, and one evening after the crush of work in the temple hosted a party for couples who had been in the original Anointed Quorum.[101]

The rush to complete the new temple ceremonies created frenzy and joy. Brigham was dismayed when men peeked behind curtains and mothers brought crying babies with them, but he was willing to work day and night to accomplish the work.[102] At the end of the day on December 30, somebody produced a violin. The music inspired Joseph Young (Brigham's older brother) to dance a hornpipe, and Brigham and Heber to commence a contra dance, taking Elizabeth Whitney and Catherine Lewis as their partners. After Erastus Snow sang "The Upper California," Elizabeth Whitney moved the company to tears with "one of the most beautiful songs in tongues that was ever heard." Her husband interpreted, explaining that the words of the song related to the building of "this House, and to the privilege we now have of meeting together in it—and of our departure shortly to the country of the Lamanites."[103]

In late December, Clayton recorded a series of sermons given in the temple that alluded to continuing tensions over the position of women. Although George A. Smith emphasized the spiritual power of a husband and wife when united in praying for their children, Brigham insisted that a woman was incapable of returning to God "unless she follow the man back," and Apostle Amasa Lyman claimed that a man was responsible for his wife's conduct as well as for his own. Heber offered a little history of the Anointed Quorum, alluding to dissenters like William Law when he said that some men, led by their wives, had apostatized, warning, "If any such cases occur again, no more women will be admitted." He insisted that, just as he was subject to God, "my wife is in subjection to me and will reverence me in my place and I will make her happy."[104]

That the authority of husbands over wives needed affirmation suggests that it had been challenged among the Saints, as of course it had. Emma had "rebelled" against her husband. But so had Augusta Cobb when she left her legal spouse to marry Brigham Young. Mormon patriarchs simultaneously sustained and challenged the old order. The law defined marriage as a contract in which a woman agreed to obey her husband in exchange for protection and material support, but Heber Kimball reflected a new sentimentalism when he said his duty was to make his wife happy. Happiness was a subjective state that could only be defined by the participants. Although social pressure and fear of damnation were powerful incentives, Mormons still believed that every woman had not only the right but the obligation to choose her own husband. How she chose depended on what she valued.

Temple sealings offered new possibilities. In these ceremonies, a woman could ratify already established relationships or forge new ones. A widow could be sealed to one man for eternity and another "for time." A man could of course be sealed to multiple spouses in either domain. What was the position of plural wives in such a marriage? Was each wife sealed only to the husband, or were the wives bound to one another as well? A later account of the ceremony used in performing plural marriages says that the first wife placed the hand of the intended wife in the hand of her husband and then linked hands with him and remained standing while the marriage was performed. The language describing the Clayton sealings suggests such an approach. According to the official record, William and his wives, Ruth, Margaret, and Diantha, went into the upper room of the temple, where they "dressed and went into room No. 1 and were *sealed to each other* on the altar by Pres B Young" (emphasis added).[105] This was not, then, a series of unions between one man and a succession of wives, but a sealing that united the entire group. Perhaps in this case, Margaret's loyalty to her sister trumped whatever feeling she may have retained for Aaron Farr.

The foundational temple ritual, the endowment, did not depend on marital status. Although Zina and Henry Jacobs went to the temple together on January 3, 1846, to receive that ordinance, they had not yet figured out what to do about Zina's previous sealing to Joseph Smith. A month later, they went back to the temple, and Henry stood by while

Zina was sealed to Joseph "for eternity" and Brigham "for time," the clerk noting that "Henry B. Jacobs expressed his willingness that it should be so."[106] Two days later, Eliza Snow became Zina's "sister wife" when she, too, was sealed to Joseph for eternity and Brigham for life.[107] Hostile accounts of plural marriage typically focus on the number of wives a man had and on the potential for conflict between them, but some marriages were held together through committed relationships among women. Zina cared about Henry, but her Nauvoo diary, as well as her later writings, attests to her close relationship with Eliza and with the other women who chose to stay with the Church and with one another after Joseph's death.

Among those embracing plurality, Heber and Vilate Kimball were either the most valiant or the most foolhardy. By the time the temple closed, Heber not only had been blessed and anointed with Vilate but had been sealed in some fashion to more than thirty women. Perhaps the majority of these "marriages" were purely ceremonial. Knowing that the Saints were about to flee Nauvoo, some women wanted assurance of a place in heaven. But in contrast to the low fertility among plural wives that existed before Joseph's death, these marriages soon produced babies. When the Kimballs left Nauvoo, five of Heber's plural wives, including Sarah Ann Whitney, were pregnant. Because Sarah Ann had been sealed for eternity to Smith, her children would belong to him rather than to Heber in the eternities.[108]

Despite her commitment to the temple, Augusta Cobb's friend Catherine Lewis declined Heber's proposal of marriage. "Mrs. K. treated me as a sister," Lewis later recalled, but she did not want to be like Hagar, the maidservant in the book of Genesis. Although aspects of Mormonism seemed enticing, she eventually decided it was a damnable heresy.[109] The exposé she composed on returning to Massachusetts has the ring of authenticity, even though its polished prose surely owes more to the Protestant minister who was her editor than to her own fluent but poorly spelled writing.[110]

In contrast, Augusta was determined to remain with the Saints.[111] She received her endowment in mid-December, then paused to consider the next step. On January 20, she wrote Brigham she could not join his other prospective wives in the temple. "The Spiret of the Lord forbids," she wrote. "Why I know not." Two weeks later, she explained that she had never for a moment doubted him as a servant of God, but only as a companion, "for I felt that our love had been like Jonah's gourd, come up in a night and perished in a night." She nevertheless expressed a willingness to submit to him "as unto a husband in the Lord" in order to ensure the exaltation of her ancestors; "it shall never be said that there is not one of my race capable of Governing a Kingdom."[112]

Latter-day Saints placed enormous faith in temple rituals. They believed that, in Kirtland, Elijah had returned the keys to the gathering of Israel, and that, by sacrificing to build a new temple in Nauvoo, they would fulfill the meaning of his promise to turn the hearts of fathers and mothers to their children, in both a literal and a symbolic sense. Uniting husbands and wives, parents and children through the generations provided not only assurance of personal salvation but the right to inherit dominions, powers, thrones, and Godhood itself. Plural marriage was many things in this period, but without question it was wound into a story about a promised life beyond the grave.

In the months after Joseph's and Hyrum's deaths, Eliza Snow pondered the nature of heaven. She knew that in Mormon theology, marriage symbolized the very essence of Godhood, the capacity for eternal increase. Did this mean that God himself must have a wife—or wives? In a poem

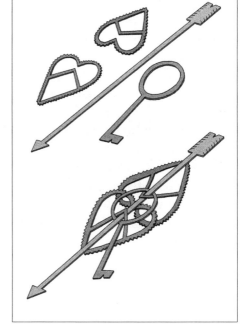

Schematic drawing of the ornamental token Eliza R. Snow made for Brigham Young and his first wife, Mary Ann. Eliza overlapped two paper hearts, then inserted a paper arrow and a key to create a love knot in the center. For a colored image of the original, see color insert 1, page 4. Drawing by Spencer Hawkes.
(Church History Library, Salt Lake City. © Intellectual Reserve.)

published just before completion of the temple, Eliza Snow answered her own question:

> In the heavens are parents single?
> No the thought makes reason stare;
> Truth is reason—truth eternal
> Tells me I've a mother there.[113]

In the closing stanza, she imagined herself being welcomed into the celestial realm by a divine Mother and Father. Eliza's poem, now the text for a beloved Latter-day Saint hymn, is characteristic of her work, which is often quietly subversive. It affirms the power—and perhaps also the invisibility—of motherhood and at the same time offers the explosive notion of a joint male-female deity.

On January 7, Eliza offered Brigham and Mary Ann Young a handmade paper emblem to honor their sealing in the Nauvoo Temple. Using a technique common in nineteenth-century valentines, she cut out two hearts with serrated edges, placing them in opposite directions so that the points overlapped, symbolizing a union of hearts. Then she cut out a paper key and an arrow, weaving their shafts into the points of the heart to create a love knot. In her poetry, as in Wilford's drawings, arrows signified death and keys priesthood authority. (See color insert 1, page 4.) With a few snips of her scissors, she had created a visual affirmation of the power of priesthood to overcome death through the turning of hearts.

The bland little verse she attached to her handmade token is more complex than it first appears: "Upon the Altar of the Lord, / Within his holy House; / Their covenants were sealed—and there / They plighted mutual vows." Her use of the term "mutual" is significant. The underlining is hers. By addressing the husband and wife with parallel titles— "President Brigham Young" and "Presidentess Mary Ann Young"—she affirmed their spiritual parity. Unlike Wilford's wreath of hearts, her token represented a couple rather than a tribe. She had not yet found a way to represent plurality, although she displayed considerable common sense by honoring Mary Ann as the presiding female in the household she was about to enter.[114]

6

"Mud aplenty"

Crossing Iowa, 1846

Patty Sessions was a midwife. She learned her trade in Maine, where in 1833 she responded to the preaching of Mormon missionaries and became a Latter-day Saint. With her family, she migrated to Missouri in 1837, suffered through the mob violence and expulsion, and settled in Nauvoo. There she became a stalwart in the Female Relief Society.[1] In the spring of 1846, she and her husband, David, were in a wagon train inching across Iowa.

"Mud aplenty the worst time we have had yet," she wrote on April 4. That night, the temperature dropped, freezing their wagon cover solid and cementing a pair of wet, muddy boots to the side of their tent. When the sun came out, the mud came back, miring their wagon wheels in thick, black goo. At 2:00 a.m. on April 7, Patty was awakened by an anxious husband begging her to attend his wife in labor. She climbed on his horse behind him and rode two miles back along the trail, "through mud and water some of the way belly deep," to an abandoned cabin where the family had found shelter. Although the baby had already arrived, Patty did what she could for the mother, then listened to her story: "She had rode 13 miles after she was in travail crossed the creek on a log after dark." As a midwife, Patty was used to arduous journeys in the middle of the night, but in this dank and dripping spring, the women she served were also in motion.[2]

As many as fourteen thousand Latter-day Saints evacuated Nauvoo in 1846. Patty and the woman she attended on that April night were among the vanguard, roughly three thousand strong, who left in February. Another ten thousand joined the hegira in June. The remainder, those too poor or stubborn to leave earlier, fled the ravaged city in autumn. The Latter-day Saints left Nauvoo because their city had lost its charter, because mob violence was escalating, because the governor of Illinois had withdrawn his protection, and because Brigham Young was determined to lead them to a new refuge beyond the borders of the United States.[3] "Brother Brigham came up with his company driving his team in the rain and mud to his knees as happy as a king," Patty wrote on April 6. Later, alone in her wagon, she prayed and wept and prayed again. "Two months today since I left home. I have been in the cold in the snow and rain with out a tent but now we are blockaded with mud and no feed for teams. . . . I never have felt so bad as now but I am not discouraged yet."[4]

Just before they left Nauvoo, her married daughter, Sylvia, had given her a new journal. On the inside front cover, in bold but uneven cursive, she had written:

A Day Book given
to me
Patty Sessions by
Sylvia P Lyon this
10th day of Feb.
1846

Farther down the page, she added the time-honored mark of rural diaries: "Patty Sessions Her Book."

The first entry in the new journal showed her poised between past and future: "Nauvoo or City of Joseph. My things are now packed ready for the west."[5] In the pages that followed, she traced her path across Iowa Territory to a Mormon refugee camp called Winter Quarters (in present-day Nebraska) and then, in 1847, to the valley of the Great Salt Lake. When the journal Sylvia had given her was filled, she started another. In terse and often cryptic entries, she tracked her life, page by page, until she had filled six thick booklets, some made of folded paper stitched together with homespun linen thread. Although there is a break in the diary beginning in 1866, she picked it up again in 1880. She made her last entry on Friday, May 4, 1888, when she was ninety-three years old, reporting for all who cared to notice that she had knitted "three pair of stockins this week."[6]

Most of Patty's entries are indistinguishable from those in any other workaday diary. "Mad[e] me a cap," she wrote on February 11, 1846, just before beginning her journey from Nauvoo, and, two days later, "made

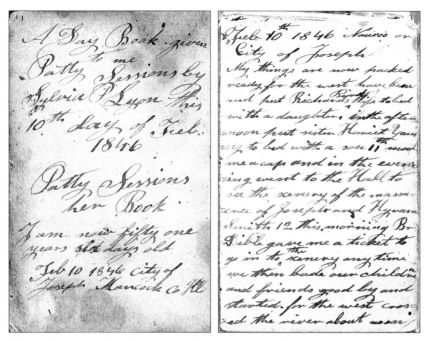

Title and opening page of Patty Sessions's diary, 1846. The bound volume, a gift from her daughter, Sylvia, measures 6 × 3¾ inches. *(Church History Library, Salt Lake City. © Intellectual Reserve.)*

me two red night caps out of some flannel Sylvia sent me." Yet amid the lists of work accomplished and women "put to bed" are glimpses of a world incomprehensible to modern readers. Patty was a religious visionary, a woman who in moments of spiritual ecstasy spoke in what was to her the pure language of Adam. She was surely the "Mrs Sessions" who in meetings of the Nauvoo Relief Society demonstrated the gift of tongues and offered blessings to the Prophet's mother and Eliza Snow. To the end of her life, she insisted that she had been sealed in 1842 to Joseph Smith, even though married to David Sessions and the mother of his children.[7]

Patty was one of a dozen diarists who chronicled the 1846 exodus from Nauvoo. These include persons we have met, such as Wilford Woodruff, Eliza Snow, and William Clayton, as well as others who, like Patty, began new journals just before leaving the city. Zina Huntington did not keep a diary in 1846, but diaries left by her father, William Huntington, and her stepsister Eliza Partridge Lyman, along with a handful of letters, continue the saga she began in Nauvoo. Among the new diarists were seventeen-year-old Emmeline Woodward, recently married to Bishop Newel Whitney, and Mary Richards, whose husband begged her to keep an account he might read on his return from a mission to England. Leonora Taylor began a new, more consistent journal. Hosea Stout, a Kentuckian who had served as a policeman in Nauvoo, continued a diary he had begun two years before, when he was ordained to a Quorum of Seventies in Nauvoo.

Trail diaries are a staple of American literature. There are so many of them and the details they record are so much alike that they tend to merge. One rainstorm, one runaway team, seems so much like another. But, unlike families who took the Oregon Trail in the same period, the Mormons had been forced to leave their homes. In that sense, they had a bit in common with the displaced Potawatomi and Omaha peoples, on whose lands they took temporary refuge once they reached the Missouri River. Unlike the better-organized Mormon migration to the Rocky Mountains that began a year later, the flight from Nauvoo was characterized by emotional as well as physical disorder. It wasn't just the weather, or the difficulty of selling Nauvoo property, or even the fear of encountering hostile Missourians along the way. It was the pressure to live up to an ideal of sainthood that had been elevated to impossible heights during the last weeks in Nauvoo.

Some sense of this buoyancy is conveyed in a scene from the diary of Hosea Stout. Shortly after crossing into Iowa, he came near the site where his first wife, Samantha, had died in 1839, after the Saints' expulsion from Missouri. "I passed by the grave which was near to the road. I found the paling still round it which I put there seven years ago as a last token of respect due to her until the first resurrection." Instead of reawakening an old sorrow, the marker reminded him of how much God had blessed him.

> When I left this place I went disconsolate and alone mourning her untimely death and my own lonesome condition. But I went to Nauvoo to keep the commandments of God. . . . Instead of being deprived of my last bosom friend I now had three equally dear and confiding to me.[8]

In Nauvoo, Stout had been sealed to three other women ostensibly without any loss in the love he had felt for Samantha. In the temple his now dead wife had been sealed to him for eternity.[9] Like Job, he had survived a devastating loss and through faith received a threefold increase.

Mormon diarists left Nauvoo with sacred promises reverberating in their souls. As they dragged their heavily loaded wagons across Iowa, they discovered how much they had to learn about pioneering, and how little they knew about the demands of establishing God's kingdom.[10]

"a perfect gale"

On February 27, William Clayton crossed into Iowa with Ruth, Margaret, Mother Moon, and the children. Diantha, who was eight months pregnant, had stayed in Nauvoo, planning to join them after her first baby was born. Although Clayton was pleased to be in a company with Nauvoo's musicians, not even the prospect of playing his violin could compensate for the relentless weariness of life on the trail. By the first week in April, he was truly ill. He revived a bit on April 4, when the "quadrille band" rallied and gave an impromptu concert near his tent. But the pleasure was brief. Lightning began before the music was done. Soon a storm "broke forth from the NW" until it was "a perfect gale," with wind so high all the tents, except his own, collapsed.[11]

Farther back, two hundred wagons lay motionless along the doughy trail. Eliza Lyman slept in her stepfather's wagon "with my head on his and Mother's bed with my feet on the front end board and my clothes wet about a quarter of a yard deep about my ankles." In such a situation, her only defense was humor: "I do not know why I did not freeze, for I had no bed and very little covering. It must be that there was not room in the wagon for the frost to get in, it was so full of folks." In the tumble of wagons, carriages, and tents, it was difficult to know where one family ended and another began. "Arose in the morning and found the mud so deep that we could not get from the wagon to the tent without getting nearly mired," she reported.[12] Mud was a mark of the deep topsoil that in future years would make Iowa an agricultural paradise. As the frontier axiom asserts, "Good soil makes bad roads."[13]

Leonora Taylor was horrified to see her seven-year-old son, Joseph, come home from tracking a lost ox covered in mud to his elbows. She was protective of him: with the death of little Leonora Agnes in Nauvoo, he had become her youngest child. In her last years in Nauvoo, Leonora had not only ended her childbearing years, she had lost some part of her identity as John Taylor's wife. Before leaving, he had been sealed to a dozen women, five of them in the month before their departure.[14] At least two of the new wives were with her on the trek across Iowa. She referred to them as "the girls," the usual term for household helpers in this era. She betrayed her annoyance when, on one miserable morning, "Mr T pact the girls things went with them and left the Children & I to scramble through the mud how we could." Yet a few days later, she seemed pleased to have their company. "Sat awhile with the girls," she wrote.[15]

Eighteen-year-old Emmeline Woodward was one of the "girls" in Bishop Newel K. Whitney's family. When her young husband, James Harris, went downriver to St. Louis to find work and never returned, she agreed to become Whitney's plural wife, having already worked as a tutor for his children.[16] Her diary entries on the trail were relentlessly upbeat, until she awoke in the middle of the night in a dripping tent with a wet pillow and quilt. On April 17, she reported her first sighting of a prairie rattler. Soon there were dozens slithering out of the muck. She quickly discovered what a molting rattler could do: "Tonight when the horses and cattle were brought up one of the horses Old Bill we call him had been bitten by a rattlesnake in three or four places about his nose." Despite the application of Indian remedies, the horse's nose continued to fester, until one day he dropped dead while trying to cross a stream on a log. Emmeline penned a eulogy: "We greatly regret his death for he has been a great use to us he was very large and strong and always true to his place."[17]

When her carriage horse was bitten, Leonora applied "Murtaher & oyle & a poltice of salt and onions."[18] Heber Kimball responded by rebuking the poison in the name of God, claiming it was "just as proper to lay hands on a horse or an ox and administer to them in the name of the Lord . . . as it is to a human being, both being creatures of His creation."[19] He might have added that without animals it was impossible to move a thousand loaded wagons across Iowa. At certain mudholes, double-teaming was essential, making it possible on the worst days to move only two or three miles.

Somewhere near the Chariton River, William Huntington became separated from his daughter Zina. Although she had been sealed "for time" to Brigham Young in the Nauvoo Temple, she was still with her legal husband, Henry Jacobs, when Eliza Lyman came across their wagon in the mud. She reported that Zina was "sick in bed on the top of the load, so near the wet cover that she could hardly raise her head, a babe in her arms but a few days old, and no other wagon near, or friends to do anything for her except her husband."[20] A week later, Zina's father found the Jacobses camped with other Latter-day Saints further along the trail. They had named their son Henry Chariton Jacobs, for his father and for the river near where he was born. Henry had been called on a mission. He left on May 31, to join Zina's brother Oliver Huntington in New York, and then would embark with him for England. He wrote Zina telling her to take good care of the cattle he had left, promising to love her for eternity, and acknowledging that though there would be "many shiftings in time and revisions in eternity" all would be made right in the end. He seems to have known that they would never again live together as husband and wife, and that Zina would soon join Brigham's family.[21]

Patty Sessions acknowledged the complexities of sealings for time and for eternity when she recorded the name of Sarah Ann Whitney's baby as "David Kimball Smith." The middle name acknowledged Heber Kimball as the baby's earthly father, the surname honored Joseph's claim in the hereafter. Patty noted that the baby had been born "in the valley of David," acknowledging the Biblical resonance in the name Heber had given to the spot. Whether intentional or not, it evoked the "valley of the shadow of death," as in the psalm.[22] Brigham had come with Heber to visit the child; Mary Ann and Vilate had blessed him.[23]

Patty officiated at fourteen births on the Iowa Trail. In all but two of these cases, she listed a payment under the name of the baby's father. In Sarah Ann's case, she forgave the fee as a gift. In the case of "Black Jane," she credited the payment to a "Brother Dikes," observing that "Jane and Isaac lives with him." Jane was Jane Elizabeth Manning, a free black woman who had joined the Church in Connecticut and in the fall of 1840 journeyed to Nauvoo, where she met and married another African American, Isaac James. Dikes paid Patty in flour, which he considered worth four cents a pound when others asked only two. Since his payment was probably on an account owed to Jane, he cheated her as well as Patty.[24]

On April 15, someone ran to William Clayton's tent to tell him that a message had arrived from Nauvoo. Diantha had safely delivered her first child, a boy, two weeks before. He was ecstatic about the baby, distressed to learn that Diantha had been ill with the ague and mumps. He settled his feelings by writing new words to a song he already knew.[25] The original words imagined the thoughts of a dying Christian:

> What's this that steals, that steals upon my frame?
> Is it death? Is it death?
> That soon will quench, will quench this mortal flame.
> Is it death? Is it death?
> If this be death, I soon shall be
> From every pain and sorrow free:
> I shall the king of glory see—
> All is well! All is well![26]

Despite the final assertion that all is well, the melodramatic opening lines gave primacy to death rather than redemption.

Clayton's lyrics transformed this dreary soliloquy by inviting a band of believers to join a holy procession:

> Come, come, ye Saints, no toil nor labor fear
> But with joy wend your way
> Tho' hard to you this journey may appear
> Grace shall be as your day.
> 'Tis better far for us to strive
> Our useless cares from us to drive;
> Do this, and joy your hearts will swell—
> All is well! All is well!

One can almost imagine the Nauvoo Brass Band rousing the Saints as they emerged from their muddy tents to continue their journey to an unknown Zion.

The new version gently rebuked those tempted to murmur or speak ill of their leaders.

> Why should we mourn or think our lot is hard?
> 'Tis not so, all is right.
> Why should we think to earn a great reward
> If we now shun the fight?
> Gird up your loins, fresh courage take,
> Our God will never us forsake;
> And soon we'll have this tale to tell
> All is well! All is well!

Clayton's words were relentlessly, even defiantly, optimistic. He assured himself that he and his weary fellows would arrive at their far-off refuge, and that when they did the world would know it.

> We'll find the place which God for us prepared,
> Far away in the West,
> Where none shall come to hurt or make afraid;
> There the Saints will be blessed.
> We'll make the air with music ring,
> Shout praises to our God and King;

Above the rest these words we'll tell
All is well! All is well!

Only in the last stanza did he acknowledge the possibility of death. Even then, he gave the final word not to the dead but to those who survived.

And should we die before our journey's through
Happy day! All is well!
We then are free from toil and sorrow too;
With the just we shall dwell.
But if our lives are spared again
To see the Saints their rest obtain,
O how we'll make this chorus swell
All is well! All is well![27]

"Come, Come, Ye Saints" has appeared in every Latter-day Saint hymnal since 1851. Today, it is known around the world as the landmark Mormon anthem. In the deluge and drizzle of 1846, it was one anxious father's heartfelt hope.[28]

Hope and despair, birth and death came together on the sodden trail across Iowa. On April 22, after a sleepless night, Patty Sessions "went and put Hosea Stouts wife to bed with a daughter." Stout's own diary completes the story. "The weather was warm, sultry with a damp heavy air & broken clouds. This was my first born in the wilderness as some of the old prophets once said and from the situation of our dwelling might be called a 'Prairie chicken.'" There was sly humor in his description, but also half-expressed fear. The next day, he weighed all three of his children. Newborn Louisa weighed a healthy eight pounds and four-year-old Hosea Jr., thirty-three, but two-year-old Hyrum, strangely out of sync with his siblings, tipped only fifteen pounds on the scale. Hyrum was probably already suffering from what his father thought was "hoping [whooping] cough and black canker." On May 9, Patty wrote, "Hosea Stouts child died with fits I went and laid it out."[29]

Nobody knows how many children died on the trek across Iowa; exposure and malnutrition may have doubled mortality rates. Children suffered not only from infectious diseases like measles and whooping cough but from ailments now only found in impoverished areas of the world. "Black canker" may have been noma, a potentially lethal disease that often began with small ulcers in the mouth, which then turned black as they ate away tissue. Although the Mormon migration was spared the cholera that ravaged communities elsewhere, they eventually encountered the horrors of scurvy as they continued to live on corn cakes and salt meat.[30]

Hosea poured his anguish into his diary: "My wife is yet unable to go about & little Hosea my only son now is wearing down with the same complaint. . . . I have fearful forboding of coming evil on my family yet. We are truly desolate & afflicted and entirely destitute of any thing even to eat much less to nourish the sick."[31] Although Patty wasn't there to record the event, little Hosea died at the end of June after experiencing such harrowing seizures that his parents thought he had been afflicted with evil spirits. Although they called in neighbors for prayer and in the solitude of their own wagon invoked the signs they had received in the temple, they were unable to save him. Stout buried him on a hill above the prairie beside another fresh grave.[32]

One morning, camped at the temporary settlement the Saints had named Mount Pisgah in memory of the spot where Moses looked over into the Promised Land, Eliza Snow looked up from the book she was reading to see a "funeral train following to its wilderness grave a little child." Since leaving Nauvoo, she had filled page after page of her diary with her own compositions, songs of affirmation and consolation. As the journey dragged on, she found it hard to keep up with the nursing and the mourning. On good days, she, like Clayton, roused herself—and others—with cheering verses.

> All at once is life in motion—
> Trunks and beds & baggage fly;
> Oxen yok'd & horses harness'd—
> Tents roll'd up, are passing by. . . .
> Camp of Israel! All is well.[33]

But on dark days, it seemed as though, in fleeing their modern-day Egypt, the Saints had taken the plagues with them. Somewhere beyond Mount Pisgah, the wagon she was driving passed a ragged clearing where someone was digging a grave. Beside it stood "a rudely constructed coffin" made from planks still covered with bark, a mark not only of the death of the body but of the loss of some essential component of the soul. "It seemed like a desolation & the wasting of the house of Israel," Eliza wrote.[34]

"not pleased with our coming"

When the first refugees left Nauvoo in February, Wilford and Phebe were on separate ships on the Atlantic, returning from their mission to England. Just before the Woodruffs left Nauvoo, Brigham Young had blessed Phebe that her children would be preserved while she was gone and that angels would watch over little Susan Cornelia as she crossed the sea with her parents. His prophecies had come true.[35] Although letters arrived from America with excruciating infrequency, all reported that Willie and Phoebe Amelia were well. Susan Cornelia's angels, who included a doting sister in the Liverpool Branch, also did their work. Wilford proudly reported that by the time they left England his two-and-a-half-year-old daughter could "read in two or three syllables quite well."[36]

To Wilford, a new baby, born in Liverpool, seemed a gift from God. "This is the first Child we have had since our endowment," he wrote. Then, invoking the language of Isaiah, he continued, "for unto us a child is born unto us a Son is given. His name shall be called JOSEPH for unto him the Priesthood belongs. He is the first fruits of the fulness of the Priesthood out of the loins of Ancient Joseph through the lineage of Ephraim given unto us in answer to our prayers."[37] In a portrait painted just before the family left England, little Joseph wears a string of coral beads and a delicate white dress that mirrors his mother's ruffled bonnet and collar. Her dark eyes peer out from the painting with a look somewhere between resolution and fear.[38] (See color insert 2, page 5, portrait of Phebe and Joseph Woodruff.)

About the same time, Phebe was struck with an episode of facial pain much like the one she had experienced after her visit to Connecticut in 1841, a malady that, as Wilford wrote, was "in England called <u>tic dileraux</u>. It causes the most excruciating pain in the face Jaw neck & sholdier. Her jaws set like the lockjaw." Tic douloureux, a recurring neurological disorder, doesn't actually cause paralysis, but the pain is so intense that any sort of motion makes it worse. Phebe's susceptibility to such attacks may explain her often dour expression in paintings and photos. Since any sudden movement of the face or jaw might trigger pain, she may have learned to keep her facial muscles still, especially when under stress.[39]

Fortunately, Phebe's pain soon subsided, and she was able to board a ship with about forty other English Saints, including Mary Ann Jackson, who had been the Woodruffs' housekeeper. Phebe's group sailed to

New Orleans, then took a steamer up the Mississippi. Wilford spent a few more days settling mission affairs, then took a packet boat to New York City. However practical, the decision to travel separately must have created anxiety for them both. Well aware that the Saints were planning to leave Nauvoo, they had no way of knowing when and where they would meet again. It was perhaps especially difficult for Phebe to bypass a visit to her father and siblings in Maine. Mother Carter had died suddenly while they were in England, a great distress for Phebe, who, as Wilford noted, "was very much attached to her Mother."[40]

Phebe's journey was apparently uneventful. Wilford's was harrowing. The storm that struck the ship in mid-February was unlike any he had ever experienced. Hurricane-force winds battered the ship through "the longest & most dismal night I ever spent at sea." Waves washed over the quarterdeck, broke the compass house in pieces, and smashed the wheel that governed the helm. "Came near washing the men overboard," he told his diary.[41] On February 22, while the passengers and crew were still recovering from the storm, a ten-year-old child died. Wilford was shaken when the little girl's coffin, though weighted with stones, failed to sink. "We saw it swimming near half a mile from the Ship."[42] He thought of his own children—Susan Cornelia and little Joseph with their mother somewhere on the Atlantic, four-year-old Phoebe with relatives in Maine, and Wilford Jr. still in Nauvoo. Would he ever see them again? On February 28, he wrote, "I dreamed last night that there was a great Storm that killed thousands of Birds that were floating upon the water. I saw many that were not quite dead. I waided in 2 or three feet of water & picked out many of them & put them under a goose that was sitting & they were warmed brought to life & run about lively & well."[43]

Even more than he wanted to convert the world, Wilford wanted to gather his family to safety, not just Phebe and the children but his parents, too. His sixty-seven-year-old father had lost his position in the Farmington mills: "turned off without any notice" in his old age after a lifetime of work, and after spending the summer getting the mills in good repair for the next season.[44] Wilford decided that baptizing his relatives wasn't enough. He wanted to take them to Zion—wherever that turned out to be.

He arrived in New York on March 5. On March 11, he was in Connecticut, helping his parents begin preparations for the journey west. On March 17, he was in Maine to collect Phoebe Amelia. Father Carter told him that Mother Carter's spirit appeared to him every night. One night, she put her arms around his neck and leaned upon him. When he asked her why she did that, she said, "Because I pitty you." When Wilford told him that Phebe's wish was that he be baptized and receive the priesthood, he seemed willing, but the next morning he had changed his mind: "It was A vary Cold day the snow over the ground And water frooze over And he Could not get an evidence that it was his duty then And thought it best to omit it." He walked with Wilford to his wife's grave and said that he would soon lie there with her. Wilford picked up a few stones from the grave to take to Phebe.[45]

Back in Connecticut to collect his parents, Wilford found his cousin Betsey Cosset ready to join the migration. By the time they left New York, there were twenty or thirty "friends," presumably church members, ready to join him. By April 13, they were in Nauvoo. Transportation in the Eastern United States had advanced so much that Wilford's thousand-mile journey by railroad, riverboat, and coach—from New York to Nauvoo with side trips to Maine and Connecticut and visits along the way—took less than six weeks. It would take him twice as long to move his family three hundred miles across Iowa.[46]

Wilford's account of the journey from Maine to Nauvoo focused on Phoebe Amelia, who never stopped asking for her mother, even though at times she wasn't quite sure who that was. "Where is my Mother," she asked after they parted with Phebe's sister Sarah Foss, who had taken them to the station in Portland.

"Which one?" Wilford answered. Phoebe Amelia said the one who had come with them to the depot. When he told her that Aunt Sarah had gone home, she cried at being left alone. At bedtime that night in Boston, she asked it again: "Where is my Mother? I want to lie with her." Wilford persuaded her to share his bed.[47]

Throughout the journey, he took responsibility for his daughter's care, getting up with her in the night, nursing her when she had a nosebleed, and devoting precious space in his diary to her words, a rare occurrence for a diarist who generally ignored children unless they were newborn, ill, or dying. He seemed charmed rather than annoyed by his daughter's relentless questions. She had been barely two and a half when her parents left her in Maine. Now she was a "large fleshy girl" with a four-year-old's curiosity. "In passing a river Phebe Asked me who Put the water there. I told Her God. She Asked me who helped him & how he got it there And several such curious questions. Many persons seemed quite interested on the journey in Phebe's conversation." Unfortunately, Wilford didn't record his own answers. Did he tell her that someday she, too, might create worlds?[48]

Azubah Woodruff, Wilford's stepmother, kept her own account of the journey. He had given her an old account book of his half brother Asahel's that he had gotten in Terre Haute after Asahel's death. At the top of the first page, Azubah wrote in a bold, clear hand: "Journey to California." More interested in her physical surroundings and her own state of health than in the people around her, she was especially impressed with the Ilus Carter house in New York, where the group stayed for a few days before embarking for the West. Phebe's brother was a merchant—in Azubah's eyes, admirably situated. "I was conducted up three or four pair of stairs all nicely carpeted & slept on a bedstead of mahogany worth I should think not far from a hundred Dollars & coverlets of damask Silk & counterpanes." Azubah's own prose aspired to such gentility. "I spent the time very agreeably with Mrs Carter & was favored with an Interview with her sisters being four in number." Later, on a boat bound for Cincinnati, she was pleased to find "quite a large company on board of Ladies & gentlemen."[49]

On a springlike morning on a different vessel, she had a quite different experience: she walked into a "Saloon" or sitting room where there had been a number of children. "I soon found to my astonishment that I was in no very pleasant fix, the bottom of my skirts were all besmirched as I found by taking hold of them to rise up in consequence of which I have had to change me throughout which has caused me some trouble of washing &c besides the jollity & laughing which the novelty of the circumstance produced."[50] She did not say who laughed at her or how her skirt became soiled. Had the children left something on the chair she sat in? Had she inadvertently dragged her long skirts through waste water or dirt before arriving in the room? Had she failed to see an earlier stain when she dressed for the day? In her journal at least, she kept her dignity.

Azubah had probably never traveled so far before. She was only eighteen when she married Aphek, a widower thirteen years her senior who had three young sons. Wilford, the youngest, was two and a half, the age Phoebe Amelia was when her parents left her in Maine. Only a year old when his mother died, he had probably been cared for by a grandmother or an aunt before he, too, learned to call another woman "Mother." Azubah was now almost fifty-four years old. She had raised Aphek's sons and given birth to six children of her own. Now all five of her boys were dead.[51] Using Asahel's account book as she retraced part of the route he had taken west, she may have felt close to him, perhaps too close to mention in writing. Eunice, her only daughter and her last surviving child, was very much on her mind. As they boarded a steamboat for the trip upriver to Nauvoo, she began to think about their reunion, wondering if Providence would favor her with finding Eunice in the land of the living. The closer she came, the more confident she felt: "A whisper sometimes assures me that I shall." Then she quickly remembered her obligation to Wilford. "I also feel much interest in the welfare of our dear son who is with us & by whose liberality through the blessing of God we are enabled to perform this journey."[52] Wilford was not only a beloved son, but at this point the main source of his parents' support.

In Nauvoo, Azubah rejoiced in finding Eunice newly delivered of a child. For Wilford the reunion with his sister was not so pleasant. "I found that Br Dwight Webster And Sister Eunice felt to turn from the Church and walk no more with us." He feared they had been influenced by a dissenter named James Strang, who offered himself and his church as an alternative to Brigham Young. Even worse, they appeared to be turning Aphek and Azubah in their direction. In a contentious meeting, Wilford spoke his mind, perhaps destroying forever the close relationship he had once had with his only sister.[53]

Although the Church had used the upper floor of the temple for endowments in the early winter, the lower floors were still unfinished. Carpenters continued to work through the winter, hoping to get it in good enough shape to dedicate and then perhaps sell, to help raise money for the migration. On April 30, Woodruff sat in the high pulpits for the dedication, taking Phebe, Mary Ann Jackson, and his parents with him. Although there is no hint of this in the diary, he may have been sealed to Jackson about this time, an action that may explain a cryptic entry in his diary for May 14: "Some of my friends at times are tried in the Celestial Law."[54] Since the term "friend" could mean almost any relative, including a wife, Phebe may have been one of those "tried." If so, Wilford was not about to admit it.

Somehow, Wilford mended whatever problem he was having with his parents, although Eunice and Dwight decided not to continue on the journey west. The Woodruffs left Nauvoo on May 16, with three baggage wagons, a carriage, six yoke of oxen, six cows, four calves, one yearling, and a pair of mules. "The Calves and cows all run various ways And while I was trying to get them together the oxen broke the tong out of my carriage," Wilford groused. Then his father drove one of the wagons into a mudhole. It took eight teams to pull it out. "This was one of the worst days of my life," he exploded.[55] More trouble followed. On May 27, "A serious Accident Happened to Father Woodruff. He went to get into the waggon while the oxen were traveling. The foreboard gave way that He took hold of & He instantly fell upon His back & both wheels of the waggon load with 25 cwt passed over his legs And arms And came near passing over his Head." Miraculously, the old man survived without a single broken bone.[56]

After that, it seemed petty to complain about mud. But this was mud such as no one had ever seen before. Wilford's superlatives mounted as he pushed across streams, swamps, and sloughs. The "exceeding bad road" they traveled on June 6, was in his view "the worst of any we had had," though not so bad as the next day's trail, which was without question "the worst peace of road on the whole journey." That night, he labored waist-deep in mud and water until 2:00 a.m., trying unsuccessfully to extricate two of his wagons from a swamp. "Cousin Betsey was in one waggon & remained all night," he wrote, adding that before daybreak he had rolled himself up in a buffalo robe and gotten a little sleep.[57]

By the time the Woodruff wagons reached Mount Pisgah, Azubah had had enough. "Mother Woodruff Handed me A lengthy epistle of complaint written in a book of 30 pages against several persons there treatment to her &c." When he referred to "several persons," Wilford was protecting Phebe, who was the target of almost all of Azubah's complaints. He refused to take his stepmother's grievances seriously. Her complaints, he wrote, were "like A tempest in a tea pot or a buble not worthy of notice. The more I have provided for Her of late the more she has Complained. She has manfiested much of a spirit of fault finding & watching for iniquity since she came to Nauvoo." He blamed it on the influence of Dwight and Eunice, "who have turned Strangites."[58]

Amazingly, Azubah's thirty-three-page manifesto survives, hidden with her travel journal in the folds of Asahel's account book. At this distance, the details do indeed seem petty—a slight over access to milk, a brusque encounter over the location of a piece of meat, disagreement over the handling of diapers (Azubah called them "shitten cloths"). All seem predictable annoyances for a group trying to keep themselves alive and well while traveling through rain and mud with animals and small children. But in Azubah's mind they amounted to something bigger. Like everyone else, she was dealing with the difficulties of being a pioneer, but her complaints offer hints of what was probably long-standing friction with Phebe, who was of course dealing with difficult adjustments of her own. Her time in England had preserved her from the radical expansion of plural marriage. Now she was having to confront it and the pioneer trail all at once.

Azubah's manifesto mentioned three other women who appeared to be traveling with the Woodruffs in addition to Phebe, herself, and Cousin Betsey—a "Mary," a "Sarah," and a woman she sometimes referred to as "Miss King."[59] "Mary" was no doubt Mary Ann Jackson. "Miss King" was Rosetta King, a woman who seemed only temporarily connected to the family. "Sarah" was probably Sarah Brown, a teenaged helper who was to play a more dramatic role a bit later on the journey. There were also several men, including Wilford and Aphek.[60]

Trying to keep some control over a limited supply of food, Phebe had given Sarah responsibility for dipping milk from the containers where it was stored after each milking. Milk cows, driven along the trail, were a major source of sustenance for adults as well as children. The issue for Mother Woodruff was status. She felt demeaned by Phebe's telling her to ask Sarah for a bit of milk for her tea, when every night she slept in a tent with milk pans all around her. She knew how to care for milk; she knew how to make butter. She thought Phebe ought to acknowledge her expertise and her good sense. "Wilford you will see at once that you need not much discernment to see that your Mother is required to take a lower seat than your Servants." She found herself reduced to begging—or to grabbing what she could, like a hungry child. She began to sneak a little milk when she wanted it, and she snatched fresh bread from the box when Phebe offered her a hard crust. But the very act of resisting diminished her in spirit.[61]

When the company halted to attend to laundry, she told Father Woodruff to give his shirts to Phebe's girls. Phebe told the girls they might wash the shirts but nothing more, not even the soiled sheet Azubah offered. The tug of war over who was going to do the laundry provoked an argument over who did or did not do laundry in Farmington five years before, when Wilford and Phebe stayed with his parents for a month. Azubah insisted that Phebe did little if any of her own washing. Phebe said she did her own and more, even though she was so ill she could barely sit up. She claimed Azubah did nothing to help her with little Willie. Azubah said she herself was ill at the time and working hard to feed a large household and prepare for Eunice's wedding; Phebe had been indifferent to her plight. She had no help "except as Wilford having some compassion on me & some of the feelings of a child offered to wash my dishes for me once & again while you was seated in the front chamber a working of muslin." The reference to working on muslin targeted Phebe's pride in being able to do the kind of white-on-white embroidery displayed in the portrait of her painted in England. Adding everything together, Azubah concluded that Phebe was "not pleased with our coming in the way we have."[62]

For Azubah, the past ten years had been a long spiral downward. Her husband had lost his mills. Her sons and stepsons had moved west, and though she initially embraced their journey as an adventure, she was uncertain whether she would ever again command a house, a kitchen, or a cow of her own. She had migrated in status as well as in body, assuming the perennially difficult position of a dependent in her own son's household. In that sense, the conflict between Azubah and Phebe was generational and archetypal. But for Phebe, the time-honored difficulty of defining status in a household with more than one adult female was now compounded by the presence of women who, though not yet acknowledged, would soon enter her world as Wilford's wives. She, too, was having to learn new rules. In the meantime, she took full control of the milk her cows produced, the bread she was forced to ration, and the labor of the still-subservient girls in her wagon.

"family discord"

On June 21, Wilford preached to a large congregation of Saints at Mount Pisgah.[63] Mary Richards, an immigrant from Lancashire who was traveling with her husband's parents while he was serving a mission in England, was grateful for the seeming formality of a Sabbath meeting even in such a temporary place. She pronounced Wilford's sermon "an exelant discorse," fascinated by the joy he expressed in being able to meet with his fellow believers "away from what is now called the Christian World."[64] Others attending that meeting had the same feeling.

When the rain came back, the feeling changed. Leonora Taylor reported "pouring down rain" nearly every day, lamenting "everything wet in the wagon."[65] On June 24, Wilford complained, "The wind has blown vary hard & cold from the east for two days."[66] Caught in the same downpour, Mary Richards wrapped herself in a quilt and hunkered down in whatever shelter she could find. "A wet gloomy morn," she wrote on June 26, and then, two days later, "I felt as gloomy as the times."[67] William Clayton, traveling back along the trail to meet Diantha, who had finally left Nauvoo, was forced to take a wagon box off its wheels and use it as a boat to float things over a swollen stream where a bridge had washed out.[68]

By the time Clayton returned to Mount Pisgah, frightening rumors were swirling through the camp. Somebody warned Eliza Snow that Lilburn Boggs, the infamous Missouri governor who had expelled the Mormons from his state in 1838, was somewhere near them on the trail, with troops ready to finish the job.[69] Clayton heard someone say that the Missourians had dispatched a committee to search for Mormon forts and cannons. "He also stated that we have got a friend in the British parliament and the British had held a private council in relation to the treatment of the U.S. towards us." Supposedly, Britain was contemplating a war against the United States and not only was sending troops to Canada and around Cape Horn to Oregon, but planned "to arm the slaves of the South and have their Agents in the Indian country . . . fight the U.S."[70] Wilford gave none of these details in his own diary, although he did mention having "an interview" with Clayton, perhaps a foolhardy thing to do with a man disposed to write everything down.[71]

When a contingent of federal officers reached Mount Pisgah and announced that they had been sent by President Polk to raise five hundred volunteers from among the Mormons to help fight the Mexican War, Wilford was skeptical. "I Had some reasons to believe them to be spies & that the president Had no hand in it."[72] Hosea Stout, still reeling from the death of his sons, was even more suspicious. He considered it a plot designed to bring trouble to the Mormons as a people. "For in the event that we did not comply with the requisition," the Americans would denounce them as enemies. If they did comply, then they would have "500 of our men in their power to be destroyed as they had done our leaders at Carthage."[73]

By the time church leaders reached Council Bluffs, they knew that the soldiers had been telling the truth. The United States government had finally responded to church appeals for help. If the Mormons would raise five hundred volunteers for the unpopular war with Mexico, the Church could collect a bounty they could use to finance their journey west and in the meantime could settle temporarily on Indian territory (near present-day Omaha, Nebraska).[74]

"We are now in the Wilderness," Leonora Taylor wrote as her family set up camp near the Missouri River. "Our Property which was worth ten thousand Dollars is gone, all except the Necessaries we have with us, we have been obliged to sacrifice it to the Mob." But as long as she had food and raiment for her family, she cared nothing about such things, or so she told her diary. She was delighted to report that the Woodruffs had "campt near us which is a great comfort to me."[75] Phebe no doubt found the arrangement pleasant as well. "We built A Bower between Elder Taylors Tent And my own," Wilford wrote, "And A large assembly of Saints met At an early hour." He spoke for an hour about his travels through the British Isles, after which Parley Pratt "reproved sin especially swareing And then addressed the people upon the subject of the Calafornia volunteers & expedition."[76]

Hosea Stout said Pratt "spoke at length in favor of sending off the 500 troops to Santa Fe and explained it to the satisfaction of most of the Saints. Indeed it needed considerable explaining for every one was about as much prejudiced as I was at first."[77] He and Wilford had both been persuaded by the "gentlemanly" manner of the army recruiter, and by the affirmations of Thomas Kane, a non-Mormon from Philadelphia, who had been shocked by the treatment of the Mormons in Missouri and Illinois and had advocated for them in Washington. Hosea found Colonel James Allen to be "a plain non assuming man without that proud over bearing strut and self conceited dignity which some call an officer-like appearance." As for Kane, he "was quite an intelligent man notwithstanding he was uncommonly small and feminine."[78]

On July 11, Wilford "spent the day in the camp assisting to gather the volunteers" for the Mormon Battalion. Leonora was more interested in the round of festivities under the hastily constructed bower in the center of the camp—a dance on July 12, then, on July 15, a wedding, and, on virtually every day up to July 16, more "Music, Voluntering, dancing."[79] The Mormons were going to send their young men off to war with as much cheer as they could manage. "Danced with Bro W Cory, W Hyde, W Kimball, and last of all with Bro Brigham," Mary Richards wrote, quickly adding that no amount of dancing could compensate for the absence of her husband, Samuel, who was in England.[80]

Patty Sessions missed the muster and the dancing. On July 16, she was camped west of the Missouri River, where her husband and son were helping to build a bridge across the Elkhorn River. She was not doing well. On August 7, she wrote, "I have lain in the waggon most all day." Then her diary stopped for almost a month. When it resumed, it was as if she had risen from the dead. "I have been very sick," she explained, "did not have my clothes on for 20 days, I vomited 4 days and nights." Nothing seemed to help. "The Doctor said I had the inflammation in the stomach and it would be a miricle if I got well." As long as she could be sure of being reunited with her loved ones on resurrection day, Patty was ready to die. When her family gathered to bid her farewell, she told them where her temple clothing was "and requested to have the latitude and longitude taken where I was lain and also to have cedar posts put down to my grave with my name cut on them so that I could be found when cald for."[81]

By late summer, Leonora Taylor's diary had become one long recital of illnesses—her own and others'. She "Doctored" one woman, made beer for another, and then, after serving "a Large Veale Pie" to five Ottawa chiefs, made soup and "took it around" to those who were ailing.[82] Mary Richards had also turned nurse. When her two-year-old niece died, she composed an awkward but heartfelt epitaph:

> Peacefull her gentle Spirit fled.
> The Heavenly Corts to adorn.
> Her body slumbers with the dead
> To wait the resurrection morn.

Then she added that the child's sickness has been "the diarrhea and canker."[83]

"The destroyer stalked forth triumphantly," Hosea Stout wrote on September 26, when his plural wife Marinda and her newborn baby died.[84] By the time Eliza Lyman recovered from childbed fever, she looked so much like a skeleton that those who had not been with her did not know her. Because of her illness, her infant was also failing.[85] Eliza Snow's diary also stopped during a fever that had "run nearly 40 days." Worse than that, she believed, was "family discord, which I think proper to call hell, reigning around me." She was horrified to witness a conversation late at night between the couple with whom she was traveling. "Revenge & retaliation seem'd the ruling spirits of each, & the pow'rs of darkness seem'd holding a jubilee around us."[86] The Saints had struggled through the mud of Iowa only to reach a worse misery. In their would-be Zion, there was never enough of anything to go around, never enough food or shelter, never enough respect or love or charity. The harder they tried to live by the dictates of their religion, the more they exposed their own lack of perfection.

Mary Richards was candid about her own limitations. When her husband wrote that he might want to add their old friend Ellen Wilding to his family when he returned from his mission, Mary responded with dismay. "I was in hopes that after your return you would have been contented to have lived with me alone for a little season. A comfort which I have never yet been permitted to enjoy although it has been the greatest desire of my heart." She liked Ellen Wilding, but she wasn't ready to share her husband's affection. "If you had seen what I have seen you would not wonder why I thus wrote for there is no such a thing as happiness known here where a man has more than one [wife]. It realy seems to me that this is a day in which Woman is destined to misery." Mary was clearly relieved when Ellen arrived in camp a few weeks later as the plural wife of Edwin Woolley. She went out of her way to welcome her.[87]

Patty Sessions's long struggle with her husband's other wife exemplified the misery Mary imagined. In Patty's view, Rosilla was nothing but trouble. She wouldn't work. She took supplies without asking. She carried tales. And worse. On November 4, Patty was distraught. "He has lain with her three nights she has told him many falsehoods and is trying to have him take her to Nauvoo and then to Maine and leave me for good I have not spoke to her to day yet she says I have quarreled with her all day I go to bed know not what to do." Finally, Patty's adult son Perrigrine intervened: "Said he had seen me abused long enough." He told Rosilla he had seen his mother cook and her sit and do nothing and then come to the table and crowd her away. Rosilla "went to the waggon saying she had nothing to do with him nor the old woman." She came and went for another month; then, on December 3, Patty reported with satisfaction, "Rosilla started for Nauvoo."[88]

By this time, most members of the Quorum of the Twelve had multiple wives. Wilford's apparent monogamy was beginning to stand out. On August 2, he wrote that Brigham had come to his tent and "delivered an interesting lecture upon the priesthood And the principal of sealing." He couldn't bring himself to admit what had actually happened, simply noting the presence of "Phebe W. Woodruff, Caroline Barton, Caroline Brown, Mary Jackson." In the margin he drew a tiny heart with keys.[89] In Jackson's case, this may have been an affirmation of an alliance made earlier. Seventeen-year-old Caroline Barton and eighteen-year-old Sarah Brown had apparently been living with the family as household helpers. That he called both of them "Caroline" suggests that he was either a bit flustered or that he had trouble telling them apart. On August 20, Wilford carried Phebe in their carriage "into a deep vale of a shaded grove to spend the day in solitude for her health." Now four months into her sixth pregnancy, she hadn't been sleeping well. Or so he said. Surely, more than one episode of family discord lay behind this retreat.[90]

More drama lay ahead. On August 27, Wilford returned from an expedition across the river to find "an evil in the camp." Certain wicked young men had been spending nights "in fiddleing & dancing And afterwards leading away young women into folley & wickedness." Among the women were Wilford's supposed wives Caroline Barton and Sarah Brown. This time, Wilford got their names right. He told them they either had to remain home at night or leave his house. Although Willard Richards warned them they would someday give their right arms to be part of the Woodruff family, they "manifested a disposition to live els whare." These purported marriages had lasted less than a month.[91]

The girls got off easy. Hosea Stout, who was serving as camp policeman, assembled a posse to track down the men. "Elder Woodruff said that they and the girls had been out for fifteen nights in succession until after two o'clock and that it was his wish & the wish of the President that I should take the matter in hand," he wrote. One man, believing the punishment for adultery was death, was relieved to discover there would only be a whipping. Another, in the midst of his eighteen stripes, cried out, "O . . . if you will only stop I'll never touch another girl again while hell's afloat." A third sassed back and got a double whipping. Hosea was careful to note that the whippings didn't draw blood, at least on the first two, and that the camp police sat the men down afterward and explained the law. When some people, including the mother of one of the men, complained that the punishment was too harsh, Brigham and Heber used their Sunday sermons to defend the police. If the Saints were to survive their sojourn into the wilderness, they said, the "Law of God" had to be enforced.[92]

Unfortunately, the law had no power over death. On November 4, little Joseph Woodruff's cold "setteled upon his lungs"; he died on November 12. "He had suffered much from convulsions during his sickness but breathed his last and fell asleep this morning 15 minutes before 6 oclok. And we took his remains to the grave at 4 oclok in the afternoon," his father wrote. The Woodruffs' child of promise was no more. Seeing the suffering around him, Wilford tried not to dwell on his own sorrow. "I have never seen the Latter Day Saints in any situation where they seemed to be passing through greater tribulations or wearing out faster than at the present time," he observed.[93] On December 8, Patty Sessions put Phebe "to bed" with a son. Baby Ezra, born six weeks early, lived only two days. "This is the second son we have buried within a short time," Wilford noted blankly. A week later, he came home from unloading supplies to find that Phebe had unpacked the portrait of herself and little Joseph that was rolled in a trunk. That and a lock of his hair was all that was left of the child who had been such a gift to them in England.[94]

Eliza Lyman had no portrait. "The baby is dead and I mourn his loss," she wrote on December 12. She and her sister Caroline had taken turns sitting up with him every night, trying to save him, "for we could not bear to part with him, but we were powerless." Eliza was thankful for friends and for the poem of consolation Eliza Snow had written, but it was hard to lose a baby, even harder to know there would be no mark of his existence. With precision and in despair, she added, "He was buried on the west side of the Missouri on the second ridge back, the eleventh grave on the second row counting from right to left, the first row being farthest from the river. This will be no guide as the place cannot be found in a few years."[95]

Birth, death, and an occasional celebration marked the ragged settlements on the Missouri as winter settled in. Patty spent December rendering tallow, dipping candles, knitting mittens, mending winter clothing, and officiating at nine births and a miscarriage. On January 1, she had a party. Eliza Snow, who had been in and out of Patty's cabin all week, was there, along with other friends. Patty marked the occasion by reading the sixtieth chapter of Isaiah, understood by the Latter-day Saints, as by other Christians, as a prophecy of the coming of the Messiah. "Arise, shine; for the light is come, and the glory of the Lord is risen upon thee." Given the struggles of the past year, she was enlivened by its promise of redemption. "Whereas thou hast been forsaken and hated . . . I will make thee an eternal excellency, a joy of many generations. . . . Violence shall no more be heard in thy land, wasting nor destruction within thy borders. . . . Thy people also shall be righteous: they shall inherit the land for ever, the branch of my planting, the work of my hands, that I may be glorified."[96]

Patty and her friends would savor the promises, knowing that their journey was not yet over.

7

"Wrote some in my earley Biography"

Camp of Israel, Winter Quarters, Omaha Nation, 1847–1848

For three evenings in a row in early February, Mary Richards sat in a smoky cabin at Winter Quarters, writing in the little packet she had labeled her "Memorandum." Since leaving Nauvoo, she had been true to the promise she had made her husband, Samuel, that she would send letters, keep a diary, and compose an account of her early life. The autobiography had gotten the least attention, but she was determined to finish it. "I Was Born in Chaidgley, In the County of Lancashire, England, Sept 8, 1825," she began.[1]

On February 18, Hosea Stout was engaged in a similar task. "Wrote some in my earley Biography," he noted in his diary. He had spent the day as usual, organizing the night guard and doing other work in an encampment surrounded by Indians hungry enough to steal cattle. When he left Nauvoo, he had been the husband of three wives. Now only Louisa and their tiny daughter were left. Writing helped him to create order out of a life that seemed to move unpredictably from joy to despair.[2]

Patty Sessions was also thinking about her past, although she had no interest in composing a memoir. It was all she could do to keep up with her daily diary. Fortunately, the "Geanalogy" her son Perrigrine began just before leaving Nauvoo helps explain the otherwise cryptic recollections she dropped into her daily entries. When she said there was more snow on the ground than she had seen since leaving Maine, that meant something. As Perrigrine explained, the Sessionses had come from a country where "the climate is cold and dreary in winter and the snow falls deep," a country "heged up on all sides by the highest mountains."[3]

Like all writing, autobiographies are products of the moment in which they were written. Mary Richards's memories of Lancashire, Hosea Stout's droll stories about Kentucky, and Patty and Perrigrine Sessions's allusions to Maine are not only windows into their early lives but reflections of their minds as they endured the winter of 1847 in a refugee camp on the western side of the Missouri River, near present-day Omaha, Nebraska. About a third of the twelve thousand Mormons who fled Nauvoo in the winter and spring of 1846 were now at Winter Quarters, the largest of the Church's temporary settlements and the designated headquarters for their projected migration west. Planted in "Indian territory" by permission of the U.S. government, it was, on paper at least, a planned community of six to eight hundred acres divided into blocks, twenty lots to the acre, with careful specifications for the placement of gardens and outhouses. In truth, it wasn't always easy to distinguish a house from a hovel, and any gardens they may have hoped for were buried in snow. People lived in dugouts, tents, wagon boxes, and rough log or sod cabins. Luxury was having a few panes of glass or a puncheon floor.[4]

Although the refugees believed they had arrived in a wilderness, the area around them had a rich and dynamic history. In the eighteenth century, the Upper Missouri was tied into the French fur trade through dense networks that connected French, Spanish, Osage, Otoe, Illinois, and Pawnee families.[5] These alliances had been disrupted but not entirely destroyed by the arrival of the British, then disturbed a bit more by the expanding United States. In 1802, English-speaking merchants planted Trader's Point at the former Pointe aux Poules. Two years later, Lewis and Clark passed through. By 1812, there was a modest U.S. military presence in the area. The first steamboat chugged upriver from St. Louis in 1819, though by the time the Mormons arrived there were still few white settlers. Potawatomi, Ottawa, and Chippewa reserves occupied the Iowa side of the river. The Omahas dominated the western bank, the area where Winter Quarters was laid out. The Omahas, too, were refugees, under pressure from the United States on one side of the river and, on the other, from the Otoes and Pawnees who challenged their claim to the land.[6]

To reassure government officials who feared they would proselytize among the Indians, church leaders built a six-foot fence around their settlement. To sustain their families, men accepted fur-hauling contracts from traders and took farm or construction work downriver, in Missouri. Women learned to raise and chink their own cabins. Bounty payments from soldiers who had gone with the Mormon Battalion provided some cash for provisions, but it was never enough, and the Missouri River bottoms were no healthier than the Mississippi had been. That old misery, chills and fever, was joined by a new scourge, blackleg or scurvy. Yet, true to form, the Saints built a Council House in the center of the settlement and cheered themselves with dancing, music, and preaching.[7]

On February 9, Mary Richards danced a cotillion with Brigham Young. "Sister Mary you have learned me I am very much obliged to you," he told her. At a party downriver in March, she danced with five different men, staying until 4:00 a.m. since she couldn't find anyone to take her home earlier.[8] Patty Sessions also loved to dance. When her husband, David, didn't feel like joining in, she accepted whoever was handy.[9] Staying out late was the norm. In early March, Hosea Stout took his wife, Louisa, to a party at the Council House. At eleven, when she complained of feeling ill, he took her home, then returned and danced until three.[10]

Hosea Stout and Mary Richards knew some of the same people and occasionally attended the same events. Yet the worlds they described at Winter Quarters were as different from each other as their childhood homes. Hosea was a man's man whose vivid stories focused on competitive and sometimes combative exchanges with other men. Mary's diary described intimate circles, both religious and domestic, that involved both sexes and people of varied ages. Hosea's wife, Louisa, is a shadowy figure

Sutcliffe Maudsley, *Hosea Stout* and *Louisa Taylor Stout*, 1845. In his Nauvoo diary, Hosea mentioned visiting "Br. Maudsley" on July 7, 1845, to "have the likeness of myself and wife taken and engraved on stone." *(Utah Historical Society, Salt Lake City.)*

Portrait based on tintype of Mary Parker Richards. Date unknown. This, the only known image of Mary Richards, was probably taken after her arrival in Utah, perhaps when her husband was on a second mission to England. *(Courtesy Maurine Ward.)*

in his diary; Mary's male kinfolk are vivid presences in hers. Although Mary, at age twenty-two, had less experience of life than Hosea, who at thirty-six had lived through both the Black Hawk and the Missouri Wars and had been married, widowed, and married again, she had seen a great deal since leaving England and had firm opinions. The two of them shared a talent for storytelling and a predilection for sentimentality nurtured by their mutual love of reading, though Hosea, unlike Mary, could spell.

Patty Sessions was a different kind of writer, or perhaps not a writer at all. Her diary measured life in tasks accomplished: "visited the sick," "made soap," "went to meeting." Unless there was something unusual in a delivery or the roof fell in, she found little point in elaborating. She was normally terse to the point of curtness. In the winter of 1847, however, she unexpectedly engaged in what can only be described as religious rhapsody. In contrast to the male gatherings recorded by Hosea Stout and the cross-gender sociability described by Mary Richards, Patty's diary reveals the formation at Winter Quarters of a visionary sisterhood prepared to carry the promises of the Nauvoo Relief Society to the Rocky Mountains. Her son Perrigrine's expressive but barely literate family history provides a context for that transformation.

The writings of Hosea Stout, Mary Richards, and Patty Sessions and her son demonstrate the ways in which their experiences at Winter Quarters helped shape their accounts of earlier periods in their lives and, conversely, how looking back helped them to find meaning in the here and now. Their writings exemplify different forms of expression and contrasting forms of sociability within the same religious community. Together, their stories reveal the dance of gender on the edge of an American frontier.

"Sometimes I wished myself back among the Shakers"

Hosea Stout's progenitors were Pennsylvania Quakers who had migrated to North Carolina before the American Revolution. As a young man, his father violated the pacifist principles of his Quaker community by enlisting in the North Carolina militia and then running away to marry Anna Smith, outside the faith. The young couple moved west, producing children along the way, first in Tennessee, then in Kentucky. In 1814, they placed all six of their surviving progeny, including four-year-old Hosea, in a Shaker community at Pleasant Hill, Kentucky. The Shakers, who were both celibate and communitarian, perpetuated themselves by taking in orphans and the offspring of indigent parents like the Stouts, allowing but not forcing the children to join the community as adults. When Hosea was eight or nine years old, his father decided to take him back, probaby because by then he was old enough to work. The child was terrified, having learned from his Shaker teachers that the "worldlings" who lived outside their community had little to eat. When he discovered this was not so, he quickly adjusted, learning to swear and play in the millrace like other boys. He soon began to resent being called a "Shaker boy."[11]

We know all this because Hosea wrote it down in the autobiography he composed at Winter Quarters. That he devoted long passages of his autobiography to his own childhood and youth cannot have been accidental. In the winter of 1847, he was serving as a commander in the Winter Quarters police. One of his many duties was keeping peace in the streets. On February 14, 1847, he raised the topic of rowdy boys at a meeting of church leaders. "A long debate ensued which resulted in good for us, for it was understood by the council for us to do our duty & they sustain us in it & stop the noise of the boys in the streets if we had to use the lash &c."[12]

Hosea acknowledged the unpleasant side of his childhood among the Shakers—the long stints of braiding straw hats, the necessity of remaining silent at mealtime, and the fear of being shut up in a dank root cellar if he disobeyed. Yet, sitting in a bleak camp on the Missouri River, he looked back with something like nostalgia on the orderliness of the place. He remembered the singing, the round dancing, the lessons in spelling and reading, and the emphasis on common courtesy. "I have often thought if fathers and those who have the charge of families would adopt some of their rules and mode of discipline, it would be a great improvement to their peace and social happiness," he observed.[13] He admitted that after leaving the Shaker community he was often lazy, disobedient, and foolish, though he never described himself as "wicked." In the autobiography, he portrayed himself as a young innocent unprepared for the ways of the world.

He experienced his father's punishments as both arbitrary and ineffective. "Sometimes I wished myself back among the Shakers, who I thought would not want me to work so hard, & if they did I would not be so solitary and alone."[14] He may have been twelve or thirteen on the day he and his father fell in with a man carrying to market two barrels of applejack, an alcoholic beverage they called "cider oil." When it began to foment and spill out of the spout, the man reduced the pressure by letting Hosea and his father take a few swigs. "It was the first I ever tasted & pleased me well. Not knowing its power I drank deep, and long before I got home was under full sail beyond the bounds of cares and sorrow."[15] In this case, as in so many others, he was left to figure things out on his own.

Hosea's mother died when he was fourteen. "By her death I lost the only unwavering friend that I had," he wrote, adding that "the loss of my mother was a misfortune which reached my heart and caused me deep and lasting trouble, which I feel to this day." This was so, he said, "notwithstanding the lapse of twenty-three years between us and the many privations, misfortunes losses in friends & perils which I have encountered since."[16] That was a remarkable claim given the sorrows he had experienced since leaving Nauvoo. Perhaps it was easier for him to write about an old pain than to deal with those that were fresh.

Hosea's stories about lessons learned in childhood sound much like those in Benjamin Franklin's autobiography. But, unlike Franklin, he filled his narrative with tears. Once, he went home on a holiday to find the house desolate, his father having taken his other children and moved without telling him. "I commenced weeping & most bitterly too It seemed that I was the most forsaken being on earth and now doomed to eternal loneliness and sorrow. . . . It seemed that I could hear the weak plaintiff voice of my departed mother admonishing me to do better and would

LEFT: Sutcliffe Maudsley, *George A. Smith,* before 1844.

RIGHT: Sutcliffe Maudsley, *Bathsheba Bigler Smith,* before 1844.

George A. Smith was Joseph Smith's first cousin. His wife Bathsheba, born in 1822, was in her early twenties when this portrait was taken. Her hair is arranged in the latest fashion, with a long loop framing her ears. Over her long life, she composed many letters as well as a brief diary. *© Pioneer Memorial Museum, International Society Daughters of Utah Pioneers, Salt Lake City.*

LEFT: Sutcliffe Maudsley, *Lt. General Joseph Smith in Nauvoo Legion Uniform,* 1840s.

RIGHT: Sutcliffe Maudsley, *Emma Hale Smith in Dark Riding Dress,* 1840s.

Emma and other Nauvoo women sometimes accompanied the Nauvoo Militia on horseback. *© Intellectual Reserve, Museum of Church History and Art, Salt Lake City.*

Sutcliffe Maudsley, *Eliza Maria Partridge,* 1840s.

Eliza Partridge and her sister Emily lived for a time in the Smith house and were sealed to Joseph Smith in 1843, greatly to Emma's dismay. © *Pioneer Memorial Museum, International Society Daughters of Utah Pioneers, Salt Lake City.*

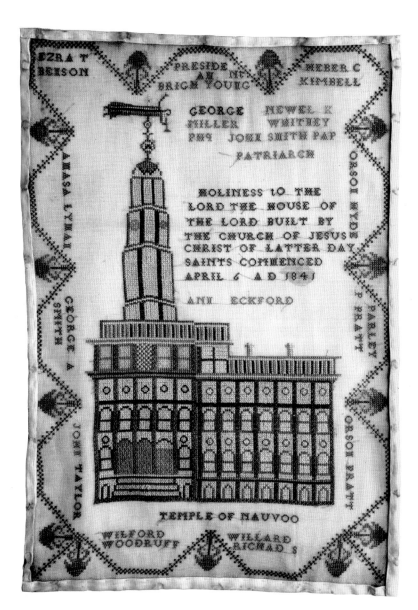

Anne Eckford, *Nauvoo Temple Sampler,* after 1846.

This silk embroidery is one of three based on the design of a Staffordshire plate commissioned by Mormon missionaries in England in 1846. © *Intellectual Reserve, Museum of Church History and Art, Salt Lake City.*

Eliza Snow, ornamental card for Brigham and Mary Ann Young, 1846.

Eliza used popular cut-paper techniques to exemplify the rich symbolism of arrows, keys, and hearts in Mormon theology. © *Intellectual Reserve, Museum of Church History and Art, Salt Lake City.*

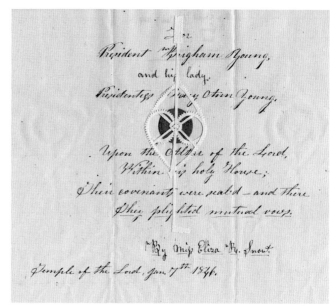

President *m* Brigham Young,
and his lady,
Presidentess Mary Ann Young.

Upon the Altar of the Lord,
Within his holy House,
Their covenants were seal'd — and there
They plighted mutual vows.

m By Miss Eliza R. Snow.

Temple of the Lord, Jan. 7th 1846.

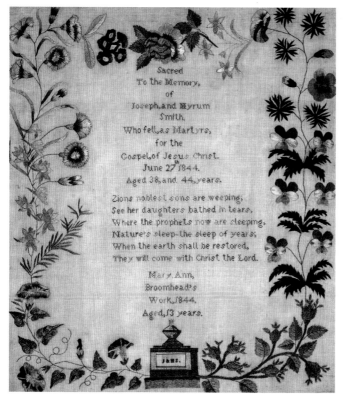

Mary Ann Broomhead, "Sacred to the Memory of Joseph and Hyrum Smith," June 27, 1844.

Thirteen-year-old Broomhead was still in England when she completed this memorial embroidery. She included an extract from an elegy written by Eliza R. Snow, embroidered the floral border in silk, and worked the text in strands of human hair. Years later, she shocked her friends by leaving Utah with soldiers bound for California. © *Intellectual Reserve, Museum of Church History and Art, Salt Lake City.*

look in the house but alas she was gone & I truly alone and where is the family."[17] It is impossible to know whether he composed these passages about his mother before or after April 23, 1847, when he wrote in his diary, "Today weighed my baby which weighed 19 pounds. I weighed all my children this day one year ago she weighed then 8 pounds and the others O! where are they now!! Hush."[18]

Hosea's father was a wanderer who alternately abandoned and retrieved his children, sometimes helping them, more often using them to fulfill his own needs. He moved through Kentucky, Ohio, Missouri, and Illinois, doing millwork, raising cabbages, castor beans, and flocks of geese, but never achieving any kind of stability. Hosea's oldest sister, Rebecca, remained among the Shakers, serving as a deaconess until she died of consumption. Hosea and his other siblings spent their youth as servants or apprentices in other men's households, occasionally taking refuge with extended family. In the autobiography, Hosea claimed that a farmer named Eli Harvey cured him of his malingering and profanity, "without any harsh words or bad feelings," by sending him to school, taking him to Quaker meetings, and eventually granting him wages as well as room and board for his labor.[19]

Hosea survived by blending in with whatever company he kept. He flirted with Quakerism and Methodism, then succumbed to the entreaties of a temperance lecturer, an episode that he considered outrageously funny. Despite his youthful encounter with applejack, he had never been a drinker. But once he signed the temperance pledge, drinking became appealing.[20] Ridiculed by his fellow millworkers, he joined them in a morning dram, admitting, "It did look foolish to me to quit that which I never did." After that, he claimed never to have troubled himself again "about the Temperance cause."[21]

In fact, a jug seems to have been essential equipment for the Winter Quarters police. One evening, Hosea got into an argument during a meeting of his men. As things heated up, Apostles Orson Hyde, Parley P. Pratt, and John Taylor came into the store where they were meeting. When Hosea paused in the middle of a sentence, Taylor told him not to stop speaking for his sake. Hosea told him it was nothing but police business and not interesting.

" 'Never mind,' says he. 'We are police men too.'

"Says, I, 'I hope you will all conform to the rules of the police then.'

" 'Certainly' says Taylor.

" 'Bring on the jug' says I, at which, they were presented with a large jug of whiskey. This was such an unexpected turn that it was only answered by a peal of laughter &c they all paid due respect to the jug. No more was said about our subject."

Hosea's gifts for storytelling and for capturing dialogue appear in this account, but so does his disdain for rigid rules. Although the Saints ostensibly followed a "Word of Wisdom" that forbade the use of "strong drink," the rules at Winter Quarters focused less on consumption than on distribution. At one point, the High Council ruled that sales of alcohol should be monitored by bishops, and profits used for the care of the poor.[22]

Learning to drink was obviously part of Hosea's initiation into manhood. Learning to fight was even more essential. As a boy, he often felt torn between the Quaker pacifism of men like Eli Harvey and the rough-and-tumble code of the settlements where he lived. When frontier toughs pushed him into a fight, he learned to win, "perfectly regardless of the consequences." Later, in a Quaker school, his classmates prodded him to take on a bully. "All the boys and girls expressed their disapprobation at his conduct and unanimously declared that he ought to be whipped." Believing that the whole school was behind him, he gave the boy "a most unmerciful beating," only to find himself threatened with dismissal. In the face of their schoolmaster's authority, his comrades backed down and testified against him. "I learned that it was not good policy to do fighting for people who had not courage or a disposition to do it for themselves and it proved a useful lessen to me in after life," he wrote.[23]

Hosea respected authority tempered by affection, themes that emerge as well in his daily diary. On March 5, he wrote, "The day was cold & dark & ground hard froze. I was around as usual and also wrote some in my Biographical history."[24] That evening, he found a policeman absent from his post on the night watch and alerted Brigham Young. Together, the two men went to the Council House, where a dance was in motion. Young told the group he and Stout had come not to dance but to look for a missing policeman. They did not expose the man, just gave what Hosea called "sarcastic slants," hoping the negligent policeman would get the point. Then they joined in a single reel and left. Hosea stayed nearby, watching to see when the policeman left the building. "He staid at the party until it broke up & came home and stayed in his house a while and came out a few minutes and went back and never appeared till one and then only to go and call up his relief." Hosea was annoyed by the behavior yet unwilling to impose harsh punishment. He administered a tongue whipping, but he allowed the man to keep his post. If he then chose to do well, all would be forgotten. If not, "he had best leave the police before he is disgraced."[25] Like Young, Stout was given to tough talk, but also to the preservation of what he called "good feelings."[26]

He had occasion to be grateful for such a policy. In March 1848, he lost his temper with a group of Mormon men who hung around a non-Mormon store, grumbling about conditions in the settlement. Annoyed by the constant backbiting, Hosea grabbed a complainer named Isaac Hill by the throat and pinned him to the counter. Within hours, he found himself called before a church council and charged with profanity and riot.[27] Wilford Woodruff, who was present at the hearing, said Young gave both men a "dressing out." He told Hill he was "no more fit for a High Priest than the police are for their office." Both men were at fault, and both needed to take responsibility for their actions. Although Young acknowledged that Hosea's anger had been driven by his love for the Church, he chastised him for overlooking an important principle—it was impossible to purge all iniquity. "We have some of the meanest spirits among us on earth. The net has halled in good and bad," but if people waited to gather until the Saints were all pure, they would never gather at all. "If I see a bad man or good man that needs reproof I will give it to him but will I go into a store & strike A man? No. Would it make him any better? No. But we should be saviors benevolent & kind & imitate the example of the savior." When both Stout and Hill admitted their faults, Young accepted their confessions and said "good would grow out of it."[28]

Composing an autobiography helped Hosea frame such experiences. He recalled how the religious enthusiasm that raged through the community where he lived in 1829 had divided people into hostile camps. The older inhabitants, mostly Quakers, "manifested a narrow, bigoted feeling towards all the rest," he recalled, adding that the attempt to enforce purity resulted in "open hostilities by and by."[29] He considered the Latter-day Saints more open-minded. His experiences with anti-Mormon vigilantism also caused him to reassess the unthinking patriotism that had led him to enlist in the Black Hawk War in 1832, a conflagration between American settlers and a band of Sauk-Fox Indians who refused to move onto a reservation. "I felt that the interest of my country was above every thing else & I must defend it at the risk of my life & supposed that every one felt the same. I did not even suspect that our rulers were full of the political intrigues which I afterwards learned."[30]

At Winter Quarters, he was constantly on guard to prevent hotheaded Mormons from going after Indians they accused of stealing their cattle.

At one point Brigham was away from the camp, and Hosea mediated when Apostles Pratt and Taylor refused to let the son of an Omaha chief and his party enter the town. "Young Elk spoke very sharp at this ill treatment & laid it to our chiefs & said that if the 'Big Red headed' chief [Brigham] was here it would not be so but he would have taken them in & fed them & spoke friendly." Hosea thought the Omaha leader's remarks "apt and just" and stepped in to prevent the police from expelling them.[31]

Relations with two men of mixed Mohawk and European heritage were more complicated. Joseph Herring, who, with his brother George, had apparently been baptized at Nauvoo, came to Stout's cabin in January 1847. He stayed all day, drinking, railing against the Twelve, and swearing "he would take Br. Willford Woodruff's life." Hosea concluded that all the trouble and expense the Church had laid out on Herring had been futile, because he did not have "integrity and stability enough." Woodruff was so shaken by the threat that he had nightmares about being attacked by Indians with knives and axes. Hosea managed the problem by befriending Herring—taking him in and putting him to bed when he had been drinking. Herring claimed that Stout was the only friend he had. Herring eventually disappeared from the diary, and apparently from Winter Quarters.[32]

In his autobiography, Hosea explained that he had come to the Church through his older sister Anna. When he heard she had married a Mormon, he vowed to rescue her, knowing nothing about the Saints except for "the common and universal slang then going about them." When he met his brother-in-law, Benjamin Jones, he discovered that he not only liked him but agreed with much of what he had to say. He hesitated before joining the Church, worrying that he would not be able to live up to its precepts, but, once committed, he became a zealous defender.[33]

The one constant in Stout's story about his early life was his love of words, an attribute that continued to sustain him at Winter Quarters.[34] "I was at home journalizing in the forenoon," he wrote in March, and, in April, "I wrote the most part of my leisure time today."[35] But words alone could not salve the wounds that life had inflicted. On August 5, he wrote: "Louisa, now my only child, who had been sick for a long time died today which seemed to complete the dark curtain which has been drawn over me since I left Nauvoo. My family then consisted of 8 members & now but two. Five of whom has died & now I am left childless but I shall not dwell on this painful subject." He stayed home the next day to bury his daughter. On the following day, he caught the nearly grown son of another church leader trying to retrieve his horse from the stray pen without authorization. Hosea gave him such a severe caning that his hickory stick broke into pieces. "He ran through the lot and cried so loud that he excited the whole neighbourhood which caused much to be said for & against us police." Hosea thought the boy "needed all he got."[36]

Hosea Stout was a man of sorrows determined to set the camp in order.

"This I said because I knew I was not mistaken"

Mary Richards began her autobiography in the usual way, with a brisk notation of the place and date of her birth. But for her, bald facts were never enough. She described a pastoral, almost idyllic childhood, in "one of the most Beautyfull valeys that my Eyes Ever Beheld. . . . The mountain Stream Ran Singing By the Door joind by the Warbleing notes of unnumbered Birds Whose melody In the Spring & Samer together with other ajoining Beautys made my Home appear Delightful."[37] Between the lines of this rhapsody was a more complex story. John and Ellen Parker raised their ten children on a tenant farm seven miles from the industrial city of Preston, England. Although its setting may have been beautiful, the land could not sustain them. They were able to keep at least some of their children at home by employing them in outwork weaving. Mary recalled that she was "larned to wind bobins" for her older sisters' looms when she was four and a half years old. When she was ten, she began to weave.[38]

Unlike Stout, she wrote about the joys rather than the burdens of work. As the youngest of her parents' children, she wanted to be recognized for her contribution to the family. She remembered standing by the side of her mother, "thinking that I was able to sew as well as She." When her mother offended her by giving her an old piece of cloth to practice on, she watched until her mother was out of the room and then added her own stitches to her mother's work. This should have been a story about an impertinent little girl learning patience after attempting something beyond her. In Mary's memory, that is not how it turned out. "On retorning & seeing what I had don. She was very willing that I should continu."[39] Mary was apparently born to hold a needle as well as a shuttle.

This same pride in work permeates the diary she kept at Winter Quarters. She lived alternately with her husband's parents, Phinehas and Wealthy Richards, and her sister-in-law Jane Richards, whose husband, Franklin, was also on a mission in the British Isles. The day before

First page of Mary Richards's
memoir, c. 1846. Although she
had little formal schooling, Mary
Richards's handwriting was neat
and legible. *(Church History Library,
Salt Lake City. © Intellectual Reserve.)*

Christmas 1846, Mary attacked the family's dirty clothes with a vengeance, spilling wash suds on everything in sight, including the rough plank floor—"the first time I have washed a floor since the first of Aprial," she wrote. There was nothing like spending seven months in a wagon to make housework appealing. That evening, the family ate supper together and "talked of several things that had passed since our leaving Nauvoo." Phinehas said something that hurt Jane's feelings. Mary was pleased when her sister-in-law "spoke noble in her own defence and made father draw in his horns and they parted still friends."[40]

In her autobiography, Mary described herself as fiercely independent. As a child, she insisted on her right to ply a needle. As a teenager, she resisted the local Anglican minister when he tried to talk her out of becoming a Mormon. According to her own self-description, she was able to withstand his arguments because she was "wilful to becoming a Mormon." She remembered defending the Mormon concept of baptism by

immersion against his charge that she was taking the scripture too liter-
ally: "I think if the Lord is not able to Speak His word as He Intends it to
be, I shall not trust to men to mend it."[41] She carried her spunkiness with
her to America, sometimes disputing with her own father-in-law. She was
especially sensitive to slights she felt as a woman. When Phinehas tried to
make her believe "that Adam never transgressed but Eve had," she argued
him down, using scripture in her own defense. When he refused to admit
defeat, she diplomatically claimed that they had difficulty understanding
each other because of her Lancashire dialect. But she confided later in her
diary, "This I said because I knew I was not mistaken, but he would have
considered me impertinent had I told him so." She added that the debate
had lasted more than an hour.[42]

Mary had only two years' formal schooling. According to her autobiography, she wound bobbins at home "until most 8 years old," being paid
four shillings a week, and then, when a change in the system relieved her
of that work, "went to scool to miss Jenneta Richards, until most 10 years
old."[43] Upon leaving school, she learned to weave. Although she tried
household service, she did not like her "Situwaytion" and quickly came
back home. When she was fourteen, she took a job as a nursemaid for a
"very respectable" family, but when she became a Mormon her employers
let her go. Once again, outwork weaving was her salvation. But as textile production increasingly moved into Preston factories, cottage weaving provided an uncertain future. Although she made no mention of the
industrial strikes of the late 1830s or the rise of Preston's radical Chartist
movement, these events as well as religious conviction surely shaped her
parents' decision to emigrate to Nauvoo.[44]

Mary's description of her own departure for America is much like
Phebe Woodruff's account of leaving Maine. Although her parents had
already emigrated, she found it difficult to part with her siblings. She
described visiting them in their own homes one by one, naming her sisters
(Ellen, Isabella, Alice, and Ann) and her brothers (Rodger, Robert, and
John). They wept. She wept. Like Phebe, she was never more bonded with
her family than when parting with them. Among the Latter-day Saints
she found a new and larger family. She considered her meeting with Ellen
Wilding at the Temperance Hall in Preston in 1840 a landmark worth
mentioning, no doubt because, as she was composing her memoir, Ellen
was an almost constant presence in her life. Mary helped nurse Ellen when
she had her first baby at Winter Quarters.[45] Ellen, in turn, introduced

Mary to her husband's brother Samuel Woolley and his wife, Catherine. Mary spent more than one evening at the Woolley house, listening to or copying Samuel's poetry.[46]

In letters to her husband, Mary playfully acknowledged her own deficiencies as a writer: "I expect you will find some excellent Spelling in this letter that will comport with the beautifull maner it is composed and placed together but as I have every reason to beleve you are high learned I have hopes you will be able to read it."[47] Despite her lack of schooling, she delighted in arranging words. During her last meeting with local church members in England, she "sung a few verses wich I had Composed as a farewell song to my Brothers & Sisters."[48] At Winter Quarters, she traded verses with fellow diarist Emmeline Woodward and with a young Scots widower, Robert Campbell, as well as with the Woolleys.[49] On a neighborly visit, she and Elsie Snyder "spent about two hours trying to see who could compose the best poetry."[50]

The diary suggests that she read almost anything she could get her hands on, from pulp novels like *The Golden Marriage, or Anne, the Orphan of St. Mary* to an almanac biography of future U.S. president Zachary Taylor.[51] Although her spelling was at points incomprehensible, her desire to become "high learned" was apparent. To her, the bluffs above the Missouri River were "magestic Piles." Taking a walk in September, she described crossing "a beautyfull roaling Praira which extended as far as the Eye could penatrate and although Autumn's Chilling Blasts had began to make its depredations among the Trees that appeard at intervails yet the Praira seemed dected in a rich livery of flowers and presented to the Eye a scene truly pleasing and interesting."[52]

Mary clearly had aspirations to learning and to gentility. Yet her diary suggests that the men who carried Mormonism to England still saw her as the good little girl who had welcomed them to her parents' home in Lancashire. On a cold day in December 1846, she was sewing at the home of Willard Richards, her husband's uncle, when he asked her if she had "grown proud." She responded that if she had she didn't know it. "Then said he come & Eat some supper with me. I did so, & eat of from his plate while conversing with him."[53]

In her autobiography, she acknowledged the many services she and her sister Alice had performed for Heber Kimball when he was recovering from illness at their home in Lancashire during his first mission to England. She recalled that he "pronounced many blessings on my head," among them that in future years she would be known as a woman who had washed the feet of the Servants of the Lord.[54] During a gathering at Winter Quarters, Kimball fulfilled his own prophecy by telling a group that when the elders first arrived in Lancashire, Mary "was then but a little girl and I used to call her My pet. . . . She would step around as quick & as light as a feather and would seem glad when she could get a chance to do any thing for me." Among other things, she helped him understand the local dialect.[55]

The day after the meeting in which he praised her, Kimball came to the Richards house to talk with her. He apparently wanted to know how she felt about plural marriage, and if Wealthy Richards, her mother-in-law, had quarreled with her husband's other wife when they lived together in Nauvoo. Mary said she had never heard them quarrel, adding that anybody who "undertook to quaril with Mother would have to do their own quariling." But she admitted that Wealthy sometimes "felt bad," justifying herself by saying "she could not help her feelings." Kimball asked why anyone would imagine she *could* help her feelings.

"Well," said Mary, "I have heard a pearson say that [a] woman could help feeling bad if they were only a mind to." Whether that "pearson" was Phinehas, she did not say.

"Pa-shaw," said Kimball. "There is not one respectable Woman in this church but what would feel bad under such sircumstances and I know there is no Woman can ever feel worse than my Wife has done and she is just as good a Woman as ever lived. And I never blamed her for feeling bad but loved her the more."[56] Kimball may or may not have realized that the little girl he had known in Lancashire had grown up and that she disdained polygamy.[57] Kimball's admission that nobody had ever felt worse than his wife Vilate could not have come as a surprise, since, just a week before, Mary had recorded in her own diary some verses that Vilate had written after her last baby was born. Mary could remember only the opening lines:

> The Lord has blessed us with another Son
> Which is the seventh I have Born
> May he be the father of many lives.
> But not the Husband of many Wives.[58]

Although plural marriage was still ostensibly hidden from "the world," it was by this time an open secret among the Saints.

In an encounter with Apostle John Taylor, who had recently arrived in Winter Quarters after visiting England, Mary demonstrated both her wit and her sensitivity to the feelings of first wives. Taylor told her that he had promised all the missionaries still in England that he would go and see their wives when he got home but that the women hadn't given him a chance, since they had all come to see him.

"Except me," said Mary, "for I came to day to see Sister Taylor and shall live in hopes that you will redeem your word and come and see me If Sister T has no objections."

Taylor responded, "I feel some afraid of going to see the Sisters for the truble is they all fall in love with me."

Mary shot back, "I expect it is some what dangerous . . . but I should be happy to have you bring Sister T with you when you come to see me. And if I should happen to fall in love with you I will try to keep it to my self."

At this point, Leonora Taylor entered the conversation. "Yes," she said. "They all ask him [to visit] and never say one word to me about going with him."[59]

It is hard to know whether Mary's exchange with Taylor was totally in fun, or whether it, like her earlier confrontation with Phinehas Richards (an encounter she described as a "confab"), was an attempt to hold her own against a powerful man.

Mary did not hide her own feelings about plural marriage. Nor did she ignore the cold, hunger, and illness she experienced at Winter Quarters. She claimed to have cured the boils that broke out on her arms and legs by anointing her limbs with sulfur and lard.[60] She was candid about bedbugs, though didn't come right out and say that in dressing Uncle Willard's hair she was looking for lice.[61] She told Samuel his mother's health was "pretty good," though admitted the "black leg," or scurvy, had affected her feet.[62] She knew he would be reading her diary as well as her letters, so worked hard to suppress discouragement. Willard Richards rewarded her by observing, "You have been a good Girl you have not come a whining around because your Husband is gone but you have endured his absence patiantly and you shall be blessed for it." Then he told her that he had been thinking about asking President Young to call Samuel and Franklin home early. Mary responded that she would rather her husband stayed ten years than that he fail to fulfill his mission with honor.[63]

In fact, it would be another year before Samuel returned. When he did, Mary's diary and her autobiography abruptly ended.

"had a good time singing praying speaking in tongues"

Patty Sessions loved a good party. In a three-day period in February 1847—a Thursday, Friday, and Saturday—she celebrated her birthday, attended a gathering of female friends, and danced in the Council House at an event honoring the "Silver Greys," the oldest members of the community. During the same three days, she officiated at three births, visited the sick, spent time with a dying woman, and had enough energy left to make a batch of soap. Here is how she wove together social events and daily work with spiritual manifestations that in her view characterized "a good time":

> February 4. my birthday fifty two years old Feb 4—1847 in the camp of Isriel Winter quarters we had brandy and drank a toast to each other desireing and wishing the blessings of God to be with us all and that we might live and do all that we came here into this world to do. Eliza Snow came here after me to go to a little party in the evening I was glad to see her told her it was my birth day and she must bless me she said if I would go to the party they all would bless me I then went and put James Bulloch wife to bed then went to the party had a good time singing praying speaking in tongues before we broke up I was called away to sister Morse then to sister Whitney then back to sister Morse put her to bed 2 oclock
>
> Friday 5 this morning I have been to see sister Whitney she is better I then went to Joanna Roundy she said it was the last time I should see her in this world she was going to see my children I sent word by her to them I then went to the Silver Grey party Eliza Snow went with us I danced with Br Knolton Mr Sessions not being well Joanna died this evening
>
> Saturday 6 made soap visited some that were sick then went put sister Whitney to bed she had a son born Eleven oclock P.M.[64]

There is plenty of evidence to confirm the broader significance of the details in these descriptions. Faithful Latter-day Saints sometimes used alcohol; speaking in tongues was an accepted practice; dancing was a common form of recreation; and Mormon midwives, like midwives in other places, attended deaths as well as births.[65]

The more subtle evidence in this segment leads us backward to Patty's early life. When Joanna Roundy said she was going to see Patty's children, she alluded to events that Patty must have shared with her earlier, events described in the autobiography that Patty's oldest son began in Nauvoo in 1845. Perrigrine Sessions, who at thirty-one was a widower with two children, started his narrative with what he called a "geanalogy," a tumble of names and dates as disordered as his spelling. Although he began in a patriarchal voice, promising to give an account of his "Father and Grandfather" in the style of Biblical or Book of Mormon lineages, he dutifully included grandmothers as well as grandfathers, and aunts, uncles, and cousins as well as siblings. Since his relatives on all sides shared names, it is almost impossible to keep them straight, but in the almost Homeric epithets he attached to them, he made his own values clear.

Perrigrine valued the practice, not the profession of Christianity. He wrote that his grandfather Sessions, who "faught for his liberty" during the Revolution, lived "an honourable liberalle piecable life with his companion and with al men" even though he never "made any pretentions to christianity." Although some relatives became Presbyterians, joined the Free Will Baptists, or "made a profession of the calvinistic religion," Perrigrine's grandfather was "never daubed with the untempered morter of sectarianism." On the other side of the family, his grandfather Bartlett never belonged to a church, yet he taught his children "to work and always to speak the truth to deal justley with all to live virtuous and to not take that that was not their own not so much as an apple from his neighbours tree with out leave." Perrigrine admired men like his uncle Asa, who was never "plastered with the creeds and crafts of the Gentile religion."[66]

It must have been a comfort to him, as he contemplated leaving Nauvoo, to rehearse his ancestors' willingness to leave their own homes to create new settlements in the little valleys that ran through the mountains of Vermont, New Hampshire, and Maine, lands wrested from the Abenaki and the French in the so-called French and Indian War. His father's father hacked out a farm in Vermont, not far from where Joseph Smith's family had failed at farming, before moving across the mountains to Maine, to a "cold mountainous cuntry" seventy miles from market. Even earlier, his mother's father had dragged family and household effects on sleds fifty miles from coastal Maine by following a line spotted on trees by his half brothers. In difficult circumstances, these resolute pioneers built houses, barns, and mills, and lived honorably with their neighbors.[67]

Woven through this story of religious simplicity and pioneer prowess

is an even more powerful theme. Nearly everyone in Perrigrine's gene-
alogy raised "a large family," though no one could match Grandfather
Bartlett, who "lived to see the fifth generation and died Sept. 1. 1825 in
the eighty third year of his age leaveing a Wife and seventeen children."
It was even more remarkable that all these children but two married and
settled within ten miles of their father's farm.[68] In this chronicle of reproductive success, there were only two exceptions—a New Hampshire uncle
and aunt who lost six of their eight children within two weeks during
an epidemic of "black measles" and "canker rash," and Perrigrine's own
parents.[69] Between 1816 and 1827, Patty gave birth to seven children. In
1823, three-year-old Anna died of "colery morbus." In 1828, baby Bartlett
died of whooping cough. In 1832, typhus fever struck the entire family,
including Grandmother Sessions and Aunt Apphia, who were living with
them. "There was Eleven that had the fever at my Fathers that summer
and many others in the neighbourhood," Perrigrine recalled. A second
sister Anna, named for the sibling who had died of cholera, succumbed to
typhus on August 10, "aged seven years and four months and twenty four
days." Although Patty lay in the same room as her daughter, she was too
ill to raise her head. Perrigrine continued:

> My Aunt Apphia and her daughter lay in an other room they were all
> helpless I had had the fever and had got so that I could set up some
> my brother David was just coming down with the fever and my Sister
> Sylvia being the second time deprived of her Only sister she morned
> and wept untill she had to go to bed at this time my feelings I could
> not discribe.

Perrigrine had just turned eighteen. On September 10, his sixteen-year-old
brother, Sylvanus, died. His nine-year-old brother, David, survived.[70]

In the aftermath of the typhus epidemic, Mormon elders came into
the community. "And as soon as my Mother herd she believed," Perrigrine
wrote, "but my Father thinking it was best to wait and examine a little
longer and she fealing that she aught to waite until he was willing and
was not baptized until the next july 1834 when he gave his consent . . .
she remained alone in the Church almost one year before any of the rest
of us joined." He portrayed his mother both as the religious leader of the
family and as a dutiful wife who deferred to her husband's wishes. When
David Sessions embraced the new faith, his son Perrigrine followed, as did
Perrigrine's bride, Julia Ann Kilgore, despite the opposition of her parents.

In June 1837, David and Patty Sessions sold their property and, with their remaining children (Perrigrine, Sylvia, and David), traveled more than a thousand miles to Far West, Missouri, where they found the Saints under siege. Patty's last child, Amanda, born shortly after their arrival, survived the exodus from Missouri but died of whooping cough in Nauvoo. Four years later, Perrigrine buried his wife, Julia Ann, in the same plot. Until he remarried, Patty cared for Perrigrine's children, ten-year-old Martha Ann and two-year-old Carlos.[71]

It would be fascinating to know what message Patty asked Joanna Roundy to take to her long-dead children on that day at Winter Quarters when she visited the dying woman. Obviously, the two women had shared stories before.[72]

During the winter of 1847, however, Patty was less concerned about the five children who had gone to the spirit world than about the one daughter who remained on earth. On February 14, she collected a group of friends, including Eliza Snow, "to pray for Sylvia and child that they might be delivered from bondage." Whether Patty's use of the term "bondage" referred to her daughter's spiritual state or to her marriage is not clear.[73] Sylvia, who had been fifteen when she wept and mourned the loss of her sister, had married a Mormon convert named Windsor Lyon in Missouri when she was not quite nineteen. In Nauvoo she had given birth to four children, only one of whom survived. She later claimed to have married Joseph Smith in 1843 while still married to Lyon, and in 1845 was sealed vicariously to Smith, with Heber Kimball standing as proxy.[74] Her friends Zina Jacobs and Presendia Buell, after such a sealing, left their legal husbands to live as plural wives at Winter Quarters.[75] Instead, Sylvia followed Windsor to Iowa City, where he had gone into business with his non-Mormon brother. This decision might have made economic sense, but it clearly worried her mother.[76]

Despairing of ever seeing her daughter again, Patty called her friends together. "We prayed sung in toungues spoke in tounges and had a good time," she wrote.[77] On April 21, 1847, the prayers of the sisters bore fruit: Perrigrine walked into his parents' cabin with Sylvia and her three-year-old daughter, Josephine. "I was almost over come with joy and gratitude to God for our preservation to see each other again," Patty wrote. The next day, her youngest son, David, arrived, and she was overcome with joy again. She noted that all her children were seated together around her table. Then she paused to insert an important correction: "all that were living." Over the next couple of days, the Sessions family participated in every form of celebration the Saints were capable of organizing: "David went to a party they prayed and danced and prayed again." More significant, Sylvia and her parents attended a meeting where they "prayed prophesied and spoke in toungues and interpreted and were refreshed."[78]

The winter had brought a pentecostal outpouring to the refugee community. According to Eliza Snow's account, it began in late December. On New Year's Day, Eliza concluded a five-day visit with women living in what she referred to jokingly as "the 2d mansion of Prest B. Young," a log house that was probably only a little bit more comfortable than others in the settlement. On New Year's Eve, the "spirit of the Lord was pour'd out and we receiv'd a blessing thro' our belov'd Mother Chase & sis. Clarissa, by the gift of tongues."[79] Phoebe Chase was, like Patty Sessions, a respected healer in the Latter-day Saint community. Her daughter Clarissa was another of Young's wives.[80] Although some Mormon leaders followed the Apostle Paul in designating glossolalia a secondary gift, Eliza defended the practice. She believed that such "sweet social music" had existed in antiquity and that the ancient mothers as well as fathers had employed it. She urged Latter-day Saints to "Redeem the gift from long abuse / When by the gentiles shar'd."[81]

Over the next six months, the practice spread. Between February 4 and June 3, 1847, Patty reported fourteen meetings at which some form of spiritual manifestation occurred. Although a few men, including David Sessions, were sometimes present, the diaries emphasize female participants. Eliza's entry for March 14 is typical:

> Spent last ev. In a very interesting manner at sis. Gheen's in com. With Mother Chase & Sessions father Kim. Call'd in & gave us much beautiful instruction, after which we had some glorious communications of the spirit of God both by way of prophecy & the gifts of tongues and our hearts were made to rejoice & praise the name of God.[82]

Patty's own account of the same meeting said simply, "Visited Sistr Gean with E R Snow sister Chase."[83] That Heber Kimball "Call'd in" at the Gheen cabin is not surprising. Esther Gheen, a widow of Quaker descent, had two daughters who became Kimball's wives.[84]

Patty routinely gave the name of the woman in whose cabin or tent they met, sometimes but not always identifying the other participants. Of the more than fifty women she and Eliza mentioned, a third were plural wives or relatives of plural wives in Young's or Kimball's families,

but though the meetings began with these women, they moved outward
to include both monogamous and polygamous wives in other households.[85] Despite Young's proscription on meetings of the Female Relief
Society, these women believed themselves entitled to the gifts of healing,
prophecy, and speaking in tongues. On one occasion, there were eighteen
women present.[86]

On April 30, Patty and Eliza "visited the girls at Brighams" and made
"arrangement to have the Mothers in Isriel meet at sister Leonards and
have a prayer meeting Saturday."[87] By then, Young, Kimball, and other
members of the Quorum of the Twelve had left Winter Quarters with the
mostly male pioneer expedition to the Rocky Mountains. Patty took Sylvia
with her to the meeting, noting that there were "none but females there."
Although the meeting had been "got up by E R Snow," Patty "presided."
Eliza noted that Vilate Kimball, Elizabeth Ann Whitney, Presendia Buell,
and Phoebe Chase were among the dozen participants. The spiritual festival continued the next day at Vilate's cabin. Eliza pronounced it as "glorious time as I ever had on earth," adding that "the pow'rs of the world to
come were truly In our midst." On Monday, they met with Mary Ann
Young.[88]

The power of such gatherings did not stop Sylvia from returning to
Iowa City. Instead of condemning her for leaving, Eliza sent her on her
way with a poem that began "Go, thou loved one, God is with thee." It
assured her that in time all the promises she had received would be fulfilled. Eliza made no reference to "bondage," unless that bondage was an
inability to leave a man who loved her. The poem continued:

> But thy husband will caress thee,
> And thy sweet, angelic child,
> With her growing charms will bless thee—
> Thus the hours shall be beguiled.

The poem ended by promising Sylvia that her friends and family would
pray for her and that angels would watch over her.[89]

Sylvia's brother David was going, too. "It is Davids birthday 23 years
old and the same time of day that he was born," Patty reminisced. She
prayed that God would speed her children safely on their journey but also
help them "keep the spirit of gathering" so that they might join the Saints
in the West. David soon did so. Sylvia waited seven years.[90]

Eliza and Patty knew that they, too, would soon be leaving Winter

Quarters. They were determined to go filled with the Holy Spirit. On June 1, Patty penned a rhapsodic description of a meeting held at the home of a Sister Miller:

> Then we blessed and got blessed & [I] blessed sister Christeen by laying my hands upon her head and the Lord spoke through me to her great and marvelous things—at the close I thought I must ask a blessing at sister Kimbals hand but it came to me that I must first bless her. . . . I obeyed layed my hands upon her head although it was a great cross and the power of God came upon me I prope I spoke great and marvelous things to her she was filed to the overflowing she arose and blessed the Lord and called down a blessing on us and all that pertained to her sister Hess fell on her knees and claimed a blessing at my hands I then blessed her sister Chase claimed a blessing of sister kimbal she blessed her with me, she spoke great things to her the power of God was poured out upon us E R Snow was there and many others thank the Lord.[91]

What is remarkable about this account is not just Patty's overpowering sense of being called to bless others but the involvement of otherwise unknown women like Miller and Hess. As female leaders grew more comfortable with their ability to call down the spirit, they began to share the gift with others. The crossed-out letters are intriguing. Had she meant to write "prophesy"? If she pulled back from that claim, she nevertheless showed her courage in obeying what she believed was a gift from God.

Shortly after they crossed the Platte River, ready to set out on their journey to the mountains, Patty and her friends encountered sisters who had not been a part of their meetings at Winter Quarters. Learning that Mary Ann Hunter was ill, they invited her husband, Edward, to join them; then the three of them laid hands on her head and "rebuk'd her illness & bless'd her." After Eliza sang in tongues, Patty responded by singing the interpretation. Their performance inspired Edward's plural wife Susannah to rise and add her voice as well.[92]

Although Patty's husband sometimes joined the women, Perrigrine always seemed to be elsewhere, herding cattle or packing wagons. Still, his family was touched by the revival. On June 14, Patty noted that his plural wives, Mary and Lucina, received the gift of tongues for the first time. Eliza had been at their house on a visit and had conversed with them about "their relationship," perhaps curious to know how the two sisters, who had asked to marry Perrigrine together after his first wife died, had adjusted.[93] At a gathering in Patty's wagon on June 27, Perrigrine's eleven-year-old daughter, Martha Ann, felt an urge to speak in tongues, but pulled back because she was afraid. After the others had gone, Patty showed Martha Ann and a friend how to have their own meeting. "We went into our wagon. She spoke in toungues and prayed. I gave the interpretation and then told them to spend their time in that way and they would be blessed."[94] Sharing her gift with another generation, Patty called down heaven's blessings.

The portrayals of life at Winter Quarters left by Patty Sessions, Mary Richards, and Hosea Stout overlap at points. Patty's references to Heber Kimball and his family enrich but do not contradict the vignettes recorded by Mary Richards. In both diaries, he appears as a benevolent patriarch comfortable in informal gatherings of women. Hosea's description of John Taylor's appearance at the meeting of the police reinforces Mary's portrait of a good-natured but somewhat self-important man, sure of himself with men but perhaps a bit insensitive with women. But neither Mary's nor Hosea's diary gives any hint of the emergence of spiritual gifts at Winter Quarters, or of the subtle leadership of the community's matrons as they attempted to bind women together in networks shaped but not dominated by the complexities of plural marriage. The meetings at Winter Quarters revived spiritual practices more common at Kirtland than at Nauvoo. These were women's meetings, but, unlike the structured gatherings of the Female Relief Society, they did not feature officers, minutes, resolutions, or petitions.

If the sisters missed Emma Smith, they did not say so. They certainly missed Sarah Kimball, the young woman whose sewing circle had stimulated their Nauvoo organization. Sarah wrote from Nauvoo that her husband, Hiram, was still settling his business and that she hoped to join them in the spring. Meanwhile, she sent the shocking news that Emma had remarried. Even worse, the ceremony had been performed by a Methodist minister. Sarah claimed that the groom, Lewis Bidamon, was looked upon "with universal contempt." A widower with two daughters, he wore a wig. Even worse, "A Mrs. Kinney, who credits him with one child, says he still loves her, but married Emy for her property. Mrs. Smith manifested the confidence she has in her intended husband by employing attorneys to execute a marriage contract and secure to her all the Property."

Sarah's mocking tone left no doubt of her contempt for Emma's decision to provide a little security for herself and her children.[95]

Sarah's lack of sympathy may have reflected her own anxieties. Hiram had invested heavily in Nauvoo's real estate and now faced financial disaster with the town's collapse. In a letter to another friend she wrote, "I thank God that there are some in this age and generation whose souls are not so contaminated with business but what they are susceptible of being clothed with garments of salvation."[96] By the time Sarah rejoined her friends, they had been long settled in Utah.

8

❧❧❧

"All are busy preparing to go either East or west"

Mormon Trails, 1847–1850

In American history, the standard narrative moves from East to West. Mormon history fits that pattern. As generally told, the action begins in New England, sweeps briefly across the Midwest, then crosses the plains to Utah, where it more or less remains. Even today, Utah and Mormonism are synonymous. Up close, the story is more complicated. Consider the iconic image of Brigham Young looking over the valley of the Great Salt Lake on July 24, 1847, and proclaiming, "This is the Place." He may well have said something like that, but a month later he turned around and went back a thousand miles to Winter Quarters, leaving a few men behind to finish laying out a settlement.[1] On the way east, he met the first really big companies of Saints heading west. He didn't join them in the Salt Lake Valley until the next year.[2] This second group of pioneers, more than fifteen hundred strong, were the ones who lived in wagon boxes and leaky cabins during the first winter, who subsisted on crows, sego roots, and thistle tops during the dank spring, and who planted, weeded, and harvested the melons that Young feasted on when he returned to the valley on September 20, 1848.[3] More than half of these intrepid pioneers were female.

Nor was Brigham the first to lead a band of Mormon pioneers beyond the then borders of the United States. That honor belongs to a mercurial newspaperman named Samuel Brannan, who sailed out of New York Harbor in February 1846 with 238 of his fellow Saints on a ship called the *Brooklyn*. They rounded Cape Horn, touched down at Juan Fernandez Island off the coast of Chile, made a brief stop at Honolulu, and landed on the coast of California on July 31, 1846, to find an American flag flying over Yerba Buena, the onetime Mexican outpost that would soon be named San Francisco. The *Brooklyn* Saints tripled the population of the town even before they were joined by veterans of the Mormon Battalion who had been mustered out at Los Angeles and come north hoping to find their families. Some of these vets took work building a mill at Sutter's Fort, where they helped make a discovery that changed the world.[4]

"All are busy preparing to go either East or west," Wilford wrote at Winter Quarters in May 1848. He had gone to the Salt Lake Valley and back with Brigham Young the year before. Now he and Phebe were about to return to New England, where for the next two years he would help manage church affairs in the East.[5] He was sitting in a rented house in Cambridge, Massachusetts, in December 1848 when he learned about the gold strike in California. "And not ownly the people of the United States but of other nations ketch the sound of Gold Gold & tens of thousands are rushing forward evry way in their power to get to the gold country as A Horse would rush to Battle," he exclaimed.[6] Although he considered the gold rush a foreshadowing of the chaos that would precede Christ's second coming, he was impressed that men from the Mormon Battalion had participated in the discovery, and he welcomed the California wealth that helped finance the migration of New England Saints to Utah in 1850.

Between 1847 and 1850, Latter-day Saint women labored to create a new Mormon kingdom. On the overland trail, in eastern houses, in tents, mud-roofed cabins, and a leafy bowery in the Salt Lake Valley, or in places in between, they prayed, testified, laid hands on the sick, stitched flags, penned poems, gathered wild roses and rattlesnake grease, prepared feasts, welcomed strangers, quieted oxen, and called down the blessings of heaven.

"Hail ye mighty men of Israel"

William Clayton was among the diarists who recorded Brigham Young's arrival in the Salt Lake Valley on July 24, 1847. He exaggerated only a little more than usual when he claimed a month later, "We as A pioneer company have accomplished more this season than can be found on record concerning any set of men since the days of Adam." The 142 men, three women, and two children who composed Brigham's company were certainly entitled to some pride. They had completed their 1,031-mile journey in 111 days. In a few short weeks, they had laid out a city two miles square, built a fort out of sun-dried brick, and planted a hundred acres of corn, potatoes, buckwheat, turnips, and garden vegetables. True, they had been reinforced by a group of men from the Mormon Battalion, who had completed their enlistment and come north from Pueblo (in present-day Colorado) to help lay out the city, but their achievement was nevertheless notable.[7]

The beauty of the valley entranced them. The apparent friendliness of the "Utahs" reassured them. Brigham didn't think the Church needed to buy land: the Lord had made enough for everyone. Nor would he claim land for himself or sell it to others. The land was the Lord's, along with everything in it. He seemed unconcerned about the details.[8]

On an evening stroll, he imagined a millennial empire in which Mormon men and native women would create a new people. As Wilford described it:

> He intended to have evry hole & corner from the Bay of Francisco to Hudson bay known to us And that our people would be connected with every tribe of Indians throughout America & that our people would yet take their squaws wash & dress them up teach them our language & learn them to labour & learn them the gospel of there forefathers & raise up children by them & teach the Children & not many generations Hence they will become A white & delightsome people.[9]

He had not as yet met any Numic women.

Pausing at the spot he had selected for a future temple, Brigham imagined a city in which each house plot would be surrounded by orchards and gardens, so that women and children would have no reason to roam in the streets. He said he had been thinking for some time of "giving a lecture to the females." Since there were only three women in the pioneer company, none of whom had joined him in the evening walk, he decided to try out his lecture on his male comrades. He wanted them to remember that, whereas a man was bound to obey God, a woman's duty was to "obey her husband." It annoyed him to see "a woman every time A man steped out be A watching him as uneasy as A fish out of water," and then, when he returned, quiz him about where he had been and why he had not returned earlier.[10]

Perhaps Brigham was trying to reassure the men with him that they need not worry about the women they had left behind—women like Phebe Woodruff, pregnant with her seventh child while mourning the loss of her fifth and sixth, busily engaged in outfitting her family for the journey west while trying to sustain them day by day. Whatever Brigham's purpose, Woodruff and the camp clerk, Thomas Bullock, were both impressed enough with his words to write them down.

Brigham hadn't planned to include women in the pioneering company. But when his brother Lorenzo refused to come along unless his wife Harriet Decker could join him, he relented. Lorenzo thought the Western air might cure Harriet of asthma. Without question, it put a thousand miles between her and the husband she had left in order to become Lorenzo's plural wife. To provide female support for Harriet, Brigham allowed two other women to join the group—Harriet's nineteen-year-old daughter, Clara, who was sealed to Brigham, and Heber Kimball's Norwegian wife, Aagaat Ysteinsdatter Bakka, better known as Ellen Sanders. Harriet and Lorenzo each brought a six-year-old son by a previous marriage. Since Harriet was pregnant with Lorenzo's child, there would soon be a his-hers-and-ours family in the valley.[11]

Harriet, who took turns entering daily updates in Lorenzo's journal, added a female voice to the otherwise all-male chronicles of the expedition. It isn't always easy to distinguish her entries from his. He appears to have written the note about Brigham's chastising the company for wickedness, and she the entry about finding the bones of an Indian child "done up very snug in skins" in a lone tree on the prairie.[12] It was she, however, who wrote, on August 26, "This day has been a lonesome one Bro Brigham and Heber with a number of the Brethren started for Winter Quarters and we feel as if we were left alone."[13] She would not be lonesome for long. Nine other companies with more than fifteen hundred Mormons, six hundred wagons, and five thousand head of livestock were on their way.[14]

This new phalanx of pioneers was divided into "hundreds," "fifties," and "tens," with a male leader at the head of each unit. Most of the time, the hundreds traveled miles apart, to avoid putting pressure on grazing and camping grounds. Because Patty Sessions, Eliza Snow, and Leonora Taylor were in different units, the diaries they kept, though related, described slightly different events. Their interests also varied.

Leonora's diary was tuned to nature. On July 4, after a rain, she was delighted to find the ground covered "with wild roses and sensitive, Briars, prickly pears and other new Flowers that are very sweet smelling." Pronouncing herself more fond of bison than of beef, she exclaimed, "Truly the Lord Has spread a Table for us in the Wilderness." Twice she went out in a carriage, once with her husband's mother, to observe the hunt.[15] Eliza was also smitten by the landscape. She used words like "picturesque," "grand," "splendid," and "romantic" to describe rock formations on the High Plains, working up to "stupendous" and "wildly magnificent" as she caught sight of the mountains.[16] In contrast, Patty scavenged for whatever was useful. She killed a rattlesnake and saved "the gall and greace" for medicine. Near Independence Rock (in what is now Wyoming), she gathered saleratus (bicarbonate of soda) from encrustations on the ground, using some of it to hull dried corn. She picked bushels of wild currants and, as they approached the valley, took up gooseberry bushes to plant.[17]

All three women were fascinated by the Plains Indians they encountered on the trail. On July 24, Eliza caught a glimpse of a Sioux village through a spyglass, and noted that "their tents or lodges" were made of skins "gaily painted." After getting closer the next day, she described women who carried their baggage on poles drawn by dogs and horses; she was impressed with their skill in fashioning carriers for their babies "by fastening skin over bows which are fix'd to the upper side of the

Seth Eastman, *Indians Traveling,* from Mary H. Eastman, *The American Aboriginal Portfolio* (Philadelphia: Lippincott, Grambo, 1853). This engraving by U.S. army officer Seth Eastman portrays a Plains Indian family using a travois to carry their baggage. As in Eliza Snow's description of a similar scene, a baby in a cradleboard is attached to the load. *(Courtesy Tozzer Library, Harvard University.)*

drays."[18] Patty and Leonora were thrilled when the Sioux women visited their encampments. "They 'sing' dance and ride round," Patty wrote. Although she put the word "sing" in quotation marks, she recognized in these strange women her own love of dancing.[19]

In their different companies, all three women built on the spiritual exercises they had developed at Winter Quarters. Eliza managed to reconnect with at least nine women who had been part of the circle at Winter Quarters and re-established or developed new friendships with perhaps a dozen others.[20] Women met as groups and as pairs. Eliza shared spiritual "treats" and pancakes with Phoebe Chase.[21] Patty bonded with Hyrum Smith's widow Mercy Thompson, whose daughter became friends with her granddaughter Martha Ann.[22] Leonora drove several miles after dark to spend time with Margaret Smoot.[23] On August 8, Eliza wrote, "The sisters of our com[pany] have a meeting—Sis Taylor & Leonard come. The Lord pour'd his spirit upon us in a copious effusion—sis. Writer [Riter] receiv'd the gift of tongues."[24]

Intentionally or not, Eliza contrasted the peace and harmony of the female meetings with the squabbling of male leaders. At the end of a frustrating morning when the men couldn't decide whether to move forward or stay put, she wrote, "After much deliberation, consultation, parleying, grumbling &c., several hunters are sent to search for the lost cattle & we move on." On another day marked by indecision, the sisters met in a grove to pray while the men dithered. "We have a time not to be forgotten," Eliza reported, suggesting that the sisters' prayers had something to do with the fact that the three leading men finally agreed on a plan. Later, she observed, "We seem to have the most difficulty when the most officers are with us. O Lord! Fill them with the spirit."[25] Patty agreed with Eliza about the power of prayer. "We did not camp until dark," she wrote on July 9. "The cattle was very uneasy I went into the wagon looked out saw them go round and round like a whirlpool the men saying they would break and runaway. I knelt down and prayed for the Lord to quiet them I arose they were quite still we went to bed heard no more from them."[26]

On September 4, Perrigrine Sessions caught sight of Brigham Young and his party coming toward them from the west.[27] A stepped series of reunions followed, as Brigham and his men moved over the next few days from camp to camp. The women in Joseph Horne's company chose Leonora "to regulate" a feast. More than a hundred persons sat down to "roast & Broiled Beef, pies, Cakes, Bisket Butter, peach sauce, Coffee, tea, Shugar, & a great variety of good things," Wilford reported. After dinner, they built "a large fire in the Willow Patches" and danced until ten or eleven at night.[28]

On September 9, twelve miles farther down the trail, Joseph Noble's hundred assembled to hear Heber and Brigham preach. The song Eliza composed for the occasion began:

> Hail ye mighty men of Israel
> Who the hiding place have found
> The eternal God has blest you,
> You have stood on holy Ground.[29]

Eliza understood how much men relied on approbation.

The next day, Brigham stopped at her carriage to offer his blessing. Eliza recorded their conversation as a dialogue:

> I ask'd who was to be my counsellor for the year to come—
> he said E.R.S.
> I said "she is not capable"—
> he said "I have appointed her president."[30]

Brigham was not calling Eliza to a church position. He was affirming her spiritual independence and her ability to preside over her own affairs. If he had doubted that, he surely would have appointed someone else to counsel her in his absence.

Brigham's casual, even playful acknowledgment of Eliza's independence exposes the contradictions built into the little sermon he had preached to the Apostles a few weeks before. Yes, women should obey their husbands. But the persons Eliza called "mighty men" were seldom home. What then? God did not need weeping willows. He wanted women who could square up their shoulders and do what had to be done. The real question was whether Eliza's "presidency" extended beyond the narrow space she inhabited in somebody else's wagon. She surely pondered that question, because somewhere, deep down, she knew that God had called her to an as yet unrealized ministry. She was already president of an invisible quorum of women empowered through poetry, prayer, and the ability to shake from their aprons feasts for body and spirit.

The rendezvous on the plains also left Wilford with unresolved questions. For years, he had struggled to bring his family of origin into the Kingdom of God. He had rejoiced at the baptism of his parents and at the marriage of his sister, Eunice, to Dwight Webster. He had gone out of his way to bring his cousin Betsey Cosset to Nauvoo and had been delighted to see his father and stepmother dancing together in the Camp of Israel. But during the months he traveled with the pioneer expedition, the rifts within his family circle widened. The bad news came in a succession of letters Phebe sent ahead. In the first, which reached him by courier shortly after he left the valley, she told him she had found a driver and a wagon for Father Woodruff and had assembled a "ton of bread stuff" to send with him, even though she feared it would almost strip them bare. She also warned that his stepmother "seames quite inclined not to go west."[31]

A second letter confirmed that Azubah had indeed gone back to Iowa with Dwight and Eunice. "It would have been better for the peace & Happiness of my family if B.C. & M.J. had been with them," Wilford confided to his diary. "B.C." was of course Betsey Cossett. "M.J." was his plural wife, Mary Ann Jackson. Jackson was surely with Abraham Smoot's hundred when Wilford met it a few days later. Although Wilford joyfully greeted his father, he said not a word about Jackson or the newborn son she had brought with her. Whether his silence was a mark of his continuing reticence about plural marriage or his anger over Jackson's behavior is uncertain. Probably it was both. Without naming names, he confessed in his diary, "I find that some persons who I have tried to do good & save, are filled with folly & the poison of Asps are under their tongue & are tatling, lying, & destroying themselves."[32] Because Wilford was returning to Winter Quarters, Jackson, like Eliza, would have to learn to be her own president.

After their meeting on the plains, Brigham's men moved east, while the big companies continued their journey west. As she prepared for the last difficult ascent, Leonora Taylor gave thanks: "I feel & know in all my tryals that the Lord is near and that he blesses and Comforts my Heart." With those words, she ended her diary.[33]

On September 24, Patty wrote, "I have drove my waggon all the way but part of the two last mts [mountains]. I broke nothing nor turned over had good luck." On her first Sunday in the valley, she delivered Harriet Young of a son. Somebody had told her five months before that her hands would be the first "to handle the first born son in the place of rest for the saints even in the city of our God." Now the prophecy had been fulfilled. She had come "more than one thousand miles to do it."[34]

Eliza emerged from Emigration Canyon on October 2 covered with grime from the trail and too ill with mountain fever to enjoy the scenery, but she was soon refreshed by a good cup of tea and a visit from "sis. Sess."[35] In contrast to the disease-ridden journey across Iowa the year before, the trip to the Rocky Mountains had gone well. Eliza's sister wife Clara Decker soon welcomed her into her cabin.

Pushing east, with their horses failing and their foodstuffs dwindling, Brigham and his men still had a month to go. As they searched for bison in the early dawn, Wilford saw a flock of swans floating on the Platte River—a harbinger of luck, perhaps. The memory of their beauty and a full stomach inspired him that night to write in detail about his own success in providing food for the company. When they spotted a herd of bison, he and another man had left their horses and walked among them. "Their is no well disciplined Army of men that are more particular to have An old experienced guard on a close look out than A herd of Buffalo," he observed. But the hunters managed to "quell their fears" until a clatter of bulls "with hundreds of cows following in the rear" emerged from the dust.

> We thought it quite time to be up & doing even for our own safety. I had a single load in my rifle & A Brace of Pistols. Br Johnson had a slide of 6 loads in his rifle. We rose. He fired twice. I reserved my fire until He had discharged his two balls. The whole body broke & run from us. He had killed none.

Wilford put a ball through a young cow, then tracked her up the ridge. He put a shot "through the hart string & lungs & she droped dead." With his manhood restored, he helped to carry home the meat.[36]

Brigham's company arrived in Winter Quarters on October 31, 1847. "I drove up to my own door & was truly rejoiced to once more behold the face of my wife & children again after being absent over six months," Wilford wrote.[37] Phebe greeted him with a three-day-old daughter they named Shuah.

"I have been to meeting 5 times this week female meetings"

Almost two months after arriving in the Salt Lake Valley, Patty and her family moved into a two-room house in the fort, a log-and-adobe structure with windowless back walls forming a stockade.[38] She delivered six babies that month, a perfectly manageable number except that births sometimes came in clusters, forcing her to rush from one woman to another and get little sleep. She still found time to stitch a coat for one of the battalion vets, quilt a petticoat for her granddaughter Martha Ann, put up curtains in her rude home, and wash and anoint Heber Kimball's pregnant wife Ellen Sanders, as he had asked her to do when she met him on the trail.[39] The washing and anointing was a healing ritual with no apparent scriptural foundation, although it surely derived from ceremonies performed in the Nauvoo Temple. When Heber asked her to anoint Ellen, he was affirming Patty's spiritual power rather than her expertise as a midwife. At this point, no one questioned the right of women to heal by the power of faith.[40]

The real issue was whether women had the right to act together in an organized way. "I have been to meeting 5 times this week female meetings," Patty wrote on November 27. She and Eliza participated in such gatherings on average every other day through October and November, and then almost daily in December. It was easy to do. Packed into the area around the fort, women who had known each other in Winter Quarters or on the trail were in constant contact. In contrast, men were often away on exploring or surveying expeditions or in the canyons cutting timber. As the women's meetings became more regular, both Eliza and Patty displayed a striking concern about who did or did not "preside."[41]

On October 31, for example, Eliza reported that Sisters Sessions, Leonard, Chase, Pierce, Young, and Hunter met in the room where she and Clara Decker were living. "Clara being mistress of the house call'd on me to preside," she noted, suggesting that women acquired authority not only through marriage but through their control of space. Although Eliza and Clara were both sealed to Brigham Young, Clara had precedence, since she had come into the valley first and was given the room by Brigham. At another meeting, Judith Higbee presided, "her hus[band] having given her permission to do so in his absence." These weren't meetings for preaching or instruction, but for personal testimony.[42]

Eliza was meticulous in acknowledging protocol, although the rules she followed were not always consistent. When Henrietta Whitney came to her cabin, Eliza told her "it was her privilege to set the pattern in the order of our meetings in honor of the household to which she belongs." Henrietta, a twenty-five-year-old widow, had been sealed in the Nauvoo Temple to Bishop Newel K. Whitney, who was still in Winter Quarters. In Eliza's terms, it wasn't just Henrietta's relationship to her husband that gave her the privilege of presiding, but her membership in a "household." That household included the bishop's first wife, Elizabeth Ann, who had been a councilor in the Nauvoo Female Relief Society. Did Henrietta derive her authority from her husband, her sister wife, or both?[43]

A woman could delegate her authority. When the sisters met at Hannah Pierce's cabin on November 29, she chose Patty Sessions to preside. When Patty was called away to a delivery, "she confer'd the authority back" to Pierce, who bestowed it on Eliza. Although there were men present at that meeting, none had authority over the mistress of the household. If the men were there to monitor the women's behavior, they seemed comfortable with what was happening. Eliza said they offered "much approbation."[44]

As on the trail, women sometimes stepped in when men fumbled. Levi and Rebecca Riter tossed authority back and forth after Orson Pratt failed to appear to give a sermon. As Patty explained it, when Pratt did not appear, "none of the men would open a meeting," so Levi Riter "gave the meeting unto his wife she called in a few sisters had a good meeting some of the men staid with us." Eliza added that Pratt's absence was caused by a meeting of priesthood leaders to deal with "an insubordinate spirit & a disposition to leave the place." She added that Rebecca Riter "wish'd me to preside for her." The following week, the sisters dined at the Riter cabin, then "arose & bless'd the mistress of the feast," who later

An undated photograph of the Levi and Rebecca Riter cabin before it was restored and installed at This Is The Place Heritage Park, Salt Lake City. One of only two surviving structures from the pioneer fort, it was the site of meeting of women during the Saints' first winter in the valley. *(Pioneer Memorial Museum, International Society of Daughters of the Utah Pioneers, Salt Lake City.)*

in the afternoon gained the courage to preside over her guests. Another sister, perhaps jokingly, dubbed the women's meetings "organiz'd parties." The term was apt. Their gatherings were both festive and organized. Eliza echoed that language the next day, when she referred to "an organiz'd visit of the little girls at Clara's."[45]

John Smith, the man Brigham had appointed as stake president, was wary. On December 27, several of the sisters met with him "so that he might understand our order." Patty presided at that meeting. Things seemed to go well, and he promised to meet with them again. The sisters assumed that, as long as God blessed their gatherings with an outpouring of spirit, they were doing nothing wrong. Interpreting a speech Eliza had given through the gift of tongues, Patty declared that it was the sisters' right "to claim for all that we bestow either spiritually & temporally."[46] Levi Jackman agreed. After attending one of their meetings, he said, "There was more intelligence in the hearts of the sis[ters] that aft[ernoon] than in the hearts of all the crown'd heads of Europe."[47]

Soon, however, there were discouraging rumors. On February 4, Eliza and Patty called on Father Smith. Clearly, some sort of conflict had arisen. Reverting to her old habit of circumlocution, Eliza wrote, "Strange that any should seek to shorten the arm that has been extended to lift them out of affliction."[48] Although Patty's entry for that day was also opaque, she eventually appended a longer explanation. The whole thing had begun when Smith declined an invitation to Patty's birthday party. He later explained that he was afraid she "was trying to take the advantage of his weakness and get him here to one of my meetings."

Smith was in a difficult position. Left to preside over affairs in the valley in Brigham's absence, he did not want to be accused of deviating from accepted practice. Patty and Eliza decided to assuage his fears by visiting him and explaining that Patty really had invited him to a *party*. As Patty described it:

> Sister Snow thought it best to go down there she took a cap that she had made. . . . I took some fried cakes and some sugar I gave that to Father Smith sister Snow gave Mother Smith the cap told him that she gave the making and that I gave the trimming he blessed me and said many good things to me and we left with good feelings.

The gift of doughnuts and a cap restored equilibrium. Father Smith gave both women blessings a few days later.[49]

Not long afterward, they learned that there was also some resentment among women. Patty mistrusted these stories. Perhaps in an effort to smooth ruffled feeling, she broadened her participation in female gatherings over the next month, attending at least fifteen meetings held at other sisters' houses.[50] She also continued her healing work. On February 13, she delivered Ellen Sanders of a son. On February 15, she and a friend met to pray for a neighbor's recovery from illness. On February 16, she "anointed and layed hands" on another sister for the same purpose, adding in her entry that the woman was healed.[51]

Meanwhile, Eliza was learning what it meant to live in a region only recently wrested from Mexico. Sometime in the fall, a Ute named Baptiste had come into the fort with two teenagers—one male, one female—and offered them for sale. When Charles Decker refused to buy them, Baptiste killed the boy. Horrified by the assault, Decker traded a gun for the girl. He gave her to his sister Clara, Eliza's housemate. The Mormons later insisted that they had bought captives only in order to save them, and that if they hadn't done so women and children would have been tortured and then sold to the "Navaho Indians or Spaniards." In the short run, this strategy kept peace with the Utes, who saw an advantage in being able to trade with the Mormons rather than carrying captives to Santa Fe, where the slave trade flourished. But purchasing captives taken from the Paiutes, Gosiutes, or other neighboring peoples helped sustain a practice the Saints claimed to despise.[52]

On March 28, Eliza ate her breakfast with rain dropping into her bowl. It had been a mild winter with little precipitation, but once the deluge began, the combination of wet snow and spring rain quickly overwhelmed the dirt-and-willow roofs on the fort, until it appeared to be raining harder inside than out. It rained constantly for ten days. Afterward, with clothes and bedding hung out to dry, the inner courtyard looked like a "variety rag fair." Years later, Eliza recalled spontaneously bursting into laughter at the sheer "romance" of it all as she sat in the dark with an umbrella over her head and soaked bedding covering her limbs. Sally, the Indian girl Charles Decker had bought from Baptiste, was rolled up in a buffalo robe, asleep on the floor. While the rain went "clink, clink" on stones laid in the mud, mice driven inside by the storm ran around the room squealing.[53]

"Not a house in the fort but what leaked but we feel to thank the Lord for the rain and snow for the land needed it very much," Patty wrote. On April 6, she acknowledged the anniversary of the organization of the Church eighteen years before, on April 6, 1830. "We females had a prayer meeting to day at Sister Adline Bensons to pray for the Brethren that were at winter quarter and elsewhere." They surely remembered to pray for themselves, knowing that their lives depended on the seeds they had begun to plant. As the weather improved and spring work began, their weekday meetings declined.[54]

Between March 4 and 22, Patty ushered eight infants into the world, including a pair of twins, pausing only for quick visits with friends. On March 20, during a brief respite in her work, she took on a surprising new project: "Commenced to finish my sampler that I began when I was a girl and went to school." As a girl in a now forgotten school in Maine, she had stitched two alphabets followed by a standard inscription: "Patty Bartlett is my name and with my needle wrought the same." In her mud-roofed cabin, she added in smaller letters immediately beneath it, "AD 1848 I commence again here in the 54th year of my age." In scattered moments over the summer, she continued her work until she was once again able to sign her name in the right-hand corner: "Patty Sessions. Salt Lake Valley North America August 22 1848."[55] (See color insert 2, page 5, Patty Sessions's sampler.)

She was a midwife, a healer, and a leader among women. In her own terms, she was also determined to bring to this strange new setting whatever refinement she could.

"with my Dear wife and Children"

In the spring of 1848, as Patty and her fellow Saints planted crops in the Salt Lake Valley and twenty-two hundred other Saints were preparing to leave Winter Quarters for the West, Phebe and Wilford Woodruff were packing for a journey to Boston. Since permission to camp on Indian lands had expired, Winter Quarters and other settlements on the western side of the Missouri River had to be abandoned. Some Mormons had already relocated to a new town called Kanesville, on the Iowa side of the river. Others found temporary homes in other Iowa settlements or in St. Louis.

On May 2, with Phebe by his side, Wilford reburied Joseph and Ezra in a single grave and placed a marker at the head. Brigham had given Phebe a blessing, promising her that she would return from the East with all her children. She had reason to worry. Nine-month-old Shuah was ill. She grew worse after they reached St. Louis and continued to decline as they hastened to reach the home of Phebe's sister Rhoda, who had recently migrated with her husband, Luther Scammon, to an Illinois town south of Chicago. The baby died on July 22. Wilford buried her in the Scammons' garden "in A good black walnut Coffin set inside of An Ash box," then, with his own hands, carved a limestone marker. On July 25, he noted, hopefully, that Phebe had "labored hard all day at the wash tubs." The next day, she collapsed in grief. "Mrs Woodruff expressed her feelings concerning the loss of her Children & refused to be comforted because of her children which were taken away," he wrote.[56]

The Woodruffs had lost four of their seven children to death. Sarah Emma's body lay in Nauvoo, Joseph's and Ezra's in a soon-to-be-abandoned settlement on the Missouri River, Shuah on a farm the Scammons might or might not sustain. Almost as grievous were divisions created by distance or loss of faith. Wilford's father and Mary Ann Jackson were in Utah; his stepmother and sister, Eunice, with her husband, Dwight, in Iowa. Phebe's family, too, was losing its center. Her mother was dead. Her father was aging and as yet unbaptized. She and Wilford did not know what their return to New England might bring.

They arrived in Boston on August 12, 1848, and were soon welcomed by Alexander Badlam, a manufacturer of coaches, pianos, and fine furniture who lived just across the river in Cambridge. Eventually, the Woodruffs rented a house at the corner of Harvard and Davis Streets, not far from the Badlams.[57] Although his headquarters were in Massachusetts, Wilford was responsible for church members throughout the Northeast. He visited branches as far south as Delaware and as far "Down East" as Miramichi, New Brunswick. Phebe and the children enjoyed an extended visit in Maine, then settled into the house in Cambridge, where she schooled the children while Wilford traveled.

He was fascinated with the material progress he saw in the East but disturbed by his sense of spiritual decline there. On November 7, 1848, he stayed home while his Cambridge neighbors went to the polls, observing, "I have not cast A vote for a President since this nation Shed the Blood of the Prophets Joseph And Hiram Smith Neither do I expect it." Still, he couldn't help marveling, "The electric telegraph has become so perfect And universal through the United States that citizens of New York received the returns of many of the States of the Union before they did the returns of the City itself."[58] In New York City, he ran into Hiram Kimball, the merchant who had been so generous in providing lots to church leaders in Nauvoo. Although Hiram had accepted baptism in 1843, he had stayed behind when the Saints left Nauvoo. Now he was in the

East, trying to rescue his failing business. Wilford was stunned to find him sympathetic to Robert Foster, one of the men involved in the schism that had led to Joseph's murder: "He was vary sorry for him & Could not help sheding tears for him. Said he could forgive him with all his heart." Wilford was disgusted that a man could take more interest "in that Class of people than in building up the Kingdom of God."[59]

The breakup in Nauvoo reinforced Wilford's longing for a safe haven where the Saints could live together without interference from others. Twice he journeyed to Philadelphia to fulfill Brigham Young's request that he meet with Thomas Kane, the patrician reformer who had befriended the Saints at Winter Quarters and had helped arrange for them to camp there and receive bounty payments for sending men to the Mexican War. Kane warned that Congress was likely to reject the petition for statehood church leaders were preparing. He thought they should withdraw it rather than risk having Congress grant territorial status, which he thought would only invite meddling from Washington. "You do not want Corrupt Political men strutting around," he warned. Wilford agreed.[60]

Although public affairs and church business dominated Wilford's diary, once in a while, thoughts of Phebe and the children produced sentimental passages. Drenched with rain after a rough voyage on Long Island Sound, he composed what passed in his diary for a poem, referring to his family as "suffering Pilgraims," and lamenting his inability to be with them. He prayed that he might reign in Heaven "with my Dear wife and Children" and with "Joseph and Hiram and all of Abrams seed." Although he was still bound by covenant to Mary Ann, he wrote "wife," not "wives."[61]

On February 4, 1849, he reported holding a Sunday meeting with his family in Cambridge, explaining: "My wife And children come to gether once A week. We sing And Pray And I teach them the things of the kingdom of God And I break bread And partake of the sacrament with them." Worried about what might happen if he was away and Phebe couldn't get to a regular meeting, he decided to ordain young Wilford to the priesthood so that he could "bless the bread And wine Administer it to the family." He laid out his reasoning in his diary.

> My ownly Son living was baptized when he was Eight years old. he is now most nine year of Age. He is A good youth And seems to be under the influence of the spirit of the Lord. He obeys his Parents in all things. I ordained him this day to the office of Priest to officiate in that

office in his Fathers household until He shall Arive At A suitable Age to officiate in the Church.[62]

Willie was of course his *oldest* but not his *only* son. James, the baby born to Mary Ann, though invisible in his father's diary, was still living.

Wilford was confident in Phebe's ability to teach their children the principles of the Gospel while he was away, but she could not administer the bread and wine. A nine-year-old boy, properly ordained, could do that. But when Willie became ill, both parents administered to him by the laying on of hands. When the cramping, vomiting, and abdominal pain returned, they gave him "pulverized charcoal in his teas to stop inflam-

Marsena Cannon, daguerreotypes of Phebe Woodruff, Wilford Woodruff, and Woodruffs with Father Carter, c. 1849. These daguerreotypes were probably taken in Boston by Cannon, who migrated to Utah with the Woodruffs in 1850 and became a prominent photographer there. *(Church History Library, Salt Lake City. © Intellectual Reserve.)*

mation," then "each bowed before the Lord & Called upon his name And Administered to him according to the order of the Priesthood And from that hour he began to recover." They performed a similar ritual when Phebe's niece Rhoda Foss was ill.[63] Whether Phebe, like her friends in Utah, joined other women in anointing and blessing the sick when her husband was absent, we do not know.

At a "family meeting" at the home of Phebe's oldest sister, Sarah Foss, Phebe "spoke in great Planeness" concerning her faith and her hopes for her family.[64] She obviously hadn't given up on bringing them into the fold. She urged her father to visit her in Cambridge.[65] On March 22, he arrived. After touring Boston, he went with the Woodruffs to the seashore, where Wilford baptized him. He was seventy-six years and three days old. Wilford considered it a great consolation to his own soul to have brought both his own father and Phebe's father into the Church.[66] In October, he baptized Phebe's sister Shuah Moulton, rejoicing that both of Phebe's parents and three of her sisters had now become Latter-day Saints, in fulfillment of a prophecy made in Kirtland many years before.[67]

In May, he ordained Father Carter to "the office of High Priest And to the office of A Patriarch in the Church of Jesus Christ of Latter Day Saints." Later, he and Phebe conversed with Father Carter "upon the subject of the Priesthood," probably an allusion to plural marriage.[68] Polygamy was surely on Wilford's mind a few days later, when he summarized an article from the New York *Weekly Herald* about an expedition to the Mandingo, a newly discovered people in Panama, noting that they had "A plurality of wives according to their means."[69] His own plural wife remained unacknowledged in his diary. Nor did Brigham Young mention Mary Ann Jackson when he wrote to tell Wilford that his father was well.[70]

Wilford followed affairs in Utah through Mormon newspapers and occasionally from pieces in the Boston papers. When someone called on him "for information to go by land to gold digings via Salt Lake," he opposed such a route. He hoped the Saints would soon get legal claim to their land, so that speculators could not move in. When Boston newspapers reported a scheme to send a balloon to California, he responded with sarcasm. If such a device flew over the Salt Lake Valley and burst its boiler and rained down "hot water, boilers, engins, Cars, Baloons, sails, dry goods & men," the inhabitants could attribute it to the "march of intellect, internal improvement, ingenuity, and yankee Notions." "Internal improvement," was a common term at the time for civic projects. It did not connote the kind of personal improvement Wilford urged as a preacher.[71]

Although he made fun of the rush to get gold, he couldn't help seeing Providence at work in its discovery. Alexander Badlam, the president of the Boston Branch, confirmed that veterans of the Mormon Battalion had indeed been involved in the discovery, and that his brother-in-law Samuel Brannan, the Mormon newspaperman, had spread the word.[72] When Badlam proposed going to the goldfields himself, Wilford was cautiously supportive. He knew that Badlam was deeply in debt, in part because he had been so generous with his fellow Saints. He blessed them when he left, praying that he would return.[73]

"This is the begining of a new era with us"

The Saints who left Winter Quarters for Utah in the spring of 1848 traveled in three big companies led by Brigham Young, Heber Kimball, and Willard Richards. A census published in the *Millennial Star* and *The Frontier Guardian* counted "623 waggons, 1,891 souls, 131 horses, 44 mules, 2,012 oxen, 983 cows, 334 loose cattle, 654 sheep, 237 pigs, 904 chickens, 54 cats, 134 dogs, 3 goats, 10 geese, 5 Bee Hives, 11 doves, 1 squirrel, 5 Ducks."[74] Caroline Crosby's diary affirms the importance of the animals. "When I first awoke this morn I imagined myself on a large farm with numerous flocks and herds about me of all descriptions, cocks crowing, cows lowing, sheep bleating, and pigs squeeling, and to crown the music, children crying."[75] Bathsheba Smith's later description of being caught in an autumn snowstorm on the trail was just as vivid, though less grammatical. Huddled inside her wagon, she lamented, "It is very greveous to heare the Children cry the Ox law the Cow ball the sheep blat the pig squeal the duck quack the Chickins cheap and we could not tell them the cause why they had to suffer thus."[76]

The Crosbys arrived in the valley on October 12, 1848. Caroline was thrilled to find her sister Louisa already planted in a cabin near the gate to the fort. She was surprised to see Louisa's husband, Addison Pratt, who "looked just as natural" as though she had seen him every day, even though he had been away for five years. He had left Nauvoo in 1843 to preach the Mormon gospel in Polynesia, had returned via California in 1847, and with some of the Mormon Battalion veterans had pioneered a trail east across the Sierra Nevada to Utah.[77] Because of Addison's adventures, the Pratt cabin became the center of attention: he exhibited shells and other curiosities and told anecdotes about his mission in the South Pacific. Caroline was delighted when Brigham came by "with 3 of his ladies or wives." She did not say which ones.[78] Catherine Woolley was delighted to visit with Rebecca Riter, who, like her, was a native of Pennsylvania and had much to report about the first year in the valley.[79]

With Brigham back, the Saints could truly begin to lay out a city. Within ten days of his return, the land office registered nearly eight hundred applicants for 9,630 acres of land beyond the fort. Following Joseph Smith's plan for the City of Zion, authorities created a grid with eight building lots of one and a quarter acres in each ten-acre square. Even though there was still nothing but sagebrush on the ground, they numbered the streets. The presidency and Apostles arranged themselves around the area designated as Temple Square. There they built an open-sided structure called a bowery for Sunday worship. Brigham established his offices and dwellings on a fifty-acre plot adjoining.[80]

There were now houses and fences to build, ditches to dig, orchards to tend, cattle to herd, and predators to destroy. In a contest against "wasters and destroyers," hunters killed eight hundred wolves, four hundred foxes, and scores of hawks, owls, eagles, and crows. They did not kill the seagulls that frequented the Great Salt Lake, finding them useful against crickets. In part because of a cricket infestation, the harvest of 1848 was too thin to sustain the massive migration of that year, even though the immigrants brought provisions with them. A harsh winter made things worse. Bishops presiding over the city's nineteen ecclesiastical wards administered poor relief, and Brigham thundered against extortioners. The Church even sought supplies from traders at the Hudson's Bay outpost at Fort Hall, to the north, in present-day Idaho.[81]

By July 1849, there were more than six thousand Saints in the valley, some of them filled with joy at having escaped the temptations of Babylon and others discouraged by the hard winter they had endured. Some packed their wagons for California. Hezekiah and Alena Thatcher were among them. They took six sons and their younger daughter with them, leaving a married daughter behind. In 1850, a census taker found them running a hotel in a mining camp at Salmon Falls. The decision to leave the valley cannot have been easy. "If you Elders of Israel want to go to the gold mines, go and be damned," Brigham roared.[82]

Those who remained in the valley reaped unexpected blessings when their crops flourished and weary forty-niners coming from the East proved willing to trade almost anything for fresh vegetables and a place to sleep before the last crossing to California. "We have had a great pleanty of the emigrents to visit us of late," one of Brigham's wives wrote a friend, adding that the California sojourners came bearing "many good things" that the Saints needed.[83]

On July 24, 1849, as wheat ripened and sweet corn, beans, beets, and squashes grew fat, the city mounted a celebration. Cannons roared, the band played, and a procession of dignitaries marched to the Bowery. After their experiences in Missouri and Illinois, they had little reason to celebrate the Fourth of July. The twenty-fourth was different. "This day 2 years ago the Pioneers arrived in this valley," Patty Sessions explained to her diary. Looking to the past, she predicted the future. "This day will be long remembered by thousands who were present. This is the begining of a new era with us."[84]

Every diarist who had pen and paper on hand had something to say about the day's events. "Tuesday the 24 came on in splendor," Zina Young cooed.[85] Eliza Lyman, who had truly suffered through the winter, was thrilled to see "plenty of victuals, music and mirth, and some good preaching,"[86] Hosea Stout recognized a tradition in the making when he called it "the first celebration of the kind ever held here."[87] Thomas Bullock produced an official account for church newspapers in Iowa and England.[88] When Wilford read Bullock's account, months later in Massachusetts, he noted only two details: that a flag or an ensign had been mounted on a "liberty pole 104 feet high," and that a feast had been spread on "2 tables 1½ miles long."[89]

The towering pole and the gargantuan table, one vertical, one horizontal, captured the impulses that animated the new holiday. In the United States, a liberty pole was a symbol of revolution. By mounting their pole on July 24 rather than on July 4, the exiled Mormons declared their own independence, embracing the ideals of the American Revolution without acknowledging allegiance to the nation they believed had abandoned them. Piling food on their mile-long tables, they invited passing emigrants and their Indian neighbors to join in another American tradition, creating an Independence Day that was also a First Thanksgiving.[90]

In her diary, Catherine Woolley also described the collaboration. Although she included most of the elements in Bullock's official account— the cannon fire, the band, the procession, the speeches, the crowd, and the way the organizers mounted awnings on the Bowery to provide shade— she caught visual and aural details he missed. She was less impressed by oratory than by the spectacle, perhaps because she understood the labor that created the banners and costumes.

> [T]here were 24 Silver Grays with staves in their right hands and with tassels on; and 24 young gents dressed in white bearing a copy in their right hands and a sword in their left; and they held a banner in hands which had written on it in large print: "Lion of the Lord," and they sang a song which had a chorus in these words: "None with us can be compared for we're of the root and branch of Joseph the bright and glorious morning star; for we are the true born sons of Zion." And there were 24 young ladies dressed in white bearing in their right hand the Bible and in the left the book of Mormon and the lines on their banner were: "Hail to our Chieftain."[91]

Although Catherine found the heat oppressive, in part because she was pregnant with her second child, she managed to stay until the end. For her, the splendor of the occasion was not so much in the historical content as in "the scenery."

Her description takes on additional significance when situated within the larger history of civic celebrations in the United States. The first thing to note is the decorous, almost genteel quality of the arrangements, which contrasted not only with the raucous atmosphere of July 4 celebrations elsewhere, but with the commercialized parades emerging in Eastern cities.[92] Middle-class women had long disdained the drinking bouts and musket firings that on Independence Day wounded or wasted their husbands and sons. By mid-century, young men added a new kind of ruckus, parades of "horribles" in outlandish costumes and sometimes in blackface. On a journey through coastal Maine on July 4, 1849, Wilford witnessed such a fête. Although invited to join a dinner set out for eight hundred men, he felt "more like fasting & praying" as he saw men "dressed in all the Horid form that the Ingenuity of man could form up. One would suppose that the inhabitants of the bottomless pit had come forth in possession."[93]

In Boston in October 1848, Wilford witnessed a parade honoring the opening of new waterworks. With a seven-mile-long procession blocking the omnibus in which he was riding, he had no choice but to watch.[94] Barnum's stuffed elephant passed by on a horse-drawn carriage. So did a fully rigged ship and "An Artificial flower manufactory drawn by 6 Horses containing 12 young girls dressed in white All busy making flowers." Although he noted the apple tree and the serpent on the Garden of Eden displayed by journeymen tailors, he declined to comment on the costumes, or lack thereof. According to a Boston newspaper, the tableau portrayed "two personages representing our primeval parents, not quite 'in puris naturalibus' but as near a representation to that as the taste of the times would admit."[95] Wilford closed his description by paraphrasing St. Matthew: "Broad is the road that leads to death & thousands flock together there while wisdom shows a narrow path with here And there A traveller."[96]

The Pioneer Day in Salt Lake City lacked the disorder of the July 4 celebration Wilford observed in Maine or the commercialism of the waterworks display he saw in Boston. In form, it was more like civic ceremonials enacted in the United States between 1790 and 1820, an era when neoclassical iconography was in vogue and establishing authority took precedence over honoring revolution. In these processions, young women in white dresses represented abstract concepts like Liberty or Justice or personified the states in the union. Male leaders, who of course managed the practical work of governance, represented themselves.[97] In the Salt Lake City parade, young men carried swords and copies of the Declaration of Independence and the Constitution. Young women held a Bible in one hand and a Book of Mormon in the other. Apparently, men were defenders of liberty, women custodians of faith. Yet both groups carried banners affirming the union of secular and religious authority in the person of their Prophet. The men's banner read "The Lion of the Lord," the women's "Hail to our Chief."

Although there had been militia parades and Masonic processions in Nauvoo, this was apparently the first public event that used both male and female participants in a symbolic performance. Years later, Eliza Snow claimed her brother, Lorenzo, devised the celebration. If so, she was surely a collaborator if not an instigator. According to her own account, she contributed two poems, one of which explicitly linked floral wreaths, like those on the brows of the female marchers, with swords in the hands of their brothers.[98] Without question, she helped make one of the two flags on display.

No one knows what the flags looked like. The one displayed inside the Bowery may have been a version of the American flag; the one displayed on the mammoth pole a now lost "Flag of Deseret."[99] "Sewed on the flag," Zina wrote on July 17, adding by way of explanation, "It is 60 feet long. Eliza R S superintends it in Sister Cobs room."[100] Augusta's room was in the newly constructed "Log Row" on Brigham Young's property. In a letter to her Boston friends Alexander and Mary Ann Badlam, Augusta wrote: "Brother Brigham has just brought in the flag which you probally purchased, for Sister Eliza Snow and my-self to make. The standard is to be raised on the 24 of this month and we expect to proclaim our Independence." Her comment about proclaiming independence reinforces the importance of July 24, rather than July 4, as the date of the celebration.[101]

Her letter also affirms the importance of women's labor in preparing for the event. While Eliza, Zina, and Augusta worked on the flag, others were busy making wreaths, scarves, banners, and tasseled scepters. According to Zina's diary, roses bloomed in the valley a month earlier. Perhaps there were still fresh flowers. If not, Utah women knew how to make what Patty Sessions called "artificials."[102] They also kept busy cooking for the feast. Eliza Lyman carried new wheat to the miller and devoted several days to baking. Hosea Stout explained that each ward prepared a table for its own members and a "very large dinner for strangers." Caroline Crosby said that the bishops of the different wards divided people into "companies" of ten families each, with captains at their heads, as they had done on the trail. She said that some "gentlemen from Boston" who sat at her table were astonished at the variety, claiming they could not have found better at home.[103]

With new houses to build and new mouths to feed, it may have seemed frivolous to expend time and resources on costumes, banners, flagpoles, broadsides, poems, songs, and speeches, and shortsighted to consume so much food when the fall harvest was still uncertain. No one seems to have questioned the decision to do so. As Caroline Crosby explained, those who came into the valley "almost famishing with fatigue and want of food" were pleasantly surprised at the welcome they received. Although later migrants complained of being gouged by Mormons eager to make a profit, at this point there was harmony. "Some expressed much gratitude, saying they [were] much disappointed in finding us to be a very different people from what they had formerly imagined." As one forty-niner wrote his wife, "They can do things up pretty strong out here."[104]

Daniel H. Wells spoke only half in jest when he toasted "the Gold Diggers" at the dinner. He welcomed the Goddess of Liberty into the valley; John Taylor lauded "The Ladies of the Lake—the lilies of the valley. Our mothers, wives, and children." Such gallantry provoked Eliza R. Snow to send a slip of paper to the stand, assuring Zion's male leaders that their women were "honored by the sentiment" and would "endeavor to prove worthy" of such praise, as if the ladies themselves hadn't been working for weeks to create the celebration, feigning submissiveness while making sure that their words and works, if not their voices, were represented.[105]

"We all got the fire of Zion"

By February 1850, the Woodruffs were actively planning their departure from New England. Toward the end of the month, they were surprised when Edwin Woolley and another Mormon merchant showed up at Sunday meeting in Cambridge. Brigham Young had sent them east to buy goods that could not be produced in the valley. "We had a glorious time. We all got the fire of Zion," Wilford wrote.[106] Phebe's brothers, Ezra and Ilus, who were now in business together in Portland, were helping Wilford acquire his own stock of goods to carry to Zion. Ilus even offered to transport their merchandise as far as Iowa.[107] Adding to Wilford's enthusiasm was Alexander Badlam's success in the goldfields. He had returned to Cambridge with "over two thousand dollars in gold for himself & considerable to cheer the Hearts of sevral indivduals & to help them to Zion." Wilford considered this a partial fulfillment of Father Smith's 1837 prophecy that he should have access "to the treasures hid in the sand" to assist him in gathering God's children.[108]

Phebe and Wilford and their children left Boston by train on April 9 with a hundred of their fellow Saints. In New York, they picked up a hundred more. Phebe's sister, Sarah Foss, and her five grown children were with them. The first part of the journey went smoothly. Although they all took the infamous portage railway over the Allegheny Mountains to Pittsburgh, either the system had been improved since Wilford was last on it or he had lost his fear. He noted simply that they made it "over the mountains in good order."[109] With Winter Quarters abandoned, the Saints had a new staging place, south of Council Bluffs. In certain seasons, it was now possible to go directly there from St. Louis by water, though that meant crossing the state of Missouri. Wilford was unfazed. "We are passing to day along the Banks of Jackson & Clay Counties whare the Saints have received such severe persecutions in former days," he wrote. "May the Lord Reward there persecuters according to their deeds."[110]

Although there was no longer any need to fear persecutions, there were new terrors to contemplate. For months, Wilford had been tracing the spread of cholera across the United States. As the gold rush began, the scourge followed the overland trail.[111] On May 2, the first death in

Wilford's company occurred. By July 18, sixteen members had perished. One family lost three persons within a single week. Passing the graves of California-bound migrants added to the terror.[112] Although Wilford attributed one of these deaths to consumption and another to lightning, the others were probably caused by cholera. Edwin Woolley, whose outfitting company followed shortly after Wilford's, was alarmed by the number of grave markers. It wasn't just the deaths that terrified them, but the way the graves clustered together, one tumbling over another, as though they would never stop. After July 18, however, the infection that threatened their journey subsided, leaving annoying but fixable problems, such as broken wheels or axles, and grumbling.[113]

Having passed through the shadow, they awakened to the wonders as well as the dangers of the trail. Wilford's diary caught Phebe looking through a spyglass to survey the country, stretching to engrave her name as high as she could reach on Chimney Rock in present-day Nebraska, and tramping with "several other Ladies" through the whole length of Devil's Gate, a geographical feature in what would become Wyoming.[114] On July 30, Wilford described her rushing into the middle of a stampede— a scene "dredded by all Emgrating Companies on the plaines." The trouble started when Willie's horse threw him and spooked another man's team. Phebe "rushed into the midst of the scene whare she was in danger of her life evry instant." Fortunately, she quickly found an opening and fled the mêlée, while Wilford rescued Susan, who hung on to the carriage, with her feet dangling between the wheels, while their horse, which had broken a leg, raced on its three good legs toward the hills. Wilford had to shoot the horse, but, to his immense relief, no other animal or person was injured.[115]

On October 14, 1850, Wilford led his little band of pioneers into the valley. He quickly went to work moving logs from the house he had hastily built in the fort in 1847 to his lot near Temple Square. Soon he was digging a cellar.[116] He said not a word about Mary Ann Jackson, though she must have been there with her son, James, who was now three and a half years old. It is easy to imagine Wilford's having a meeting with James much like the one Addison Pratt had with his youngest daughter, who turned away in fear when someone told her he was her father. Perhaps Wilford, like Addison, took "curiosities" or new shoes or a hat from his bag and told the boy these things were for him. Perhaps not. That he did not describe such a meeting doesn't mean it didn't happen, although it might mean that he was still having trouble recognizing that he had more than one son.

Nine months later, on July 19, 1851, Phebe gave birth to a healthy baby girl, Beulah Augusta. When the baby was five days old, the city held its third annual Pioneer Day celebration. The cannons roared, and, in Wilford's words, the brass band sent forth "on the wings of the Morning its sublime straines of martial & cheering Music." While Phebe suckled her baby at home, Wilford, Aphek, and the three oldest Woodruff children joined the procession. "In many respects this was the most interesting day of my life," Wilford exclaimed. "My Father, myself, & my Children making three generations . . . in the Grand Escort to Honor the Holy Prophets of God." Hosea Stout pronounced it "the greatest celebration ever held here."[117]

The newly launched *Deseret News* carried a full story. Once again, the "24 young ladies" sang a song with words composed by Eliza R. Snow. In the morning of life on earth, she wrote,

> God and angels talked with men,
> And woman too was free;
> For both were pure and sinless then,
> In perfect liberty.

Eliza's tight little verses exposed both her deepest yearning for a world where women were free and her surprisingly orthodox interpretation of the Biblical passage in which God told Eve, "Thy desire shall be to thy husband, and he shall rule over thee." In this poem, Eliza placed all her hopes on heaven:

> For woman, if submissive here
> To God and man's decree,
> Restor'd, will fill a nobler sphere
> In glorious liberty.[118]

9

"My pen is my only weapon"

The Log Row, Salt Lake City, 1850–1851

When the first National Woman's Rights Convention met in Worcester, Massachusetts, in October 1850, Eliza Snow was living in Brigham Young's Log Row, on the hill two blocks beyond Temple Square. She learned about the convention months later, when Eastern newspapers arrived with the overland mail. *The New York Herald,* a Mormon favorite, dismissed the convention as an "Awful Combination of Socialism, Abolitionism, and Infidelity" got up by "fanatical and crazy mongrels in breeches and petticoats."[1] Eliza had a more ladylike response. In a poem published in Salt Lake City's *Deseret News,* she acknowledged the desire of reformers to create a better world but warned those agitating for female rights that they might as well attempt to realign the stars and planets as to remove woman from the sphere assigned to her by God. Then she issued an invitation:

> Let those fair champions of "female rights"
> Female conventionists, come here. Yes, in
> These mountain vales. . . . here are noble men
> Whom they'll be proud t'acknowledge to be far
> Their own superiors, and feel no need
> Of being Congressmen.[2]

Eliza had no idea that, twenty years later, champions of women's rights would indeed come to Utah, not to acknowledge the superiority of Mormon men, but to investigate the newly acquired rights of Mormon women. Nor did she imagine that in time she, too, would become a "conventionist."

Eliza sought liberty through submission to the men she considered God's vicars on earth.[3] Her housemate Augusta Cobb was different. Writing to Brigham Young in the autumn of 1850, Augusta mused, "Is there any such a thing as an independent woman in the economy of God? If there is, I want to be that woman." Although she was Brigham's wife, she insisted that she so seldom saw him that she had no alternative but to address him in writing. "My pen is my only weapon that God has given me to fight my way through this unfriendly World," she wrote. For Eliza, a pen could also be a weapon. She used it to defend Zion and to secure her own place within it. Augusta pointed her pen directly at Brigham. Her letters matter not because she was representative of Mormon women or typical of Brigham Young's wives, but because her audacious attacks expose stress points easily overlooked in the writing of more compliant women.[4]

Eliza was not being entirely fanciful in her description of affairs in Zion. If female conventionists had come to Utah in 1850, they would have discovered that Mormon lawmakers had already addressed, in a topsy-turvy way, some of the very grievances they discussed in their conventions. One of these was the continuing use in many American states of the common-law notion of *coverture,* which declared married women civilly dead and denied them control of their own earnings and the property they brought into marriage. Another was framing the laws of divorce without regard "to the happiness of women."[5] In its first session, the Utah legislature abolished use of the common law, not because of a concern for women's rights, but to protect themselves from its strictures against bigamy. By refusing to pass any marital legislation at all, they remanded governance of marriage to the Church, which meant that divorce became freely available, especially to women, Brigham Young having embraced the radical notion that a marriage without mutual affection was a form of adultery.[6]

Utah legislators inadvertently eliminated other kinds of inequality. Out of disdain for doctors and lawyers, they opened courts to anyone who wanted to plead a case and created a Council of Health that included midwives and lay healers.[7] In principle at least, they also embraced coeducation. The University of Deseret opened its doors to women in its second year. Unfortunately, in its third year it collapsed for lack of resources.[8] In Utah, women had more opportunity because nearly everybody had less.

Of necessity Utah pioneers revived household production and exchange, allowing informal participation by women in what was still an undeveloped economy. For Augusta, that was precisely the problem. She wondered whether a wife's ability to manage her own earnings mattered if she was forced to live in poverty. Although in principle she embraced plural marriage, she asked whether deference to other women was any improvement over obedience to a husband.

Her letters take us beyond issues of law to more mundane queries about what it meant to live day to day inside a utopian dream. Her letters not only deflate Eliza's portrayal of Mormonism's superior men; they provide an intriguing contrast to the writings of Patty Sessions, Zina Jacobs Young, Vilate Kimball, and Bathsheba and Lucy Meserve Smith. More urbane than they, she was also less prepared for pioneering and less skilled at circumventing male authority.

"I would like to be a Mother of Mother's and Queen of Queen's!"

Augusta claimed to have sacrificed more to marry in plurality than any other woman in the Church. She may have been right. Although others left legal husbands, few faced the ignominy of a divorce on grounds of adultery. While her friends were trekking across Iowa and chinking cabins at Winter Quarters, she was in Massachusetts trying to win the support of her children against her husband's sensational charges. In Massachusetts, a conviction of adultery allowed an immediate and absolute divorce, known as a divorce *a vinculo,* whereas a charge of desertion yielded only a divorce *a menso et thoro,* usually called a "divorce from bed and board," a kind of legal separation. Not surprisingly, half of the divorce suits in Suffolk County, Massachusetts, in this period included adultery among the charges. Because he wanted to remarry, Henry Cobb took the only means at his disposal.[9]

His children were horrified. "Oh! that a <u>Father</u> could so lose sight of the best interests of his children," twenty-year-old Ellen wrote to a friend in Philadelphia. She said that when she saw her father "bending his head in prayer at Church," she imagined "dark & Evil designs" that not even "that Garb of hypocrisy" could conceal. Although she did not share her mother's faith, she said she would stake her life on her innocence. With the support of her siblings, Ellen appealed to her father's lawyer, portraying her mother as a "victim of a misguided Faith."[10]

When Augusta refused to play the victim's part, Henry's lawyer collected statements from Catherine Lewis and George Adams, old associates who were now Mormon dissidents. (Adams had himself been excommunicated for attempting to seduce Mormon girls employed at a Lowell mill.)[11] Although the testimony Lewis and Adams provided was damning, it was hardly watertight. For one thing, the dates were wrong. If Augusta slept with Brigham in Boston, it wasn't on August 10, 1844, because he was by then in Nauvoo, claiming his right to lead the Church. They were no doubt correct, however, in quoting Augusta as saying "that the doctrine taught by Brigham Young was a glorious doctrine for if she did not love her husband it gave her a man she did love."[12]

Brigham, who had little sense of the obstacles Augusta faced, wrote from Winter Quarters, urging her to remain faithful to her covenants. "Mary ann is verry kind to all of the Famely," he assured her, then added, "You must excuse my mestakes in my letter. I send my own hand wrighting for I think you would rather See it than eney other."[13] Fearing that the Saints were about to leave Winter Quarters for the Rocky Mountains, she chose to flee before the trial, taking Charlotte with her. That decision was not unusual: in ten of the eleven divorce cases heard in the same session, the defendants failed to appear. As a consequence, Henry got his divorce, and newspapers throughout the region carried the sensational story of the Boston matron who, having been converted to the "spiritual wife" doctrine, had "gone to live with Brigham Young."[14]

Augusta was encamped on the Missouri River when her oldest son, a junior at Harvard, died suddenly in Boston. Her other children wrote plaintive letters imploring her to come home. Seventeen-year-old Albert even promised to support her if she would return. She responded with a poem inviting her children to "Come unto Christ."[15] Yet by this point, she was having second thoughts about her sealing to Brigham in the Nauvoo Temple. On February 21, 1847, she signed a "Last Will and Testament" asking that, in the next temple to be built, she be sealed by proxy to Joseph Smith "if it is not my privelige to be sealed to Jesus Christ." She added that she was willing to have Brigham perform the role of proxy for Joseph, if he was willing. She closed "in the name of the Lord Jesus Christ and by virtue of the Holy Preisthood vested in me," signing with her maiden name, "Augusta Adams," and adding a paper heart with a red wax seal.[16]

Augusta's request to be sealed directly to Jesus was no more audacious than her use of the phrase "by virtue of the Holy Priesthood vested in me." That was the phrase men used while performing ordinances such as baptisms or sealings. Although she, like other women, had been clothed in the "robes of the Priesthood" in the temple, she had not been ordained to any office. For her that distinction did not matter. Although prepared to meet God, she quickly recovered from her illness and was with Brigham's company when he returned to the valley in the spring of 1848.

Augusta had married Brigham believing she would share equally with Mary Ann. In the Salt Lake Valley, she found herself submerged in a crowd. Eighteen of Brigham's wives appeared in the Utah Census for 1850. Only Mary Ann was listed under his name.[17] Anyone with eyes to see knew that polygamy was being practiced, but it was not to be acknowledged in any document going to Washington. Mary Ann lived on the hill leading to

Map of Salt Lake City, 1850–1852, with the location of some dwellings. *(Samantha Van Gerbig.)*

Daguerreotypes of Mary Ann Young
(top left), Eliza Snow (bottom left),
and Brigham Young (top right), 1850s.
These photographs of Mary Ann and
Eliza reflect their determination to
maintain respectability even in a frontier
environment. Brigham, who is about to
begin twiddling his thumbs, seems a bit
bored. *(Church History Library, Salt Lake
City. © Intellectual Reserve.)*

City Creek, a rushing stream that separated Brigham's property from that
of Heber Kimball. Her adobe house served as both a residence and the
seat of territorial and church government. Because it had been plastered
and painted, people called it the "White House." Below it sat the Log
Row. Constructed somewhat like a modern motel, it had doors opening
outward from individual apartments into a courtyard. An adobe kitchen

attached to one end served double duty as a site for family meetings. Eliza, Zina, and Augusta worked on the Pioneer Day flag in Augusta's room.[18]

At forty-eight, Augusta was the oldest of Brigham's wives. Mary Ann was forty-seven and Eliza forty-six. Three of the others were in their thirties, the remaining twelve in their twenties.[19] Augusta was furious when anyone referred to her as one of the "girls." She told Brigham, "I would like to be a Mother of Mother's and Queen of Queen's! I do not like to call Mary Ann Young Mother or Queen; neither do I like to call Emma Smith or Eliza R Snow so either."[20]

Augusta's problems were in part economic. Although she had apparently kept boarders in Boston, she had no experience in frontier life. In this rough new settlement, she seemed incapable of begging, borrowing, or manufacturing the things she needed. She did admit to stealing. In one of her cheekiest letters, she asked Brigham to inform whatever church council was interested "that Augusta the Wife of Brigham stole a bushel of corn from the tithing crib to pay for some meat in the year 1850, and contemplates stealing some more to buy some tea, having seen that her Husband has been sending it round to others and forgetting her."[21] Since Brigham insisted that church leaders support their families with their own labor, this was a stinging attack. Augusta knew that goods in the tithing house were meant for the poor. She insisted *she* was poor.

When criticized for burning a length of wood too big for her small stove, she countered that she had no choice because she didn't have an ax "for an Indian to chop some." Chastised for gathering kindling from a pile of laths used in construction, she shot back, charging that no one objected when Brigham's little boys broke up laths in playing. Castigated for the way she was feeding her pig, she retorted that it was "quite a piece of condescension to be willing to boil the offal and wait on a pig at all. . . . Think of it servant to a hog. O my God how much lower will thou have me descend."[22] She kept watch on what other people got and demanded the same or more. When Brigham sent her fabric for a dress, she thanked him but asked also for "a plain linen gingham like Zina's."[23] In another missive, she asked him to take back the "thin" fabric and "ordinary" bonnet he had sent and "in lieu thereof give me a bolt of sackcloth. I have plenty of ashes on hand."[24]

Once, Brigham had been impressed by her genteel ways and had sent his daughter to live with her in Massachusetts. Now the whole family had turned against her, "because foresooth some body has said I wanted to bring Charlotte up a <u>Lady</u>."[25] Having traded social status, a comfortable house, and grown children to marry Brigham, she wanted recompense. She had not yet figured out that, on a day-to-day basis, women controlled the flow of resources and distribution of work in the Log Row. When she refused to be one of the "girls," she took herself out of the system.

In an expansive letter to Brigham in October 1851, she complained that all she heard around her was "work, work, work, gusset, and seam, and shirt, spinning wheels, . . . &c." Anybody who wanted to teach Charlotte how to spin might do so. As for herself, she had no intention of taking up household manufacturing. She had neither a wheel nor wool and did not want them. She had another plan for making herself useful in the world: "I am going to turn Mid Wife as I cannot be any other kind of wife." True to form, she soon moved into the middle of a controversy between a newly arrived physician and the botanic healers who dominated health care in Salt Lake City.[26]

The Council of Health was a bit like one of the "Friendly Botanic Societies" created in the early United States by followers of Samuel Thomson, a lay healer who patented a system designed to restore bodily balances through the use of herbal teas, sweating, and hot peppers and by single-minded devotion to the herb lobelia.[27] Willard Richards, a licensed Thomsonian practitioner, gave ecclesiastical sanction to such practices. His brother Phinehas was president of the Council, with Dr. Samuel Sprague, a Brigham Young favorite, as his counselor. Phoebe Angel, Patty Sessions, and Susanna Richards (Willard's and Phinehas's sister) presided over a parallel Female Council as well as participating in the broader organization.[28] Although Utah legislation mandated fines of up to a thousand dollars and a year at hard labor for the use of mercurial compounds and other remedies favored by regular physicians, the Council operated primarily through social pressure. Patty noted only two cases where a person was formally "cut off." Both involved Augusta.[29]

The trouble began when she attended a meeting to discuss charges against Dr. Jeter Clinton, who had apparently offended the others by claiming to know more than they did. Augusta told Brigham, "I think the rottenness is in Mother Sessions, the nose skinning is in Dr Sprague and the egotism in Dr P. Richards." As for Dr. Clinton, he was a "Saint and Gentleman [who] bore their abuses in a most humble and God like Spiret."[30] When Augusta continued to defend Clinton after he was voted off the Council, she found herself facing discipline. "I have yet to learn that I must use hot medecines on every occasion," she wrote in an appeal, insisting that, because she had been "called into the field of action by the Speret of God," the group had no right to restrain her. On November 12, Patty reported without comment, "I went to the counsel of health cut sister Cobb off."[31]

Augusta blamed Brigham for not being there when she needed him.[32] On December 10, he delivered a rambling discourse in a meeting of the Council, dismissing most doctors as "Ignoramuses" and "Scoundrels," and reaffirming his own faith in "mild herbs" and in female management of births. Drawing his examples from the animal kingdom and from Native American practice, he argued that nature provided its own remedies. "The practice of Doctors in visiting women in childbirth is damnable. When the time has come Nature will deliver her of her child without a Doctor."[33]

Augusta agreed that women should care for one another rather than calling in doctors, but she was appalled that Brigham would compare women to animals: "And is not a woman's life more valuable than a beast's?" In her view, Indian women's apparent ease in childbirth was easily explained. "Degrade us like them and compel us to travel all our life time on foot as they do and to bear the burdens of our Lord instead of their bearing ours, together with the early habit of rideing astride on horseback and marying very young . . . we probably might bring forth as they do. But we believe in a different way from that." Augusta told Brigham she was committed to "ascending not descending." She was happy to have an Indian chop her wood, but she did not want to live like a squaw.[34]

In another of her pungent parodies, she challenged the gender division of labor in church service. At every general conference, Brigham called men on missions. Why not women?

My Dear Husband.
    We the undersigned your Humble suppliants beg in the name
of Joseph that you will send us on a mission to the states or Islands
or some where else, for we are so heartily tired and sick of our dear
Companions, that we can hardly live. Unless we can arise and shake
ourselves from the dust, and put on our beautiful garments . . . We do
not fear Cholary or any thing else so much as we dread to encounter
cold heartless Husbands. All else seems as nothing, but this has
become almost insupportable. Yours as ever stripped for the race and
harnessed for the battle.
                                                          Onward.[35]

Augusta Cobb letter, January 31, 1851. Although addressed to "My Dear
Husband," Augusta's letter asking to be sent on a mission was cosigned by
two of her friends, Harriet Russel and Ruth Vose. *(Church History Library, Salt
Lake City. © Intellectual Reserve.)*

Once again, Augusta used scriptural metaphors to needle Brigham. Interestingly, in the Book of Mormon, the passage that in the Bible reads "Put
on thy beautiful garments, O Jerusalem" reads "Put on thy beautiful garments, O daughter of Zion."[36]

Augusta was using a classic feminist strategy, applying to her own sex a
standard intended for men. Although a few women in this era did indeed
serve missions, as Phebe Woodruff had done, they did so as adjuncts to
their husbands. In 1848, Catherine Woolley helped organize a going-away
party for Francis and Mary Jane Hammond, who were going to the Sandwich Islands (Hawaii). A bit later, Parley Pratt took one of his wives with
him to Peru.[37] Augusta's proposal was more directly inspired, however, by

the departure of her friends Louisa Barnes Pratt and Caroline Crosby for Tahiti.

Addison Pratt, Louisa's husband, had been a bit of a celebrity in the Salt Lake Valley after returning from his mission to the South Pacific. He spoke in meetings, gave lessons in Tahitian, and displayed his curiosities at social gatherings.[38] But, to his wife's dismay, he volunteered in the autumn of 1849 to accompany a group of men back to California and then, with Brigham's blessing, returned to the Pacific, promising that Louisa could follow if she chose. She agonized over that decision, uncertain about whether he really wanted her to come. Sometime in March 1849, Mary Ann Young visited her, acknowledging that Brigham had sent her to find out whether she wanted to join her husband. Still unsure of herself, Louisa consulted Willard Richards, who only smiled when she complained that if she were an elder she would never consent to leave her family for so long. She then asked her female friends to pray for her, not knowing whether to be pleased or worried when "their prophesies were that I would go to the Islands of the seas, to join my companion." She was shocked when, on the first day of the April conference, she heard several men "in whose society I could not foresee much pleasure" called to accompany her to the islands. At intermission, she sought out Mary Ann, begging her to use her influence to arrange for her sister Caroline to join her.[39]

So it was that, in the spring of 1850, Jonathan and Caroline Crosby and their son Alma joined Louisa Pratt and her four daughters on a journey to Tahiti. A year later, Louisa wrote Augusta and Eliza, noting that, since they lived so near together, she thought one letter might do for both. "Let all the good substantial Mormon Sisters read it if they wish to; and be sure and tell them I have great faith in their prayers." She concluded with a few words in the language she was trying hard to acquire, "ia ora na oua (that is, peace be with you two)."[40]

Alas, Augusta had no husband to follow her into the field. Her sardonic request to be sent on a mission was yet another demonstration of her frustration in trying to become "an independent woman in the economy of God."

"mercy mercy O mercy is all that I can say"

Like Augusta, Zina Jacobs had left a legal husband to become part of Brigham Young's household. Unlike Augusta, she had come to the valley with her extended family. Although she appreciated Brigham's support, she did not rely on his attention. Perhaps she avoided it. Her closest emotional bonds were with her sister Presendia and her brothers Dimick and Oliver Huntington. Having been raised on the frontier, she took pride in being able to sustain herself, although she understood that, in a society that depended for its survival on common effort, no one was truly independent.

During their first winter in the valley, she relieved Brigham of any responsibility for her support by living and teaching school in a two-room log house that her brother Dimick provided in the fort. On one winter day, she packed fifty-six children into her sixteen-foot-square room; by the end of the term, the class had grown to sixty-nine. To earn extra income, she sometimes held spelling and writing classes after school. She was thrilled when a little "Lamanite" or Indian girl named Adalade joined her class. Zina called her students "schollars," even though she wasn't much of a scholar herself. She earned just enough to keep her own little boys, Zebulon, age seven, and three-year-old Chariton, in clothing and shoes.[41]

For a time, Presendia, who was pregnant, lived with her, but she could not bear the smoking chimney and the noise of the children. On the day she moved out, Zina noted it had been seven years to the day "since Presendia was sealed to Joseph Smith."[42] Presendia went into labor a month later. "The babe came near perishing but survived," Zina reported. Patty Sessions, who was in attendance, said that Heber came into the room after supper and "Great ware the blessing sealed upon the childs head." The baby's name, Presendia Celestia Kimball, was appropriate. Although she belonged to Heber on earth, in the Celestial Kingdom she would be Joseph's.[43]

Three days after Presendia's delivery, Brigham came to Zina's cabin and accompanied her to a party. "On our walk home we had a few words concerning Josephs kingdom," she wrote cryptically. Presendia had done her part to increase Joseph's progeny. Perhaps Brigham believed it was Zina's turn.[44] On March 15, he visited her again and stayed the night. "A new era of things awates me," she wrote. Then she paused to summarize what she had achieved over the past few months: "I have rolled through the winter. The Lord hath given me strength for which I trust I shall ever be grateful to Him. 33 dollars have I pade for wood this winter. I earned it my self. My school bill amounted to 75 dollars and 86 cts. I fell truly thankful for evry blessing and mercy."[45]

Her entry for March 17, the day she moved up the hill to Brigham's compound, was wistful: "Many are the reflections of my minde. My Father & mother is not. Joseph is not. BY is very kinde indeed." She said nothing about Henry Jacobs, who was now said to be living with a new wife in California. "My Wagon was set near Emiline and Margret's door," she continued.[46] She was soon engaged as a teacher for Brigham's children. On her first day, she had only fifteen scholars, but five small boys, perhaps the same ones who broke up laths outside Augusta's cabin, kept her very busy.[47]

Zina enjoyed listening to Brigham expound scriptural mysteries at family meetings. Sometimes there were as many as seventeen women gathered in the adobe kichen. Although she judged most meetings "first rate" or "comforting," she was not so sure about the one on January 6, 1850. "The children were blest & BY gave the females there due. O there weakness Lord have mercy mercy O mercy is all that I can say do I pray."[48] She did not explain who among the females was in such dire need of mercy. Perhaps Augusta was among them. In a letter to Brigham written about the same time, she said he had wounded her feelings by telling her that there was an open door before her and she could walk through it if she chose.[49]

Zina did not tell tales, though she hinted at recurring conflict in the Log Row. In an unusually candid entry, she acknowledged that she had witnessed many scenes "common to the vicissitudes of this life. Some very pleasant and others perplexing that I will pass by."[50] A squiggly line in a diary entry probably pointed toward something unsavory or disturbing that she chose not to record.

Zina relished the opportunity to use her nursing skills. Louisa Beaman, whose twin babies had died shortly after arriving in the valley, was now suffering with a tumor or an abscess on her breast. Margaret Alley, another of Brigham Young's wives, was also ill, apparently threatening to miscarry.[51] On Sunday, March 27, 1849, both women needed Zina's attention. As if Providence had willed it, Phoebe Angel, the family midwife, walked by, and in about two hours, Zina reported, "Margaret was relieved of 2 months sickness—perfect form occasioned by a hurt." In a two- or three-month pregnancy, the embryo would have been only an inch or two long, small enough to fit in the palm of the hand, its developing shape and attached umbilical cord identifiable by an experienced midwife like Mother Angel and perhaps by Zina as her reference to "perfect form" suggested. She did not explain how Margaret had been "hurt."[52]

That afternoon, Zina gave Louisa an emetic. In the evening, she summarized her ministrations, referring to Louisa, Margaret, and Clarissa, another inhabitant of the Log Row, by their initials:

> I had a buisy day and it seemed quite a day of little events M's misfortune, L's emetic, and her hen hatched & C's cat came on the bed when she was asleep and had 2 fine kittens which I hope will prosper as the mice are very troublesome.[53]

Babies, mice, hens, and kittens. For Zina, there had been no unraveling of mysteries on this Sabbath, no thundering sermon from Brigham. It had been "a day of little events," the kind of day that gave her satisfaction.

At its best, her work as a healer allowed her to merge practical service with spiritual ministry. "With the tenderness of a mother," a dying woman put her arms around her "and whispered a blessing to me in tongs." When Zina asked her if she would return from the dead for a visit if she could, the woman said she would. Zina was thrilled. "Ah blessed thought— O Glorious hope," she wrote. "My heart leaps forward at the thought when we poor mortals shall be free from pane and sin and vanity." Her request to the dying woman may have been inspired by Patty Sessions's account of a visit to another woman, who reported visiting over an hour with a sister who had been dead more than two years. Confident that life continued beyond the grave, Zina mourned with those who mourned and, like Patty, comforted those who were facing death.[54]

Yet she relished earthly pleasures. One May morning, she reported that her schoolroom was perfumed with roses, the little girls having celebrated the coming of spring by decking themselves with wild blossoms. "It is truly cheering to see what the Lord has here growing spontaneaous to please the eye and gladden the hart."[55] She marked the success of almost any event by the food, praising God for mince pie, gooseberry tarts, rice pudding, pancakes with butter and molasses, and green peas fresh from the garden.[56] At a party organized by her brother's quorum, she praised both the "comforting instructing encourageing" speeches and "an execelent supper & beer to drink." At a party where someone played an accordion and a fiddle, she "arose and sung some," having covenanted with God to obey the voice of the spirit when it called her to do so. She added that both Brigham and Heber were at that gathering. When she rose to sing a song of Zion at another such event, a brother "dansed the time."[57] She understood the Book of Mormon passage that said, "Adam fell that men might be; and men are, that they might have joy." She may or may not have recognized the unspoken addendum: "And women are that they might provide it."[58]

On a June day, just as the sun set, she sat singing with her children, rocking her younger son, Chariton. Suddenly she found herself singing in tongues, and the spirit told her to go bless Clarissa Decker, another of Brigham's plural wives. Since Zina had promised God that she would always follow such impressions, she went to Clary's cabin and blessed her. Then, after blessing two other women, she noticed Sally, the Indian captive that Brigham's son-in-law had bought from the Ute trader Baptiste. Zina wrote:

> I lade my hands upon her hed and my language changed in a moment and when I had finished she said she understood [e]very word. I had talked in her mother tongue. The speret bore testimony but there was positive proof that could not be denied. I told her that her mother and sisters ware coming, and She must be a good girl. It was to her understanding. It was a great cross but the Lord crowned it with joy for which I fee[l] to praise his name.[59]

It is not entirely clear what Zina considered "a great cross," perhaps her willingness to leave her own cabin and offer a blessing uninvited.

She might also have been thinking of the "great cross" borne by Sally, who had been taken from her mother and then placed in a home among people who could not speak her language. For a moment at least, Zina believed that the spirit of God had connected her with the little Shoshone girl. If Sally did experience Zina's babblings as affirmation in her own language that her mother and sisters would soon come to get her, how disappointed she must have been when they failed to appear.

In the spring of 1850, Zina left a glaring blank in her diary. At the top of a page, she wrote "April 1850," then stopped. When she picked up her daily entries on June 8, she started a new page, as though she intended to go back and fill in what she had left out. That did not happen. Perhaps she could not bring herself to write about the tumult and sorrow that had unfolded around her.[60] On April 3, she gave birth to a daughter, Zina Presendia. A month later, her sister Presendia's sixteen-month-old daughter, Presendia Celestia, drowned in City Creek. Presendia's only remaining child by her first husband, ten-year-old Oliver Buell, had turned his back for a minute, and his little sister was gone. Presendia was inconsolable. One night, as she lay wakeful in her room with a single candle burning, the door seemed to open and her father, long dead, walked into the room with Joseph Smith. She thought they had come to take her with them. She would have welcomed that. But, thinking of Oliver, she vowed to live for the sake of her remaining child.[61] (See color insert 2, page 4.)

On May 15, Louisa Beaman died. If she did have breast cancer, as some thought, her death was both disfiguring and excruciatingly painful.[62] Perhaps Zina attempted to help with the nursing, even though she was caring for her own tiny baby and dealing with Presendia's distress. Sometime later, Zina went back to an earlier entry to note that Louisa had left her room for the last time in late February to attend a birthday party in Zina's honor. The blank page Zina left in her diary between April and June was an eloquent reminder of the loss of her friend and her niece.[63]

On June 27, the anniversary of Joseph's and Hyrum's martyrdom, Zina "had all of Joseph's family together that could meet in the vally." Eleven attended. "Praise the Lord that so many are continueing in well doing and striving to hold out faithful to the end."[64] This was not the first time Joseph's wives had assembled to remember him. Sometimes they met on December 23, the anniversary of his birth. On one such occasion, Eliza "read Joseph's lectures," presumably the sermons recorded in her minute book.[65]

If this had been an ordinary community, a gathering to memorialize a dead leader would have included his publicly acknowledged widow and children, but, despite repeated invitations to join the migration, Emma remained in Nauvoo. On Joseph's birthday in 1847, she had shocked her former friends by marrying Lewis Bidamon, a jovial widower with no apparent interest in religion.[66] Joseph's mother, Lucy Mack Smith, had also remained in Nauvoo, ostensibly because she was too feeble to travel. Nor did any of Joseph's surviving siblings—his brother, William, and sisters, Sophronia, Katherine, and Lucy—go west. Hyrum's widows, Mary and Mercy Fielding, made the trek, as did Joseph's cousin George Albert Smith, but none of Joseph's immediate family.[67]

When Zina said that eleven members of Joseph's family had gathered, she was talking about a shadow family composed of fifteen women sealed to Smith who had managed to reach the Salt Lake Valley by 1850. These included Brigham's wives Eliza Snow and Emily Partridge; Emily's sister Eliza, who had married Amasa Lyman; Heber Kimball's wives Sarah Ann Whitney and Presendia Buell; his daughter Helen Mar Whitney; Melissa Lott, who had married Ira Willes after Joseph's death; and several others. Elvira Holmes and Patty Sessions missed this meeting because they were out of town.[68] Zina may not have included women posthumously sealed to Joseph, but that list was growing. In 1852, Brigham served as proxy for Joseph Smith when Amanda Barnes Smith went to the Endowment House to be sealed. Although her first husband died a martyr at the Haun's Mill Massacre in 1838, she chose not to be sealed to him, or to her second husband, whom she divorced when he became abusive. She later told her children about a powerful spiritual manifestation that convinced her Joseph was her rightful husband.[69]

However Zina defined it, "Joseph Smith's family" intersected with other men's families. It was a surprisingly diverse group, united not by legal bonds or biological kinship but by religious faith and commitment to a man and his memory. When Augusta proclaimed in one of her letters to Brigham, "I have Called on the Spiret of Joseph to rest on me," she reflected a larger impulse among women to see in Joseph—or in the community of women looped around him—an answer to earthly disappointment.[70]

"I am . . . determined to find a good substantial tree to cling fast to"

Patty Sessions was as independent as a woman could be in the Salt Lake Valley. As a midwife, she had an occupation that kept her steadily employed. As a member of the Council of Health, she was a recognized leader in her community. As a woman of God, she blessed and anointed other women, seemingly at will. But in January 1850, she felt rejected and discouraged. At the age of fifty-nine, her husband David had married nineteen-year-old Harriet Teeples, a woman who had already been married and divorced and had a little son. David's first adventure in plural marriage had ended at Winter Quarters, when Rosilla Cowan left him after tangling with Patty for months. Patty was determined to avoid that kind of trouble. "I wish to do right but I fear I shall fail through sorrow," she wrote. "Oh Lord give me thy spirit to guide me safe in the right way." The new marriage lasted exactly eight months. In August, David died, leaving Patty to care for Harriet, who was pregnant.[71]

Legally, Harriet had the right to inherit a portion of David's property. Yet Patty effectively controlled family resources. She told Harriet that she would not pay for her board elsewhere, and that if she chose to leave after the baby was born, she could not come back. When Harriet decided to go, Patty made her admit in front of witnesses that she had had a good home there. In December, Patty moved into a new house outside the fort.

"Oh if my husband was with me as he was once how happy I could be," she lamented. She had apparently forgotten the grief he and his plural wives had caused her. A year later, she reported dryly, "I was married to John Parry and I feel to thank the Lord that I have some one to cut my wood for me." Parry, a Welsh widower, exceeded Patty's somewhat modest expectations. He turned out to be good company until he, too, married a younger woman.[72]

Independence was not all a woman needed. Augusta Cobb wanted a soulmate. "Yes Brigham, with all your neglect of me I love the[e] still," she wrote. She not only loved him, she wanted him to reciprocate her passion. "I am from this moment determined to find a good substantial tree to cling fast to," she threatened. She compared herself to a vine that had again and again been "dashed to the Earth." What a vine needed was "a good sturdy oak to cleave to."[73] In a blank space in Heber's diary, Vilate Kimball employed the same image:

> Like the frail ivy to the oak
> Drawn closer by the tempest riven
> Through sorrows flood he'll bear me up
> And light with smiles my way to heaven.[74]

The concept of a wife as a vine entwined around a sturdy tree originated in Latin poetry from the first century B.C.E. and was adapted by scores of writers from Shakespeare and Milton onward. Sometimes the tree was an elm, sometimes an oak.[75] Perhaps the image was popular because, like a vine, it could be twisted in so many directions. In a famous passage in *A Vindication of the Rights of Woman,* the eighteenth-century feminist Mary Wollstonecraft ridiculed the idea of a wife as "graceful ivy, clasping the oak," arguing that "husbands, as well as their helpmates, are often only overgrown children." Yet, in a letter to her lover Gilbert Imlay, she imagined herself throwing out "tendrils to cling to the elm by which I wish to be supported."[76]

The negative connotation of a wife as a "clinging vine" may derive from the substitution of ivy, a parasite, for the original grapevine. In ancient viniculture, the elm lifted the vine toward the sun, producing fruit. In the earliest poem, the image of sexual union—and its rejection— were explicit. A maiden who fled "the fond embrace" withered.[77]

In letters written during the summer of 1850, Augusta was surprisingly explicit about her own sexual needs. With so many fruitful vines around her, she could hardly avoid noticing who was receiving Brigham's attention, and she felt neglected. As usual, she wrote in an acerbic style that makes it almost impossible to tell when she was being satirical. "I am thank[ful] you are going to have such a delightfull excursion with your Lady," she wrote him. "But I expect I should be still more thankfull If you were going to sow holy seed." With her? Two weeks later, she spelled out her meaning. She intended to claim her privilege to bear children, and if Brigham did not want to further her goal, she asked that he appoint a proxy.[78] She said she would be happy to accept Apostle Ezra Taft Benson, as long as he followed her directions. "Which will be to keep himself entirely for me as long as wisdom may dictate, and be devoted to me as long as I may desire whether longer or shorter. . . . Then when we separate I shall not feel defrauded and it will be with Consent."[79]

Serious or not, Augusta's "directions" merged a practical understanding of conception (it didn't always happen immediately) with a sentimental understanding of male gallantry (a good man would not abuse a woman's feelings). Perhaps in her mind the latter was more important. Alluding to the Latter-day Saint notion of childbearing as creating earthly bodies (or tabernacles) for pre-existing spirits, she wrote:

> I do not marvel that I have not borne children to you, and I should have been much astonished if we had been blessed with posterity. For certain it is to my mind that no Noble Spiret would have been willing to have taken a tabernacle under such ignoble circumstances.

As for Brigham's claim that she was too old to have children, she did not think she was much older than Vilate Kimball.[80] She was, in fact, four and a half years older.

She may or may not have been serious about wanting another child. In a postscript, she said she had given Brigham "another fine opportunity for having a little sport." But she had made her point. She had married Brigham because she loved him, and she did not want to be cast aside like a withered vine. Her letters pushed toward a more expansive critique of plural marriage, especially in the form it took in very large households like Brigham's and Heber's. In a household with so many wives, even a woman who wanted to bear children might not be able to do so. She also exposed the marginal position of older women in a system that defined a woman's worth by her reproductive potential and, by extension, her sexual attractiveness.

The latter issue appears explicitly in an undated poem in Vilate Kimball's papers. Framed as an address from a devoted wife to her husband, it pleads for his continuing fidelity.

> Forget me not though brighter eyes
> May beam with sparkling fire
> Forget me not though fairer forms
> May cause thee to admire.

Other verses remind him of her devotion to him through "fear and wild alarms," concluding, "You should not drive a faithful wife / Forever from your arms!"[81]

Some of Vilate's descendants believe she wrote this poem shortly after arriving in the valley, in a moment of despair over plural marriage. Although she may have copied it then, the poem was actually written by a forgotten Ohio poet named Lyman Walbridge Trask sometime in the 1830s. It appeared in newspapers and anthologies with the title "A Lady to Her Husband."[82]

Whatever Vilate's motivation for copying it, it links the concerns of polygamist wives, readers of sentimental poetry, and advocates for women's rights. The Seneca Falls Declaration, for example, deplored the existence of a sexual double standard that condemned women for behaviors "not only tolerated but deemed of little account in men."[83] Lucretia Mott gave a slightly different twist to this complaint in her speech at Worcester in 1850, saying that when a society valued women primarily for their physical appearance, what people today would call their sex appeal, it undermined the value of older women, "for an old woman is simply an object of ridicule, and anything that is ridiculous or foolish is said to be only fit for an old woman."[84]

Vilate had without question done her part in bringing spirits to earth. On January 20, 1850, at the age of forty-three, she delivered her tenth and last child. Her prodigious fertility had allowed her to remain "a Mother of Mother's and Queen of Queen's." But her household was filled with younger women. In 1850 and 1851, Heber fathered nine children, including a pair of twins, by eight plural wives, two of whom were in their thirties, six in their twenties.[85] He knew that his attentiveness to the other wives wounded Vilate. In February 1849, while sitting in a meeting with other church officials, he wrote her a letter bluntly addressing the issue. He admitted that she had been called to make a great sacrifice by sharing her husband, but assured her that her reward in heaven would be worth it. "What I have done is according to the mind and will of God for his glory and mine so it will be for thine," he wrote.[86]

A few sentences later, he again used the phrase "what I have done." This time he seemed to be addressing his sexual relations with the other women, although it is not entirely clear whether he was defending himself for sleeping with them, or for sleeping with them on the sly, so that Vilate was forced to discover their pregnancies by hearsay.

> Let me say unto you V. K. every son and daughter that is brought forth by the wives that are given to me will add to your glory as much as it will to them. They are given to me for this purpus and for no other. I am a Father of lives to give lives to those that wish to receive. Woman is to receive from Man. What I have done has been by stolen moments for the purpus to save your feelings. And that alone on the account of the love I have for you.

He assured her he had received power from God "for the purpus to get honor to my self and those that he has given me." Her duty was to look after her children and teach his other wives how to mind their own business, hold their tongues, treat one another well, respect their husband, and leave his business alone. "Now I say 'God bless you my dear Vilate with peas and love and every good thing.'" He signed himself "your true friend and husband in Christ."[87]

Heber refused to concede any asymmetry in men's and women's reproductive roles. Sexuality was not about personal pleasure or even about creating a bond between husbands and wives. It was about bringing spirits to earth and raising them to inherit the Kingdom of God. By virtue of the New and Everlasting Covenant and ordination to the priesthood, men received power from God to give lives to those who wished to receive them. A woman's role was to receive those lives, by conceiving, bearing, and rearing righteous children.

Shortly after her last child was born, Vilate received an impertinent letter from her sister-in-law, Laura Murray, a non-Mormon who lived in upstate New York. Murray said she had heard from visitors to the West that the stories about polygamy were true, that Heber had more than one wife, and that Brigham Young had twelve sons born to him in one night. In her answer, Vilate ignored the comment about Heber but said that the story about Brigham was "to[o] absurd a saying to be believed

Portrait of Heber and Vilate Kimball and Two Children (above) and *Portrait of Heber and Ann Alice Gheen with One Child* (below). Dates unknown. Very few early Mormon portraits portray a man with more than one wife. In the first portrait, Heber Kimball is pictured with his first wife, Vilate, and the youngest of their children. *(Pioneer Memorial Museum, International Society of Daughters of Utah Pioneers, Salt Lake City.)*

by any rational person. It was no doubt told by some mischievous person to see how big a ly they could stuff down people and make them believe it." Neither denying nor confirming the existence of plural marriage, she assured her sister-in-law that there was "no principle believed, practiced, or upheld by this people, that is not virtuous, pure, and holy."[88] Vilate suffered because of polygamy, but she was not going to admit that to anyone who showed disrespect for her faith. That the doctrine came from God did not make it any easier to explain to outsiders.

"I have to work hard for it"

On June 15, 1851, Brigham stood in the pulpit in the open-sided Bowery on Temple Square and uttered a few words on the priesthood, a few more on treating Indians well, and a great many on the nature of household authority. "The man is the Head of the family and should Govern it," he began, as though there were anyone in the congregation who did not know it. "Let the wife rule the Husband & she will keep him tied to the dish cloth & kitchen all the days of his life." That would indeed be a curse. Men had their duties, and women had theirs. "Do you know your calling as Mothers?" he asked. "It is your duty to Brace up your feelings as men have to do & Be Mystress of your House."[89]

At one level, Brigham was repeating standard nineteenth-century ideas about gender. Men's calling was governance, women's was motherhood. But his language betrayed a more specific agenda. He was not just a pastor offering a homily. He was a prophet, a head of state, and a commander in chief. When he said he did not want men tied to a dishcloth, he was talking about competition between domestic duties and the demands of an emerging empire. To build God's kingdom on earth, he needed men willing to leave their wives and children to serve missions, lead exploring expeditions, lay out new settlements, build roads and bridges, and negotiate with and fight Indians. He did not want trailing vines in beribboned bonnets. He wanted women who could brace up their feelings like men and take charge of things at home, women who could function with or without a husband, who were capable of supporting themselves and their children, who could teach school, take in sewing, plant a garden, milk a cow, press a cheese, and weave a carpet out of old clothes. "Is there a woman in this valley who will make me a suit of clothes?" he asked.[90] These were the kind of women Zina and Patty admired and Augusta feared she might become.

"I spun 126 knots and carded about half of it in one week and one day," George A. Smith's wife Lucy wrote him in July 1851, adding, "In the mean time I have made three cheeses."[91] It wasn't preaching that kept Lucy at work. It was a social system that elevated communal effort over private needs. Plural marriage complicated but did not create that phenomenon. The spinning bees of the American Revolution and the female-manned factories of World War II mobilized women's labor in a similar way, and, of course, in any situation where an authority outside the family—an army, a corporation, or a political movement—demands male allegiance, women are often left to pick up the pieces. That is the way of the world. Among the Mormons, additional women provided social and economic support for each other as long as the number of children did not multiply disproportionately.

In that regard, George Smith's family was ideally situated. Bathsheba later claimed that she willingly gave George five plural wives in the eighteen months after Joseph Smith's death. She was only twenty-two when he married the first of them. All but one of the new wives were in their late twenties; Sarah Libby was seventeen.[92] In Utah, the George A. Smith wives were renowned for unusually harmonious relations. That may or may not have had something to do with the fact that, after Winter Quarters, they never attempted to live all together in one house. Collectively, they also produced an unusually small number of children. When Brigham called George to oversee the establishment of an iron industry 250 miles south of Salt Lake City, he took Zilpha Stark with him. Childless, she had recently lost her second baby. Bathsheba and her two children, nine-year-old George and seven-year-old Bathsheba, moved in with George's parents in a house near Temple Square. Hannah and Sarah Libby, each of whom had a three-year-old son, lived in an old adobe house nearby. Lucy, whose first baby had died before his first birthday and the second at birth, moved in with another family, working as a wet nurse for a time, then keeping a school with forty-five little "scholars."[93]

Perhaps because their families were small, the Smith women became prodigies in economic production. "I am quite comfortable this winter but I have to work hard for it," Bathsheba wrote her husband in February, while he was away on church duties. She had recently earned seven dollars writing out blessings given by George's father, the church patriarch. With the money, she had paid off a debt, purchased logwood to dye the warp for a carpet, paid a cobbler for mending her children's shoes, bought a broom, and still managed to save a few pennies. With another small payment, she had purchased door handles and a lock for their unfinished house. She expected to have the "Carpet ready for the Loom by the first of next week." At the end of her letter, she confessed to having gone with a friend to visit a woman who told fortunes. "Mine was a good one I was to be vary rich and have 13 Children and have you as long as I lived which was fifty six years." She decided to "believe her when all comes to pass."[94] By June, she was managing several cows, spinning, dyeing and knitting wool for stockings, and taking in sewing to pay for the children's schooling and small furnishings for the now finished house. She soon acquired two boarders.[95]

Letters from Lucy were just as upbeat. While continuing to teach, she, too, was engaged in dairying. She told George that seven little girls from her school had been chosen to march in the July 24 parade, costumed in "palm leaf or chip hats with a blue ribbon [and] a white dress with a pink ribbon across the shoulder." Maybe she was joking when she added that "24 second wives with coars straw hats" would also be in the parade. As a second wife herself, she took pride in household industry and laughed rather than complained if others had better things than she. Sarah and Hannah were not so resilient. Bathsheba admitted that, when one of George's creditors gave her twenty dollars, she didn't share it with them, believing they had not managed their other resources very well.[96]

Little wonder. Sarah was ill, perhaps with consumption. By summer she was fading fast. Hannah, who had never lived apart from her sister, seemed desperate. She had a "breaking out" of sores around her mouth and, worse, a habit of lashing out at Bathsheba and her children whenever they visited.[97] Bathsheba nevertheless took turns with Lucy and the neighbors in sitting up with Sarah at night, and then, when she died, helped dress her. "She was Cloathed in her Robes vary beautifully I put roses in her bosom and each side of her face." Little John Henry, Sarah's son, "would often run and uncover his mothers face through the course of the day and say Mother they hant buried you up yet." Then he would go and play with the other children.[98]

Lucy and Bathsheba both assured George they had done everything within their power for Sarah. But Hannah was inconsolable. After the funeral, she told Bathsheba "she did not want me ever to come in her house." She seemed afraid that somebody was going to take Sarah's son, John Henry, away from her. Perhaps she was wise to worry. Bathsheba, who had lost her youngest child at Winter Quarters, had only two children and showed no sign of being pregnant again. Did she seem perhaps too kind to John Henry? Recognizing Hannah's despair, Lucy went to live with her. The two of them were soon spinning and weaving together. "I feel as though I could do all most any thing if I can be blessed with good health," Lucy assured their husband.[99]

Adept at whatever work lay before them, Lucy and Bathsheba managed essentially separate lives. Each wrote to George as though she were his own special love. At the end of a long day, Bathsheba told him she had two more tasks before she went to bed—to pray for the family, and to contemplate his portrait, which hung on the wall behind their bed. It was the last thing she saw at night and the first thing she looked at in the morning.

> Oh it is sutch a comfort to me; it always looks pleasant and kind as you do and seems to say when I feel bad Cheer up all is well and you will return and we will be more happy than if we had been togeather if possible and many other Comforting things I will not write when the shades of night falls upon it it does look so much like you that it makes the tears fall fast sometimes when I think it is not realy you.[100]

As a first wife, Bathsheba had pride of place, and she knew it.

As a second wife, Lucy may sometimes have felt neglected, but if so she handled it with humor. When an expected letter from George did not arrive, she teased, "You need not think to make me believe that you don't want to see me by not writing to me for I know better you want to see me so bad you dare not tell it for fear some boddy will have the blues." She did not say who it was who might have the blues. Then she added, with apparent confidence and a hint of romantic ardor:

> I should not dream such good dreams about you if you did not feel right towards me there is better days for you and me George I think we have suffered about enough to learn wisdom and patience and perseverance &c Good bye my dear til we meet again this is from our affectionate wife Lucy Smith.[101]

Her language is telling. She did not say better days for the family but "for you and me George." Although she felt a responsibility to the others, she considered her relationship with him intimate and particular—at least in the imagined world of letters. For Bathsheba and Lucy Smith, writing was a tool deftly managed.

"They only of themselves bereft us"

In 1851, the legislature passed what Wilford called "a liberal charter" protecting religious liberty in Utah. Brigham explained that if the "Shaking quakers" were to come into the territory, they would have the right to deny marriage to their members. In the same way, the Latter-day Saints could have as many wives as they chose. He said that, though some denied that they practiced plural marriage, he did not deny it. "I am perfectly willing that the people at Washington Should know that I have more than one wife & they are pure before the Lord and are approved off in his sight."[102] He and Heber had an opportunity to pursue this new transparency when the first federal appointees arrived from Washington.

"We have some officers here Judges I believe," Lucy wrote George. "There was a ball at the Bath House maid on purpose for them and the President and Br Kimball took three or four wives each with them and interduced them to the judges one of them was an old Batch I have understood."[103] The old bachelor, whoever he was, was apparently shocked. Only one of the appointees, Broughton Harris, brought a wife with him. Years later, she reported meeting Vilate Kimball, whom she considered a pleasant and intelligent woman until, at a tea held in the officials' honor, Vilate introduced six of Heber's other wives, three of whom were carrying babies. Sarah Harris was so shocked by such behavior that she insisted on moving out of the Mormon home in which she and her husband were boarding.[104]

If the judges were shocked by plural marriage, the Mormons were appalled by the judges. Even before he arrived, gossip about Perry Brocchus reached the valley. A Virginian who had practiced law in Alabama, he had spent years trying to secure a judgeship in one of the Western territories. News spread that he had solicited a maid in St. Louis, cast a wandering eye on Mormon women in Iowa, and told lewd stories on the trail. Almost as bad, he welcomed company in an unlaundered shirt. When he abruptly decided to leave the territory, apparently because he was disappointed at not being chosen as its delegate to Congress, he asked if he might give a farewell speech at a church conference.[105] Displaying a sprig of myrtle plucked from the cemetery at Winter Quarters, he assured the congregation that he sympathized with their past suffering, then proceeded to give them a lecture on patriotism. He addressed "the ladies," and expressed his hope that the Mormons might become "a virtueous people." They were understandably insulted.[106]

Within weeks, all four of the federal appointees had left the territory, taking Congress's appropriation with them and claiming they feared for their lives. Thanks to skilled lobbying by friends of the Saints, they ended up looking foolish for leaving so quickly and for providing so little documentation of their grievances.[107] For Pioneer Day in 1852, Eliza wrote a song about the "Runaway Judges" to the tune of "Old Dan Tucker." The audience was so pleased with the chorus, they asked to have it repeated:

> Tho' Brocchus, Day, and Brandebury,
> And Harris too, the Secretary;
> Have gone!—they went—but when they left us,
> They only of themselves bereft us.[108]

Struggling to negotiate their new system of marriage, Latter-day Saint women were not about to let other people question their virtue. Even Augusta Cobb, in the presence of federal agents several years later, claimed that in Utah she had "known nothing but liberty."[109]

⚜

"the revelation on plurality of wives was read"

Salt Lake City, Hong Kong, Hindoostan, Liverpool, 1852

Samuel Woolley was a taciturn diarist. "At the store as usual. Clear," he wrote on August 24, 1852. And on August 25, 26, and 27. On August 28, he had a bit more to say: "went to Conference at 10 oclock. about 200 Elders Chosen to go to foreign Missions among whom I was one to go to Calcutta in Hindoostan. a good meeting. Clear."[1] That was the way things happened in Utah. You could be an ordinary man, dutifully tending your brother's store. Then, all of a sudden, you were sent off to save the world.

Samuel thought there were "about 200" called on foreign missions. Hosea Stout estimated eighty or ninety. Patty Sessions didn't bother to count. For her, the important news was that her son Perrigrine would be going to England.[2] Wilford Woodruff, who kept the minutes of the meeting, knew that precisely one hundred men were on the list. Forty-two were going to Great Britain, still the most productive site of Mormon preaching; seven to continental Europe; and nine to the Sandwich Isles (Hawaii).[3] The remaining forty-two were to be scattered across the British Empire, from Nova Scotia to the Cape of Good Hope. Hosea Stout was slated for Hong Kong. "I feel well pleased with the mission allotted to me and feel in the name of my master to full[fill] it to the honor and glory of God," he wrote.[4]

Apostle George A. Smith assured the congregation that "probably from 3 to 7 years will be as long as any man will be absent from his family." He insisted that if a man declined to go his wife would surely leave him, "for there is not a Mormon sister who would live with a man a day, who would refuse to go on a mission." Heber Kimball went further: "I say to you who are elected to go on missions, *go, if you never return,* and commit what you have into the hands of God—your wives, your children, your brethren and your property. Let truth and righteousness be your motto, and don't go into the world for anything else but to preach the Gospel, build up the kingdom of God, and gather the sheep into the fold."[5]

On the second day of the conference, church leaders raised the stakes even higher. The newly called missionaries were going into the world not only to preach repentance but to defend the arguably least defensible aspect of their faith—plural marriage. "Orson Pratt preached on the plurality of wives the first that it has been made public," Patty Sessions told her diary.[6] Samuel Woolley, newly energized by his own mission call, reported that when "the revelation on plurality of wives was read to the Conference the house was filled to overflowing."[7] At long last, the document the Prophet had dictated to William Clayton in secret in 1843 was to be shared with the world. Hosea Stout was ecstatic that Latter-day Saints could now "publickly declare the true and greatest principle of our holy religion."[8]

Strangely, the one diarist who said nothing at all about the public avowal of polygamy was Wilford Woodruff. Although a few months before he had added forty-nine-year-old Mary Webster to his family, he could not quite admit that to his diary. On the day of their sealing, he simply noted that President Brigham Young had spent a little time at his house in the evening and that Webster had taken up "her abode with us as a Boarder." Later, he or someone else added, "And was sealed to W Woodruff for time & Eternity."[9]

In Wilford's diary, polygamy was still unmentionable. To the world at large, it would soon be an acknowledged reality. The *Deseret News* printed Pratt's sermon and Joseph Smith's 1843 revelation in a special edition that elders carried with them as they departed the valley. Pratt himself headed to Washington, D.C., where he launched a newspaper called *The Seer,* in which he marshaled Biblical and sociological evidence for the virtues of plurality, citing the writings of Martin Luther and other reformers in its defense, and even flirting with the idea that the Muslim prophet Muhammad might have been inspired. Mormon missionaries in San Francisco, Liverpool, Cape Town, and Calcutta followed Pratt's lead, publishing extracts from his writings and defenses of their own.[10]

Pratt began with a seemingly conventional point, that God com-

manded Adam and Eve to "multiply and replenish the earth." By accepting the new order of marriage, righteous men could not only fulfill that
commandment but inherit the promise God gave to Abraham, that their
posterity would be as numberless as the stars in the heavens or the sands
of the sea. Even in the next life, he argued, a man's posterity would "con-
stitute his glory, his kingdom, and dominion." Righteous women would
achieve exaltation by preparing bodies for pre-existent spirits that were
clamoring to come to earth and by raising them in faith. Pratt estimated
that fewer than one-fifth of the nations of the earth embraced monogamy,
and in doing so they showed themselves to be contracted in spirit and in
mind. Furthermore, the promulgation of monogamy had brought hor-
rendous evils on the earth, including the prostitution, degradation, and
misery of women.[11]

Latter-day Saints had contradictory ideas about sex. They simultaneously glorified reproduction and urged sexual restraint. Although they
accepted the nineteenth-century notion that women were inherently
less troubled by sexual passion than men, they vehemently denied that
polygamy was an outlet for male lust. A man who married multiple wives
in order to indulge his lascivious impulses was as guilty of adultery as a
monogamist who strayed from his marital vows. Mormons understood
that human beings were imperfect and that they lived in a fallen world.
How, then, was prostitution to be prevented? In Pratt's words, "It is to
be prevented in the way the Lord devised in ancient times; that is, by
giving to His faithful servants a plurality of wives, by which a numerous
and faithful posterity can be raised up, and taught in the principles of
righteousness and truth." A righteous man understood that his bodily
desires originated in a Godlike drive to populate worlds. Latter-day Saint
theology liberated male sexuality by transforming lust into responsibility, and by giving every woman an opportunity to marry and become a
mother.[12]

The missionaries who went forth to preach this strange new gospel
were mostly mature men. At thirty-eight, Perrigrine Sessions hit the average. Hosea Stout and thirty-one others were in their forties, eight in their
fifties. Fourteen, including Samuel Woolley, were under thirty. Although
most were married, only a third had more than one wife.[13] Samuel later
claimed that he first heard the doctrine of plurality expounded when he
was a teenager in Nauvoo and believed it instantly, but at twenty-eight he
was married only to Catherine, the diarist who had so vividly described

the first Pioneer Day celebration in the valley. In 1851, he had served a five-month-long mission helping to lay the foundation for a settlement at Parowan, two hundred miles south of Salt Lake City. Now he was headed for India, leaving Catherine and three children under five behind. The children wouldn't recognize him when he returned.[14]

For the moment, Hosea was also monogamous. Having survived the horrors of Winter Quarters, he and Louisa had managed to establish a new life for themselves in Salt Lake City, where he had achieved some success as a self-taught lawyer. When he received his mission call, they had three children, ages five, three, and one. Louisa was expecting a fourth in the winter.[15]

Lucina and Mary Sessions, the sisters Perrigrine married in Nauvoo, now had three children between them, an infant, and a boy and a girl, both age four. Ten-year-old Carlos, Perrigrine's son by his first wife, also lived with the family. Seventeen-year-old Martha Ann, the granddaughter Patty had taught to speak in tongues, had recently married. Perhaps her departure provoked Perrigrine to take a third wife, fourteen-year-old Fanny Emorett Loveland. For her, childbearing would wait until his return.[16]

Measured by the number of converts made in relation to the effort expended, all three men failed dismally. Because illness forced Perrigrine to return early, he spent more time going and coming than preaching. Hosea's record was even worse. After taking ten months to get to Hong Kong, he and his companions spent only two months in the field. Not only did they fail to baptize anyone; they were unable to find a venue for meetings. Samuel had a bit more success, but after a year in India, he lamented that he had "traveled near 3000 miles . . . trying to make a proclamation of the Gospel but pretty near to no effect."[17] Upset by the inequality and cruelty as well as by the prostitution and debauchery they saw in the cities they visited, the missionaries invited those who were willing to live by God's rules to gather to Utah, that they might prosper and experience goodness. Yet their ideas about goodness horrified their would-be converts, their own non-Mormon relatives, and church members just becoming aware of plurality.

Gathering converts was not the only purpose of a mission. Although a minority of the 1852 missionaries had been polygamists before they left, nearly everyone adopted the practice on return. Men who were willing to brave shipwrecks, smallpox, cholera, and public opprobrium proved willing to practice what they preached.[18] That was apparently the point.

"We've left our Wives & friends most dear"

Before leaving for their missions, the newly called missionaries needed to settle debts, prepare "outfits" for overland travel, and make arrangements for their families while they were gone. Those who planned to embark from the Eastern United States left in mid-September, traveling by wagon train across the Great Plains to Kanesville, Iowa, then by wagon, riverboat, and rail to New York City. The Asian and Pacific missionaries, who would travel south and west toward California, had more time to prepare, since they had less fear of early snow. On October 16, they met at the Council House, where they were rebaptized and then blessed by the laying on of hands.

"Went up to our Blessing meeting," Samuel wrote with typical economy. "Had a good time. We all got good blessings."[19] In contrast, Hosea copied into his diary the entire blessing Wilford Woodruff gave him, taking special note of the allusion to the missionary heroes of the Book of Mormon: "When snares are set for thy feet thou shalt have power to escape them, and be like Nephi and Alma who over came their enemies and every obstacle through their faith and the power of God," the Apostle said. Hosea was so filled with the spirit that when his son fell ill the next day he recorded a prayer of his own in his diary, rebuking the Destroyer and vowing that his family should prosper until his return.[20]

By collecting money from the territorial government for the work he had done preparing legislative records for printing, Hosea was able to pay his back tithing and give the public-works department an almost full payment for building a new house. He raised more cash by selling his carpentry tools and some books.[21] Although Samuel was less successful at calling in debts, he nevertheless managed to add a new room to his house by hauling, mud, rock, and "dobies" himself, and by helping to lay a foundation, chimney, floor, and roof.[22] Hosea's new house wasn't finished when it came time to leave, but he felt certain that, given all he had done, Louisa would be able to manage on her own. In a long entry summarizing the preparations he had made, he wrote, "I feel to dedicate my family, my self and my all to the God of Israel invoking his blessings upon them for it will be verily so."[23] Samuel's entry for the same day was typically succinct: "Loded up and started for Calcutta."[24]

The first part of the journey south was like a royal procession. The little Mormon settlements along the way fed the missionaries, housed them, and listened to their preaching. On October 23, traveling toward a place called Willow Creek, Hosea saw a man "standing in the road with a Sheaf of wheat under his arm, waiting for us to come as he said for our animals to eat his grain for he had more than he knew what to do with."[25] At Parowan, Samuel found the house he had helped to build the year before and sat down and wrote Catherine a letter.[26] By today's standards, distances were strangely skewed. It actually took a few days longer for Hosea to get from Salt Lake City to San Francisco than from San Francisco to Hong Kong. The worst part of the journey was through the remote parts of southern Utah and across the Mojave Desert to a new Mormon settlement at San Bernardino, California.[27]

The missionaries rested up at San Bernardino, then pushed on to San Pedro (now part of present-day Los Angeles), where they hoped to get a ship for San Francisco. Hosea was thrilled when they reached the coast— "Now for the first time in my life, the roaring Surges of the ocean saluted my ear like the distant sound of a coming storm"—but he was disgusted by "the loathsome, lousy and miserable excuse, for convenience," that San Pedro offered.[28] "This place contains 4 houses & is a dirty filthy place the people cursing & swearing," Samuel concurred. He and and the other Hindoostan missionaries revived themselves by going to a nearby mountain to sing hymns and pray.[29]

Practicing their singing was a good idea. When Samuel's group got on board a brig headed to San Francisco, the captain was rude to them until they "went on the poup & sung the Gallant Ship & How often in sweet meditation my mind." After that, he treated them well. Little matter. Samuel was soon so seasick that he was unable to eat anything but a bit of cake Catherine had tucked into his trunk. He comforted himself with the thought that, unlike some of his fellow passengers, he was not "after Gold silver or precious stones" but was setting out "to preach the everlasting gospel to the inhabitants of the earth," a theme reflected in the songs he had just sung.[30]

Unfortunately, gold and silver turned out to be essential. With no means of support, the missionaries were forced to go door to door in San Francisco, soliciting contributions to pay for their tickets to Asia.[31] Samuel thought it was "stooping rather lower than I ever stooped before to go the street of a city begging money," but he joined his companions in canvassing "doctors Lawyers Ministers Merchants Bankers & all most all classes gamblers not excepted." By the end of the first day, they had collected $7.75. They needed almost a thousand times that much.[32]

Fortunately, some of the Mormons who had come to California on the ship *Brooklyn* in 1846 had prospered. Samuel was astounded when a brother dropped a hundred dollars into his hand. Non-Mormons with little means were also amazingly generous. He was surprised when an unnamed "black man" offered him a dollar.[33] Hosea found Jewish merchants "more believing & friendly towards our religion than any other people here," giving the missionaries presents "& otherwise favoring us in trading."[34] He was also impressed with the kindness of the Chinese, some of whom spoke good English and proved "affable and friendly."[35]

Both men were puzzled by the strange mixture of roughness and refinement they found in San Francisco. "Strolling around the city," Hosea observed, "churches, gambling houses, Houses of ill fame, Hotels, Hawkers, brokers, Bankers, Law offices and innumerable other establishments all mingled and all mixed & inter mixed . . . as though all classes and grades of society were of one heart and mind & in full fellowship with each other and all trades, professions, misteries and occupations were equally honorable."[36] Woolley was more blunt. "This place is full of corruption & is about fit to be cleansed by fire or some other way."[37]

Poised on the rim of the Pacific, the missionaries imagined themselves as harbingers of a better world. They had not chosen to leave home, but were willing to do so because even more than earthly comfort they craved salvation. A song Samuel copied into his journal conveyed that vision:

> We've left our Wives & friends most dear
> But this with us don't matter
> We've gone because the Lord we fear
> Our homes we'll have hereafter.[38]

Should they die, they would have that assurance.

The Hong Kong missionaries were the first to leave San Francisco. Just before departing, Hosea received word that Louisa had given birth to a son and was doing well. The vision of his little family sustained him on the voyage. On April 23, 1853, as the ship lay becalmed in the Pacific, he imagined it resting "like a smiling infant in her sleeping mother's arms." The blue of the water met the blue of the sky as he conjured up comforting scenes of home:

> Now my wife & my little ones, dance playfully before my imagination. Now the scenes of home reveal themselves. Now the saints in peaceful Utah roll by, busy in their different avocations. Now their fervent

prayers ascend on high in my behalf . . . while the wicked howl and prepare themselves for the doom which awaits them.

Then, as if awakening to the excesses of his own prose, he grew somber: "O the future opens too wide."[39]

Four days later, with the wind in its sails, the ship arrived in Hong Kong Harbor. It had "scarcely dropped anchor" when it was filled with Chinese women. Some wanted work as washerwomen. Others offered "to bargain off their professional sex to the crew and all whom it concerned at the lowest possible rates, which seemed on board to range at about one dollar each. The custom far exceeding the patronage even at that reduced rates." Somebody had already told him, "In the city such services could be procured for from ten to twenty cents."[40] Hosea displayed neither horror nor compassion at the sight. To him, the prostitutes and their patrons represented the same sort of cupidity he found among humans everywhere.

He had plenty of scope for irony in the two months he spent in Hong Kong. Although a Presbyterian missionary they met in San Francisco had warned them that it would be almost impossible to survive as itinerants, they had come anyway, trusting that God would open the way.[41] They were surprisingly successful in attracting crowds to the first two meetings they held on the parade ground at the center of the city. Hosea thought that as many as two hundred people turned up at the first meeting, about half of them British soldiers. There were even more soldiers at the second meeting, though fewer civilians. But the next few meetings were rained out, and by the time they were able to schedule a third, the *Hong Kong Register* had printed an editorial suggesting that, rather than attack the Mormons, respectable citizens should just ignore them. The audience was smaller at the next meeting, and to the final three nobody came at all.[42]

The missionaries were no more successful in maintaining informal contacts. For a time, they met with a group of Methodist soldiers who were holding daily meetings for study and prayer, but here, too, initial interest petered out.[43] Hosea was both amused and annoyed by British politeness. The few citizens who had approached them after their public meetings had done so with "an assumed modest bashfulness like the false modesty of a tickelish flaunting coquette wanting to talk and not be seen."[44] He would have preferred a good debate, but he did not get it. On May 11, "two Chinamen one of them a Taylor in this place" came to their lodgings. One "had been raised under the fostering care of the London missionary society" and had become skilled in flattening out all differences in religion, "reconciling all sects and parties in love and unity, and construing the Scriptures accordingly." With such an approach to truth, Hosea concluded, the man was incapable of recognizing that God had once again established true authority on the earth.[45]

At the local theater, a group of Persians approached the elders and asked about plural marriage. Hosea considered this good news. "We never had mentioned the subject but it has been humbuged to day through this city in consequence of what came out in the papers."[46] He believed that opposition aroused interest and allowed people to find things out for themselves. Once again, he was disappointed: the Persians disappeared. By June 9, the missionaries had to admit that their work had come to nothing. "And as to our staying here to learn the chinese language without one friend or one possible recourse to us appears totally impracticable and Paul-like we can truly say that the spirit speaketh expressly, that we preach the gospel no more in Asia for the present." Because of an expanding rebellion on the mainland, Hong Kong was the only port where they could safely live, and in Hong Kong they could neither work legally nor rely on the largesse of the local population. Since they had enough money to pay for a passage home, they had no choice but to leave.[47]

Departing Hong Kong, Hosea again observed women crowding into the ship, this time as passengers. He concluded that they were "going to California under charge to opperate professionally for those who will most likely get all the profits." He understood their plight but pitied their ignorance. "Some of them are very free to converse on their anticipations of future enjoyments and the golden harvest which awaits them."[48] Later, when the ship was becalmed, he was amused by the sight of the "Chinese *courtesan* ladies" placating the wind gods by burning incense and tossing paper charms into the air. To "the great joy of all," the breeze lifted the very next day.[49] When the captain, during another period of calm, tied a goose to the mast and organized a shooting contest, Hosea composed a parody on the "Fowl-tastophe." Mostly, he simply noted the passing of time. To counteract boredom, he read novels.[50]

When the ship landed at San Francisco on August 23, he rushed ashore, eager for a letter from Louisa. Instead, he received "the inconsoleable intelligence of her death and the death of her child." For the first time he admitted to his diary that he had been "Baffled & disappointed" by his mission. Drawing upon a full stock of ready-made phrases to express his grief over Louisa's death, he lamented not having been there to experience the "blissful sorrow of soothing the last agonies of her death" or witness "her immortal Spirit drop the mortal coil." He crossed out words and added others to capture the fulsome formality he thought appropriate, finally ending a three-hundred-word lamentation with a brisk reminder: "Let me not forget from whence comfort & consolation comes."[51] Perhaps he found comfort as well in steadily making entries in his diary.

The Saints in San Francisco took up a collection to help pay his expenses home. Rumors of Indian trouble kept him in San Bernardino through September and into October. On October 20, he wrote: "To day completes one year since I left home where I was surrounded by all the endearing ties of an affectionate wife, whose ashes now lies mouldering in the dust and my children lonely orphans, my home, with all its kindred ties, no more. I feel a disconsolate blank." In early November, he was finally able to assemble a company willing to brave the journey across the desert. They made him their captain.[52]

The vicissitudes of lost cattle, dry water holes, broken wagon wheels, and incompetent teamsters helped him recover his sardonic humor. His mood lifted further when he teamed up with George A. Smith at Payson for the last leg of the journey. Despite his sorrows, Hosea enjoyed the Apostle's "agreeable social <u>yarning</u>" and his talent for launching rural

Hosea Stout's house, Salt Lake City. Date unknown. In 1852, Hosea left this house before it was finished to serve a mission in Hong Kong. When he returned in 1853, he found strangers living in it. *(Utah Historical Society, Salt Lake City.)*

Mormons into a state of "connubial bliss." After his long journey, he was also grateful for the food these rural weddings provided. On December 7, he wrote: "I forgot to state that while at American Creek, I had the satisfaction to witness the triumph of Mormonism over the traditions of our fathers for George A. sealed Arza Adams to an old maid aged 48 as withered and forbidding as 4 Doz. Years of celibacy might naturally be supposed to indicate. She joyfully took his hand and consented to be part of himself as number two."[53]

On December 8, he faced his own desolation. English immigrants who knew nothing of his wife and children had moved into his house. Eventually, with help from his sister Anna, he found his children living north of the city with their grandmother Taylor. "How can I attempt to describe my emotions when I embraced those three dear pledges which Louisa had left me of her love and fidelity," he wrote. He steeled himself for a visit to her grave:

> How calmly, sadly, happily, seemed to rest her ashes. How quiet seemed that heart which once beat for me so warmly. Her smiling countenance, but all now rests in death's embrace while I remain as a blank on earth, a monument of disappointed hopes. I have followed three wives to their graves and behold the earth enclose seven of my own children yet I had hopes of better days but now hope vanished & I must give myself up to inconsolable sorrow.[54]

He spent the next two weeks working on his still unfinished house.

On December 30, he opened a can of sardines with a friend, then stayed alone in the house, attempting what he called "the first lesson in my meditated Bachelorship." The next morning, feeling solitary and alone, he had "commenced the solemn ceremony" of getting breakfast when, to his joy, Anna stopped by and "finished the job a thing which I was wholy incompetent to do for myself."[55]

Hosea's "meditated Bachelorhood" lasted just ten days. On January 9, 1854, out of desperation as much as conviction, he married a widow named Aseneth Gheen, introducing her to his children as their "new mother." But when the Church called him to serve six months as a military guard on the eastern border of the territory, Aseneth went back to her own house, refusing to care for his children as well as her own. "I can not see one bright ray of future happiness," he complained. When Grandmother Taylor refused to help, the ever-faithful Anna kept the children.[56] It apparently never occurred to Hosea to refuse the mission. Men had their duties, and women theirs.

"Some were drunk, some sober, others mad and others glad"

A week before he received his mission call, Perrigrine Sessions dreamed that he was about to take a long journey. In the dream, he dressed in his best clothes, had his wife tie his cravat, and then traveled through a beautiful green plain until he reached a neat and prosperous town with a single street leading to its center. At the end of the street he saw a door open into a remarkably clean blacksmith shop, where a young man dressed in good clothing displayed a set of splendid tools. Hearing singing, Perrigrine walked through the shop into a large, pleasant room, where he was greeted by a tall woman who had long hair hanging down over her shoulders and a brush and combs in her hand. She motioned him to a fine sofa. The entire room "seamed filled with Wiming," he wrote. His mother was there "and whole generations looking like her from youth to old Age." His friends and neighbors were there, too; those who had died looked "in the vigor of life and health." Perrigrine was charmed when the congregation began to sing "Oh! Susanna," and when a man stood at a pulpit and began preaching in English, Perrigrine said to himself, "That is the Gospel." But as he followed the crowd out of the room, he abruptly woke. "I wakened my Wife and told her the dreem and lay and thought on the dream and wished to my self that I could in reality see the same."[57] He did not say which wife he awakened.

In another man's dream, the woman with the fine sofa and uncombed hair might have presided over a brothel. To Perrigrine, the woman in the dream conveyed a welcoming and righteous domesticity. He could imagine nothing better than an afterlife surrounded by women who looked a lot like his mother. But now he was going to leave them all—his wives Lucina, Mary, and Emorett; his mother; his daughter Martha, and the little children, a boy and two girls. On September 15, 1852, in the very first entry in his new missionary journal, he wrote, "Left the city of the saints at four Oclock with my family going several miles with me in a carriage. I then took leave of them and left them in the hands of the Lord."[58]

By December 12, he was in New York. On Christmas Day, he woke on board ship to a sea that looked "like mountains covered with snow." Inside, the vessel looked like the belly of hell: "We spent the day with some Catholicks and al kinds of men and wimin hores and Masters curs-

ing and swareing & drinking . . . with severil fites [fights] to mak it interesting . . . some sick and groneing Vomiting and so thick that the room
smelt like a pig pen more then the home of human being."59 Perrigrine
had never been to sea. Nor, it seems likely, had he spent much time in
school. Indifferent to spelling and entirely unaware of punctuation, he
wrote in a jumbled syntax that had its own kind of power. He must have
been a great storyteller. The unexpected images and rhythms in his prose
capture the disorder and pathos that he often found in the world. He was
shocked and at the same time entranced by the wonders and horrors he
encountered.

One of his favorite spots in the industrial town of Manchester, England,
where he spent part of his mission, was a massive zoological park called
Belle Vue that featured fireworks and theatrical pageants. He marveled at
the brass band, and the hundred-foot-long pavilion where people could
"dance and make themselves Merry," and at the broad lawns and lanes
where a person might "jump and run foot races with men or dogs or cats
or any thing you please." Here the beasts of the field and the fowl of the
air were "in subjection to Man," and the arts and sciences flourished. If
humans could erect such a pleasure garden in only forty years, what might
they do in the thousand years that would follow Christ's second coming,
"when this Mortal has put on Imortality when this corruption shall have
put on Incoruption And Sickness and earth is no More"? He considered a
visit to Belle Vue Place "a shilling well spent," since it called up reflections
on human destiny.60

Sessions may have been especially sensitive to the corruptions of mortality because his own body was failing. Since arriving in Liverpool, he
had been unable to shake a debilitating cough that rattled his frame at
unexpected moments and at night. As president of the Manchester Conference, he was responsible for 3,048 members in thirty-three branches of
the Church, yet gastrointestinal distress that he called the "cholery morbus" pursued him. Determined to do his work, he dragged himself from
town to town, shaking with fever in one borrowed bed after another, until
he had traversed his assigned circuit and could begin again.61

The England described in his diary seems stranger and more exotic
than Hosea Stout's Hong Kong. Visiting a medieval church at Ashton-
under-Lyne, he was shocked by the "Auful looking faces" and "hideous
looking serpents" carved on the façade, and disturbed at the thought that,
all around the church's yard and beneath its stone floors, "thousands of
the human family are laid low packed down a vault dug some forty feet

deep," while above them a priest in a white dress performed strange cer-emonies. "My heart sickened while I stood and looked on and witnessed the blindness of the people with out the gifts of God and I felt to say Oh Lord God how long shal the blind leed the blind and polute the Earth for within one hundred yards of the church more than five hundread Prostitutes live and in the night time it would be imposable to approach this church with out being insulted with these caracters."[62] To him, the specter of dead bodies, stone gargoyles, and rude women merged into a single nightmare.

More disturbing was the evidence he saw all around him of violence and disorder in families. His descriptions swung between compassion and disdain, as he simultaneously identified with and pushed himself away from the victims. As a minister of God, he had been called to save the world, but what was he to do when all the forces of that world seemed to conspire against his message?

Constantly moving, he saw the lives of the working men and women around him mostly through the windows of the houses where he stayed. One evening, he saw three women drag a younger one into the street and beat her until they were out of breath. Then they ran back into the house and locked the door behind them. To Sessions, the girl they had beaten looked like a sheep torn by a wolf, a circumstance he had probably witnessed more than once in frontier Maine or Utah. But in this alien set-ting, the girl also took on the form of one of the frightful carvings he had seen outside the church in Ashton. "She stood half bent or sqot [squat] and the water run from her like running from an eye spout." The sight of the urinating girl twisted and bent like a gargoyle both confused and dis-gusted him. Making inquiries, he discovered that it was the girl's mother and sisters who had beaten her, and that she had outraged her family by giving birth to a "chance child." To him, such violence was further evi-dence of the corruption around him: "This is one among the many such fights that I have seen here I have seen too [two] Wives beet near to death in one night and one killed by her husband by nocking her down stairs when about to bee confined with her twenty third child by him this hap-pened acrost the street from whare I staid over night."[63]

He liked to say, when describing the alternately dazzling and horrific spectacles around him, "Some were drunk, some sober, others mad and others glad."[64] In Manchester, he stumbled onto what seemed to him a riot but may actually have been a political demonstration. He was certain there were no fewer than two hundred thousand people crowded into the streets and on the tops of buildings. Although police were everywhere, they seemed incapable of holding back the crowd, which responded with loud hurrahs to speeches he could not comprehend.

> Here I stood and looked on with many reflections thinking that I was in the Midst of one of the largest cities in the world and to see the spirit that governed the Multitude that surrounded me and if I had told them that I was Messenger caled of God and sent to this mighty city to preach the Gospel to them they would have been redy to have stoned me here my heart sickened and could all most say like Paul I could all most wish my Self in the high corts of heaven and leave the wicked to go their Own way when my word has so little effect on this mighty People.

The only way he knew to absolve himself of responsibility for these people ("to rid my garments of their Blood") was to preach, but to preach was to be ignored, laughed at, or stoned, or so he feared.[65]

Meeting with his fellow Saints, he struggled to fit what he saw and heard into familiar frameworks. Early in his mission, he reported a gathering where the conversation had presumably turned to childbirth, perhaps because he mentioned that his mother was a midwife. He thought it worth noting that a woman he met there, an Englishwoman, reported walking "eleven miles after being sick and had her child on the road and brought it in her arms five miles."[66] Women like these would certainly make good Saints. At home, he had seen women drive teams, plant crops, and harvest grain, yet to him they had remained women. Not so the female miners laboring in an open-pit coal mine near Wigan. To avoid tripping on their clothing, they had hiked up their petticoats until the buttons on the men's pants they were wearing were fully visible. "I should not have thought of their being females by their dress or their bodies they were so black and ragid [ragged] if it had not have been for their long hare and some of them had some Old bunnets on their heads here they were climeing about like men this beet me out to see these females dressed like men."[67]

Surely, it wasn't just the cross-dressing that disturbed him. He was amused rather than scandalized when, at a church member's home, "Old sister Doncle came in as I was writeing with Brother John Whitehead he drest in Womens Clothes and her in mens clothes." That was all in good fun, a masquerade. The two were followed into the room by "bout a dozen more of the Saints and another dish of fun like it would be hard to get up."[68] Among the Saints, he knew when to laugh and when to cry, he knew who he was and what role he was expected to play. But among the working-class people of Lancashire, he was often confused, uncertain of his place. What was a man to do when his landlord burst into his room dressed in nothing but his shirt and then, just as abruptly, "went in to another room and commenced a row with his Wife"? Perrigrine lay awake, wondering if he had been taken for a seducer, "as I had never been in the house before & knew not what the result would bee." He was relieved when he got up in the morning and learned that the man had come home drunk and entered the wrong room.[69]

He was on surer ground in assessing the spirit of a Latter-day Saint congregation. If people listened attentively to his preaching and displayed unity and love, he knew he was in the right place. He was especially pleased when his own efforts produced results—as at Wigan, where, after a little nudging, Saints who had been "all by the ears and ready to devour each other" had, after a little encouragement, "agreed to forgive each other and burey all their troubles."[70] Far too often, however, there was backsliding or worse. At Malton, he attended a church trial "Against Tom Jackson for being intimate and keeping Sister Mary Ann Grundy in his house."[71] In Hyde, he heard charges against William Potts "and a man by the Name of Verity" who had been caught staying all night with two young women and "not being at home with their families."[72] He found a member's house in Manchester "in an uproare as a small lad had stole too dollars in money and spent it this money belonged to a dead child and the Mother All most in fits as the father of the child it was a chance child was about to get Maried to another Women both of these made her frantick."[73] Adultery and stealing were bad enough, but it was physical violence that really upset him. Called to settle "a fight between brother Turnball and his Lover," he gave the man a "tung lashing" when he discovered that out of jealousy the man had given his supposed sweetheart "a good malling." Men like that ought to be cut off from the Church.[74]

In June 1853, he dreamed of being pursued by a "large black snake about 10 feet long" that was in turn being pursued by an immense gray one that seemed "big with young." He chased the two serpents under a barn, but two more snakes, both gray, appeared. When a church member told him that "a cirtin man was intangled with three Wimin," he decided the dream had been prophetic. A few weeks later, he was present when a fellow missionary, Thomas W. Treat, was tried for adultery. Treat openly acknowledged that, while teaching others to be pure, he himself had committed sin. He begged church leaders to show mercy on the women, claiming that he had led them astray. The next issue of the *Millennial Star* reported that he had been excommunicated "for his whoredoms and abominations."[75]

Had Treat been a bit too earnest in preaching plurality to the women of Lancashire? Perrigrine did not say. But at Saddleworth, he reported having "a great deal of talk upon the doctrine of a plurality of Wives."[76] Little wonder. While missionaries in other parts of the world were combatting press reports about debauchery in Utah, church leaders in England were struggling to control their own members. At another church council, he was distressed to hear "about a man trying to make covinants with the Sisters."[77] Didn't people know that polygamy was not an excuse for sexual license, and that only the president of the Church had the power to authorize plural marriages?

In the midst of all this turmoil, William Clayton, who had arrived in England about the same time as Sessions, tangled with a former church member over polygamy and found himself thrown out of the house. On the way to the train, he decided he needed a bit of comfort. Later, he claimed that, in his weakened state, a single cup of gin overwhelmed him so that he appeared drunk when he showed up at a church meeting. Anxious to avoid any more scandals, Samuel Richards, who was now the mission president, sent him home.[78] Perhaps stories about Clayton's transgression were in Mary Richards's mind when she wrote Samuel, assuring him that she had as much confidence in him "as any man living," yet prayed that he would not go astray; she had known "good worthy men who possessed my confidence who proved that they had not ability and strength to resist temptations." Then, fearing that she had gone too far, she excused her "outburst," explaining that she could not help "feeling anxious for you I am desirous that you should excel all in goodness and could wish my self perfect for your sake that I might ever find favor in your sight."[79] Mary was surely not worried that her husband would get drunk, but, as later events showed, she was more than a little anxious that he might embrace polygamy.

In the midst of all these problems, Perrigrine began to dwell on days gone by. On the anniversary of his first marriage, he remembered, "This day nineteenth yeares ago I Maried with Juliann Killgore but Alass she is gone the way of all the Earth yet her Memory lasts and will while time and Eternities rolls on with Me for her Virtues and life of humilities in the Kingdom of God." The next day, his thoughts turned to the birth of his first child: "This day Eighteen years My Eldest Child was born that I called Marthann and when I reflect that the Mother is dead and the Daughter is Maried and is a Mother My mind is filled with reflecions that gives me strong fealings to reflect on the scenes that have passed with me in the last nineteen yeares of my life here I am in England some seven thousand miles from my family & halth poor but the God of Jacob is my healp & my refuge and in him do I put my trust as I have all my life Long."[80] Strangely, he never referred to his present wives, Lucina and Mary, by name, or composed sentimental reveries about them. He did buy each of them a Scotch-plaid dress and two shawls.[81]

As his health declined, the English Saints brought him preserves, cakes, and little pies; packed hot bricks around him to induce a sweat; and sang cheering songs. Nothing seemed to work. He continued to cough. The vomiting and diarrhea grew worse, until, staring out the window at the smoke and fog, he "almost wished to die." Richards decided it was time to send him home.[82] Just before he left, a woman who did not belong to the Church paid him a visit, bringing him oranges as a treat. Ever the missionary, he showed her "likenesses of all my family and had a long talk with her that will not bee forgotten by her." Her willingness to sit by his bedside and look at his pictures cheered and encouraged him. He was sure he had planted gospel seeds that would "spring up and grow."[83] He did not say whether he identified the women in the pictures as his wives.

As Perrigrine prepared to leave England, he learned that a church member had been among the ninety miners killed in an explosion when their lamps ignited gas in the shaft; "this was a horid scene but one that Often Ocurs in the coleries this pit is twelve hundread feet deep."[84] He was pleased that thousands of English Saints were now preparing to escape such a living hell by gathering to Zion. After another nightmarish Atlantic voyage, he arrived in Portland, Maine, on March 17, 1854.[85] Despite his cough, he immediately took a train to Bethel, Maine, where he visited his "old Granmother 86 years Old" and other friends and relatives, even though it meant trudging through drifts with "the snow flying like feathers."[86] His next stop was Iowa City, where his sister, Sylvia, and her four children were preparing to join him on the journey across the plains. Sylvia's husband provided teams and money for the journey, even though he declined to join her; he seemed resigned to a separation, although he hadn't entirely given up on the idea that she might at some point return.[87]

The roads across Iowa were better than they had been in 1846, but it was still a muddy, rainy trek. Perrigrine was philosophical: "This looked like squaley times for a man with no better health then mine but I have ever found as yet by the Blessing of God that I have been Able to indure the fatigues of a Mormons life which is one of trial."[88]

"I walk like the Mormon Elders always do"

When the missionaries arrived in Calcutta on April 25, 1853, after eighty-six days at sea, Samuel Woolley prayed that they would "come off victorious." By his count, it had been six months and six days since he left home. He couldn't be sure, however, because the ship had crossed the international date line. After a little thought, he concluded that there had been "no Tuesday this week."[89] It wasn't just time that seemed awry. His first forays into the city confirmed all the stereotypes he had about colonial India: the imperial English were ostentatious and idle; the natives couldn't be trusted; there was no middle class. In the dining area of the first house he visited, he was disgusted to see a man pulling a string on a six-foot-wide ceiling fan to keep guests cool as they ate. Even more shocking was the practice of having grown men carried about the streets. "The natives have a machine they call Palankeen for carrying folks." No one would catch him indulging in such a foolish practice. "I walk like the Mormon Elders always do," he wrote.[90]

Samuel admitted that the Indian climate produced marvelous fruit, but in general he didn't care much for the food. "This country is all curry & rice for dinner & generally for Breakfast & supper."[91] As an experienced storekeeper, he was appalled by the seeming chaos of Calcutta's markets. "It is a perfect odity to trade with them & to see their manner," he began, noting the diminutive buildings made of bamboo and mud crowded along streets only four or five feet wide. Shops were nothing but stalls with an old chest or two and a few shelves stacked along the street. "When one is trying to buy anything there is about a half a dozen has hold of him at once, saying come buy of me & another says buy of me don't buy of him he tells you a lie & makes so much Noise that I could hardly hear my self think." To him, the scanty clothing of the hawkers marked their degradation. "They look up to a white man as their superior," he wrote, "& the Natives do all the work." Still, the people of India were part of the human family, people he had come to save.[92]

The Indian missionaries faced many of the same problems as those in Hong Kong—the indifference of polite colonials, legal restrictions on proselytizing, and the inability to speak to local people in their own languages. But the men in Calcutta had an advantage those in Hong Kong did not: a small cadre of local members. The first Mormon elders had come to Calcutta in 1851, at the request of English soldiers based there. One of the first converts, a man named James Patrick Meik, had leased land and built a small lecture hall for the Church. By May 1852, there were reportedly 189 members in the general area, a mixture of English colonials and local families. But hopes of English-style growth were dashed. As Samuel put it, "Most of them that had been baptized had apostertised."[93]

There were many reasons for this, including competing expectations about what church membership entailed. New members were expected not only to consecrate their resources, time, and talents to the Church, but to gather to Zion. Although as many as eleven Calcutta converts eventually migrated to Utah, there was little hope that many would be able to do so.[94] Polygamy was a divisive issue. Because news of the 1852 pronouncement reached India before the missionaries themselves, Samuel faced

Photographs of Samuel Woolley and of Catherine Mehring Woolley and daughter. Dates unknown. A close look at Samuel's portrait reveals a ring in his earlobe. Some believe he was following a tradition that gave sailors the right to wear an earring once they had circumnavigated the globe. He had done that by leaving for India in 1852 from San Francisco and returning in 1855 via Boston to the East. The child in Catherine's picture may be Rachel, who was a baby when her father left. *(Church History Library, Salt Lake City. © Intellectual Reserve.)*

questions almost as soon as he arrived in his own field of labor, in Chinsura, a town thirty miles north of Calcutta. Members expected Samuel to explain as well as defend the practice. He reasoned from the scriptures as best he could, then, in desperation, told them "it was their privelage to know of the truth of it for themselves."[95] Samuel was an earnest advocate of the principle, but he had little practical experience to share. In truth, Catherine was not fully convinced it was right.

Communication with home was daunting. For months, he dutifully sent letters without receiving even "the screech of a pen from anyone in the valley." Finally, on August 14, ten months minus five days after he left home, a letter from Catherine arrived. Apparently, six others had been lost.[96] He immediately sat down to compose an answer. Although her letter has not survived, his response makes clear that he had somehow offended her in one of his letters by alluding to the commandment that a wife obey her husband. He assured her that he loved her, but hadn't the Apostle Paul said "the man is the head of the Woman as Christ is the head of the Church"? Didn't she want to join him "in the celestial Kingdom of our God with Abraham, Isaac, Jacob, Joseph, Hyrum, Brigham Heber Wilard & all the rest"?[97]

Samuel was sorry if he had hurt her feelings, but he was not going to apologize for things that he had not said. Using the Quaker pronouns he had been taught as a child, he wrote, "Thee says thee has always labored for my interest I did not say any thing to the contrary, did I. Nor I did not say thee was disobedient either to my recollection." Then he addressed what was clearly the bigger issue between them, the prospect that he might take another wife, a person he refers to in his letter as a "co," perhaps short for "cohab," an adaptation of the legal term "unlawful cohabitation." His thoughts tumbled out helter-skelter: "Thee says I wish to have thee trained by the time I get home if I should lead home a co and quite a number of them [of] the fairer sex." He assured her he had no plans to do such a thing, but he hoped she would be just as willing to obey him if he had. He reminded her that in time all good men would have multiple wives. Then, having established his right to govern his family, he told her she could do just as she liked with the property she wanted to sell. He knew that, half a world away, he had little control over what Catherine did in Utah.[98]

Meanwhile, he was struggling to keep a widow named Charlotte Thompson active in the Church in Chinsura. Perhaps he contemplated making her a wife. She was a kind and generous woman who fed the missionaries, paid for their laundry, and shortly after his arrival gave Samuel six new shirts carefully marked with his name. He in turn blessed her when she was ill, loaned her books and pamphlets, and spent time listening to her children recite their lessons.[99] But, try as he might, he could not assuage her doubts about plural marriage. She thought it "was hard on the women." Samuel responded that, since Joseph Smith and Brigham Young were called of God, it must be true.[100] She was not convinced. Although she regularly came to church and on at least one occasion stood to give her testimony, she was also reading anti-Mormon tracts supplied by an Anglican minister.[101] Her greatest concern was for her children. She thought Mormonism would be "a hard thing for them to go into when they grow up."[102] When Samuel prepared to leave Chinsura, she presented him with five rupees and a very fine umbrella. As soon as he was out of sight, she sent a letter to the branch president asking to be cut off from the Church.[103]

Aside from the family of the branch president, Brother Sankey, Woolley had few other serious contacts in Chinsura. He made liberal use of consecrated oil to bless a "native woman" whom he never honored with a name, but he made no effort to follow through when she invited him to her village.[104] He was pleased when an Armenian priest showed curiosity about the Church. The man seemed comfortable with the idea that Joseph Smith might have found truth through dreams and visions, and there were some follow-up meetings, but the man's interest soon faded, perhaps because of the difficulty they had communicating through a translator.[105]

Samuel was encouraged when he visited a Church of England meeting and discovered that the preacher on that day had fewer listeners than the Mormons.[106] But, despite the missionaries' best efforts to attract new prospects, only the handful of existing church members attended. In informal contacts with nonmembers, Samuel tried to model patience, long suffering, and kindness, but he sometimes failed. He was annoyed by an English schoolmistress who considered herself "some Pumpkins" even though, in his view, she was ignorant about everything that really mattered, and when two men told him only fools or asses would believe Mormonism, he shot back that only fools and asses would swallow the anti-Mormon diatribes they were distributing.[107]

In August 1853, he and a companion set out on an arduous three-thousand-mile journey to Agra and back, hoping to get permission to preach at military compounds along the way. In the end, they held few meetings and converted no one.[108] Back in Chinsura, he fasted and prayed that Brother Sankey's married daughter would accept baptism. To his

Friendship album with locks of hair, Nauvoo, Illinois, 1840s.

This little scrapbook features locks of hair, some of it loose, some tightly woven into fans or circles. © *Pioneer Memorial Museum, International Society Daughters of Utah Pioneers, Salt Lake City.*

Inscription of Sarah Kimball, Nauvoo, Illinois, March 22, 1841.

Someone pasted this loose sheet into an album that Sarah Kimball gave Eliza Snow in 1842. It exemplifies the nineteenth-century practice of collecting autographs enhanced with drawings, poems, or mottoes.
© *Intellectual Reserve, Museum of Church History and Art, Salt Lake City.*

Fourteenth Ward album quilt, Salt Lake City, 1857.

This quilt features autographed squares from sixty-seven women. Some quilters signed in ink, others in stitchery. Some ornamented their squares with patchwork, others with wool and silk embroidery, freehand appliqué, or images cut from printed fabric. When the quilt was cut in half in the late nineteenth century, Phebe Woodruff's signature was severed from the buzzing bees surrounding her appliquéd beehive. *Courtesy of Dan and Carol Nielson and Shirley Mumford. Photograph by Dan Nielson.*

Clockwise from upper left are squares by Phebe Woodruff, Ester Ann Hoagland, Leonora Taylor, and Kezia Pratt. *Courtesy of Dan and Carol Nielson and Shirley Mumford. Photograph by Dan Nielson.*

LEFT: Artist unknown, *Celestia Kimball,* c. 1850.

ABOVE: Eliza Sorsey Ashworth, patchwork baby dress, 1856.

Presendia Kimball's daughter Presendia Celestia drowned in City Creek in 1850, Eliza Ashworth's son in Mill Creek a few years later. The patchwork dress, like the portrait, became a memorial.
© *Pioneer Memorial Museum, International Society Daughters of Utah Pioneers, Salt Lake City.*

C. C. A. Christensen, *Weighing the Baby,* 1872.

This genre painting by a Danish immigrant portrays the father of a newborn baby entering a room inhabited by five women, two toddlers, and two infants.
© *Springville Museum of Art.*

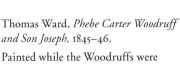

Patty Sessions, sampler, silk on linen.

Patty began this sampler as a girl in Maine in 1811 and finished it in the Salt Lake Valley in 1848. *Courtesy of Suzanne Brown Anderson.*

Thomas Ward, *Phebe Carter Woodruff and Son Joseph*, 1845–46.

Painted while the Woodruffs were in England, this portrait later helped Phebe Woodruff cope with the death of her son Joseph, who died at Winter Quarters in 1846. © *Intellectual Reserve, Museum of Church History and Art, Salt Lake City.*

William Warner Major, *Kono-sa. Chief of the Pervants near Filmore,* watercolor, 1852.

Kono-sa (or Kanosh) wears a shirt made of hickory, a striped fabric commonly used for worker's clothing and purchased in bulk by the so-called Indian Relief Societies in Salt Lake City. © *President and Fellows of Harvard College, Peabody Museum of Archaeology and Ethnology, PM# 41-72-10/426.*

BOTTOM RIGHT: William Warner Major, *Walker, War Chief of the Utahs,* watercolor, 1852

BELOW: Pima figured belt, wool and cotton.

Walker (Walkara) has wrapped his head in a woven band much like the brightly colored strap in the inset image. © *President and Fellows of Harvard College, Peabody Museum of Archaeology and Ethnology, [Walkara] PM# 41-72-10/427; [woven band] PM# 78-35-10/14722, gift of John R. Bartlett.*

Spoon made from the horn of a mountain sheep and winnowing tray, Paiute, southern Utah, c. 1877. These objects, collected by Edward Palmer, are similar to those described by Mormon missionaries in the 1850s. © *President and Fellows of Harvard College, Peabody Museum of Archaeology and Ethnology, [spoon] PM# 77-23-10/12151; [winnowing tray] PM# 77-23-10/12115.*

Amanda Barnes Smith, patchwork quilt. 1860–70.

Amanda Smith was secretary of the first Indian Relief Society. According to family tradition, Smith made this quilt from fragments of old clothing, including a brown overcoat traded by an officer who came to Utah with federal troops in 1858.

© *Pioneer Memorial Museum, International Society Daughters of Utah Pioneers, Salt Lake City.*

Sunburst from Old Salt Lake Tabernacle, 1852.

The face and background were originally painted bright yellow, the rays orange.
© Intellectual Reserve, Museum of Church History and Art, Salt Lake City.

Eliza R. Snow, embroidered square from the Twentieth Ward album quilt, 1870.

Eliza's embroidery references a passage in Isaiah about the lamb and the lion living peacefully together. Did it also allude to her own residence in Brigham Young's Lion House? *© Pioneer Memorial Museum, International Society Daughters of Utah Pioneers, Salt Lake City.*

great joy, she and her stepsister did.[109] Still, given the sluggish pace of the work, the Church simply did not need the nine missionaries they had sent to Hindoostan. After eighteen months in India, Samuel boarded a steamer for Boston.[110]

On his journey across the Atlantic, he dreamed that Catherine came into a room in his brother Edwin's house in Salt Lake City. She did not recognize him until others told her who he was. Then "she clung her arm around me & kissed me over & over again as I did her." He told her that it was all a dream and that he "would not be home in reality until next August. . . . This seemed to peeve her a little but still she was reconciled to it. I then thought I left the house . . . to return to this ship & I expected to fly or waft myself right through the air as soon as I got out of sight of every body."[111] Samuel wanted to go home, but he also wanted to believe that his mission had been a success. The world seemed to him ripe with iniquity, as in the days of Noah.[112]

He landed in Boston on February 12, 1855, and immediately headed south to Wilmington, Delaware, where he hoped to borrow money from his aunt Sarah Woolley, a single woman who was now leader in the Society of Friends. She welcomed him to her home, fed him, took him with her to Quaker meeting, listened to his stories, and resolutely refused to give him a loan. Samuel was despondent. Here he was, two thousand miles from home, having been gone more than two years, and a beloved relative had refused him. She surely knew he would repay her.[113]

The news from his relatives in Pennsylvania was no more encouraging. They "held a convention at West Chester a few days ago to see if they would give me money to go home," he explained. Writing to Aunt Sarah, they claimed that their refusal was a matter of principle. They feared he would pay tithing on any sum they offered, and since they were "opposed to spreading Mormonism," they did not want even 10 percent of their means to go to such a cause. Aunt Sarah had a somewhat different reason for rejecting her nephew's entreaties. She thought that, because Samuel had had such a difficult time on his mission, his church would now consider him entitled to take another wife, and she considered that practice "licentious, degrading, and Abominible." Perhaps she thought that, by keeping him in Delaware, she could persuade him to abandon what she called "his Delusion." She nevertheless gave him two dollars and told him to buy himself a new carpetbag, because his was "about worn out and does not look decent."[114]

Samuel postponed his homeward journey for another year and

accepted a call to serve as president of the Delaware Conference of the Eastern States Mission. His job was to preach, to teach, and to help place English immigrants in temporary jobs so they could earn money to complete their journey to Utah. Everywhere he went, people were talking about polygamy. One man told him he would happily migrate to Utah if he could have half a dozen wives, but he "thought it was not expedient & would prove the LDS overthrow." Another went around telling people that if a man was sick for eighteen months Samuel would be willing to "jump" his wife. Samuel was horrified. He had never said such a thing, "to him or any man."[115]

Perhaps controversy helped. His preaching eventually attracted crowds. In Centreville, in March 1855, he had "quite a good turn out especially of the fair sex." A female member of the audience, not wishing to speak in public, modestly passed him a note asking that he consider II Timothy 3:6, which in the King James translation reads, "For of this sort are they which creep into houses, and lead captive silly women laden with sins, led away with divers lusts." At the next meeting, Samuel addressed the scripture, explaining that it was monogamy, not polygamy, that led to "divers lusts." "I made the womans own stick whip herself nicely," he gloated.[116]

Although he got plenty of catcalls, he also got help. A Delaware crowd that included mostly non-Mormons sided with him against a heckler, even giving him money to take him to his next appointment.[117] Church members went out of their way to support him with food, lodging, and small gifts. A Pennsylvania Mormon added a "fine Ivory knob" to the top of his cane; a sister refused to charge him for doing his laundry, even though that was "the way she gets her living"; another woman performed hairdressing service, washing Samuel's head with gin and combing dandruff out of it.[118]

He was for the most part successful in finding work and lodging for newly arrived immigrants, though occasionally frustrated by their demands. He was stunned when, after he arranged for the purchase and delivery of a stove to one family, they wanted him to take it back, because they had found one they thought was a better deal. "This kind of game rather vexed me, & I was not sufficiently on my guard, so I showed it a little," he confessed.[119] Yet, despite occasional friction, he took pride in his work with church members, and was pleased when some of them joined him on his journey home. Unlike Hosea Stout and Perrigrine Sessions, he had the satisfaction of bringing a few Saints to Zion.

"Where we're meeting and parting and parting and meeting"

An undated poem in Eliza Snow's works captures the rhythm of family life among those whose men were called to serve missions.

> Our life is a cup where the sweet with the bitter,
> And bitter with sweet oft commingle again;
> Where we're meeting and parting and parting and meeting,
> Pain changes to pleasure and pleasure to pain.[120]

For Hosea Stout, returning from Hong Kong brought only pain. His hasty attempt to provide a new mother for his children had failed miserably. He was somewhat reconciled to his situation by the time he came home from his second, shorter mission into the mountains: "Aseneth as I had expected had obtained a Divorce and all was well." A few weeks later, he spent a Sunday morning visiting Louisa's grave.[121]

Perrigrine Sessions's return in August 1854 was more pleasurable. Patty, Lucina, Perrigrine's son Carlos, and his brother David took a wagon over the big mountain and camped, so they could meet his company at the mouth of Echo Canyon the next day. "A happy meeting it was," Patty wrote. "My son had been gone almost two years and been very sick the most of the time and I had not seen my daughter for over seven years we wept for joy and rejoiced exceedingly." They camped together for the night, then rolled into the valley together.[122]

Samuel Woolley's family had to wait two more years for such a reunion. Because his company was one of the first to reach the valley in 1856, it seemed that the whole city had come out to greet them. His eight-year-old son, Samuel Henry, was one of the first to arrive. Samuel said that he "did not know him at first sight being absent so long, & he having grown so much." As they ascended the big mountain, the final obstacle of the journey, Samuel caught sight of his sister Sarah Davis in a wagon with her sons. She had six-year-old Mary Pamelia with her. About halfway down the other side, he spotted Catherine with four-year-old Rachel Anna, who had been just a baby when her father left. Catherine was riding in style in a carriage belonging to Apostle Ezra Taft Benson, "which his good wife kindly loaned to mine." After a feast of melons brought from the valley, Samuel turned his team over to another man, boarded the carriage, and drove into the city with his family.[123] He had no co-wife beside him—nor, if Catherine had anything to do with it, would there be one anytime soon.

11

"Synopsis of my labors"

Wilford Woodruff Household, 1853

Wilford awoke on January 1, 1853, with a joyous sense that he lived in an era more significant than any other in the history of mankind. "The deeds of the last thousand years sink into insignificance in comparison to the work of a year at the present time," he exulted. The Prophet Daniel had foreseen it all. A "little stone cut out of the mountain without hands [would] roll forth until it became a mountain & filled the whole Earth & broke in peaces & subdued all other kingdoms." That stone, Wilford believed, was the Church of Jesus Christ of Latter-day Saints. Any nation or kingdom that attempted to oppress it would face the judgments of God.[1]

He knew something about stones cut out of a mountain without hands. The canyons opening to the east of the city were filled with them. Today, geologists call these gatherings "boulder fields" or "talus."[2] Wilford had gone to such a place to gather rocks for the foundation of the house he now lived in. With the help of his nephew Ezra Foss, he had "tumbled rock from the top of the Hill," drawing wagonload after wagonload to the corner of South Temple and First West.[3] Although he built the walls of his house of adobe rather than fired brick, it had a foundation as strong as the mountains around it. Standing only a few rods from Temple Square, the house would be worthy of one of the Lord's Apostles, a dwelling with the dignity of the one he and Phebe had left behind in Nauvoo.[4]

At 8:00 a.m. on January 1, he walked out the front door and strolled one block east to the Council House on the corner of East Temple Street, where other members of the Twelve were waiting. Surely, it was some kind of portent that so many were able to celebrate the New Year together in the valley after years dispersed across the earth on missions. Only Orson Pratt, who was still in the East defending polygamy, was missing. Two brass bands were already playing when the Apostles reached Brigham's compound on the hill above South Temple. The Apostles wished Brigham a Happy New Year and received his blessing, then paraded up the hill to Heber Kimball's dwelling, where they repeated the ceremony. All over the city, people were greeting the new year "with open ears & Harts of Joy." Open ears were inevitable. "God bless the bands," Wilford wrote.[5]

Three hundred sixty-four days later, he looked back on the year that

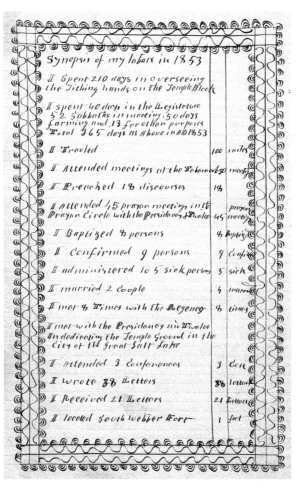

Wilford Woodruff, "Synopsis of my labors in 1853." Wilford composed summaries at the end of every year, focusing on church service. *(Church History Library, Salt Lake City. © Intellectual Reserve.)*

had begun so auspiciously. On a new page in his diary, he created a "Synopsis of my labors in 1853," tallying the baptisms, confirmations, and marriages he had performed, the sermons he had preached, the blessings he had given, and the prayer meetings he had attended with the First Presidency and the Twelve. He had spent fifty-two Sabbaths in church, forty days in the territorial legislature, fifty days farming, and 210 supervising the "tithing hands," who donated one day in ten to excavating and building a foundation for the temple they hoped to build on Temple Square.[6]

His synopsis did not include landmarks in the history of his family. Had it done so, it might have noted that:

On January 26 Phebe gave birth to a son who died two hours later.

On March 13, Sarah Brown and Emma Smith became his wives.

On December 13, he and Mary Ann Jackson signed a certificate of divorce.[7]

In his daily entries, Wilford briefly acknowledged the baby's birth and death and the two marriages. He did not mention the divorce. In fact, all the references to his family in the 1853 diary absorbed less than a sixth of the space he devoted to his march around town with his fellow Apostles on January 1. Wilford cared about his wives and children. He probably would have argued that everything he did in 1853, from cutting hay to laying the foundation for a temple, was to ensure their happiness and salvation. But he did not say so in his diary. When it came to family affairs, he kept a tight grip on his pen.

By the time Wilford completed his 1853 synopsis, the journal he had been using for several years was almost full. He used the remaining pages to summarize data from the end-of-the-year summaries he had kept for the previous nineteen years. There were more than forty categories on his list. Since 1834, he had traveled 80,588 miles, preached 1,395 sermons in public meetings, baptized 696 persons, and assisted in the baptisms of thousands of others. Had he included family events, he could have written: "I have married seven women. I have fathered ten children." He might or might not have added that only three of those wives and four of those children were now with him. Perhaps some things were better left uncounted.

Yet, if family relationships were at the core of Wilford's faith, as he surely would have claimed, the hope and the despair expressed in those numbers mattered. Gathering together the things he included in his summaries with those he did not allows us to interpret the births and deaths of his children and the comings and goings of his plural wives within the broader history of Latter-day Saint and nineteenth-century American family life. The Woodruff household was both like and unlike those created by other Latter-day Saints, including the Apostles who marched with him behind the brass band on January 1, 1853.

"I felt it to be quite a loss to us"

Aphek Woodruff was the last of Phebe's nine children. Born at 1:00 a.m. on January 26, 1853, he died at 3:00. Wilford buried his son in the garden and penned a brief lament: "I felt it to be quite a loss to us." Two days later, Phebe remained "quite poorly."[8] She would soon be forty-six years old. Her reproductive labors had ended. His had only begun. The two young women he married a few weeks later, joined by another in 1857, would eventually give him twenty-three children.

Some Latter-day Saints argued that this was exactly what nature intended. In an 1854 pamphlet, Belinda Marden Pratt explained that the differing reproductive capacities of males and females required polygamy. "The strength of the female is designed to flow in a stream of life . . . till mature age and approaching change of worlds, would render it necessary for her to cease to be fruitful." In other words, until she reached menopause. In contrast, a male had no fixed limit on his ability to propagate.

> If God shall count him worthy of an hundred fold in this life, of wives and children, and houses and lands and kindred, he may even aspire to patriarchal sovereignty, to empire; to be the prince or head of a tribe, or tribes; and like Abraham of old, be able to send forth for the defence of his country, hundreds and thousands of his own warriors, born in his own house.

With only one wife, a man could not achieve that glory.[9]

Belinda's treatise, originally written as a letter to her sister in New Hampshire, was among the most widely distributed of the pro-polygamy defenses that emerged after the public announcement of 1852. Belinda's husband, Apostle Parley P. Pratt, pronounced it "one of the Little entering wedges of a worlds Revolution." Belinda was herself a bit of a revolutionary. She had left a legal husband in Massachusetts in 1844 in order to join the Saints in Nauvoo, then married Parley in secret. There is no record that she and her first husband were ever divorced. Parley's relationship with Belinda, including his precipitous decision to take her with him to New York in the autumn of 1844, provoked a long-standing conflict with his legal wife, Mary Ann, who despite her initial enthusiasm for plural marriage, eventually left Parley. In contrast, Belinda portrayed her relationship with Parley's remaining wives as one of "mutual affection" and "long continued exercises of toil, patience, long-suffering, and sisterly kindness."[10]

Wilford was one of the last of the Apostles to take a plural wife. Phebe later admitted that she opposed polygamy until she became "sick and wretched." Only when convinced that it was a revelation from God did she accept it. She did not say how long that took.[11] In sharp contrast to other church leaders, Wilford fathered only one child by a plural wife during Phebe's childbearing years. Because his union with Mary Ann Jackson was difficult and his marriage to Mary Webster ended within a few weeks because of her death, his relationship with Phebe was, until 1853, for all practical purposes monogamous. Phebe was thirty years old when she and Wilford married. Her age did nothing to inhibit her fertility. She gave birth to her first child fifteen months later and was still having babies into her forties.

Phebe's fertility is all the more remarkable when we consider how often she and Wilford were apart. Whether consciously or not, conceiving a child became a way of marking his departure or return from a mission. Sarah Emma was conceived just before Wilford set out for the Fox Islands; Willie before he left for his first British mission; Phoebe Amelia just after his return; Susan Cornelia after his recovery from the illness he contracted during a harrowing journey to St. Louis; Joseph in Maine, just before they left for England; Ezra in Nauvoo, soon after their return; Beulah within days after their arrival in the Salt Lake Valley; and Aphek after Wilford's return from a journey to southern Utah with Brigham Young.[12] The arrivals of the Woodruff children marked the rhythm of their father's missions. Interestingly, three of the children were conceived at the Carter home in Maine, perhaps in the upper chamber that Wilford wrote about so fondly when he visited without Phebe.

Shuah is one exception to this pattern. Phebe conceived her at Winter Quarters, two months after burying Ezra and Joseph. That Shuah also died in infancy is consistent with a demographic study based on slightly later Utah records, showing that the risk of infant death was significantly higher when the previous infant had died, suggesting that the mother had not fully recovered from the earlier pregnancy or that common environmental circumstances were at play.[13] After Shuah's death, Phebe did not become pregnant again for three years. This could be a consequence of aging, but intentional delay seems more probable. After Shuah's death, Wilford wrote, Phebe "refused to be comforted." She had left two dead babies at Winter Quarters and was now about to leave another in Illinois. To heal in body and spirit, she required relief from childbearing, and presumably from sexual relations.[14]

The timing of pregnancies provides the best evidence we have concerning conjugal relations in times past. Such data tell us what people did, not what they did *not* do. If there was a baby, the parents had obviously slept together. If there was not, they may or may not have engaged in sexual intercourse. In the nineteenth-century United States, some couples attempted contraception, but for most people abstinence in combination with breast-feeding was the most common method of spacing children.

Demographers argue that a reduction in the frequency of sexual intercourse actually brought a decline in the overall birthrate in the nineteenth-century United States. That is, the desire to limit the number of children actually preceded the development of effective forms of contraception. In this regard, Mormons are a fascinating case study, because they were strongly pro-natalists. In their theology, the more babies the better, and they were in a hurry. They believed that bringing pre-existent spirits to earth was essential in the preparation of the second coming of Jesus.

Yet Latter-day Saints accepted the ideas of secular reformers who argued that too frequent intercourse was damaging to parental health and a danger to the health and moral character of infants if practiced during pregnancy and lactation. When asked what was the right frequency of sexual intercourse, William A. Alcott, a physician who was among the moderates, said that, although he did not want to be doctrinaire, once in a lunar month was probably what God intended. He declined to say that all congress between the sexes should be avoided during pregnancy, but he thought restraint was definitely in order—not because of concern over moral damage to the child, but because of the danger of miscarriage.[15]

Mormon preachers had varied approaches to the problem. Brigham Young recommended abstaining from sexual intercourse until seven days after the cessation of menstrual discharge, but as for the question of what to do during pregnancy, people could suit themselves.[16] Some Latter-day Saints embraced more radical notions. Apostle Orson Hyde once told a mixed audience of Saints in Springville, Utah, that human propagation was much like gardening. "You wouldn't plant even a squash seed in the *Fall*," he said. In like manner, there were times and seasons for sexual intercourse.[17] He said husbands should let their wives alone during pregnancy and lactation. "It is true that goats it is said will have sexual intercourse within fifteen minutes of the moment when the kid is born. Monkeys also, as some writers affirm are as debased in their practices, but most of the lower animals, may give us a lesson." What was at stake was not just the health of the mother and the safety of the child, but the spiritual authority of the father. "I say suppose a family, where there is no intercourse of this kind, only with the prospect of having children born,— *That family can be governed.*"[18]

The assumption was that sexual excitement might be communicated to a child through the umbilical cord or through breast milk, inculcating a tendency toward lasciviousness or rebellion. Belinda Pratt seems to have embraced some such notion; she explained to her sister that when a woman was engaged in the formation and growth of an infant, her "heart should be pure, her thoughts and affections chaste, her mind calm; her passions without excitement." Although a kind husband should comfort and sustain her during such seasons, "he should refrain from all those untimely associations which are forbidden in the great constitutional laws of female nature." She expected her sister, who was not a Latter-day Saint, to know what she meant.[19]

One way to determine whether Latter-day Saints accepted or rejected such taboos might be to explore intervals between births. Because breast-feeding retards ovulation, birth intervals in societies without other forms of contraception tend to average around twenty-four months, unless the death of a previous baby ends breast-feeding.[20] In Phebe Woodruff's case, her son Ezra's death at birth explains why Shuah could be born only ten months later. More interesting is that, aside from the long gap between Shuah and Beulah, only one interval in her birth record reached a full two years. Willie was born eighteen months after Sarah Emma; Susan sixteen months after Phoebe Amelia; Ezra seventeen months after Joseph; and Aphek eighteen months after Beulah. When she conceived each of these children, she had another baby in arms, between seven and nine months old. Either she was weaning her babies somewhat earlier than usual, or she and Wilford were engaging in sexual relations during lactation. Either conclusion is possible. Perhaps the Woodruffs were more moderate in their attitudes toward sex than Orson Hyde or Belinda Pratt. Perhaps Phebe's milk failed, and she had no choice but to turn to cow's milk or other foods.

In sixteen years of marriage, Phebe gave birth to nine children. That works out to one baby for each 1.7 years—a crude measure of fertility, to be sure, but an indication of what it meant to be swept along by what Belinda Pratt called the "stream of life." In contrast, Parley Pratt's childbearing wives averaged three years per child, a comparison that points toward the argument of some demographers that, whereas polygamy increases the number of children per father, it actually decreases the number per mother.[21] In the Pratt family, six childbearing plural wives produced twenty-four children between 1844 and 1856. Two other wives, who did not have children, helped to raise and support them.[22] The Pratt family was a reproductive collective that produced an impressively large number of children for the father while making fewer demands on the mothers than was the case with the Woodruffs.

In 1851, Parley took two of his plural wives, Elizabeth Brotherton and Phebe Soper, with him when he served a mission in California. Soper, who had already lost a baby shortly after birth, seemed determined to have another, and she soon became pregnant. Brotherton, who was by then in her late thirties and seemed destined not to bear children, soon secured work sewing. Meanwhile, in Salt Lake City, Belinda, Hannahette, Sarah, and Agatha all gave birth. Fearing that Mary, who was the only one not already pregnant when Parley left, would be disappointed in not being among them, Parley promised in a letter that it would be "her turn next, and She shall have a great boy, as handsome as a picture, and the verry Image of his father and mother." Mary did give birth after his return—to a girl![23]

In his own defense of polygamy, Parley's brother Orson argued: "God is the Author of sexual or conjugal love, the same as He is of all other kinds of pure love. . . . God has ordained that pure and virtuous love should be incorporated with sexual love; that, by the combination of the two, permanent union in the marriage covenant may be formed, and the species multiplied in righteousness." Parley followed the same logic, claiming that the purpose of sexual union was not just for propagation but for "mutual affection."[24] Pratt's own letters fizz with enthusiasm for all kinds of love.

"I am now inclined to believe that our father in heaven never associated in this Lower world of fallen nature, spirits more conjenial, Lovely and happy in each other, than we are as a family," he wrote while away from them. He praised Sarah for her improved writing, told Agatha that her letter was like herself, "all Love and affection," and admitted that he had recently dreamed about Mary. "O Could I get my mouth as near her lips as I did in a dream, I would immediately snatch one good Long hearty kiss. Lest in stoping to smile into her eyes I should awake with my mouth within about an inch of hers and go without a kiss as I did in my dream." He also dreamed about Belinda. Troubled that in the dream she seemed vexed about something, he remembered that the last time he saw her she was "seting in my lap with her arms around my neck in a meak and humble spirit and she said: 'comfort me.' And I did comfort her, with kind words while I enfolded her in my arms and pressed her to my heart."[25]

A non-Mormon couple who spent some time in Utah during this period observed that, when introducing their wives, some Mormon men had a kind of "hang-dog look." Not Parley. Self-confident and suave, he blithely introduced "five Mrs. Pratts in succession" without embarrassment.[26] Openness was part of Pratt's personality, but it also had something to do with the fact that none of the wives who remained with him after Mary Ann's departure had ever had exclusive claims to his attention. Since he married so many women in such quick succession, he found it easy to extend virtual hugs and kisses to all of them.

Pratt family stories describe Parley balancing multiple toddlers on his lap and singing. In truth, much of his parenting happened in absentia. During a second California mission, he created a humorous letter, embellished with a decorative border on four sides. The salutation took up most of the space, which was of course the point of its humor.

> Dear Mary and Belinda, and Sarah, and Hannahette, and Keziah,
> and Agatha, and Phebe, and Parley, and Alma, and Nephi, and
> Helaman, and Julia, and Belinda Jun'r, and Abinadi, and Cornelia,
> and Lucy, and Agatha, Junr and Malona, and Teancum, and Ette,
> and Lehi, and Mary Jun'r, and Phebe Junr, and Moroni, and so many
> more as there be, etc.
>
> I am well and very lonesome. I would give more to see you than I
> would, to be delivered from the Rathole of a Garret where I live.
>
> I cannot think ~~of any think~~ of any thing more to write. Elzabeth
> sais: this is a curious mess of Sheff [Chaff?] And Br Morris sais it is a
> long catalogue of names: for one family circle. I say the Lord increase
> it a hundred fold while I yet Live.
>
> I am yours, as ever P.P. Pratt.[27]

For Pratt, listing the members of his family was a pleasure, even if he had to resort to "etc."

Perhaps the disappointments Wilford and Phebe experienced made it difficult for him to elaborate his feelings about them in his diary. Phebe's labors were more difficult to summarize than his own.

"sealed at the Counsel House in Great Salt Lake City"

Beneath his diary entry for March 13, 1853, Wilford drew a strange spiral of overlapping circles, a slightly smaller version of an image he had used ten years before in Nauvoo, when he and Phebe went to John and Leonora Taylor's house and listened to Hyrum Smith expound on some "principles of the celestial world." The ink in the text that followed is lighter than what surrounds it, suggesting that he wrote it in another sitting, spacing it out to fill a gap left on the page:

> *Wilford Woodruff born March 1st 1807 in Farmington Hartford County Connecticut.*
>
> *Phebe Whitmore Carter born March 8th 1807 Scarborough Cumberland County Main.*
>
> *Wilford Woodruff and Phebe Whitemore Carter was Sealed for time & Eternity By President Hiram Smith in Nauvoo at 9 oclok P.M. Nov. 11th 1843. (it was not recorded)*
>
> *Wilford Woodruff and Phebe Whitmore Carter was sealed at the Counsel House in Great Salt Lake City for time & Eternity by President Brigham Young at 7 oclock March 13th 1853.*

There is a comfortable symmetry to these entries—Wilford's birthday and Phebe's just one week apart; their sealing in Nauvoo (which apparently was not recorded in any official document at the time, but was recorded in Wilford's diary); and the carefully matched sealing in Salt Lake City, now formally on the records of the Church. Phebe and Wilford had reaffirmed their vows in an upper room in the Council House, which was now serving as a substitute for a temple.

Beneath this record, he added two more items, perhaps not quite complete when originally written (there are parentheses around the two girls' names, and smudges where words have been erased):

Wilford Woodruff & (Emma Smith born March 1st 1838 at Diahman Davis County Missouri) was Sealed for time & Eternity by President Brigham Young at 7 oclock P.M. March 13, 1853.

Wilford Woodruff and (Sarah Brown born in ~~Henderson County New York~~ Jefferson County New York May 1st 1834) was sealed for time and Eternity By President Brigham Young at 7 oclock PM March 13, 1853.[28]

Wilford and Phebe had just turned forty-six. Emma was fifteen, Sarah almost nineteen. Had they married at the usual age, the Woodruffs could have been both girls' parents.

The new wives arrived in the diary unannounced except for a telltale sign in a seemingly routine entry on February 19: "My Children Willford, Phebe & Susan Also Emma & Sarah were all present at the breaking of the ground for the foundation of the Temple." Grouping "Emma & Sarah" with his children implied that they, too, were dependents in his household—wards or household helpers. Given their family circumstances, they may well have been. Both had lost their fathers during journeys to the Salt Lake Valley. As the oldest children of widowed mothers, they were perhaps in need of a home and an opportunity to work for their own support.

In this they were not unlike other young women in Utah in the 1850s. In one town, 36 percent of women marrying for the first time married into polygamy. These women—or girls—tended to be economically disadvantaged or to have migrated without fathers. Some were foreign-born. In contrast, brides who initially married monogamously and who eventually accepted additional wives into their families had the advantage of being "first wives," with whatever privileges that accorded them. They also had some say in whether or when their husbands married again. Usually, they were close in age to their husbands. Young women married to older men in polygamy were in a far different position.[29]

Although there was a slight surplus of women over men in some parts of Utah (a striking contrast to the situation prevailing in the West generally), polygamy would have been difficult without an expanding population. Because Utah was growing by natural increase as well as migration, the number of persons at lower levels of the age pyramid exceeded those above, allowing men to choose plural wives from among women much younger than themselves. Although polygamy ensured that virtually every woman in the territory married, it also created competition in the marriage market, guaranteeing that women married at younger and younger ages. By 1860, the mean age at marriage in one Utah town had fallen to sixteen years for both monogamous and polygamous brides.[30] It is important to note, however, that younger wives usually lived with their plural families for a time before having children, their husbands perhaps delaying conjugal relations. Although Sarah Brown had her first baby about a year after marriage, Emma's first child was born more than three years later, when she was well past nineteen.[31]

In comparison with some of the men who paraded with him on January 1, 1853, Wilford had not been very successful in putting plural marriage into practice. George Smith had managed to keep four wives in addition to Bathsheba for almost a decade. Amasa Lyman had retained the loyalty of seven women, and in 1853 he added an eighth—Lydia Partridge, whose older sisters Eliza and Caroline were already members of his family. Meanwhile, Patty Sessions was kept busy attending the births—and in one case a miscarriage—of Lorenzo Snow's wives Charlotte, Adeline, Harriet, Sarah, and Eleanor.[32] In contrast, Wilford's hasty marriages at Winter Quarters had ended within days. His marriage to Mary Ann Jackson had produced a son at the cost of much unhappiness. His marriage to Mary Giles Webster, who died shortly after they were sealed, was so brief as to be virtually unnoticeable.

In choosing Sarah Brown and Emma Smith, Wilford hoped for a better outcome. Although he said nothing about the new wives' earlier histories in recording their sealings, a probing of previous entries in his diary and other records explains why, of all the fatherless young women who came to the valley in the early 1850s, they became part of his household. He (and perhaps Phebe) had first met their parents early in their years in the Church and were eventually linked to them through bonds of kinship, friendship, and misfortune.

Wilford became acquainted with Emma Smith's parents, Samuel and Martisha Smith, during his mission in Kentucky in 1835. Martisha's brother, Abraham Smoot, was Wilford's missionary companion. Like the Smoots, the Smiths migrated to Missouri. To write, as Wilford did, that Emma was born in "Diahman Davis County Missouri" was to connect her to a spiritual legacy of immense proportions. "Diahman" was short for Adam-ondi-Ahman, a site in northern Missouri that Joseph Smith identified as the very place where Father Adam, at the end of his days, gathered his posterity together to bless them, and where the righteous would once again gather before the second coming of Jesus. Brigham Young dedicated a site for a temple at Adam-ondi-Ahman in 1838, shortly before the Saints were expelled from Missouri. Emma was born there on March 1, 1838, in what was then still called Spring Hill, Missouri. She became a refugee before she had reached her first birthday.[33]

For Wilford, the site of Emma's birth may have had even richer meaning, because at a secret meeting in Missouri in which he was ordained to the Quorum of the Twelve, before leaving for his English mission, the congregation sang a song composed by William W. Phelps called "Adam-ondi-Ahman."[34] The hymn began with a pastoral vision:

> This earth was once a garden place,
> With all her glories common;
> And men did live a holy race,
> And worship Jesus face to face,
> In Adam-ondi-Ahman.

The song continued with a promise that Adam's ancient garden spot would also be a site of glory during the millennium.[35]

Phelps's hymn appeared in the first Latter-day Saint hymnbook, the one edited by the Prophet's wife Emma, the woman for whom Martisha and Samuel Smith's daughter was surely named, even though the Kentucky Smiths and the New England Smiths were not kin. Wilford and Phebe surely knew Emma as a child. Phebe of course lived with the Smoots for a time when Wilford was on his first mission to England. Martisha, like Phebe, became a member of the Female Relief Society in Nauvoo, and in 1845, she and Samuel were endowed in the Nauvoo Temple.[36]

The Smiths remained in Iowa after the expulsion from Nauvoo. In 1850, they joined Wilford's company on the journey west. On June 28, 1850, Emma father's died of cholera. With the help of others, Wilford dressed him in his temple robes, then laid him on the ground inside his tent in preparation for burial. "But we had but Just got it done until A tremendious thunder Storm over took us. Blew the tent down. We had to cover over the corpse & let it lie until morning." They buried him the next day and, because they had no choice, continued the journey.[37] Emma was twelve, her younger sister eight, one brother six and another, named Abraham Owen for his uncle, not quite two. Twelve days later, Martisha Smith gave birth to another girl. Wilford didn't mention the birth in his diary, perhaps because he was too absorbed by the deaths from cholera all around them.[38]

Although Wilford said nothing about the Smiths after they arrived in Utah, the Federal Census taken in 1851 counted Martisha Smith and her family but misidentified her as a white farmer named "Melatiah." Obviously, whoever entered the names into the roster had not seen her. She and her children were surely on the guest list when Wilford and Phebe held a party on February 26, 1852, for those who had traveled with them to the valley. There is no way of knowing whether they attended, nor when Emma first came to live with them, but she was surely not a stranger when she first showed up in the diary.[39]

Sarah Brown's connection to Wilford also went back to his earliest years in the Church. In the opening pages of the first volume of his diary, Wilford explained how Harry Brown, Sarah's father, came through the New York town where he was living on a preaching expedition with Parley Pratt and convinced him to travel to Kirtland to join others in an expedition to Missouri, to relieve the Saints who were suffering under mob violence. After the Missouri expedition broke up, Brown returned to his family in Kirtland and remained there until the early 1850s, when he rediscovered his Mormon faith and decided to bring his family to Utah.[40]

When the Browns arrived in St. Louis, they booked passage on the *Saluda,* a riverboat that had supposedly been refurbished after sinking during an earlier journey.[41] Abraham Smoot, who was passing through the same area at the time, later claimed to have warned people that the vessel was unsafe, but the emigrants were eager to get moving and ignored him. Spring had come late that year. There were still ice floes in the river, and it was difficult to navigate around the narrowest part of the channel. When a piece of debris from fallen trees damaged its flywheel, the *Saluda* stopped in Lexington, Missouri, for repairs.[42]

As Sarah recalled in an autobiography she wrote as an adult, "The boat captain's patience gave out as we had been on the boat nine days . . . so on the third of April 1852 he said we will start today if we blow the old boat to Hell, and in a few minutes it was blown somewhere with the poor captain blown all to atoms."[43] *The Cleveland Herald* pronounced it one of the worst disasters on record, and "the result of the most criminal recklessness." The dying engineer admitted he had caused the explosion by following the captain's foolhardy instructions. Wanting to build up a quick head of steam, he had turned off the water to the boiler, hoping to heat it quickly. But it boiled dry, turned red hot, and burst. Witnesses said the bodies of the captain and second clerk were blown over the warehouses on the shore and halfway up the bluff. *The Natchez Courier* thought between 100 and 125 persons had died, including most of the crew. The reporter for the *Missouri Courier* found it impossible to describe the carnage, though he made an attempt, writing of scalded bodies, mangled corpses, frantic mothers, and crying orphans.[44]

Smoot, who witnessed the explosion from the shore, dispatched a letter to Salt Lake City reporting the loss of seventy-five persons, only twenty or twenty-five of whom were Latter-day Saints. He did not have a final death count, because many of the victims were still being nursed by "the citizens of Lexington, who have proved themselves in this case as noble hearted and generous a people as I have ever seen."[45] Sarah's memoir fills in that story. When the explosion hit, her father had been standing over the provision box to get a piece of bread for her little brother, who was whimpering for something to eat. He and the baby were both blown into the hold in a tangled mass of debris. Although her father found the baby unhurt amid the rubble, he himself was injured. Her fourteen-year-old brother, Ira, had his front teeth knocked out and his right leg broken.[46]

The family remained in Lexington for three weeks, then boarded another riverboat headed to Council Bluffs. On the way, Sarah's father's injuries grew worse, and he died. Her mother left her alone to guard the body while she went ashore for help. Sarah would never forget the drunken man who terrified her by raising the sheet covering her father's face and laughing, or the kind man who took him by the collar and sent him away, then watched over her until her mother returned.[47] The Browns stayed six weeks at Council Bluffs. Then, on July 12, as Sarah recalled, they "crossed the river and started on the plain." Because of his injured leg, Ira had to lie in the wagon, making space so tight that Sarah was moved to another company. "Ira's leg did not heel," she later explained, "and it was so hot traveling it mortified and all his toes dropped off, so mother had to stay with him and the children at Fort Laramie and have his leg amputated at the hip." Sarah arrived in the valley without her family. Her younger sister married a soldier she had met at the fort. Her mother and the other children eventually came to the valley, but did not stay long.[48]

Perhaps Abraham Smoot had some role in uniting Wilford with his two teenaged brides. Emma was, of course, his niece. He had also been a witness to the disaster that had devastated Sarah's family. However it happened, Sarah Brown and Emma Smith became Wilford's wives on the same day. Sarah conceived her first child four months after the sealing, during July haying. She gave birth on April 4, 1854, to a son they named "David Patten," after the Apostle who had died in Missouri. Unlike Sarah, Emma appeared more like a daughter than a wife. (She was exactly the age the Woodruffs' first daughter, Sarah Emma, would have been had she lived.) Together, Sarah and Emma were integrated into the family economy, learning to spin, weave, sew, and tailor men's clothes under the expert supervision of the woman they called "Aunt Phebe."[49]

"to dissolve all the relations which have hitherto existed between us"

Although Wilford neglected to mention his divorce from Mary Ann Jackson in his diary, a copy of the divorce certificate survives in Brigham Young's papers. Dated December 13, 1853, it contains both Wilford's and Mary's signatures, as well as those of two witnesses—Brigham Young's counselor, Willard Richards, and his clerk, Thomas Bullock. Although Brigham issued these certificates, he did not sign them. As the pre-printed document makes clear, the couple themselves contracted the divorce, filling in their names on a form claiming they did "mutually covenant, promise, and agree to dissolve all the relations which have hitherto existed

Mary Ann Jackson, c. 1870s, after Jackson remarried. *(Courtesy of Linda Andrews.)*

between us, as Husband and Wife; and to keep ourselves separate and apart from each other from this time forth." The signed and witnessed statement then gave them a complete divorce with "liberty to marry whomsoever they will."[50]

In sharp contrast to divorces granted elsewhere in the United States, plural marriages were dissolved by "mutual consent" rather than by civil authority and did not require a judgment of guilt. That the certificate Wilford and Mary signed was printed rather than handwritten is compelling evidence that the procedure was common. Historians now know that, in much of the United States and in Britain, informal and extra-legal separations and bigamous remarriages occurred far more frequently than either legal records or prescriptive literature would imply. Marriages broke up because wives as well as husbands ran away, and because increased mobility and multiple jurisdictions allowed them to do so.[51] The Mormon system brought such practices within a system of church law. During his administration, Brigham Young authorized at least 1,645 divorces, three-fourths of those before 1866. Divorces among women married in polygamy were three times as common as among those in monogamous marriages. Because high church officials contracted so many plural marriages, they were especially vulnerable. Divorce was perhaps the safety valve that made polygamy work.[52]

The December 13 certificate made divorce look easy. A December 30 letter Wilford sent to Mary Ann shows that it was no easier in the nineteenth century than today to dissolve a relationship fully, especially when a child was involved. The formal agreement ostensibly removed all obligations between the spouses, but fathers were required to continue supporting their children. Wilford's letter showed a continuing struggle over the distribution of resources. Although he reminded Mary Ann that, at the time they signed the bill, he had "made you no promise what amount I would do for you," he had apparently promised to continue providing for her in some way. He complained that "the more I do for you the more ungrateful you are, and the wors you act, which is a poor incouragement to bestow favors upon anyone."[53]

Then he raised an issue that had surely been a source of contention between them—her inability to live peaceably with Sarah Brown. Perhaps Sarah's change in status from household helper to wife helped precipitate the divorce. Sarah had apparently been living with Mary Ann in the old house, the one made from logs moved from the fort. He continued, "Your constant ill treatment to Sarah is very unbecoming in you and you will not gain any favors with me by continuing in it. She has as good a right in that house as you have & you are ownly injuring yourself by continuing your ill treatment to her." Given the divorce, one would think that Sarah actually had a greater right to the house than Mary Ann. But Mary Ann had a child and Sarah did not—at least not yet. Wilford considered himself responsible to support James. As for Mary Ann, she would have to beg "favors." His promise to give her enough broadcloth to make James two coats and a pair of pants, as well as a pair of pants cut out for Willie that had proved too small, suggests Phebe's involvement. She was, of course, an expert tailor. Turning the cloth into clothing would now be Mary Ann's problem.[54]

The issues raised in this acrimonious and one-sided encounter sound a great deal like those raised in Augusta Cobb's letters to Brigham, with the wife complaining about a lack of support and the husband insisting that the wife—or in this case the ex-wife—do more for herself. As in other cases, the marriage appears to have foundered not just over distribution of basic resources but over the harmony or lack thereof in the family. "Concerning your threat of complaining of me to President Young I would say that does not alarm me. For he is better qualified to judge both man & woman and their spirits than either of us," Wilford wrote.[55] Given his church position, maintaining dignity mattered. When, a year later, he heard that Mary Ann had been spreading tales around the neighborhood, he exploded:

> Mary A Jackson I wish to say that I have been informed [by] Orson Pratts family & several Other Sources that you are reporting to people as you have an opportunity that president Young . . . sharply reproved me saying that I had treated you ill, if you have made any one of these statements to any person you have lied & stated falshoods. President Young did not reprove me Neither did He require or advise me to feed, cloth, or help you one day or give you a dime what I have done for you Since I gave you a Bill I have done out of Charity not because I was compelled to do it And I will now say if you do not [stop] your lying I shall expose you & you need not [come] to me for any further support untill I am satisfyed that you Have recalled those fals statements where you have made them. W. Woodruff[56]

Orson Pratt's house was directly across the street from Wilford's. If Mary was still in the old house, she had easy access to its inhabitants. Perhaps

Sarah Pratt, who later became totally disaffected from Orson, was a willing listener.[57]

Brigham once told Wilford that "there was No law in Heaven or in Earth that would Compel a woman to stay with a man either in time or Eternity."[58] What Brigham did not say was that economic need and an inability to provide for herself might compel a woman to do what the law could not. On March 7, 1857, Wilford received a note from Mary Ann. It took him almost two months to answer it, disingenuously claiming that a "multiplicity of business" had prevented him. In truth, he had spent most days in those weeks in his office, "reading and writing," and most nights "at home." He must have thought long and hard about what he should say.[59]

Mary Ann had apparently apologized for having "gone astray" and asked his forgiveness. His answer was carefully worded.

> In reply I would say I feel to freely forgive you & all men who have in any wise sin[n]ed against me. I lay nothing up against you but with regard to Entering into the bonds of Matrimony I do not feel prepared to take that step for we have had a long experience in that & the past has fully shown that we have not rendered each other happy.

He did not say that a covenant was meant to be kept, not broken, that once married a man and a woman should strive to be true to their promises. He said marriage was about happiness—mutual happiness. They had not made *each other* happy. This was a strikingly modern concept. Wilford was a patriarch, to be sure, but in his self-presentation he insisted that his goal was not social order but happiness, eternal happiness, but happiness nonetheless.

He continued in the same vein. "Even after being separated for years I again provided you with a home but our spirits for some cause were not congenial." He reminded her that she was the one who had asked for a divorce. Then he briefly exposed what was probably an even more crucial issue, his relationships with other members of his family. Phebe may have been the unseen presence here.

> Our marriage has caused us both a good Deal of unhappiness which has been felt throughout my whole family. At Present I have peace & union with every member of my family I would not wish to take any

~~step to~~ for they are all subject to me & all strive to abide my counsel &
act for each other's interest & welfare.

There are many ways to read between the lines of this intriguing letter.
That he quickly shifted from "peace and union" to his own authority,
after excising a sentence about taking any step that would disturb his
family, suggests a concern for Phebe. It is impossible to know whether it
was Jackson's unwillingness to follow his "counsel" or the lack of harmony
among the women that mattered. Maybe it was both. Wilford diplomatically concluded, "I do not feel that it is wisdom to take the steps which
you suggest lest we should both be rendered unhappy instead of bettering
our condition."[60]

Wilford added that he was ready to take James into his household at
any time and "do as well as I can by him as soon as He is old enough He
should go to some useful trade." Jackson kept her son, and within a few
months married David James Ross, by whom she had two more children.
Six years later, James returned to live with his father.[61]

In the sermons on family life that became plentiful after the public announcement of polygamy, the core assumption was that men were
responsible not just for governing their households but for saving them.
Wilford recorded from memory a pungent sermon in which Lorenzo Snow
exclaimed, "Almost any fool can go & preach the gospel but it requires a
vary wise man to be a patriarch & save his own household." To do that, a
man must do more than provide physical necessities; he had to be a model
of gentleness, kindness, and peace.[62] Yet, in the same sermon in which he
enjoined men to be more Christlike, Lorenzo reinforced common stereotypes about the vanity, frivolity, and contentiousness of women. If a man
did not work hard to save his family, he might face a stampede of wants
and demands.

> This woman wants a gown that one a Bonnet the next one Shoes &
> their Children clothing & one thinks she Has to do more than her
> part & this one will not do what she should &c & the man has got to
> stand in the midst of his family like a God in order to calm the troubled
> waters & safe [save] them.[63]

In Lorenzo's view, a Godlike man was supremely self-confident, perfectly
in control of his emotions, and irresistible to righteous women. That made
things difficult for men who had not been endowed with such gifts.

"cruel I must say to leve me"

Wilford's divorce from Mary Ann Jackson provides insight into one aspect of plural marriage in early Utah. His relationship with Mary Webster offers another. He may or may not have known that she was still married when Brigham sealed her to him on the day she came into his house as a "boarder." When they lived in Boston, Wilford and Phebe were acquainted with Mary and her husband, Nathan. Although her name doesn't appear on the list of those who were in their company when they left for Utah, she was probably with them.[64] She died at the Woodruff house on October 3, 1852. Three weeks later, Woodruff noted that he had written to "Mr Webster," presumably to send news of his wife's death. By then he had certainly read the letter found in her papers.[65]

Webster had written in stages in June and July 1850, not long after Mary left home. He mentioned hearing about cholera deaths in St. Louis, sent news from friends in Boston and Salem, and asked her to send a chronicle of her journey. He mostly wanted to assure her that he loved her. Apparently, they had quarreled over his refusal to join her on the journey west. He worried that she had forgotten her "once dear friend" and apologized for inquiring in an earlier letter about some of his shirts that were missing. He never thought she had taken them; he had given her permission to take anything she wanted from the house. "I hope you will forgive me for this one falt and I will endever not to offend you again." His letter was a tumble of penitence and recrimination.

> O Mary cruel I must say to leve me. I never would ov left you I would
> [have] died by your side first, but my once kind Mary I will for give
> you and I do pray night and morning for you that God will bless you
> and give you strength to meet any evle and every temptation and if we
> never meet again in this world I hope that I shall so conduct my self
> hear in the world to come to part no more.

He paused to provide a little news from her friends, then continued his lamentation:

> O Mary you cannot tell how much sorrow you have caused me. Have
> I been unkind to you. do i deserve to be forsacon by my only dear
> friend. I cannot for get you allthou you have forsacon me you are not
> out of my mind five minutes in a day. O the tears I have shed for you.

they are precious drops you will find some future day. . . . I cannot
forget you whilst life and reason remains.

He then assured her that if, in this uncertain world, she was ever short of
money and wished to return to Boston, he would leave in care of a banker
two hundred dollars that she could have simply by calling for it.

That his next passage alluded to Mormon concepts of the hereafter
suggests that he was, or at some point had been, a Latter-day Saint. He
prayed that their Heavenly Father would bless her with every blessing, and
added, "If we never meat a gain in this world may we meet in the Celestial
kingdom to part no more where tears shall be wiped from every eye and
our happiness be complete." He held on to the letter; when he received one
from her on July 10, he picked his up again, promised to write as often as
he could, and then, once again, begged her not to forget him. As if uncertain whether he had made his point, he added, "Mary as it respects my
filings [feelings] towards you you no [know] them as well as I do my self
I have got a peace of your bread in my Buro [bureau] to remember you
with was made by your kind hands." He added that he had been reading
the Book of Job.[66]

Mary Webster belongs to a larger group of women who, when forced to
choose between gathering to Zion or remaining with their legal husbands,
chose Zion. Belinda Marden Pratt, Augusta Cobb Young, Sarah Noon
Kimball, Zina Huntington Jacobs, and Presendia Buell Kimball all took
that course. So, eventually, did Sylvia Sessions. Although she remained
with her first husband, Windsor Lyon, until his death, she eventually left
her second to join her family in Utah. She seems not to have been reinte-
grated into Heber Kimball's family, even though in the Nauvoo Temple
she had been sealed to him for time and to Joseph Smith for eternity.

The surprising thing is how few of the abandoned husbands chose to
fight back. Henry Cobb appears to have been unique in suing his wife
for adultery. Most of the other men simply faded away. A few sent plaintive letters. In its sentimentality and its sense of hopelessness, the one
Henry Jacob sent to "Dear Zina and beloved Children" is very much like
Webster's. Although Henry and his new wife, Aseneth, had resettled in
California, he could not forget his former wife and their two sons. He
opened the letter with reference to the boys, adding an awkward allusion
to Zina's tiny daughter by Brigham Young: "Oh how happy I should be
if I only could see you and the little Children bone of my bone and flesh
of my flesh. I mean all[.] I would like to see the little babe." Although he

knew that Zina Presendia was not bone of his bone, for Zina's sake he still wanted to see her. He told Zina that his feelings were "indiscrieable." He had no peace. His comfort had vanished.

"The glory of day has fled like the fog before a pleasant morning," he wrote, reflecting his own confusion in the awkward simile: in California, it was usually the fog that vanished as the sun rose, not the reverse. Little matter. His brain and spirits were socked in. He was befuddled by nostalgia:

> I have had meny a good dream about you and the little ones I have imagin myself at home with you and the Little Boys upon my kneese a singing and playing. . . . What a comfort what a Joy to think upon those days that are gone by O heaven Bless me even poor me shall I ever see them again.[67]

When his second wife, Aseneth, left him in November, Henry blamed interference from her mother, whom he called "the ole woman."[68] His continuing longing for Zina must also have been an issue.

Caroline and Jonathan Crosby, who had found work in San Jose after returning from their mission to Tubuai, were surprised to see Henry at a church meeting on December 12, 1852. "He has been 3 or 4 years in Cal— has passed through a variety of fortunes, and has at last been burned out by the great fire at Sacramento." Caroline said Henry had "got his mind quite awakened again to the subject of the gospel, made quite an exciting speech in our meeting." He spent Christmas Day with the Crosbys, telling Caroline she "reminded him so much of Zina his first wife that it revived all his past trials on her account." He went home and returned with his fiddle. He and Jonathan Crosby "had fine times playing together," such fine times that he stayed another night, and then another. "Tuesday being rainy he staid all day, and all night again," Caroline continued. That night, the two men played for a dance at a neighbor's new house. When it rained again the following day, they decided to have another party. Caroline cleaned up the house and "went to cooking." The crowd danced through yet another night.[69]

To Caroline's astonishment, Henry returned three days later to say he planned to get married and asked her to plan a party. Over the next few weeks, Henry and his new wife, Mary Clawson, called frequently. Toward the end of March, Mary came alone. "She looked very sad, said she had been weeping gave us an account of her late husband Henry B Jacobs,

Zina Huntington Jacobs Young with daughter, Zina Presendia, c. 1856. Zina Presendia was born in 1850. When the Lion House was completed, she lived with her mother there. *(Pioneer Memorial Museum, International Society of Daughters of Utah Pioneers, Salt Lake City.)*

leaving her in consequence of his old wife coming and claiming her previous right." The old wife was apparently Aseneth. Caroline said nothing more in the diary about their fiddling friend, except that at a church conference on April 9, 1853, he was "disfellowshiped in consequence of unlawful conduct in regard to matrimony." Among the Mormons, he was certainly able to take another wife, but he had to have church authority to do so, and he had apparently not bothered to secure it.[70]

Caught as they were in the utopian drama of early Mormonism, it was sometimes difficult to know what was and what was not "unlawful."

When Wilford Woodruff and his fellow Apostles perambulated their neighborhood on New Year's Day in 1853, they were celebrating the establishment of a new Zion. Yet each of them was also building a personal kingdom. After Phebe's last baby died early in 1853, Wilford made decisions with enormous consequences. By bringing two fatherless young women into his household, he paid debts to old friends and at the same time reinvigorated his reproductive potential. By signing a bill of divorce with Mary Ann Jackson, he also ensured peace, at least for a time. Sometimes, random entries in a man's diary, when read alongside seemingly inert references to births, deaths, and marriages, can yield dynamic stories.

12

"we now must look after the poor"

Utah Territory, 1852–1855

Patty Sessions was a joiner. She joined the Female Relief Society when it was organized in Nauvoo in 1842. When it was disbanded, she worked to keep its spirit alive. In Utah, she became an officer in the Council of Health, attended meetings of the Deseret Agricultural and Manufacturing Society, joined Lorenzo Snow's "Polysophical Society," signed up for dancing school, and enrolled in classes to learn the Deseret Alphabet, a system of writing designed to make learning English easier for Indians and immigrants. On June 10, 1854, she became "Presidentess" of a society to cut out and stitch clothing for Southern Paiute women and children.

Six months later, she wrote, "I have been to see the Bishop. He told me he would appoint a meeting for the sisters next week as the Presd had called on us to do somting for the poor said we had clothed the squaws and children first rate we now must look after the poor in each ward."[1] Patty's reference within a single entry to the "presd," the "ward," the "bishop," the "sisters," the "poor," "squaws," and "children" mapped a complex set of relationships that extended from the most to the least visible inhabitants of Mormon Utah. The "presd" was, of course, Brigham Young, who was both governor of the territory and president of the Church. The "bishop" was Shadrach Roundy, the presiding officer in Salt Lake City's Sixteenth Ward, the nine-block area where Patty lived. The "sisters" were members of what in other wards became known as the Indian Relief Society because of their work making clothing for Southern Paiute families ("squaws" and "children"). Now, it seemed, Patty's group was to switch its attention from the Paiutes to the "poor" in their own neighborhood.

A casual reading of this entry suggests a smoothly running ecclesiastical organization in which Brigham Young issued instructions, bishops passed them on, and obedient women carried them out. But what if the active agent was actually Patty? Suppose she went to the bishop's house not to receive instructions but to make a request for help in responding to a call Brigham had given, not to the bishops, but to the women themselves. In Sunday sermons, Brigham often made direct requests to members. Perhaps it was he, not the bishop, who said the women had clothed the squaws and children first-rate. The text can be reread in that way.

> I have been to see the Bishop. He told me he would appoint a meeting
> for the sisters next week as the Presd had called on us to do somting for
> the poor said we had clothed the squaws and children first rate we now
> must look after the poor in each ward.

Such a reading acknowledges Patty's agency. But it still leaves Brigham in control.

Pushing the story backward in time changes that emphasis. On June 4, 1854, Brigham had indeed asked Salt Lake city women to "form themselves into societies" to "clothe the Lamanite children and women."[2] But when he stood in the Tabernacle to issue that request, women had already been meeting for eighteen months to do just that. In a fascinating replay of the history of the Nauvoo Relief Society, Brigham simultaneously validated their work and absorbed it into an ecclesiastical and hierarchical system at least formally under his control.[3]

Shortly after arriving in the valley, church leaders had divided Salt Lake City into wards, each with a bishop at its head. Although bishops gradually assumed pastoral responsibilities, they were at first primarily concerned with practical matters. They supervised construction of fences and irrigation ditches, and during periods of dearth they oversaw the rationing of grain. They also arranged housing for new immigrants and assumed general responsibility for those in need within their ward boundaries.[4] Asking women to clothe Indians didn't infringe on ward bishops' responsibilities, but giving them responsibility for the poor in their own wards introduced the potential for confusion over who really was in charge of such practical matters. The bishop of the Thirteenth Ward, Edwin Woolley, hesitated before organizing a Female Relief Society in his ward, and, when he did, he insisted that female leaders defer to him.[5]

Patty's relations with Shadrach Roundy were less rigid. For years they had worked together with little concern about lines of authority.[6]

From the outside, everything that happened in Utah in the 1850s appeared to be under Brigham Young's control. From the inside, his genius lay in an ability to embrace what he could not command. The story of women's organizational activities in early Utah exposes both the strength and the limitations of their seemingly marginal position within the Church.

"one of the best meetings I ever had"

Women participated both in a general Council of Health, organized at Willard Richards's house in 1849, and in a separate Female Council, established shortly thereafter. In the summer of 1851, Patty Sessions became first counselor to Phoebe Angel, the "Presidentess" of the Female Council.[7]

Patty kept minutes of a meeting held on August 14, 1852. In her opening remarks, she "told the reason of this separate counsel, which was in consequence of a slackness of attendance of the females, which was supposed to be caused by there being present Male Members." The sisters then proceeded to choose a man to take minutes of the meeting and give Dr. Sprague permission to come and go as he pleased, since he was responsible for opening the door to the building.[8] That the doctor asked permission showed respect for the sisters. That they so quickly granted it suggests they were less concerned about the presence of males than Patty's introduction implied. Apparently, this was a women's meeting, not so much because women outnumbered men as because a woman presided. Their effort to reach out worked. Fifty-three new sisters joined the Council; eventually, there were as many as three hundred members.[9]

The Council of Health, like other Mormon associations, had both spiritual and practical goals. Phoebe Angel set the tone for the August 14 meeting by sharing an experience she had in Nauvoo when everyone seemed to be suffering from chills and fever. "She cried to the Lord that he would show her something to do them good," and in the night, she received, as if by revelation, a recipe for a medicine composed of the herbs boneset and lobelia steeped in vinegar. The remedy worked so well that over the summer she used a full bushel of boneset. For her, this was evidence that the sisters needed to "see to the Lord for wisdom."[10] Other women offered cures for ant and snake bite, piles, erysipelas, dyspepsia, and intestinal worms in children. Although some recipes, like Angel's, contained the Thomsonian favorite lobelia, others featured such common herbs as catnip, tansy, rue, yarrow, goldenseal, and barberry. References to "desert root" and "squaw root" suggested acquaintance with local plants.[11]

A discussion of preventative health care also merged medical and spiritual goals. "Spoke much on the subject of taking care of our health to avoid tight laceing cold or wet feet to take care of our infants and how to train up our children that they may be prepared to be saints and fill the measure of their creation in ritchcousness." Patty worked with a "Sister Smith" (Amanda?) to produce gowns "more conducive to health than the long tight waisted dress filed with whale bone & hickery that they ware now."[12]

This was of course the very moment when woman's rights activists in the East were scandalizing their neighbors by adopting a costume named for the Seneca Falls editor Amelia Bloomer.[13] Although there is no evidence that Mormon women actually wore bloomers (loose pantaloons gathered in at the ankle), they without question reduced the length and breadth of their skirts and the amount of boning in bodices. Zina Young became both an advocate for and a designer of such clothing. She was pleased when a notice was read at Sunday meeting "for the ladies that wore or approved of the Deseret costume" to meet at the Social Hall the next day. Through the week, Zina was busy cutting and fitting dresses according to the new style.[14]

In her diary, Patty used the same phrase—"had a good meeting"—in describing Council of Health meetings and earlier gatherings where glossolalia was welcome. When Phoebe Angel "sung a song in toungues" at a Council meeting, Patty interpreted. When a lecture by Heber Kimball inspired Dr. Sprague to indulge the same gift, she again provided an English interpretation of his words. In Patty's opinion, a meeting of the Female Council on June 5, 1852, was "one of the best meetings I ever had sister granger spoke toungues beautiful."[15]

To outsiders, glossolalia was almost as shocking as polygamy. It contributed to the disdain of men like Benjamin B. Ferris, who served for a time as territorial secretary in Utah. He considered Mormonism "a continuing illustration of the prodigious power of religious fanaticism over the mind." His wife, Elizabeth, elaborated the point in the chatty letters she sent home to Ithaca, New York, during her time in Utah in 1852. Her letters, which made fun of practices the Latter-day Saints considered sacred, eventually appeared in serial form in an Eastern periodical, and then as a book.[16]

Daguerreotypes of Patty Sessions (left), and Zina Young with her sister Presendia Kimball (right), c. 1858. Although the dresses on the three women reflect the general trend in the late 1850s for fuller skirts and bigger sleeves, the cross-over or wrapped bodice on Zina's dress is unusual and may represent the cut of the "reform dress" she was promoting in this period. Certainly, the clothing she and her sister are wearing contrasts with the tight bodices of the late 1840s and early 1850s. *(Pioneer Memorial Museum, International Society of Daughters of Utah Pioneers, Salt Lake City.)*

She described Vilate Kimball as "care-worn and sad," and Eliza Snow as a "delicate woman with raven hair and piercing black eyes" whose poetry "would scare the Muses out of their senses." She said Lorenzo Snow, "a small, neatly-dressed, dapper-looking man," kept six wives in two little huts.[17] Although she did not mention the Woodruffs, her husband insisted that Wilford had "a regular system of changing his harem. He takes in one or more young girls, and so manages, after he tires of them, that they are glad to ask for a divorce, after which he beats the bush for recruits."[18]

Elizabeth's favorite character was "Aunty Shearer," a person better known among Latter-day Saints as Vienna Jacques, one of the first Boston converts to gather with the Saints at Kirtland. Elizabeth described her as a "queer specimen of severe angularity of mind and body," who, had she remained in the States, "would have blossomed out early, as a Woman's Rights champion," a charge that to Elizabeth was no compliment. "On most points, except that of the Mormon Superstition, her ignorance is gross, like darkness, so thick that you can cut it with a knife and dull the edge."[19] Shearer's clothing merited special attention. A dress that was "some of her own handiwork in spinning and weaving" was just wide enough to cover her gaunt form. It was also "Bloomer enough to display a serviceable pair of brogans." Thus attired, she went out each evening to look for her cow, "armed with a stout stick, bidding defiance alike to the tawny digger and the grizzly bear."[20]

Among the Saints, Vienna Jacques was known for both her piety (in Kirtland, she consecrated everything she owned to the Church) and her independence. Although married long enough to acquire the surname Shearer, she clearly preferred the role of old maid. In 1852, she declined Orson Hyde's invitation to join his family as a plural wife, writing Brigham that she wanted a building lot of her own, preferably near the center of the city. "My wagon cover is so rotted that I can't live under it another winter," she complained. Brigham apparently complied with her request because she was living on her own in the Twelfth Ward in 1854, when she joined the Indian Relief Society.[21] That same year, she attested to a story her friend Jane Neyman contributed to the Church Historian's Office. Neyman claimed that when she heard Joseph's first comments on baptism for the dead at Nauvoo, she immediately enlisted an elder to administer the rite on behalf of her deceased son, Cyrus. Since Joseph had not yet told anyone how to perform proxy baptisms, this was an audacious act. Fortunately, Vienna Jacques was on hand to reassure the Prophet that everything was done properly. According to testimony the two women gave to George A. Smith in 1854, Jacques "rode into the water on horseback from Curiosity to hear the Ceremony & she assents that it was Precisely the Same as was afterward used by the Elders."[22]

Just before leaving the valley, Elizabeth Ferris accepted Aunty Shearer's invitation to attend a meeting of the Council of Health, which Ferris described as "a sort of female society, something like our Dorcas societies, whose members have meetings to talk over their occasional various aches and pains, and the mode of cure." Her description suggests that she attended a general meeting of the Council rather than one of the female meetings, although her focus was very much on the women. Judging from "physiognominal indications," she assigned almost all of them to "the lowest class of ignorance." The older ones were of the "wrinkled, spiteful, hag-like order." The younger ones were "more repulsive still—there was no youthful vivacity of appearance or manner. They were stupid, and sensuality had swallowed up all pure womanly feelings."[23]

The men were no better. Although in appearance the speaker, who she thought was Willard Richards, might have passed for a church deacon, he was in fact a "hoary-headed old sinner." Dr. Sprague, who had "a look of vulgar dissipation," made commonplace remarks on health, alternately boring and annoying the women. As soon as he sat down, one of the women "bounded up like a cork" to claim that Latter-day Saints should not be subject to disease or pain, since those conditions belonged to the Gentiles. That inspired a performance by Susanna Lippincot, "one of Dr. Richards's houris, and a fair specimen of the degraded class of spiritual wives."

> She fastened her red, gooseberry eyes upon me, and made some ill-natured remarks about the Gentiles. She finally broke forth into an unknown tongue, and, as near as I can recollect, those were the words: 'Eli, ele, elo, ela—come, coma, como—reli, rele, rela, relo—sea, selo, sele, selum.' This gibberish was repeated over two or three times. Sister Sessions then arose and translated these mysterious words. The interpretation proved to be a mere repetition of what the inspired Susanna had before said in murdered English.[24]

Stirred by this performance, a pale and sickly young woman holding a large baby on her lap came forward to be healed. "The sisters crowded around, and, with the two brothers, laid their right hands upon her, and prayed very much like the Catholics repeating their Aves and Pater Nosters over their beads." (Ferris obviously shared with other nineteenth-century Americans a prejudice against Catholics as well as Mormons.)[25]

Ferris claimed to have given a faithful account of the meeting except for softening language she considered "too gross to be repeated." She said that, as the proceedings ended, "Sister Sessions again took the floor, and related a dream of the night before, of a remarkable fight between the Lord and the devil. His sooty majesty came pretty near obtaining the mastery, but was finally overcome, and, as the moral of the affair, the Lord advised her to use lobelia in curing disease, as that would drive the evil away." Ferris left the meeting filled with "a superstitious dread" that she might be forced to remain even longer in a place she considered a "region of human depravity."[26]

Despite her obvious exaggerations and her caustic tone, Ferris captured elements in the operations of the Council of Health also apparent in Patty's diary. Clearly, the meetings' format was very much like that of the "blessing meetings" conducted among the Saints from Kirtland onward, with participants offering spontaneous contributions as the spirit moved. Although no Latter-day Saint source explicitly mentioned the performance of healing rituals in Council meetings, Ferris's description of men and women "laying hands" on the distraught young woman conforms to what we know of general LDS practice. Patty referred to laying on hands both in blessings she performed independently and in those she did jointly with her husband.[27] Wilford Woodruff recalled that on one occasion, after Willard Richards was stricken with what may have been a stroke, "the Twelve and all his wives were administering to him at the same time."[28]

Ferris's letters portrayed the Council only through a single meeting, one that reinforced every prejudice she had already formed. Patty's diary documented it in the context of a broader system of cooperative care focusing on female responsibility for women's and children's bodies. Recognizing that poverty or lack of help in the home sometimes made recovery from illness impossible, the Female Council began to act more and more in the spirit of the Nauvoo Relief Society, collecting funds for the poor, and carrying medicines and food to those they knew were in need. They eventually appointed one woman from each ward to collect and distribute contributions. The leaders met with these agents after regular meetings to give instruction. Patty occasionally joined in such calls. On a day when she wasn't feeling well herself, she reported being none the worse after walking three miles round-trip to deliver relief. "The Lord has strenthened me," she concluded.[29]

Participation in the Council also encouraged consultation among practitioners. Patty kept separate notes on cases that she thought might become controversial. One of these concerned Isabella Forsyth, an emigrant from Scotland whose baby Patty had delivered a year before. Although five persons in the family were ill, Patty was most worried about Isabella, who seemed consumptive and particularly vulnerable, especially since the dirt floor in her cabin was wet. She urged the family to call a doctor "lest I should be blamed." Isabella refused, not wanting anyone else but Patty to see "what a fix they were in" with four sick persons sharing the same bed. Patty agreed that they were "badly situated" but thought preserving their dignity less important than getting help. She kept notes of her visit on a separate sheet of paper that she eventually folded and pasted into her diary. Just as she feared, Isabella and her youngest child died. The rest of the family recovered.[30]

A few months later, she encountered a more dramatic case. Mary Miranda Rogers had been in Patty's company coming west in 1847.

After Miranda's husband died at Sutter's Mill in California, she married Thomas Rhodes, famous for leading a party of miners from California to the valley in 1849 with a reputed fortune in gold. Her husband's prominence in part explains the attention Miranda's case attracted.[31] She was in desperate condition by the time Patty arrived. Susanna Richards was already there. They soon summoned Vienna Jacques Shearer. No one could help. The infant's arm was in the birth canal, and it seemed impossible either to move it back or to facilitate delivery. The midwives suggested calling a doctor, but Miranda "said she had been butchered once by Dr Vaughn and she would not have a Dr neither would she take any lobelia." When labor stopped, she alternately rallied and talked of dying, saying something similar had happened when her twins were born. The day passed. Her attendants washed her body and changed her clothes. She ate her supper. When her pains returned, the child's arm was still "in the birth place."[32]

Sometime between ten and eleven at night, Miranda clutched her left side and cried out. The midwives tried to summon Willard Richards, but he could not come. Dr. Sprague was ill. Brigham was nowhere to be found. At 1:00 a.m., they called Wilford Woodruff, who brought Franklin Richards. The men gave her a blessing shortly before she died. Wilford closed her eyes. Within an hour, the First Presidency, several other Apostles, and a Dr. Andrews arrived to perform a postmortem. According to Wilford, who took notes in shorthand, the "child had torn the womb to bits with his feet." Preaching the funeral sermon the next day, Brigham said, "Women were not made to die in child bed as sister Rhodes has done." He assured her friends and family that she lived still. If they could escape their own bodies, they could see her and shake hands with her in spirit. Patty thought it a "great discourse," especially the part about no one being to blame. Days later, she found what she thought were "mortification sores" on her own hands, caused, she thought, from touching blood on the sheet when the body was opened. As Brigham said, "It is death that has caused it. Death is in the land around us. It is here."[33]

For a few years, the Council of Health was a focal point in Patty's life. She recorded seven meetings in 1850, ten in 1851, and twenty-seven in 1852. Although she noted fewer meetings in 1853 and 1854, in part because other activities entered her diary, by 1855, meetings of the Council, which now included separate "midwives meetings," had resumed their 1852 level.[34] But there were many others things to do. In 1854, Lorenzo Snow organized the Polysophical Society, where would-be writers and intellectuals dressed in their best clothes could share poetry, essays, and music. Patty occasionally attended, perhaps because her friends Eliza and Zina were involved.[35] More to her liking was the "dancing school." The exercise—and the joy—sustained her. In January and February 1854, in addition to continuing work as a midwife, she attended parties at the Social Hall and a public meeting concerning the possible route of a railroad.[36] In May, she "went to school to learn the new alphabet." The Deseret Alphabet, which was loosely based on a form of shorthand, simplified English spelling and pronunciation.[37] Patty had a passion for learning in whatever form. The next year, she regularly attended a series of lectures by Dr. William France, a graduate of the University of Glasgow, who had joined the Church and immigrated to the Salt Lake Valley.[38]

Ultimately, her most important activity in 1854 was her presidency of what became known as the Indian Relief Society.

"the organizeing of Relief Soceitys in all the Wards"

The new organization was inspired by two related developments: a violent conflict between Mormon settlers and a band of Utes led by the Mormons' former ally Walkara, or Walker; and a movement to send missionaries to Paiute communities in central Utah.[39] "Quite a fuss with the Indians," Patty noted in late July 1853, as reports came in of mounting violence.[40] Brigham tried to tamp down panic, assuring anxious settlers that everything was happening according to God's will. If the Indians had grown restive, people had only themselves to blame. They had moved into new areas too quickly and had not prepared for the possibility of war. If they wanted peace, they should have built forts, protected their cattle, and refused to trade rifles. Other talks given in the Tabernacle that fall made the same argument.[41]

Brigham was quite willing to use arms to subdue Walker, but he thought the neighboring Paiutes could be more easily conquered through religion. Turning to Book of Mormon prophecies, he told the Saints that God had brought them into "the midst of the Lamanites" precisely so they could save them. The "poor, ignorant Lamanites who surround us, and are in our midst, at our own doors . . . are a remnant of the House of Israel, they are of the seed of Abraham, and the Book of Mormon, and all the prophecies concerning that people declare that the gospel shall be preached unto them. And we have it to do, and it is time for us to begin." Men should learn tribal languages. They should teach Indians to work rather than steal. Above all, they should "deal with them honestly and righteously in all things. Any man who cheats a Lamanite should be dealt with more severely, than for cheating a white man."[42] Although God had cursed Lamanites with a dark skin for their sinfulness, those who repented would help prepare the earth for the second coming of Jesus.[43] Parley Pratt suggested that the Saints provide clothing for the Lamanites. He acknowledged that when the pioneers arrived in the territory they had all they could do to clothe themselves; now that things were a bit better, they could share what they had. If the Saints did their part to "redeem the children of Nephi and Laman," they, too, would receive rich blessings.[44]

On January 24, 1854, eighteen women met at the home of Matilda Dudley, a thirty-five-year-old convert from Pennsylvania, to organize a society for Indian relief. No one told them to do it. They were, to all appearances, ordinary women and girls, ranging in age from fifty-seven to thirteen. None kept a diary, though they took care to keep and preserve minutes of their meetings. Nor were any of them married to prominent men. They were born in New England, New York, Pennsylvania, Ohio, and Tennessee, and in the British Isles—four from England and one each from Ireland and Wales. Three were single, ten were married in monogamy, five in polygamy, although the number of polygamists increased by the end of the decade. The secretary, Amanda Smith, who was known for having survived the Haun's Mill Massacre in Missouri, was the only one of the founders to have otherwise made a ripple in church history. She was now single, having been granted a divorce from her second husband.[45]

Although the minutes did not describe the textile work the women did during meetings, they did give the names of those who attended and indicated at whose homes they met. Sometimes they listed the hymns the sisters sang.[46] On April 14, 1854, the choice was "Redeemer of Israel," an adaptation by William W. Phelps of an eighteenth-century English text by Joseph Swain. While Swain's verses focused on a solitary Christian addressing his savior, Phelps described a group led, like the children of Israel, through a wilderness, an experience that for these women must have seemed real.[47] Dropping Swain's "I" for the plural "we," the song looked forward to the second coming.

> We know he is coming
> To gather his sheep;
> And plant them in Zion, in love,
> For why in the valley

> Of death should they weep,
> Or alone in the wilderness rove?[48]

These women were confident that the Redeemer of Israel would not just save but *gather* his people.

On June 7, they chose another song by Phelps. It, too, described a wandering people in need of God's care, but it imagined, instead of a band of believers affirming their faith, a White Man querying a Red Man.

> O stop and tell me, Red Man,
> Who are ye? Why you roam?
> And how you get your living?
> Have you no God—no home?

Decked in "feathers, paints, and broaches," Phelps's imagined Red Man answered that he, too, was a son of Jacob, but his fathers had lost their blessings and fallen into darkness. For a thousand moons they had wandered, living by hunting instead of artful labor, succumbing to "idle Indian hearts."

The Red Man, as imagined by the White man, believed that with God's help his people might "quit their savage customs" and break the "Gentile yoke."

> Then joy will fill our bosoms,
> And blessings crown our days,
> To live in pure religion,
> And sing our Maker's praise."[49]

Phelps's texts, though first published in the 1830s, had resonance in 1854, as Utahns began to reach out to the people whose land they had seized.

Although Brigham Young's famous slogan "It is cheaper to feed them than to fight them" did not prevent him from sending out the Nauvoo Legion to subdue combative Utes, he then turned to diplomacy.[50] Matilda Dudley's group was still meeting in the spring of 1854, when Wilford Woodruff witnessed Brigham's meeting with Walkara. Three years earlier, Wilford had briskly dismissed the Ute leader as "an ugly cunning chief."[51] Now he watched the play of power on both sides as Walkara accepted Brigham's gifts of tobacco and beef. Wilford seemed moved when a Ute leader named Tulpridge spoke through tears, saying that his wife had been killed and that he now wanted to live in peace. Assured by the Ute leaders that there "would be no blood in their path," the Mormons departed, taking with them two children, probably Paiute rather than white, who had been Ute prisoners.[52]

In the little Mormon settlements along the way, Brigham preached about the importance of reaching out to "the remnants of the House of Israel who are our brethren." At Fillmore and again at Parowan, he asked the sisters to think of times when they had spoken in tongues and prophesied about the redemption of the Lamanites.[53] At Parowan, he said he planned to propose that the sisters in Salt Lake City make clothes for the Indians, and he enjoined women in the new settlements to do so as well, especially for "little children & the women, the men I don't care so much about."[54] Perhaps he saw greater hope for converting those who were most vulnerable to being captured by enemy bands and who, not coincidentally, could be most easily integrated into Latter-day Saint households.

On his first Sunday back in the valley, Brigham made good on his promise. According to Eliza Lyman's diary, he not only preached "on the subject of the Lamanites becoming converted," he explicitly "requested the sisters to form societies for the purpose of making clothing for the squaws and their children." Lyman was present, two days later, when the sisters of the Fourteenth Ward met with their bishop, Abraham Hoagland, to organize. Although she herself was quite poor, she contributed five yards of factory cloth to the cause, almost immediately vowing to take in sewing, washing, ironing, or other work to earn money for more.[55]

Lyman's response suggests that although Mormons shared many racial assumptions with other Americans, their reading of the Book of Mormon nourished compassion. Even Elizabeth Ferris, who had little sympathy for Indians, noticed that Utah's inhabitants were "very charitable" toward the "wretched-looking objects" she often saw "squatting down in the very middle of the streets, devouring their food like dogs." She did acknowledge that the "papooses, with eyes glittering like little snakes, have humanity about them, for I can make them smile, like other babies, by chirping to them." Benjamin Ferris had no doubt that the Indians would soon disappear.[56] He would have been pleased to think that the Mormons would do the same.

Although Brigham's engagement greatly expanded Indian relief, it also ended the independent society Matilda Dudley had led. The final entry in the minutes explained, "This was the last meeting of the Society as Brother Brigham Young Counceled the organizeing of Relief Soceitys in all the Wards of the City and each member joined the society in their own wards and our President was called to preside in her own Ward the 13th by Bishop Woolley."[57] Bishop Woolley was, of course, the merchant Edwin Dilworth Woolley. Although an effective leader, Woolley was notorious for wanting to have things done his own way. One mark of his influence was the covenant the women approved unanimously at the first meeting, promising that they would "speak no evil of each other nor of the Authorities of the church but endeavor by all means in our power to cultivate a spirit of union humility and love." That pledge might have been a challenge for Dudley's newly appointed counselor, Augusta Cobb, but she seconded the motion when Dudley offered it.[58]

At least one woman in the Sixteenth Ward was apprehensive about the emergence of the new organization. When Dudley proposed calling it the "Female Indian Relief Society," Martha Coray objected: "No association could be virtually sustained by females but must of necessity be kept by their Husbands Father or Guardians." Dudley replied that the name was proper, since "the labor required was female Labor." Her proposal passed unanimously "with one exception."[59]

Amanda Smith, who had served as secretary in Dudley's group, became president of the Indian Relief Society in the Twelfth Ward, and Patty Sessions in the Sixteenth.[60] Phebe Woodruff helped spread the word beyond Salt Lake City when she joined Wilford on an excursion to a newly established settlement at South Weber, where she "spoke to the sisters about forming a female society."[61] By the end of the summer, there were at least twenty-four ward Relief Societies. Within a few months, their members had contributed nearly nine hundred items of clothing, valued at over fifteen hundred dollars. At the peak of activity, women in Dudley's ward contributed the equivalent of one day a week to the project.[62]

Patty's diary gives a good sense of what took place in her ward. As soon as local stores received their spring shipment of fabric, she bought lengths of from twenty-five to fifty-five yards, then cut the fabric for others to assemble and stitch. She purchased both calico and a heavier fabric called "hickory," a cotton twill with a fine blue stripe, favored by men in the goldfields and by laborers generally.[63] The sisters constructed simple garments—shifts, shirts, aprons, and child-sized pantaloons, clothing that could be cut along the lines of the fabric, leaving few wasteful scraps.

Two watercolor portraits completed in 1852 by the Mormon artist William Major show that Ute leaders, if not their Paiute neighbors, were already wearing a mixture of European and native-style clothing. The leader of the Pahvant band, Kono-sa, wears a hickory shirt, much like those made by the Relief Societies. In contrast, "Walker, War Chief of the Utahs," appears in a tailored suit of buckskin cut in European fashion but with deep fringe along the legs and arms and tooled or beaded decoration. His power as a trader in California, New Mexico, and the Rockies is exemplified in the mixture of accessories he sports—a woven head wrapping, a fringed and beaded sash, and both black and red silk bandannas. Barely visible beneath his coat is what appears to be a fine cotton or linen shirt. Kono-sa's modest hickory shirt shows the different resources available to the proud Ute and the more humble Pahvant. Both men, however, display a similar hairstyle, a single braid wrapped in silk ribbon.[64] (See color insert 2, page 6.)

In written sources, Paiute women are shadowy figures who, when approached, clutch their children and disappear. Given the threat of being captured for the Ute slave trade, this is hardly surprising. But not all of them were standoffish. A rare description left by the Mormon missionary Thomas Brown provides a closer glimpse of their lives. In the very week in which Salt Lake City women were organizing to make clothing, Brown and his fellow missionaries camped with a small band on the Santa Clara River. Earlier that day, the men delayed their own breakfast, not wanting to violate hospitality by eating in front of a Paiute visitor, but also fearful that if they shared their flour they might end up without enough for themselves.[65]

In contrast, when the missionaries approached a Paiute camp, they found the people "liberally kind with their wine, wheat & seed flour porridge & berries." Brown, a Scots immigrant, described the women carrying firewood, water, and their own children on their heads "as the Fish women of Edinburg carry their loads of fish." An old woman engaged in crushing berries "called aloud for me to come and sup, she handed me a large spoon made of the horn of a mountain sheep that would hold about a pint, full of this home made wine, she then set down a large bowl made of small willows & pitched within full of this wine to our men and we all partook freely of this sweet and nourishing fluid." When the missionaries responded to an invitation to sing hymns, "a good spirit prevailed and their fears gave way to confidence and love." As he listened, one Indian kept grinding seeds for more porridge, putting it into a large earthen pot of red clay.[66] (See color insert 2, page 7.)

Church leaders expected the missionaries to use clothing shipped from Salt Lake City to pay for Paiute labor on church farms. In this way, they would teach Lamanites European agricultural techniques and integrate them into the white exchange economy, ridding them of the habit of "stealing."[67] No one seemed to have noticed that taking horses and cattle was a way of pushing back against the incursion of alien animals on land the Indians depended on for the wild grains and berries they had so generously shared. It was also a way of compensating for loss of their own corn patches and watering places as whites moved onto fertile areas in the arid Great Basin.

In December, Brown reported that they had sold little clothing. "The few that have been steady and regularly employed in the settlements have been clothed, those that still prefer an outside & offish course . . . are fully engaged hunting our Small game—rabbits for their food. And the many almost naked we find on the Santa Clara & surrounding country have nothing to give in return for this clothing."[68] That they were "almost naked" may have had something to do with the desert climate. In warm weather, there was little reason to wear clothing. During cold desert nights, they wrapped themselves in intricately stitched mantles made from the skin and fur of the rabbits used for food. Still, Brown was hopeful about the reformation of the Paiutes, more hopeful, in fact, than about the reform of some of his fellow Mormons. He was especially harsh in his judgment of John D. Lee, a man given to dreams, visions, and resentments.[69]

Latter-day Saints who had accepted the call to settle in the beautiful but harsh valleys of southern Utah were often impoverished themselves. They looked with envy on the clothing arriving from the north. Isaac Haight, president of the stake at Cedar City, was responsible for distribution. Frustrated by his inability to supply all the needs of workers at the newly opened ironworks, he cast an eye at the Indian goods and wrote Brigham, "I think it would be better to let the Sisters have many articles that were made up for the Indians as they are altogether unfit for the Indians." He complained that even the best clothing would bring little return if distributed as payment for work. As a consequence, some of the clothing probably ended up in the hands of white settlers.[70]

When it became clear that the Indian Relief Societies had produced more than the missionaries could distribute, Brigham asked them to make rag carpeting for the newly constructed Salt Lake Tabernacle and assist bishops in relieving the poor in their own wards, including immigrants pouring into the valley.[71] This was the moment when Patty met with Shadrach Roundy to plan a meeting for sisters in her ward. They embraced their new duties with enthusiasm. Surviving minutes record thirty-one meetings between June 17, 1854, and December 1855. Meetings sometimes featured speakers, but mostly the women gathered materials, cut and stitched clothing or carpet rags, and distributed goods to those in need. People contributed old clothes—nightgowns, shirts, vests, and hoods—and they organized to spin, color, reel, knit, and weave new ones. They also contributed meal, flour, potatoes, salt, soap, onions, cabbages, and occasionally cash. When the carpet for the Tabernacle was finished, they held a celebration at the bishop's house.[72]

Activities in the Thirteenth Ward were similar. One of the most earnest contributors was Mary Ann Young, Brigham's legal wife, who wasn't above going door to door to solicit funds from her neighbors. Augusta Cobb was also an active member, at one point acting as supervisor for collective work when Matilda Dudley left a meeting early. Whoever kept the records was more systematic than circumstances actually required, however, since most people seemed to prefer working at home. Although there were lots of blanks in the carefully constructed tables for recording hours, cash contributions were steady, perhaps because the neighborhood was wealthier than most. On one excursion to identify needy members in the ward, Matilda Dudley found only two, which may explain why they were able to give a quilt to "Brother Brigham" and another to "Bishop Woolley," neither a logical target for charity. Honoring their male mentors nevertheless seemed like a wise thing to do.[73]

Taken together, the minutes of these young societies seem flat compared with those Eliza kept in Nauvoo. Although meetings sometimes lasted all day, the secretaries usually summarized them in two or three sentences. Hannah Tapfield King, a recent emigrant from Oxfordshire, gave a fuller account of a meeting she attended on March 3, 1855. She said that she "went with Sister Wilkin to the Bishop's to work for the poor as we are told to do." As the work proceeded, her companion fell silent.

> I smiled and said, were there wine on the table, I should propose Sister Wilkin's health in her absence! This set her talking and she spoke of her early days in this church, of her speaking in tongues and I asked her to do so now. After a time she consented, but first desired us all to join in prayer, first laying all our work away.

Another woman followed Wilkin, who rose and began to bless the sisters, laying her hands on Hannah's head and speaking to her in tongues. She promised her she should become great in the Church, should herself gain the gift of tongues and interpretation. "Indeed it was a rich blessing," Hannah wrote. The two walked home together and took tea.[74]

The newly revived Relief Societies are sometimes portrayed as successors to the Female Council of Health, but that was not so. The Council persisted, and when Phoebe Angel died, late in 1854, Patty took her place as "Presidentess."[75] Through 1855, Patty continued to work on multiple fronts. During a six-day period in late February, for example, she attended a meeting of midwives and another of the general council, presided over her ward's Relief Society, sought out winter clothing for "old sister Wilson," attended to a sick baby and a crippled child "with a bunch on its back," conferred with a local physician on some topic she failed to mention, sent a Book of Mormon to relatives in Maine, and responded to a call from a sick man who had apparently just arrived in the valley and whose name she did yet know. "I had to get an interpretor to go with me they were French I found them destitute of food I boiled some flour potatoes & me[a]t carried to them for their supper." It is impossible to know whether Patty attended the French family as an independent healer, a member of the Council of Health, president of the Female Relief Society, or a good neighbor. In daily life, her many opportunities to serve flowed one into another.[76]

"I red over several of the old sermons of Joseph"

A diary is a record of daily happenings. An album is a repository of precious fragments—often autographs, drawings, and poems. (See color insert 2, page 1.) The albums of Sarah Kimball and Eliza Snow offer different perspectives on female associations in Salt Lake City during this period. Sarah's album, which contains almost nothing in her own hand, documented friendship. Eliza's album, which had been a gift from Sarah, contained her early Nauvoo diary, but soon became a place for keeping selections from her own poetry, including poems that she recited at meetings of her brother Lorenzo's Polysophical Society. Taken together with fragments from other sources, these two quite different albums show how ideas about women's place in the social order developed alongside the more practical work recorded in Patty Sessions's diary.

Sarah Kimball arrived in Salt Lake City in September 1851 with her two sons, ages nine and four, her widowed mother, Lydia Granger, two unmarried brothers, and a young woman who had lived with the family for almost a decade and would eventually marry one of the brothers. Sarah's husband, Hiram, who was in New York attempting to rescue his failing business, came to the valley the next year, "financially ruined and broken in health." To sustain the family, Sarah taught school, first in the Fourteenth Ward and then in the house she exchanged for the "fit out (team, .etc)" that had brought the family west. When her youngest son was born, in April 1854, she took only three months' leave from teaching. Sarah's mother became president of the Relief Society in the Fifteenth Ward; there is no record of Sarah's involvement. She did, however, take in "a nine years old wild Indian girl" whom she named Katie. Katie lived with the family until her death, ten years later.[77]

Sarah brought her autograph album from Nauvoo. In Utah Eliza Snow added two inscriptions. The second, dated April 4, 1854, was effusive.

> Sarah, I love you—I have lov'd you long
> With love that can't be utter'd in a song—
> That will not perish with life's hopes and fear,
> But lives and strengthens with increasing years.[78]

By then, Sarah had accumulated autographs from Leonora and John Taylor, Eliza and Amasa Lyman, Heber, Vilate, and Presendia Kimball, and Zina Young. Zina's inscription, identical to the one she added to Mary Woolley's album, was somewhat morbid.

> *Say, would it afford you*
> *A Pleasing Sensation*
> *Some trace of a Friend*
> *To behold*
> *When the heart*
> *That now dictates*
> *Has Ceast*
> *Its pulsation*
> *And the hand that now*
> *Writes this is Cold.*[79]

In October of that year, Phebe and Wilford Woodruff added their inscriptions. With impeccable penmanship, Phebe offered a comfortingly sentimental verse:

> *May guardian angels their kind wings display*
> *And be your guide through every dangerous way. . . .*

In ev'ry state may you most happy be
And somemes may you think of me.

She or one of her daughters may have drawn the winged bird grasping a floral wreath across which Wilford added his name.[80]

In contrast to these highly stylized invocations of love and friendship, Heber Kimball's rhyme was strikingly personal, suggesting that at some point his friendship with Sarah had not been so smooth. He dated his little verse July 31, 1854:

> Sarah, thou mayst know I love thee
> For I once chastised thee sore
> Thou didst bare it like a christian,
> Now I love thee ten times more.

At the top of the page he wrote, "Whom the Lord loveth he chasteneth."[81] Sarah's allegiance to her sometimes backsliding husband, a man who shared a surname but little else with his cousin Heber, may have been one cause of that earlier chastisement.

Although Wilford also remained wary of Hiram, he was impressed with Sarah's abilities as a teacher. When he attended a recitation at her school in the Fifteenth Ward, he described it as "a Juvinile polosophical society," noting that it was the "same kind of a school" conducted by a male teacher in the Fourteenth Ward whom he admired. By 1856, Hiram seems to have recovered his health and equanimity, wisely demonstrating his loyalty to the cause of Zion by turning over his contract to carry the U.S. mail to Brigham Young as "trustee in trust" for the Church. The next year, Sarah succeeded her mother as president of the Fifteenth Ward Relief Society.[82]

Meanwhile, Eliza Snow was engaged in private efforts to reaffirm the importance of Joseph's teachings to Latter-day Saint women. In February 1854, ten days after Matilda Dudley gathered her friends into the Indian Relief Society, she and Elizabeth Whitney called on the Woodruffs. As Wilford described it:

> We talked over the days of Kirtland & other times. I red over several of
> the old sermons of Joseph not record any whare ownly in my Journal.
> We spent a plesant evening. Before they left Sister Whitney sung in
> tongues in the pure language which Adam & Eve made use of in the

garden of Eden. . . . It was as near heavenly music as any thing I ever herd.[83]

Wilford's brief description acknowledged three forms of remembrance—conversation among friends, the preservation of written records, and the recapitulation of spiritual gifts.

These same activities characterized other encounters involving Eliza and her friends. One of the few legible entries in Zina's now fragmentary diary described how, in the midst of a heavy rainstorm, she, Elizabeth Whitney, and Eliza met to share "a heavenly exertation in tongues by Eliza and a few words from unworthy me." A few days later, Zina "went over to see the President about the relief society, met him in the new room he greeted me with more kindness than he has for years I truly feel to acknowledge the hand of God in all things and help me o Lord to prophet by all things."[84] It would be interesting to know what she and Brigham talked about. Her misspelling of "profit" as "prophet" is intriguing, but inscrutable.

Although Eliza had by this point entirely given up keeping a diary, the poems she entered in her album provide a month-by-month, if not day-by-day, record of her thoughts. On January 30, 1855, she treated the Polysophical Society to a long poem on the topic of "Woman," explaining that, since a male speaker had previously addressed that subject, she thought:

> That a woman's self might speak of woman too;
> But not for "Woman's Rights" I plead or claim—
> No! that, in Zion, I should blush to name.

Once again, she dismissed the efforts of "Gentile Ladies" to improve the position of women.

> But all their efforts to remove the curse
> Are only making matters worse and worse.
> They could as well unlock without a key,
> As change the die of man's degeneracy,
> Without the holy priesthood. . . .[85]

Twenty lines later, she returned to the word "key," but not before offering a sardonic critique of romantic love as the basis for female power.

Eliza argued that, by focusing too exclusively on winning a man, a woman reduced her own potential as a human being.

> The season's gone when she could set her stake
> To which the will of man must bow or break—
> The time is past for her to reign alone,
> And singly make a husband's heart her throne:
> No more she stands with sovereignty confess'd;
> Nor yet a play-thing dandled and caress'd.

The word "singly" in this passage is a subtle reminder of Eliza's commitment to plurality. A few lines down she makes a more explicit allusion to Mormon doctrine when she praises the woman "Who thro' submission, faith, and constancy; / Like ancient Sarah, gains celebrity." Such a woman, she argues, becomes equal to man, and "with him . . . holds the key / Of present and eternal destiny."[86]

Meanwhile, George A. Smith and his clerks in the Church Historian's Office were working on a history of Joseph Smith, to be published in installments in the *Deseret News*. When they asked Brigham about including Joseph's sermons to the Female Relief Society, "he referred them to Sister Eliza Snow, who delivered them the original Sermon in the Female R.S. Record also delivered up one of her own Journals." Eliza's minutes, written in her own hand at the time the sermons were given, were apparently not good enough. Smith and three assistants worked until ten o'clock that evening, reporting that when Heber Kimball stopped by the office that day to hear Joseph's sermons read, he "liked it better as revised."[87]

The version of Joseph's speeches that they published in the *Deseret News* that fall, with Brigham's approval, not only added a new awkwardness to the Prophet's prose but reversed his cherished promises to the Relief Society.[88] In Eliza's version, Joseph said "he was going to make this Society a kingdom of priests as in Enoch's day—as in Paul's day." George A. Smith and his clerks changed that to "The Lord was going to make of the Church of Jesus Christ a kingdom of priests, a holy people, a chosen generation, as in Enoch's day. . . ." In Eliza's version, Joseph "spoke of delivering the keys to this Society and to the church." In the revised version, he "spoke of delivering the keys of the Priesthood to the church, and said that the faithful members of the Relief Society should receive them in connection with their husbands."

Whereas the speech Eliza recorded enjoined the sisters to place confidence in the leaders they had chosen to lead their organization, the revised version told them to "place confidence in their husbands, whom God has appointed for them to honor, and in those faithful men whom God has placed at the head of the Church to lead his people." In the original version, Joseph said, "I now turn the key to you in the name of God and this Society shall rejoice and knowledge and intelligence shall flow down from this time." In the revised version, Joseph said, "I now turn the key in your behalf in the name of the Lord, and this Society shall rejoice, and knowledge and intelligence shall flow down from this time henceforth: this is the beginning of better days to the poor and needy, who shall be made to rejoice and pour forth blessings on your heads." The day Brigham approved the revision of Joseph's speeches, he gave instructions for building a fireproof vault for church records. Eliza's minutes were not among those preserved.[89]

In a fascinating poem presented to the Polysophical Society in March 1855, Eliza imagined a seraphlike figure appearing at twilight, gently asking how he might help her. She asked the seraph, whose name was "Priesthood," why people suffered. He answered—*disobedience*. The poem's emphasis was not on original sin, however, but on the eternal destiny of those who, through obedience, became joint heirs with Christ. Eliza seems to have imagined herself as Everywoman in the person of Eve on a journey through a lone and dreary world toward celestial glory, as in the Mormon temple ceremony. Her allusion to polygamy toward the end of the poem is surprisingly candid:

> And what to Eve, tho' in her mortal life
> She'd been the first, the tenth, or fiftieth wife?
> What did she care when in her lowest state,
> Whether by fools, consider'd small or great?
> 'Twas all the same to her—she prov'd her worth—
> She's now the Goddess and the queen of earth.[90]

If earthly life brought abasement, submission brought eternal glory. The insight was deeply Christian. Eliza believed that ordinary women, like Jesus, learned "obedience by the things which [they] suffered."[91]

When she wrote, "I felt my littleness, and thought, henceforth / I'll be, myself, the humblest saint on earth," she expressed ideas associated in this period not only with women but with slaves, as in Harriet Beecher

Stowe's *Uncle Tom's Cabin,* published just two years before. There is at the same time a slant rebellion in her comment that feels more like Emily Dickinson's "I'm nobody! Who are you?" In Eliza's poem, the priesthood was neither an ecclesiastical position nor the power given to men to act in the name of God. It was a revelatory essence, a source of illumination. The poem ends, not with the words of the male seraph, but with an effusion of light emanating from "the queen of night."[92]

Similar themes appear in two unpublished poems that she copied into her old Nauvoo journal. The first is an epistle to an unnamed lady. Here, as in her earlier poem on "Woman," she betrayed her own struggle between a desire for eminence and her painful embrace of subservience. She reminded her unnamed friend that God knew what was good for her and that all she had to do was "obediently pursue / His Priesthood leadings." She did not say "leaders," but "leadings." "Leaders" ascended pulpits. "Leadings" were to be discerned through the spirit.[93] The second poem argued for complete self-abnegation:

> Though we keep every other commandment,
> In the one, we may be lacking still;
> Not to sell and impart our possessions,
> But to lay on the altar, the Will.[94]

Eliza surely believed that males must also give up their own ambitions in order to fulfill the commandments of God, but in her poetry, renunciation was woman's burden, woman's glory.

The assault on the Relief Society minutes did nothing to impede female participation in the practical work of relieving the poor. In a testimony meeting in the Eighteenth Ward on September 6, 1855, a few days before the Church Historian's Office published their expurgated version of the Nauvoo Relief Society minutes, Eliza gave "an Exho[r]tation to the Sisters." The minutes do not report the content of her speech, but it surely had something to do with the bishop's comments "in regard to organizing a society to make up clothing for the Poor." He set apart Eliza and several other women to continue that work.[95] As new immigrants poured into the territory, and drought and a scourge of grasshoppers threatened the city's survival, their work was sorely needed, and the bishops knew it.

13

"What a life of wandering"

San Bernardino, California, 1856–1857

Entering a makeshift structure in California that smelled like a stable, Caroline Crosby consoled herself by thinking that if the baby Jesus could dwell in such a place she could, too.[1] During twenty-one years as a Latter-day Saint, she had moved in and out of thirty dwellings—shanties, log and adobe cabins, a Polynesian cottage, a "cellar kitchen," rooms in an old Spanish mission, a house made of green lumber plastered with paper, and at least four covered wagons. On January 5, 1856, her forty-ninth birthday, she opened her diary and wrote: "What a life of wandering for 21 years; previous to that time I lived in the one town, scarcely knowing a change. I scarcely know which was the most agreeable, for the Lord has comforted me in my travels, and I have realized his guardianship in thousands of instances."[2]

Born in 1807 in Dunham, Lower Canada, an English-speaking settlement just over the Vermont border in Quebec, Caroline began her life of wandering after she married Jonathan Crosby, who had briefly visited her town, then faithfully corresponded with her for two years. He was already a Mormon. When she accepted the faith, they "set our faces as a flint Zionward."[3] In Kirtland, Caroline gave birth to a boy they named Alma after a Book of Mormon prophet. Jonathan worked on the temple, gaining woodworking skills that would sustain them as they moved with their fellow Saints from Ohio to Illinois, Iowa, and then, in 1848, to the Salt Lake Valley. After spending eighteen months on the French-held island of Tubuai with Caroline's older sister Louisa and her husband, Addison Pratt, they returned to California, where Jonathan found work as a carpenter in San Jose and San Francisco. In 1856, they moved to San Bernardino, a Mormon settlement east of Los Angeles.[4]

There is poignancy in Caroline's claim that she did not know which was most agreeable, the settled world of her childhood or her twenty-one years as a *wanderer*. Her use of that term is intriguing. Cows, children, and Indians wandered. A *traveler* knew where she was going. A *pioneer* settled. A *wanderer* lived in uncertainty. Caroline understood the words

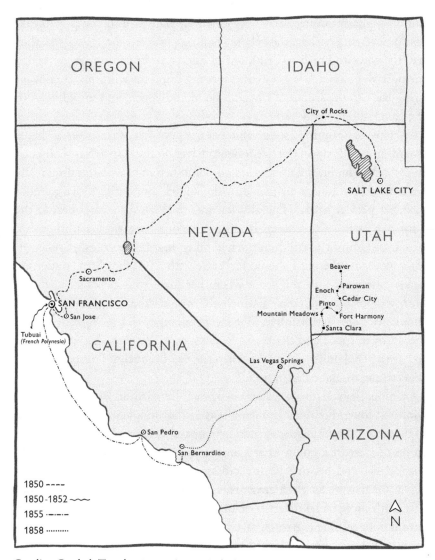

Caroline Crosby's Travels. *(Samantha Van Gerbig.)*

of a beloved Mormon hymn: "How long we have wander'd / As strangers in sin / And cried in the desert for thee!"[5] Recording her life day by day gave structure to an existence that might otherwise have seemed aimless.

She kept her first diary on the overland trail. Although she wasn't a self-conscious writer, she knew how to capture a moment. Sightseeing on the High Plains, she exchanged looks with a bison, engraved her name in a cave, and washed her hands and face in clear, cool water caught in the hollow of a rock. She was both amused and relieved when, after staying out all night searching for cows, Jonathan walked into camp at break-fast time saying he and the others "had not suffered for victuals as they had the cows and bells to drink out of." For Caroline, distance awakened memories of home; "almost every morning I find my spirit has been wan-dring back to the scenes of my childhood and youth, and mingling with the companions of my early days."[6]

Scraps of scripture, song, and poetry gave her wandering a shape. Boarding a sailboat on the Sacramento River on the way to San Francisco in 1850, she "found the musketoes on board before us and standing ready with open jaws to devour us." But, she added, "we desire to let patience have her perfect work." The allusion was to the Epistle of James, in the Christian Bible.[7] On Tubuai in 1851, left alone for a week with her son, Alma, and four little children she had taken into her home, she "reflected for a moment whether I should feel safer with a pistol or knife under my head." She went into the room where her niece sometimes slept, found both weapons, contemplated which she would take, then concluded, "I should feel safer with neither." She awoke saying with the Psalmist, "I laid me down in peace and slept." A few days later, however, she was grateful to have a pistol under her pillow when she heard someone "round my win-dow, trying to make discoveries."[8]

Unlike Tubuai or San Francisco, San Bernardino was ostensibly a Mormon town. Founded in 1851, it was initially populated by a company of pioneers led by Apostles Amasa Lyman and Charles Rich. It was meant to be the last in a chain of settlements leading from Salt Lake City to the Pacific, and became both a crossroads for Mormon travelers and a haven for mavericks. As a crossroads, it acquired a mildly cosmopolitan cast, with more racial diversity than in most Anglo towns. As a Mormon community outside the reach of Utah law, it sheltered Saints who chafed against authority or who lacked the resources or faith to complete a jour-ney to Deseret. While there were a few high-status polygamists in town (four of Lyman's eight wives regularly lived there), most marriages were monogamous.

Although Jonathan Crosby seems to have been sealed to a second wife in the last tumultuous months in Nauvoo, that marriage ended when the new wife declined to go west.[9] As far as we know, the Crosbys never again attempted plurality. Thus, Caroline's diary offers a useful counterpoint to those kept by polygamous wives. When combined with a series of letters between Caroline's niece Ellen Pratt and a friend living as a plural wife in Salt Lake City, it creates a dialogue between two marriage systems. Caroline's description of her own efforts to care for other people's children, and the searing stories that other women told her, allow us to see monogamy in conversation with polygamy during a time of crisis for both Utah and California Saints. Beyond that, Crosby's diary provides a glimpse of racial, ethnic, and religious diversity on the edge of the Mormon kingdom. It helps us to understand Mormonism as an oasis of meaning in a world of wanderers.

"full of strangers"

On an evening in the autumn of 1855, Caroline noted that all the Mormon houses in San Francisco were "full of strangers, saints just arrived from foreign lands. 'Flocking like clouds and doves, to their windows.'" The reference was to a passage in the book of Isaiah that to her signified the gathering of new converts to the restored church. California was indeed filled with strangers and "the sons of strangers," as the scripture said.[10] It was also filled with old friends and with people who in other circumstances might have been friends.

Caroline seems not to have recognized, for instance, that the "Mr Bidaman from Nauvoo," who entertained Utah travelers in 1850 under a bower made of pine boughs in a camp near the goldfields, was Emma Smith's second husband. (Lewis Bidamon's sojourn in California was brief. He returned home, with no more wealth than when he left.)[11] She was quite aware, however, that the "Sister Pickett" she met in San Francisco was the former Agnes Coolbrith Smith, the sister-in-law whose rumored relationship with Joseph had created a fuss in the Nauvoo Relief Society. When Agnes and her daughter visited Caroline in San Bernardino, Caroline gave her one of her precious seashells from Tubuai.[12]

In northern California, over the course of a few weeks, Caroline conversed with a ship captain from Sweden, haggled with Polish and Russian peddlers, enjoyed a "sociable chat by the kitchen fire" with a Portuguese cook, and prepared food for "Spanish boys" who worked for her landlord. Meanwhile, she cared for seven-year-old Alfred Tahinevai Layton, the son of a Mormon missionary and a Polynesian convert. In her diary, she referred to him as "our Tahitian boy." Later she would use the term "half-breed" to describe a child brought to San Bernardino from the Sandwich Isles (Hawaii).[13]

The names in Caroline's diary mapped a world in motion. In the two years she lived in San Bernardino, she amassed 650 references to 180 persons and families.[14] Repeated references folded out into full stories; single sentences hinted at what lay behind. When John Eldridge stopped in San Bernardino on his way home from a mission to Australia, Caroline and her sister Louisa were pleased to see him, for they had known him in Nauvoo. After dinner, he offered "a very minute account of his journeyings and shipwreck on his passage home." Other sources tell us that he had been with a company of twenty-eight Australian Saints on the sailing ship *Julia Ann* when it struck a coral reef two hundred miles west of Tahiti. Two little girls were washed overboard, and two women and a five-week-old baby trapped in the cabin drowned. The rest of the passengers managed to get footing on the reef, where they stood all night in waist-high water. Using a salvaged rowboat, the captain and crew ferried the survivors, along with a few tools and a chest of clothing, to a nearby island, where they survived for weeks on turtle eggs, fish, and coconuts, until they were able to row to Tahiti for help.[15] "It was a very exciting story," Caroline wrote.

A few months later, another visitor offered an equally compelling but darker history. "Negro Phill called in the evening," Caroline wrote. "Told us many anecdotes of the southern states, and the slaves." Philemon was one of twenty-six African Americans brought to Utah by Mormons from Mississippi. Listed as slaves in the 1851 Utah census, they were technically free on arrival in California, which had come into the Union as a free state under the Compromise of 1850. But "hands" claimed by Bishop William Crosby (no relation to Jonathan) continued to work for their former master, as did Philemon, who in Utah was listed as the property of Daniel Thomas, a judge. That Caroline called him "Negro Phill" shows that she saw him through the lens of race. That she acknowledged his "anecdotes" in her diary suggests that he captured her attention. Philemon's former master said he left "of his own free will and accord" to work as a bootblack in Los Angeles.[16]

Caroline mentioned a "colored woman" who was helping with the food at a quilting, but she did not refer to her by name. The most famous of San Bernardino's freedwomen was Bridget, or Biddy, Mason. Robert Smith, a member of the stake presidency who became disillusioned with Mormonism, tried to take her, another woman, and eight children with him to Texas to re-enslave them. Biddy surely would have had powerful stories to tell. She and Hannah, the other woman Smith sequestered in a Santa Monica canyon while waiting for a ship to take them to Texas, were listed as "Black" on the Utah slave schedule, but seven of their eight children were described as "mulatto" or "yellow." In a famous case, a California court freed them all. In Los Angeles, Biddy supported herself as a nurse and midwife, invested in real estate, and amassed more property than any other African American in the town. She eventually helped fund the city's first African American Episcopal church.[17]

Caroline was in San Francisco in August 1855 when a small group of Mormons arrived from India. Among them were a red-haired Scot named William Tait and his two-year-old son, Johnny. That such a tiny child was traveling without his mother surprised everyone. The father told Caroline that he had boarded a ship in Calcutta, bringing his son and all the family's luggage with him, expecting his wife, who was native to India, to join him. At the very last minute, he got word that his wife's mother would not let her come. When he reached China, he received a letter saying she would leave on the next vessel. Unfortunately, the next ship went to New York, rather than San Francisco, and William and Elizabeth Xavier Tait ended up on opposite sides of the continent and were forced to take separate journeys to Utah. William asked Caroline to care for his son while he worked in the harvest north of the city to earn money to continue his journey.[18]

She took Johnny into her home and her heart. When he cried at night, she let him into her bed. When the father was ready to leave, she washed, starched, and ironed both his clothing and Johnny's, determined to send them off to San Bernardino in style. "Johny kept in good spirits," she wrote, "but I could not refrain from tears when I reflected upon his being separated from a second mother, to whom he was as much attached as almost any child to a mother. I believe his father was almost tempted to leave him with me, but though[t] if his mother should come from Indie that she would feel bad to find he had left him among strangers." To her joy, Johnny and his father were in San Bernardino when she and her family arrived in November. Once again, she became the child's second mother, while the father, fearful that the winter journey would be too hard on the boy, set out for Utah to meet his wife.[19]

The father's journey went well enough, but Johnny's mother had the misfortune to join the Willie Handcart Company when it left Iowa City on July 15, 1856, far too late in the season for such a journey. Faulty equipment, a disastrous stampede of cattle, and early snow overcame them before they could reach the valley. Circumstances in the Martin Handcart Company, which followed about ten days later, were even worse. Despite a massive rescue effort, two hundred of the thousand emigrants died, by far the worst disaster in Mormon immigration history, and one of the worst in the annals of the West.[20]

Johnny's mother survived. In letters that reached San Bernardino on January 23, 1857, she "told of her journey in the handcart company, and of burying her little girl in Iowa." Her husband wrote about "going out to meet her, and of the sufferings of the company."[21] In April, Caroline learned that the Taits had settled in Cedar City, Utah, 250 miles south of Salt Lake City. They asked a friend who was leaving San Bernardino to bring Johnny to them. Caroline was of course pleased that Johnny would be reunited with his parents, but sad at the thought of once again losing a child who had grown dear. "It struck me very sensibly at the arrival of the time for his departure. How many times he had asked me to sing Do they miss me at home. . . . He kissed us all around and set off very cheerfully. But left sad hearts behind him."[22]

Caring for the children of "strangers" was Caroline's way of filling a void in her life. Although she only once mentioned having a miscarriage, she obviously longed for more children. In Tubuai, she had become a second mother to a little boy named Darius, the son of "Queen Pitomai," and a little girl namd Luna, the child of a white mariner married to an island woman. She mourned when their island relatives refused to let her bring them to the United States.[23] Had Jonathan Crosby been a polygamist, there might have been a ready-made solution to Caroline's problem: polygamist wives routinely became "second mothers" to one another's children. Caroline and Jonathan were both willing to defend plural marriage when asked about it during their time in northern California. On one occasion, Caroline even found herself in the middle of a debate, "Myself on one side" and three other Mormon women "all engaged against me, and very warmly too."[24] But in their years of wandering, they were either unable or unwilling to attempt it.

By the time Johnny left, Caroline was deeply engaged with problems besetting another family. Abraham and Olive Coombs came to California in 1846 on the ship *Brooklyn,* then, after several years in northern California, moved to San Bernardino, where Caroline employed their thirteen-year-old daughter, Helen, as a household helper.[25] In December 1856, Olive gave birth to her sixth child, her fifth daughter. When the baby was only six weeks old, Olive told Caroline she was thinking of going to the mountains to cook for the men at the sawmill. Although that came to nothing, in March 1857 she said she was thinking of leaving her husband. Caroline advised her against it.[26]

The next day, at Helen's request, Caroline went to the Coombs house to find Olive "prostrate on the bed her babe crying by her side" and three little girls, the oldest only ten, "standing around, looking very sad and forsaken." Olive had obviously been drinking. Caroline "seized the babe and the one next to it and brought them home," telling ten-year-old Emily to take care of her next youngest sister and to come to her house if they got hungry. The children soon learned to come to the Crosby house whenever they needed something. Sometimes their mother sent them, saying she had nothing to feed them.[27] Caroline offered to take the two-year-old into her own home and "do a mothers part by her." For a time, both parents appeared to consent. Caroline was delighted when her friends admired her new "baby." She believed she had done the right thing in taking the child, since a local physician told her that when he went to the Coombs house he had "found the mother in a state of intoxication."[28]

Just when things seemed settled, Olive changed her mind about giving her child away. She said she and her husband expected to leave soon for northern California, and she wanted to take all of the children with her. She admitted that her child was better off with Caroline but said "she was very unhappy without her." Caroline encouraged her to pray about her decision instead of being "guided solely by her impulses." Olive went home, sent her ten-year-old to the store for brandy, and drank it. Her husband was distraught. Jonathan told him that he had to make a decision, that he and Caroline would keep the child only if they had a firm agreement. Jonathan also told Helen, who was still living with them as a household helper, that unless she was resolved to stay when her parents went north, she had better leave their house immediately. Helen left.

Caroline packed up all the Coombs children's clothing, "regulated things in her mind," and admitted to her diary that she felt free again.[29]

Although her involvement with the Coombs family was stressful, Caroline had effective ways of coping. One day, she stayed behind while her family and friends went on a picnic in the mountains.

> I felt rather lonely after they were gone, and somewhat inclined to murmur at my poverty, and lack of the enjoyments which many of my brethren and sisters were blessed with. But finally took down a piece of select poetry which I had previously pinned to the wall, and sung it several times over. The text is "It is all for the best." I found much consolation from reading it, and my spirits became cheered and enlivened thereby.[30]

Her reference to a "piece of select poetry" suggests she had copied from one of several anthologies popular at the time a verse by the English poet Martin Farquhar Tupper that began, "All's for the best! be sanguine and cheerful, / Trouble and Sorrow are friends in disguise." One edition recommended singing it "To the Same Music as 'Never Give Up.' "[31] Despite a potential contradiction between the resignation implied in "All's for the best" and the determination expected from "Never Give Up," both mottoes seemed to work in Caroline's life.

"she sighs to be relieved from her bondage"

The same issue of the *Los Angeles Star* that reported on Robert Smith's attempt to take Biddy and Hannah back to slavery contained a whimsical story from gold country about runaway wives:

> The Placerville *American* says that out of nineteen families upon Reservoir Hill and vicinity, no less than six wives have left their husbands within the last six months; not because they were ill-treated by their husbands, but because they were treated by other men that they liked just a little better, and perhaps more so. We think it must have been the more so. Reservoir Hill is in the vicinity of Upper Placerville, but nowhere near our city. And beside, they have preaching there every Sunday.[32]

The reference to the town's having preaching every Sunday was a way of saying that the presence of a church in a town did not guarantee good behavior.

Caroline did not need anyone to remind her of that. San Bernardino produced more than its share of preaching and, judging from her diary, its own quota of runaway wives as well. Perhaps, from the men's point of view, the preaching was the problem, because it highlighted female religiosity by exposing the deficiencies of their husbands. For the faithful who had landed in San Bernardino, the question was whether to stay or to move on. Could one be a good Mormon in California? Or was it necessary to migrate to Utah?

Semi-regular mail delivery brought church newspapers to wandering Saints. Caroline and Jonathan probably subscribed to the *Deseret News* and the *Western Standard,* a Mormon newspaper published in San Francisco. For Caroline, getting a letter from Eliza Snow added another layer of identification with the Church. It not only "cheered and comforted" her heart, but gave her some renown among their friends. One day, a neighbor came to Caroline's house to hear a letter from Eliza read. Then she and Caroline carried the letter to a gathering at the Pratt house, where Louisa and half a dozen women "thought it quite a pleasure to hear from our beloved poetess."[33]

None of Eliza's letters to Caroline survive, but on June 28, 1856, Caroline copied one of her own letters to Eliza in her diary. It assured Eliza that there were sisters in San Bernardino who felt blessed "to receive a word of consolation, and counsel, from one of Zions daughters whose experience, and faith, command our sincerest respect and esteem." The formality suggests Caroline was a bit in awe of her accomplished friend. She knew she lived in a supposed backwater, and that remaining too long in California might create suspicion about her piety. She admitted she did not know why she and Jonathan had been unable to find a way to return to Salt Lake City, but she tried not to be uneasy. "I hear many complain that they cannot, or do not, enjoy as much of the Spirit of God here as they did at headquarters, but where the fault lies is difficult to determine. Perhaps it is reasonable that we should not, as we are certainly deprived of many privileges which are there enjoyed. But if I am capable of judging there are many good kind people here, who apparently enjoy the Holy Spirit."[34]

One Sunday morning, two of Caroline's friends called on the way to church. Having just received the *Deseret News,* she read a bit to them, "and they became so interested, that they declined going to meeting, and listened very attentively." She read three or four sermons from Brigham Young and some of the Apostles. Whether by happenstance or intention, small gatherings of this sort flourished. At another, the hostess brought out a large Bible containing the Apocrypha, a collection of books found in Catholic but not Protestant Bibles. Caroline read aloud from several chapters, enjoying "interesting stories which some of the company had never before heard." At another, the sisters "talked of past days, when the Church of Christ was small and could all assemble under one roof, to hear the words of eternal life, from the mouth of the prophet of the Lord. And our hearts burned within us, as we conversed upon the great work of the last days." On August 13, 1857, Caroline reported, they "related dreams visions &C. While I read to them, sister Snows letter, and the Salt lake catechism."[35]

The catechism was a list of questions asked of the faithful during the autumn of 1856, a period sometimes referred to as the Reformation. Believing there were too many lukewarm believers among the Saints, Brigham Young had called for stringent preaching and had instructed bishops to appoint home teachers or missionaries in each ward who would catechize their neighbors. The catechism wasn't a statement of doctrinal principles but a list of behavioral questions. It included explicit references to the Ten Commandments, as in "Have you committed murder, by shedding innocent blood, or consenting thereto?," but it added practical issues of concern to a rural society, such as "Have you taken water to irrigate with, when it belonged to another person at the time you used it?" or "Have you taken up and converted any stray animal to your own use?" For women an important question was "Do you teach your family the gospel of salvation?" Persons who found themselves in error were enjoined to repent, make restitution, and submit to rebaptism.[36]

Caroline was helping a neighbor nurse a sick child when a leader in the ward told her that Jonathan "had been appointed to the office of teacher, in this district. Said they wished him to go around, and take the census, and report at conference. . . . Said the council thought he was getting very worldly, and concluded to try him in Spiritual things, or his faithfulness, in spiritual things." Given Jonathan's steady attendance at church and apparent performance of his duties, this was an odd statement. Perhaps Jonathan had been a bit too outspoken in meetings or perhaps simply less eager than others to accept Priesthood callings. Over the next year, Caroline dutifully noted his attempts to fulfill his duties as a "teacher." He made the rounds of families in his district, responding promptly to need. One day, he left his work to give a blessing to a dying woman. A few hours later, Caroline helped prepare the body for burial.[37]

In their meetings, Caroline and her friends may have been conducting their own reformation by attending to their own spiritual condition and providing encouragement to those burdened with unbelieving husbands. In the letter she sent to Eliza, Caroline conveyed greetings from Roxana Repshar, now Roxana Patten, who "earnestly requested me to remember her love to you, and ask you to pray for her. She is a very unhappy women. Her husband is very cross and unkind to her at times, and has lately taken a part with the dissenting party. . . . I believe she tries to be as patient as she can, but she sighs to be relieved from her bondage."[38] Caroline expected Eliza to know whom she meant. Roxana had briefly attracted attention at Kirtland when she showed sympathy for noncanonical revelations. In Nauvoo, Joseph Smith chastised her for leaving her first husband, saying he was a moral man and a gentleman. Later, he changed his mind and sealed her to James Adams as a plural wife. When Adams died, Roxana married Andrew Patten, who was probably not a Mormon.[39]

Caroline frequently referred to him as "Old Man Patten." He had old-fashioned ideas about a husband's rights. "He advertised her, forbidding any one to harbor or trust her on his account," Caroline wrote. In early America, as in England, "advertising" was a form of self-divorce in which a man published his wife's name in a newspaper and said that she had "eloped from his bed and board" and that he would not pay any debts she had contracted in his name. Whether Patten had actually "advertised" his wife is uncertain, but he was resolute about not wanting to support her. Roxana responded by consulting a Mormon lawyer, Quartus Sparks. Caroline witnessed an attempt at mediation in which Patten told his wife he "did not want her about him" and said "she might have her clothes, and what little she brought there from Great Salt Lake," but nothing else.[40]

She stayed with Caroline for a couple of weeks, and by some means "effected a reconciliation with the old man," probably because he was ill and wanted her to care for him. For a time, his behavior improved, especially when others were present. The Crosbys began buying milk from him, and he helped Jonathan with plowing.[41] But he was still stingy with his resources. One evening, Roxana came to the Crosby house to say that her husband had gone to the mountain and left her alone without food or wood for a fire. She said she "had eaten very little through the day, Asked me if I had cold coffee or anything to give her." Caroline immediately prepared her supper. Although Caroline and her sister did what they could for their friend, they were honest in their response when, a few weeks later, Roxana confessed to feeling some coolness from them. Caroline assured her that she and Louisa had the same feelings toward her as they always had, but that they had a great many persons to "sympathize with besides herself." She added that they had "sometimes thought and said that were we in her place we would not complain as much as she does of her husband, but as long as she lived with him as his wife, should try to make him appear as respectable as possible." Roxana thanked her for the counsel and promised to heed it.[42]

On the surface, things seemed to be improving, but Roxana was anxious. The edifying literature she and her friends had sought out was not always comforting. She told Caroline she feared "she had deprived herself of the blessings promised to the righteous, by marrying an unbeliever, after she had been sealed by the Priesthood, to a good man. She read in the Seer, the law of the Lord concerning such persons." *The Seer* was the newspaper Orson Pratt edited, defending plural marriage.[43] In July, the Crosbys had been in bed about an hour when someone rapped on their door. Caroline found Roxana at the threshold. "She said she wished to put some articles into a chest which Mr C had made for her, and which was in our new chamber. And that she took the advantage of the night and her husbands absence as she did not wish it known that she had things secreted."[44] She was clearly preparing to leave. As long as her husband maintained the appearance of fulfilling his responsibilities, she had no grounds for divorce. Nor did she have money for a lawyer.

Desertion by one spouse or the other was probably still the most common form of marital separation, especially in areas of high migration. Caroline's diary offers some information on three friends, other than Roxana Patten, who embraced that solution. In her letter to Eliza, she mentioned a "Sister Sherwood" (probably Jane Sherwood) who had left her husband and now lived alone with her children, although she believed the "old gent is relaxing his temper a little, and shows symptoms of reconciliation towards the church." In this case, as in others, it was not just bad temper but religious disaffection that was at issue. Henry Sherwood, a surveyor who had laid out Salt Lake City as well as San Bernardino, was eventually excommunicated from the Church.[45]

Justus Morse, another long-term church member, was one of the few San Bernardino residents who had two wives, although it is not certain that both were in the city. His problem appeared to be alcohol. One of his friends said he was a good enough man when he wasn't drinking, but when he was he would "abuse his best friend"—that is, his wife. One evening, Eleanor Morse came to Caroline's house and asked if Caroline would come stay with her for a while, since her husband had been gone all day and "she was alone and very lonely." She may have been afraid as well as lonely. Eventually, he consented to give her a yoke of oxen so that she and her nine-year-old daughter, Charlotte, could join a wagon train going to Salt Lake City.[46] Mary Folks was not so fortunate. On December 10, 1857, she came to the Crosby house with her two youngest children, wishing to leave them with Caroline until she "could get them off to Salt Lake." She said her husband had been drinking and was very abusive. Though she soon sent for the children, saying he was "enraged at their absence," she told Caroline she "would sooner die than live in her present situation."[47]

Only one of the unhappy marriages Caroline wrote about ended in a formal divorce. Ironically, it involved Quartus Sparks, the lawyer Roxana had asked for help in resolving her own marital difficulties. Six months before, Mary Sparks had spoken to Caroline and Louisa "concerning her troubles with her husband." When they were called to testify in court, they hesitated, "as it had been represented to us to be a place unfit for the appearance of ladies." But they went and, in Caroline's view, were treated "very civilly" by the judge and lawyers. That evening, one of the lawyers came to the Crosby house with additional questions, and Caroline consulted both her memory and her diary. The diary must have been useful only for dates, because she did not record details about Mary Sparks's "troubles" anywhere in it.[48]

According to the *Los Angeles Star*, Mary sued for divorce on the grounds of her husband's adultery with "one Jane Coburn." He countered by charging that she had been intimate with a doctor in San Francisco. The *Star* claimed that most of the evidence "was of a nature that would hardly bear publication," though noted that the court considered a "most interesting question as to the legitimacy of the youngest child, which gave an opportunity to investigate the arcana of midwifery." That may have been where Caroline's diary was useful. She had seen both Mary and Quartus Sparks in San Francisco at various times, and the timing may have been crucial. The testimony of his adultery must have been damning, because Mary received not only a divorce, but custody of her four children, "peaceable possession of the dwelling house until further order," and thirty dollars in monthly support. The court guaranteed payment by putting a hold on notes Sparks held against three prominent church leaders. The behavior of Jane Coburn added to the story. According to the *Star,* she refused to return certain items of personal property belonging to Mary Sparks, and when the sheriff attempted to arrest her, resisted with a sword, a pistol, and a bowie knife.[49]

Caroline's diary reminds us that divorce records are an insufficient measure of family disruption, even in a setting where divorce was relatively easy to secure. The Sparks case emphasizes the need for a woman to have community support and a good lawyer, but it also highlights the importance of wealth. Without significant property to fight over, there was really no reason for a divorce. For ordinary people, leaving town was often a better solution.

As plans to evacuate San Bernardino proceeded, the relationship between Roxana Patten and her husband continued to deteriorate. She no longer felt safe being alone with him. When she told Caroline that he had been talking about trading a wagon and yoke of oxen for one of the houses the Mormons were leaving, Caroline said she thought Jonathan would make such a trade. After several days of haggling, he and the Crosbys agreed on the trade—a remarkable bargain for Patten, since Jonathan had worked hard on the house, even installing a special bathing room with a "patented shower system" to accommodate Caroline's interest in the currently popular water cure.[50] The Crosbys also agreed to share their house with the Pattens until they left.

One day, Roxana became very ill "with nervous headache." Caroline helped her into a warm bath "and after ward, anointed her with consecrated oil." Then she and Jonathan jointly laid their hands on Roxana's head for a healing blessing. Relieved of pain, Roxana praised God for his mercy and set about getting breakfast, saying she felt like a new creature. Soon Caroline began to feel pain in her back and lower limbs. "I did not realize for some time that I had taken her pains upon myself, until she spoke of it," she wrote. "My husband told me that it was wrong for me to lay hands on a stronger person than myself. But after breakfast I felt much better, and by degrees my pains wore away."[51] Both women felt stronger after this experience.

Just before Christmas, "Old man Patten" reported that he was ready to deliver the promised oxen. He seemed eager to get rid of his wife, and at the same time loath to see her go. He dealt with his own indecision by drinking.[52] On Christmas Day, the women prepared dinner together, but as everyone sat down to eat, "old Mr P— came in quite intoxicated." Even though his wife "was accustomed to seeing him in that situation, yet on that occasion when we were trying to enjoy each other society, perhaps for the last time, it was doubly mortifying to her, as well as us." Another female guest calmed him down by talking back to him "in his own style," and he left the room. That evening, cursing his wife, he came to the Crosby fireside and exclaimed that "she might go to Salt lake as soon as she pleased, but that he would not give her a cent." Caroline made him a cup of tea. Roxana left San Bernardino, and a few months later was admitted to the Female Relief Society in Cedar City, Utah.[53]

"Love fancies"

Throughout her time in San Bernardino, Caroline was closely involved with the lives of her sister Louisa Pratt and Louisa's daugthers, Ellen, Lois, and Ann Louisa. (Their sister Frances was often in San Francisco.) On August 14, 1856, Caroline wrote, "Went this morning to see the new Daguean, which takes likeness on an improved plan. Called Ambrotype and Photographick, admired his pictures. Lois P— had her likeness taken. Sister and I think of having ours taken <u>togather</u>." Although a photograph of Lois, taken about the same time, is now in the Pratt family collection, no image of Caroline with her sister Louisa has survived, nor does there

J. M. Ford, *Lois Barnes Pratt Hunt,* c. 1855 (above), and *Crosby Family Portrait,* 1855 (right).

Lois was the youngest daughter of Addison and Louisa Barnes Pratt. In 1855, she was eighteen years old. The damaged photograph of the Crosby family includes Ann Louisa Pratt with Jonathan, Caroline, and Alma. *(Special Collections and Archives, Merrill-Cazier Library, Utah State University)*

appear to be an existing image of Ellen. There is, however, a damaged daguerreotype of Caroline, Jonathan, and Alma Crosby with Ann Louisa. In truth, all three Pratt girls were very much part of Caroline's family.

Caroline was busy sewing and caring for hatching chickens when her sister Louisa announced, on a Sunday evening, that her daughter Ellen and William McGary were thinking of getting married that night. They wanted Jonathan to perform the ceremony. When Jonathan protested that it would take time to get permission from the presiding authorities, they agreed to wait until Monday. Caroline knew how to celebrate a wedding. Over the years, she had organized a party or "infare" for a friend in her little cabin in the fort in Salt Lake City, had provided space in her chamber in San Jose for a Catholic ceremony, had attended a genteel event in San Francisco in which the bride and her bridesmaid were dressed in similar white dresses and the room was filled with flowers, and would later help mount a Fourth of July wedding for Ellen's younger sister Lois. She also knew how to decorate a cake, even if she did not have all the right materials. Later, in Utah, she ornamented a cake with "wild roses and prickly pear blossoms in place of candies and sugar plums." So, when Louisa summoned her the morning of the wedding to help make a cake, she willingly complied.[54]

The wedding party assembled at ten that evening. "After the refreshment we danced one French four, and one cotillion," Caroline wrote. "We then escorted the bridegroom and bride home." John Eldridge, the returning Australian missionary, promised to carry the news to Salt Lake City for publication in the *Deseret News*. Jonathan said he would send it to the *Western Standard*.[55] Ellen announced it herself in a letter to her friend Ellen Clawson, who lived in Salt Lake City.

> Since I commenced this I have changed my name. Would you believe it? I can hardly convince myself of it but I suppose it is so. John Eldridge was here on his way home from Australia, so we thought we would have it over while he was here. He was all the one present beside the relations nobody heard a word of it for a week and when they did you never saw such a surprised set of folks as there were there.[56]

Intentionally or not, Ellen's brief description of her marriage set up a number of jokes between herself and her friend, jokes that exposed differences between Utah and California and between a woman deeply involved in plural marriage and one who had so far been able to avoid it.

Until she read "Mrs William McGary" at the end of the letter, Ellen Clawson thought her friend had married John Eldridge. Reading his name, her first thought was, "Well, that's always the way with girls that are so particular, and can't find anybody good enough for them, they are very apt to flat out at last." She quickly added that there was nothing wrong with Eldridge, except of course that he already had two wives. (She might have added that he had left those wives to serve a mission in Australia and had suffered shipwreck on his return.) Clawson was also amused by her friend's plan to have their real celebration on their first anniversary. "I suppose you had so few relatives present at the ceremony, you thought you would wait and increase them, before you made a wedding," she quipped. "I guess your mother can find room in the corner for the cradle." Her prediction came true. Ten months after her marriage, Ellen gave birth to a daughter.[57]

Ellen Spencer and Ellen Pratt met in Nauvoo in 1841, when they were nine years old. Their fathers soon left on missions, Orson Spencer to Europe, Addison Pratt to the Pacific. When her mother died in 1846, Ellen Spencer became, at the age of fourteen, a virtual mother to her younger siblings. Both Ellens were in Brigham Young's company going west in 1848; they lived near each other in the Old Fort until the Pratts and the Crosbys left for Tubuai. They had a great deal to report by the time they reconnected, via letters, in 1856. Still unmarried at the age of twenty-four, Ellen Pratt was admired as a teacher and a musician in San Bernardino. In contrast, her namesake was now a well-placed matron with three living children and more to come. Her husband, Hiram Clawson, was both well-to-do and rising in the Church, so it is not surprising that, shortly after she gave birth to their second child, he took his first plural wife, and would soon also marry one of Brigham Young's daughters.[58]

Ellen C. wrote her monogamous friend that Salt Lake City had "improved greatly since you left it, and is very much like a city of the world, except in wickedness, but we are not entirely free from that, for you know where there is good, ther is always evil also. I expect you hear a great many bad reports about this place." She had a particular scandal in mind. In the spring of 1855, several Mormon women had left the city with federal troops under the command of Colonel Edward Steptoe, who had wintered in the valley while investigating the murder of a government surveyor. Clawson wondered what her California friends knew about "Mrs Wheelock" and "Miss Potter," women who had been guests in her house.[59]

Female involvement with the soldiers had indeed sent many "bad reports" flying out of Utah. Heber Kimball was outraged. He claimed church leaders had treated the officers "as gentlemen should be treated and invited them to our parties and habitations and feasted them and tried to make something of them. While doing this, they began to play with some of the skitty wits, alias whores."[60] Among the officers was a flamboyant young lieutenant named Sylvester Mowry, whose letters to a friend suggest that, had all his plans succeeded, things might even have been worse. Delighted to learn that Mormons liked dancing, he fixed his sights on Brigham Young's twenty-year-old daughter-in-law, Mary Ayers Young, whose equally youthful husband was serving a mission in England. "She is as hot a thing as you could wish. I am going to make the attempt and if I succeed and don't get my head blown off by being caught shall esteem myself some," he wrote. When his conquest failed, he blamed the city's "damnable system of espionage—better than that of the old Inquisition or Napoleon's police." He told his friend that church leaders seemed "afraid we were going to f—k our way through the town." He considered the Mormon hierarchy "jealous lecherous and revengeful in all that concerns women."[61]

An anti-Mormon pamphlet published in England in 1857 claimed that "over one hundred of the Mormon women begged of the soldiers to take them to California."[62] In truth, the number of known runaways was closer to a dozen, but that was more than enough to create a scandal.[63] When the company's northern contingent reached Sacramento, a local newspaper debunked claims that forty or fifty Mormon women were with them, reporting that, with the exception of "a Mrs. Broomhead and three daughters," only one of whom was a Mormon, and perhaps two or three others, all of the other women with the soldiers had been with them when they arrived in Salt Lake City.[64]

The issue was not that women had left the valley, but that women of some renown had done so. Broomhead's daughter, Mary Ann Wheelock, was known for her theatrical performances in the newly opened Social Hall and had been intimate with a circle of women connected to Brigham Young's family, including the Clawsons. As Ellen C. explained: "I know the authorities of this Church, are very particular in regard to womens conduct with the Gentiles, and some of the girls that left here in company with the officers and soldiers, were so willful that they commenced with the officers just out of spite, thinking they could resist all temptation and flattery, but they missed the mark in doing so, and repented when too late."[65] (See color insert 1, page 4.)

"I suppose your greatest fear of this place is, the plurality of wife System, being so popular," she wrote in her second letter to Ellen McGary, "but if your heart was right, you would be willing to be tried, if necessary, in order that you might 'rise above all things.'" The mixture of piety and humor in this passage was characteristic. In her first letter, she joked that Hiram was willing to rescue her California friend from "Old Maiddom," if she chose. In the second, she sent his equally lighthearted apology for presuming to woo a married woman. The tone was light, but the implications were clear. Mormonism allowed a man multiple spouses while confining each woman to one—unless enlisting one's husband to wed a best friend counted.[66]

In November, Ellen Clawson's tone shifted. No more preaching about getting one's heart right, just an astonishingly open acknowledgment of her own feeling of loss when her husband took a third wife.

> I never thought I could care again if Hiram got a dozen wives, but it seems as though my affections return with double force, now that I feel as if I had lost him but I expect he thinks as much of me as ever, only in a different way you know a new wife is a new thing, and I know it is impossible for him to feel any different towards her just as present, still it make[s] my heart ache to think I have not the same love, but I console myself with thinking it will subside into affection, the same as it is with me for you know the honey-moon cannot always last at least if you don't know it now you will sometime perhaps.[67]

She admitted that her heart ached because of her loss, but she considered such a transition inevitable. Honeymoons ended; a settled "affection" followed.

But what was it that had come before? Passion? Infatuation? Romance? Though she did not name it, she acknowledged that it was a feeling a husband might experience again and again. He could not help it: "A new wife is a new thing." But for her the honeymoon came only once. Watching Hiram's relationship with young Alice Young deepened her understanding of what it meant to be a wife in a system in which new wives might appear in succession. She suddenly felt wiser, older, and more melancholy. Was this what it meant to "rise above all things"? She thought that Hiram's second wife, Margaret, might feel even worse, because she had been last to experience the "newness." Yet she insisted that Hiram was kinder than ever, if possible. "I do <u>know</u> one thing certain, there never was a <u>better</u>

husband in this world, and I know he means to do right, and I want to help him to do so all that lays in my power I do not want him to think so much more of me, that he cannot treat the rest as he aught, although it is womans nature to be jealous."[68] Ellen had embraced the tangled dictum of nineteenth-century womanhood—that women achieved moral superiority by asking nothing for themselves.

Ellen McGary tried to sympathize with her friend's situation, but she was too wrapped up in her own happiness to understand it fully. She and William were "as happy as clams at high water" or "as cozy as pigs in clover." It did not matter that he had few connections and little wealth. He was "one of the kindest of husbands and what more need woman ask in this vale of caprice and frowns?" Because he was a musician, she had access to all the parties she wanted, and they had "some very nice ones" in San Bernardino. "Those who think I have not done so well as I had ought must remember that happiness is not always an inmate of 'guilded halls' alone. 'Love in a cottage' you know is the most romantic and fully as apt to be enduring." She supposed that her friend was thinking, "Ah well those fancies will all vanish in air by and by." If so, she would enjoy them while they lasted and then let them go. "Love fancies are not the only things that vanish thus." She had already seen enough of the world to know that.[69]

"There is quite a reformation going on here at present. all the true hearted Mormons are being baptized over again, those who are not, are not considered members of the church. I think it is doing great good the meetings are more fully attended than before and they are more lively," Ellen Clawson reported. She wondered whether the reformation had taken the same effect in San Bernardino "in regard to getting more wives." If it had, then she might have to send "the comforting words 'grin and bear it'" to her friend. The mania for marrying had grown so intense that some men married two girls at once. Her uncle Daniel took four. She thought that if Hiram had not married Alice Young before the Reformation, he would have been asked to take one or two more. She supposed "the hand of the Lord must be in it," because the attitude of young women had changed so that they no longer thought of refusing. Still, there may have been more dismay than affirmation in her report that a girl Ellen had once taught "was married the other day to a man with two wives, and is'nt sixteen yet." She added, "but that is not so bad as thirteen."[70]

Ellen McGary responded that the Reformation hadn't made a change in attitudes toward plurality in San Bernardino, in part because anyone who had more than one wife was "threatened pretty strongly by the opposers"—that is, the growing body of disaffected Mormons, including Henry Sherwood and Quartus Sparks, who threatened to use plural marriage as a chip in their struggle for political authority. Given California law, Ellen did not think there would be a cause to send condolences to her as long as she stayed there. "William thinks there will <u>never</u> be any cause for it," she continued. She admitted that men changed their minds and that someday she might be forced to "'grin and bear it' or in other words 'suffer and be strong.'" Later, she apologized for joking. "My earnest desire, and ever has been to do right and to obey the will of my heavenly Father in <u>all things</u> when I can be made to <u>feel</u> that it is his will and <u>know</u> it for myself and not for another." The underlined words suggest that the six years she had spent wandering had given her a streak of independence.[71]

She was more defensive about her own parents. In earlier letters, she had somewhat casually noted that, after her father returned from yet another attempt to preach in Tahiti, he had remained in San Francisco, where her sister Frances had joined him. In February 1857, Ellen Clawson responded, "If you would not take it amiss, I should like to know why your Father and Mother live separate." By the time that letter arrived, her father had returned to San Bernardino, looking "fleshy and hearty (or more so)" than she had ever seen him. She explained that he had stayed in northern California because he was in debt. Although that was probably true, it also represented her own wishful thinking. Later, she admitted that her parents didn't agree about moving to Utah. "Mother has better courage to live in a hard place."[72]

Hints of trouble between Addison and Louisa had been building for months, and Ellen must have known it. While Addison was still in San Francisco, Louisa told Caroline he had sent a strange letter directed to his daughters rather than to her. A few weeks later, they received another "and not a word to herself."[73] Although Addison never engaged in open dissent, his conflict with Louisa, which may have begun years before over differences in life choices, was now entangled with a crisis of faith. In April, a San Bernardino leader took Jonathan Crosby aside to tell him he had had a private conversation with Addison in which he "denied the faith in some important points and spoke lightly of others." On a teaching visit to the Pratt house, Jonathan confirmed that report, finding his brother-in-law "extremely skeptical, and full of vain philosophy."[74] Yet, in June, Caroline reported a family dinner with the Pratts and other friends during which they sang Tahitian and English hymns and enjoyed one another's company. Addison was present for his daughter Lois's Fourth of July wedding to John Hunt, but in September, Louisa took a walk with Caroline and told her "of her trials with her husband, his hard Speeches, and the disunion that existed between them." Having heard such stories from others, Caroline was sorry to hear that her sister was also unhappy.[75]

Perhaps knowing that his daughters and their husbands were going to Utah freed Addison to make a difficult decision. Shortly after Christmas, he brought his wagon to the Crosby yard for repairs, saying he was preparing it for Louisa and their youngest daughter "but thought he should go another way." Like Jonathan, he sold his house and land for half of what it was worth, using the proceeds to prepare Louisa for the journey. She was distraught at the prospect of being left "to lead her family again, without a head." William and Ellen McGary were also despondent. Although Caroline tried to cheer them, they could barely smile.[76]

Addison stayed with Louisa until she crossed the first mountain, then left a letter addressed to Ellen, defending his decision to turn back. He told his daughter that if he had ever been warned by "the whisperings of the spirit," it was at that moment. He knew without a doubt that he should not continue the journey. He told her that the polygamy system had long been "an abomination to my feelings." It wasn't just religious differences that stood in his way, however, but his inability to reconcile with Louisa. He told Ellen that he had tried "every humiliating and condescending proposition that the case demanded," but had only met with disdain. If old friends asked when he was coming, he told her to tell them, "The time is not yet."[77]

On December 17, 1857, Caroline wrote, "2 years ago this day we sailed from San Francisco for this place. I little thought then, that we should stop here as long as we have. . . . But now the word of the Lord from the Prophet is to come to the valley of the mountains, as soon as possible, or consistent." On New Year's Day 1858, she and Jonathan finished loading their wagon and "set off, with our faces zionward."[78]

The wagon they had gotten from Old Man Patten was now outfitted in style; somebody compared it to a steamboat. They soon discovered, however, that, even with fresh oxen, they could not get it over the first mountain. While waiting for help, Caroline joined with others in melting snow in order to water their animals. The next day, with help from another company of Saints, they unloaded some of their baggage and carried it up "by hand . . . a very hard job," then used double-teaming to get the wagon to the top. At 10:00 p.m. on January 5, as Jonathan and Alma settled into their beds, Caroline opened her diary to write, "This is my 51st birthday, and here I am on the high mountains in the cold of winter, pursueing our course to the valleys of the saints. The Lord only knows what we may be called to pass through."[79]

They reached Las Vegas Springs on February 1. There, surrounded by Paiutes and shifting companies of San Bernardino emigrants, they paused to recuperate their animals. Three weeks later, they resumed their journey. On March 3, as they passed by the red rock cliffs at Santa Clara, Utah, Caroline imagined a wall stretched from cliff to cliff to create a safe haven for the Saints. Although she and Jonathan were pointed "zionward," she knew their ultimate destination was uncertain. They settled briefly at Pinto, then at a place called Johnson's Fort, before moving on to Beaver, a town two hundred miles south of Salt Lake City that would become their home.[80]

To understand why their journey was so uncertain requires turning back to events unfolding in Salt Lake City during the Crosbys' last year in California.

14

"The house was full of females"

The Fourteenth Ward, 1857–1858

I attended the female relief society at the 14th ward. The house was full of females quilting sewing etc.," Wilford Woodruff wrote on February 11, 1857.[1] He had sat in countless meetings since becoming a Latter-day Saint and had preached at more than fifteen hundred of them. Yet this was apparently the first time he had participated in a meeting where women not only filled the benches but presided.[2] Phebe was now president of the Salt Lake City Fourteenth Ward Relief Society. He and the bishop had come to bless her and her counselors. "We laid hands upon them & ordained them & set them apart to their office & calling," he reported. He was delighted with the progress of the society. In June, he found more than fifty women at his own house, sewing, knitting, stitching carpet rags, and quilting. "It is a laudable undertaking," he exclaimed. "I wish all go & do like-wise."[3]

In the United States in 1857, nothing was more ordinary than a gathering of white women to sew for the poor. But this was no ordinary setting. Phebe and her sisters worked on their quilts in the midst of a roiling conflict. Congress had not only rejected Utah's petitions for statehood but was considering ways of stamping out polygamy. Benjamin B. Ferris, the federal official whose wife, Elizabeth, had produced such vivid caricatures of the women of Salt Lake City, laid down the essential argument: Latter-day Saints were not just sexual deviants; they were aliens. Although God had allowed polygamy to exist among the ancient Jews because of the "hardness of their hearts," no modern civilized nation allowed a practice that "belongs now to the indolent and opium-eating Turks and Asiatics, the miserable Africans, the North American savages, and the Latter-day

Saints." The only solution was the "ultimate disorganization of the Mormon community."[4]

Francis Lieber, soon to be elevated to the first chair in history and political science at Columbia, built upon Ferris's analysis. The real question for Congress was whether granting statehood to Utah would infuse "a foreign and disturbing element" into the American system. It wasn't an issue of religious freedom—Mormons could believe anything they wished. It was a question of whether they should be allowed to undermine "one of the elementary distinctions—historical and actual—between European and Asiatic humanity." Unless Congress stood firm, the foundation of the nation might collapse. Another state or territory might adopt French communism or "become so filled with Chinese that the whites were absorbed," or worse yet "become *bona fide* Africanized."[5]

To Eastern reformers, Mormonism represented virtually anything and everything that appeared "un-American"—Islamic and Hindu religion, African and ancient Jewish religious practice, slavery in the American South, savagery on the American frontier, and heterodox ideas that to all appearances emanated from civilized countries. One of the characters in Metta Victor's novel *Mormon Wives,* which sold more than forty thousand copies in the 1850s, found it easy to accept Mormonism after she had "tainted the sweetness of womanhood, by yielding a belief to the philosophy of Socialism."[6] A character in another anti-Mormon novel blamed her acceptance of polygamy on the "mystical magical influence" of the Mormon Prophet, who had supposedly learned the art of mesmerism (a form of hypnotism) from a German peddler.[7]

A writer in *Harper's Illustrated Weekly* in the spring of 1857 raised an even more alarming possibility—that, in addition to the dangers of mesmerism, socialism, and mental magnetism, Mormon women may also have been tainted by what later generations would call feminism. Describing a purported visit to Utah, he said that among Brigham Young's wives were homely creatures "dressed in a kind of Bloomer costume, with pantaloons like those of the men, dresses made like a man's over-coat, tall straw hats with broad ribbons." In Utah, he concluded, strong-minded women actually helped their husbands get more wives. "What a lesson for Miss Lucy Stone!" he exclaimed, presuming his readers would recognize Stone as the woman who kept her own name and refused a vow to obey when she married fellow reformer Henry Blackwell.[8]

In the previous two years, the Saints had survived a series of crises. Wintering soldiers had produced drunken riots and made attempts on

Mormon women.[9] Then grasshoppers fell like black snowflakes from the sky. Drought followed, bringing near famine in the late winter of 1856. Finally, two companies of Mormon immigrants pushing handcarts to the valley had nearly perished on the High Plains. All of this reinforced a flourishing "reformation," which sent Apostles like George A. Smith into the southern settlements preaching the Mormon version of hellfire and damnation.[10]

Things had just begun to settle down when more bad news arrived from Washington. "All hell is boiling over," Wilford exclaimed on May 20, 1857, after reading Eastern papers. On June 23, word reached the city that Apostle Parley P. Pratt had been gunned down in Arkansas. On July 24, exhausted riders interrupted Pioneer Day festivities to report that "the United States had taken away the mail Contract & that a New Govornor & Judges & 2,500 troops would start for Utah soon." With radical Republicans in an uproar over the Dred Scott decision and his own party deeply divided over slavery, President James Buchanan had decided to tackle the one issue on which everyone seemed to agree—something had to be done about the Mormons. On August 15, Wilford put a new handle on the sword that Joseph Smith had carried in Zion's Camp. By the end of September, Hosea Stout was preparing "to go meet Uncles troops."[11]

In early October, amid all the hubbub, the sisters of the Fourteenth Ward won first prize at the territorial fair for their "album quilt."[12] When we look at the quilt today, it is hard to imagine it emerging from such turmoil. But it did. The quilt takes us beneath headlines to the symbolic language through which Phebe Woodruff and her sisters defended their faith, their civility, and their patriotism. This was not the language of indignation, but of quiet dignity. Interpreted alongside their own fragmentary writings, the quilt exposes the complexity of their decision to behave as ladies when assaulted from without by threats of invasion and from within by their own complex feelings about plural marriage.

"the desert shall rejoice, and blossom as the rose"

Album quilts were all the rage in the United States in the 1840s and 1850s. Like autograph albums, they brought together signatures, mottoes, and images from many sources. The Fourteenth Ward quilt exemplifies techniques and images used elsewhere during the same period. Its historical significance comes from the interplay of these seemingly conventional images with its own peculiar setting.[13] Because so many squares feature flowers, the quilt looks a bit like a garden, with plain blue strips, like paths, separating and unifying all the plots. No two squares are exactly alike. When two quilters used the same pattern, they employed differ-ent fabrics; when they used common fabrics, they developed alternative designs. As in ornamental gardening, each patch was meant to be unique yet contribute to an overall harmony.[14]

The finished quilt also looks like the street plan of Salt Lake City, which, following the general outlines of Joseph Smith's design for the City of Zion, was laid out on a grid, with house lots set at opposite angles on each side of the extra-wide streets. Since houses were generally small and individual plots large (about an acre and a half, with ten lots to a block), there was plenty of room for outbuildings, gardens, and orchards. Irriga-tion ditches bordered each block.[15] An admiring traveler wrote in 1858, "Probably no other city in the world of this size presents to the approach-ing voyager so magnificent a prospect." He saw "streets set as it were in a jewel of rippling brooks," with "rows of young verdant trees," "beauti-ful gardens and orchards," and "small fields thick covered with flowing wheat."[16] Obviously, he had not visited the city during a year when grass-hoppers had decimated crops and drought had drained ditches.

For Latter-day Saints, the ability to grow fruit and flowers in the sagebrush-covered valley was a fulfillment of Biblical prophecy: "The wilderness and the solitary place shall be glad for them; and the desert shall rejoice, and blossom as the rose." In an inscription, now almost too faint to read, one quilter embroidered the last part of that passage on the flowerpot she appliquéd on her square.[17] Given a decade-long struggle for survival and the near famine in 1856, the Saints' commitment to flowers as well as foodstuffs was significant. The Agricultural and Manufacturing Society announced prizes to be given not only for field crops, vegetables, and fruit, but for ornamental plants such as roses, dahlias, and asters.[18] In their mountain fastness, Latter-day Saints were bent on creating beauty as well as plenty.

Mary Isabella Horne used a stylized pattern for her appliquéd pot of flowers. Although scarcity limited her choice of fabrics for the foliage, she cut carefully so that the pattern on a now blue but once green print sug-gested veins in the leaves. She embellished her abstract roses with embroi-dered pistils and stamens. Sarah Ann Church's free-form cucumber plant is less elegant but more original. It portrays all the stages of gestation and development, from the bright yellow and orange blossoms on the vine, to the tiny green bulges emerging as fruit begins to form. Her green cucumbers have prickles. Her single ripe one has yellow flecks on its bright-orange skin, just like a real cucumber. The motto she wrote across the top of the square—"The tree is known by its fruit"—describes her own situation as well. She was about to give birth to her fourth child.[19]

Phebe Woodruff's square, now unfortunately split, once stood in the center of the quilt. Beneath an old-fashioned bee skep she embroidered "By industry we thrive," a motto by which she lived. In August 1856, when famine threatened, she took her daughters into the field to glean wheat, sleeping over and coming home wet after it rained. Things were more promising in 1857. In the first two weeks of March, her husband sowed gooseberry, currant, and cherry seeds, set out grapevines, transplanted almond, peach, apricot, and plum seedlings, and began grafting apples and pears. On April 14, he enumerated twenty-three varieties of apples in his orchard. The appliquéd fruit on Phebe's square acknowledged her faith in his efforts, although his diary gives no hint of her labor in gathering and processing the fruit their garden and orchard yielded.[20] (See color insert 2, pages 2–3, for illustrations of the quilt and individual squares.)

Although Salt Lake City women were still spinning and weaving homemade fabrics, they dedicated precious scraps of store-bought cloth to the quilt. All the materials except bits of carded wool in the filling had traveled more than a thousand miles by wagon train. One square, an intricately pieced patchwork, displayed sewing-machine stitches around the borders of the central patch, announcing to the world that, though its maker lived in the middle of nowhere, she had access to the latest technology.[21]

The quilters, too, had traveled. Elizabeth Cain, the owner of the sewing machine, was one of twenty quilters born in England. Another five came from Scotland, and one each from Wales, Canada, and Switzerland. Of the thirty-four quilters native to the United States, thirteen were born in New England, nine in the Mid-Atlantic, seven in the Midwest, and five in the South.[22] But a simple identification of birthplace does not tell the whole story. Phebe Soper Pratt left her rural Long Island home to seek tailoring work in New York City before migrating to Nauvoo, Illinois. By 1850, she was a plural wife of Apostle Parley Pratt and on her way to San Francisco, then Chile; in Valparaiso, she gave birth to her second child.[23] Willmirth East, born in Georgia, moved with her family to Texas when she was twelve, then, after marrying a former Texas Ranger, lived in Kansas before migrating to Utah in 1855.[24] Josephine Marie Augustine de la Harpe Ludert, identified as "Josephine Richards" on her square, was born in Switzerland to a family of diplomats and educated in St. Petersburg, where she met and married a German who was serving as the tsar's consul in Havana. After her husband died, she returned to Switzerland and alternately flirted with Catholicism and French socialism before becoming a Latter-day Saint.[25]

There is little evidence of these diverse origins in the designs employed. Phebe Pratt's needlework skill is apparent in her neatly stitched chintz appliqué, but nothing of her peripatetic past. The same is true for others. The one self-consciously ethnic square was made by Jane Ballantyne Taylor, the Scots-born wife of Apostle John Taylor, who created a thistle and a butterfly with plaid wings.[26] Suppression of regional and national identity may have been deliberate. In a poem recited at the Polysophical Society in 1855, Eliza Snow acknowledged both the diversity of the Mormon gathering and its insistence on unity:

> For none I cherish a partiality. . . . I'm not
> Italian, Hindoo, English, German, Scot;
> Neither American, Swiss, Welsh, or Dane,
> Nor any Islander from ocean's main,
> Nor Spanish, French, Norwegian, nor Swede—
> I claim no country, nation, kingdom, creed
> Excepting Zion; this I proudly name—
> This is the home I fondly love to claim.[27]

Eliza's litany of nations ignored the native place-names that she and her fellow Saints used every day—Utah, Parowan, Paragonah, Tooele, Wasatch, Sanpete.[28] She nevertheless captured one of the most distinctive attributes of Mormonism, its emphasis on gathering. Although most immigrants to Utah, as to other parts of the United States, came from Northern Europe, that didn't guarantee ease of communication. To take just one example, the Welsh immigrants Henry Hugh and Mary Rees Harries left Liverpool on a Mormon immigrant ship that carried 725 passengers who among them spoke nine different languages.[29]

By 1860, more than half of the household heads in the Fourteenth Ward were foreign-born.[30] Although the majority came from the British Isles, there were class differences among them. Eliza's friend the Oxfordshire poet Hannah Tapfield King was especially sensitive to the "hinting—and dabbing" on that issue from other women during her first months in the city. "Silly Women they only exposed their ignorance, and ill-manners," she complained.[31] Institutionally, at least, the quilters were committed to equality. According to its quarterly report for May 1857, the Fourteenth Ward Relief Society contributed $126, more than half of its total disbursements, to the Perpetual Emigrating Fund, a rolling loan system for poor immigrants. At a time when skilled carpenters, joiners, blacksmiths, and masons earned from two to three dollars per day, this was not an insignificant amount.[32]

Measured by real-estate valuation, the Fourteenth Ward was the second-wealthiest in the city, and Wilford Woodruff the second-richest man in the ward. No matter how prosperous a man was, however, Mormons believed he was meant to be a worker.[33] The old-fashioned bee skep on Phebe's square symbolized that ethic. The original name of Utah Territory was Deseret, a term derived from a Book of Mormon term for "honey bee." Although there wasn't much honey raised in early Utah, bees flourished as a symbol. The Fourteenth Ward quilters embellished their squares with everything but the buzz.[34] For Joseph Cain, whose wife, Elizabeth, was one of the quilters, bees symbolized the wanderings of the Latter-day Saints. In Utah, he believed, they had at last found a hive. If their enemies dared to follow them there, they would discover that, like "the bees who work and sing, / The Saints of God can also sting."[35]

As federal troops approached the territory, the Fourteenth Ward quilters insisted they were patriotic Americans. Kezia Pratt (one of Parley Pratt's wives), who cut her dignified American eagle from pre-printed fabric, proclaimed her allegiance to the United States even though she had been born in England. The print she used was probably a decade or two older than the quilt, suggesting that it had been saved for years in someone's scrap bag for just such an important project.[36] Using plain bright cottons, Aura Annette Cummings constructed a jaunty bird with flamboyant striped legs, a folk adaptation of the spread eagle in the Great Seal of the United States.[37] For Latter-day Saints, eagles represented both patriotism and resistance. Eliza Snow once described her country's treatment of her people as a "foul stain on the Eagle's crest." Other writers insisted that Latter-day Saints were the true custodians of liberty, and that with them the American eagle had "fled to the mountains."[38]

The Fourteenth Ward quilt was not only a garden and a banner of liberty, it was a diagram of social relationships. The quilters were joined by birth, marriage, and shared experiences as well as by membership in the Relief Society. The diagram on page 345 highlights squares contributed by Phebe Woodruff's daughters, her sister Sarah Foss, her niece Rhoda Richards, and all three of Wilford's plural wives—including Sarah Delight Stocking, who married him in July. Other relationships looped backward in time. Ester Ann Hoagland, whose maritime compass is one of the most spectacular images on the quilt, and her sister Caroline Snyder, who stitched an equally striking Rose of Sharon, were born on the Fox Islands of Maine. With their parents and grandparents, they had joined Wilford and Phebe when they set out from Scarborough in 1838. Leonora Taylor, who shared so many experiences with Phebe in the Old Fort at Montrose and later in Nauvoo and Winter Quarters, also made an impressive square. Scores of similar relationships can be traced among the quilters.

There is nothing peculiarly "Mormon" about flowers, bees, baskets of fruit, eagles, or a mariner's compass. Yet, brought together in a quilt made in Utah in 1857, these seemingly innocuous motifs carried a political charge.

"we discussed the Plurality Doctrine from first to last"

There is an earnest, almost defiant cheerfulness about the quilt, an attitude captured as well in letters and diaries written by Salt Lake women about the same time. "I can hardly wait until next week I want to put in seed in the garden, so bad," Bathsheba Smith wrote George.[39] Margaret Smoot was as enthusiastic about spinning and weaving as her friend was about gardening. She warned Abraham, who was on a buying expedition in the East, that her progress in household manufacturing might mean poor sales for his merchandise, boasting, "I am making a pice of woolen carpet for the exhibition. I expect to take the Diploma on it."[40] Optimism was the default mode for women who had faced so much adversity. "I'm happy, I'm cheerful I am merry and gay / From years end to years end [so] time glides a way," Bathsheba trilled, borrowing lyrics from a popular ballad. Then, in a move common in women's letters, she apologized for her poor handwriting.[41]

Cheerful on demand, Latter-day Saint wives were also skilled at self-deprecation. In a letter to Wilford, Phebe confessed, "I get cross sometimes among my many cares," adding that she hoped her "friends" (that is, the members of her family) would overlook her faults.[42] Margaret Smoot wrote in a similar mode, using the productivity of the younger wives as a marker of family harmony. Emily was "working away spinning," Diana was "busy with her work and tending [children]," and Anna, though troubled with toothache, "was able to attend to her work as usual." With mild

Illustration of quilt with identification of quilters (facing page). The shaded squares mark the contributions of Phebe Woodruff, her sister, niece, daughters, and sister wives. *(Samantha Van Gerbig.)*

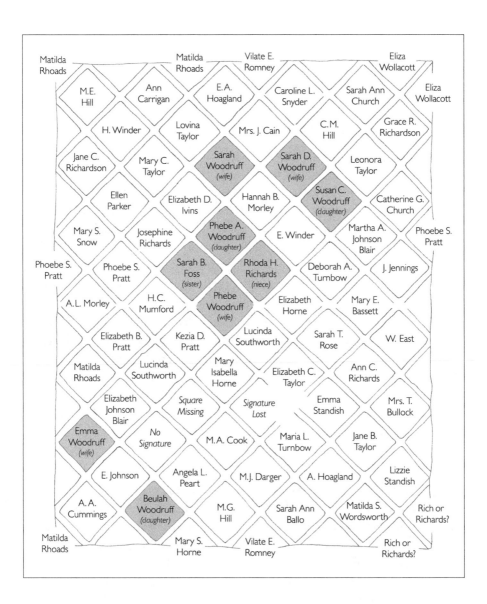

humor, she acknowledged her own faults: "As for Margaret it is about as usual with her, however, I do not think that is a very good recommend."[43] Relentlessly productive but never good enough, these pioneer women carefully avoided disparaging comments about polygamy—at least in public, or in letters to their absent husbands. But they talked about it among themselves, as their spouses knew. "I believe I will not tell you all," Bathsheba taunted in a letter to George, after noting that she had spent the evening with Phebe.[44]

There had been more opportunity for talk in the winter of 1855–56, when members of the legislature spent six weeks in Fillmore, a town 160 miles south of Salt Lake City that had briefly been designated as the territorial capital. The men departed Salt Lake City on December 2, leaving their families to celebrate Christmas and New Year's alone. In a letter written on December 26, 1855, Bathsheba reported that the neighbors had had "a fine lot of fun about Br Pratts getting married."[45] She did not say which "Br Pratt" had caused such hilarity. Parley Pratt's marriage to Eleanor McLean, who had left a husband in San Francisco, was great fodder for gossip, but since that marriage had taken place a month before, it may already have been old news. The more immediate target was Orson Pratt, who on December 14 married sixteen-year-old Juliett Phelps in Fillmore.[46] In his description of Christmas in Fillmore, Hosea Stout wrote, "No guns firing no boys hooping No petty fandangos, No brilliant cotillion parties Every man minding his own business, and perhaps some few wife hunting or rather hunting the raw material."[47]

Back in the city, Bathsheba's letter continued, "Sister Woodruff had a visiting party . . . and we discussed the Plurality Doctrine from first to last." She told George the women decided "that the men had the worst of [it] any how," and that they also "partly concluded to say to our Husbands to take all the wives they pleased as we know that they would anyhow perhaps." Her use of the words "partly" and "perhaps" suggests there may have been some disagreement on that point.[48]

In the next two weeks, Phebe wrote Wilford twice. In both letters, she dropped references to plural marriage into the middle of comments about other things. On January 2, she wrote, "Well if you felt like getting 1 or 2 of the &c, and see any one or two that will answer your purpose please do so I do not wish to prevent it any way,"[49] Presumably "the &c" was a euphemism for "plural wives." (Had Wilford at some point begun a letter to her, "Dear Phebe &c"?) Her letter continued with a bit of gossip: "L. Hardy has got him another wife Harriet Blair." Then she added,

"Don't let me stand in your way in regard to that."[50] Leonard Hardy and his new wife had both been in the Woodruff company when they came west in 1851. Wilford probably already knew that Harriet had divorced Seth Blair, a prominent member of the Fourteenth Ward. Since two of Harriet's sisters were already married to Hardy, she had some idea of what she was getting.[51]

A week later, Phebe wrote again. "We hear that all of the members of Congress are getting themselves new wives if so I hope you will not be an odd one among them." Without more context, it is impossible to know whether her comments were supportive or sardonic. "Don't let me stand in your way" might mean "Don't let my struggles keep you from doing what you think is right."[52] Her hope that he not be "an odd one" may reflect her understanding of the kind of pressure he was under. Yet neither allusion to plural marriage was in any sense reverential, and both are consistent with Bathsheba's summary of the discussion at the "visiting party": a wife might as well give her permission, since men did what they wanted regardless.

Mary Richards was neither teasingly supportive, like Bathsheba, nor cryptic, like Phebe. She was openly angry, perhaps even indignant. She had agreed to Samuel's first plural marriage since she was already close to his intended wife, her niece Mary Ann Parker. But when she learned he had promised himself to Helena Robinson, a woman she believed he had fallen in love with while serving as mission president in England, she was outraged.

> You speak of our feeling happy. Do you expect when you plant a
> thorn in your gardin; that it will bring forth peaches and Apples. If so
> then may you expect when you willingly plant the seeds of sorrow and
> mistrust on the hearts of those who love, confide, and look up to you
> that this will yeald Joy and happiness O alas I fear this world has none
> but little in store.

She was unable to understand how he could be so obtuse as to wonder what he had done to hurt her feelings; "light as you make of it dear Samuel it has built a wall between me, and the one for whose sake you have done it."[53]

When he wrote suggesting that she invite the intended bride to tea, she shot back, "You must think I have A very Child like spirit to hint such a thing." He had neglected her in order to court Helena. Did he really think she "should condescend to invite her here to gl[oa]t over my humiliation. Never." She claimed to be a slave to his wishes as long as he treated her with respect, but if he did not do so, he would get few favors: "tread on a worm and it will turn."[54] Samuel continued to write in an effusive, sentimental mode, as though refusing to acknowledge her pain would make it go away. Perhaps that strategy worked. On February 16, 1856, both Mary and Mary Ann were present when Samuel married Helena *and* her friend Jane Mayer. Wilford Woodruff was a witness.[55]

Plural marrage had a way of blurring distinctions between members of a family. In his diary, Wilford usually honored Phebe as "Mrs Woodruff," referring to the other members of his family by their first names, as in "I wrote 7 letters to my family to Mrs Woodruff to Phebe, Susan, Bulah, Moroni, Emma & Sarah." Phoebe Amelia, Susan, and Beulah were his daughters; Moroni was the twelve-year-old Paiute boy he had purchased the previous May. Emma and Sarah were his wives. But wives sometimes behaved like children. He stayed awake one night in Fillmore, writing a "lengthy letter to Emma upon the principle of obeying counsel."[56]

The letters Wilford received from his younger daughters during the time he spent in Fillmore were whimsical and childlike. Beulah reported that Willie had gotten a lamb from their neighbor Bathsheba Smith, and Susan told him, "Some little birds are building their nest under the Cornish [cornice] of our house the locust trees are all in bloom and the peach trees are heavely covered with peaches and the plumb trees have got some plums on them." Both asked their father about the Paiutes who lived near the new capital, Beulah begging him to "bring me a little Indian to play with." Wilford met that request a year later, when he paid forty dollars for a second Paiute child, a six-year-old boy named Saroquetes. "He appears like a smart active good boy," he wrote. Although he planned to rename him Nephi and educate him so that he might become a preacher to the Piedes, he became known in the family as "Keets."[57]

It took Wilford much longer to add a third plural wife to his family. In July 1857, in the midst of the furor over the coming army, he married nineteen-year-old Sarah Delight Stocking, who grew up near the herd ground in Fort Harriman where he kept his cattle.[58] According to a family legend, Delight's father asked Wilford to marry her because local boys were giving her too much attention. The story is plausible. Just a few months before, Wilford had offered his fifteen-year-old daughter Phoebe Amelia to Brigham Young, perhaps for similar reasons. Brigham rejected the offer, telling Wilford that he "did not wish to take any more young

wives but would see that she was take[n] up in due time." In the heat
of the Reformation, the marital age for girls, already low, fell so far that
even Brigham became concerned. He told Wilford that a man had come
to him with three girls, twelve to thirteen years old, but he refused to
marry them, since they "would not be equally yoked together." He did not
explain what being "equally yoked" might be.[59]

On the quilt, there is no way of distinguishing a Woodruff daughter
from a plural wife. Phoebe Amelia, who was fifteen, and Emma Smith,
who was nineteen, cut and appliquéd almost identical roses from the same
printed chintz. Susan Cornelia, who was thirteen, and Sarah Delight
Stocking, the newest wife, constructed similar birds from plain bright
fabrics. (Beulah, who was six, portrayed a cat on a cushion.) Wilford's
wife Sarah Brown, who at twenty-three was the oldest of them all, displayed both skill as a needleworker and originality in design, using scraps
from different pieces of printed chintz to create two birds hovering over
a nest containing three eggs. Perhaps she, like Susan and Delight, was
inspired by the birds in the cornice of the house. But the eggs in the nest
reflected her own position and Emma's as polygamous wives. Sarah gave
birth to her second child in January 1857, Emma to her first in October.
On the original chintz, two birds might have represented an avian mother
and father. In the Woodruff house, they were perhaps two young mothers
sharing the same nest.[60]

Bathsheba Smith's claim that men had the worst of it in plural marriage had some foundation. Men with any aspiration to leadership were
pressured into taking multiple wives whether they wanted to or not.
Shortly after Samuel Woolley returned from his mission, Brigham came
up to him and another man at a meeting and told them "to go & get us a
couple more wives each." Samuel ignored him. His wife, Catherine, may
have had something to do with that. In contrast, his older brother, Edwin,
who already had three wives and sixteen children, married a forty-year-old
widow and her daughter in 1857. A year later, both women left him for
California.[61]

Samuel heard Heber Kimball say that another man was released as
bishop because he "allowed his wife to rule him."[62] Samuel soon faced a
similar charge from his brother, John, who claimed that Samuel and Catherine hadn't visited much with him and other relatives since he returned
from India. John also charged Samuel "with being controlled, governed,
or influenced by my wife." Samuel denied the first charge but only "partially" denied the second.[63] In truth, his diary documents far fewer visits

with John, Edwin, and other relatives than with Sarah and Nathan Davis, who often hosted Samuel and Catherine for Sunday dinner. Sarah, who was Samuel's older sister, was the one who met him in the canyon when he returned from his mission. Her daughter Rachel Hannah was especially close to Catherine. But the tension in the family surely wasn't about where people dined. Nathan, like Samuel, had not yet taken a plural wife. John and Edwin may have considered him a bad example. But, unlike Edwin, Samuel didn't have to worry when Brigham at a Sunday meeting "told the sisters that were dissatified with their Husbands" that they were free to leave. Samuel didn't take a plural wife until 1867, when he married a fifteen-year-old English immigrant. By then Catherine was worn out by childbearing. She had lost an infant son a few weeks before and would lose two others by the time Samuel's second wife had her first child.[64]

In 1856, religious fervor inspired sixty-year-old Abraham Hoagland, bishop of the Fourteenth Ward, to begin a diary. On the title page he wrote: "Abraham Hoagland History, not very perfect."[65] His wives might have agreed. On January 22, 1857, Woodruff preached a sermon in the Fourteenth Ward in which he reminded the congregation to sustain their bishop, adding, "A mans family was his throne & kingdom & no man had a right to interfere with him." He wasn't really talking about interference from *men*. His real complaint was with women who "would spin street yarn & go from house to House & try to turn away women from their Husbands & stir up strife in families."[66] Soon Agnes charged her husband before the presidency and the Twelve: "He did not pay attention enough to her & provide well enough for her."[67]

Agnes Hoagland had been converted to Mormonism around the same time as her brother Apostle John Taylor. She joined Hoagland's family as a plural wife in 1847, after leaving her first husband, a non-Mormon who reportedly tried to put her in jail to keep her from going west, and a second, John Benbow, who was unable to consummate the marriage. (That divorce was granted on the overland trail.) In 1857, she had six living children, ranging in age from seventeen to one. She was clearly overwhelmed.[68] Brigham had little sympathy. He was weary from counseling disgruntled couples, who lined up at his doors all hours of the day.[69] He said, "There is many women that care more about their Husband sleeping with them than they do about God or his kingdom," adding that "if a man was to submit to such women he would not be worth shucks in building up the kingdom of God." He said Agnes wanted "pillow council instead of ward council." He told her that if she never again got "pillow council," she should simply "go home & do right."[70]

A square inscribed "A. Hoagland" is without question the least accomplished piece on the quilt. Perhaps Agnes made it in haste or despair. Maybe her seven-year-old daughter, also named Agnes, did the work. Whatever its origins, it contrasts with the perfectly pieced mariner's compass made by the bishop's childless third wife, Ester Ann. Ester assembled forty-eight perfect points, then added eight-pointed stars and delicate buds in the four corners of her square. In the center, she embroidered the comforting words: "Father is at the helm. All is right." She surely meant God the Father, not any earthly man. (See color insert 2, page 3.)

In 1861, Agnes Hoagland succeeded in divorcing her husband. The next year, at the age of forty-one, she married a twenty-four-year-old German immigrant named Wilhelm Schwartz, and gave birth to three more children. She did not leave Utah or the Church. Her story is unusual, but not unique. Eight of the fifty-nine married quilters (14 percent), including Agnes's sister wife Ester Ann, eventually divorced or separated from their spouses.[71] The beautifully ordered quilt, with its jaunty flowers and delicate embroidery, gives little sense of the anger, ambivalence, confusion, instability, and anxious acceptance that characterized plural households in this period. It does, however, convey the cooperative spirit, resilient faith, and pride of its makers.

"United We Stand"

When Parley Pratt was murdered in Arkansas on May 13, 1857, newspapers from New York to San Francisco described him as a seducer who perverted his own demonstrable talents to devious purposes. While living in San Francisco, he had supposedly enticed Eleanor McLean to desert her husband and become his ninth "concubine." They claimed that when Hector McLean sent his children to their grandparents in New Orleans for protection, she followed them there, kidnapped them, and sped to a rendezvous with Pratt in Arkansas. Although McLean tracked them down and had Pratt arrested, an Arkansas court dismissed the case. McLean felt he had no choice but to kill Pratt.[72] "Thus did the hoary old villain meet a just retribution at the hands of a man whom he had most outrageously injured!" declared the writer for the San Francisco *Daily Evening Bulletin*.[73] The *Fort Smith Herald* admitted, "We are pleased to see that such men—not men, demons—pursuing such a course cannot, with impunity, come into our midst, in Arkansas."[74]

It must have surprised readers to find a rejoinder from Eleanor a few days later. The press had portrayed Pratt as a seducer; she lauded him as an apostle of light. They pictured McLean as an aggrieved husband; she condemned him as a drunken brute. They described her as a fallen woman; she insisted on her virtue. "I am free to declare, before angels and men, that Parley P. Pratt was innocent of the charges made against him."[75] After returning to Salt Lake City, she began a sixty-two-page handwritten account that, in its intensity and detail, reads like a pro-polygamy novel that never got published. In it, she sketched out a heroic struggle conducted in a world of duplicity and danger. She said that, in an Arkansas courthouse, awaiting Pratt's trial, "the gentlemen apologized for crowding to see me, by saying they had never seen a Lady from Utah. . . . I told them I was aware a living Mormon woman who had been so fortunate as to escape from Salt Lake City was a great curiosity, but they must not take me as a fair specimen for they had so nearly killed me that I could not be like myself."[76] Her sarcasm betrayed her anger at the self-righteousness of those who claimed to be protecting Latter-day Saint women by assaulting their choices.

To the judge who asked if Pratt had lured her away from her family, she responded that, long before she heard of Mormonism, McLean had driven "happiness from our home by imbibing that spirit that comes in bottles. . . . Who but a wife knows bedroom scenes. It is true if I had gone for my neighbours and brought them to see him lying with his head hanging nearly off the bed, one coat sleeve off, and the other on, one boot off and the other on, and the vomit over his boots and all richly perfumed with old bourbon, (or some other well known beverage that adorns the shelves of the fashionable saloon) then I might have hundreds of witnesses to what I now state." But she was ever a faithful wife, keeping her husband's failings to herself, cleaning up after him, and providing clean clothing and a warm breakfast before he left for the day. And if he chose to preach a temperance sermon to his fellow lodge members at night, no one would know his secret.[77] When challenged that polygamy was unjust by giving one man sixty wives and leaving fifty-nine others without, she had a quick response: What virtuous woman would not prefer one-sixtieth of a man like Pratt to all of a husband like McLean?[78]

Although there is no way of knowing when the ladies of the Fourteenth Ward began to work on their album quilt, the few dated squares indicate a flurry of activity in July and August, after word of Pratt's murder arrived in the valley and as the threat of war became most evident.[79] Three of Pratt's eleven widows—Kezia, Elizabeth, and Phebe—contributed to the quilt. All three were especially close to Eleanor. Although the women of the Fourteenth Ward had a range of attitudes toward plural marriage, they seem to have considered the issues with their own husbands to be private matters. When others threatened their Church, they were ready to rally in its defense.

On August 16, Brigham told a congregation in the Tabernacle that the "United States had turned mob & were breaking the Constitution of the United States & we would now have to go forth & defend it." He asked if the Saints were willing to give up all they had accomplished in the past ten years, lay waste to their own homes and farms, and flee into the mountains if necessary. "The shout of Yes rent the air of the assembled thousands." Harriet Thatcher, who had just arrived with her family from California, said she had never seen such unity in her life. Unity was also the quilters' theme. "United we Stand," Elizabeth Johnson Blair wrote. Hannah Morley's square echoed that pledge.[80]

On August 30, John Taylor gave a powerful sermon on the relationship of the Latter-day Saints to the American tradition of natural rights. The first part of his narrative could have come from any Fourth of July oration in the country. The second elaborated a Mormon theme: "We have turned this desert into a flourishing field, and the desert has blossomed as the rose, and God has blessed our labours. And whom have we interfered with? Have we gone over to the States and interfered with them?" Just as monarchs had abused the rights of their subjects and Americans had cheated and oppressed their Indian neighbors, the U.S. government was now denying Mormons their rights. "What are we going to do, then?" he asked. His answer was firm: "We are going to establish the kingdom of God upon the earth."[81] On the Fourteenth Ward quilt, his wife Leonora made the same point more succinctly. She built the first five letters of her motto from eighty-nine pieces of cloth, the smallest only one-quarter-inch square, then finished the sentence in embroidery: "In God Is Our Trust."[82] (See color insert 2, page 3.) Through the month of September, somebody stitched all the blocks together with bright-blue sashing. By the end of the month, the Fourteenth Ward album quilt was ready for display.

At six in the morning on September 30, 1857, the citizens of Salt Lake City awoke to the sound of drums. Four hundred men who had been in the mountains were returning to the city. Eight hundred more were out on the plains, destroying supply wagons and stampeding and steal-ing cattle belonging to the oncoming army. "It is a solum time," Wilford wrote. "The Armies of the Gentiles are making war upon us because of our religion & we have to defend ourselves against a Nation of 25,000,000 of people." He told Brigham he was himself ready at any moment to go into the mountains with the militia. Instead, he went to the Agricultural and Manufacturing Society Fair, to judge the fruit and flowers.[83] If he saw the quilt Phebe and her sisters had made, he did not mention it. According to the *Deseret News,* the First, Second, Third, Seventh, Ninth, Thirteenth, and Fourteenth Wards all displayed album quilts. The Thirteenth Ward won for workmanship, the Fourteenth Ward for design. Sarah Kimball's Fifteenth Ward sisters won a certificate for their cow-hair blanket. Patty Sessions won third prize for her plums.[84]

Over the next few weeks, Mormon troops continued to bring in cattle. Their spies reported that the federal army was on quarter-rations, and men were deserting.[85] Like other armies in this period, these troops had women among them. On October 13, Eliza Snow published a poem enti-tled "The Ladies of Utah to the Ladies of the United States Camp." It asked:

> Why are you in these mountains,
> Expos'd to frost and snows,
> Far from your shelt'ring houses—
> From comfort and repose?
> Has cruel persecution,
> With unrelenting hand,
> Thrust you from home and kindred
> And from your native land?

No, she answered, the women of the army had joined a crusade against a people they did not know. Perhaps, through suffering, they would dis-cover that "All satan's foul devices / 'Gainst Zion will be foil'd."[86]

The crusade against the approaching army did not defeat it, but it slowed its progress. With winter approaching, the troops had little choice but to hunker down. They did indeed suffer. Elizabeth Cumming, wife of the man President Buchanan had sent to replace Brigham Young as governor, had frostbite so extreme that for weeks she could not walk. Yet she wrote relentlessly cheerful letters home and, as spring approached, reported on rumors flying back and forth across the mountains. Peace negotiations facilitated by Thomas L. Kane, an old friend of the Mormons, seemed promising. Perhaps the conflict between the Saints and the national government would be resolved by diplomacy.[87]

Unfortunately, in another part of Utah Territory, events had already taken a violent turn.

"The scene of Blood has Commenced"

On September 29, 1857, John D. Lee, a church leader from the little town of Harmony in southern Utah, arrived in Salt Lake City with news that on September 11 a band of Paiute Indians had ambushed a company of emigrants passing through a place called Mountain Meadows on their way to California, and had massacred all the adults and most of the children. He told Wilford Woodruff that local Mormons had pacified the Indians, rescued eight or ten children, and buried the dead. In truth, Lee, with other Mormon leaders in the southern settlements, had orchestrated the massacre and enticed the Paiutes to participate. As if constructing his own alibi, Lee blamed the carnage on the victims themselves. Some "belonged to the mob in Missouri & Illinois," he told Wilford, adding, "He did not think their was a drop of innocent Blood in their Camp for he had too [two] of their Children in his house & he Could not get but one to kneel down in prayer time & the other would laugh at her for doing it & they would sware like pirates." Wilford seems to have believed Lee's story, interpreting the slaughter as the beginning of apocalyptic events prophesied in scripture: "The scene of Blood has Commenced & Joseph said we should see so much of it that it would make our hearts sick."[88]

We do not know how Salt Lake City women who had spent so much of their own time and energy making clothing for the Southern Paiutes responded to the news of the massacre. It is hard to read the minutes of the quite different Female Benevolent Society, founded in Cedar City in 1856, with a neutral eye knowing that the men whose voices dominated the minutes also ordered the slaughter. What is striking is not the content of the speeches but the near absence of women's voices. Stake president Isaac Haight reminded the sisters, "As Christ is the head of the Church and it is subject to him, so is the woman subject to her own husband." His counselor John Higbee warned that any women who "would speak or go against the Plurality were in darkness." A Sister Whittaker responded defensively, explaining that she always spoke positively "on the principles of the new and Everlasting covenant" and that she was not aware that "any of the members disbelieved the Principle." But in these minutes female engagement was rare. In March, Elias Morris admonished the women, "When your husbands are called on duties either by day or by night, mind your own business, and ask no Questions."[89] Although Isaac Haight and Elias Morris were not at the massacre, they helped to plan it. John Higbee, the third member of the stake presidency, led troops to the site, gave the order for the slaughter to begin, and participated in the looting of the bodies.[90]

Whether their wives would have asked questions had they the opportunty to do so, we do not know. At a female meeting on September 10, Sister Haight told the sisters "that these were squally times, and we ought to attend to secret prayer on behalf of our husbands, sons, fathers, brothers." She urged the sisters to teach their children principles of righteousness and "to implant a desire in their hearts to avenge the blood of the Prophets," an allusion perhaps to the false rumor that some of the emigrants were from Missouri.[91]

The news of the slaughter reached San Bernardino on September 30, one day after John D. Lee arrived in Salt Lake City with the same gruesome tale. Caroline Crosby's informant told her that the migrants enraged the Indians "by poisoning a dead ox, which the indians ate, and several of them died immediatly." Perhaps Caroline, like Wilford, considered the Paiute ambush just another "sign of the times." Two weeks later, her sister Louisa Pratt shared "particulars of the terrible insurrection in India," the so-called Kanpur Massacre or Mutiny of 1857. The *Los Angeles Star* reprinted details from another newspaper. Its descriptions of violated women and dismembered children were almost pornographic, and its call for the British to wreak revenge "on the inhuman monsters" of Delhi echoed some Californians' cries against the Paiutes and Mormons. Although no one in San Bernardino had a credible account of either event, Quartus Sparks joined a mass meeting in Los Angeles charging the Mormons "and their allies, the Indians," with "fiendish atrocities."[92]

Caroline and her sister probably took note of the turmoil in India because of her friendship with William Tait, the Mormon convert and former British soldier from Calcutta who had met her in San Francisco and entrusted her with the care of his son, Johnny. Caroline surely would have been horrified to learn that Tait, who now lived with his family in Cedar City, had, by virtue of his experience in the British Army, helped train the militia that conducted the assault at Mountain Meadows. (Like many of the participants, he later claimed that he had killed no one.)[93]

Tait had escaped one horror only to become involved in another. Although the circumstances that provoked the East Indian and southern Utah massacres were different, both ratified already confirmed notions about the perpetrators. In the minds of many Americans, there was little difference between an American Indian, an East Indian, and a Mormon.[94]

Thus, when the Crosbys began their journey to Utah in January 1858, they had reason to be wary of both government soldiers and Paiutes. When they heard army bugles shortly after leaving San Bernardino, they were relieved to discover that the soldiers were only looking for stolen cattle. Indians were a more constant presence. At each watering place, their more experienced companions scrutinized moccasins to discern who was and was not friendly. They were relieved as they approached the southern border of Utah Territory to meet Paiutes who joined in Mormon hymns. Still, every Native American they met wanted something. Caroline dutifully handed out flour and biscuits while the men fussed if one of their animals went missing. When one Paiute attempted to steal a baby's diapers, the leader of the band "rather justified him in taking small things, and said that they thought the Mormons ought to provide for them shirts pants and other clothing That they had to go to the mountains for food where it was cold, and they needed warm clothing."[95] Benjamin Hulse, the Mormon missionary stationed at Las Vegas, tried to protect the travelers from theft, but since his job was to "plead the cause of the Lamanites," he expected travelers to share what they had. "Begging" was the toll the Paiutes exacted for passing through their land.

The Crosbys were at Las Vegas on February 13, when Apostle Amasa Lyman arrived at their camp with a man whom he introduced as "Dr. Osborn." Caroline afterward learned he was Thomas L. Kane, the Pennsylvanian who had befriended the Mormons at Winter Quarters. Kane had sailed to California at his own expense and was now traveling incognito toward Salt Lake City in hopes of mediating the conflict between his friend Brigham Young and the federal government. Caroline and her niece Ellen McGary had spent the day doing laundry. When Kane saw them sitting beside their camp stove "ironing clean white clothes," he was stunned. He told Caroline he "should about as soon have expected to see his mother behind a bar in San Bernardino." Caroline found his comment amusing. She had always found ways of being at home while wandering.[96]

As the Crosbys moved into the southern settlements, Caroline discovered that Utah Mormons were as varied as Mormons anywhere. At Pinto, Jane Hulse, the wife of the Las Vegas missionary, admitted she was an "unbeliever in polygamy." But at Johnson's Fort, Susan Johnson came out to greet them with two sister wives. They "seem to enjoy themselves well together," Caroline observed, although she was surprised to discover that their husband, Joel Johnson, had been away in "the States" for more than a year. In his absence, she noted, "Sister Susan and Nephi seem to have charge of home affairs." At Pinto, she had been distressed "by hearing sis H relate circumstances concerning the massacre of emigrants, by the Indians, last summer." She had no way of knowing that Nephi Johnson, the grown son who was managing affairs for his absent father, had served as an interpreter for the Paiutes and given them the order to attack.[97]

There would be time enough to worry about the massacre. For the moment, the bigger worry was the U.S. Army. On June 18, Caroline reported that Nephi and the Parowan militia commander, William Dame, were headed to Salt Lake City. "The report is that the soldiers are coming in, and that the city will be burned."[98]

"I think I can take the spoiling of my things with joy"

Thomas Kane's journeys to Salt Lake City and then out onto the plains to confer with the approaching army eventually produced a compromise, though it took time for the news to reach southern Utah. To the relief of everyone, Brigham agreed to surrender the governorship, but he refused to allow troops to occupy Mormon towns. If they attempted to do so, he vowed to exercise the "Sebastopol option," a strategy employed in the Crimean War, when the Russians destroyed their ships and city rather than let them be occupied by their enemies. In late winter, Brigham had issued orders for an evacuation of Salt Lake City and other northern Utah towns, proposing to leave a small body of men behind to set fire to everything should the army attempt to enter. Moving thirty thousand people and their cattle was no easy task, even for leaders with decades of experience on the overland trail.[99] For one thing, the enticements to remain in the valley were immense. "I am in a fair way to have the most excellent garden I ever had," Hosea Stout lamented. Ultimately, he concluded he really had no choice but to sacrifice his own interest, for "such is the fate and always has been with those in every age who would dare to worship the true God."[100]

Wilford began packing up his goods at the end of March, transferring Sarah, Emma, and their tiny children to Provo in early April. Moving back and forth to the city, he saw a continuous line for almost fifty miles, with animals, women, and children wading through water, snow, and muck. When he returned to collect Phebe on May 17, he found his orchard "loaded with fruit strawburies beginning to get ripe Currants loaded peach Apricotts & Aple trees bearing full." He spent the next day pruning his orchard, then, just before leaving, picked three quarts of strawberries.[101]

Patty Sessions alternated between anxiety and resolve: "I feel first reate cheerful and happy I think I can take the spoiling of my things with joy Oh Lord help me so to do." When her granddaughter's husband walked through her garden and orchard, he said "he never saw such a [b]eautiful sight in his life so many trees so full of fruit." But Patty packed up the medicine she had been making and left. On May 29, living in a little shanty her son Perrigrine had built for her in American Fork, she attended a birthday celebration for Susanna Richards, the woman who had worked with her for so many years on the Council of Health. Patty considered it the "fulfillment of a prediction" that forty or fifty persons were able to gather under a bowery to eat a delicious meal. Five years before to the day, Willard Richards had told his sister Susanna, who was then living in a small room in a rude log cabin, "that in five years more she should have a plenty of room to set as big a table as she wanted and plenty to put on it and room enough to accommodate all that she wished to have present."[102] In a way no one expected, the prophecy had come true. Susanna did indeed have room for forty or fifty friends, all willing to rejoice together in a common exile.

On June 26, 1858, federal troops marched through an eerily silent Salt Lake City and established a temporary camp safely beyond its limits. "When we git the news good and solid we will go home," Brigham told a congregation in Provo.[103] Within a few weeks, most of the inhabitants had returned to take up their lives and their long struggle over whose God, whose economy, and whose families mattered.

The carriage in which Heber Kimball's plural wife Mary Ellen was riding reached home about 9:00 p.m. on July 22. "The moon shone brightly and I never saw the city look more lovely in my life," she wrote. "Every thing was peaceful and quiet while the shrubery and gardens looked luxurient and rich as if they would yield their bounties with gladness to the returning husbandman. It seemed a hallowed spot to me, and I thought as I passed a long the streets how could the army feel otherwise when they passed through and beheld the industry of the saints." Heber met Mary Ellen's group at the gate and conducted them through the lane to the house, where they found two of his other wives exhausted from restoring the house to its normal state. Mary Ellen ended the day's entry with a prayer: "O Lord how shall I be sufficiently greatful for all thy tender mercies and blessing unto me."[104]

By then, word had reached the southern settlements that the new governor, Alfred Cumming, had issued a message of conciliation. There was relief, but little cause for celebration. In Caroline Crosby's dry account, the governor "assured us that we were all forgiven of our sedition and treason, and exhorted us to be quiet, and law abiding, etc."[105]

15

"The records of this House"

Utah Territory, 1858–1872

Historians like to say, "No source, no history." Or, put another way, "If nobody wrote it down, it didn't happen." Because Eliza Snow wrote things down, the Nauvoo Relief Society has a history. Because she and others kept records at Winter Quarters and in early Salt Lake City, we know that, even without the Relief Society, women continued to meet together to speak in tongues, bless one another, and heal the sick, and that they participated in the Council of Health, the Polysophical Society, and the Indian Relief Society. Because Wilford Woodruff took notice, we know that in 1857 the Fourteenth Ward Relief Society met once a week on Wednesdays, and that sometimes as many as fifty women attended. Because the members of that society signed their names to a quilt, we know something about their skill, their connections to one another, and their patriotism. Because Caroline Crosby wrote things down, we know that, even in faraway San Bernardino, women gathered together to support one another and to read letters from Eliza Snow and newspapers from Utah. These things have a history because someone wrote them down.

Yet, strangely, the female societies that seemed so vibrant and thriving in 1857 disappeared. Did they really go away, or did people stop writing? Without question, the sources thinned out. As Margaret Smoot observed, "The year fifty eight I intirely neglected and it was the most important year since we have been in this valley." Caroline Crosby blamed "the great scarcity, and high price of paper," for lapses in her diary after 1863. But for busy women that was not the only explanation. As Mary Ellen Kimball acknowledged, "Writing is easier laid a side than any thing else."[1] A great deal of what women did has been lost because no one wrote it down.

Yet there is evidence that formal meetings really did decline if not disappear in the period after the Utah War. Although Patty Sessions continued to make daily entries through 1866, she said nothing at all about the female organizations that had been such an important part of her life in the decade before. Then, on January 23, 1868, in a calendar of notable events that succeded her diary, she wrote, "I went to the female relief society and joined."[2] In his Sunday sermon six weeks before, Brigham Young had instructed ward bishops, "You have smart women for wives, many of you; let them organize Female Relief Societies in the various wards." Samuel Woolley, who was now a bishop, followed instructions, naming his wife Catherine as president in his ward.[3]

The few historians who have noticed the collapse of Relief Societies after 1858 have blamed the war.[4] But, though the exodus south was disruptive, most other things quickly revived. Immigration picked up, settlement expanded, ceremonies in the Endowment House flourished; new meetinghouses, social halls, and an impressive Salt Lake Theatre rose.[5] Why would Relief Societies disappear? One explanation might be that in the early 1860s Brigham Young no longer needed them, and that by 1867 he did. In short, the rise and fall of women's activities was driven by Brigham Young. But that story seems too simple. Anyone who knows the role of women in the organization of the Nauvoo Relief Society in 1842, or the Indian Relief Societies in 1854, will wonder if in 1868 "smart women" had already begun to revive organizations that had lagged.

The patchwork of diaries available for the early sixties, when combined with the speeches, minutes, and correspondence that emerged afterward, provides a richer picture of a seemingly lost decade, suggesting that too earnest a focus on formal institutions can blind us to enduring practices. The Relief Society was in some respects an epiphenomenon, a manifestation of a deeper and more pervasive female culture that existed with and without formal structure. For Brigham Young, the reorganization of ward Relief Societies was a way of dealing with immense changes facing Utah after 1867—the imminent completion of the transcontinental railroad, the growing threat of a Reorganized Church of Jesus Christ of Latter-day Saints supported by Emma Smith and her sons, and a newly powerful anti-polygamy movement. In his case, external forces pushed for more engagement by women.

This was also a moment, familiar in the larger woman's rights movement, when opportunity met a cadre of female leaders who, having survived years of bearing and rearing children, now had skills, energy, and a vision they believed worth promulgating. It is no accident that the revived Relief Society was led by women who had been part of the first Relief Society in Nauvoo. A key factor was a renewed collaboration between Eliza Snow and Sarah Kimball, the woman who, as a young mother, had invited a group of neighbors to join her in a sewing circle. Now approaching fifty and a widow, Sarah took up the work with vigor. Less than eight months after assuming the presidency of the Fifteenth Ward Relief Society, she laid the cornerstone for a building to house its operations. Eliza wrote a hymn for its dedication. In ten crisp verses, she invoked the presence of the Holy Spirit, pledged the building to God, prayed for unity in its operations, and committed its resources to Zion's welfare. In the eighth verse, she gave a shout-out to history.

> The records of this House shall prove
> We're neither slack nor slow.[6]

Eliza knew the power of records. For twenty-five years she had preserved the minutes of the Nauvoo Relief Society. She was determined that, as she and her sisters moved into a new era, their work would be remembered.

Fifteenth Ward Relief Society Hall. From Emmeline Blanche Woodward Wells, *Charities and Philanthropies: Woman's Work in Utah* (Salt Lake City: G.Q. Cannon, 1893). This photograph, taken for a pamphlet prepared for the Woman's Conference at the Chicago World's Fair, shows the hall as it looked late in the nineteenth century. The motto, "Holiness to the Lord," is on the façade. *(Photograph Courtesy Harvard University Library.)*

"The spirit of the god of Joseph rested upon us"

Relief Societies may have declined after the Utah War because women had better things to do. The specific goals that had led to their establishment, such as providing clothing for Indians or rag carpets for the Salt Lake Tabernacle, were quickly met. Without specific assignments, there was little impetus to continue formal meetings, especially if other strategies for supporting the poor or furnishing buildings were available. The presence of the military and the opening of mines in nearby territories offered new opportunities for selling local produce. As the First Presidency explained, "There is no sin in selling grain to the army, but the sin is in disposing of it for less than it is worth." Increased income for members meant increased revenue in the tithing office.[7]

The Civil War raging in the states was also a factor. Like other Americans, Mormons valued the colorful printed cottons that came from Eastern factories, but disrupted trade and high prices during the war kept them busy spinning and weaving. Bathsheba Smith's sister wife Lucy bragged that, whether living in Salt Lake City, Provo, or Parowan, "I make the cloth come off the beam in a hurry."[8] When Caroline Crosby attended a spinning bee at Johnson's Fort in 1858, she found the buzzing of wheels combined with the noise of a dozen children too confusing, so carried her wheel home and spun thirteen knots in silence. Yet later, in Beaver, she frequently attended spinning bees at other women's houses, and on one occasion brought ten sisters to her own house to help clean raw wool. "We enjoyed ourselves finely," she wrote.[9] In May 1864, she noted that she had neglected her journal for over a year because "carding, spining, and weaving" had taken so much of her time. She found spinning Utah-grown cotton "a very slow process," perhaps because of the quality of the fiber. Local production had expanded with the opening of the "Cotton Mission" in the southern part of the state, an area that became known as "Utah's Dixie." Caroline noted that streams of migrants passed through her town on the way to the cotton settlements.[10]

No one was more engaged in textile production than Patty Sessions. Sometimes for days at a time her diary entries read simply "spun." Then she would shift to dyeing, warping, and weaving. She usually specified the end product of this work, as in "warped my carpet" or "sized and spooled my dresses." She was, of course, warping her loom in order to weave her carpet, and sizing and spooling the thread from which she would weave fabric for dresses.[11]

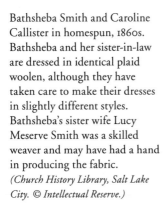

Bathsheba Smith and Caroline
Callister in homespun, 1860s.
Bathsheba and her sister-in-law
are dressed in identical plaid
woolen, although they have
taken care to make their dresses
in slightly different styles.
Bathsheba's sister wife Lucy
Meserve Smith was a skilled
weaver and may have had a hand
in producing the fabric.
*(Church History Library, Salt Lake
City. © Intellectual Reserve.)*

Through the summer and early fall, Patty's attention shifted to her
orchard. "I have worked very hard gathering and seling my peaches," she
wrote in October 1862. A few weeks later, she took two bushels of apples
into town and "sold them to sister Ruff for eight Dollars." Sister Ruff
bought three more bushels a few weeks later. She may have been resell-
ing them, drying them, or preserving them some other way. Patty paid
tithing in apples, peaches, and plums, and she prospered because fruit
was in great demand. She planted apple seeds and peach pits and sold the
seedlings. She built a scaffolding for drying fruit and sometimes stayed up
all night to prevent it from being stolen. One summer, she helped a man
sack up 460 pounds of dried peaches to take to the mines. That year, an
Eastern visitor reported that Utahns sold two hundred thousand pounds
of dried peaches to the mines in Idaho and Montana.[12] Some families
engaged newly arrived immigrants to help with the work. Anna Sorine
Anderson, a Norwegian immigrant who had arrived with a company led
by Samuel Woolley, worked at rubbing the fuzz off peaches to prepare
them for drying.[13]

When Abraham Smoot was in the East on a merchandising mission, Margaret was employed in both textile production and farming, or, as she put it, in "various kinds of business of housewifery and some husbandry." One day she reported twisting carpet warp; on another she set the younger wives to work "Pulling wheat." (Pulling, rather than cutting, preserved the full length of the stalk for braiding.) She was fortunate in having a mechanical threshing machine. On a weekday set aside for church meetings and fasting, she and her helpers stayed home to thresh thirty-two bushels of wheat and 158 of oats, "the greatest days work ever done on the machine." When the harvest was over, she vowed to work no more on fast days or on Sundays. Because she was interested in agricultural improvement, she sometimes attended meetings of the manufacturing society.[14]

As their households expanded, polygamous husbands sought out new sites for grazing cattle and sheep. In 1859, Wilford took his youngest wife, Delight Stocking, home to Fort Harriman, southwest of the city, where he kept some of his cattle. He rented a room from Delight's father and left her for the summer, "to keep house by herself to milk the Cows make Butter take Care of the Calves &c." Later, he and a hired hand built a milk house up one of the canyons, a place infested with rattlesnakes and scorpions. Confident that she could cope, he carried her "out to the fort to take Charge of our Cows."[15] In the Kimball family, Vilate managed dairying. In summer, she often took one of her sister wives with her into a canyon east of the city to make butter and cheese. In May 1863, she invited Mary Ellen to join her. Together, Mary Ellen wrote, they made "time pass agreeably" while engaged in "useful employment."[16]

Responsibilities for child care also expanded as the proliferation of plural marriages in the 1850s produced a population explosion in the next decade. The Woodruff household is a case in point. Between 1858 and 1870, Wilford recorded fourteen births, one miscarriage, and three infant deaths in the family. He listed children born to his plural wives Sarah, Emma, and Delight, and to his grown daughters, Phoebe Jr., Susan, and Beulah, each of whom married during this period.[17] The Utah census of 1870 tallied more babies per capita than in any other state or territory in the nation. Almost 20 percent of the population was under five years of age, roughly 60 percent under twenty.[18] Eliza Snow proclaimed demographic truth in the chorus of a song she composed in 1867: "In our lovely Deseret, where the saints of God have met, / There's a multitude of children all around." Children had to be educated as well as fed and clothed.[19]

Any of these factors may have played a role in the decline of weekly

Wilford Woodruff and Sarah Brown with three of their eight children. Date unknown.
(Pioneer Memorial Museum, International Society of Daughters of Utah Pioneers, Salt Lake City.)

meetings. Still, aspects of Relief Society activity persisted, especially for women whose children were grown. The most direct evidence comes from Wilford's diary. On December 24, 1861, he walked to the new Fourteenth Ward Meeting House, where he found Phebe "and several others of the Sisters." They had been at work almost around the clock for several days "in making the Curtains & trimings for the windows and doors." When Wilford offered the dedicatory prayer for the building, he followed a conventional format, mentioning each element in the building, the stones in the foundation, the adobes, the joists, boards, nails, rafters, shingles, lath, plaster, pulpit and benches, and the doors with their screws, locks, and latches. He did not forget "the curtains with the trimings thereof and the shades that they may be Holy unto the Lord."[20] With or without weekly meetings, Phebe and her sisters were still doing work very similar to what they had done in the 1850s, when they furnished carpet for the Tabernacle—and before that in the Kirtland and Nauvoo Temples.

Wilford added an even more intriguing bit of information in April 1864, when he reported attending a gathering at the ward schoolhouse, where he "presented the Quilt of the Female Relief Society to be sold for $140 dollars to purchase an organ for the meeting purposes of the ward."[21]

Was this a new quilt or the prize-winning one that the sisters had made in 1857? If a new quilt, then the Fourteenth Ward Relief Society was still meeting and making things. If an old one, then someone had preserved it for just such an occasion. According to a Horne family tradition, the 1857 quilt was "raffled" at a fund-raising event, but nobody gave a date. It is hard to imagine such a raffle occurring in the autumn and winter of 1857, when people were preparing for war, or in 1858, when they were trying to put themselves back together after the exodus. Although seven years seems like a long time to keep something in reserve, this quilt was special. Richard Stephen Horne, who won the raffle, was thirteen years old in 1857. In 1864, he was the twenty-year-old teacher of the Fourteenth Ward School. If the quilt was raffled off in that year, he was an appropriate person to win it.[22]

In Beaver, Caroline Crosby became engaged in another form of church service—feeding Brigham Young and his entourage when they passed through the village. In June 1861, Maria Lyman served as "presidentess" when sixteen or eighteen women met at her house to plan the meal. By noon the next day, the sisters had four long tables ready. Caroline, who stood beside Brigham's place, found him "very sociable while eating." She was pleased when he said that "two East Indie sisters" were of the pure blood of Israel and entitled to receive their endowments. When Brigham's party passed through the town the next year, the ladies' committee crowned the feast with "a tumbler of honey the production of bees in Utah, which was an entirely new thing, and much admired."[23]

Women also contributed to the Perpetual Emigrating Fund, an enterprise that allowed poor immigrants, such as Emma Jackson, to come to America sooner than they might have done. Traveling with the Daniel Robison Handcart Company, Emma met a widowed ship carpenter named Robert Siddoway, and shortly after arriving became his wife. There were hundreds like her. Perhaps it was the sight and sound of the city's brass bands welcoming such folks into the city that inspired Patty Sessions to put twenty dollars into the PEF on August 23, 1859. In May 1862, she contributed dried peaches and beans "for the boys that go to the states after the poor." Although the last few handcart companies had come through without major problems, the Church in the early sixties discovered a better method of helping the poor come to the valley, the so-called out-and-back method. Each spring, the bishops offered tithing credit to those willing to take teams and wagons to the Missouri River to bring immigrants back. In July 1861, an English brick maker named

Charles Turner wrote from Florence, Nebraska, to friends back home, "It whould do you good to see this Company of teams that have arived from the Valley to take home the Saints who have not means to take themselves." He urged those still in England to "be faithful and help to role on the work for the kingdom must be built up & the work Acomplished." Those were sentiments Patty shared.[24]

Surviving records from the early sixties affirm that women persisted in the spiritual and temporal work they had been engaged in since Nauvoo. They testified in weekly "fast meetings." They maintained friendships through "social visiting." They blessed and anointed the sick. When Margaret Smoot's horse shied and threw her from her carriage, she "was washed and anointed under the hands of Sister Whitney and Sister Eliza Snow and then administered to by Mother Chase." She concluded her account, "The spirit of the god of Joseph rested upon us to an overflowing the house and all that were in it was filled with the spirit of God."[25] Female healers administered to men as well as women, and to new arrivals as well as old friends. Patty Sessions anointed her second husband, John Parry, when he feared he was dying, then, along with his second wife, "laid hands on him," claiming that "he was healed instantly."[26] In 1863, she took in an immigrant named Naomi Debenham, who suffered both from physical illness and despair. When doctors' remedies seemed to make her worse, Patty called in an elder, who offered both an herbal emetic and prayer, reporting that the girl "seemed a little better." But when Zina washed and anointed her, Patty judged her "desidedly better."[27]

Zina and Eliza appear everywhere in these stories. When Patty appeared to be dying, it was Zina who did the anointing.[28] When Wilford had "a tremendious raging Lung fever," Zina stayed with him through the day and Eliza at night. When his cough "seemed to rend my left Lung in peaces," Eliza remained with him, giving him "20 drops of the strongest Hemlock oil," which went through his whole system and checked his fever.[29] When Phebe had a severe allergic attack with hives and difficulty breathing, the two women again came to the rescue.[30] They were both present when Phoebe Amelia delivered her first child, a daughter. Although an unnamed midwife revived the baby, who appeared to be stillborn, by breathing into her lungs and putting her alternately in warm and cool water, she soon failed. Zina revived her until she began to nurse. When she died, Eliza laid her out.[31]

Such ministrations occurred even in new settlements like Beaver, two hundred miles south of Salt Lake City. When Caroline rushed to the home of her niece Ellen McGary, who was ill, "Mother Nayman was there anointing her. She requested us to lay our hands upon her, in the order of the priesthood, which we did, and afterwards she seemed better." "Mother Nayman" was Jane Neyman, the woman who had testified in 1854 that she had instigated the first baptism for the dead in Nauvoo. Neyman read Caroline some poetry said to have been written by a near-blind woman named Margaret Morgan, who said "she received the gift by the spirit of God, which when I heard the verses, I believed to be true." Later, Caroline copied out some of Margaret Morgan's verses for another neighbor.[32]

Heber Kimball's plural wife Mary Ellen was uncertain about the validity of such rituals. After joining Presendia in washing and anointing another woman, she asked Heber if it was mockery for sisters to wash and anoint the sick. "He replied, inasmuch as they are obedient to their husbands, they have a right to administer in that way in the name of the Lord Jesus Christ, but not by authority of the priesthood invested in them, for that authority is not given to women. He also said they might administer by the authority given to their husbands inasmuch as they were one with their husband."[33] There was less contradiction than may appear between Heber's interpretation and Mother Neyman's request that women lay on hands "in the order of the priesthood." Neyman was referring to the form of prayer used in the temple or the Endowment House. Women who had participated in those rituals were by definition "one" with their husbands, having been sealed to them for eternity.

Mary Ellen's concern about overstepping bounds is nevertheless surprising, considering how many years she had spent alongside Presendia and Zina. The nature of her record may explain this reluctance: Heber seems to have assigned her and her sister wife Laura Pitkin the job of keeping notes on his sermons to the family; he sometimes read and corrected what she had written. A male writer later claimed that attending one of Heber's family meetings was the closest that he ever felt to God, and that Heber's prayers brought the deity "down into that room."[34] In contrast, Mary Ellen's portrait of her husband, though meant to be admiring, portrays an overbearing and insensitive man.

A classic example is the blessing he gave her when, after years of disappointment, she became pregnant:

> I bless the child that it may be perfect in its brain, in its limbs and joints
> and vitals, possessing all the energy, strength, and fortitude of his father
> and be free from the desponding spirit which has often had power over

its mother. And may it be like a lion, energetic in all its movements . . . and like its father ever ready to listen to the words of life and be blind to the wickedness and corruption of the world.

When the child died before his second birthday, Mary Ellen blamed herself for not having "enough of the spirit of the Lord to save him from his early grave." She was still struggling with depression in July 1861, when she visited relatives in a settlement outside Salt Lake City. There she attended a female prayer meeting in which "the spirit of the Lord was poured out upon the sisters. They prayed for the recovery of my health, and I felt benefited by their prayers both temporally and spiritually. It seemed to add another effort to the prayer that Mr. Kimball offered before I left."[35]

"Had a good time," Caroline Crosby wrote after she and her sister Louisa attended a Sunday evening meeting together in the little settlement of Johnson's Fort. "Only 4 brethren present. Quite a number of sisters and children. They nearly all spoke around, and bore testimony to the truth."[36] Caroline's phrase "had a good time" is familiar from earlier diaries that describe outpourings of glossolalia. Reporting on a visit from Laura Pitkin Kimball, Zina used a related term—"had a very good season." She continued, "Yes the spirit of the Lord was with us to comfort and edify."[37] What looked to the world like social visiting could become something more—an opportunity for prayer, comfort, and the exercise of spiritual gifts, like speaking or singing in tongues. During the years she kept her diary, Margaret Smoot mentioned frequent visits from Phebe Woodruff, Eliza Snow, Vilate Kimball, Elizabeth Ann Whitney, Leonora Taylor, and others, singly or in tandem. Phebe Woodruff and Patty Sessions were both at the Smoot house when Margaret's sister wife Emily gave birth. When Zina Young learned that Emily had named the baby after her, she, too, paid a visit. Margaret and Phebe found a great many friends when they went together to "Brother Brigham's" family prayer circle. It seems likely that they were interested not only in what Brigham had to say but in how his wives reacted.[38]

As the Civil War in the States accentuated concern over the imminence of the second coming, work in the Endowment House also expanded.[39] Women served as officiators and also performed the essential though less visible tasks of constructing, marking, and laundering ceremonial clothing. In August 1859, for example, Eliza Snow made Patty Sessions a temple apron, a job that involved ornamental embroidery as well as plain sewing. Patty, like other women, made her own ceremonial undergarments, often out of fabric she wove herself. She also constructed a complete temple suit for her second husband, John Parry, who disappointed her by not inviting her to attend the session where he was sealed to another woman. In his defense, Patty had married him only "for time."[40] In Beaver, Caroline Crosby's former San Bernardino associate Roxana Patten developed a little business painting temple aprons for those fortunate enough to go to Salt Lake City to be married in the Endowment House.[41]

Given the intense engagement of Latter-day Saint women in spiritual and temporal activities of so many kinds, it is difficult to understand what the formal reorganization of the Relief Society might have offered. What we can know is how the major leaders in the newly revived organization understood their work. Although they embraced Brigham Young's economic goals, they had more ambitious aims of their own.

"after the Order of Heaven"

Brigham Young framed his support for the Relief Society in practical terms: the Relief Society would help the Saints resist foreign fashions and Gentile merchants; it would encourage home manufacture; it would assist bishops in caring for the poor. Eliza Snow's vision was broader. For her, the reorganization of the Relief Society was the culmination of a decades-long effort to affirm the religious authority of women, an authority she believed derived from their innate spiritual power, from their willingness to sacrifice, from the sealing ordinances that bound them to righteous men, and from the unfulfilled promises Joseph Smith had made to them in Nauvoo.

Years later, she claimed, "Pres. Young commissioned me to assist the Bishops in organizing Branches of the Society in their respective Wards, for, at that time, the Bishops had not acquainted themselves with the movement, and did not know how to proceed."[42] This is a rare example of Eliza's actually claiming credit for the work she did behind the throne. She had no official position in the new Relief Societies. In none of his public speeches did Brigham mention her, nor did he suggest that the bishops needed instruction. In 1867, as in the past, she went about her work quietly but with great effectiveness. Her influence is visible in the way the minute books of the new societies reflected the form of the Nauvoo minutes. It shows up as well in letters of instruction, such as the one she sent the newly called Relief Society president in the town of Fillmore.

She explained that female presidencies "should preside just as the first Presidency presides over the church," an almost direct quote from the Nauvoo minutes. She added that their Relief Society callings were "a portion of the Order of Heaven."[43]

Eliza's renewed alliance with Sarah Kimball sustained her. When Sarah organized the sewing circle that became the Nauvoo Relief Society in 1842, she was the twenty-four-year-old wife of an ambitious merchant. Now she was a forty-nine-year-old widow with the confidence born of successfully handling multiple sorrows and losses. She had brought her family to Utah and taught school to support them until Hiram recovered his equanimity and health. She had raised three sons to adulthood and along the way acquired valuable experience in teaching and business. The only surviving document that gives any hint of her internal struggles during these years suggests that in her early forties she began to worry about having rejected plural marriage when Joseph Smith attempted to teach her about it in Nauvoo. When she told him to "teach it to someone else," he looked at her "reprovingly, and said 'Will you tell me who to teach it to? God requires me to teach it to you, and leave you with the responsibility of believing or disbelieving.'"[44]

At some point after her arrival in Utah, that responsibility began to weigh upon her. Although she and Hiram had both received their endowments in the Nauvoo Temple, they had not been sealed for eternity. Hiram was apparently contemplating taking a plural wife. Sarah now pondered her own eternal fate. Should she be sealed to Hiram for eternity? Or did she belong to Joseph?[45] If so, who would be her proxy?

In May 1858, the Kimballs were living in Springville, fifty miles south of Salt Lake City, when Sarah wrote Brigham to retract what she now believed was a hasty rejection of a solution he had offered when she met with him to discuss her situation. "In Sister Snow's room, You observed that if you should talk with Hiram and counsel him to stand proxy in a certain case he would do it and feel satisfied. I replied from the impulse of the moment that he would take your counsel but I <u>feared</u> that he would not at all times feel satisfied."[46] She now believed that Hiram would accept Brigham's counsel and that asking him to serve as proxy for her sealing to Joseph would satisfy her earthly obligations as a wife:

Again my Patriarcal Blessing reads that I shall be a comfort and a blessing to my Companion all <u>his days</u> and if I understand correctly the above course would prevent the necessity of my being sealed to another to obtain what I desire, ie, Eternal lives in the Kingdom of Our Father.[47]

Fourteen years after his death, Joseph was still claiming new wives.

No one knows how Hiram felt about this. Perhaps he pushed back by renewing his own commitment to the Church in order to claim Sarah for eternity. In 1863, he accepted a mission call to the Sandwich Islands (Hawaii). Wilford Woodruff was astonished. "This is the first time Hiram Kimball Ever attempted to take a Mission to Preach the gospel since he has been member of the Church," he wrote. Although Hiram did manage to get as far as California, he drowned in a steamship accident off the coast of San Pedro in April 1863, as he was preparing to embark for the islands. Not long after Hiram's death, Sarah's nineteen-year-old Indian daughter, Katie, also died. Her sons were grown. Her own mother had died in 1861. She was now unexpectedly free, yet bereft of those who had been such an important part of her life for so many years.[48]

In 1867, when the sisters of the Fifteenth Ward elected her president of their Relief Society, she moved into a new life. According to the minutes Hattie Jones kept, Sarah composed her first speech on March 17, 1868, the anniversary of the founding of the Nauvoo Relief Society, explaining to the sisters that though their organization was new it rested on the same principles as the old. She asked them to join her in laboring "for our own advancement as well as the good of others," hoping to "secure for us a name and a place that will live after we have passed away."[49] Like Eliza, she had her eye on history.

Together, she and Eliza drafted a constitution that laid out the duties of officers from the president and her counselor to teachers and deaconesses arranged in quorums. Like corresponding offices in the male Aaronic Priesthood, these women had discrete responsibilities: the teachers for visiting their assigned blocks "to inquire after the prosperity and happiness of the members," the deaconesses to care for the hall and make sure that the rooms were in proper order and that members were provided with water, lights, and fire as needed during meetings. Even though there were no ritual responsibilities associated with these callings, and Relief Society duties were practical, they were not insignificant. The Constitution put an emphasis on record keeping, providing not only for a secretary but for a historian who "should survey the past and present condition of the Society and make a faithful record that will be worthy of preservation and useful for reference."[50]

Sarah's most ambitious goal was building a Relief Society Hall. When the Fifteenth Ward bishop offered to donate the land, she declined, insisting that the sisters wanted to be fully independent. She found a lot in the center of the ward, borrowed money to pay for construction, hired a builder, and signed a contract complete with a drawing of the promised structure.[51] In November 1868, she presided at the groundbreaking. With a silver trowel and mallet borrowed from a Master Mason, she stood atop the cornerstone and told the assembled crowd that she had been present at the dedication of the Kirtland Temple and at the laying of the cornerstone of the Nauvoo Temple and of the Salt Lake Temple "now in progress of erection" a few blocks away. Although, in comparison with the others, this building was an "unpretending Edifice," the stone on which she stood was a "consecrated rock," a stepping stone to greater things. It would offer "a more extended field of useful labor for female minds and hands."[52]

In a set of statements that would have been welcome at any woman's rights convention in the East, she continued:

> It will readily be admitted that woman's allotted sphere of labor is not sufficiently extensive, and varied to enable her to exercise all her God-given powers and faculties in a manner best calculated to strengthen and develop the perfect woman. Nor are her labors made sufficiently remunerative to afford her that independence compatible with true womanly dignity.

Sarah knew that she and the members of the new society would face criticism for what they were about to do, but she was confident that their efforts were "in the direction of human progress and universal good." She graciously thanked the "gentlemanly citizens" who had assisted them.[53]

In February 1869, Brigham Young spoke in the Fifteenth Ward Meeting House to members of Relief Societies from throughout the city and beyond. He praised the women for their efforts, then laid out his view of women's duties. He offered a grandfatherly lecture, full of sentiments found in advice literature from the early nineteenth century. By cultivating patience, kindness, and temperance, women would bring forth and rear well-behaved children. They should teach their daughters just enough etiquette to allow them to mingle among strangers and deport themselves as ladies, but not so much as to undermine their ability to keep house and knit their own stockings. Brigham departed from the thinking of many men of his generation, however, by acknowledging "the same variety of taste and character among the female portions of the community as among the males," and arguing that girls should be allowed to follow their own interests, whether they chose to become artists, musicians, mathematicians, naturalists, or bookkeepers.[54]

He then launched into a complaint made by many before and after—that young women were unstable employees. Although the territory had trained many girls to operate the telegraph line, it was forced to employ more men than they wished because "women are brought up in such ignorance that they know nothing about their duty; they do not seem to know but that it is perfectly right, without leave of absence, to run off to a party, or visit here and there for two or three days together."[55] Brigham blamed lack of education. He did not understand that persons raised to respond to household rhythms might have difficulty obeying the demands of a clock. The organizers of Relief Societies in the 1850s and 1860s faced the very same problem. Women signed up but then came to meetings only when there wasn't someone or something at home that needed tending—an infant, a sick sister, a soap leach, a newborn calf, or an unexpected visitor. Meetings were time-specific. Nature's clock was different. One of the things that made rural women so effective as caregivers was their capacity to integrate work and sociability. Thus, when Eliza cautioned the president of the Fillmore Relief Society to fill up the agenda of meetings to prevent "idle talk," she may have been making those meetings less attractive to those she hoped would come.[56]

In time, Eliza and her compatriots would succeed in modernizing their sisters, encouraging them in educational, economic, and political enterprises they had never before imagined. At the moment, they had a more insistent task—defending plural marriage against a new coalition of dissenters who had come together in Iowa to re-establish what they believed was the true Church of Jesus Christ of Latter-day Saints. In 1859, Joseph and Emma's oldest son, Joseph Smith III, agreed to lead the new movement, which in 1863 sent missionaries to Utah to announce that Brigham Young lacked legal and spiritual authority, that the doctrine of plural marriage was akin to slavery, and that Joseph III was the true heir to his father.[57] Brigham knew whom to blame. In a sermon preached in the Tabernacle in October 1866, he exclaimed, "Emma Smith is one of the damnedest liars I know of on the earth; yet there is no good thing I would refuse to do for her, if she would only be a righteous woman."[58]

The fight over polygamy became a family squabble, pitting Joseph Smith III against Joseph F. Smith, Hyrum's son, who had come to the Salt Lake Valley with his mother, Mary Fielding Smith, in 1848. Even more important to the unfolding debate was the presence in Utah of more than a dozen women who claimed to have been Joseph's wives. Between May and August 1869, Joseph F. secured notarized statements from ten of them.[59]

These were legal documents, not oral histories. Eliza Snow's affidavit gives a sense of their character.

> Be it remembered that on this Seventh day of June A.D. 1869, person-ally appeared before me, James Jack, a notary public, in and for said county, Eliza Roxcy Snow, who was by me Sworn in due form of law and upon her oath Saith, that on the twenty-ninth day of June A.D. 1842, at the City of Nauvoo, county of Hancock, State of Illinois, she was married or sealed to Joseph Smith, President of the Church of Jesus Christ of Latter Day Saints by Brigham Young, President of the Quo-rum of the Twelve Apostles of Said Church according to the laws of the same regulating marriage, in the presence of Sarah M. Cleaveland.[60]

Eliza was precise about the date, perhaps because the diary she began on that day helped her remember it. Even though she had been known for years as "Eliza Snow," she reinforced the power of her statement by signing herself "Eliza R. Snow Smith."[61]

Eliza's affirmation of her sealing to Joseph Smith sustained her church's argument about their founding Prophet's role in establishing plural mar-riage. It also strengthened her authority to lead other women in the reor-ganization of the society Joseph had helped establish in Nauvoo.

"shall we obey God or Congress?"

After 1868, the Female Relief Society emerged more powerfully in Wilford Woodruff's diary than it ever had before. He noted when Relief Society reports were read at general conference, acknowledged meetings of Relief Society teachers at his house, and on a journey south enjoyed a Relief

Society meeting at Battle Creek and a supper prepared by Relief Society sisters at Beaver. In his own ward, he witnessed the dedication of a new Relief Society Hall, one of 140 such structures that would eventually be built in Utah.[62]

"The Ladies of Salt Lake City held a Mass meeting in the Tabernacle at 1 oclok to Express their indignation at the Course Congress was taking," he observed on January 13, 1870. Because men were not invited, he could not have heard the "many vary interesting speeches" that were given. Presumably, Phebe gave him a report.[63] On January 9, he had preached a sermon at a large Sunday meeting in the Salt Lake Tabernacle, replaying a sentence he had already polished in his diary. "The Lord has Revealed the Law of the Patriarchal order of Marriage & the Lord says we shall be damned if we do not obey it & Congress says we shall be damned if we do." He asked, "Now which shall we obey God or Congress?" The congregation responded by acclamation, "We will obey God."[64] Women had always voted in church meetings, although on this occasion, as on most, they were not participating in a democratic process so much as affirming decisions already made by church leaders. That must have been what church leaders—and their opponents—believed would happen once woman suffrage was adopted.

But women were not so passive as outsiders assumed. At a meeting to plan the indignation meeting, Bathsheba Smith had proposed "that we demand of the Gov the right of franchise." After that resolution passed, Lucy Kimball said "she felt that we had borne in Silence as long as it was our duty to bear, and moved that we be represented at Washington." The group elected Sarah Kimball and Eliza Snow to fill that role.[65] Since the resolutions adopted at the indignation meeting were directed at Congress, not at the Utah governor or legislature, there was no reason to introduce the proposal for woman suffrage at the mass meeting, especially since raising the specter of suffrage might undermine their main objective, which was to attack the Cullom Bill. But the proposal to enfranchise women did reach the legislature.

As a member of the upper house, Wilford attended the sessions in which it was debated. He did not offer details in his diary about this bill or any other. He did note several evening parties during this period, at least two at his own house, as well as a pleasure excursion on a newly completed track of railroad and evenings at the theater, all involving wives as well as members of the legislature.[66] Legislative debates, evening parties, and meetings to plan and evaluate the indignation meeting all took place within a few blocks in downtown Salt Lake City, in the neighborhoods where members of the legislature and their families lived.

Relief Society leaders planned their mass meeting in the upper room of the new Fifteenth Ward Hall, which was situated on the same block as Sarah Kimball's house. A month later, they gathered in the same building, ostensibly to talk about "Retrenchment," a movement to encourage simplicity in housekeeping and apparel, but the minutes of that meeting show they had even bigger issues in mind. Eliza Snow began by reading the account of the indignation meeting published in *The Sacramento Union*. She thought the story was a "very fair one." She also suggested forming a committee to write a letter to the non-Mormon governor thanking him for signing the woman suffrage bill. Sarah Kimball then took the floor. She said "she had waited patiently a long time" but, now that Utah women had been granted the right of suffrage, "she would openly declare herself a womans rights woman." Calling on the others to back her up, she said she had sometimes entertained "ideas that appeared wild that she thought would yet be considered woman's rights." She warned the group that they would have to overcome the prejudices of women as well as men, but she believed that all they had accomplished in recent days was a foreshadowing of better things to come.[67]

Phebe Woodruff said she, too, had been waiting for years for just such reform, but she warned against moving too quickly. She said that, since God had "moved upon our brethren to grant us this privilege," she did not want to lose what they had gained by acting hastily. Still, she was confident. "Great and blessed things are ahead. All is right and will come out right and woman will receive her reward, in blessings and honor." Bathsheba Smith said that she had no objection to anything that had been said, that she "had never felt better, nor never felt weaker." She was determined to do the best she could, feeling that woman was coming up in the world, "for there is nothing required of us that we cannot perform." Presendia Buell said she was grateful to be numbered with the others in moving forward this reform. "I am glad to see our daughters elevated with man and the time come when our voices will assist our leaders and redeem ourselves . . . from the curse placed upon Eve." She added, "Our daughters who are in polygamy will be the first redeemed."[68] Since Presendia had no living daughters of her own, she obviously meant younger women mentored collectively in the plural households of church leaders.

Margaret Smoot was less comfortable than the others with the call for woman's rights. Although she said she had always voted in conference, she

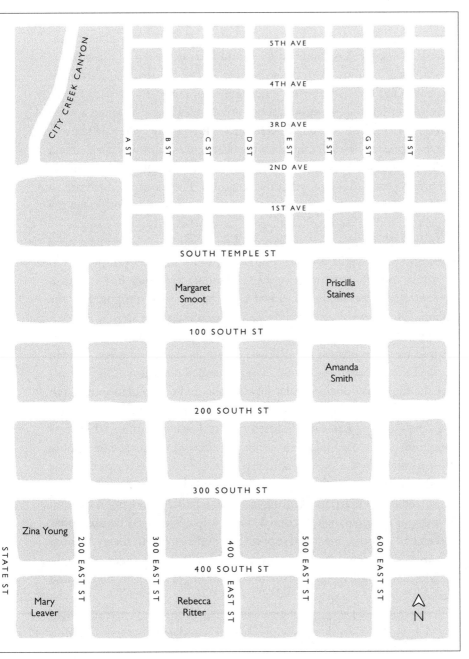

Map showing major buildings and locations of residences of named planners and participants in the indignation meeting. *(Samantha Van Gerbig.)*

insisted, "I have never had any desire for more rights than I have. I have always considered these to be beneath the sphere of woman." She, too, expressed her support for polygamy, and said that, though its practice had been difficult, she was thankful for it and had "never felt to dissolve ties thus formed." Willmirth East, a member of the Fourteenth Ward, said she "could not quite agree with sister Smoot in regard to womans rights. I have never felt that woman had her privileges. I always wanted a voice in the Politics of the Nation, as well as to rear a family." She said she was "much impressed" by a poem by another Latter-day Saint woman that had begun by asking, "Who cares to hear a womans thoughts?" Her answer was firm: "I wish to hear a womans thoughts." The meeting ended with a vote to send Bathsheba Smith on a mission to southern Utah to preach the gospel of territorial self-sufficiency and "woman's rights if she wished."[69]

In March, the *Deseret News* reported that Utah women had held mass meetings in fifty-eight towns, from Logan in the north to tiny Pinto in the south, and that as many as twenty-five thousand women had attended. At Tooele, Elizabeth Clegg claimed that the measures proposed in the Cullom Bill were worse than those "enforced against the serfs of Russia." In Provo, the president of the Fourth Ward Relief Society said she "could not find words to express her disgust." In small towns and large, women attacked the proposed legislation. They defended polygamy. They excoriated the hypocrisy of those who howled about the degradation of Utah women and then indulged in illicit sex. In the tiny town of Providence in Cache County, a speaker boasted that in her community "there had never been a case of child-birth out of the circle of wedlock, nor a house of prostitution, nor a case of adultery known since its settlement, some eleven years before."[70] That argument was unlikely to convince those who considered plural marriage nothing more than prostitution, but it built on the logic of reformers who believed prostitution flourished because poor women had no other means of support and were unable to marry because men used them for their own purposes and abandoned them. In Utah, the Mormons argued, every woman had an opportunity to be honored as a wife.[71]

Relief Society leaders not only defended polygamy, they sustained Brigham Young's economic agenda, which urged reduced consumption ("Retrenchment") and cooperative production and marketing as antidotes to encroaching capitalism. Underlying the furor over plural marriage were deep-seated economic issues that disturbed relations between

Mormon and non-Mormon merchants and that led to a short-lived but significant rift in the Church. Among the dissidents were William Godbe and T. B. H. Stenhouse, two educated British converts who had been especially close to Brigham Young. Through private meetings and in the pages of the independent *Utah Magazine,* Godbe argued that the Church ought to welcome mineral development and cultivate good relationships with Gentile merchants. He and Stenhouse both believed that Brigham's economic policies were too coercive and the Church too authoritarian and rigid. Eventually, both men were involved in a so-called New Movement that took them out of the Church.[72]

In the late 1860s, they were still in good enough graces to court young women raised in the Lion House. Stenhouse, who already had two wives, attempted to add Zina Young's sixteen-year-old daughter, Zina Presendia, to his family, much to the dismay of his first wife, Fanny. Known for her performances in the Salt Lake Theatre, Zina Presendia could probably have married any leading man in the territory. She later claimed that she broke off the engagement after receiving a warning in a dream. When Stenhouse left the Church, she felt vindicated.[73]

William Godbe chose Augusta Cobb's thirty-year-old daughter, Charlotte, for his fourth wife. A skilled pianist and charming conversationalist, she had waited a long time to choose a mate and may have thought she had met her match. William's excommunication eventually led to a divorce, perhaps because Charlotte chose to remain with the Church, but also because Godbe began to question plural marriage. When Elizabeth Cady Stanton and Susan B. Anthony arrived in Salt Lake City in June 1871, William Godbe met them at the station. During their weeklong visit they spoke at the Liberal Institute, a new lecture hall constructed by the dissenters, as well as to big audiences in the Tabernacle. Charlotte, who had become interested in woman suffrage while visiting with relatives in Boston, may have been in both meetings.[74]

Some Mormon women brought their babies with them when they crowded into the Tabernacle to listen to a five-hour discourse from the two suffragists. Stanton did not appreciate the babies. In the account she wrote for *The Revolution,* the weekly newspaper she and Anthony had founded, she suggested that the Church appoint several humane bishops to dish out soothing syrup to anyone under three—not for the babies' sake, but for the comfort of those who wanted to hear the speakers. Still, she was impressed that so many Mormon women had come to hear her speak. With a bit more self-confidence than the situation warranted, she assured readers that the intelligent among them abhorred the Church's marital system.[75]

On July 2, Anthony attended a meeting at the Liberal Institute and asked to say a few words. As she later recalled, "I asked those men around me, bubbling over with the divine spirit of freedom for themselves, if they had thought whether the women of their households, (many of them still in polygamy) were today rejoicing in like manner?" She said some women in the audience began to weep.[76] Perhaps Fanny Stenhouse was one of them. She had tolerated her husband's first plural marriage, but was deeply distressed when she discovered love letters he had exchanged with Zina Presendia. Perhaps the speech Stanton gave, assailing the power of religion to keep women in thrall, propelled Fanny to break with the Church she had long supported. In 1872, she published a memoir that, when reissued in 1874 with a preface by Harriet Beecher Stowe, launched her career as an anti-Mormon lecturer.[77]

Ironically, it wasn't dissenters like Fanny but leaders within the Relief Society who formed the strongest alliance with Eastern suffragists. The *Woman's Exponent,* founded in 1872, became a relentless defender of both plural marriage and suffrage. Because the dissenters and their non-Mormon allies were badly outnumbered at the polls, they gave up any hope of eliminating plural marriage through the ballot and began to see federal intervention as their only hope of breaking Mormon power.[78]

In March 1872, Bathsheba Smith sent two letters to the editor of *The Woman's Journal,* a Boston periodical published by Lucy Stone's wing of the women's rights movement. Utah had included women on the committee to draft a constitution associated with a new petition for statehood, and women as well as men had voted on its ratification. Bathsheba enclosed a copy of what she believed was "the first American Constitution . . . recognizing the equal right of Suffrage" to all citizens, male or female, age twenty-one and over.[79] Henry Blackwell, the editor of the *Journal,* agreed with her. Although he laid out the concerns of those opposed to Utah statehood, he considered them wrong in both principle and policy. He argued that if polygamy was a problem, the proposed Constitution had put the power to change it into the hands of women. If dissenters were unable to convince the majority that they were wrong, then trying to impose force seemed injudicious. "It is a strange spectacle—this rejection of the State Constitution of Deseret," he concluded. *"For it is the only State Constitution that was ever framed by the representatives of the whole people, since the creation of the world."* (The emphasis was his.) He believed the Latter-day Saints had done everything possible to accommodate their critics except "ceasing to be Mormons," and that was something no conscientious American would ask.[80]

Congress rejected Utah's petition.

For the next quarter century, Latter-day Saints struggled to retain both the rights of citizenship and an ability to practice their religion. Brigham Young died in 1877. His successor, John Taylor, carried on the fight, sometimes while in hiding from federal marshals. When the Supreme Court ruled in 1879 that anti-polygamy laws were constitutional, Congress passed even stricter measures, culminating in the Edmunds-Tucker Act of 1887, which disincorporated the Church, abolished the Perpetual Emigrating Fund, dissolved the territorial militia, and rescinded the 1870 act on woman suffrage. Male polygamists had already lost the right to vote.[81]

During the long fight over plural marriage, nothing outraged Mormon women more than the notion that they were simply pawns of the patriarchy. At a mass meeting of women held in the Tabernacle in 1886, they emphatically denied "that we vote otherwise than according to our own free choice, and point to the fact that the ballot is absolutely secret in Utah as proof that we are protected in voting for whom and what we choose with perfect liberty." They had already seen neighbors, husbands, and brothers imprisoned. Now they were about to lose the right to vote. "And why are we thus persecuted?" Mary Isabella Horne asked. She had quilted with the Fourteenth Ward in 1857, had spoken at the indignation meeting in 1870, and had exercised the right to vote for the past seventeen years. They were being persecuted, she said, "because we choose to unite ourselves to honorable, God-fearing men."[82]

In 1889, Wilford Woodruff succeeded John Taylor as president of the Church. He was eighty-two years old. In 1885, he had watched from a window in a nearby building as Phebe's funeral procession passed along South Temple Street, unable to show himself in public lest he be arrested. Now, as rumors circulated that federal marshals were about to confiscate the laboriously constructed temples where Latter-day Saints had for the past ten years performed vicarious baptisms, endowments, and sealing ordinances, he earnestly prayed for God's help. His diary entry for September 25, 1890, was a long one. It began, "I have arrived at a point in the History of my life . . . where I am under the necessity of acting for the

Temporal Salvation of the Church." The next day, he issued the "Official Declaration" or "Manifesto" that began the arduous process of eradicating a social practice that had been part of the Church's teachings for more than fifty years. Years before, he had roused a congregation in the Salt Lake Tabernacle by telling them that they had to choose between obeying God or Congress. Now he appeared to have no choice but to advise the Saints to obey the law of the land.[83]

Some Latter-day Saint women rejoiced. Others wept. Many were simply confused. Whatever their feelings, those who had for so long led the defense of polygamy were determined that the Church's capitulation would not be in vain. Their work ensured that when Utah achieved statehood in 1896 its Constitution gave women not only the right to vote but the right to hold office. Since only two other states, Wyoming and Colorado, had by then adopted woman suffrage, their cause was almost as anomalous in 1896 as it had been in 1870. Although the support of high church officials, including Wilford Woodruff, helped, the real key to their success was their political experience and their grassroots work in the Relief Society. Religious commitment and political experience worked together to produce a definable result. Given their long struggle for political rights, it is not surprising that the first woman elected to a state senate in the United States was a female physician who had married in polygamy, or that, by 1900, Utah had a far higher proportion of its population affiliated with the national woman suffrage movement than any other state or territory in the nation.[84]

Ten of the women who launched the indignation meeting in 1870, including Sarah Kimball, lived to see Utah become a state. Lydia Alder, who had served as Kimball's secretary, attended international congresses of women in London in 1899, Berlin in 1904, and Rome in 1914. When Susan B. Anthony celebrated her eightieth birthday in 1900, Utah women sent her a length of brocaded silk they had raised and spun themselves. Anthony sent personal notes to all those who had contributed, concluding that her pleasure in the gift was "quadrupled because it was made by women politically equal to men." Many Utah suffragists, like their Eastern counterparts, were blessed with the gift of longevity. When Eliza Snow died in 1887, Zina Young succeeded her, and when Zina died in 1902, eighty-year-old Bathsheba Smith took up the cause.[85]

This book has focused on the earliest years and on the writings of ordinary people who between 1835 and 1870 translated the dissenting religions of Lancashire, upstate New York, and the Ohio Valley into Mormonism and carried its principles to the American West. Latter-day Saint women built the Church that claimed their loyalty. They sustained its missionary system, testified to its truths, and enhanced its joyful, performative, and playful elements—its July 24 processions, its feasts and dances, its theatrical festivals, its quiltings and spinning bees, and its exchanges of poetry, locks of hair, and cut-paper works. Without earnest female converts, Mormonism's meetings would have been less colorful and its revelations less intimate and personal. Mormon women blessed and healed one another in leaking log cabins, cried over unmarked graves left on plains and prairies, and wove motifs taken from sentimental annuals and the writings of upstart women into sacred discourse. They gave birth to the children who sustained the kingdom.

Certainly, there could have been no such thing as plural marriage if hundreds of women had not accepted "the principle" and passed it on to new generations. Some did so because they believed plural marriage was a glorious doctrine, others out of a hope for future exaltation or because conforming seemed a lesser evil than abandoning their homes and faith. Later generations of Latter-day Saints sometimes claimed that their pioneer ancestors lived "a higher law." If so, that higher law was not polygamy but a constellation of virtues—patience, forgiveness, and love—that allowed them to live together in peace. When those virtues failed, divorce or a separate house let them try again.

Mormonism has always been a faith of second chances. How else did its early adherents persist in building one promised Zion after another, even when the early ones failed? In the same way, confidence in new beginnings allowed earnest female leaders to turn the other cheek when officious men disparaged their religious gifts or denied the promises they believed God had given them. Living their religion, they learned wisdom by the things that they suffered, and when the opportunity came in 1870, they defended the right to speak for themselves.

Acknowledgments

All eight of my great-grandparents and four of my great-great-grandparents migrated to Utah before 1860. I grew up knowing their names and a few of their stories. I did not find it odd that my father had both a grandmother who sometimes lived with his family and a "Grandma on the hill." In personal essays over the years, I have explored some of this material. This book is my first attempt to approach early Mormonism as a work of scholarship.

When I began graduate school in the 1970s, I briefly considered writing about Mormonism, but Colonial and Revolutionary America captured my attention, and I took another path. I have spent the last eight years learning how little I actually knew about Latter-day Saint history. Years ago, Claudia Bushman, Maureen Ursenbach, Jill Derr, Carol Madsen, Linda Newell, and Lavina Fielding Anderson, with many others, created the field of LDS women's history. Again and again I came back to their work as I attempted to say something new.

I could not have completed this project without the expert assistance of Brittany Chapman at the Church History Library in Salt Lake City. I am especially grateful to Richard Turley for connecting me with her on the second day the library's new building on North Temple Street opened to the public. Brittany has been my guide ever since. I also appreciate the help of Jennifer Reeder, Robin Jensen, Emily Utt, Ronald Esplin, Carrie Snow, Bill Slaughter, Christy Best, Janelle Higbee, and Kate Holbrook, and many others. I am grateful as well to archivists and librarians at Brigham Young University, Utah State University, the University of Utah, and the Huntington Library. At the Utah Historical Society, Melissa Coy accomplished the seemingly impossible task of finding Caroline Crosby's diary. Kari Main became my guide to the treasure trove of images and artifacts collected by the Daughters of the Utah Pioneers and held at their Pioneer Memorial Museum. I also appreciate the generosity of Ron Fox, who showered me with marvelous images from his collection. I only wish I could have used more of them. At the last minute, the staff at the Springville Utah Art Museum kindly located the painting that now graces the cover of the book and then made arrangements to show it to me on a Saturday. Early in the project, Erica McGinnis and Elizabeth Hammond helped with periodical research. Working with Samantha Van Gerbig on maps and other graphics was a delight.

My source notes only hint at what I owe to conversations and e-mail exchanges with my fellow laborers in Mormon history—Jill Derr, Kathleen Flake, Richard Bushman, Kathryn Daynes, John Turner, Gary Bergera, Richard Jensen, Connell O'Donovan, Matt Grow, Jennifer Mackley, Barbara Jones Brown, and many others. Claudia Bushman read my first long draft, as did Ann Braude, Janet Polasky, and Sarah Pearsall, whose perspectives from outside the field of Mormon history were immensely helpful. Seemingly casual conversations with my family have also influenced my thinking. Gael Ulrich continues to be my best reader.

I gave my first paper on a chapter of this work at the Center for Pacific and American Studies at the University of Tokyo in May 2009. Subsequently, I shared bits of my work in progress with audiences at the University of Missouri, the University of Nebraska–Lincoln, Claremont Graduate School, Indiana University–Bloomington, the Milwaukee Art Museum, the DeWitt Wallace Gallery at Colonial Williamsburg, the New England Quilt Museum, the LDS Church History Museum, and at conferences of the American Association for State and Local History, the Mormon History Association, the Association of Living History and Farm Museums, and the Society for the Scientific Study of Religion. I appreciate the generosity of commentators and audiences at these events.

This work is better for my having subjected it to the very helpful criticism of students and colleagues in the American Studies Program at Harvard, at a remarkable soirée conducted by Michael Zuckerman and Sarah Barringer Gordon in Philadelphia, at the Harvard Divinity School's North American Religion Colloquium (NARC), and at material culture symposia organized by Ivan Gaskell and Sarah Ann Carter at Bard Graduate School and by Ruth Phillips at Harvard.

My presidential addresses at the 2009 American Historical Association Meeting and the 2015 Mormon Historical Association Conference in 2015, and the Sterling W. McMurrin Lecture that I gave at the University of Utah in 2012, have been published as "An American Album, 1857," *American Historical Review* 115 (Feb. 2010): 1–25; "Remember Me: Inscriptions of Self in Nineteenth-Century Mormonism," in *Women and Mormonism: Historical and Contemporary Perspectives,* ed. Kate Holbrook and Matthew Bowman (Salt Lake City: University of Utah Press, 2016), 41–55; and "Runaway Wives, 1830–1860," *Journal of Mormon History* 42 (April 2016): 1–26.

Jane Garrett, my longtime editor at Knopf, was an early advocate for this book. I appreciate the many persons at Knopf who helped see it through production after she retired, including senior editor Victoria Wilson and her assistant Ryan Smernoff. I am also grateful for the thoughtful and thorough copyediting of Anne Zaroff-Evans and for the patience of all those who facilitated my many revisions.

This is only a partial list of those who have helped me with this work. I thank one and all and blame no one.

—*Laurel Thatcher Ulrich, August 2016*

Abbreviations Used in Notes

Archives and Databases

CHL   Church of Jesus Christ of Latter-day Saints, Church History
Library, Salt Lake City, Utah

JSP   The Joseph Smith Papers, josephsmithpapers.org

HBLL   Harold B. Lee Library, Brigham Young University, Provo,
Utah

MOT   Mormon Pioneer Overland Travel, 1847–1868, history.lds.org
/overlandtravels/

Diaries, Letters, Affidavits, Minutes

AAC Family   Augusta Adams Cobb Family Papers, in Theodore Schroeder
Collection, 1845–1901, Microfilm, CHL.

AAC Letters   Augusta Adams Cobb Letters in Brigham Young Office Files.
CR 1234 1, Box 66, Folders 7–9, CHL.

Affidavits CM   Affidavits About Celestial Marriage, MS 3423, CHL. This
collection includes both bound volumes, which will be cited
by volume number, and loose documents, which will be cited
by folder.

AOS Papers   Abraham O. Smoot Papers, L. Tom Perry Special Collections,
HBLL.

AP   *The Journals of Addison Pratt,* ed. S. George Ellsworth (Salt
Lake City: University of Utah Press, 1990).

BWS Diary   Diary of Bathsheba W. Bigler Smith, George A. Smith Family
Papers, J. Willard Marriott Library, University of Utah, Salt
Lake City.

BWS Letters   Bathsheba W. Smith Letters, Family Correspondence,
George A. Smith Papers, 1322, CHL.

CBC   Diary of Caroline Barnes Crosby, Utah State Historical
Society MSS B-89, with transcription by S. George Ellsworth.
The diaries before 1857 have been published as *No Place to Call
Home: The 1807–1857 Life Writings of Caroline Barnes Crosby,*

ed. Edward Leo Lyman, Susan Ward Payne, and S. George Ellsworth (Logan: Utah State University Press, 2005).

CBC2   Diary of Caroline Barnes Crosby, Typescript, Utah Historical Society, Salt Lake City. MSS B-89, with transcription by S. George Ellsworth. For entries after 1857, I have cited page numbers in the Ellsworth transcript.

CMW   Catherine Mehring Woolley diary, transcribed and published by J. Cecil Alter, in his column "In the Beginning," *Salt Lake Telegram,* January 7–March 2, 1935.

EPL   Eliza P. Lyman Journal, MS 1527, CHL, published as *Eliza Maria Partridge Journal,* ed. Scott H. Partridge (Provo, Utah: Grandin Book Company, 2003).

ERS1   Eliza R. Snow Journal, 1842–1844, MS 1439, CHL, published in *The Personal Writings of Eliza Roxcy Snow,* ed. Maureen Ursenbach Beecher (Salt Lake City: University of Utah Press, 1995), 47–99.

ERS2   Diary of Eliza R. Snow, 1846–1849, Huntington Library, San Marino, Calif., published in *The Personal Writings of Eliza Roxcy Snow,* ed. Maureen Ursenbach Beecher (Salt Lake City: University of Utah Press, 1995), 109–230.

ERS3   Eliza R. Snow Smith, "Sketch of My Life," April 13, 1885, Bancroft Library, Berkeley, Calif., published in *The Personal Writings of Eliza Roxcy Snow,* ed. Maureen Ursenbach Beecher (Salt Lake City: University of Utah Press, 1995), 6–45.

ERS *Poetry*   *Eliza R. Snow: The Complete Poetry,* ed. Jill Mulvay Derr and Karen Lynn Davidson (Provo, Utah: Brigham Young University Press; Salt Lake City: University of Utah Press, 2009).

HCK   *On the Potter's Wheel: The Diaries of Heber C. Kimball,* ed. Stanley B. Kimball (Salt Lake City: Signature Books, 1987).

HS   Hosea Stout Papers, MSS B-53, Box 1, Utah Historical Society, Salt Lake City, and Hosea Stout Journal, 1844–1845, MS 1910, CHL published as *On the Mormon Frontier: The Diary of Hosea Stout, 1844–1889,* ed. Juanita Brooks (Salt Lake City: University of Utah Press and Utah State Historical Society, 1964).

HS Autobiography   Hosea Stout Papers, MSS G-53, Box 1, Utah Historical Society, Salt Lake City, published as *The Autobiography of Hosea Stout,* ed. Reed A. Stout (Salt Lake City: University of Utah Press, 2010).

KFL   Kimball Family Letters, ed. Pat Geisler, Heber C. Kimball Family Association, typescript, CHL.

LCT 1 and 2   Leonora Cannon Taylor Diary, 2 vols., George John Taylor Papers, MS 2936, CHL. Parts of the second journal have been published in Carol Cornwall Madsen, *Journey to Zion: Voices from the Mormon Trail* (Salt Lake City: Deseret Book, 1997), 197–216.

LMS Letters   Lucy Meserve Smith Letters, Family Correspondence, George A. Smith Papers, 1322, CHL.

MEK   Mary Ellen Harris Kimball Journal, MS 4218 2, CHL. A version of this with additional biographical materials has been published as *Journal of Mary Ellen Kimball* (Salt Lake City: Pioneer Press, 1994).

MPR   Mary Haskin Parker Richards Diary and Letters, published as *Winter Quarters: The 1846–1848 Life Writings of Mary Haskin Parker Richards,* ed. Maurine Carr Ward (Logan: Utah State University Press, 1996).

MPR Mem   Mary Parker Richards, "Memorandum," published as a separate chapter in *Winter Quarters: The 1846–1848 Life Writings of Mary Haskin Parker Richards,* ed. Maurine Carr Ward (Logan: Utah State University Press, 1996), 53–63.

MTS   Diary of Margaret T. Smoot, Abraham O. Smoot Papers, MS 896, box 2, folder 3. L. Tom Perry Special Collections, HBLL.

MTS Letters   Extracts from Margaret T. Smoot letters, in Olive Smoot Bean, "Life Sketch of Margaret T. Smoot," Abraham O. Smoot Papers, MS 896, box 2, folder 7. L. Tom Perry Special Collections, HBLL.

NRS Minutes   Book of Records, containing the proceedings of the Female Relief Society of Nauvoo, CHL; also online at JSP.

PGS   *Exemplary Elder: The Life and Missionary Diaries of Perrigrine Sessions, 1814–1893,* ed. Donna Toland Smart (Provo, Utah: Joseph Fielding Smith Institute, 2002).

PS   Patty B. Sessions, diaries and account book, 1846–1866, 1880, 8 vols., CHL, published in *Mormon Midwife: The 1846–1888 Diaries of Patty Bartlett Sessions,* ed. Donna Toland Smart (Logan: Utah State University Press, 1997).

SW   Samuel Amos Woolley Diaries, MS 1556 (Dec. 1850–Aug. 1853; Jan. 1856–Oct. 1857); MS 11996 (Aug. 1853–March 1854); MS 7468 (April 1854–Dec. 1855), CHL.

WC1   *Manchester Mormons: The Journal of William Clayton, 1840–1842,* ed. James B. Allen and Thomas G. Alexander (Santa Barbara and Salt Lake City: Peregrine Smith, 1974).

WC2   Journal of William Clayton, 1842–1846, Manuscript, 3 vols., CHL.

WC Smith   *An Intimate Chronicle: The Journals of William Clayton,* ed. George D. Smith (Salt Lake City: Signature Books, 1991).

WW 1–9   Wilford Woodruff Journals, 1828–1898, 15 vols., MS 1352, CHL, published as *Wilford Woodruff's Journal: 1833–1898,* 9 vols., ed. Scott G. Kenney (Midvale, Utah: Signature Books, 1983–85).

WW Collection   Wilford Woodruff Collection, 1830–1898, MS 5506, CHL.

WW Corr   Wilford Woodruff Journals and Papers, 1828–1898, MS 1352, CHL.

WW Letters   Wilford Woodruff Collection, 1831–1905, MS 19509, CHL.

WW Misc   Emma Smith Woodruff Collection, 1832–1919. CHL.

Z1   Zina D. H. Young Collection, MS 6240, CHL, published as "'All Things Move in Order in the City': The Nauvoo Diary of Zina Diantha Huntington Jacobs," ed. Maureen Ursenbach Beecher, *BYU Studies* 19 (Spring 1979): 285–320.

Z2   Zina C. Brown Collection, MS 4780, CHL, published as "'A Weary Traveler': The 1848–50 Diary of Zina D. H. Young," ed. Marilyn Higbee, *Journal of Mormon History* 19 (1993): 86–125.

Z3   Zina C. Brown Collection, MS 4780, CHL, loose pages.

Other Frequently Cited Works

Alexander, *Woodruff*   Thomas G. Alexander, *Things in Heaven and Earth: The Life and Times of Wilford Woodruff, a Mormon Prophet.* Salt Lake City: Signature Books, 1991.

Allen, *No Toil nor Labor*   James B. Allen, *No Toil nor Labor: The Story of William Clayton.* Provo, Utah: Brigham Young University Press, 2002.

Arrington, *BY*   Leonard J. Arrington, *Brigham Young: American Moses.* New York: Alfred A. Knopf, 1985.

Arrington, *Great Basin*   Leonard J. Arrington, *Great Basin Kingdom.* Urbana and Chicago: University of Illinois Press, 2005; orig. pub. 1958.

Arrington, *Woolley*   Leonard J. Arrington, *From Quaker to Latter-day Saint: Bishop Edwin D. Woolley.* Salt Lake City: Deseret Book, 1976.

Bennett, *WQ*   Richard E. Bennett, *Mormons at the Missouri: Winter Quarters, 1846–1852.* Norman: University of Oklahoma Press, 1987.

Bradley and Woodward   Martha Sonntag Bradley and Mary Brown Firmage Woodward, *Four Zinas: A Story of Mothers and Daughters on the Mormon Frontier.* Salt Lake City: Signature Books, 2000.

Bushman, *RSR*   Richard L. Bushman, *Joseph Smith: Rough Stone Rolling.* New York: Alfred A. Knopf, 2006.

Daynes, *Wives*   Kathryn M. Daynes, *More Wives Than One: Transformation of the Mormon Marriage System, 1840–1910.* Urbana and Chicago: University of Illinois Press, 2001.

Doctrine and Covenants   *The Doctrine and Covenants of the Church of Jesus Christ of Latter-Day Saints.* Salt Lake City: Church of Jesus Christ of Latter-day Saints, 1989. To find cited passages in earlier versions, see "Correlation of Current Doctrine and Covenants with Earliest Sources on the Joseph Smith Papers Website," josephsmithpapers.org.

EOM   *Encyclopedia of Mormonism,* ed. Daniel H. Ludlow. New York: Macmillan, 1992. Digital ed., Brigham Young University, 2007, eom.byu.edu.

First Fifty Years   *The First Fifty Years of Relief Society: Key Documents in Latter-day Saint Women's History,* ed. Jill Mulvay Derr, Carol Cornwall Madsen, Kate Holbrook, and Matthew J. Grow. Salt Lake City: Church Historian's Press, 2016.

Givens and Grow   Terryl L. Givens and Matthew J. Grow, *Parley P. Pratt: The Apostle Paul of Mormonism.* New York: Oxford University Press, 2011.

Hales, *Polygamy*	Brian C. Hales, *Joseph Smith's Polygamy,* vols. 1–3. Salt Lake City: Greg Kofford Books, 2013.
KJV	King James Version of the Bible. All citations are to individual books and verses.
Madsen, *In Their Own Words*	Carol Cornwall Madsen, *In Their Own Words: Women and the Story of Nauvoo*. Salt Lake City: Deseret Book, 1994.
Madsen, *Journey to Zion*	Carol Cornwall Madsen, *Journey to Zion: Voices from the Mormon Trail*. Salt Lake City: Deseret Book, 1997.
Newell and Avery, *Mormon Enigma*	Linda King Newell and Valeen Tippetts Avery, *Mormon Enigma: Emma Hale Smith*. Garden City, N.Y.: Doubleday, 1984.
O'Donovan, *Boston Mormons*	Connell O'Donovan, *Boston Mormons*. Online, connellodonovan.com/boston_mormons.
Tullidge, *Women*	Edward W. Tullidge, *The Women of Mormondom*. New York: Tullidge and Crandall, 1877.
Turner, *BY*	John Turner, *Brigham Young: Pioneer Prophet*. Cambridge, Mass.: Belknap Press, 2012.

Notes

Introduction: An Indignation Meeting

1. Minutes of a Ladies Mass meeting, Jan. 6, 1870, in Relief Society Minutes and Records, vol. 1, 1868–1873, Fifteenth Ward, Salt Lake Stake, CHL; Lola Van Wagenen, *Sister-Wives and Suffragists: Polygamy and the Politics of Woman Suffrage, 1870–1896* (Provo, Utah: Joseph Fielding Smith Institute for Latter-day Saint History and BYU Studies, 2003), 6, 7; Arrington, *Great Basin,* 356, 357; C. Mark Hamilton, *Nineteenth-Century Mormon Architecture and City Planning* (New York: Oxford University Press, 1995), 57–60. Although the new, domed-roof Tabernacle was complete, it had not yet fully replaced the old structure, in part because the architects had not solved the problem of poor acoustics.

2. Justin S. Morrill, "Utah Territory and Its Laws—Polygamy and Its License," Feb. 23, 1857, U.S. Congress, House, appendix to the Congressional Globe, 34th Cong., 2nd Sess., 284–90, quoted in *At Sword's Point, Part I: A Documentary History of the Utah War to 1858,* ed. William P. MacKinnon (Norman: University of Oklahoma Press, 2008), 87; "Republican Party Platform of 1856," June 18, 1846, in Gerhard Peters and John T. Woolley, *The American Presidency Project,* www.presidency.ucsb.edu; Kelly Elizabeth Phipps, "Marriage and Redemption: Mormon Polygamy in the Congressional Imagination, 1862–1887," *Virginia Law Review* 9 (April 2009): 435–64; Nancy F. Cott, *Public Vows: A History of Marriage and the Nation* (Cambridge, Mass.: Harvard University Press, 2000), 72–76, 111–31; Sarah Barringer Gordon, *The Mormon Question: Polygamy and Constitutional Conflict in Nineteenth-Century America* (Chapel Hill: University of North Carolina Press, 2002), 29–54.

3. Gary L. Bunker and Davis Bitton, "Illustrated Periodical Images of Mormons, 1850–1860," *Dialogue: A Journal of Mormon Thought* 10 (Spring 1977): 82–94; Terryl L. Givens, *Viper on the Hearth: Mormons, Myths, and the Construction of Heresy* (New York: Oxford University Press, 1997); Megan Sanborn Jones, *Performing American Identity in Anti-Mormon Melodrama* (New York: Routlege, 2009); Nancy Bentley, "Marriage as Treason: Polygamy, Nation, and the Novel," in *The Futures of American Studies,* ed. Donald E. Pearse and Robyn Wiegman (Durham, N.C.: Duke University Press, 2002), 341–70; and Bruce Burgett, "On the Mormon Question: Race, Sex, and Polygamy in the 1850s and the 1990s," *American Quarterly* 57 (March 2005): 75–102.

4. Michael E. Woods, " 'The Indignation of Freedom-Loving People': The Caning of Charles Sumner and Emotion in Antebellum Politics," *Journal of Social History* 44 (2011): 689–95; Fredrika Bremer, *The Homes of the New World,* trans. Mary Howitt (New York, 1853), vol. 2, 153; Nancy Isenberg, *Sex and Citizenship in Antebellum America* (Chapel Hill: University of North Carolina Press, 1998), 69–70, 129.

5. *Proceedings in Mass Meeting of the Ladies of Salt Lake City to Protest Against the Pas-*

sage of Cullom's Bill ([Salt Lake City], 1870), 4, 6, 7. See also "Great Indignation Meeting," *Deseret News,* Jan. 19, 1870, 5; *Daily Evening Bulletin* (San Francisco, Calif.), Jan. 18, 1870; *New York Times,* Feb. 8, 1870; Tullidge, *Women,* 400.

6. "Polygamy: Mass Meeting of Mormon Women in Salt Lake City," *New York Herald,* Jan. 23, 1870; *Daily Evening Bulletin,* Jan. 18, 1870; "The Mormon Women and the Anti-Polygamy Bill," *Daily Cleveland Herald,* Jan. 29, 1870.

7. T. A. Larson, "Woman Suffrage in Wyoming," *Pacific Northwest Quarterly* 56 (1965): 57–66; Virginia Scharff, *Twenty Thousand Roads: Women, Movement, and the West* (Berkeley and Los Angeles: University of California Press, 2003), 67–92; Dean May, "A Demographic Portrait of the Mormons, 1830–1980," in *The New Mormon History,* ed. D. Michael Quinn (Salt Lake City: Signature Books, 1992), 125; Lowell C. Bennion, "Plural Marriage, 1841–1904," in *Mapping Mormonism: An Atlas of Latter-day Saint History,* ed. Brandon S. Plewe (Provo, Utah: Brigham Young University Press, 2012), 122–25; Daynes, *Wives,* 100–102.

8. I have not been able to find the original *New York Times* piece, which was reprinted in part in "The Female Suffrage Question," *Deseret News,* Jan. 15, 1868. For similar arguments in favor of enfranchising Utah women and responses to the territorial passage, see Beverly Beeton, "Woman Suffrage in Territorial Utah," *Utah Historical Quarterly* 46 (Spring 1978): 100–120, reprinted in *Battle for the Ballot: Essays on Woman Suffrage in Utah, 1870–1896,* ed. Carol Cornwall Madsen (Logan: Utah State University Press, 1997), 116–35. The New Jersey writer's response is in *Centinel of Freedom* (Newark, N.J.) LXXIV, issue 7 (Feb. 15, 1870): 1.

9. "Mrs. Stanton on Mormon Women," *Daily Evening Bulletin,* July 25, 1871; Elizabeth Cady Stanton, "Overland Letters: The City of the Saints," *Revolution* 8, no. 2 (July 13, 1871): 1, 2.

10. In addition to Jill Mulvay Derr, Janath Russell Cannon, and Maureen Ursenbach Beecher, *Women of Covenant: The Story of Relief Society* (Salt Lake City: Deseret Book, 1992), and Madsen, ed., *Battle for the Ballot,* foundational works on these topics include Carol Cornwall Madsen, *An Advocate for Women: The Public Life of Emmeline B. Wells, 1870–1920* (Provo, Utah: Brigham Young University Press, 2006), and essays by Carol Cornwall Madsen, Linda King Newell, and Jill Mulvay Derr in *Sisters in Spirit: Mormon Women in Historical and Cultural Perspective,* ed. Maureen Ursenbach Beecher and Lavina Fielding Anderson (Urbana and Chicago: University of Illinois Press, 1987).

11. E.g., Joan Iversen, "Feminist Implications of Mormon Polygyny," *Feminist Studies* 10 (1984): 505–22; Anne Firor Scott, "Mormon Women, Other Women: Paradoxes and Challenges," *Journal of Mormon History* 13 (1986): 3–19; Julie Roy Jeffrey, *Frontier Women: "Civilizing" the West, 1840–1880* (New York: Hill and Wang, 1998), 191; Patricia Lyn Scott and Linda Thatcher, eds., *Women in Utah History: Paradigm or Paradox?* (Logan: Utah State University Press, 2005). Margaret Toscano and Paul Toscano, *Strangers in Paradox: Explorations in Mormon Theology* (Salt Lake City: Signature Books, 1990), and Terryl L. Givens, *People of Paradox: A History of Mormon Culture* (New York: Oxford University Press, 2007), have applied the same term to Mormonism as a whole.

12. The involvement of women in pubic appeals began in the aftermath of the expulsion from Missouri and continued in Nauvoo. On the broader significance of such activities for women's political development in the antebellum United States, see Isenberg, *Sex and Citizenship in Antebellum America,* 41–74.

13. Minutes of a Ladies Mass meeting Jan. 6, 1870; "To His Excellency, the Acting Governor of the Territory of Utah, S. A. Mann," *Deseret News Weekly,* March 2, 1870.

14. The names appear in *Proceedings in Mass Meeting of the Ladies of Salt Lake City.* For biographical information, I relied on life sketches in Tullidge, *Women,* 63–67, 121–32, 150–55, 201–14, 403–6, 423–24, 456–57, 490–95; Steven P. Pratt, "Eleanor McLean and the Murder of Parley P. Pratt," Jared Pratt Family Association website; MOT; FamilySearch .org. Some but not all of these women are among those described as "leading sisters" in

Maureen Ursenbach Beecher, *Eliza and Her Sisters* (Salt Lake City: Aspen Books, 1991), 129–47.

15. *Proceedings in Mass Meeting.*

16. Daynes, *Wives,* 31. Attempts to identify plural marriages in Nauvoo include Todd Compton, *In Sacred Loneliness: The Plural Wives of Joseph Smith* (Salt Lake City: Signature, 1997); George D. Smith, *Nauvoo Polygamy* (Salt Lake City: Signature Books, 2008); Gary James Bergera, "Identifying the Earliest Mormon Polygamists, 1841–1844," *Dialogue: A Journal of Mormon Thought* 38, no. 3 (Fall 2005): 1–74; and Hales, *Polygamy.*

17. NRS Minutes, 22 (March 30, 1842). On the complex Mormon concept of priesthood, see Kathleen Flake, "The Emotional and Priestly Logic of Plural Marriage," Leonard J. Arrington Lecture, Utah State University, 2009, and her forthcoming book on that subject.

18. On the numbers, see Maurine Carr Ward, " 'This Institution Is a Good One': The Female Relief Society of Nauvoo, 17 March 1842 to 16 March 1844," *Mormon Historical Studies* 3 (Fall 2002): 90.

19. Joseph Smith, "Discourse," April 7, 1844, as reported by William Clayton, JSP; ERS *Poetry,* 376, 377. For variant interpretations of these themes, see Bushman, *RSR,* 420–23, 533–37; Samuel Morris Brown, *In Heaven as It Is on Earth: Joseph Smith and the Early Mormon Conquest of Death* (New York: Oxford University Press, 2012), 146–49, 224–41; Taylor G. Petrey, "Toward a Post Heterosexual Mormon Theology," *Dialogue: A Journal of Mormon Thought* 44, no. 4 (Winter 2011): 106–43; and Laurel Thatcher Ulrich, "Remember Me: Sensibility and the Sacred in Early Mormonism in *Oxford Handbook of History and Material Culture,* ed. Ivan Gaskell and Sarah Anne Carter (forthcoming).

20. W. Randall Dixon, "The Beehive and Lion Houses," in *Brigham Young's Homes,* ed. Colleen Whitley (Logan: Utah State University Press, 2002), 128–31; Thomas Carter, "Living the Principle: Mormon Polygamous Housing in Nineteenth-Century Utah," *Winterthur Portfolio* 35 (2000): 223–51.

21. Lowell C. Bennion and Thomas R. Carter, "Touring Polygamous Utah with Elizabeth W. Kane, Winter 1872–1873," in *Colonel Thomas L. Kane and the Mormons, 1846–1883,* ed. David J. Whittaker (Salt Lake City: University of Utah Press, 2010), 163–66, 179–82; Lowell C. Bennion et al., *Polygamy in Lorenzo Snow's Brigham City: An Architectural Tour* (Salt Lake City: Western Regional Architecture Program, University of Utah, 2005), 26; Marie Cornwall, Camela Courtright, and Laga Van Beek, "How Common the Principle? Women as Plural Wives in 1860," *Dialogue: A Journal of Mormon Thought* 26 (1993): 149; Daynes, *Wives,* 101, 130–33.

22. Biographical information on the Dorius family is from FamilySearch.org supplemented by U.S. Census information for 1860 and 1870 from Ancestry.com.

23. Ruth Christensen Forslund, Gunild Ryerson Togerson, familysearch.org/photos /stories/2141233.

24. Carol Holindrake Nielson, *The Salt Lake City 14th Ward Album Quilt, 1857: Stories of the Relief Society Women and Their Quilt* (Salt Lake City: University of Utah Press, 2004), 7–11, 203, 206. Dan Nielson and Shirley Mumford, who inherited the two segments, are both descendants of Richard Henry Horne, the winner of the raffle. I thank Carol for showing me the quilt, for answering many questions, and for providing illustrations for my first attempt to write about the quilt, "An American Album," *American Historical Review* 115 (2010): 1–25.

25. WW 5:36–37 (March 17, 1857).

26. WW 4:445 (Sept. 6, 1856).

27. Maureen Ursenbach Beecher, Introduction, "The Life Writings of Ordinary Women," in *The Personal Writings of Eliza Roxcy Snow,* ed. Maureen Ursenbach Beecher (Salt Lake City: University of Utah Press, 1995), xv.

28. For example, there are only five diaries kept by women among the 114 missionary diaries recently digitized by the Brigham Young University Library. "About the Collec-

tion," Mormon Missionary Diaries, Digital Collection, HBLL, http://lib.byu.edu/digital /mmd/about.php.

29. MEK, Sept. 16, 24, Oct. 5, Dec. 19, 1858; March 3, April 7, 1859; May 19–June 1, 1862.

30. Beecher, ed., *Personal Writings of Eliza Roxcy Snow,* 47–48.

31. Z1, 1–2; Martha Sonntag Bradley and Mary Brown Firmage Woodward, *Four Zinas: A Story of Mothers and Daughters on the Mormon Frontier* (Salt Lake City: Signature Books, 2000), vii, viii.

32. BWS Diary. The granddaughter was apparently Margaret May Merrill Fisher (1872–1946), the great-granddaughter Josephine Abby Fisher Affleck (1908–1992). See "Margaret May Smith Merrill Fisher" entry in Find a Grave online (www.findagrave.com), and "Margaret May Merrill Fisher," Springville Museum of Art website.

33. On the history of the manuscript minutes, see Jill Mulvay Derr and Carol Cornwall Madsen, "Preserving the Record and Memory of the Female Relief Society of Nauvoo, 1842–92," *Journal of Mormon History* 35 (Summer 2009): 88–117. I have a photocopy of a transcription given to me by a friend sometime after 1982 with a note explaining that the microfilm could be consulted by researchers in the Church Archives but that the typescript was for my files only, and "Under no circumstances is it, or any portion of it, to be copied or loaned." A digital edition of the Nauvoo Relief Society Minutes was made available in 2011 in JSP. The minutes are now in print in *The First Fifty Years of Relief Society: Key Documents in Latter-day Saint Women's History,* ed. Jill Mulvay Derr, Carol Cornwall Madsen, Kate Holbrook, and Matthew J. Grow (Salt Lake City: Church Historian's Press, 2015), a meticulously edited collection that includes other important early records.

34. WW 4:200 (Feb. 15, 1853).

1. "Wonder on wonder strikes my sense"

1. WW 1:106–8 (Nov. 25, 1836); Bushman, *RSR,* 286, 297. On the display of Egyptian antiquities in the early United States, see. S. J. Wolfe and Robert Singerman, "Admission Twenty-Five Cents—Children Half-Price: Exhibiting Egyptian Mummies in Nineteenth-Century America," in *Life on the Streets and Commons, 1600 to the Present,* ed. Peter Benes, Proceedings of the 2005 Dublin Seminar on New England Folk-Life (Boston: Boston University Press, 2007), 124–41.

2. James Harrison Kennedy, *Early Days of Mormonism: Palmyra, Kirtland, and Nauvoo* (New York: C. Scribner's Sons, 1888), 131–32; Bushman, *RSR,* 215–19; Elwin C. Robison, *The First Mormon Temple: Design, Construction, and Historic Context of the Kirtland Temple* (Provo, Utah: Brigham Young University Press, 1997), 33–39, 79, 113, 114; Mark Lyman Staker, *Hearken, O Ye People: The Historical Setting for Joseph Smith's Ohio Revelations* (Salt Lake City: Greg Kofford Books, 2009), 410–13, 425, 426, 437, 455 n8, 456 n17. Contrary to legend, Latter-day Saint women didn't add their best china to the stucco; the ceramics came from nearby trash heaps.

3. *Doctrine and Covenants,* 88:119. Lest there be any doubt about the name, the Saints had inscribed its name on a plaque mounted just beneath the roof: "House of the Lord, built by the Church of the Latter Day Saints, a.d. 1834." Although begun in 1834, the building was completed in 1836.

4. Steven C. Harper, " 'A Pentecost and Endowment Indeed': Six Eyewitness Accounts of the Kirtland Temple Experience," in *Opening the Heavens: Accounts of Divine Manifestations, 1820–1844,* ed. John W. Welch and Erick B. Carlson (Provo, Utah: Brigham Young University Press; Salt Lake City: Deseret Book, 2005), 327–71; "Pentecost Continued: A Contemporaneous Account of the Kirtland Temple Dedication," *BYU Studies* 42, no. 2 (2003): 4–22.

5. WW 1:56, 57, 58, 60, 61, 62 (Feb. 1, 15, 16, 27, March 11, 12, 1836).

6. WW 1:109 (Nov. 27, 1836); Isaiah 56:3–5.

7. Wilford inserted birth and death dates for his siblings in an undated section of his 1837 diary; WW 1:160, 161. Also see Alexander, *Woodruff,* 6–10, 15–22.

8. Wilford summarized his early life at the beginning of his first diary. WW 1:5, 6.

9. WW 1:17–106 (Jan. 13, 1835 to Nov. 14, 1836), passim; Alexander, *Woodruff,* 35.

10. *Doctrine and Covenants,* 68:4.

11. This analysis is based on a physical examination of the manuscript diaries. See also Alexander, *Woodruff,* 10–22, 35–43.

12. WW 1:113–14 (Dec. 31, 1836).

13. "Wilford Woodruffs Day Book & Journal Containing an Acount of my travels in the Ministry as a member of the church of Latter Day Saints of 1835," CHL 5506, box 1, folder 4.

14. WW 1:110, 122, 123; *Early Patriarchal Blessings of the Church of Latter-day Saints,* comp., H. Michael Marquardt (Salt Lake City: Smith-Pettit Foundation, 2007), 152.

15. Bushman *RSR,* 310–15; Exodus 30:30, 40:12–15; Exodus 30:22–25.

16. WW 1:129–31 (April 4, 1837).

17. George A. Smith, "Gathering and Sanctification of the People of God," sermon delivered March 18, 1855, *Journal of Discourses* 2 (Liverpool: F. D. Richards, 1855), 215.

18. Tullidge, *Women,* 99, 207, 208. See also Newell and Avery, *Mormon Enigma,* 59; Linda King Newall, "Gifts of the Spirit: Women's Share," and Carol Cornwall Madsen, "Mormon Women and the Temple: Toward a New Undestanding," in *Sisters in Spirit: Mormon Women in Historical and Cultural Perspective,* ed. Maureen Ursenbach Beecher and Lavina Fielding Anderson (Urbana and Chicago: University of Illinois Press, 1987), 113, 81.

19. See *The Journals of William E. McLellin, 1831–1836,* ed. Jan Shipps and John W. Welch (Provo, Utah, and Urbana and Chicago: BYU Studies and University of Illinois Press, 1994), 34; and the essay by William G. Hartley, "The McLellin Journals and Early Mormon History," in the same volume. Other descriptions appear in excerpts from the writings of Caroline Barnes Crosby and Mary Fielding Smith, in *Women's Voices: An Untold History of the Latter-day Saints, 1830–1900,* ed. Kenneth W. Godfrey, Audrey M. Godfrey, and Jill Mulvay Derr (Salt Lake City: Deseret Book, 1982), 48–51, 61. Crosby suggests that "Mother Smith" confirmed the blessings her husband gave.

20. WW 1:121 (Jan. 6, 1837); Staker, *Hearken,* 244, 245, 248 n14.

21. WW 1:126 (March 23, 1837).

22. Bushman, *RSR,* 144–55; Staker, *Hearken,* 147–68. Both Bushman and Staker cite *Doctrine and Covenants,* 52:12–19, as related to this controversy. The original text can be found in *The Joseph Smith Papers: Revelations and Translations: Manuscript Revelation Books* (Salt Lake City: Church Historian's Press, 2009), 149.

23. WW 1:126, 127 (March 23, 1837).

24. Bushman, *RSR,* 218; C. Mark Hamilton, *Nineteenth-Century Mormon Architecture and City Planning* (New York: Oxford University Press, 1995), 34–38.

25. WW 1:141 (April 13, 1837).

26. "Ezra Carter's Family Record," in WW 1:200, 201.

27. *Doctrine and Covenants,* 88:70.

28. Alexander, *Woodruff,* 52; "Phebe W. Carter Woodruff," in *Representative Women of Deseret,* comp. Augusta Joyce Crocheron (Salt Lake City: J. C. Graham, 1884), 35, 36.

29. Based on searches for the two phrases in http://www.forgottenbooks.com/word data/.

30. PW to "Beloved Parents," c. 1836, WW Letters.

31. "Phebe W. Carter Woodruff," 35.

32. ERS3, 6, 10; CBC, 35–37.

33. Bradley and Woodward, 53.

34. Without more genealogical research, it is difficult to give precise numbers. By my

count, Joseph Smith, Sr., gave blessings to 129 males, 33 females, 73 couples, and 12 family groups. I arrived at these numbers simply by counting the names in *Early Patriarchal Blessings,* 21–179.

35. *Early Patriarchal Blessings,* 22, 110, 113, 121: *Joseph Smith Papers: Journals* (Salt Lake City: Church Historian's Press, 2008), 1:73, 420 (Oct. 25, 1835).

36. *Early Patriarchal Blessings,* 146.

37. *Early Patriarchal Blessings,* 126; *Joseph Smith Papers: Journals,* 1:109–10, 419 (Nov. 24, 1835); William G. Hartley, "Newell and Lydia Bailey Knight's Love Story and Historic Wedding," *BYU Studies* 39, no. 4 (2000): 6–22; M. Scott Bradshaw, "Joseph Smith's Performance of Marriages in Ohio," *BYU Studies* 39, no. 4 (2000): 23–69; Lydia Goldthwaite to Dear Papa and Mama, June 22, 1833, in Letters and Papers of Lydia Knight and Newel Knight, typescript, 1–2, L. Tom Perry Special Collections, HBLL; Newell Knight, Autobiography and Journal, typescript, CHL.

38. ERS *Poetry,* xxiv, xxv, 6–70; ERS3, 10, 259 n19; "Great is the Lord" and "The Glorious Day Is Rolling On," in *A Collection of Sacred Hymns for the Church of the Latter-day Saints,* selected by Emma Smith (Kirtland, Ohio: F. G. Williams, 1835), 92–94. Although dated 1835, the hymnbook was probably printed early in 1836, with W. W. Phelps assisting Emma Smith as editor. See Michael Hicks, *Mormonism and Music: A History* (Urbana and Chicago: University of Illinois Press, 1989), 19–20. On desertion as "self-divorce," see Nancy F. Cott, *Public Vows: A History of Marriage and the Nation* (Cambridge, Mass.: Harvard University Press, 2000), 38; Henrik Hartog, *Man & Wife in America* (Cambridge, Mass.: Harvard University Press, 2000), passim.

39. *Early Patriarchal Blessings,* 179; "John Harvey Ballard," www.biographicwiki.com /index.php/John_Harvey Ballard (1825–1891).

40. *Early Patriarchal Blessings,* 121.

41. *Early Patriarchal Blessings,* 113.

42. *Early Patriarchal Blessings,* 84.

43. *Early Patriarchal Blessings,* 92, 93.

44. Wilford copied Phebe's blessing as well as his own into an undated section of his 1837 diary (WW 1:144–45). Both also appear in *Early Patriarchal Blessings,* 86, 87, 155, 156.

45. ERS3, 10.

46. WW 1:10, 118 (Dec. 20–27, 1836; Jan. 3, 1837); Milton Homes, in Reference/People, JSP.

47. Nathaniel Milliken was born in Buxton, a town just inland from Scarborough. Mary's hometown of Saco, Maine, shares a border with Scarborough. See *Early Patriarchal Blessings,* 130, 131; Nathaniel Milliken, Reference/People, JSP. I found only six other persons from Maine in this Kirtland blessing book, among dozens from the other New England states.

48. Kathleen Flake, "The Development of Early Latter-day Saint Marriage Rites, 1831–53," *Journal of Mormon History* 41, no. 1 (2015): 77–102. Some writers interpret an allusion in an 1838 slander trial against Oliver Cowdery as evidence that Smith had an extramarital relationship with Fanny Alger, a young woman living in his household in Kirtland. Much later, some Mormons began interpreting this as an attempt at plural marriage. For the Alger story, see Newell and Avery, *Mormon Enigma,* 64–67; Bushman, *RSR,* 323–27; and the early chapters in Hales, *Polygamy,* 1:85–152.

49. M. Scott Bradshaw, "Joseph Smith's Performance of Marriages in Ohio," *BYU Studies* 39, no. 4 (2000): 60.

50. *Joseph Smith Papers: Journals,* 1:165–66 (Jan. 20, 1836).

51. WW 1:140–41 (April 13, 1837).

52. WW 1:140–41 (April 13, 1837).

53. WW 1:147–49 (May 30–31, 1837).

54. WW 1:149–50 (June 4–5, 1837).

55. WW 1:155–58 (June 22, 28, 1837).

56. Alexander, *Woodruff,* 11, 12.

57. WW 1:159–61 (July 6, 1837).

58. WW 1:163 (July 12, 1837).

59. PW to WW, Canaan, Conn., July 9, 1837, WW Letters.

60. WW to PW, Kingston, Upper Canada, June 14, 1837, WW Letters.

61. WW 1:164–67 (July 14–Aug. 8, 1837).

62. Augustus F. Moulton, *Grandfather Tales of Scarborough* (Augusta, Maine: Katahdin Publishing Company, 1926), 3–8, 21–22. Moulton's mother, Shuah Carter Moulton, was Phebe Woodruff's younger sister.

63. In his first reference, Wilford called his brother-in-law Joseph F., but he soon learned to call him "Fabyan," the name commonly used by the family. WW 1:168 (Aug. 8 and 11, 1837).

64. Sarah Brackett Fabyan died in Scarborough in 1820, and Phebe Whittemore Carter in New Hampshire in 1823.

65. WW 1:167–68 (Aug. 8, 10, 1837); "Ezra Carter's Family Record," WW 1:200, 201. Rhoda Carter married Luther Scammon on Nov. 12, 1837. Although Wilford, who had by that time left Phebe at her parents' house and gone preaching, did not note it, the next time he mentioned Rhoda, she was "Rhoda Scammon," and when he and Phebe visited her, it was at "Luther Scammon's house" in Saco (WW 1:244 [May 4, 1838]; 1:282 [Aug. 31, 1838]). The date of Rhoda's marriage in Kenney's transcription of the family records is wrong: the 1839 should be 1837.

66. In 1810, Connecticut, Maine, and Ohio each had between 225,000 and 250,000 inhabitants. In 1840, Connecticut had 310,015, Maine 501,793, and Ohio 1,519,467. Massachusetts had 472,000 in 1810 and 737,699 in 1840. See "Historical Census Browser," University of Virginia Library, mapserver.lib.virginia.edu.

67. WW 1:168 (Aug. 11, 1837).

68. WW 1:170 (Aug. 20, 1837).

69. WW 1:172, 174, 173 (Aug. 22, Sept. 3, Aug. 27, Sept. 4, 1837).

70. WW 1:135 (March 30, 1838); Linda King Newell, "Gifts of the Spirit: Women's Share," in *Sisters in Spirit,* ed. Beecher and Anderson, 111–50; Jonathan A. Stapley and Kristine Wright, "Female Ritual Healing in Mormonism," *Journal of Mormon History* 37, no. 1 (Winter 2011): 1–85.

71. Entries on Joseph Ball in O'Donovan, *Boston Mormons.* In this period, there was no restriction on the ordination of African Americans to the LDS priesthood. On Ball's father, see *Laws of the African Society* (Boston: For the Society, 1796), 7. On his sisters, see Debra Gold Hansen, *Strained Sisterhood: Gender and Class in the Boston Female Anti-Slavery Society* (Amherst: University of Massachusetts Press, 1993).

72. WW 1:191, 193, 234, 235 (Dec. 20, 23, 31, 1837; March 29, 1838); PW to WW, Vinalhaven, Maine, March 1, 1838, WW Letters.

73. WW 1:191, 228, 234, 235 (Dec. 20, 23, 31, 1837, Jan. 21, March 29, 1838); Alexander, *Woodruff,* 60, 61. Although the Baptists had a meetinghouse by 1810, they had difficulty keeping clergy. See Joshua Millet, *A History of the Baptists in Maine* (Portland: Charles Day, 1845), 189–90.

74. WW 1:221, 225, 180, 224 (Jan. 13, 16, Feb. 1, 1838; Oct. 30, 1837; Jan. 31, 1838); 2 Kings 2:23–24.

75. Bushman, *RSR,* 328–32, 336–41; Staker, *Hearken,* 519–40.

76. PW to WW, March 2, 1838, WW Letters; Alexander, *Woodruff,* 74; Milton V. Backman Jr., "Kirtland, Ohio," *EOM.*

77. WW 1:240 (April 17, 1838).

78. WW 1:240–43 (April 17–30, 1838).

79. WW 1:247 (May 11, 1838).

80. WW 1:247–49 (May 11–14, 1838). On the role of Boston women in the early Church, see Christopher M. B. Allison, "Layered Lives: Boston Mormons and the Spatial Contexts of Conversion," *Journal of Mormon History* 41, no. 2 (April 2016): 168–213.

81. WW 1:258–69 (June 10–July 8, 1858).

82. WW 1:263 (July 1, 1838).

83. WW 1:265–69. Wilford placed this clearly retrospective account on two facing pages to set them off from his regular diary entries, dating them both July 1, 1838.

84. Alexander, *Woodruff*, 70; WW 1:267 (July 1, 1838).

85. WW 1:143 (April 15, 1837).

86. WW 1:271 (July 14, 1838).

87. WW 1:276–77 (Aug. 9, 1838).

88. WW 1:283, 288 (Sept. 5, 6, 13, 1838).

89. WW 1:282, 283, 284, 288 (Aug. 28, 29, 31, Sept. 9, 14, 1838).

90. WW 1:285–87, 290–91 (Sept. 11, 24, 25, 1838).

91. WW 1:293, 294 (Oct. 3, 4, 1838).

92. WW 1:295 (Oct. 4, 1838).

93. WW 1:304–6 (Nov. 27–Dec. 4, 1838); *Wilford Woodruff: History of His Life and Labors as Recorded in His Daily Journals,* ed. Matthias F. Cowley (1909; Salt Lake City: Bookcraft, 1964), 97–98.

94. WW 1:299, 201, 203, 204–5, 307–11 (Nov. 3, 16, 20, 23, Dec. 8–11, 1838).

95. WW 1:309 (Dec. 12, 1848).

96. WW 1:312–14 (Dec. 19–31, 1838).

2. *"There was many Sick among the Saints"*

1. Bushman, *RSR,* 222–27, 235–47; Jackson County Manifesto, in *History of the Church of Jesus Christ of Latter-day Saints,* ed. B. H. Roberts (Salt Lake City: Deseret Book, 1957), vol. 1, 374–76.

2. See Stephen C. LeSueur, *The 1838 Mormon War in Missouri* (Columbia: University of Missouri Press, 1987); Thomas M. Spencer, ed., *Missouri Mormon* (Columbia: University of Missouri Press, 2010); Jeffrey N. Walker, "Mormon Land Rights in Caldwell and Daviess Counties and the Mormon Conflict of 1838," *BYU Studies* 47, no. 1 (2008): 4–55.

3. Leland H. Gentry, "Missouri," and Max H. Parkin, "The Mormon Conflict," in *EOM,* 927, 931, estimate twelve thousand. William G. Hartley, "'Almost Too Interolerable a Burthen': The Winter Exodus from Missouri, 1838–39," *Journal of Mormon History* 18 (1992): 7, suggests eight thousand, but "Missouri's 1838 Extermination Order and the Mormons' Forced Removal to Illinois," *Mormon Historical Studies* 2 (Spring 2001): 22, says "more than ten thousand."

4. WW 1:347 (July 22, 1839). Later variants include "History of Wilford Woodruff [From His Own Pen]," *Millennial Star,* May 27, 1865, 326, 327; Wilford Woodruff, *Leaves From My Journal,* 2nd ed. (Salt Lake City: Juvenile Instructor Office, 1882), 62–65; "Autobiography of Wilford Woodruff," *Tullidge's Quarterly Magazine* 3 (April 1884): 126; *Wilford Woodruff: History of His Life and Labors As Recorded in His Daily Journals,* ed. Matthias F. Cowley (1909; Salt Lake City: Bookcraft, 1964), 104–6; Roberts, ed., *History of the Church,* vol. 4, 3–5; Debbie Birch, "A Day of God's Power," *New Era,* March 1971; "A Day of God's Power," *The Friend,* Feb. 2009 (with comic-book-like illustrations); *Teachings of Presidents of the Church: Joseph Smith,* Melchizedek Priesthood and Relief Society Course of Study (Salt Lake City: Church of Jesus Christ of Latter-day Saints, 2007), 379–81.

5. WW 1:325–29 (April 8–26, 1839); *Doctrine and Covenants,* 118:4; Arrington, *BY,* 69–72; Larry C. Porter, "Brigham Young and the Twelve in Quincy: A Return to the Eye of the Missouri Storm, 26 April 1839," *Mormon Historical Studies* 2, no. 1 (Spring 2001): 29–58; Alexander, *Woodruff,* 74, 82.

6. Givens and Grow, 165, 166; Samuel W. Taylor, *The Kingdom or Nothing: The Life of John Taylor, Militant Mormon* (New York: Macmillan, 1976), 61–62; Breck England, *The Life and Thought of Orson Pratt* (Salt Lake City: University of Utah Press, 1985); Theodore Turley, Journal, vol. 1, 1839–1840, Special Collections, HBLL.

7. Stanley B. Kimball, *Heber C. Kimball: Mormon Patriarch and Pioneer* (Urbana and Chicago: University of Illinois Press, 1981), 40–54; Robert Bruce Flanders, *Nauvoo: Kingdom on the Mississippi* (Urbana and Chicago: University of Illinois Press, 1965), 58; Leonard J. Arrington and Davis Bitton, *The Mormon Experience: A History of the Latter-day Saints* (New York: Alfred A. Knopf, 1979), 129.

8. 1 Nephi 5:2–3; Jacob 2:32–35.

9. Randall M. Packard, *The Making of a Tropical Disease: A Short History of Malaria* (Baltimore: Johns Hopkins University Press, 2007), 19–23. See also "Malaria," Earth Institute, Columbia University, http://www.earth.columbia.edu/articles/view/43.

10. Packard, *Making of a Tropical Disease,* 17–18.

11. WW 1:348 (July 25, 29, Aug. 6, 1839).

12. WW 1:349–50 (Aug. 7, 10, 11, 1839); Erwin H. Acherknecht, *Malaria in the Upper Mississippi Valley, 1760–1900* (Baltimore: Johns Hopkins Press, 1945; New York: Arno Press, 1977), 107. For a short biography of Sappington and an image of an advertisement for his "fever and ague pills," see Historical Society of Missouri website, shs.umsystem.edu /outreach/mohist/may15.

13. WW 2:50 (Feb. 20, 1842).

14. PW to WW, Sept. 19, 1839, WW Letters.

15. Leonora Taylor to John Taylor, Sept. 9, 1839, CHL.

16. The most important American transmitter of malaria, a mosquito with the scientific name *Anopheles quadrimaculatus,* doesn't multiply rapidly enough to have been a serious problem, but in areas with an abundance of stagnant water, such as the Illinois river bottoms, serious outbreaks have developed. As recently as 2003, a breakdown in routine maintenance of irrigation canals caused an epidemic in Palm Beach County, Florida. (Packard, *Making of a Tropical Disease,* 6, 7, 61–63.) For the impact of malaria in another early settlement, with particular attention to high mortality among childbearing women, see Darrett B. and Anita H. Rutman, "Of Agues and Fevers: Malaria in the Early Chesapeake," *William & Mary Quarterly,* 3d ser., 33 (1976): 31–60.

17. Vilate to Heber Kimball, Sept. 21, 1839, and Heber C. Kimball to Vilate, Oct. 25, 1839, KFL.

18. PW to WW, Sept. 19, 1839, CHL.

19. Leonora Taylor to John Taylor, Sept. 9, 1839, CHL. On organized efforts to get the poor out of Missouri, see Glen M. Leonard, *Nauvoo: A Place of Peace, a People of Promise* (Salt Lake City: Deseret Book; Provo, Utah: Brigham Young University Press, 2002), 275–77.

20. Leonora Taylor to John Taylor, Sept. 9, 1839, CHL.

21. Stanley B. Kimball, "Nauvoo West: The Mormons of the Iowa Shore," *BYU Studies* 18 (Winter 1978): 132–42; Anne F. Hyde, *Empires, Nations & Families: A History of the North American West, 1800–1860* (Lincoln: University of Nebraska Press, 2011), 478; Thomas Burnell Colbert, "'The Hinge on Which All Affairs of the Sauk and Fox Indians Turn': Keokuk and the United States Government," in *Enduring Nations: Native Americans in the Midwest,* ed. R. David Edmunds (Urbana and Chicago: University of Illinois Press, 2008), 56–59; John W. Hall, *Uncommon Defense: Indian Allies in the Black Hawk War* (Cambridge, Mass.: Harvard University Press, 2009), 77, 107; Willis B. Hughes, "The First Dragoons on the Western Frontier, 1834–1846," *Arizona and the West* 12, no. 2 (Summer 1970): 115, 117, 122, 123.

22. Flanders, *Nauvoo: Kingdom on the Mississippi;* WW 1:332, 333 (May 18, 30, 1839).

23. WW 1:334, 339, 346 (May 24, June 20, July 10, 1839); Phebe Woodruff, Montrose, Iowa, to Wilford Woodruff, May 9 and Sept. 8, 1840, WW Letters.

24. Leonora Taylor to John Taylor, Jan. 2, 1840, CHL.

25. PW to WW, Sept. 19, 1839, WW Letters. Phebe provided additional details on her illness in PW to WW, July 2, 1840, WW Letters.

26. Leonora Taylor to John Taylor, Sept. 9, 1839, CHL.

27. PW to WW, Sept. 19, 1839, WW Letters.

28. John Taylor to Leonora Cannon, Jan. 30, 1840, CHL.

29. Compare Journal, 1838–Jan. 1839, WW Corr, with Journal, Aug. 8, 1839–Jan. 12, 1840, WW Collection. In both versions of the diary, he originally dated this entry Oct. 8 rather than Aug. 8. Later, he, or someone else, corrected it.

30. "Phebe's Supplication," WW Letters. Phebe's note referred to "the mysterious thing which was hid in the draw," suggesting that she may have fashioned the hair into some sort of ornament. On that practice, see Lauren Hewes, "My Hairy Valentine," *Past Is Present: A Blog from the American Antiquarian Society,* Feb. 11, 2010, http://pastispresent .org/2010/curatorscorner/my-hairy-valentine/, and, for a more general discussion of the practice, Helen Sheumaker, *Love Entwined: The Curious History of Hairwork in America* (Philadelphia: University of Pennsylvania Press, 2007).

31. WW 1:374, 401–3, 588–89 (Dec. 20, 1839; Jan. 1, 11, 1840), and "A Synopsis of the travels of W. Woodruff in A.D. 1840").

32. WW 1:488 (May 12, 1840); Alexander, *Woodruff,* 91–94.

33. WW 1:414–15, 446–47, 452, 533–36 (Feb. 7, May 8, 22, Oct. 19, 1840).

34. WW 1:471 (June 26, 1840); WW 2:31, 36 (Jan. 23, Feb. 2, 1841).

35. WW 1:405, 419–21 (Jan. 14, Feb. 18, 19, 1840).

36. WW 2:74, 69 (March 17, 22, 1841).

37. WC1, 22; Rebecca Bartholomew, *Audacious Women: Early British Mormon Immigrants* (Salt Lake City: Signature Books, 1995), 84–85; WW 1:406, 431 (Jan. 14, April 4, 1840).

38. WW 1:435–39 (April 13, 15, 1840); Givens and Grow, 176–79.

39. "Duties of Women," *Millennial Star,* Aug. 1840, 100–101.

40. "Duties of Women," quoting 1 Timothy 5:14; Ephesians 5:22–29; Titus 2:2–6; 1 Peter 3:1–7.

41. Later issues praised female piety in similar terms as in *Millennial Star,* March 1841, 191–92, 299–301; Aug. 1841, 49–51, 64; May 1842, 1–12, 14–15; Aug. 1842, 69–70, 78–79.

42. E.g., WW 1:470, 483 (June 23, July 11, 1840); WW 2:37, 40, 65, 66 (Feb. 4, 7, 8, March 18, 20, 1841).

43. WW 1:505 (Aug. 31, 1840).

44. WW 1:529–30 (Oct. 15, 1840); Alfred Cordon's Journal, Oct. 14, 1840, in "Ahlstrom Family History," ahlstrom.weebly.com.

45. WW 1:530 (Oct. 15, 1840). In Feb. 1841, Wilford noted receiving a letter from Bromley "containing a remarkable dream," but though he answered the letter he did not record this dream. (WW 2:35, 42 [Feb. 1, 12, 1841].)

46. Theodore Turley, Diary, Special Collections, HBLL, 38, 41, 43, 48, 76, 87, 92 (April 18, 19, 21, 25, May 2, June 16, July 10, 18, 1840).

47. Cordon, Journal, April 28, 1842 ("I went to Brittle lane to Brother Bullocks, father Rushtons son in law from Leek, Mother Rushton had gone to live with him, all the rest of the family had gone to the land of Joseph"—i.e., Nauvoo). Ancestry.com shows Richard and Eliza Rushton in St. Louis in the U.S. Federal Census of 1860. Other members of the Rushton family, including Richard's brother-in-law Thomas Bullock, migrated to Utah. See *The Pioneer Camp of the Saints: The 1846 and 1847 Mormon Trail Journals of Thomas Bullock,* ed. Will Bagley (Spokane, Wash.: Arthur H. Clark, 1997), 344.

48. WW 1:527, 529 (Oct. 11, 15, 1840).

49. WC1, 117.

50. WC1, 135, 136, 110. For a general account of this relationship, see WC1, "Introduction," 32–35; and James B. Allen, *No Toil Nor Labor Fear: The Story of William Clayton* (Provo, Utah: Brigham Young University Press, 2005), 23–26.

51. WC1, "Introduction," 1–3, 20–35.

52. WC1, 73.

53. WW 1:411, 412 (Jan. 26, 1840).

54. WW 1:428 (March 26, 1840).

55. WW 1:502, 520, 580 (Aug. 28, Sept. 21, Dec. 20, 1840).

56. WW 1:429–30; WW 2:24 (March 28, 1840; Jan. 6, 1841).

57. WW 1:475–77 (July 2, 7, 1840); Ronald O. Barney, "Letters of a Missionary Apostle to His Wife: Brigham Young to Mary Ann Angell Young, 1839–1841," *BYU Studies* 38 (1999): 178–81.

58. WW 1:475–77.

59. Bushman, *RSR,* 421; Alexander L. Baugh, " 'For This Ordinance Belongeth to My House': The Practice of Baptism for the Dead Outside the Nauvoo Temple," *Mormon Historical Studies* 3 (Spring 2002): 47–58.

60. PW to WW, Oct. 6, 1840, WW Letters.

61. Vilate Kimball to Heber Kimball, Oct. 22, 1840, KFL.

62. WW 1:478. Although Wilford dated this dream Oct. 25, 1840, it is out of sequence in the diary, following his account of Ann Booth's vision.

63. Book of Mormon, 1 Nephi 8:10–13.

64. PW to WW, April 1, July 2, Sept. 1, 1840, WW Letters.

65. PW to WW, July 2, Sept. 1, 1840, WW Letters.

66. PW to WW, April 1, 1840, WW Letters.

67. PW to WW, March 24, April 1, 1840, WW Letters.

68. PW to WW, April 1, 1840, WW Letters.

69. PW to WW, May 9, 1840, WW Letters.

70. PW to WW, April 2, 1840, WW Letters.

71. PW to WW, May 9, 1840, WW Letters.

72. PW to WW, May 9, 1840, WW Letters.

73. Givens and Grow, 158–60; Morris Calvin Phelps, "Life History of Laura Clark," www.morrisphelps.org; Antone Clark, *Noble Pioneer: A Biography of Ezra Thompson Clark,* 77, www.ezratclark.org.

74. PW to WW, July 2, 1840, WW Letters.

75. PW to WW, July 18, 1840, WW Letters.

76. PW to WW, July 18, 1840, WW Letters.

77. Four days before getting the letter, Wilford heard about his daughter's death from George A. Smith. Wilford copied parts of Phebe's letter and Margaret Smoot's poem into his journal. (WW 1:537, 541, 542 [Oct. 22, 26, 1840].)

78. PW to WW, Sept. 1, 1840, WW Letters.

79. PW to WW, Sept. 8, 1840, WW Letters.

80. PW to WW, Oct. 6, 1840, WW Letters.

81. PW to WW, Oct. 6, 1840, WW Letters.

82. PW to WW, Oct. 25–Nov. 2, 1840, WW Letters.

83. PW to WW, March 8, April 1, 1840, WW Letters; Clark V. Johnson, ed., *Mormon Redress Petitions: Documents of the 1833–1838 Missouri Conflict* (Provo, Utah: Brigham Young University Religious Studies Center, 1992), 282, 417–18.

84. Johnson, ed., *Redress Petitions,* 558.

85. Johnson, ed., *Redress Petitions,* 144, 145.

86. Johnson, ed., *Redress Petitions,* 351, 352.

87. Johnson, ed., *Redress Petitions,* 168, 169.

88. William O. Clark to "Dear Relitives and Friends," Caldwell Co., Mo., March 13, 1839, CHL.

89. Johnson, ed., *Redress Petitions,* 329, 499.

90. Johnson, ed., *Redress Petitions,* 475.

91. Johnson, ed., *Redress Petitions,* 157. Several women pleaded loss of citizenship: e.g., Louisa Follet, 201; Mary Ann Gilbert, 215; Sophia Higbee, 235; Elizabeth Munjar, 502.

92. Johnson, ed., *Redress Petitions,* 157, 197.

93. PW to WW, Dec. 6, 1840, WW Letters.

94. PW to WW, Jan. 10, 1841, WW Letters.

95. WW 2:114 (Aug. 6, 1841).
96. WW 2:121–22 (Aug. 24–28, 1841).
97. WW 2:128–34 (Sept. 31–Oct. 19, 1841).

3. "I now turn the key to you"

1. WW 2:133–39 (Oct. 11–Nov. 24, 1842).
2. WW 2:157 (March 4, 1842); *Wilford Woodruff: History of His Life and Labors as Recorded in His Daily Journals,* ed. Matthias F. Cowley (1909; Salt Lake City: Bookcraft, 1964), 690.
3. WW 2:153, 154 (Feb. 3, 4, 7, 8, 9, 10, 11, 1842); Terence A. Tanner, "The Mormon Press in Nauvoo, 1839–46," in *Kingdom on the Mississippi Revisited: Nauvoo in Mormon History,* ed. Roger D. Launius and John E. Hallwas (Urbana and Chicago: University of Illinois Press, 1996), 106, 107; *The Joseph Smith Papers: Journals* (Salt Lake City: Church Historian's Press, 2011), vol. 2:38 (Jan. 28, 1842).
4. WW 2:143 (Dec. 19, 1841); *Joseph Smith Papers: Journals,* 2:45, 53, 54, 54 n198 (March 15, May 4, 1842).
5. WW 2:158 (March 15, 1842). Marvin S. Hill, "Religion in Nauvoo: Some Reflections," in *Kingdom on the Mississippi Revisited,* ed. Launius and Hallwas, 93.
6. Through the spring, he performed vicarious baptisms for seventeen deceased persons—his mother; his brothers Philo and Asahel; his grandparents, great-grandparents, several aunts, uncles, and cousins; and a charismatic Connecticut preacher named Robert Mason, who had first awakened his interest in religion. On April 21, Phebe joined him in the river to be baptized for her grandparents Ezra and Phebe Whittemore Carter. (WW 2:164–65, 171, 175, 177, 178 [March 26, 27, April 21, May 7, May 29, 30, 1842], and a summary of Wilford's baptisms added to the diary by a later clerk, WW 2:204, 205 . This list incorrectly gives the year 1841 for baptisms performed in 1844.) On Mason, see Alexander, *Woodruff,* 18–20. In contrast to current-day practice, which requires that males be baptized for males and females for females, early Saints were baptized regardless of the sex of the deceased.
7. WW 2:172–74; Jeremy L. Cross, *The True Masonic Chart, or Hieroglyphic Monitor* (New Haven, Conn.: Lagg & Gray, 1819), 3, 10; W. Kirk MacNulty, *Freemasonry: Symbols, Secrets, Significance* (London: Thames & Hudson, 2006), 144, 156, 157, 164, 162; *Masonic Symbols in American Decorative Arts* (Lexington, Mass.: Scottish Rite Museum of Our National Heritage, 1976), 8, 13, 51, 52, 76.
8. WW 2:154–56. The first installment of the Prophet's translation appeared in the *Times and Seasons* on March 1. The second included a fold-out of the circular illustration from the ancient papyri that may have influenced Wilford's earlier drawing. (*Times and Seasons* [Nauvoo, Ill.] 3, no. 9 [March 1, 1842]: 703–6; 3, no. 10 [March 15, 1842]: 719–22, fold-out 720a; 3, no. 14 [May 15, 1842]: 783, 784).
9. WW 2:175 (May 7, 1842).
10. Cross, *Masonic Chart,* 26; MacNulty, *Freemasonry,* 160, 161.
11. Matthew 16:19; Revelation 3:7; 9:1; 20:1; *Doctrine and Covenants,* 6:28; 7:7; 13:1; 27:5, 9, 12, 13; 28:7; 35:18, 25; 42:69; 64:5; 65:2; 68:17, 18; 78:16; 81:2; 84:19, 26; 90:2, 3, 6, 7; 97:14; 107:15, 16, 18, 20, 35, 70, 76; 110:11, 16; 112:15, 16, 32; 113:6; 115:19; 124:34, 92, 95, 97, 123, 128, 143; 128:10, 11, 14, 18, 20, 21; 129:49; 130:11; 132:7, 19, 39, 45, 59, 64. For early editions, see "Corresponding Section Numbers in Editions of the Doctrine and Covenants," JSP. On overcoming death, see Samuel Morris Brown, *In Heaven as It Is on Earth: Joseph Smith and the Early Mormon Conquest of Death* (New York: Oxford University Press, 2012), 164–69; 190–91; 195–201.
12. "Be Not Discouraged," "To the Saints," "The Invocation," "The Nauvoo Legion," "The Temple of God," ERS *Poetry,* 130–35, 161–63, 169–71; NRS Minutes 41 (April 28, 1842).

13. ERS1, 52 (June 29, 1842); Eliza R. Snow Smith, Affidavit, June 7, 1869, in Affidavits CM.

14. WW 2:179, 180 (June 18, 1842).

15. John C. Bennett, *The History of the Saints: Or, An Expose of Joe Smith and Mormonism* (Boston, 1842; Urbana and Chicago: University of Illinois Press, 2000), 257.

16. "Lines," ERS *Poetry*, 187–88; Oliver Granger in Reference/People, JSP.

17. WW 2:143, 144 (Dec. 25, 1841); Robert Bruce Flanders, *Nauvoo: Kingdom on the Mississippi* (Urbana and Chicago: University of Ilinois Press, 1965), 31, 52, 53, 164.

18. "Sarah M. Kimball," in Augusta Joyce Crocheron, *Representative Women of Deseret* (Salt Lake City: J. C. Graham, 1884), 24–25.

19. Nancy F. Cott, *Public Vows: A History of Marriage and the Nation* (Cambridge, Mass.: Harvard University Press, 2000), 50–55; Michael Grossberg, *Governing the Hearth: Law and the Family in Nineteenth-Century America* (Chapel Hill: University of North Carolina Press, 1985), 234–47.

20. Bushman, *RSR,* 154–55, 181–83, 414.

21. Sarah M. Kimball, "Auto-biography," *Woman's Exponent* 12 (Sept. 1, 1883): 51. In this version, she (or a typesetter) misdated the founding to 1843. Kimball used the correct date in her manuscript history, Record of the Relief Society from First Organization to Conference, April 5, 1892, bk. 11, 29, 31, CHL. For modern uses of the story, see Jill Mulvay Derr, Janath Russell Cannon, and Maureen Ursenbach Beecher, *Women of Covenant: The Story of Relief Society* (Salt Lake City: Deseret Book, 1992), 26, 27; *Daughters of My Kingdom: The History and Work of Relief Society* (Salt Lake City: Church of Jesus Christ of Latter-day Saints, 2011), 11.

22. John 2:1; *Doctrine and Covenants,* 25:3, 6–12.

23. Newell and Avery, *Mormon Enigma,* 102–4; Bushman, *RSR,* xvii.

24. NRS Minutes, 6 (March 17, 1842). Richards reinforced this meaning of "elect" in the entry provided in Joseph Smith's official journal, *The Joseph Smith Papers: Journals,* 2:45 (March 17, 1842); Maurine Carr Ward, "'This Institution Is a Good One': The Female Relief Society of Nauvoo, 17 March 1842 to 16 March 1844," *Mormon Historical Studies* 3 (Fall 2002): 87–203, provides biographical information, including birth dates for 1,010 of the 1,341 women who appear as members in the minutes. Only two other women in the room were over forty. Nine were in their thirties, five in their twenties, and possibly two in their teens. Six, like Eliza, were single. Leonora Taylor, whose husband, John, was also present, was the only Apostle's wife among the twenty. Phebe Woodruff, whose baby was less than two weeks old, didn't join the society until April.

25. This paragraph is based on examination of the original document and on the source note provided in the digital edition at JSP.

26. Ward, "This Institution Is a Good One," 89–90.

27. NRS Minutes, 10–12 (March 17, 1842).

28. NRS Minutes, 16 (March 24, 1842).

29. Richards's one-sentence record reads (writing in the voice of his employer Joseph Smith): "[I] waited on the members of the Female Relief Society & entered a complaint against Clarissa Marvel for Slander." (*Joseph Smith Papers: Journals,* 2:46 [March 24, 1842].)

30. But the evidence is by no means certain. Hales, *Polygamy,* 1:22–25, 259, 268–69, 272; 2:326.

31. NRS Minutes, 17 (March 24, 1842).

32. NRS Minutes, 23 (March 30, 1842).

33. NRS Minutes, 24, 86–89 (March 30, 1842). Eliza copied Marvel's certificate into the minute book in the space after her minutes from the Sept. 28, 1842, meeting. For variant accounts of the investigation of Clarissa Marvel and its relation to Agnes Smith, see Newell and Avery, *Mormon Enigma,* 108–10; Compton, *In Sacred Loneliness,* 153–56, 178–80, 675; and Smith, *Nauvoo Polygamy,* 104–10. Compton, who concluded that Durfee was by then a plural wife, finds this exchange almost comic. The editors of Joseph Smith's

journal conclude that while Agnes "may have" been a plural wife, Durfee was not. See *Joseph Smith Papers: Journals,* 2:439, 472, 481.

34. NRS Minutes, 24, 86–89 (March 30, April 2, 1842). Eliza also inserted this document, which was dated April 2, in the minutes of the Relief Society at the end of September, noting that it had been read at the earlier meeting.

35. Hales, *Polygamy,* vol. 2, app. B, 323–41, lists possible plural wives chronologically. Note that some sealing dates are conjectural or unknown and that very few sources are contemporary to the sealings. But on the list of those who may have been sealed by the end of March 1842 are four women (Louisa Beaman, Zina Huntington Jacobs, Presendia Huntington Buell, and Patty Sessions), who with Eliza became central to later groups formed around Joseph's memory.

36. NRS Meetings, 88 (April 2, 1842).

37. NRS Minutes, 7, 8 (March 17, 1842).

38. NRS Minutes, 22 (March 30, 1842).

39. NRS Minutes, 36–38 (April 28, 1842).

40. NRS Minutes, 40 (April 28, 1842).

41. NRS Minutes, 41 (April 28, 1842).

42. NRS Minutes, 30, 31 (April 19, 1842).

43. NRS Minutes, 31, 32 (April 19, 1842).

44. Compton, *In Sacred Loneliness,* 4, 120–24; Bradley and Woodward, 87, 88, 96, 116. On uncertainties about the dating of plural marriages, see Gary James Bergera, "Memory as Evidence During Joseph Smith's Plural Marriages to Louisa Beaman, Zina Jacobs, and Presendia Buell," *Journal of Mormon History* 41, no. 4 (Oct. 2015): 95–131.

45. NRS Minutes, 32, 33 (April 19, 1842). The minutes refer to Sessions either as "Martha" or as "Mrs Sessions." There was no Martha Sessions in Nauvoo, and since "Patty" was often considered a nickname for "Martha," I am assuming that Eliza jumped to the conclusion that "Martha" was her formal name. Reinforcing the conclusion that the "Mrs Sessions" who appears in the Minutes was Patty, is that she was both generous with her means, assertive in speaking, and given to spiritual gifts, all qualities characteristic of the midwife whose diary will be featured in Chapter 5.

46. NRS Minutes, 20, 45–46 (March 24, May 13, 1842).

47. WW 2:287 (Sept. 9, 1843). On one of his own missionary journeys, Kimball wrote to his wife about purchasing fabric for his own pantaloons, probably using money provided by members (Heber C. Kimball to Vilate Kimball, Aug. 13, 1843, KFL). On the symbolic important of pantaloons as the mark of American democracy, see Michael Zakim, "Sartorial Ideologies: From Homespun to Ready-Made," *American Historical Review* 106, no. 5 (Dec. 2001): 1575–80.

48. NRS Minutes, 94 (July 7, 1843).

49. "One of Time's Changes," ERS *Poetry,* 190–91, originally published in *Times and Seasons,* March 1, 1842. On the idealization of household production in nineteenth-century America, see Laurel Thatcher Ulrich, *The Age of Homespun: Objects and Stories in the Creation of an American Myth* (New York: Alfred A. Knopf, 2001).

50. NRS Minutes, 94.

51. "The Tatler" and "The Female Relief Society of Nauvoo: What Is It?," ERS *Poetry,* 202–5, originally published in *The Wasp,* June 21, 1842, and *Times and Seasons,* July 1, 1842.

52. For a detailed discussion of the creation and later use of the record, see Jill Mulvay Derr and Carol Cornwall Madsen, "Preserving the Record and Memory of the Female Relief Society of Nauvoo, 1842–92," *Journal of Mormon History* 35 (Summer 2009): 88–117.

53. ERS1, title page. I thank Jill Mulvay Derr for pointing out the importance of the inscriptions and for suggesting the relationship between the two volumes.

54. ERS 1, Eliza made sporadic entries in this journal from June 19, 1842, until April 14, 1844, then used it until 1882 to record poems.

55. Eliza R. Snow Smith, Affidavit, June 7, 1869, in Affidavits CM. I arrived at the

number six by including only those for whom there is either contemporary documentation or first-person affidavits providing dates. Other sources add a number of additional women based on a variety of sources and assumptions about the order of sealings. For some of these lists, see Hales, *Polygamy*, vol. 2, app. B, 323–41; Compton, *In Sacred Loneliness*, 4–7; George D. Smith, "Nauvoo Roots of Mormon Polygamy, 1841–1846: A Preliminary Demographic Report," *Dialogue: A Journal of Mormon Thought* 37 (Spring 1994): 1–72; Smith, *Nauvoo Polygamy*, 36, 138, 195, 102; Gary James Bergera, "Identifying the Earliest Mormon Polygamists, 1841–1844," *Dialogue: A Journal of Mormon Thought* 38, no. 3 (Fall 2005): 1–74; Bushman, *RSR*, 437–46, 490–99; Richard Lloyd Anderson and Scott H. Faulring, "The Prophet Joseph Smith and His Plural Wives," *FARMS Review*, no. 2 (1998): 67–104, maxwellinstitute.byu. Since the purported marriage to Fanny Alger did not occur in Nauvoo, I have omitted her in my count. In Anderson and Faulring's list, Eliza is tenth; in Compton's, twelfth; in Smith's and Bergera's somewhat different lists, thirteenth.

56. On the difficulties in defining such a marriage, see Daynes, *Wives*, 30, 31.

57. ERS1, 52 (June 29, 1842).

58. ERS1, 52 (June 29 1842).

59. Bushman, *RSP*, 461; *Joseph Smith Papers: Journals*, 2:67 (June 17, 1842); NRS Minutes, 69 (June 23, 1842); WW 2:179, 180 (June 18, 1842).

60. *Joseph Smith Papers: Journals*, 1:120 n420 (Aug. 26, 1842); Bushman, *RSR*, 60–65; Andrew F. Smith, *Saintly Scoundrel: The Life and Times of Dr. John Cook Bennett* (Urbana: University of Illinois Press, 1997), 99–141.

61. Bennett, *History of the Saints*, 8–9.

62. "Conference Minutes," *Times and Seasons* 3, no. 12 (April 1842): 763. See also B. H. Roberts, ed., *History of the Church of Jesus Christ of Latter-day Saints* (Salt Lake City: Deseret Book, 1966), vol. 4, 585.

63. Bennett, *History of the Saints*, 236–40. Brotherton's affidavit first appeared in the *American Bulletin* (St. Louis, Missouri), July 16, 1842. On her family and their migration to Nauvoo, see Paul B. Pixton, "The *Tyrian* and Its Mormon Passengers," *Mormon Historical Studies* (Spring 2004): 40–46, http://mormonhistoricsitesfoundation.org.

64. Bennett, *History of the Saints*, 236; "Testimony of J. McIlwrick," in *Affidavits and Certificate Disproving the Statements and Affidavits Contained in John C. Bennett's Letters*, broadside, Nauvoo, Aug. 31, 1842; "Apostacy," *Millennial Star* 3, no. 4 (Aug. 1842): 73–74; Mary E. Fissell, "Hairy Women and Naked Truths: Gender and the Politics of Knowledge in 'Aristotle's Masterpiece,'" *William & Mary Quarterly* 60 (2003): 43–74.

65. WW 2:179, 180 (June 18, 1842); NRS Minutes, 69 (June 23, 1842).

66. Newell and Avery, *Mormon Enigma*, 114–15, 134.

67. ERS1, 52, 53, 269 n1 (July 29, 1852); Bushman, *RSR*, 462, 463; Smith, *Saintly Scoundrel*, 110.

68. NRS Minutes, 80, 81 (Aug. 31, 1842).

69. WW 2:187 (Aug. 10, 1842).

70. ERS1, 53–58 (Aug. 3, 9, 14, 18, 22, 25, 28, Sept. 4, Oct. 9, 12, 1842).

71. ERS1, 54, 55 (Aug. 18, 25, 28, 1842).

72. ERS1, 55–56 (Sept. 4, 1842).

73. *Joseph Smith Papers: Journals*, 2:124, 125, 444, 445, 464; Bushman, *RSR*, 310, 339–40, 350, 440, 479.

74. Revelation, July 27, 1842, MS 4583, CHL; Joseph Smith Jr., "To the Whitneys, August 18, 1842," in *The Personal Writings of Joseph Smith*, ed. Dean C. Jessee (Salt Lake City: Deseret Book, 1984), 539–40. Kathleen Flake, "The Development of Early Latter-day Saint Marriage Rites, 1831–53," *Journal of Mormon History* 41 (January 2015): 77–101, argues that priesthood was not only the means of this marriage but its object and that it conveyed a familial form of priesthood, unassociated with Church office, that included women as well as men.

75. For a succinct summary and discussion of the many documents associated with the Whitney sealing, see Hales, *Polygamy,* 1:502–10.

76. "Your Portrait," ERS *Poetry,* 215–16, composed Aug. 20, published in *The Wasp,* Aug. 27, 1842. It may have been the full-length profile prepared by an English convert and former textile engraver named Sutcliffe Maudsley, to be lithographed for inclusion on a Nauvoo map. Her point about its inadequacies was well taken. Contemporary descriptions of Smith uniformly describe him as a handsome man, over six feet tall, with a genial and unpretentious personality. Maudsley's stylized portrait emphasizes his ample belly, sloping forehead, and prominent nose. (Richard G. Oman and Robert O. Davis, eds., *Images of Faith: Art of the Latter-day Saints* [Salt Lake City: Deseret Book, 1995], 6–7, and plates 6, 7, 8.)

77. ERS1, 57, 58 (Oct. 9, 12, 1842).

78. "The Bride's Avowal, Inscrib'd to Miss L. for the Bridal Morning," ERS *Poetry,* 210–11.

79. ERS1, 52, 57 (June 29, Sept. 23, 1842).

80. WW 2:177 (May 27, 1842). For Willard Richards's notations on these events, see *Joseph Smith Papers: Journals,* 2:63 (May 24, 25, 26, 1842).

81. For a discussion of competing sexual "frameworks" in this period, see Helen Lefkowitz Horowitz, *Rereading Sex: Battles over Sexual Knowledge and Suppression in Nineteenth-Century America* (New York: Alfred A. Knopf, 2002).

82. Testimonies in Nauvoo High Council Cases, MS 24557, CHL. Although Joseph Smith had already signed a certificate disfellowshipping Bennett, he had not yet delivered it (Bushman, *RSR,* 460–61).

83. John S. Dinger, ed., *The Nauvoo City and High Council Minutes* (Salt Lake City: Signature Books, 2011), 417.

84. Testimonies in Nauvoo High Council Cases.

85. Dinger, ed., *Nauvoo City and High Council Minutes,* 415 n40.

86. Hales, *Polygamy,* vol. 1, table 15.1, 428; Gary James Bergera, "'Illicit Intercourse,' Plural Marriage, and the Nauvoo Stake High Council, 1840–1844," *John Whitmer Historical Association Journal* 23 (2003): 59–91.

87. Orson Pratt, Letter (Nauvoo, Ill.), July 14, 1842, CHL.

88. Breck England, *The Life and Thought of Orson Pratt* (Salt Lake City: University of Utah Press, 1985), 78–81; Bushman, *RSR,* 466–68.

89. Compare the verses in Bennett, *History of the Saints,* 253, 255, 257, with *Hamlet,* act I, scene 4 ("Angels and ministers of grace defend us"), *Richard II,* act II, scene 4 ("Ah, Richard"), *Henry V,* act II, scene 2 ("God quit you in his mercy"), and *Henry VI, Part II,* act III, scene 2 ("Would curses kill, as doth the mandrake's groan"), in *Complete Works of William Shakespeare* (London: Scott, Webster, and Geary, 1838), 827, 431, 364, 490.

90. Compare the verses in Bennett, *History of the Saints,* 256, 254, with *Don Juan by Lord Byron* (Philadelphia: R. W. Pomeroy, 1841), vol. I, canto I, stanzas CXVI, CXIX, CXCIX, 34, 116, and vol. II, canto VIII, stanza XXV, 14; and compare passages in Bennett, *History of the Saints,* 219, 220, 221, 223, 224, 231, 235, 242, 243, 254, with verses from *The Poetical Works of Thomas Moore* (Paris: A. and W. Galignani, 1829), 3, 125, 180, 244, 286, 299, 317. 360.

91. Bennett, *History of the Saints,* 221–25, 227. He used the word "Cyprian" to describe the Mormon system. In this period, the word "Cyprian" was a polite term for lewdness, perhaps because the Island of Cyprus was associated with the worship of Aphrodite.

92. Smith, *Saintly Scoundrel,* 127–32; quotes on 124, 126.

93. *Joseph Smith Papers: Journals,* 2:120.

94. WW 2:183–86 (July 30–Aug. 20, 1842).

95. WW 2:212 (Jan. 18, 1843); *Joseph Smith Papers: Journals,* 2:236, 243, 245–46 (Jan. 7, 11, 18, 1843); WC2 (Jan. 18, 1843).

96. The day after the party, the Quorum of the Twelve assembled at the river, broke through the ice, and rebaptized Orson and Sarah. Joseph then confirmed them and

ordained Orson to the Apostleship, restoring him to his former calling (WW 2:212–13 [Jan. 19, 1843]).

97. ERS *Poetry*, 232. There is no entry in Eliza's diary for Jan. 18.

4. *"a favor which I have long desired"*

1. I have based this count on a conservative reading of the information contained in the appendix to Gary James Bergera, "Identifying the Earliest Mormon Polygamists, 1841–44," *Dialogue: A Journal of Mormon Thought* 38, no. 3 (Fall 2005): 52–74; and on related material in Todd Compton, *In Sacred Loneliness: The Plural Wives of Joseph Smith* (Salt Lake City: Signature, 1997), 5–9, and Hales, *Polygamy*, 1:24–25; 2:268–73. Although marriages for Reynolds Cahoon, Joseph Knight, and Heber Kimball have been surmised, Young's is the only documented plural marriage by July 1842. The seventy-six women include the thirty-three Joseph Smith wives listed by most scholars and the nineteen legal and forty-three plural wives sealed to the other men.

2. When Leonora copied a blessing Isaac gave Eliza, she signed herself A. L. Morley. ERS1, 89–90 (Dec. 19, 1843).

3. John Taylor, April 9, 1882, in *Journal of Discourses* 23:64; Lucy Walker in Lyman Omer Littlefield, *Reminiscences of Latter-day Saints: Giving an Account of Much Individual Suffering Endured for Religious Conscience* (Logan: Utah Journal Co., 1888), 46–48; Brigham Young, in *Journal of Discourses* 3:266, quoted in Hales, *Polygamy*, 3:268, 216.

4. Lorenzo Snow Notarized Statement, Aug. 28, 1869, in Affidavits CM, folder 4; Eliza R. Snow Smith Affidavit, June 7, 1869, in Affidavits CM, 1:25. Also see Hales, *Polygamy*, vol. 1, table 8.1, 188–91.

5. Bushman, *RSR*, 437–40; Bradley and Woodward, 113–14.

6. This story, which Helen Mar Whitney first published in the *Woman's Exponent* 10 (Oct. 15, 1881): 74, is reprinted in *A Woman's View: Helen Mar Whitney's Reminiscences of Early Church History*, ed. Jeni Broberg Holzapfel and Richard Neitzel Holzapfel (Provo, Utah: Religious Studies Center, Brigham Young University, 1997), 138–39.

7. Tullidge, *Women*, 295. See also ERS3, 16, 17.

8. Catherine Lewis, *Narrative of Some of the Proceedings of the Mormons; Giving an Account of Their Iniquities* (Lynn, Mass.: The Author, 1848), 5.

9. WC2, vol. 1, March 7, 1843.

10. Allen, *No Toil nor Labor*, 4–10, 33.

11. WC1, 214–19 (Aug. 17, Sept. 11, 1841; Feb. 10, 1842); Allen, *No Toil nor Labor*, 67–71.

12. WC2, vol. 1, Jan. 13, 15, 28, Feb. 12, 20, 24, March 1, April 16, 19, 1843; Allen, *No Toil nor Labor*, 1, 44–45, 63, 166, 263.

13. WC2, vol. 1, Feb. 27, March 3, 1843; Allen, *No Toil nor Labor*, 66, 67.

14. WC2, vol. 1, March 7, 1843.

15. WC2, vol. 1, Feb. 12, March 9, 1843; William Clayton Affidavit, Feb. 16, 1874, in Affidavits CM, folder 1. A transcription of the affidavit also appears in WC Smith, app. C, 555–59. There are slight differences between the account in the affidavit and the account in the diary, but they tell roughly the same story.

16. WC2, vol. 1, April 24, 27, 1843. At this point, Clayton switched to a second notebook (WC2, vol. 2). A slightly different entry for April 27 in the new book reads, "Was m to M.M." On Mormon concepts of sealing, see Samuel Morris Brown, *In Heaven as It Is on Earth: Joseph Smith and the Early Mormon Conquest of Death* (New York: Oxford University Press, 2012), 146–49, and on an early legal definition, Alexander Mansfield Burrill, *A New Law Dictionary and Glossary* (New York: John S. Voorhies, 1850), 672, 757.

17. WC2, vol. 2, May 31, June 3, 1843.

18. Melinda Evans Jeffress, "Mapping Historic Nauvoo," *BYU Studies* 31 (1992): 274, 275.

19. WC2, vol. 2, June 11, 13, 22, 1843.

20. On the sealings, see Emily D. P. Young Affidavit, May 1, 1869, in Affidavits CM, 1:11, 13, and copies of Eliza Maria Lyman Affidavit, July 1, 1869, in Affidavits CM 2:30, 32, 33. For more on these affidavits, see chapter 15.

21. Newell and Avery, *Mormon Enigma*, 132–39, provide an overview of affairs in the Smith house, relying to a large extent on retrospective accounts. Bushman, *RSR*, 494–95, stays closer to Clayton's account.

22. WC2, vol. 2, May 23, 1843.

23. WC2, vol. 2, June 23, 1843.

24. WW 2:244–55 (June 25–July 1, 1843); Bushman, *RSR*, 504–8.

25. ERS1, 78 (June 30, 1843).

26. WW 2:245–46; ERS1, 76–80 (June 18, 20, 23, 25, 27–30, 1843); WC2, vol. 2, June 1–July 1, 1843; Bushman, *RSR*, 504–8. A somewhat garbled version of this event appears in some detail in *History of the Church of Jesus Christ of Latter-day Saints*, ed. B. H. Roberts (Salt Lake City: Deseret Book, 1967), vol. 5, 431–35, 438–60.

27. WW 2:247 (June 30, 1843).

28. ERS1, 77 (June 27, 1843); WW 2:252 (June 30, 1843).

29. ERS1, 78–79 (June 30, 1843); ERS *Poetry*, 244–46. Eliza entered the poem in her journal on June 30, perhaps after sharing it with Emma. Published in the *Nauvoo Neighbor* on July 26, 1843, it was anthologized a century later in Charles O'Brien Kennedy, *A Treasury of American Ballads* (New York: McBridge Co., 1954).

30. WC2, vol. 2, July 12, 1843; WC Smith, 557–58; Bushman, *RSR*, 442–46. Although published in church newspapers in 1852, it did not become part of the Church's *Doctrine and Covenants* until 1876. See Richard E. Turley Jr. and William W. Slaughter, *How We Got the Doctrine and Covenants* (Salt Lake City: Deseret Book, 2012), 88.

31. *Doctrine and Covenants*, 132:7.

32. *Doctrine and Covenants*, 132:20, 30, 31.

33. *Doctrine and Covenants*, 132:31, 32.

34. *Doctrine and Covenants*, 132:52, 54.

35. *Doctrine and Covenants*, 132:61–66.

36. WC 2, vol. 2, July 12, 13, 15, 1843.

37. ERS1, 80 (July 20, 1843).

38. WC2, vol. 2, Aug. 21, 1843.

39. ERS1, 81 (July 30, 1843).

40. WC2, vol. 2, July 16, 22, 23, 24, 1843.

41. WC2, vol. 2, July 23–26, 1843.

42. WC2, vol. 2, July 29, 30, Aug. 5, 1843.

43. WC2, vol. 2, Aug. 5, 11, 13, 1843.

44. WC2, vol. 2, Aug. 13, 1843; Roberts, ed., *History of the Church*, vol. 5, 529–31.

45. WC2, vol. 2, Aug. 18, 1843.

46. WC2, vol. 2, Aug. 18, 19, 1843.

47. Clayton's comment on April 30, 1843, that he "walked out with Margaret and accomplished a good object" may have been his way of acknowledging their intimacy. Working backward from the birth of the baby (WC2, vol. 2, Feb. 18, 1844), I computed the probable time of conception by using a conception calculator at www.baby2see.com.

48. Hales, *Polygamy*, 1:66, 73, 77, 298–300, 375–76, citing published and unpublished work by geneticist Ugo A. Perego.

49. Hales, *Polygamy*, 1:296–302; Bergera, "Identifying the Earliest Mormon Polygamists," 50–51, and app., 52–74. Bergera arrived at an average interval of twenty-four months by leaving out a handful of births with extraordinarily long intervals. I saw no reason to exclude those, which is why the interval in my set is twenty-six. It is also worth noting that many women who entered plurality in this period never had a child. A few women were past childbearing age, some died or left, and other alliances may have been celibate. Neither Bergera nor I included those women in our calculations.

50. Brigham Young's younger brother was charged with claiming "that poor men

ought not to raise up seed or children," a statement that echoes ideas in Owen's writings from the same period. See Minute Book 1, Sept. 29, 1835, JSP, and, on Owen's teaching, Helen Lefkowitz Horowitz, *Rereading Sex: Battles over Sexual Knowledge and Suppression in Nineteenth-Century America* (New York: Alfred A. Knopf, 2002), 56.

51. For the new emphasis on female purity and male restraint, see William A. Alcott, *The Young Husband: Or, Duties of Man in the Marriage Relation* (Boston: G. W. Light, 1839), 241–52; *The Physiology of Marriage: By an Old Physician* (Boston: John P. Jewett, 1856), 114–20. Classic secondary works on this topic include Daniel Scott Smith, "Family Limitation, Sexual Control, and Domestic Feminism in Victorian America," *Feminist Studies* 1 (Winter–Spring 1973): 40–57; Nancy F. Cott, "Passionlessness: An Interpretation of Victorian Sexual Ideology, 1790–1850," *Signs* 4 (Winter 1978): 219–36.

52. WC2, vol. 2, Aug. 16, 1843.

53. WC2, vol. 2, Aug. 11, 1843.

54. The legal responsibility of male household heads both for minors in their families and for their wives remained powerful in American law, despite some changes in family law after the Revolution. In law, a wife was not legally responsible for herself in either criminal or civil law, nor could she herself sue or be sued—hence the responsibility of fathers to protect their daughters before marriage and husbands to protect their wives thereafter. The general concept survived despite the growing availability of divorce in the early United States. For a brief overview, see Nancy F. Cott, *Public Vows: A History of Marriage and the Nation* (Cambridge, Mass.: Harvard University Press, 2000), 9–16, 52–55.

55. *Doctrine and Covenants*, 132:61–62.

56. WC2, vol. 2, Aug. 24, 1843.

57. WC2, vol 1, Feb. 12, March 7, 9, April 30; vol. 2, May 2, 31, June 2, 4, 13, Aug. 16, 1843; April 18, June 28, July 8, 1844; Allen, *No Toil nor Labor*, 192–93.

58. WC2, vol. 2, Sept. 15, 17, 31, 1843.

59. WC2, vol. 2, Oct. 19, 20, 1843.

60. WC2, vol. 2, Oct. 1, 7, 1843.

61. WW 2:228, 233 (April 19, May 22–26, 1843); Jeffress, "Mapping Historic Nauvoo," 274, 275. The Woodruffs' old house may have been on the same lot, though "on the corner." During construction, they seem to have moved temporarily to quarters in the printing office. See WW 2:340, 348 (Jan. 16, Feb. 6, 1844). Woodruff said the new house would be "fronting Durfee street on the east." William Clayton seems to have moved into his house in early June. See WC2, vol. 2, June 4, 10, 1843.

62. WW 2:234, 237, 238, 243 (May 24, 25, 26, 29, 30, 31, June 2–10, June 13, 17, 19, 1843).

63. WW 2:246, 259–60, 278 (June 27, 29, July 5–7, 25, Aug. 24, 1843).

64. WW 2:278–85 (Aug. 24–Sept. 8, 1843).

65. Vilate Kimball to Heber C. Kimball, June 29, 1843, KFL; WC2, vol 2, May 11, Aug. 20, 27, 1843. Despite complications, Pratt soon married Elizabeth Brotherton, a sister of the Martha Brotherton who had signed an affidavit in 1842 accusing Heber Kimball and Brigham Young of trying to teach her polygamy. On the complexities of Pratt's entrance into plurality, see Givens and Grow, 204–7.

66. Vilate Kimball to Heber C. Kimball, KFL, June 29, 1843. Descendants of Noble have long claimed that the son Alley delivered on Feb. 2, 1844, was the first child born to a plural wife in Nauvoo. See Hazel Noble Boyack, *A Nobleman in Israel* (Cheyenne, Wyo.: Pioneer Printing Company, 1962), 69, cited in David L. Clark, *Joseph Bates Noble: Polygamy and the Temple Lot Case* (Salt Lake City: University of Utah Press, 2009), 86.

67. The family legend, which appears to derive from Helen Mar Whitney's story about her parents' introduction to plural marriage, is repeated in Stanley B. Kimball, *Heber C. Kimball: Mormon Patriarch and Pioneer* (Urbana and Chicago: University of Ilinois Press, 1981), 93–95, 311–12, and in most other accounts of Kimball's life.

68. Vilate Kimball to Heber C. Kimball, June 29, 1843, KFL; Registers of Vessels Arriving at the Port of New York from Foreign Ports, 1789–1919, National Archives M237, rolls 1–95, Ancestry.com; *The Wasp* (Nauvoo, Illinois), April 26, 1843, 3; Fred E. Woods,

"The Cemetery Record of William D. Huntington, Nauvoo Sexton," *Mormon Historical Studies* 3, no. 1 (Spring 2002): 138; Alfred Cordon Journals, April 12, 1841, June 1, 1842, in "Ahlstrom Family History," ahlstrom.weebly.com; Roberts, ed., *History of the Church*, vol. 4, 558–64.

69. Vilate Kimball to Heber C. Kimball, June 29, 1843, KFL.

70. HCK, 50–53 (June 23, July 12, 28, 1843); Heber C. Kimball to Vilate Kimball, Oct. 16, 1842, July 25, 1843, KFL. Bathsheba and George Albert Smith also alluded to eternal bonds. See Bathsheba Smith to George A. Smith, Aug. 14, Sept. 5, 1843; George A. Smith to Bathsheba W. Smith, July 21, 1843, BWS Letters.

71. Heber Kimball to Vilate Kimball, Oct. 16, 1842, KFL.

72. Heber Kimball to Vilate Kimball, Sept. 3, 1843, KFL.

73. Heber Kimball to Vilate Kimball, Aug. 17, 1843, KFL.

74. Dorothy W. Peterson, *All Things Right: A Biography of Vilate Murray Kimball* (Privately published, 2009), 116–19, captures the emotional neediness in Heber's letters. He recognizes what plural marriage will require of him and Vilate, and seems genuinely concerned about losing the oneness that he cherishes.

75. WW 2:310 (Sept. 20, 1843).

76. WW 2:305–6 (Sept. 13, 14, 1843).

77. WW 2:304–10 (Sept. 12–18, 1843).

78. Wilford Woodruff to Phebe Woodruff, Oct. 8, 1843, Emma Smith Collection, CHL, MS 2081, folder 1.

79. WW 2:319–22 (Oct. 19, 1843); William Sipes, Thomas Moran, and James W. Louderbach, *The Pennsylvania Railroad: Its Origin, Construction, Condition, and Connections* (Philadelphia: Passenger Department, 1874), 8, 139. There is now a National Historic Site near Altoona, Pennsylvania, commemorating the railroad, which operated from 1834 to 1854; see www.nps.gov/alpo/.

80. WW 2:326 (Oct. 25, Nov. 5–10, 1843).

81. Udney Hay Jacob, *An Extract from a Manuscript Entitled The Peacemaker, or the Doctrines of the Millennium* (Nauvoo, Ill.: J. Smith, [1842]). For the publication history of the pamphlet, see Peter Crawley, *A Descriptive Bibliography of the Mormon Church*, vol. 1: *1830–1847* (Provo, Utah: Religious Studies Center, Brigham Young University, 1997), 211, 212, 412, 413.

82. John Regan, *The Emigrant's Guide to the Western States of America, or, Backwoods and Prairies* (Edinburgh: Oliver & Boyd, [1852]), 270–72; *The Mormon Vanguard Brigade of 1847: Norton Jacob's Record*, ed. Ronald O. Barney (Logan: Utah State University Press), 19, 21, 56, 65, 66, 73, 77, 89, 252, 278, 281, 302, 309, 310, 313–16; Kenneth W. Godfrey, "A New Look at the Alleged Little Known Discourse by Joseph Smith," *BYU Studies* 9 (1968): 5–6; Janice Atterholt to Laurel Ulrich, e-mail, April 24, 2012. Joseph Johnstun kindly put me in touch with Mrs. Atterholt, who is a descendant of Jacob's son Stephen.

83. *Times and Seasons* 4, no. 2 (Dec. 1, 1842): 32; Dean Jesse, "John Taylor's Nauvoo Journal," *BYU Studies* 23 (Summer 1983): 84; "A Base Calumny Refuted," and "Beware of the Apostates Doom," *Millennial Star* 12 (March 15, Sept. 15, 1850): 92, 93, 280–83.

84. The many discussions of Jacob's pamphlet include, in addition to Godfrey, "A New Look," Lawrence Foster, "A Little-Known Defense of Polygamy from the Mormon Press in 1842," *Dialogue: A Journal of Mormon Thought* 9, no. 4 (1974): 21–34; Richard S. Van Wagoner, *Mormon Polygamy: A History*, 2nd ed. (Salt Lake City: Signature Books, 1989), 50, 60; B. Carmon Hardy, "Lords of Creation: Polygamy, the Abrahamic Household, and Mormon Patriarchy," *Journal of Mormon History* 20 (1994): 138. The oft-cited notion that Smith published Jacob's work as "as a feeler among the people, to pave the way for celestial marriage" comes from *Mormonism Unveiled; or The Life and Confessions of the Late Mormon Bishop John D. Lee (Written by Himself)* (St. Louis: Bryan, Brand & Company, 1878), 146. On the purported link between Jacob's tract and modern fundamentalist practice, see Anne Wilde, "Response to Under the Banner of Heaven," paper presented at Sunstone, Aug. 16, 2003, available as an audiotape at www.sunstonemagazine.com.

85. Henrik Hartog, *Man & Wife in America: A History* (Cambridge, Mass: Harvard University Press, 2000), 123, 137, 150.

86. Susan Klepp, *Revolutionary Conceptions: Women, Fertility, and Family Limitations in America* (Chapel Hill: University of North Carolina Press, 2009), 101–5.

87. "Woman's Rights," *Littell's Living Age* XVIII (1848): 424.

88. For an accessible summary of this story, see Carol Berkin, "Angelina and Sarah Grimké: Abolitionist Sisters," *History Now: Newsletter of the Gilder Lehrman Institute,* gilderlehrman.org.

89. Jacob, *Extract from The Peacemaker,* 27.

90. Quoted in Klepp, *Revolutionary Conceptions,* 102. Klepp associates the changing meaning of the phrase with changing attitudes toward sexuality and reproduction.

91. "A Favourite Song, Sung at Vauxhall by Mr. Vernon, Set by Mr. Brewster," in *Essex Almanack for the year of our Lord Christ, 1771* (Salem, Mass., 1771), n.p.

92. *Notes and Queries,* 3d ser., II (July–Dec. 1862): 410, 436.

93. Jacob, *Extract from The Peacemaker,* 2, 4.

94. Jacob, *Extract from The Peacemaker,* 30–34.

95. Rebecca Looney, "Migration and Separation: Divorce in Kane County, 1837–1869," *Illinois Historical Journal* 89, no. 2 (Summer 1996): 70–84; Daniel W. Stowell, "Femes UnCovert: Women's Encounters with the Law," and Stacey Pratt McDermott, "Dissolving the Bonds of Matrimony: Women and Divorce in Sangamon County, Illinois, 1837–60," in *In Tender Consideration: Women, Families, and the Law in Abraham Lincoln's Illinois,* ed. Daniel W. Stowell (Urbana and Chicago: University of Illinois Press, 2002), 20–23, 71–103.

96. Jacob, *Extract from The Peacemaker,* 15–17.

97. Jacob eventually embraced Mormonism, and in 1845 took a plural wife, who promptly left him. He then wandered around Illinois, peddling his pamphlet, until he migrated to Utah, where he died in 1860. His legal wife, Elizabeth, lived out her life in Illinois. Although he considered himself a prophet, his descendants have mostly forgotten him. (Janice Atterholt, e-mail to Laurel Ulrich.)

98. For an overview of this theme, see my Mormon History Association Presidential Address, published as Laurel Thatcher Ulrich, "Runaway Wives, 1830–1860," *Journal of Mormon History* 42 (April 2016): 1–26.

99. Entry on Augusta Cobb in O'Donovan, *Boston Mormons.*

100. WW 1:248–49 (May 1838); WW 2:110 (July 10, 1841).

101. Elizabeth Brooks Thompson to Augusta Cobb, Philadelphia, Sept. 14, 1843, AAC Family.

102. WW 2:314 (Sept. 30, 1843).

103. WW 2:374 (Sept. 30, 1843); "O'Donovan, *Boston Mormons,* citing the *Nauvoo Neighbor,* Nov. 8, 1843, and an essay by Augusta's great-granddaughter in *American Heritage* 16 (Feb. 1965): 54.

104. Augusta Adams Young Affidavit, July 12, 1860, in Affidavits CM, 1:50, 52, and copy of Harriet Cook Young Affidavit, March 4, 1870, in Affidavits CM 2:12, 14.

105. Ellen Cobb to Augusta Cobb, Rocheport, Mo., March 27, 1844; Henry Cobb to Ellen Cobb, April 15, 1844, AAC Family.

106. Lewis, *Narrative,* 5.

107. Elizabeth Brooks Thompson to Augusta Cobb, March 21, 1841, AAC Family; Jean L. Silver-Isenstadt, *Shameless: The Visionary Life of Mary Gove Nichols* (Baltimore: Johns Hopkins University Press, 2002), 29–44.

5. "Menny females was recieved in to the Holy Order"

1. WW 2:326–40 (Nov. 13, 1843–Jan. 16, 1844). The cellar in question may or may not have been in the new house. He had cleaned it out and installed gangways on Dec. 1,

perhaps moving some of the family's supplies from the printing house where they were living, even though the house itself was not yet finished.

2. WW 2:344 (Jan. 28, 1844); Ivan Blumenthal, "Carbon Monoxide Poisoning," *Journal of the Royal Society of Medicine* 94 (June 2001): 270–72; Mayo Clinic, "Carbon Monoxide Poisoning," www. mayoclinic.org; Iowa State University Extension, "Charcoal Grills Can Emit Deadly Carbon Monoxide," www.extension.iastate.edu.

3. HCK, 55–56 (January 1844).

4. WW 2:332–33 (Dec. 23, 1843). For a succinct overview of the history of the Anointed Quorum, see Devery S. Anderson and Gary James Bergera, "Editor's Introduction," in *Joseph Smith's Quorum of the Anointed 1842–1845: A Documentary History* (Salt Lake City: Signature Books, 2005), xiii–xliii. Bushman, *RSR,* 496–99, also summarizes interpretations originally developed in Andrew E. Ehat, "Joseph Smith's Introduction of Temple Ordinances and the 1844 Succession Question," M.A. thesis, Brigham Young University, 1982, and Michael D. Quinn, *The Mormon Hierarchy: Origins of Power* (Salt Lake City: Signature Books, 1994), 491–502.

5. WW 2:326–27 (Nov. 11, 1843).

6. WW 2:329 (Dec. 2, 3, 23, 24, 1843). Wilford explicitly mentioned the anointings, but referred more vaguely to "blessings" received the next day. Presumably, this meant the endowment.

7. Newell and Avery, *Mormon Enigma,* 172–75. Anderson and Bergera, in *Quorum of the Anointed,* xxxv, note, "No plural wife received the ordinance prior to Joseph's death," a point that I believe has received too little attention.

8. Carol Cornwall Madsen, "Mormon Women and the Temple: Toward a New Understanding," in *Sisters in Spirit: Mormon Women in Historical and Cultural Perspective,* ed. Maureen Ursenbach Beecher and Lavina Fielding Anderson (Urbana and Chicago: University of Illinois Press, 1987), 80–110; Margaret and Paul Toscano, *Strangers in Paradox: Explorations in Mormon Theology* (Salt Lake City: Signature Books, 1990), 179–91; Todd Compton, "Preface," in *Quorum of the Anointed, Quorum,* xi–xii.

9. For a current Latter-day Saint description of the ritual undergarment, see "Mormon Underwear," at www.ldschurchtemples.com.

10. On the evolution and interpretation of the new rituals, see, in addition to the accounts cited in note 4 above, David John Buerger, "'The Fulness of the Priesthood': The Second Anointing in Latter-day Saint Theology and Practice," *Dialogue: A Journal of Mormon Thought* 16 (Spring 1983): 10–47; Michael Homer, "'Similarity of Priesthood in Masonry': The Relationship Between Freemasonry and Mormonism," *Dialogue: A Journal of Mormon Thought* 27 (Fall 1994): 67–75; Kathleen Flake, "'Not to Be Riten': The Mormon Temple Rite as Oral Canon," *Journal of Ritual Studies* 9 (Summer 1995): 1–21; Devery S. Anderson, "The Anointed Quorum in Nauvoo, 1842–43," *Journal of Mormon History* 29 (Fall 2003): 137–57; Samuel Morris Brown, *In Heaven as It Is on Earth: Joseph Smith and the Early Mormon Conquest of Death* (New York: Oxford University Press, 2012), 183–88.

11. Later, he used similar initials to mark the anointings of others, as in WW 2:340, 344, 346, 348, 350 (Jan. 20, 27, 30, Feb. 4, 18, 26, 1844). The use of paired initials highlighted the absence of plural wives from the quorum. During Joseph's lifetime, eleven of the nineteen male participants (58 percent) had plural wives; the remaining eight, including Wilford, did not. (Anderson, "Anointed Quorum," 152–53.) Phebe used her middle initial (for Whittemore), hence PWW.

12. For examples of such things, see Jane Katcher, David A. Schorsch, and Ruth Wolfe, eds., *Expressions of Innocence and Eloquence: Selections from the Jane Katcher Collection of Americana* (New Haven: Yale University Press, 2006), vol. 1, 84–91, 95–99; vol. 2, 326–29; Peter Benes, "Family Representations and Remembrances: Decorated New England Family Registers, 1770–1850," in *The Art of Family: Genealogical Artifacts in New England,* ed. D. Brenton Simons and Peter Benes (Boston: New England Historic Genealogical Society, 2002), 15–59.

13. References to Elijah appear in the Book of Mormon and in five sections of the present-day *Doctrine and Covenants,* although some of these revelations were as yet unpublished in 1844. See 3 Nephi 25:5; *Doctrine and Covenants,* 2:1; 27:9; 35:4; 110:13–16; 128:17 (section 128 was added in 1845, sections 2 and 110 in 1875); Richard E. Turley Jr. and William W. Slaughter, *How We Got the Doctrine and Covenants* (Salt Lake City: Deseret Book, 2012), 85, 136 n20. On Joseph's sermons, see WW 2:342, 359–66 (Jan. 21, March 10, 1844).

14. HCK, 56–57 (February 1844); John 12:3–8, KJV.

15. WW 2:293 (April 26, 27, 29, 30, May 1, 2, 3, 4, 5, 9, 1844). Apparently, he and Phebe had been living in the printing office, but when Taylor bought the press, the Woodruffs moved out and returned to the old house at Durphy and Hotchkiss Streets, the site where he was building his new one (WW 2:340, 348 [Jan. 16, Feb. 5–7, 1844]).

16. Bushman, *RSR,* 508–12.

17. Bushman, *RSR,* 512–17.

18. Bushman, *RSR,* 517–25.

19. WC2, vol. 2, Jan. 16, 30, 1844; WW 2:355 (March 7, 1844).

20. WC2, vol. 2, March 23, 1844.

21. Bushman, *RSR,* 494–99; Hales, *Polygamy,* 2:115–19, 247–49.

22. Newell and Avery, *Mormon Enigma,* 172–75; WW 2:357 (March 7, 1844); W. W. Phelps, "The Voice of Innocence from Nauvoo," copy made by Thomas Bullock with corrections by Emma Smith, CHL, printed in *Nauvoo Neighbor* 47 (March 20, 1844): 2.

23. NRS Minutes, 122–27 (March 9, 16, 1844).

24. Hyrum Smith, in *History of the Church of Jesus Christ of Latter-day Saints,* ed. B. H. Roberts (Salt Lake City: Deseret Book, 1957), vol. 6, 298; "Nauvoo Conference Minutes," *Millennial Star,* Nov. 6, 1844, 85, reprinted from *Times and Seasons,* Aug. 1844.

25. Anderson and Bergera, ed., *Quorum of the Anointed,* xli, 48–49, 51–52; Lyndon W. Cook, "Biographical Essay," and William Law, "Record of Doings in Nauvoo in 1844," in *William Law,* ed. Lyndon W. Cook (Orem, Utah: Grandin Book Company, 1994), 1–34, 37–56; WW 2:392, 393 (April 18, May 6, 1844).

26. WW 2:393 (May 6, 1844).

27. *The Words of Joseph: The Contemporary Accounts of the Nauvoo Discourses of the Prophet Joseph,* comp. and ed. Andrew F. Ehat and Lyndon W. Cook (Provo, Utah: Religious Studies Center, Brigham Young University, 1980), 376. On Joseph's awareness of Phelps's work, see *An American Prophet's Record: The Diaries and Journals of Joseph Smith,* ed. Scott H. Faulring (Salt Lake City: Signature Books, 1987), 448. This appears to come from *History of the Church,* vol. 6, 480–512.

28. *Nauvoo Expositor,* June 7, 1844, 1; Law, "Record of Doings in Nauvoo," 54–61.

29. *Warsaw Signal,* June 12, 1844, quoted in Bushman, *RSR,* 541.

30. Bushman, *RSR,* 537–50.

31. Bradley and Woodward, 107–14. Other accounts include Todd Compton, *In Sacred Loneliness: The Plural Wives of Joseph Smith* (Salt Lake City: Signature Books, 1997), 71–113; Allen L. Wyatt, "Zina and Her Men: An Examination of the Changing Marital Status of Zina Huntington Jacobs Smith Young," www.fairlds.org; and Hales, *Polygamy,* vol. 1, chapters 12–16.

32. Vilate Kimball to Heber C. Kimball, June 9–24, 1844, in Ronald K. Esplin, "Life in Nauvoo, June 1844: Vilate Kimball's Martyrdom Letters," *BYU Studies* 19 (1979): 2–3.

33. Vilate Kimball to Heber C. Kimball, June 9–24, 1844.

34. Vilate Kimball to Heber C. Kimball, June 9–24, 1844.

35. Phebe Carter Woodruff to Wilford Woodruff, Nauvoo, June 16, 1844 (inserted in a letter from Bathsheba to George A. Smith, June 15, 1844, BWS Letters.

36. Bathsheba Smith to George A. Smith, Nauvoo, June 15, 1844. BWS Letters.

37. Vilate Kimball to Heber C. Kimball, June 9, 1844, in Esplin, "Life in Nauvoo," 3–4.

38. Z1, 5, 6. (June 24, 25, 26, 27, 1844).

39. Z1, 6, 7 (June 28, July 1, 4, 15, 1844).

40. Mary Ann Angel Young to Brigham Young, June 30, 1844, Brigham Young Papers, CHL, in Madsen, *In Their Own Words,* 141–42.

41. Vilate Kimball to Heber C. Kimball, June 30, 1844, in Espin, "Life in Nauvoo," 6–7.

42. Phebe W. Woodruff to Dear Parents, July 30, 1844, CHL, transcribed by Bruce A. Carr. When Phebe came to the end of her paper, she reversed it and continued writing in the opposite direction, between lines.

43. HCK, 64–65 (June 6, 1844).

44. WW 2:413 (June 27, 1844). For a brief summary of the Philadelphia riots, see Zachary M. Schrag, "Nativist Riots of 1844," *The Encyclopedia of Great Philadelphia,* philadel phiaencyclopedia.org.

45. WW 2:416 (July 1, 1844).

46. WW 2:419, 421, 422, 423 (July 9, 11, 13, 16, 17, 1844).

47. WW 2:422–31 (July 17–23, 1844).

48. Z1, 7 (Aug. 8, 1844); WW 2:434–40; HCK, 79 (Aug. 7, 8, 1844).

49. They also called on Mother Lucy Smith, who asked Wilford for a blessing (WW 2:441–42, 449–50, 453–54 [Aug. 14, 15, 21, 23, 1844]).

50. WW 2:197–203. Because he used a blank page in an earlier section of the diary, this entry is out of chronological order.

51. WW 2:456–57 (Aug. 27, 1844).

52. Z1, 19 (March 31, 1845).

53. Z1, 14 (Jan. 25, 1845).

54. Z1, 27 (June 7, 1845).

55. Z1, 20 (April 19, 1845).

56. Z1, 26 (July 14, 15, 16, 1845).

57. Z1, 10 (Nov. 13, 1844).

58. Z1, 13 (Dec. 31, 1844).

59. Z1, 9 (Sept. 20, 1844).

60. Z1, 24 (June 16, 1845).

61. Z1, 20 (April 15, 1845).

62. Z1, 16, 19, 25, 27 (Feb. 15, March 25, July 2, Aug. 1, 8, 1845).

63. Z1, 10 (Nov. 13, 1844).

64. Z1, 14, 17, 19, 23 (Jan. 22, March 22, 27, June 2, 1845).

65. Z1, 29 (Sept. 11, 1845).

66. See comment by Maureen Ursenbach Beecher, Z1, 3.

67. Z1, 17 (March 7, 1845).

68. Z1, 12 (Dec. 20, 1844).

69. Z1, 14, 15, 17 (Jan. 19, Feb. 5, 11, March 1, 13, 1845).

70. Z1, 21 (May 3, 1845).

71. Job 17:11, KJV. Modern translations substitute "desires" or "wishes" for "thoughts," smoothing out the seeming contradiction. See also Alma 18:20, Book of Mormon. A similar construction in Isaiah 10:7, KJV (repeated in 2 Nephi 20:7, Book of Mormon), reads "neither doth his heart think so." The Revised Standard translation reads, "But he does not so intend" (Michael D. Coogan, ed., *The New Oxford Annotated Bible* [Oxford and New York: Oxford University Press, 1989], 745, 993).

72. Z1, 21 (May 9, 1845).

73. Z1, 23 (June 10, 11, 1845).

74. WC2, vol. 2 (Jan. 26, 1845).

75. William had been initiated in Feb. 1844, before Joseph Smith's death, but at that time neither of his wives had been included (WC2, vol. 2 [Jan. 22, Feb. 3, 4]; vol. 1 [Dec. 22, 1844; March 29, 1846]).

76. Edward Leo Lyman, *Amasa Mason Lyman: Mormon Apostle and Apostate* (Salt Lake City: University of Utah Press, 2009), 90–93, 496–97.

77. Stanley B. Kimball, *Heber C. Kimball: Mormon Patriarch and Pioneer* (Urbana and Chicago: University of Illinois Press, 1981), 307–16; Arrington, *BY*, 420–21; Hales, *Polygamy*, 2:304–5.

78. Z1, 24 (June 14, 1845) and 34 n44.

79. Z1, 22 (May 24, 1845).

80. Z1, 21, 25, 28 (April 26, June 27, July 14, 1845).

81. Z1, 26 (July 6, 1845).

82. Z1, 25 (June 26, 1845).

83. Z1, 30 (Sept. 18, 20, 1845).

84. Z1, 29 (Sept. 13, 15, 1845); Robert Bruce Flanders, *Nauvoo: Kingdom on the Mississippi* (Urbana and Chicago: University of Illinois Press, 1965), 323–35.

85. WC2, vol. 3 (Aug. 24, 1845).

86. Flanders, *Nauvoo*, 193–98; ERS1, 76 (June 13, 1843); Bushman, *RSR*, 448–53; Ronald K. Esplin, "The Significance of Nauvoo for Latter-day Saints," in *Kingdom on the Mississippi Revisited: Nauvoo in Mormon History*, ed. Roger D. Launius and John E. Hallwas (Urbana and Chicago: University of Illinois Press, 1996), 19–38; Lisle G. Brown, comp., "Chronology of the Construction, Destruction, and Reconstruction of the Nauvoo Temple," users.marshall.edu.

87. *Millennial Star* 5, no. 1 (June 1844): 15; *MS* 6, no. 5 (Aug. 15, 1845): 75; *MS* 6, no. 7 (Sept. 15, 1845): 103.

88. Catherine Lewis to Brigham Young, Lynn, Mass., Nov. 17, 1845, Brigham Young Office Files, box 20, folder 7, CHL.

89. WC2, vol. 1, Feb. 18, Aug. 17, 1844; Jan. 12, 14, 25, 27, 28, 1845.

90. WC2, vol. 1, Feb. 10, 1845; Dec. 8, 9, 11 23, 26, and year-end summary for 1844; Jan. 9, 13, 14, 19, 31, 1845; Allen, *No Toil nor Labor*, 185–218.

91. WC2, vol. 3, July 1, July 16, 17, 1845.

92. WC2, vol. 3, Aug. 24, 1845.

93. Brigham Young, Discourses, March 9, 1845, in *The First Fifty Years of Relief Society: Key Documents in Latter-day Saint Women's History*, ed. Jill Mulvay Derr, Carol Cornwall Madsen, Kate Holbrook, and Matthew Grow (Salt Lake City: Church Historian's Press, 2016), 171.

94. HCK, 151–65 (Nov. 26–Dec. 8, 1845).

95. Heber C. Kimball Journal, kept by William Clayton, in WC Smith, 199–258. This journal is also used in *The Nauvoo Endowment Companies, 1845–1846: A Documentary History*, ed. Devery S. Anderson and Gary James Bergera (Salt Lake City: Signature Books, 2005), the most comprehensive source for this period.

96. Anderson and Bergera, eds., *Endowment Companies*, xxxvii–xxxviii, 109, 115, 150, 191, 192, 197, 232, 313.

97. LCT1.

98. LCT1.

99. This interpretation first appears in W. Wyl [Wilhelm Ritter von Wymetal], *Mormon Portraits, or the Truth About Mormon Leaders from 1830 to 1886* (Salt Lake City: Tribune Printing, 1886), 245. It has been picked up by many writers since.

100. LCT1; John Taylor Family, FamilySearch.org.

101. Anderson and Bergera, *Endowment Companies*, 7, 44, 57, 73–80, and passim; on Leonora's party, 343, 346.

102. Anderson and Bergera, eds., *Endowment Companies*, 190–91.

103. Anderson and Bergera, eds., *Endowment Companies*, 94, 98, 194–95, 231–32.

104. WC Smith, 221–27, 239.

105. WC2, vol. 3, Jan. 26, 1846.

106. Anderson and Bergera, eds., *Endowment Companies*, 295–98, 313, 564–65.

107. Anderson and Bergera, eds., *Endowment Companies*, 51–58, 607; Arrington, *BY*, 120–21.

108. Kimball, *Heber C. Kimball*, 122–23, and family history data in app. A, 307–16.

Four were conceived between April 29 and July 23, 1845, and the fifth between Jan. 12 and Jan. 19, 1846. Frances Swan, Clarissa Cutler, and Emily Cutler left him. Lucy Walker, the other woman who had been married to Smith, remained. Other than occasional references to Sarah Ann Whitney Kingsbury, there is no hint in Kimball's diary of his association with these women.

109. Catherine Lewis, *Narrative of Some of the Proceedings of the Mormons; Giving an Account of Their Iniquities* (Lynn, Mass.: The Author, 1848), 12–13.

110. Lewis, *Narrative,* 6–7; Anderson and Bergera, eds., *Endowment Companies,* 128, 132, 137; HCK, 72 (July 5, 1844).

111. Elizabeth Adams Henderson to Augusta Cobb, Sept. 25, 1845, AAC Family.

112. Anderson and Bergera, eds., *Endowment Companies,* 24, 56–58, 60, 364; Augusta Cobb to Brigham Young, City of Joseph, Jan. 20, Feb. 2, 4, 1846, AAC Letters.

113. ERS *Poetry,* 314.

114. Eliza R. Snow to B. Young and Mary Ann Young, Jan. 7, 1846, Brigham Young Papers, box 44, folder 21, CHL.

6. "Mud aplenty"

1. PS, Intro, 13–14, 16–17.

2. PS, 40–41 (April 4–7, 1846).

3. Robert Bruce Flanders, *Nauvoo: Kingdom on the Mississippi* (Urbana and Chicago: University of Illinois Press, 1965), 323–41; Bennett, *Winter Quarters;* Marshall Hamilton, "From Assassination to Expulsion," in *Kingdom on the Mississippi Revisited: Nauvoo in Mormon History,* ed. Roger D. Launius and John E. Hallwas (Urbana and Chicago: University of Illinois Press, 1996); Susan Sessions Rugh, "Conflict in the Countryside: Rural Communities in the 1840s Mormon War," *Illinois Heritage* 10, no. 3 (2007): 6–9. In 2004, the Illinois House of Representatives issued a kind of apology for the expulsion, the sponsors finding it difficult to understand how such religious persecution could exist. (See Melissa Sanford, "Illinois Tells Mormons It Regrets Expulsion," *New York Times,* April 8, 2004). In a country where "removal" had been a long-standing solution to confict with American Indians, it may have seemed quite rational.

4. PS, 41, 44 (April 6, 12, 1846).

5. PS, 32 (Feb. 10, 1846).

6. PS, 394 (May 3, 1888).

7. PS, 19–22, 24, 25, 276 (Feb. 10, 13, 1846, June 16, 1860); NRS Minutes, 33 (April 19, 1842).

8. HS, 122, 127 (Feb. 13, 26, 1846).

9. HS, 127 (Feb. 26, 1846).

10. Bennett, *WQ,* 26–45; Stanley B. Kimball, *Heber C. Kimball: Mormon Patriarch and Pioneer* (Urbana and Chicago: University of Illinois Press, 1981), 129–42.

11. WC Smith, 260, 267, 268 (Feb. 27, 28, April 1, 4, 6, 1846); Allen, *No Toil nor Labor,* 221, 225.

12. EPL, 24, 25 (April 9, 10, 1846); Edward Leo Lyman, *Amasa Mason Lyman: Mormon Apostle and Apostate* (Salt Lake City: University of Utah Press, 2009), 116–20.

13. For a short but vivid description of the problem with mud, see Kimball, *Heber C. Kimball,* 132. For an early use of the axiom, see George Monro Grant, *Ocean to Ocean: Sanford Fleming's Expedition Through Canada in 1872* (London, 1872; New York: R. Worthington, 1877), 136, 176.

14. George D. Smith, *Nauvoo Polygamy* (Salt Lake City: Signature Books, 2008), 286, 287, 627, 628. Samuel W. Taylor, *The Kingdom or Nothing: The Life of John Taylor, Militant Mormon* (New York: Macmillan, 1976), 99, 100, lists ten wives by the time Taylor left Nauvoo.

15. LCT 2, 199 (March 6–12, 1846). It is difficult to know how many plural wives trav-

eled with them. Elizabeth Kaighan, whom Taylor married in 1843, apparently remained in Nauvoo, where she gave birth to her first child on March 15. In her trail diary, Leonora mentioned Jane Ballantyne and Mary Ann Oakley by name, using their surnames to identify them, but there are no explicit references to the others.

16. Emmeline B. Wells Journals, vol. 1, L. Tom Perry Special Collections, HBLL. All but a few small sections of this volume have been published in Madsen, *In Their Own Words,* 43–49, which contains the brief Nauvoo section, and Madsen, *Journey to Zion,* 113–29, which contains the trail diary.

17. Wells, in Madsen, *Journey to Zion,* 115, 117 125, 127, 129 (March 3, 11, April 16, 23, May 4, 1846).

18. LCT 2, 200 (April 24, May 5, 1846).

19. Kimball, *Heber C. Kimball,* 235, quoting a memoir by Kimball's daugher Helen Mar Whitney, in *Woman's Exponent* 12 (Jan. 15, 1884): 127.

20. EPL, 22–23 (April 2, 3, 1846).

21. William Huntington, in Madsen, *Journey to Zion,* 134, 136, 138 (March 20, 26, April 8, 1846); PS, 52 (June 1, 1846); Henry B. Jacobs to Zina D. Jacobs, Aug. 19, 1846, CHL, MS 3248. On variant accounts of their separation, see Allen L. Wyatt, "Zina and her Men," FairMormon Conference 2006, at www.fairmormon.org.

22. PS, 36 (March 8, 1846), 42 (Accounts for Attendance at Deliveries).

23. Wells, in Madsen, *Journey to Zion,* 117 (March 8, 1846).

24. PS, 41, 54, 54 n78 (June 10, 1846).

25. WC Smith, 170 (April 15, 1846); Allen, *No Toil nor Labor,* 198–200. Clayton, who was passionate about music, may have discovered the song in the published version. More likely, he had heard it sung in some now lost setting.

26. The original words and the first published version of the tune appear in *Revival Melodies, or Songs of Zion* (Boston: John Putnam, 1842), 18.

27. Karen Lynn Davidson, *Our Latter-day Saint Hymns: The Stories and the Messages* (Salt Lake City: Deseret Book, 1988), 58–59.

28. Davidson, *Our Latter-day Saint Hymns,* 59.

29. HS, 155, 160 (April 22, 23, May 8, 1846); PS, 48 (May 9, 1846).

30. Bennett, *WQ,* 134–42; Maureen Ursenbach Beecher, "Women in Winter Quarters," *Sunstone Magazine* 40 (July–Aug. 1983): 16, 19 n42; Evan L. Ivie and Douglas C. Heiner, "Deaths in Early Nauvoo, 1839–46, and Winter Quarters, 1846–48," and "Medical Terms Used by Saints in Nauvoo and Winter Quarters, 1839–48," *Religious Educator* 10, no. 3 (2009): 152–62, 164–72.

31. HS, 160, 161 (May 8, 10, 1846).

32. HS, 170–71 (June 25, 27, 28, 1846).

33. ERS2, 115 (March 1, 1846).

34. ERS2, 142 (Aug. 26, 1846). This is apparently a misdating for Aug. 25.

35. WW 2:458–59 (Aug. 28, 1844).

36. WW 2:623 (Dec. 25, 1845).

37. WW 2:581, 584–86 (July 18, July 25, 1845).

38. WW 2:624 (Dec. 27, 1845). The implication of Wilford's entry ("Elder Ward Commenced to draw the portrait of Mrs Woodruff with little Joseph in her arms") is that he had just begun the work. The finished portrait is in oil and quite complex, but he must have completed it before Wilford's departure on Jan. 23, if not Phebe's on Jan. 16.

39. WW 2:120–21, 623, 624 (Aug. 24, 1841; Dec. 30, 1845); WW 3:5 (Jan. 16, 1846); "Trigeminal Neuralgia Fact Sheet," National Institute of Neurological Disorders and Stroke, National Institutes of Health, www.ninds.nih.gov; "Trigeminal Neuralgia," U.S. National Library of Medicine, PubMed Health, www.ncbi.nlm.nih.gov; George Woollam, "Case of Traumatic Tetanus, Successfully Treated by the Sesquicarbonate of Iron," *Provincial Medical Journal and Retrospect of the Medical Sciences* 4, no. 4 (April 30, 1842): 72.

40. WW 2:599–600 (Sept. 16–20, 1845).

41. WW 3:18–20 (Feb. 18–19, 1846).

42. WW 3:20–21 (Feb. 22, 1846).

43. WW 3:22–23 (Feb. 28, 1846).

44. WW 2:486 (Nov. 17, 1844).

45. WW 3:25–30 (March 7, 11, 17–18, 1846).

46. WW 3:8–38, 48–65 (March 7–April 13, May 16–Aug. 4, 1846).

47. WW 3: 31 (March 18, 19, 1846).

48. WW 3:28, 35 (March 16, April 2, 1846).

49. Azubah Woodruff Journal, in Asahel H. Woodruff Daybooks, vol. 1, 51, MS 9333, CHL. The pagination is not consistent. I have indicated it only where numbers were visible.

50. Azubah Woodruff Journal, 56–57.

51. See Family Record in WW 1:199–211.

52. Azubah Woodruff Journal, 55.

53. WW 3:38–40 (April 13, 14, 18, 1846).

54. WW 3:48 (May 14, 1846).

55. WW 3:48 (May 17, 1846).

56. WW 3:50 (May 27, 1846).

57. WW 3:51–52 (June 6, 7, 1846).

58. WW 3:53 (June 20, 1846).

59. Azubah Woodruff Journal, 63, 81, 83.

60. WW 3:55 (June 27, 1846); Rosetta King entry, MOT.

61. Azubah Woodruff Journal, 72, 81, 83.

62. Azubah Woodruff Journal, n.p.

63. WW 3:54–55 (June 21, 1846).

64. MPR, 66 and Afterword.

65. Madsen, *Journey to Zion,* 207.

66. WW, 3:54 (June 24, 1846).

67. MPR, 67.

68. WC Smith, 283–84 (June 26, 1846).

69. ERS2, 137 (June 24, 1846).

70. WC Smith, 284–85 (June 28, 1846).

71. WW 3:55 (June 28, 1846).

72. WW, 3:54–55 (June 26, 1846).

73. HS, 172 (June 28, 1846).

74. Turner, *BY,* 148–52.

75. LCT2, 208–9 (July 5, 1846).

76. WW 3:59 (July 12, 1846).

77. HS, 172–73 (June 28, 30, 1846).

78. HS, 175, 176, 177 (July 5, 11, 1846).

79. LCT2, 84 (June 12–16, 1846).

80. MPR, 1–10, 78 (July 15, 1846).

81. PS, 58, 60, 61 (July 16, Aug. 7, Sept. 2, 1846).

82. Madsen, *Journey to Zion,* 210, 211, 212, 213.

83. MPR, 89–92 (Aug. 16–28 , 1846; letter to Samuel, Sept.–Oct.).

84. HS, 202 (Sept. 26, 1846).

85. EPL, 32 (Aug. 9, 1846).

86. ERS2, 143–44 (following entry for Aug. 29, 1846).

87. MPR, 30, 78, 88, 89 (July 15, Aug 12, 13, 14, 15, 1846).

88. PS, 56, 62, 63, 65–67 (June 22, 23, Oct. 13–19, 25–30, Nov. 4, 28, 1846).

89. WW 3:64–65 (Aug. 2, 1846).

90. WW 3:66, 67 (Aug. 8, 20, 1846).

91. WW 3:71, 72 (Aug. 26, 29, 1846); Alexander, *Woodruff,* 135.

92. HS, 190–93 (Sept. 4, 5, 6, 13, 1846).

93. WW 3:94–96 (Nov. 4–13, 21, 1846); Alexander, *Woodruff,* 122.

94. PS, 67 (Dec. 8, 1846); WW 3:97 (Dec. 8, 9, 10, 11, 1846).

95. EPL, 34, 41 (Dec. 12, 1846; Jan. 29, 1847); ERS2, 149 (Dec. 14, 1846). The poem appears in both diaries.

96. PS, 69 (Jan. 1, 1847); ERS2, 151 (Jan. 1, 1847).

7. "Wrote some in my earley Biography"

1. MPR, 53–63, 108 (Feb. 1–5, 1847). I'm guessing that she added to her autobiography in Feb. Although her letters and diary are more extensive than her "Memorandum," all three were clearly written during the same period.

2. HS, 136 (Feb. 18, 1847).

3. PGS, 21–22.

4. Bennett, WQ, 72–74, 77, 90, 137–40, 143–45; MPR, Introduction, 25–30. Fragments of a manuscript census taken in Dec. 1846 showed 3,483 "souls" distributed in twenty-two wards, and counted 538 log houses, 83 sod houses, and 814 wagons. The emphasis in the census on wagons, horses, oxen, and mules shows the concern for continuing the migration. There were at this point 502 "well men" and 117 "sick men," but censuses from individual wards show that many men were absent—usually in Missouri, getting provisions. (Bishop's Reports, Camp of Israel, Winter Quarters, Omaha Nation, Dec. 20, 1846, LR 6359, folder 2, CHL.)

5. Anne F. Hyde, Empires, Nations, and Families: A History of the North American West, 1800–1860 (Lincoln: University of Nebraska Press, 2011), 27, 41, and chapter 1 passim.

6. Bennett, WQ, 72, 96, 97, 254 n13; MPR, Introduction, 20, 24.

7. Arrington, Woolley, 163–73; Bennett, WQ, 112–28, 134–37, 141 (table 7), 279 n8, 170–71; MPR, Introduction, 28.

8. MPR, 109, 113 (Feb. 9, 11, March 4, 1847).

9. PS, 71 (Feb. 5, 1847).

10. HS, 239 (March 2, 1847).

11. HS Autobiography, 2–8.

12. HS, 236 (Feb. 14, 1847).

13. HS Autobiography, 5–6.

14. HS Autobiography, 9, 10.

15. HS Autobiography, 13.

16. HS Autobiography, 15.

17. HS Autobiography, 19.

18. HS 251 (April 23, 1847).

19. HS Autobiography, 22.

20. HS Autobiography, 40.

21. HS Autobiography, 41.

22. HS, 259, 260 (June 3, 1847); Bennett, WQ, 181–82.

23. HS Autobiography, 17, 19.

24. HS, 239 (March 5, 1847).

25. HS, 240 (March 5, 6, 1847).

26. HS, 241 (March 13, 1847).

27. HS, 305, 306 (March 17, 1848).

28. WW 3:331–33 (March 17, 1848).

29. HS Autobiography, 35.

30. HS Autobiography, 47, 48.

31. HS, 256–57 (May 25, 1847).

32. HS, 224, 229, 308, 308 n72 (Jan. 8, 9, 17, 1847; April 7, 1848); WW 3:116 (Jan. 9, 1848). Juanita Brooks thinks Herring may have been the "half-breed Indian" William Hickman later claimed to have scalped.

33. HS Autobiography, 49–52.

34. HS Autobiography, 45, 46.

35. HS, 240, 245 (March 8, April 2, 1847).
36. HS, 268, 269 (Aug. 5–7, 1847).
37. MPR Mem, 53.
38. MPR Mem, 55–56.
39. MPR Mem, 55.
40. MPR, 103 (Dec. 24, 1846).
41. MPR Mem, 57.
42. MPR, 192, 193 (March 2, 1848).
43. MPR, 55, 265. Jennetta married Samuel's uncle Apostle Willard Richards.
44. David Hunt, *A History of Preston* (Lancaster, Eng.: Carnegie Publishing, 1992), 152–55, 173, 184–87.
45. MPR Mem, 58; MPR, 100, 104, 150, 151, 156, 165, 183–85 (Dec. 1, 1846; Jan. 3, June 27, July 9, Aug. 27, Oct. 30, Dec. 10, 28–31, 1847; Jan. 1–7, 1848.
46. MPR, 122, 192 (May 2, 1847; Feb. 19, 1848). On other encounters with the Woolleys, see 147, 149, 150, 179, 186 (June 13, 20, 26, Nov. 5, 30, 1847; Jan. 7, 1848).
47. Mary Richards to Samuel Richards, Jan. 1847, in MPR, 131.
48. MPR Mem, 59.
49. MPR, 191, 228 (Feb. 20, 22, 23, 1848).
50. MPR, 104 (Dec. 29, 1846).
51. MPR, 114 (April 1, 1847).
52. MPR, 151, 159 (July 9, Sept. 17, 1847).
53. MPR, 104 (Dec. 31, 1846).
54. MPR Mem, 57, 58.
55. MPR, 110 (Feb. 14, 1847).
56. MPR, 110, 111 (Feb. 17, 1847).
57. Mary Richards to Samuel Richards, July 18, 1846, in MPR, 78.
58. MPR, 109 (Feb. 10, 1847).
59. MPR, 121 (April 19, 1847).
60. MPR, 113 (March 17–23, 1847).
61. MPR 149, 191 (June 20, 1847; Feb. 20, 1848).
62. Mary Richards to Samuel Richards, June 8, 1847, in MPR, 167.
63. MPR, 116–17 (April 5, 1847).
64. PS, 71, 72 (Feb. 4–6, 1847).
65. Eliza Snow, Mary Richards, Hosea Stout, and Wilford Woodruff all commented on the dances that took place during this week, Snow and Woodruff specifically on the Silver Greys, a party for older people. Wilford was pleased that his parents attended. (ERS2, 154, 155 [Feb. 3, 4, 5, 1847]; MPR, 109 [Feb. 10, 1847]; HS, 235, [Feb. 9, 11, 1847]; WW 3:125, 126 [Feb. 5, 1847].)
66. PGS, 17, 18, 21.
67. PGS, 18, 19, 21.
68. PGS, 21.
69. PGS, 18.
70. PS, 14; PGS, 22–25.
71. PGS, 24–25, 78.
72. Shadrach Roundy, Joanna's father-in-law, had been with Wilford and other members of the twelve when they met in secret at the Temple Site in Far West in 1839. Joanna apparently lived for a time in Joseph Smith's house at Far West, where she may first have met Patty. Perhaps Patty delivered her first child, born in Nauvoo in 1845. (WW 1:327; Biographical Register, byustudies.byu.edu).
73. PS, 72 (Feb. 14, 1847).
74. Anderson and Bregara, eds., *The Nauvoo Endowment Companies, 1845–1846: A Documentary History* (Salt Lake City: Signature Books, 2005), 496–97 (Jan. 26, 1846).
75. Bradley and Woodward, 145–69.
76. Cylvia [*sic*] Lyon, unsigned affidavit, Affidavits CM, 1:60. For different attempts

to untangle Sylvia's marital history, see Todd Compton, *In Sacred Loneliness: The Plural Wives of Joseph Smith* (Salt Lake City: Signature Books, 1997), 171–204; Hales, *Polygamy*, 1:349–77.

77. PS, 72 (Feb. 14, 1847).

78. PS, 78–79 (April 21–25, 1847).

79. ERS2, 151 (Jan. 1, 1847).

80. ERS2, 157–58 (March 7, 1847).

81. ERS2, 153–54 (Jan. 26, 1847); ERS, *Poetry*, 334–36.

82. ERS2, 159 (March 14, 1847).

83. ERS2, 74 (March 13, 1847).

84. ERS2, 239–40.

85. Exact identification is impossible, because she usually gave only surnames. In addition to Eliza Snow and "Zina," she listed Sisters Allen, Benson, Beamon, Brown, Buell, Hickenlooper, Higbee, Kimball, Knight, Leavitt, Leonard, Markham, Miller, Noble, Taylor, Thomson, Van Cott, Whitney, and Young. For possible identifications, see Maurine Carr Ward, "'This Institution Is a Good One': The Female Relief Society of Nauvoo, 17 March 1842 to 16 March 1844," *Mormon Historical Studies* 3 (Fall 2002).

86. PS, 81 (May 19, 1847).

87. PS, 79 (April 29, 30, 1847).

88. PS, 79 (May 1, 2, 3, 1847); ERS2, 170 (May 1, 2, 1847).

89. Patty and Eliza both copied the poem into their diaries (PS, 80 [May 5, 1847]; ERS2, 171 [May 2, 1847]). It also appears in ERS *Poetry*, 257–58.

90. PS, 81, 147, 148, 207 (May 9, 1847; June 9, 25, 1850; Aug. 4, 1854); PGS, 253 (May 3, 1854).

91. PS, 83 (June 1, 1847). For readability, I cut a short section from this entry which in Smart's transcription read: "and show Herber [probably Heber's] girl the order that duty called them to perform to get any blessings from him upon them." In other words, she was not just fulfilling a spiritual calling to "bless" Vilate Kimball. She was trying to teach a younger member of the Kimball circle how to go about getting blessings. The "him" is ambiguous but likely refers to God rather than to Heber.

92. ERS2, 180 (June 19, 1847). Patty did not mention this event, perhaps because she was absorbed in writing a letter to Syvia (PS, 85 [June 19, 1847]).

93. PS, 85 (June 14, 1847); ERS2, 178 (June 14, 1847).

94. PS, 88 (June 27, 1847).

95. Sarah M. Kimball to Marinda Hyde, Nauvoo, Jan. 2, 1848, CHL; Newell and Avery, *Mormon Enigma*, 247–48.

96. Sarah M. Kimball to Sarepta Heywood, Nauvoo, n.d., Joseph L. Heywood Letters, CHL. On legal devices for protecting property from a husband's debts, see Nancy F. Cott, *Public Vows: A History of Marriage and the Nation* (Cambridge, Mass.: Harvard University Press, 2000), 52–54.

8. *"All are busy preparing to go either East or west"*

1. According to Woodruff, who was with him on July 24, "President Young expressed his full satisfaction in the Appearance of the valley as A resting place for the Saints" (WW 3:134, July 24, 1847). Turner, *BY*, 169, believes he used the famous words on July 28. Arrington, *BY*, 145, 459 n81, claimed that if Brigham Young did say, "This is the place," he did so on July 24.

2. WW 3:233, 234, 263, 265–69 (July 24, Aug. 26, Sept. 4–10, 1847); Alexander, *Woodruff*, 141–45, 149, 150.

3. PS, 118 (Sept. 20, 21, 1858).

4. Kenneth N. Owens, *Gold Rush Saints: California Mormons and the Great Rush for Riches* (Norman: University of Oklahoma Press, 2004), 32–55, 58–61, 96–105. A number

of unofficial LDS organizations celebrate the California roots of Mormonism. See, for example, "Ship Brooklyn: The Forgotten Voyage," at http://shipbrooklyn.com/; California Heritage Foundation at http://californiapioneer.org/.

5. WW 2:228, 233 (May 19, 23, 1843); Alexander, *Woodruff*, 156, 383 n46.

6. WW 3:392 (Dec. 20, 1848).

7. Allen, *No Toil nor Labor*, 227–31, 243–46; *The Pioneer Camp of the Saints: The 1846 and 1847 Mormon Trail Journals of Thomas Bullock*, ed. Will Bagley (Spokane, Wash.: Arthur H. Clark Company, 1997), 112, 137 (July 24, 1847); WW 3:233–35, 262–63 (July 24, Aug. 25, 1847); WC Smith, 362–63 (July 22, 1847); "Diary of Lorenzo Dow Young," *Utah Historical Quarterly* 14, no. 1–4 (1947): 163, available online at digitallibrary.utah.gov.

8. WW 3:236, 245 (July 25, 31, 1847).

9. WW 3:341 (July 28, 1847).

10. WW 3:341; Bagley, ed., *Pioneer Camp*, 241–42 (July 28, 1847).

11. James Amasa Little, "Biography of Lorenzo Dow Young," *Utah Historical Quarterly* 14 (1946): 79–80; Stanley B. Kimball, *Heber C. Kimball: Mormon Patriarch and Pioneer* (Urbana and Chicago: University of Illinois Press, 1981), 122, 124 n11, 129, 146–47, 150–51; Turner, *BY*, 102; Arrington, *BY*, 120–21, 130–31. Sobieski Young's name apparently derived from a celebratory history of the seventeenth-century Polish king who was said to have saved Europe from the Turks. See "Lorenzo Sobieski Young (1841–1924)," http://www.geni.com/people/Lorenzo-S-Young/.

12. "Diary of Lorenzo Dow Young," 160 (May 26, 27, June 1, 1847). This is not the first reference in Lorenzo's diary to disturbing Indian burials. See also 146, 159 (Aug. 4, 1846, May 23, 1847).

13. "Diary of Lorenzo Dow Young," 163.

14. WC Smith, 383–84 (Aug. 17, 1847).

15. LCT 2, July 4, 15, Aug. 6, 7, Sept. 2, 1847.

16. ERS2, 187, 188, 190, 193, 194, 201 (July 29, 30, 31; Aug. 9, 20, 24; Sept. 14, 19, 27, 28, 1847).

17. PS, 94, 96, 97, 99 (July 30, Aug. 1, 24, 30, Sept. 22, 1847).

18. ERS2, 186, 187 (July 24, 25, 26, 1847).

19. PS, 92 (July 23, 1847); LCT 2, July 23, 1847.

20. E.g., ERS2, 178, 179, 180, 181, 182, 183, 184, 185 (June 14, 15, 16, 17, 18, 27, 30, July 4, 11, 17, 19, 20, 1847).

21. ERS2, 190, 199, 202 (Aug. 6, Sept. 9, 22, 1847).

22. PS, 90, 92, 93, 97 (July 11, 18, 29, Sept. 8, 1847).

23. LCT 2 (July 19, Aug. 1, 8, 1847).

24. ERS2, 190 (Aug. 8, 1847). For similar entries, see 185, 191 (July 19, Aug. 14, 1847).

25. ERS2, 185, 192, 193 (July 21, Aug. 17, 19, 1847).

26. PS, 92 (July 9, 1847).

27. WW 3:262–64 (Aug. 25–Sept. 4, 1847); PS, 97 (Sept. 4–5, 1847).

28. LCT 2 (Sept. 7, 1847); WW 3:268 (Sept. 7, 1847); Bagley, ed., *Pioneer Camp*, 281 (Sept. 7, 1847). Leonora didn't say who came up with the idea for the dinner. M. Isabella Horne, "Pioneer Reminiscences," in *The Young Woman's Journal*, ed. Susan Young Gates (Salt Lake City: George Q. Cannon & Sons, 1902), vol. 3, 292–93, said it was "Bishop Hunter and Brother John Taylor," and that Hunter offered a fat steer.

29. WW 3:269 (Sept. 9, 1847); ERS2, 199 (Sept. 9, 1847). For complete text of the poem, see "Hail to the Twelve and the Pioneers," ERS *Poetry*, 363–64. See also Hannah Harvey Peirce Journal, Mormon Pioneer Travel database, 51–53. This otherwise dry diary bursts into life in describing the celebration on Sept. 9, noting that the hymn composed by Eliza R. Snow, although the words she included deviate slightly from those Eliza later published.

30. ERS2, 199 (Sept. 10, 1847).

31. Phebe Woodruff to Dear Wilford, Winter Quarters, [May 16,] 1847, WW Corr.

32. WW 3:263–64, 267–68 (Aug. 29, Sept. 7, 1847). On the birth of James to Mary Ann Jackson, see the biographical sketch of Mary Jackson in Jennifer Mackley, "Wilford Woodruff's Witness," www.wilfordwoodruff.infowives. On Jackson's journey west, see two reminiscences of her son, no doubt based on stories that she told him: James Jackson Woodruff, "A Brief Sketch of the Life of James Jackson Woodruff," in *Chronicles of Courage,* 8 vols. (1990–97), 2:127–29; and James Jackson Woodruff and Mary Ann Woodruff, biographical sketch, April 1917, 1–2, MOT.

33. LCT 2, Sept. 19, 1847.

34. PS, 99 (Sept. 26, 1847).

35. ERS2, 204 (Oct. 2, 1847).

36. WW 3:279–80 (Oct. 3, 1847).

37. WW 3:268 (Oct. 31, 1847).

38. PS, 102–5 (Oct. 20, Nov. 1, 2, 18, Dec. 24, 1847).

39. PS, 102–3 (Nov. 3–30, 1847).

40. Secondary works on female healing in early Mormonism include Claudia Lauper Bushman, "Mystics and Healers," in *Mormon Sisters: Women in Early Utah,* ed. Claudia L. Bushman (Cambridge, Mass: Emmeline Press, 1976), 1–24; Linda King Newell, "A Gift Given, a Gift Taken: Washing, Anointing and Blessing the Sick Among Mormon Women," *Sunstone* 6 (Sept.–Oct. 1981): 16–25; Linda King Newell, "Gifts of the Spirit: Women's Share," in *Sisters in Spirit: Mormon Women in Historical and Cultural Perspective,* ed. Maureen Ursenbach Beecher and Lavina Fielding Anderson (Urbana and Chicago: University of Illinois Press, 1987), 111–50; Susanna Morrill, "Relief Society Birth and Death Rituals: Women at the Gates of Mortality," *Journal of Mormon History* 36 (Spring 2010): 128–59; Jonathan A. Stapley and Kristine Wright, "The Forms and the Power: The Development of Mormon Ritual Healing to 1847," *Journal of Mormon History* 35 (Summer 2009): 41–87, and Stapley and Wright, "Female Ritual Healing in Mormonism," *Journal of Mormon History* 37 (Winter 2011): 1–85.

41. According to my count, Eliza used the term "visit" nine times in Oct., referred once to a "treat," twice to one of the sisters "administering," and only once to a "meeting." But in Nov., eleven of the fourteen references to women getting together used the term "meeting," and for the first time Eliza became concerned with the question of who presided.

42. ERS2, 211, 213 (Oct. 31, Dec. 2, Nov. 2, 1847).

43. ERS2, 212 (Nov. 15, 1847). On Henrietta Whitney's sealing to Whitney, see D. Michael Quinn, "The Newell K. Whitney Family," *Ensign,* Dec. 1978, www.lds.org /ensign/.

44. ERS2, 213 (Nov. 29, 1847); PS, 103 (Nov. 29, 1847).

45. ERS2, 213–15 (Dec. 4, 23, 25, 1847); PS, 104 (Dec. 1–8, 16, 1847).

46. PS, 105 (Dec. 27, 1847); ERS2, 212, 215 (Nov. 14, Dec. 27, 1847).

47. ERS2, 216 (Jan. 1, 1848).

48. ERS2, 213–14, 218 (Dec. 12, 1847; Feb. 4, 1848).

49. PS, 107, 108, 122 (Feb. 4, 6, 18, 1848).

50. PS, 1–7, 109 (Feb. 6, 9, 10, 12, 13, 14, 15, 17, 24, 25, 27, March 2, 4, 5, 1848).

51. PS, 108–9 (Feb. 13, 15, 26, 1848).

52. Ned Blackhawk, *Violence over the Land: Indians and Empires in the Early American West* (Cambridge, Mass.: Harvard University Press, 2006), 227–44; Martha C. Knack, *Boundaries Between: The Southern Paiutes, 1775–1995* (Lincoln: University of Nebraska Press, 2001), 51–58; Sondra Jones, *The Trial of Don Pedro Leon Lujan* (Salt Lake City: University of Utah Press, 2000), 48–52; Brian Q. Cannon, "Adopted or Indentured, 1850–1870: Native Children in Mormon Households," in *Nearly Everything Imaginable: The Everyday Life of Utah's Mormon Pioneers,* ed. Ronald W. Walker and Doris R. Dant (Provo, Utah: Brigham Young University Press, 1999), 341–57.

53. ERS2, 222–23 (March 28, 29, 31, 1848); PS, 110 (March 25–April 1, 1848); Mary

Isabella Horne, "Home Life in the Pioneer Fort," *Juvenile Instructor* 29 (March 25, 1894), 181–85, quoted in C. Mark Hamilton, *Nineteenth-Century Mormon Architecture and City Planning* (New York: Oxford University Press, 1995), 107; ERS3, 30–31.

54. PS, 109–18 (March 5–Sept. 24, 1848). Patty "went to meeting" twelve of twenty-four Sundays in this period. She noted six female meetings in March and four in April; then they appear to have stopped.

55. PS, 110, 113, 1145, 117, 188 (March 20, May 27, June 26, Aug. 22, 29, 1848); Patty Bartlett Sessions, Sampler, courtesy Suzanne B. Anderson.

56. WW 3:343, 345, 346, 358, 359, 360 (April 13, 22, May 2, June 21, July 19, 22, 23, 25, 26, 31, 1848).

57. WW 3:362, 389 (Aug. 12, Nov. 22, 1848).

58. WW 3:387 (Nov. 7, 1848).

59. WW 3:496 (Nov. 26, 1849).

60. WW 3:375, 495–97, 513–16 (Oct. 7, 1848, Nov. 26, 1849). For Kane's own attempts to negotiate partisan conflict during this period, see Matthew J. Grow, *"Liberty to the Downtrodden": Thomas L. Kane, Romantic Reformer* (New Haven: Yale University Press, 2009), 93–112.

61. WW 3:377–80 (Oct. 18, 1848).

62. WW 3:414–15 (Feb. 4, 1849). Eventually, they began to hold church meetings in Cambridge, sometimes at their house (WW 3:492, 528 [Oct. 21, 1849; Jan 13, 1850]).

63. WW 3:415–16, 436 (Feb. 4, 6, 7, March 30, 1849).

64. WW 3:370 (Sept. 21, 1848).

65. Phebe Woodruff to Ezra Carter, Sr., Feb. 23, 1849, WW Letters.

66. WW 3:433–34 (March 22, 1849).

67. WW 3:484, 489 (Sept. 25, Oct. 10, 1849).

68. WW 3:447 (May 16, 1849).

69. WW 3:448–49 (May 19, 1849).

70. WW 3:485–87 (Oct. 2, 1849). Young's letter, dated July 25, 1849, had taken a bit over three months to reach him.

71. WW 3:419 (Feb. 15, 1849). On the proposed scheme, see "The First Balloon from New York for California," *Daily National Intelligencer,* Feb. 15, 1849; and a note about a picture of such a device in a shopwindow in Boston, reported in *Boston Courier,* March 19, 1849.

72. WW 3:391–92, 412–13 (Dec. 19, 20, 1848; Jan. 21, Feb. 1, 1849). Woodruff could have read about the gold discovery in *the Boston Daily Atlas,* Nov. 29, Dec. 11, 1848, and the *New York Weekly Herald,* Dec. 2, 9, 16, 1848, but though the *Herald* mentioned "Mormon Diggings" on the American River, it did not include details. Woodruff must have learned about the Saints' involvement from Badlam. On the importance of the Mormon Battalion veterans in the discovery, see Owens, *Gold Rush Saints,* 94–97; David L. Bigler, ed., *The Gold Discovery Journal of Azariah Smith* (Salt Lake City: University of Utah Press, 1990); Kenneth N. Owens, "Gold-Rush Saints: The Mormon Beginnings of the California Gold Rush," in *Riches for All: The California Gold Rush and the World,* ed. Owens (Lincoln: University of Nebraska Press, 2002).

73. WW 2:412–13, 537–38 (Jan. 27, 31, Feb. 1, 1849; March 12, 14, 1850).

74. WW 3:405, 410 (Jan. 11, 24, 1849).

75. CBC, 74 (July 8, 1848).

76. BWS Diary, Oct. 14, 1849.

77. *AP,* 324–60; HS, 327 (Sept. 24, 1848).

78. CBC 86, 87 (Oct. 12, 18, 1848).

79. CMW, Jan. 11, 12, 23, March 27, 30, 1849; Preston Woolley Parkinson, *The Utah Woolley Family* (Salt Lake City: Privately published, 1967), 52.

80. HS, 327, 332 (Sept. 23, 24, 30, 1848); Arrington, *Woolley,* 225–35; Brandon S. Plewe, ed., *Mapping Mormonism: An Atlas of Latter-day Saint History* (Provo, Utah: Brigham

Young University Press, 2012), 84–85, 92, 98, 114; Martin Mitchell, "Gentile Impressions of Salt Lake City, Utah, 1849–1870," *Geographical Review* 87 (1997): 334–52.

81. Arrington, *Great Basin,* 57–62.

82. Arrington, *Great Basin,* 4–49, 59, 64–71; Brigham Young quotation on 65. Different branches of the Thatcher family tell this story differently. Some believe Brigham Young actually called Hezekiah to go to California, others that he became disaffected with something on the overland trail and vowed to leave even before he got to the valley. That the Thatchers returned in 1857 suggests they hadn't totally abandoned the faith. They are listed in the Winter Quarters First Ward in 1846, where their newborn son died, and in Perrigrine Sessions's part of the Daniel Spencer Company coming west. See "Statistics of the Winter Quarters First Ward," winterquarters.byu.edu; entries for Hezekiah Thatcher, MOT; and Hezekiah Thatcher, U.S. Census *1850*: *Salmon Falls, El Dorado, California,* Ancestry.com.

83. Louisa Beaman to Marinda, Martha, and Mary Ann Hyde, Salt Lake Valley, July 14, 1849, in " 'Remember Me in My Affliction': Louisa Beaman and Eliza R. Snow Letters, 1849," ed. Todd Compton, *Journal of Mormon History* 25 (1999): 55.

84. PS, 133 (July 23, 24, 1849).

85. Z2, 113 (July 24, 1849).

86. EPL, 56 (July 24, 1849).

87. HS, 355 (July 24, 1849); "Utah State Holiday—Pioneer Day," Utah State Library, pioneer.utah.gov/research/.

88. ERS2, 230 (July 24, 1849); CMW, July 24, 1849; *Millennial Star* 11, no. 23 (Dec. 1, 1849), 359, 360. For a brief biography of Woolley, see Jay W. Burrup, " 'All Is Well and Peace With Us Dwells': Catherine Elizabeth Mehring Woolley," in *Women of Faith in the Latter Days,* vol. 2, ed. Richard E. Turley Jr. and Brittany A. Chapman (Salt Lake City: Deseret Book), 413–28.

89. WW 3:471, 526 (July 24, 1849; Jan. 7, 1850).

90. On the trek as a rite of passage, see Wallace Stegner, *The Gathering of Zion: The Story of the Mormon Trail* (New York: McGraw-Hill, 1964), 1–13. On the development of Pioneer Day and the myths associated with it, see Richard C. Poulsen, " 'This Is the Place': Myth and Mormondom," *Western Folklore* 36 (1977): 246–52; Steven L. Olsen, "Celebrating Cultural Identity: Pioneer Day in Nineteenth-Century Mormonism," *BYU Studies* 36 (1996–97): 159–67. Although Thanksgiving was not yet a national holiday, it was widely celebrated in New England and in Midwestern communities with New England roots. See Elizabeth Pleck, "The Making of the Domestic Occasion: The History of Thanksgiving in the United States," *Journal of Social History* 32 (1999): 773–89.

91. CMW, July 24, 1849.

92. Len Travers, *Celebrating the Fourth* (Amherst: University of Massachusetts Press, 1997), 167, 215, 221, 252; Mary P. Ryan, *Civic Wars: Democracy and Public Life in the American City During the Nineteenth Century* (Berkeley and Los Angeles: University of California Press, 1997), 69–73; Sean Wilentz, *Chants Democratic: New York City and the Rise of the American Working Class, 1788–1850* (New York: Oxford University Press, 1984), 88–92.

93. WW 3:463–64 (July 4, 1849). On mock militias elsewhere, see John Thomas, "Questioning Authority: The June Training of the University Invincibles," in *New England Celebrates: Spectacle, Commemoration, and Festivity,* ed. Peter Benes and Jane Montague Benes, vol. 25 of *Annual Proceedings of the Dublin Seminar for New England Folklife* (Boston, 2002), 105–19.

94. WW 3:382–84 (Oct. 25, 1848); Carl Smith, *City Water, City Life: Water and the Infrastructure of Ideas in Urbanizing Philadelphia, New York, and Boston* (Chicago: University of Chicago Press, 2013).

95. "The Water Celebration," *Boston Daily Atlas,* Oct. 27, 1848.

96. WW 3:384 (Oct. 25, 1848), paraphrasing Matthew 7:13–14.

97. Laurel Thatcher Ulrich, *A Midwife's Tale: The Life of Martha Ballard Based on Her Diary, 1785–1812* (New York: Alfred A. Knopf, 1990), 31–32; Simon Newman, "Principles

or Men: George Washington and the Political Culture of National Leadership," *Journal of the Early Republic* 12 (1992): 482–84; Cynthia A. Kierner, "Genteel Balls and Republican Parades: Gender and Early Southern Civil Rituals, 1677–1826," *Virginia Magazine of History and Biography* 104 (1996): 186, 196, 201, 204, 210; Harry S. Laver, "Rethinking the Social Role of the Militia: Community-Building in Antebellum Kentucky," *Journal of Southern History* 79 (2002): 791.

98. Eliza R. Snow Smith, *Biography and Family Record of Lorenzo Snow* (Salt Lake City: Deseret News, 1884), 95–101; ERS *Poetry*, 153–54, 1,082. The poem appeared in Bullock's account in *The Frontier Guardian*, Sept. 19, 1849, 4, as "Ode to Liberty." In a similar celebration held two years later in England, the men carried scriptures, the women flowers (*The Programme of the London Conference Festival, to Be Held in the Freemasons' Hall, Monday June 2, 1851* [London: J. B. Franklin, 1851]).

99. As the pioneer company set out on their first journey to the valley, Wilford recorded Brigham Young's comments about "the standard & ensign that would be reared in Zion, to govern the Kingdom of God," and included a little drawing. Although the drawing probably had symbolic meaning for Woodruff, it appears to be a doodle, rather than a design (WW 3:188 [May 29, 1847]; D. Michael Quinn, "The Flag of the Kingdom of God," *BYU Studies* 14 [1973]: 1–6; Ronald W. Walker, " 'A Banner Is Unfurled': Mormonism's Ensign Peak," *Dialogue: A Journal of Mormon Thought* 26 [1993]: 71–91; "Flags of the State of Utah," North American Vexillological Association, www.loeser.us/flags/utah).

100. Z2, 113 (June 17, 1849).

101. Augusta Cobb to Alexander and Mary Ann Badlam, July 20, 1849, CHL.

102. PS, 126, 127, 128, 129, 132 (Jan. 1, 23, Feb. 1, 12, 15, March 30, June 22, 1849); "Paper Flower-Making: The Poppy," *Godey's Lady's Book and Magazine* 56 (May 1858): 418; "Knitted Artificial Flowers: White Garden Lily," *Godey's Lady's Book and Magazine* 62 (March 1861): 62; Bradley and Woodward, 255.

103. PS, 133 (July 23, 1849); EPL, 56 (July 21, 22, 24, 1849); HS, 355 (July 24, 1849); CBC, 89–90 (Summer 1849).

104. CBC, 89–90 (Summer 1849); A. P. Josselyn to Dear Wife, printed in the Zanesville (Ohio) *Courier*, Oct. 8, 1849, in *Among the Mormons: Historic Accounts by Contemporary Observers*, ed. William Mulder and A. Russell Mortensen (New York: Alfred A. Knopf, 1967), 236.

105. *Millennial Star* 11, no. 23 (December 1, 1849), 360.

106. WW 3:534 (Feb. 24, 1850). Woolley had the additional incentive of retrieving a son whose mother, a plural wife, had chosen to remain in the East and had recently died. On the Heywood/Woolley outfitting journey, see, Arrington, *Woolley*, 250–75.

107. WW 3:460 (June 18, 1849).

108. WW 3:531, 535–38 (Feb. 12, March 2–3, 6, 12, 14, 1850).

109. WW 3:545 (April 15, 16, 1850).

110. WW 3:549 (May 9, 1850).

111. E.g., WW 3:457 (June 8, 9, 1849). The classic study of the epidemics is Charles E. Rosenberg, *The Cholera Years: The United States in 1832, 1849, and 1866* (Chicago: University of Chicago Press, 1962, 1987). See also Patricia Rushton, "Cholera and Its Impact on Nineteenth-Century Mormon Migration," *BYU Studies* 44 (2005): 123–44.

112. Sophia Lois Goodridge Journal, June 26, 27, 30, July 1, 1850, MOT.

113. WW 3:547–50 (May 1, 2, 5, 11, 12, 1850); Wilford Woodruff Company List, MOT; Arrington, *Woolley*, 269.

114. WW 3:562, 568, 572, (July 19, Aug. 13, Sept. 8, 1850).

115. WW 3:563–65 (July 30, 1850).

116. WW 3:577–78, 582, 588 (Oct. 14, 19, Dec. 6, 17, 19, 21, 28, 1850); WW 4:3–7 (Jan. 2, 3, 10, 11, 13, 20–24, 1851).

117. WW 4:48, 49–51 (July 19, 24, 1851); PS, 167 (July 24, 1851); HS, 402 (July 24, 1851); *Deseret News*, July 27, 1851, 1.

118. *Deseret News*, Aug. 19, 1851, 308; ERS *Poetry*, 409–11; Genesis 3:16, KJV. On the

complicated discourse over the theology of Eve in later Mormonism, see Boyd Jay Petersen, " 'Redeemed from the Curse Placed upon Her': Dialogic Discourse on Eve in the Woman's Exponent," *Journal of Mormon History* 40, no. 1 (Winter 2014): 135–74.

9. *"My pen is my only weapon"*

1. *New York Herald,* Oct. 25, 26, 1850, 1.
2. ERS *Poetry,* 419–22.
3. *Deseret News,* Aug. 19, 1851, 308; ERS *Poetry,* 409–11.
4. Augusta Cobb to Brigham Young, Sept. 19, 1850, Nov. 18, 1850, AAC Letters. Aside from in Connell O'Donovan's work, Augusta has not received much attention in Mormon history. She doesn't appear in any of the anthologies of women's writings from early Utah, is mentioned only as one of Young's wives in Arrington, *BY,* and, though mentioned, doesn't merit a place in the index to John Turner's more recent biography of Young. On a recent controversy over the interpretation of her writings, see Connell O'Donovan, "Augusta Adams Cobb Young: Priesthood Holder," letter to the editor, *Journal of Mormon History* 38 (Spring 2012): vii–ix; J. Stapley, "Responding to O'Donovan on Augusta Adams Cobb Young and Priesthood," *Juvenile Instructor,* April 12, 2012; "Women, the Priesthood, and Augusta Adams Cobb: Connell O'Donovan's Response to Jonathan Stapley," *Juvenile Instructor,* April 13, 2012, juvenileinstructor.org. In his blog post, Stapley twice referred to Cobb and her writings as "anomalous," although he agreed that that was no reason to ignore them.
5. "Declaration of Sentiments and Resolutions," Woman's Rights Convention, Seneca Falls, July 19–20, 1848, in Elizabeth Cady Stanton and Susan B. Anthony Papers Project, ecssba.rutgers.edu/docs/Seneca; "Historical Library," Worcester Women's History project, wwhp.org/Resources; Nancy F. Cott, *Public Vows: A History of Marriage and the Nation* (Cambridge, Mass.: Harvard University Press, 2000), 4–8, 50–55; Hendrik Hartog, *Man & Wife in America: A History* (Cambridge, Mass.: Harvard University Press, 2000), 12–15, 64–77; Norma Basch, *Framing American Divorce: From the Revolutionary Generation to the Victorians* (Berkeley and Los Angeles: University of California Press, 1999), 43–65.
6. Michael W. Homer, "The Judiciary and the Common Law in Utah Territory, 1850–61," *Dialogue: A Journal of Mormon Thought* 21 (1988): 98–108; Carol Cornwall Madsen, " 'At their Peril': Utah Law and the Case of Plural Wives, 1850–1900," *Western Historical Quarterly* 21 (1990): 425–43; Daynes, *Wives,* 83–87, 143–46, 160–64. Some scholars believe that a quarter of polygamous wives divorced their husbands, though most remarried, often to another polygamist. On an unloving marriage as a form of adultery, see Wilford's summary of Brigham Young's sermon, WW 4:38 (June 15, 1851).
7. "Declaration of Sentiments and Resolutions," 3; Madsen, " 'At their Peril' "; J. Cecil Alter, "The Council of Health," *Utah Historical Quarterly* 10 (1941): 37–40.
8. When the university opened again in 1867, it admitted women, although the curriculum for either sex was limited. See Maureen Ursenbach Beecher, *Eliza and Her Sisters* (Salt Lake City: Aspen Books, 1991), 109–28; "Deseret University, 1850–1892," University of Utah Sesquicentennial, 1850–2000, J. Willard Marriott Library, www.lib.utah.edu; Grethe Ballif Peterson, "University of Deseret," *EOM,* 1498; Samuel C. Monson, "Deseret Alphabet," *EOM,* 373–74.
9. *Cobb v. Cobb,* Records of the Supreme Judicial Court of Suffolk County (March–Nov. 1847), 252–53, Massachusetts State Archives; Elizabeth Blair Clark, "The Inward Fire: A History of Marital Cruelty in the Northeastern United States, 1800–1860" (Ph.D. diss., Harvard University, 2006), 17–19, 337. In 1857, full divorce for desertion became possible after five years.
10. Ellen and Augusta Adams Cobb to Elizabeth Brooks Thompson, Jan. 30, 1847; Ellen Augusta Cobb to Abraham Annis Dame, March 1, 1847, AAC Family; Augusta Cobb to Brigham Young, Jan. 20, 1846, AAC Letters.

11. Entries on Catherine Lewis and George Adams in O'Donovan, *Boston Mormons;* Givens and Grow, 229–30, 442 n39, n40; Peter Amann, "Prophet in Zion: The Saga of George J. Adams," *New England Quarterly* 37 (1964): 477–500.

12. Divorce Libel, *Cobb v. Cobb;* George Adams Deposition, 8; Catherine Lewis, *Narrative of Some of the Proceedings of the Mormons; Giving an Account of Their Iniquities* (Lynn, Mass.: The Author, 1848), 6–7, 12–13; WW 3:431–41 (July 24–Aug. 13, 1844); Turner, *BY,* 112–13.

13. Brigham Young to Augusta Adams Cobb, Winter Quarters, Feb. 27, 1847, AAC Family.

14. *Cobb v. Cobb,* 252–53, and file 44, 1847, Massachusetts State Archives; "Fruits of Mormonism," *Vermont Chronicle,* Dec. 22, 1847, quoted in O'Donovan, *Boston Mormons.*

15. Cobb Children to Augusta, Dec. 16, 1847; Albert Adams Cobb to Augusta, Sept. 30, 1847; and poem, n.d., AAC Family.

16. Last Will and Testament of Augusta Adams, Winter Quarters, Feb. 21, 1848, AAC Letters.

17. *1850 United States Federal Census, Salt Lake City,* Ancestry.com.

18. Judy Dykman and Colleen Whitley, "Settling in Salt Lake City," in *Brigham Young's Homes,* ed. Colleen Whitley (Salt Lake City: University of Utah Press, 2002), 90–104; Louisa Beaman to Marinda, Martha, and Mary Ann Hyde, April 8 and July 14, 1849, in "'Remember Me in My Affliction': Louisa Beaman and Eliza R. Snow Letters, 1849," *Journal of Mormon History* 25 (1999): 52, 54; ERS2, 229 (June 28, 1849); Z2, 113 (July 17, 1849).

19. Computed from list of Brigham Young's wives in Arrington, *BY,* app. B.

20. Augusta to Brigham, Feb. 14, 1851, AAC Letters.

21. Augusta to Brigham, Jan. 13, 1851, AAC Letters.

22. Augusta to Brigham, June 23, 1850, Feb. 25, 1851, AAC Letters.

23. Augusta to Brigham, July 30, 1850, AAC Letters. Zina's diary, Z2, 120 (July 28, 1850), confirms that Brigham had in fact given her nine yards of linen gingham three days before.

24. Augusta to Brigham, March 1, 1851, AAC Letters.

25. Augusta to Brigham, Aug. 11, 1851, AAC Letters.

26. Augusta to Brigham, Oct. 6, 1851, AAC Letters.

27. Thomas J. Wolfe, "Steaming Saints: Mormons and the Thomsonian Movement in Nineteenth-Century America," in *Disease and Medical Care in the Mountain West,* ed. Martha L. Hildreth and Bruce T. Moran (Reno: University of Nevada Press, 1998), 18–28. Earlier studies include N. Lee Smith, "Herbal Remedies: God's Medicine?," *Dialogue: A Journal of Mormon Thought* 12, no. 3 (Autumn 1979): 37–60; and three works by Lester E. Bush, "The Word of Wisdom in Early Nineteenth-Century Perspective," *Dialogue: A Journal of Mormon Thought* 14 (Autumn 1981): 47–65; "The Mormon Tradition," in *Caring and Curing: Health and Medicine in the Western Religious Traditions,* ed. Ronald L. Number and Darrel W. Amundsen (New York: Macmillan, 1986), 397–420; and *Health and Medicine Among the Latter-day Saints: Science, Sense, and Scripture* (New York: Crossroads, 1993), 69–93.

28. W. W. Phelps, *Deseret Almanac* (Salt Lake City: Willard Richards, 1852), 34; PS, 166, 168, 170, 176, 210, 214, 215 (July 8, Sept. 16, Dec. 10, 20, 1851; May 12, 1852).

29. J. Cecil Alter, "Health Laws," *Utah Historical Quarterly* 20 (1942): 40; Linda P. Wilcox, "The Imperfect Science: Brigham Young on Medical Doctors," and N. Lee Smith, "Herbal Remedies: God's Medicine?," *Dialogue: A Journal of Mormon Thought* 12 (1979): 27–28, 31–32, 45–47; PS, 140, 169, 176, 215 (Dec. 3, 17, 1849; Oct. 15, 29, Nov. 12, 1851; May 22, 1852).

30. Augusta to Brigham, Oct 20, 1851, AAC Letters.

31. Augusta to Brigham, Nov. 4, 1851, AAC Letters; PS, 168 (Oct. 15, 29, Nov. 12, 1851).

32. Augusta to Brigham, Nov. 23, 24, 1851, AAC Letters.

33. WW 4:81–85 (Dec. 1851); PS, 170 (Dec. 10, 1851). Wilford gave the month but not the day.

34. Augusta to Brigham, Dec. 16, 1851, AAC Letters.

35. Augusta to Brigham, Jan. 31, 1851, AAC Letters.

36. Cf. Isaiah 52:1, KJV, with Book of Mormon, Moroni 10:31. Three other passages in Latter-day Saint scriptures adapted Isaiah's passage (2 Nephi 8:24, 3 Nephi 20:36, and *Doctrine and Covenants* 81:14), but only Moroni used the word "daughter."

37. CMW, Nov. 19, 1848; Givens and Grow, 304.

38. HS, 332, 333 (Sept. 28, Oct. 15, 1848); *The History of Louisa Barnes Pratt: Mormon Missionary Widow and Pioneer,* ed. S. George Ellsworth (Logan: Utah State University Press, 1998), 105–7; AP, 363–67, 378; WW 3:329 (March 20, 1848); HS, 327, 332, 333 (Sept. 24, Oct. 1, 15, 1848); PS, 119, 136 (Oct. 1, 1848; Sept. 21, 1849); Z2, 95 (Nov. 28, 1848).

39. Ellsworth, ed., *History of Louisa Barnes Pratt,* 107–8; CBC, 90–91.

40. Louisa Barnes Pratt to Augusta Cobb and Eliza R. Snow, April 8, 1851, AAC Family.

41. Z2, 94, 95–96, 97, 98, 99, 100 (Dec. 17, 18, 22, 1848; Jan. 2, 4, 10, 14, 18, 21, Feb. 1, 3, 4, 6, 22, 1849). Bradley and Woodward, 175, indicate that the room was sixteen feet square. If so, it had an area of 250 square feet. Today's standards for elementary-school classrooms suggest three to four times that much for a class of twenty (National Clearinghouse for Educational Facilities, "Space Requirements for School Facilities," July 15, 2014, www.ncef .org).

42. Z2, 92–93 (Dec. 11, 1848).

43. Z2. 97, 97 n25 (Jan. 8, 9, 1849); PS, 126–27 (Jan. 9, 1849).

44. Z2, 97 (Jan. 12, 1849).

45. Z2, 102, 119 n71 (March 16, 1849); Bradley and Woodward, 183–84.

46. Z2, 102 (March 16, 17, 1849).

47. Z2, 106 (May 13–14, 1849).

48. Z2, 100, 101, 103, 104, 105, 106, 107, 116 (Feb. 5, 25, April 6, 20, 15, May 3, 12, 26, Dec. 30, 1849; Jan. 6, 1850).

49. Augusta to Brigham, January 22, 1850, AAC Letters. In this letter, she is still protesting her love and her desire to be with him.

50. Z2, 114–15 (Oct. 7, 1849).

51. Louisa to Dear Sisters Marinda Martha and Mary Ann, April 8, 1849, in "Remember Me in My Affliction," 51; Z2, 107–8 (May 18, 20, 24, 1849); PS, 140, 146 (Dec. 10, 1849; May 7, 1850); EPL, 62 (May 18, 1850). Although it is impossible to diagnose Louisa's breast problems from such sparse entries, the reference to erysipelas, known today to be caused by a streptococcus infection, is intriguing. At least one contemporary physician linked it with puerperal fever. It occurred concurrently with abscesses and scarlet fever in other places. Charles Knowlton, "Erysipelas and Puerperal Fever," *Boston Medical and Surgical Journal* 30, no. 5 (March 6, 1844): 89–95; Emily Baumrin, William Corbett, Amita Kulkarni, and Lee A. Witters, M.D., "The Most Unspeakable Terror," *Dartmouth Medicine* (Winter 2009), dartmed.dartmouth.edu; Laurel Thatcher Ulrich, *A Midwife's Tale: The Life of Martha Ballard Based on Her Diary, 1785–1812* (New York: Alfred A. Knopf, 1990), 40–46.

52. In some religious traditions, being able to identify the presence of a developing child in an apparent miscarriage is important. A website containing images that might be used in identification can be found at "Lost Innocents: Practical Helps for Miscarriage from an Orthodox Christian Perspective," lostinnocentsorthodox.blogspot.com.

53. Z2, 108 (March 26, 27, 1849).

54. PS, 118, 132 (Sept. 29, 1848, June 24, 29, 1849); Z2, 98, 111 (Jan. 14, June 29, 1849).

55. Z2, 107, 108 (May 20, 29, 1849).

56. Z2, 97, 98, 102, 112 (Jan. 13, 17, March 14, 15, 16; July 3, 1849).

57. Z2, 93, 97, 117 (Dec. 16, 1848, Jan. 13, 1849; Feb. 28, 1850). Zina said the party on Jan. 13 was at Addison Pratt's house and that some of their "connexions" were there. That

has to have meant Caroline and her husband, who seemed always to be in the center of any musical evening. Caroline was Louisa Pratt's sister.

58. Book of Mormon, 2 Nephi 2:25. The "addendum" is a Mormon joke that I first heard from the renowned LDS historian Leonard Arrington.

59. Z2, 109 (June 16, 1849).

60. Z2, 118, 120 (March 28, June 8, 1850).

61. This story is told in Bradley and Woodward, 192–93, and Emmeline B. Wells, "A Venerable Woman," *Woman's Exponent* 12 (Aug. 6, 1883): 43.

62. Usher Parsons, "Dissertation on Cancer, Which Obtained the Boylston Prize for the Present Year," *Boston Medical and Surgical Journal* 13, no. 5 (Sept. 16, 1835): 69–90; "Some Diseases of the Breast: From Sir B. C. Brodie's Clinical Lectures at St. George's Hospital," *Boston Medical and Surgical Journal* 31, no. 2 (Aug. 14, 1844): 31–35; "Cancer of the Breast," *Boston Medical and Surgical Journal* 37, no. 4 (Aug. 25, 1847): 70–75.

63. Z2, 118 (Feb. 27, 1850).

64. Z2, 118 (June 27, 1850).

65. PS, 88, 121, 132 (June 27, 1846; Dec. 23, 30, 1848; June 27, 1849); ERS2, 229 (June 27, 1849). The protective cover on the manuscript Nauvoo Minute Book appears to be made of fabric commonly used in lining dress bodices in the nineteenth century. Since Eliza was a dressmaker, it is not improbable that she covered it, though that is of course only a guess.

66. Newell and Avery, *Mormon Enigma,* 247–48.

67. Short biographies of members of the Smith family can be found at Reference/People, JSP. Lucy Mack Smith, the Prophet's mother, died in Nauvoo in 1856. His sisters Sophronia, Katherine, and Lucy became members of the Reorganized Church of Jesus Christ of Latter-day Saints in 1873. See chapter 15 for more information on the role of his son Joseph Smith III in reorganizing the Church in the Midwest.

68. PS, 148 (June 27, 1850); EPL, 62 (Dec. 3, 1849); Z2, 105, 116 (April 18, 23, Dec. 15, 1849; July 6, 1850).

69. Amanda Smith to Brigham Young, Sept. 10, 1850, Feb. 16, 1852, BY Office Files, CHL; Hulda Cordelia Thurston Smith, "O My Children and Grandchildren: An Account of the Sealing of Amanda Barnes to Joseph Smith," *Nauvoo Journal* 4 (1992): 5–8; Turner, *BY,* 238, 439 n21, 22.

70. Augusta to Brigham, June 4, 1850, AAC Letters.

71. PS, 141–42 (Dec. 1, 30, 1849; Jan. 13, 14, 15, 27, 31, 1850). On Rosilla, see chapter 6.

72. PS, 151, 152, 153, 170 (Oct. 7, Dec. 1, 1850; Dec. 1, 9, 14, 1851).

73. Augusta to Brigham, July 10, Dec. 28, July 10, 1850, AAC Letters.

74. HCK, 55, undated. An apparent allusion to eternal marriage in the final stanza of the poem suggests it may have been original, although it was laden with phrases common in early-nineteenth-century popular poetry as revealed in a search on forgottenbooks.com /worddata). On the phrases "vaulted arch," "plighted vow," "altar laid," "clinging vine," and "tempest driven": All but "tempest driven" were common from the late eighteenth to the early nineteenth century, a period that produced reams of poetry and prose used in nineteenth-century school readers and gift books. "Tempest driven" peaked a couple of decades later. I did not find "tempest riven" on this website, but it definitely appeared in late-eighteenth-century poetry. Although editors have added a "d" to Vilate's poem, I suspect that she actually meant "riven." She was clearly a consumer if not a producer of popular poetry.

75. Anya Jabour, "Albums of Affection: Female Friendship and Coming of Age in Antebellum Virginia," *Virginia Magazine of History and Biography* 107 (Spring 1999): 125–58; Andrea R. Foroughi, "Vine and Oak: Wives and Husbands Cope with the Financial Panic of 1857," *Journal of Social History* 36 (Summer 1003): 1009–32; Mandy Green, "'The Vine and Her Elm': Milton's Eve and the Transformation of an Ovidian Motif," *Modern Language Review* 91 (1996): 301–16. A key text throughout the nineteenth century was Washington Irving, "The Wife," in his *History, Tales & Sketches* (New York: Library of America, 1983), 739, first published in 1820, and quoted approvingly in [Thomas Roder-

ick Dew], "Dissertation on the Characteristic Differences Between the Sexes, and on the Position and Influence of Woman in Society," *Southern Literary Messenger,* Aug. 1835, 673, which was picked up and reused by others.

76. Mary Wollstonecraft, *A Vindication of the Rights of Woman* (1792; Oxford: Oxford University Press, 1999), 87; Janet Todd, *Mary Wollstonecraft: A Revolutionary Life* (London: Bloomsbury Reader, 2014), 250.

77. "Youth," in *The Poems of Caius Valerius Catullus,* trans. George Lamb (London: John Murray, 1821), vol. 2, 8, 112–13. Relations between grapevines and elm trees were still showing up in horticultural books in the early twentieth century ("Grape Vine Growing on an Elm Tree," *Meehans Monthly: A Magazine of Horticulture, Botany and Kindred Subjects* [1901]: 70).

78. Augusta to Brigham, July 30, Aug. 13, 17, 1850, AAC Letters.

79. Augusta to Brigham, Aug. 17, 1850, AAC Letters.

80. Augusta to Brigham, Aug. 17, 1850, AAC Letters.

81. Dorothy W. Peterson, *All Things Right: A Biography of Vilate Murray Kimball* (Privately published, 2009), 173–74.

82. Lyman Walbridge Trask, "Forget Me Not: A Lady to Her Husband," *Philadelphia Visitor* (Philadelphia: A. Weikel, 1835), vol. 1, 160; Lyman Walbridge Trask, "Forget Me Not: A Lady to Her Husband," *Atkinson's Casket of Literature, Wit and Sentiment (*Philadelphia, 1835), no. 1, 15; "The Lady to Her Husband," *Liberator* (Boston, Mass.), June 13, 1835, 96; "A Lady to Her Husband," *Onondaga Gazette,* July 11, 1848, 1.

83. *Report of the Woman's Rights Convention, Held at Seneca Falls, N.Y., July 19th and 20th, 1848* (Rochester, N.Y.: John Dick at the North Star Office, 1848), online at www.nps.gov/.

84. "Woman's Rights Convention: Awful Combination of Socialism, Abolitionism, and Infidelity," *New York Herald,* Oct. 25, 1850, 1.

85. Derived from data in familypedia.wikia.com/wiki/Heber Chase Kimball (1801–1868).

86. Heber C. Kimball to Vilate Kimball, Feb. 12, 1849, Stanley B. Kimball Collection, quoted in Peterson, *All Things Right,* 175–76.

87. Heber C. Kimball to Vilate Kimball, Feb. 12, 1849.

88. Quoted in Peterson, *All Things Right,* 179–81.

89. WW 4:38 (June 15, 1851).

90. WW 4:31 (June 1, 1851).

91. Lucy Meserve Smith to George A. Smith, LMS Letters, July 16, 1851.

92. Bathsheba Wilson Bigler Smith, Autobiography, typescript, HBLL; Ancestral Files, FamilySearch.org.

93. Lucy to George, LMS Letters, June 10, 1851; Lucy Meserve Smith Autobiography, Special Collections, University of Utah; 1850 United States Federal Census, Great Salt Lake, and Iron, Utah Territory, Ancestry.com.

94. Bathsheba to George, BWS Letters, Feb. 14, 1851.

95. Bathsheba to George, BWS Letters, June 1, 8, 1851.

96. Lucy to George, LMS Letters, June 10, 1851; Bathsheba to George, BWS Letters, Feb. 14, 1851; WW 4:50 (July 24, 1851).

97. Bathsheba to George, BWS Letters, June 8, 1851.

98. Bathsheba to George, BWS Letters, June 12, 13, 1851.

99. Bathsheba to George, BWS Letters, June 13, 1851; LMS Letters, June 10 and following, 1851.

100. Bathsheba to George, BWS Letters, Feb. 14, 1851.

101. Lucy to George, LMS Letters [June 1851?].

102. WW 4:11–12 (Feb. 4, 1851).

103. Lucy to George, LMS, Letters, July 17, 1851.

104. Ronald W. Walker, "The Affair of the 'Runaways': Utah's First Encounter with the Federal Officers, Part 1," *Journal of Mormon History* 39, no. 4 (Fall 2013): 17–18, 25–26.

105. Walker, "Affair of the 'Runaways,'" 26–29.

106. WW 4:61–63 (Sept. 8, 1851).

107. Walker, "Affair of the 'Runaways,'" 1–43; Ronald W. Walker and Matthew J. Grow, "The People Are 'Hogaffed or Humbugged': The 1851–52 National Reaction to Utah's 'Runaway' Officers," *Journal of Mormon History* 40 (Winter 2014): 1–52; quotation on 38.

108. ERS *Poetry*, 432–34.

109. Discourse of April 25, 1858, in Letterpress Copybook 4, 167–68, Brigham Young Papers, CHL, cited in Turner, *BY*, 295. Although the source does not give Augusta's name, her comment about having left the territory twice to visit her family fits her biography. I thank John Turner for providing this information and confirming her identity.

10. "the revelation on plurality of wives was read"

1. SW, Aug. 24–28, 1852.

2. PS, 179 (Aug. 28, 29, 1852).

3. PS, 179 (Aug. 28, 1852).

4. SW, Aug. 28, 1852; HS, 450 (Aug. 28, 1852); WW 4:144 (Aug. 28, 1852); *Deseret News,* Sept. 18, 1852, 1, 4.

5. *Deseret News,* Sept. 18, 1852, 1.

6. PS, 179 (Aug. 29, 1852).

7. SW, Aug. 29, 1852.

8. HS, 449–50 (Aug. 29, 1852).

9. WW 4:103 (March 28, 1852).

10. Breck England, *The Life and Thought of Orson Pratt* (Salt Lake City: University of Utah Press, 1985), 174, 175, 178–80; David J. Whittaker, "Early Mormon Polygamy Defenses," *Journal of Mormon History* 11 (1984): 43–64. For excerpts from some of these defenses, see *Doing the Works of Abraham: Mormon Polygamy, Its Origin, Practice, and Demise,* ed. B. Carmon Hardy (Norman, Okla.: Arthur H. Clark, 2007), 74–110. Other Mormon preachers picked up on Pratt's comment about Muhammad. On this point, see S. Spencer Wells, "Muslims Under the Mormon Eye: Theology, Rhetoric, and Personal Contacts, 1830–1910," *Journal of Mormon History* 42, no. 1 (April 2016): 74–79.

11. Orson Pratt, "Celestial Marriage," *Journal of Discourses* 1 (1852): 53–66; a condensed version can be found in *Doing the Works of Abraham,* ed. Hardy, 76–79.

12. Pratt, "Celestial Marriage," 61–62; Julie Dunfey, "'Living the Principle' of Plural Marriage: Mormon Women, Utopia, and Female Sexuality in the Nineteenth Century," *Feminist Studies* 10 (1984): 527–30; B. Carmon Hardy and Dan Erickson, "'Regeneration—Now and Evermore!': Mormon Polygamy and the Physical Rehabilitation of Humankind," *Journal of the History of Sexuality* 10, no. 1 (2001): 40–61; Jeffrey D. Nichols, "Polygamy and Prostitution: Comparative Morality in Salt Lake City, 1847–1911," *Journal of Mormon History* 27, no. 2 (Fall 2001): 1–39; Robert E. Riegel, "Changing American Attitudes Toward Prostitution (1800–1920)," *Journal of the History of Ideas* 29, no. 3 (July–Sept. 1968): 437–41; Joan Iversen, "Feminist Implications of Mormon Polygyny," *Feminist Studies* 10, no. 3 (Autumn 1984): 510.

13. Using Family Search, Ancestry.com, and other genealogical sources, I was able to locate birth dates for eighty-eight of the hundred men, and marital information for eighty-two. Six were unmarried, fifty-one had one wife, nineteen had two, four had three, and two had four. This contrasts, of course, with the multiple marriages of men at the top of the church hierarchy. By 1852, the fifteen members of the presidency and Quorum of Twelve Apostles all had several wives, though some, like Woodruff, had experienced divorces as well as multiple marriages. See D. Michael Quinn, *The Mormon Hierarchy: Origins of Power* (Salt Lake City: Signature Books, 1994), 552, 561, 569, 571, 581, 582, 597, 631; and Quinn, *The Mormon Hierarchy: Extensions of Power* (Salt Lake City: Signature Books,

1997), 465, 538, 557, 561, 569, 571, 575, 581, 597. In his brief biographies of church leaders, Quinn lists all possible wives, a method that potentially inflates the number of wives per man but does not undermine the broader point about polygamy being associated with high church position.

14. SW, April 10, 1852; CMW, Dec. 13, 1850, Feb. 1, 18, March 9, 1851; Preston Woolley Parkinson, *The Utah Woolley Family* (Salt Lake City: Privately published, 1967), 180.

15. HS, 454 n6.

16. PS, 180, 181, 403 (Sept. 1, 6, 7, 13, 15, 1852).

17. SW, April 26, 1854.

18. Of the eighty-two, I found only six who appear never to have taken a plural wife. For a recent iteration of the idea that plural marriage and the opposition against it bound Mormons together, see Omri Elisha, "Sustaining Charisma Mormon Sectarian Culture and the Struggle for Plural Marriage, 1852–1890," *Nova Religio: The Journal of Alternative and Emergent Religions* 6, no. 1 (Oct. 2002): 45–63.

19. SW, Oct. 16, 1852.

20. In his diary, Woodruff wrote, "Spent the day teaching 44 Elders that were going on Foreign Missions to China, Australia, Siam, Hindustan, the Isles of the Sea," adding, "They will do a great work & gather many saints & much wealth to Zion." See also HS, 454, 455 (Oct. 15, 16, 17, 1852); WW 4:150 (Oct. 16, 1852).

21. HS, 452, 453 (Sept. 28, Oct. 4, 11, 13, 14, 1852).

22. SW, Aug. 30, Sept. 9, 10, 13, 14, 15, 17, 18, 21, 22, 27, 1852.

23. HS, 455 (Oct. 19, 1852).

24. SW, Oct. 19, 1852.

25. HS, 457 (Oct. 23, 1852).

26. SW, Nov. 3, 1852.

27. Travel in the nineteenth century was far from predictable, depending on winds, weather, and the condition of wagons, animals, and ships. It actually took Samuel Woolley a few days longer to get from San Bernardino to San Francisco than it did Perrigrine Sessions to sail from New York City to Liverpool. Samuel left San Bernardino Dec. 17, 1852, and arrived in San Francisco on Jan. 8, 1853. Perrigrine Sessions left New York City on Dec. 17 and arrived in Liverpool on Jan. 5. It took Hosea Stout forty-three days to travel from Salt Lake City to San Bernardino, and Perrigrine Sessions forty-six days to travel from Salt Lake City to Kanesville. It took the Western group almost as long to travel from Salt Lake City to San Bernardino as it did the Eastern group to go from Salt Lake City to Kanesville, Iowa (near present-day Omaha), though the distance from Salt Lake City to Kanesville was almost 50 percent greater.

28. HS, 466, 467 (Dec. 24, 1852; Jan. 3, 6, 9, 1853).

29. SW, Dec. 22–25, 1852.

30. SW, Dec. 30, 1852; Jan. 1, 1853. Both "The Gallant Ship" by W. W. Phelps and "How Oft in Sweet Meditation" by Parley P. Pratt appear in *A Collection of Sacred Hymns,* selected by Emma Smith (Kirtland, Ohio: F. G. Williams, 1835), 65–66, 107–9.

31. HS, 468, 469 (Jan. 20, 21, 25, 1853); SW, Jan. 21, 1853.

32. SW, Jan. 12, 14, 1853.

33. SW, Jan. 8, 22, 1853.

34. HS, 468 (Jan. 13, 16, 1853).

35. HS, 468, 470, 471 (Jan. 15, 19, Feb. 13, March 3, 1853).

36. HS, 468 (Jan. 17, 1853).

37. SW, Jan. 8, 12, 13, 16, 1853.

38. At San Bernardino, he copied several songs apparently composed by fellow elders during the journey from Salt Lake City.

39. HS, 475 (March 1, April 23, 1853).

40. HS, 476 (April 27, 1853).

41. HS, 472 (March 3, 1853).

42. HS, 479–82 (May 18, 20, 23, 25, 27, 31, June 3, 4, 7, 1853).

43. HS, 478–80 (May 6, 9, 13, 23, 1853).

44. HS, 479, 480 (May 20, 21, 24, 1853).

45. HS, 478 (May 11, 1853).

46. HS, 480 (May 21, 1853).

47. HS, 482 (June 9, 1853).

48. HS, 484 (June 22, 1853).

49. HS, 487 (July 26, 27, 1853).

50. HS, 485, 486, 487 (July 2, July 16, Aug. 4, 1853).

51. HS, 488 (Aug. 23 1853).

52. HS, 491–93 (Sept. 19, 27–30; Oct. 3, 5, 17, 19, 20, 26; Nov. 3–5, 1853).

53. HS, 498 (Dec. 5, 7, 1853).

54. HS, 498, 499 (Dec. 8, 9, 14, 1853).

55. HS, 499, 500 (Dec. 15, 16, 17, 19, 23, 25, 28, 30–31, 1853).

56. HS, 504, 509, 510–11, 514 (Jan. 9, March 18, 21, 30, 31, May 1, 1854). Anna, who had spent her childhood and teens in a Shaker village, married Benjamin Jones, a Mormon widower with five children. She left him, perhaps after he took another wife, was briefly reconciled, then divorced after what Hosea said had been seventeen years of marriage. She seems to have lived with Hosea for several years. (HS 265, 303, 362, 669, 669 n37 [July 8, 1847; Feb. 26, 1848; Feb. 7, 1850; April 17, May 1, 1848; Nov. 22, 1858].)

57. PGS, 145–46 (Aug. 20, 1852).

58. PGS, 152 (Sept. 15, 1852).

59. PGS, 171–73 (Dec. 12, 17, 25, 1852).

60. PGS, 208–10 (Aug. 8, 1853). For an engaging visual history of the park, which closed in the 1980s, see "Belle Vue Revisited," manchesterhistory.net.

61. William Hartley, "LDS Pastors and Pastorates, 1852–55," in *Mormons in Early Victorian Britain,* ed. Richard L. Jensen and Malcolm R. Thorp (Salt Lake City: University of Utah Press, 1989), 195, 205.

62. PGS, 204, 205 (July 19, 1853).

63. PGS, 205, 206 (July 22, 1853). This may have been the same murder he mentioned in PGS, 196 (May 11, 1853).

64. PGS, 196, 233 (May 18, Oct. 14, 1853).

65. PGS, 223, 224 (Oct. 14, 1853).

66. PGS, 191 (March 16, 1853). Sessions's habit of jumbling stories with little sense of chronology makes it impossible to know whether the birth had occurred that same week or years before. It was the story that seems to have mattered. Given his mother's occupation, he was no doubt tuned to stories of harrowing births. His story makes clear, however, that such stories were told in mixed company as well as among women.

67. PGS, 206, 207 (July 17, 1853).

68. PGS, 216 (Aug. 19, 1853).

69. PGS, 221 (Sept. 20, 1853).

70. PGS, 185 (Feb. 12, 1853). See also PGS, 185, 191, 227 (Jan. 12, March 16, Nov. 23, 1853).

71. PGS, 208 (Aug. 7, 1853).

72. PGS, 227 (Nov. 23, 1853).

73. PGS, 216 (Aug. 30, 1853).

74. PGS, 223 (Oct. 20, 1853).

75. PGS, 198, 200, 201, 201 n56 (June 9, 25, 1853).

76. PGS, 226 (Nov. 9, 1853).

77. PGS, 226 (Nov. 10, 16, 1853).

78. Allen, *No Toil nor Labor,* 292–99. Although the details are murky, Clayton obviously became a liability to the mission. He appears to have had a drinking problem and perhaps was a bit too enthusiastic in preaching plurality.

79. Mary Richards to My Dear Samuel, May 29, 1854, Samuel W. Richards Papers, box 1, folder 8, CHL.

80. PGS, 221 (Sept. 21, 1853).

81. PGS, 244 (Feb. 8, 1854).

82. PGS, 228–31, 233, 241, 242 (Dec. 6, 8, 13, 14, 18, 30, 1853; Jan. 8, 17, 1854).

83. PGS, 230, 231 (Dec. 14, 1853).

84. PGS, 245 (Feb. 24, 1854).

85. PGS, 244, 246–48 (Feb. 14, 15, March 2–17, 1854).

86. PGS, 249–51 (March 18–April 2, 1854).

87. "Letter from Ezekiel Clark to Sylvia Clark," PGS, 237–40. Clark wrote that he presumed his children were happy in Utah at the time but worried that "when they arrive at years of discretion and reflection they will be very unhappy and fear they will hate me."

88. PGS, 254 (May 16, 1854).

89. SW, April 25, 1853.

90. SW, April 27, 1853.

91. SW, April 25, May 12, June 3, 15, 16, 1853.

92. SW, April 28, 1853.

93. SW, April 27, 28, 1853; R. Lanier Britsch, "The Latter-day Saint Mission to India: 1851–1856," *BYU Studies* 12, no. 3 (1972): 1–14; Britsch, *From the East: The History of the Latter-day Saints in Asia, 1851–1996* (Salt Lake City: Deseret Book, 1998), 8–42.

94. Britsch, *From the East,* 25–28.

95. SW, May 13, 1853; Whittaker, "Early Mormon Polygamy Defenses," 45–47.

96. SW, May 19, 23, June 3, July 19, Aug. 14, 1853.

97. Samuel Woolley to My Dear Beloved Catharine, Calcutta, Aug. 14 [1853], MS 77007, CHL.

98. Samuel Woolley to My Dear Beloved Catharine. He had raised the issue of polygamy in an earlier letter when he assured her that he still loved her just as he did when they were first engaged and that, whether or not he someday had "more," she would still keep the same place in his heart.

99. SW, May 21, June 9, 18, 19, 21, 24, July 2, 4, 5, 10, Aug. 2, 1853.

100. SW, May 18, 21, July 8, 1853.

101. SW, May 29, July 11, 12, 29, Aug. 7, 1853.

102. SW, July 15, 1853.

103. When he returned from his journey, he participated in the council that cut her off (SW, Aug. 18, Aug. 24, 1853; April 5, 23, 1854).

104. SW, April 18, 19, 20, 26, 1854.

105. SW, May 13, June 18, 1853.

106. SW, Aug. 14, 1853.

107. SW, April 18, 27, 1854.

108. SW, April 26, 1854.

109. SW, April 13, 20, 22, 1854.

110. SW, July 29, Nov. 4, 1854.

111. The month before, he had written, "I had a singular dream about being married to my Wife &c." (SW, Jan. 13, 1855; Dec. 4, 1854.)

112. SW, Dec. 31, 1854; Jan. 20, 1855.

113. SW, Feb. 24, 1855.

114. SW, April 18, 1855.

115. SW, Feb. 15, 17, 19, 21, 26, March 4, 5, Dec. 1, 1855.

116. SW, March 3, 4, 1855.

117. SW, March 17, 1855.

118. SW, April 9, 11, 14, 1855.

119. SW, July 21, 1855.

120. ERS *Poetry,* 195, 196, originally published in Eliza R. Snow, *Poems, Religious, Historical, and Political* (Liverpool: F. D. Richards, 1856).

121. HS, 522, 523 (July 7, 23, 1854).

122. PS, 206–7 (July 31, Aug. 1, 1854).

123. SW, Aug. 11, 12, 13, 1856. HS, 599 (Aug. 13, 1856) notes that this was "the advance train of the Mormon Emmigration this season."

11. "Synopsis of my labors"

1. WW 4:175–76 (Jan. 1, 1853). Wilford was alluding to Daniel 2:34–35, in a chapter offering Daniel's interpretion of a dream related by the Babylonian king Nebuchadnezzar. For many Christians, this passage remains an important text for predicting the "end-times" or what Latter-day Saints call "the last days." For an LDS version, see "Daniel 2: Nebuchadnezzar's Dream," Old Testament Seminary Student Study Guide, 2002, 176–77, www.lds.org.

2. Julie B. Willis and Grant C. Willis, *Geology of Wasatch Mountain State Park,* Utah Geological Association Publication 29 (2000), 30, 31, 32, 33, 40.

3. WW 3:378–79 (Oct. 19, 22, 23, 26, 1850); 4:14 (Feb. 18, 1851).

4. WW 4:4, 7, 14–19, 32, 41, 43, 47–49, 90, 103 (Jan. 2, 3, Feb. 16, 18, March 4, 8, 10, 11–15, 17–22, 25, June 3, 23, 28, July 1–3, 7–12, 21–23, 1851; Feb. 13, 15, 1852).

5. WW 4:175–78 (Jan. 1, 1853).

6. WW 4:228. He obviously perused his daily entries to arrive at this summary. It is not clear whether or how he categorized his activities on the nineteen days in the year when he simply noted that he had been "at home" or "at home writing" (WW 4:181, 183, 186, 187, 189, 190, 204, 221, 226 [Jan. 22, 25, 26, 28, 31, Feb. 3, 4, 5, 8, 9, 10, 17, 19, Sept. 3, 5, 6, 7, 9, 10, 1853]).

7. WW 4:183, 210–11 (Jan. 26, March 13, 1853); Certificate of Divorce, BY Office Files, CHL.

8. WW 4:183 (Jan. 25, 26, 28, 1853).

9. [Belinda Marden Pratt,] *Defence of Polygamy* (1854), 6.

10. Givens and Grow, 327–31; David J. Whittaker, "Early Mormon Polygamy Defenses," *Journal of Mormon History* 11 (1984): 53–57; [Pratt,] *Defence of Polygamy,* 9.

11. Tullidge, *Women,* 413.

12. The relevant diary entries correlated with probable dates of conception are: WW 1:182–83, 340–42 (Oct. 17–25, 1837; June 25–July 3, 1839); WW 2:105–6, 190–91, 476–78 (June 7–15, 1841; Oct. 8–26, 1842, Oct. 21–29, 1844); WW 3:38–39, 125–26, 378–80 (March 13–21, April 13, 1846; Jan. 31–Feb. 8, 1847; Oct. 22–30, 1850); WW 4:183 (April 23–May 21, 1852). Matching probable conception dates with information from Wilford's diary suggests that Ezra and Aphek, the two sons who died within hours of birth, were most likely premature. Wilford would not yet have been in Nauvoo at the time of Ezra's conception had he been full-term, nor was Wilford in Salt Lake City at the time Aphek, if full-term, would have been conceived. In both cases, he was reunited with Phebe about a month later. Wilford did in fact refer to Ezra's birth as "untimely."

13. Lee L. Bean, Geraldine P. Mineau, and Douglas L. Anderton, "High-Risk Childbearing: Fertility and Infant Mortality on the American Frontier," *Social Science History* 16 (1992): 337–63. See esp. 345–46.

14. WW 3:349–60 (July 26, 1848); WW 4:48 (July 16, 17, 18, 19, 1851).

15. [William A. Alcott,] *The Physiology of Marriage. By an Old Physician* (Boston: John P. Jewett, 1856), 114–20, 156.

16. Journal History of the Church, April 29, 1849, quoted in Lester E. Bush Jr., *Health and Medicine Among the Latter-day Saints* (New York: Crossroads, 1992), 141.

17. Orson Hyde, in Luke William Gallup, Reminiscences and Diary, Feb. 11, 1857, LDS Archives, 193–95, quoted in *Doing the Works of Abraham: Mormon Polygamy, Its Origin, Practice, and Demise* (Norman, Okla.: Arthur H. Clark, 2007), 133–35.

18. Hyde, in Gallup, Reminiscences and Diary.

19. [Pratt,] *Defence of Polygamy,* 4.

20. Sally McMillen, "Mothers' Sacred Duty: Breast-Feeding Patterns Among Middle-

and Upper-Class Women in the Antebellum South," *Journal of Southern History* 51 (1985): 333–56. For abstracts of modern obstetrical research on this topic, see R. V. Short, P. R. Lewis, M. B. Renfree, and G. Shaw, "Contraceptive Effects of Extended Lactational Amenorrhoea," *Lancet* 337 (1991): 715–17; K. I. Kennedy and C. M. Visness, "Contraceptive Efficacy of Lactational Amenorrhoea," *Lancet* 339 (1992): 227–30, U.S. National Library of Medicine, www.ncbi.nlm.nih.gov/pubmed/.

21. For a recent version of this argument, see Jacob A. Moorad, Daniel E. L. Promislow, Ken R. Smith, and Michael J. Wade, "Mating System Change Reduces the Strength of Sexual Selection in an American Frontier Population of the 19th Century," *Evolution & Human Behavior* 32 (2011): 147–55, an article that received a lot of attention on the Internet when a popular-science magazine compared polygyny among humans to the behavior of fruit flies.

22. Analysis based on Pratt records on FamilySearch.org.

23. Givens and Grow, 293; Pratt records, FamilySearch.org.

24. Orson Pratt, in *The Seer*, 1:37–39, and Parley P. Pratt, *Key to the Science of Theology*, 173, quoted in Bush Jr., *Health and Medicine*, 149.

25. Givens and Grow, 293, 304, 305.

26. Benjamin G. Ferris, *Utah and the Mormons* (New York: Harper, 1854), 288–89; Givens and Grow, 327.

27. Parley P. Pratt to wives, San Francisco, Calif., July 29, 1854, Mary Jean Freebairn Collection, MS 4337, CHL.

28. WW 4:210–11 (March 13, 1853).

29. Daynes, *Wives,* 116–27.

30. Daynes, *Wives,* 93–95, 101–2, 107.

31. WW 4:258 (April 4, 1854); WW 5:105 (Oct. 4, 1857).

32. Givens and Grow, 316–24; Bathsheba W. Smith, "Autobiography," typescript, HBLL; Edward Leo Lyman, *Amasa Mason Lyman: Mormon Apostle and Apostate* (Salt Lake City: University of Utah Press, 2009), 495–99; PS, 121, 128, 137, 140, 142, 152, 184, 194, 199 (Dec. 17, 1848; Feb. 19, Oct. 14, Dec. 9, 1849; Jan. 16, Oct. 21, 1850; Dec. 4, 1852; July 7, 1853; June 1, 1854). Although there are inevitable errors in the patron-submitted files on FamilySearch.org, I have found this source useful in comparing the marital records of the other men who were part of Wilford's quorum. In 1853, they were Orson Hyde, Parley Pratt, Orson Pratt, John Taylor, George Smith, Amasa Lyman, Ezra Benson, Charles Rich, Lorenzo Snow, Erastus Snow, and Franklin D. Richards. All had more wives with them in Utah in 1853 than Wilford did, with the exception of Orson Hyde, whose plural wife Martha apparently left him just before he, Marinda, and Mary Ann emigrated. On Hyde's wives, see Myrtle Stevens Hyde, *Orson Hyde: The Oliver Branch of Israel* (Salt Lake City: Agreka Books, 2000), 496–507.

33. *Doctrine and Covenants,* 107:53–54; 116; Adam-ondi-Ahman, Missouri in Reference/Places, JSP; "Adam-ondi-Ahman Temple," www.ldschurchtemples.com; Karen Lynn Davidson, *Our Latter-day Hymns: The Stories and the Messages* (Salt Lake City: Deseret Book, 1988), 78–79.

34. WW 1:327 (April 26, 1839).

35. *A Collection of Sacred Hymns for the Church of the Latter-day Saints,* selected by Emma Smith (Kirtland, Ohio: F. G. Williams, 1835), 29–30.

36. WW 1:27 (April 20, 1835); Maurine Carr Ward, " 'This Institution Is a Good One': The Female Relief Society of Nauvoo, 17 March 1842 to 16 March 1844," *Mormon Historical Studies* 3 (Fall 2002): 183; Devery S. Anderson and Gary James Bergera, eds., *The Nauvoo Endowment Companies, 1845–1846: A Documentary History* (Salt Lake City: Signature Books, 2005), 190; Sarah Brown, Henry Miller Company, MOT.

37. WW 3:559 (June 28, 29, 1850).

38. FamilySearch.org.

39. 1850 Census, Great Salt Lake, Utah Territory, Ancestry.com; Autobiography of Silas Richards Heritage, wayneandbonniegenealogy.net; WW 4:90 (Feb. 16, 1852).

40. WW 1:7. The brief reference to Harry Brown in Wilford's memoir didn't even merit an entry in the index to the Kenney edition of the diaries, perhaps because Brown was so quickly overshadowed by Wilford's description of Pratt's preaching. On Brown's calling to accompany Pratt, see Minute Book 1, March 17, 1834, JSP.

41. "Life Sketch of Sarah Brown Woodruff," Smithfield, Utah, April 15, 1909, Family Search.org.

42. William G. Hartley, "'Don't Go Aboard the *Saluda!*': William Dunbar, LDS Emigrants, and Disaster on the Missouri," *Mormon Historical Studies* (Spring 2003): 41–70; L. Douglas Smoot, "Abraham O. Smoot and the Steamboat Explosion, 9 April 1852," *Mormon Historical Studies* (Spring 2004): 143–47.

43. "Life Sketch of Sarah Brown Woodruff."

44. *Cleveland Herald,* April 24, 1852; "The Explosion of the Saluda," *Missouri Courier,* April 22, 1852; *Natchez Courier,* April 27, 1852.

45. "Terrible Accident—Explosion of the Steamer Saluda—Seventy-Five Lives Lost," *Deseret News,* May 29, 1852. Smoot also noted that Ilus Carter, "br. Woodruff's brother-in-law, was on board, on his way to the valley, but was not hurt." This might be in error. Phebe's brother arrived at the Woodruff house on June 25, 1852. He stayed for five days, settling accounts with Wilford over their joint business ventures. On June 30, Wilford baptized him, and on July 1 accompanied him for the first six miles of his journey to California. (WW 4:140–41 [June 25, 28, 29, 30, July 1, 1852].)

46. "Life Sketch of Sarah Brown Woodruff."

47. "Life Sketch of Sarah Brown Woodruff."

48. "Life Sketch of Sarah Brown Woodruff"; "Mary Brown Blakely," FamilySearch .org. Mary's descendant said her sister became estranged from Sarah because of her marriage. Apparently, Sarah's mother, Rhoda, went back to Ohio. That Rhoda North Brown was born in Farmington, Conn., suggests that Wilford's connection with the family may initially have been through her.

49. "Life Sketch of Sarah Brown Woodruff."

50. Brigham Young Papers, CR 1234/1, box 67, folder 7, CHL.

51. Lawrence Stone, *Road to Divorce: England, 1530–1987* (Oxford and New York: Oxford University Press, 1990), 143–48; Olive Anderson, "Emigration and Marriage Break-Up in Mid-Victorian England," *Economic History Review,* new ser. 50, no. 1 (1997): 105; Beverly Schwartzberg, "'Lots of Them Did That': Desertion, Bigamy, and Marital Fluidity in Late-Nineteenth-Century America," *Journal of Social History* 37, no. 3 (Spring 2004): 573–600; Schwartzberg, "Grass Widows, Barbarians, and Bigamists: Fluid Marriage in Late Nineteenth-Century America" (Ph.D. diss., University of California, Santa Barbara, 2002); and Henrik Hartog, *Man & Wife in America: A History* (Cambridge, Mass.: Harvard University Press, 2000), 87–92; Nancy F. Cott, *Public Vows: A History of Marriage and the Nation* (Cambridge, Mass.: Harvard University Press, 2000), 29–39; Michael Grossberg, *Governing the Hearth: Law and the Family in Nineteenth-Century America* (Chapel Hill: University of North Carolina Press, 1985), 120–21.

52. Jessie L. Embry, *Mormon Polygamous Families: Life in the Principle* (Salt Lake City: University of Utah Press, 1987), 176, 177; Daynes, *Wives,* 160–70. See also Richard S. Van Wagoner, *Mormon Polygamy: A History,* 2nd ed. (Salt Lake City: Signature Books, 1989), 92, 93; Eugene E. Campbell and Bruce L. Campbell, "Divorce Among Mormon Polygamists: Extent and Explanations," in *The New Mormon History,* ed. D. Michael Quinn (Salt Lake City: Signature Books, 1992), 181–200.

53. W. Woodruff to Miss Mary A. Jackson, Great Salt Lake City, Dec. 30, 1853, Woodruff Papers, MS 1352, box 6, folder 5, item 7, CHL.

54. W. Woodruff to Miss Mary A. Jackson.

55. W. Woodruff to Miss Mary A. Jackson.

56. WW to Mary Jackson, Jan. 9, 1855 [1854?], WW Corr.

57. Breck England, *The Life and Thought of Orson Pratt* (Salt Lake City: University of

Utah Press, 1985), 185, 270–71. It is difficult to date Sarah Pratt's disaffection, which didn't become public until the 1870s.

58. WW 5:56 (June 2, 1857).

59. WW 6:30–50 (March 7–April 30, 1857).

60. WW to Sister Jackson, Great Salt Lake City, April 30, 1857, WW Corr.

61. WW 6:113 (May 29, 1863).

62. WW 5:14–16 (Feb. 20, 1857).

63. WW 5:15 (Feb. 20, 1857).

64. WW 3:480 (Sept. 9, 1849).

65. She was still in Boston in January 1850, when a friend wrote her from St. Louis, but her husband assumed she was on her way to the valley when he wrote her in June 1850 in care of "Wilford Woodruff, Salt Lake City." She was definitely in the valley on Nov. 23, 1850, when John Smith gave her a patriarchal blessing. The census taken in 1851 found her living in Salt Lake City with Ruth Sayers, one of the more visible former members of the Boston Branch. See Patriarchal Blessing for Mary Webster, Nov. 23, 1850; Anne E. Wilson to Sister Webster, St. Louis, Jan. 19, 1850; Nathan Webster to My Dearest Mary, June and July 1850, all in Papers of Mary Webster, WW Misc; WW 4:151 (Oct. 30, 1852).

66. The idea of tucking a piece of bread into his bureau is not so bizarre as it seems. A Boston museum still has a piece of bread found in a bureau drawer and labeled by an antiquarian in the middle of the nineteenth century. He claimed that it had been brought to Boston on an English ship in 1630. (Nancy Carlisle, *Cherished Possessions: A New England Legacy* [Boston: Society for the Preservation of New England Antiquities, 2003], 26–27.)

67. Henry B. Jacobs to Zina Diantha Young, Sept. 2, 1852, Zina D. H. Young Collection, quoted in Bradley and Woodward, 198.

68. Bradley and Woodward, 200.

69. CBC, 176–77 (Dec. 12, 25, 27, 1852).

70. CBC, 17, 178, 179, 181, 184, 186 (Dec. 27–31, 1852; Jan. 3, 10, 18, Feb. 1, 3, 17, March 20, April 9, 1853).

12. "we now must look after the poor"

1. PS, 211–12 (Jan. 19, 1855).

2. Minutes of Meeting, Salt Lake City, June 4, 1854, Thomas Bullock Minutes Collection, CHL, quoted in Richard L. Jensen, "Clothing the Indians and Strengthening the Saints: Organized Activity of Mormon Women During the 'Lapse' of the Relief Society, 1844–1867," *Task Papers in LDS History,* no. 27, Church Historical Department, 10–11.

3. Jill Mulvay Derr, "The Relief Society, 1854–1881," in *Mapping Mormonism: An Atlas of Latter-Day Saint History,* ed. Brandon S. Plewe (Provo, Utah: Brigham Young University Press, 2012), 102–3; Richard Jensen, "Forgotten Relief Societies, 1844–67," *Dialogue: A Journal of Mormon Thought* 16 (1983): 105–25; Jill Mulvay Derr, Janath Russell Cannon, and Maureen Ursenbach Beecher, *Women of Covenant: The Story of Relief Society* (Salt Lake City: Deseret Book, 1992), 75–82.

4. Brandon S. Plewe, "Emergence of Modern Stakes and Wards," in Plewe, *Mapping Mormonism,* 128–29; Arrington, *Great Basin,* 30, 51–59, 148–60.

5. Arrington, *Woolley* (Salt Lake City, Utah: Deseret Book, 1976), 338–39.

6. During their first crucial months in the valley, both Roundy and his counselor, Levi Jackman, praised the meetings Patty and Eliza organized, and she remained close to both of them (PS, 105, 107, 161, 163, 164, 165, 166, 167, 212 [Jan. 1, Feb. 2, 1848; Feb. 11, March 20, April 1, April 15, April 30, May 14, May 16, August 15, 1851]; "An Autobiographical Sketch of the Life of Levi Jackman," www.boap.org; "Letter to the Reunion," majackman.com).

7. PS, 166, 168 (July 8, Sept. 17, 1851). Phoebe Ann Morton Angel was Brigham

Young's mother-in-law. Her daughter Mary Ann was Young's legal wife; her son Truman was the designer of many important LDS buildings.

8. Female Council of Health Minutes, Aug. 14, 1852, MS 3195, CHL.

9. Female Council of Health Minutes; PS, 174 175, 180 (April 28, May 24, Aug. 31, 1852); Thomas J. Wolfe, "Steaming Saints: Mormons and the Thomsonian Movement in Nineteenth-Century America," in *Disease and Medical Care in the Mountain West*, ed. Martha L. Hildreth and Bruce T. Moran (Reno: University of Nevada Press, 1998), 26; *Deseret News*, May 15, 1852.

10. Female Council of Health Minutes.

11. Female Council of Health Minutes.

12. PS, 175 (April 17, 21, 24, 1852).

13. On the complex origins and competing meanings attached to these new costumes, see Robert E. Riegel, "Women's Clothes and Women's Rights," *American Quarterly* 15 (Fall 1963): 390–401; Ann Kesselman, "The 'Freedom Suit': Feminism and Dress Reform in the United States, 1848–1875," *Gender and Society* 4 (1991): 495–510; Marion Tinling, "Bloomerism Comes to California," *California History* 61 (Spring 1982): 18–25; Gayle V. Fischer, *Pantaloons and Power: A Nineteenth-Century Dress Reform in the United States* (Kent, Ohio: Kent State University Press, 2001), 75–77. Fischer discusses Mormon clothing, in Utah and among the Strangite movement, in the context of other communitarian and utopian movements.

14. Z3, Aug. 25, 26, 17, 28, 1855. Zina's diary entries are scattered during this period, so it is impossible to know how long she continued with this work, but clothing reform was clearly a focus in the late summer of 1855. Mrs. B. G. Ferris, *The Mormons at Home* (New York: Dix & Edmunds, 1856), 154–56, found Vienna Shearer's clothing odd but did not mention pantaloons. Shearer's homespun dress, she wrote, was "just wide enough and none to spare" to cover her gaunt form, and was "Bloomer enough to display a serviceable pair of brogans." The author of "Scenes in An American Harem," *Harper's Weekly* 1:41 (Oct. 10, 1857): 648–50, claimed that the Utah bloomer costume had been invented by Eliza Snow. The artist who illustrated this story had not visited Utah and seems to have relied on illustrations of "Bloomer costumes" from other periodicals. Contemporary writers usually ridiculed reformist dress. See, for example, Richard Francis Burton, *City of the Saints, and Across the Rocky Mountains* (New York: Harper, 1862), 91, which includes a description of a non-Mormon "lady" in such clothing.

15. PS, 169, 173, 176, 177, 212 (Nov. 5, 1851; March 10, May 26, June 5, 1852; Feb. 14, 1855).

16. Benjamin F. Ferris, *Utah and the Mormons* (New York: Harper, 1854), 156, 167; Nina Baym, *Women Writers of the American West, 1833–1927* (Urbana, Chicago, and Springfield: University of Illinois Press, 2012), 103–279; Martin Mitchell, "Gentile Impressions of Salt Lake City, Utah, 1849–1870," *Geographical Review* 87 (1997): 334–52, chart 336; "Life Among the Mormons," *Putnam's Monthly Magazine* 6 (1855): 144–48, 262–66, 376–81, 501–5; Mrs. Ferris, *Mormons at Home*.

17. Mrs. Ferris, *Mormons at Home*, 157–58, 146, 137, 148, 127.

18. Ferris, *Utah and the Mormons*, 255.

19. Mrs. Ferris, *Mormons at Home*, 124. On her biography, see "Vienna Jacques Dead," *Deseret News*, Feb. 13, 1884, in O'Donovan, *Boston Mormons;* and on her significance in Mormon history and memory, Christopher M. B. Allison, "Layered Lives: Boston Mormons and the Spatial Contexts of Conversion," *Journal of Mormon History* 42, no. 2 (April 2016): 168–213.

20. Mrs. Ferris, *Mormons at Home*, 155.

21. Amanda Barnes Notebook, June 10, 1854, MS 2005, CHL; Vienna Jacques to Brigham Young, Oct. 16, 1851, Brigham Young Office Files, CHL.

22. Jane Neyman Statements, Nov. 29, 1854, in Joseph Smith History Documents, 1839–1860, CHL. See also Alexander L. Baugh, "'For This Ordinance Belongeth to My

House': The Practice of Baptism for the Dead Outside the Nauvoo Temple," *Mormon Historical Studies* 3, no. 1 (Spring 2002): 47–48 n5; Ryan C. Tobler, "'Saviors on Mount Zion': Mormon Sacramentalism, Mortality, and the Baptism for the Dead," *Journal of Mormon History* 39 (2013): 182–238. For the 1854 context of the statements by Neyman and her friend Vienna Jacques, see Dean C. Jessee, "The Writing of Joseph Smith's History," *BYU Studies* 11 (1971): 470–73.

23. Patty noted a meeting "of the council" on March 10 and a "female meeting" on March 19. Ferris could have attended either, but since she and Patty both mention Dr. Sprague's speaking in tongues, it was likely the March 10 meeting, even though Patty says Heber Kimball spoke and Ferris identified the speaker as Willard Richards. Mrs. Ferris, *Mormons at Home,* 199–200; PS, 173, 174 (March 10, 19, 1852).

24. Mrs. Ferris, *Mormons at Home,* 201–2.

25. Mrs. Ferris, *Mormons at Home,* 203–4.

26. Mrs. Ferris, *Mormons at Home,* 204.

27. PS, 77, 78, 112, 119 (April 1, 15, 1847; April 30, Oct. 23, 1848).

28. WW 4:241–43, 254–55 (Jan. 22–31, March 12, 1854).

29. PS, 181, 182, 203 (Oct. 13, 26, 29, Nov. 9, 13, 1852; April 26, 1854).

30. PS, 168–69, 181–84 (Sept. 25, Oct. 1, 1851; Nov. 15, 21, 23, 15, Dec. 1, 2, 3, 6, 7, 13, 14, 15, 16, 1852, and loose sheet pasted in); Stephen Markham Company 1850, MOT; FamilySearch.org.

31. PS, 189–90 (Feb. 9, 10, 11, 1853); Perrigrine Sessions Company and Thomas Rhoads Company, MOT; J. Kenneth Davies, "Thomas Rhoads, Forgotten Mormon Pioneer of 1846," *Nebraska History* 64 (1983): 81–95; "Pedigree Resource File," FamilySearch.org.

32. PS, 190–91 (Feb. 11, 1853).

33. PS, 190–91 (Feb. 11, 27, 1853); WW 4:190 (Feb. 11, 1853).

34. PS, 146, 147, 149, 151, 153 (May 8, 22, June 5, 31, Aug. 28, Sept. 11, Nov. 6, 1850); PS 163, 164, 166, 168, 169 (March 22, April 19, May 28, July 8, Sept. 16, Oct. 15, 29, Nov. 5, Dec. 10, 20, 1851); PS, 172, 173, 176, 178, 180, 181 (Feb. 7, 25, March 10, 24, May 12, 22, 26, June 5, 9, 19, 23, July 14, 21, 31, Aug. 4, 14, 17, 31, Sept. 14, Oct. 12, 13, 16, 20, 26, 29, 30, Nov. 13, 1852); PS, 188, 189, 191, 192, 193, 194, 195, 197, 198 (Jan. 8, 22, Feb. 5, 19, March 5, 19, April 1, 16, 30, May 14, 18, June 1, 29, July 27, Sept. 6, 21, Oct. 5, 19, Dec. 3, 31, 1853); PS 200, 201, 202, 203, 205, 206, 208 (Jan. 14, 28, Feb. 25, March 11, 25, April 15, June 6, July 1, Sept. 19, Oct. 17, 31, Dec. 28, 1854); PS, 211, 212, 214, 215, 216, 217, 218, 220 (Jan. 17, 25, Feb. 8, 14, 22, March 14, 22, 24, April 5, 14, 28, May 3, 11, 16, 26, 31, June 9, 14, 23, July 7, 21, 26, Aug. 4, 23, Sept. 1, Dec. 13, 1855).

35. PS, 215, 216 (April 16, 25, May 2, 8, 1855).

36. PS, 199–202 (Jan. 3, 11, 20, Feb 3, 8, 11, 17, 22, 25, 1854).

37. PS, 204 (May 2, 1854); Samuel C. Monson, "Deseret Alphabet,"*EOM,* 373–74.

38. PS, 216, 216 n50, 217, 218 (May 5, 14, 18, June 2, 4, 16, 19, 30, July 9, 14, 31, 1855); "William France," MOT.

39. Amazingly, the descendants of both secretaries preserved copies of the minutes. See Record of the Female Relief Society, Louisa R. Taylor Papers, MSS SC 23, CHL L. Tom Perry Special Collections, HBLL; Amanda Barnes Smith Notebook, 1854–1866, MS 2005, CHL. See also Jensen, "Forgotten Relief Societies," 105–25; Derr et al., *Women of Covenant,* 75–82.

40. PS, 194 (July 25, 1853).

41. *Deseret News,* Oct. 15, Nov. 24, 1853. In a sermon given at General Conference on Oct. 7, George A. Smith warned that Walker might take white women captive, as he had done with Paiute women. In what appears to have been a bad joke, he said that Walker had been teasing for a white wife, and that if any woman in the congregation wanted to marry him, he could arrange it.

42. *Deseret News,* Nov. 24, 1853.

43. On the complex racial configurations in the Book of Mormon, see Jared Hickman,

"*The Book of Mormon* as Amerindian Apocalypse," *American Literature* 86 (Sept. 2014): 429–61; Max Perry Mueller, "Black, White, and Red: Race and the Making of the Mormon People, 1830–1880" (Ph.D. diss., Harvard University, 2015).

44. *Deseret News,* Oct. 15, 1853, 3.

45. Matilda Dudley, the founder of the society, became the second wife of Joseph Busby. Jane Capener married Ephraim Hanks, whose first wife was her fellow Relief Society member Amelia Decker. Clarissa Homiston's husband, Lyman, age seventy-eight, took as his plural wife Amelia Milner, age fifty-two. (He died a year later.)

46. Record of the Female Relief Society, Taylor Papers; Amanda Barnes Smith Notebook. Barnes used the unused part of her minute book to copy her own autobiography, including an account of the attack at Haun's Mill, Missouri, in 1838.

47. Karen Lynn Davidson, *Our Latter-day Hymns: The Stories and the Messages* (Salt Lake City: Deseret Book, 1988), 35–36.

48. *A Collection of Sacred Hymns for the Church of the Latter-day Saints,* selected by Emma Smith (Kirtland, Ohio: F. G. Williams, 1835), 12.

49. *Collection of Sacred Hymns,* selected by Smith, 83–84.

50. Turner, *BY,* 210–17, 246, 343–49.

51. WW 4:262–80, 20 (May 3–30, 1854; April 25, 1851).

52. WW 4:262–80 (May 3–30, 1854).

53. Brigham Young Sermon, May 14, 1854, Fillmore, Miscellaneous Minutes Collection, CHL, quoted in Jensen, "Clothing the Indians," 8.

54. Jensen, "Clothing the Indians," 9.

55. EPL, 71–72 (June 4, 6, 9, 17, 1854).

56. Mrs. Ferris, *Mormons at Home,* 193; Ferris, *Utah and the Mormons,* 29.

57. Record of the Female Relief Society, Taylor Papers; Amanda Barnes Smith Notebook.

58. Thirteenth Ward Relief Society Records, vol. 1, 1854–1857, June 14, 1854, LR 6133 21, CHL.

59. Thirteenth Ward Relief Society Records (June 7, 1854).

60. Amanda Barnes Smith Notebook, June 10–Aug. 16, 1854; PS, 205, 343 (June 10, 1854).

61. WW 4:281 (June 15, 16, 1854).

62. Jensen, "Forgotten Relief Societies," 113–15.

63. PS, 205, 206, 207, 208 (June 10, July 12, 18, 22, Aug. 14, 26, 28, 30, 1854).

64. William Major Watercolors, 41-72-10/424-427, Peabody Museum of Archaeology and Ethnology, Harvard University. On "hickory," see "Hickory-shirt," *Oxford English Dictionary,* new ed. (New York: Oxford, 2000), online.

65. Thomas D. Brown, *Journal of the Southern Indian Mission,* ed. Juanita Brooks (Logan: Utah State University Press, 1972), 53 (June 10, 1854).

66. Brown, *Journal,* 53–54 (June 11, 1854).

67. Brigham Young to Dear Brethren, July 26, 1854, in Brown, *Journal,* 85–86 (Aug. 28, 1854).

68. Brown, *Journal,* 103–4 (Dec. 22, 1854).

69. Brown, *Journal,* 30, 117–19 (May 18, 1854; March 18, 1855).

70. Jensen, "Clothing the Indians," 15–18; "Forgotten Relief Societies," 115–17.

71. Jensen, "Forgotten Relief Societies," 118.

72. Minutes of the Sixteenth Ward Relief Society, Patty Sessions Papers, CHL.

73. Thirteenth Ward Relief Society Records, July 12, 1854; Oct. 18, 25, Nov. 1, 1855; Oct. 22, 1856.

74. Hannah Tapfield King, Autobiography, circa 1864–1870, typescript, MS628, CHL, March 3, 1855.

75. PS, 210–12 (Nov. 16, 1854; Jan. 17, 19, 27, 1855).

76. PS, 212–13 (Feb. 19, 22–27, 1855).

77. "Auto-biography," *Woman's Exponent* 51 (Sept. 1, 1883): 2.

78. Autograph Book of Sarah M. Kimball, MS 131, 15, CHL; ERS *Poetry,* 443.

79. Autograph Book of Sarah M. Kimball, 40.

80. Autograph Book of Sarah M. Kimball, 54, 55.

81. Autograph Book of Sarah M. Kimball, 38.

82. Derr, *Sarah M. Kimball,* signaturebookslibrary.org/sarah-m-kimball/; Emmeline B. Wells, "President Sarah M. Kimball," *Woman's Exponent,* Dec. 15, 1898; Arrington, *Great Basin,* 164; WW 4:401 (Feb. 12–16, 1856).

83. WW 4:245 (Feb. 3, 1854).

84. Z3, June 12, 13, 18, 1854.

85. "Woman," ERS *Poetry,* 474–75.

86. "Woman," ERS *Poetry,* 474–79.

87. Historian's Office Journal, vol. 17, 361, 362 (March 29, 31, 1855), CR 100, CHL.

88. Historian's Office Journal, vol. 18, 97 (Aug. 8, 1855).

89. Jill Mulvay Derr and Carol Cornwall Madsen, "Preserving the Record and Memory of the Female Relief Society of Nauvoo, 1841–92," *Journal of Mormon History* 35 (Summer 2009): 88–117; Source Note, NRS Minutes.

90. ERS *Poetry,* 491–96.

91. Hebrews 5:8, KJV.

92. ERS, *Poetry,* 495, 496.

93. ERS *Poetry,* 496–500.

94. ERS *Poetry,* 501; Derr et al., *Women of Covenant,* 74–75.

95. Eighteenth Ward, Salt Lake Stake, General Minutes, 1854–57, Sept. 6, 1855, 9, quoted in Derr et al., *Women of Covenant,* 79–80.

13. "What a life of wandering"

1. CBC, 251 (March 23, 1854). For descriptions of some of the other houses, see CBC, 43–48, 50, 53, 54, 55, 56, 59, 67, 87, 90, 121, 170–71, 229, 237, 245. On Polynesia, see *The History of Louisa Barnes Pratt,* ed. S. George Ellsworth (Logan: Utah State University Press, 1998), 125.

2. CBC, 381 (Jan. 5, 1856).

3. CBC, 28–30, 38–39, 50–51.

4. CBC, 4, 17–18, 28, 35, 38–39, 46, 60, 63, 67, 68, 90–91.

5. William W. Phelps, "Redeemer of Israel," *A Collection of Sacred Hymns for the Church of the Latter-day Saints,* selected by Emma Smith (Kirtland, Ohio: F. G. Williams, 1835), 12.

6. CBC, 76, 78, 81, 83, 84 (July 22, Aug. 4, 21, Sept. 6, 22, 1848).

7. CBC, 95–120, (May 7–Oct. 19 1850); quotes on 106, 113–14; James 1:4, KJV.

8. CBC, 140, 142 (Feb. 1, 12, 1852).

9. CBC, 4, 64, 65, 66, 194, 243, 256, 259, 515 n9 (Sept. 1845; Sept. 1846; June 19, 1853; April 19, May 9, 1854).

10. CBC, 351 (Sept. 17, 18, 19, 1855); Isaiah 60:8–10, KJV.

11. CBC, 109, 110 (July 10, 1850); Newell and Avery, *Mormon Enigma,* 252–55.

12. CBC, 236, 256, 259, 264, 265, 267, 268, 391, 436, 469, 470, 471 (Jan. 22, 23, May 8, 29, June 6, 19, 20, 1854; Feb. 19, Nov. 31, 1856; May 25–30, June 4–8, 13, 15, 1857). On Agnes's situation in Nauvoo, see Chapter 3.

13. CBC, 174–75 (Nov. 17, 18, 22, Dec. 2, 6, 7, 1852). On the child, see CBC 156, 216, 527 n33 (June 6, 1852; Nov. 5, 1853). On the "half-breed," see CBC 431 (Oct. 16, 1856).

14. Edward Leo Lyman, *San Bernardino: The Rise and Fall of a California Community* (Salt Lake City: Signature Books, 1996), 255–56.

15. CBC, 405, 407, 408, 540 n19 (May 9, 25, 26, 27, 1856); Marjorie Newton, *Southern Cross Saints: The Mormons in Australia* (Laie, Hawaii: Institute of Polynesian Studies, 1991), 145–48, 151–53.

16. CBC, 423 (Aug. 11, 1856); "Slave Schedule," 1850 Federal Census, Utah Territory, trans. Maggie Stewart, USGenWeb, www.usgencensus.org, 2008; Lyman, *San Bernardino,* 276, 289–92; Ellsworth, ed., *History of Louisa Pratt,* 231–32; "Suit for Freedom," *Los Angeles Star,* Feb. 2, 1856.

17. Dolores Hayden, "Biddy Mason's Los Angeles, 1856–1891," *California History* 68 (1989): 85–99; Marne L. Campbell, "African American Women, Wealth Accumulation, and Social Welfare Activism in 19th-Century Los Angeles," *Journal of African American History* 97 (2012): 383–89; Campbell, "'The Newest Religious Sect Has Started in Los Angeles': Race, Class, Ethnicity, and the Origins of the Pentecostal Movement, 1906–1913," *Journal of African American History* 95 (2010): 6; CBC, 428 (Sept. 4, 1856). I thank Cori Tucker-Price, whose work in History 1410 inspired me to learn more about Biddy Mason.

18. CBC, 347–49, 352 (Aug. 27, 30, Sept. 22, 1855). On Johnny's descent, see CBC, 432, 542 n46 (Oct. 5, 1856).

19. CBC, 352, 355, 377 (Sept. 22, 29, 30, Oct. 1, Dec. 16, 17, 1855).

20. WW 4: 483–84 (Oct. 31, 1856); LeRoy R. Haven and Ann W. Haven, *Handcarts to Zion* (Lincoln: University of Nebraska Press, 1960), 91–141.

21. CBC, 448 (Jan. 23, 24, 1857). The roster for the James G. Willie Company, MOT, lists Ann Tait, age thirty-one, born Aug. 21, 1824, died Oct. 20, 1856, without further information. Elizabeth Xavier Tait, age twenty-three, born Dec. 23, 1832, survived. Four-year-old Johnny Tait was in Amasa Lyman and Charles Rich's company when it left San Bernardino on April 18, 1857.

22. CBC, 460 (April 12, 1857). *Songs of the Civil War,* ed. Irwin Silber (New York: Columbia University Press, 1960), 119, dates "Will They Miss Me at Home" to 1852.

23. CBC, 125, 131, 135, 139, 141, 144, 145, 148, 149, 150, 157 (Feb. 18, July 10, Oct. 12, 1851; Jan. 7, Feb. 1, 23, 24, 26, March 1, 20, 22, 31, June 12, 1852).

24. CBC, 4, 296, 312, 318, 353, 354, 370, 371 (Dec. 12, 1854; March 21, April 12, Sept. 23, 24, 27, Nov. 21, 1855).

25. "Passengers on the Ship Brooklyn in 1846," Utah Chapter of the Ship Brooklyn Association, http://shipbrooklyn.com/passengers.html; CBC, 338–39, 340, 380, 396, 398, 430, 435, 440 (July 18, 23, 1855; Jan. 1, March 19, 29, Oct. 23, 27, Dec. 6, 1856).

26. CBC, 441, 442, 443, 448, 449, 450, 456 (Dec. 16, 17, 21, 1856; Jan. 19, 26, 27, Feb. 1, 11, March 22, 1857).

27. CBC, 147 (March 29, 30, 31, April 1, 1857).

28. CBC, 458–60 (April 2, 4, 7, 14, 1857).

29. CBC, 462, 464, 465, 466, 467 (April 18, 23, May 2, 4, 11, 25, 16, 1857).

30. CBC, 463–64 (May 1, 1857).

31. "All's For the Best," in Edward Hughes, *Select English Poetry* (London: Longman, Brown, Green, and Longmans, 1851), 310–11; C. Gough, *The Cruet Stand: Select Pieces of Prose and Poetry* (London: Wertheim and Macintosh, 1853), 71; Martin Farquhar Tupper, *Hactenus* (Boston: Charles H. Peirce, 1848), 9.

32. *Los Angeles Star,* Feb. 2, 1856, 1.

33. CBC, 251, 295, 379, 404, 405, 413–15, 422, 474, 479–80 (March 22, Dec. 1, 1854; Dec. 30, 1855; May 3, 6, 1856; June 28, Aug. 7, 1856; July 1, Aug. 2, 7, 1857).

34. CBC, 413–15 (June 28, 1856).

35. CBC, 397, 477, 479–80, 481 (March 27, 1856; July 10, Aug. 2, 7, 13, Sept. 5, 1857); on San Francisco, see CBC 274 (July 27, 1854); on Tubuai, CBC 136 (Nov. 30, 1851).

36. Paul H. Peterson, "The Mormon Reformation of 1856–1857: The Rhetoric and the Reality," *Journal of Mormon History* 15 (1989): 69–72.

37. CBC, 431 (Sept. 26, 1856), and references to his work as a teacher on 431, 437, 439, 447, 452, 453, 459, 462, 463, 464, 467, 468, 474, 484 (Oct. 26, 1856–Sept. 25, 1857).

38. CBC, 413–15 (June 28, 1856).

39. NRS Minutes, 11 (Aug. 31, 1842); Z1, 9 (Oct. 26, 1844); Gary James Bergera, "Identifying the Earliest Mormon Polygamists, 1841–1844," *Dialogue: A Journal of Mormon*

Thought 38, no. 3 (Fall 2005): 5; *Journal of the House of Representatives of the State of Missouri* (Jefferson City: James Lusk, 1851), 65; *Frontier Guardian,* Aug. 8, 1851, 2; Roxsena Rachel Adams, Affidavits About Celestial Marriage, July 11, 1843, MS 3423, CHL. In 1860, she appears as "RR Patten," age fifty-five, living in Salt Lake City's Twelfth Ward (*Great Salt Lake City Ward 12, Great Salt Lake, Utah Territory,* Ancestry.com). In 1870, she was listed in Cottonwood, Salt Lake City, as "Roxana Adams," age sixty-nine.

40. CBC, 375, 384, 385 (Dec. 4, 1855; Jan. 15, 16, 1856).

41. CBC, 387, 392, 396, 397, 400, 406, 407, 410, 422, 426–27, 442, 451, 472, 474, 484 (Jan. 28, Feb. 26, March 18, 26, April 19, May 9, 25, June 8, 13, Sept. 29, Dec. 25, 1856; Feb. 11, June 19, July 1, 16, Sept. 6, 29, 1857).

42. CBC, 409–10, 453, 454, 461 (June 6, 1856; March 1, 10, April 16, 1857).

43. CBC, 465 (May 7, 1857).

44. CBC, 477–78 (July 17, 1857).

45. CBC, 413–15 (June 28, 1856); Lyman, *San Bernardino,* 15, 40, 90, 104, 113, 122, 147, 315–16, 332.

46. CBC, 413, 455, 461 (June 24, 1856; March 15, April 15, 1857); Lyman, *San Bernardino,* 287.

47. CBC, 502 (Dec. 10, 1857).

48. CBC, 376, 409, 410, 411 (Dec. 13, 1855; June 4, 6, 9, 12, 1856).

49. CBC, 288, 289, 290 (Oct. 19, 28, 30, 31, 1854); Lyman, *San Bernardino,* 135, 136, 267, 330, 407–8; *Los Angeles Star,* June 21, 1856, 2.

50. CBC, 498, 499 (Nov. 17, 18, 19–23, 1857).

51. CBC, 500 (Nov. 28, 29, 1857).

52. CBC, 501, 505 (Dec. 5, 21, 1857).

53. CBC, 506 (Dec. 25, 1857); "Cedar City Ward Relief Society, Minutes, September 20 and December 10, 1857, and March 11, 1858," *First Fifty Years,* 235, 235 n28, 236.

54. CBC, 89, 180, 258, 475 (June 1849; Feb. 7, 1853; May 1, 1854; July 4, 1857; CBC2, 829 (June 22, 1859).

55. CBC, 407 (May 23, 24, 25, 26, 27, 1856).

56. *Dear Ellen: Two Mormon Women and Their Letters,* ed S. George Ellsworth (Salt Lake City: University of Utah Library, 1974), 20.

57. Ellsworth, ed., *Dear Ellen,* 22–23; CBC, 454 (March 8, 1857).

58. Ellsworth, ed., *Dear Ellen,* 3, 5, 7, 10, 11, 14; CBC, 411, 422, 460, 472, 473, 488, 502 (June 25, Aug. 5, 1856; April 6, 9, June 19, 22, Sept. 20, Dec. 7, 1857); Lyman, *San Bernardino,* 267–68.

59. Ellsworth, ed., *Dear Ellen,* 23, 24.

60. The most detailed account of this event is William P. MacKinnon, "Sex, Subalterns, and Steptoe: Army Behavior, Mormon Rage, and Utah War Anxieties," *Utah Historical Quarterly* 76 (Summer 2008): 227–46; the Heber C. Kimball quote is on 239. I thank Bill MacKinnon and Polly Aird for helping me locate additional sources.

61. Mackinnon, "Sex, Subalterns, and Steptoe," quotes on 231–32.

62. *Mr. Hathornwaite's Adventures Among the Mormons as an Elder* (Manchester, England: For the Author, 1857), 12.

63. PGS, 259–60, 262 (March 25, 26, 1855); HS, 388, 512 (Jan. 19, 1852; April 9, 1854).

64. *Sacramento Daily Union,* July 13, 1855; Heber C. Kimball to William Kimball, May 29, 1855, Journal History of the Church, CHL, quoted in MacKinnon, "Sex, Subalterns, and Steptoe."

65. Ellsworth, ed., *Dear Ellen,* 23, 28; John S. Lindsay, *The Mormons and the Theatre: Or, The History of Theatricals in Utah, with Reminiscences and Comments Humorous and Critical* (Salt Lake City, 1905); for Broomhead and Wheelock biographies, see MOT.

66. Ellsworth, ed., *Dear Ellen,* 22, 23, 25.

67. Ellsworth, ed., *Dear Ellen,* 33.

68. Ellsworth, ed., *Dear Ellen,* 33.

69. Ellsworth, ed., *Dear Ellen,* 30, 31, 45.

70. Ellsworth, ed., *Dear Ellen,* 38, 39.

71. Ellsworth, ed., *Dear Ellen,* 41, 45.

72. Ellsworth, ed., *Dear Ellen,* 31, 34–35, 39, 40, 41.

73. CBC, 421, 424 (July 29, 30, Aug. 20, 1856).

74. CBC, 462–63, 464, 543 n7 (April 23, May 3, 1857).

75. CBC, 473, 475–77, 487 (June 28, July 4, 5, Sept. 12, 1857).

76. CBC, 507 (Dec. 27, 28, 29, 1857).

77. S. George Ellsworth, "Editor's Essay: His Last Years, 1851–1872," in *Journals of Addison Pratt,* ed. Ellsworth (Salt Lake City: University of Utah Press, 1990), 514–16.

78. CBC, 498 (Nov. 17, 1857); CBC2, 693 (Jan. 1, 1858).

79. CBC2, 697–98, 724 (Jan. 4–5, Feb. 23, 1858).

80. CBC2, 729, 736, 742, 788–89 (March 3, 7–8, April 3, Nov. 17–19, 1858).

14. "The house was full of females"

1. WW 5:20 (Feb. 11, 1857).

2. WW 4:235, 298, 377, 526 (end-of-decade and end-of-year summaries from 1834 to 1856). I can find no evidence in the diary that Wilford had ever attended a meeting of the Female Council of Health or the Female Relief Society. His comment about finding the "house full of females" suggests that at some level he found the gender imbalance novel.

3. WW 5:20, 25–26, 59–60 (Feb. 11, 21, June 17, 1857).

4. Benjamin G. Ferris, *Utah and the Mormons* (New York: Harper, 1854), 246, 249, 253, 257, 258.

5. "The Mormons: Shall Utah Be Admitted to the Union?," *Putnam's Monthly* 5, no. 27 (March 1855): 225–36. On the continuing use of racial tropes in attacking polygamy, see Nancy F. Cott, *Public Vows: A History of Marriage and the Nation* (Cambridge, Mass.: Harvard University Press, 2000), 73–76, 88–89, 92.

6. Metta Victoria Fuller Victor, *Mormon Wives: A Narrative of Facts Stranger Than Fiction* (New York: Derby and Jackson, 1856), 313; Bruce Burgett, "On the Mormon Question: Race, Sex, and Polygamy in the 1850s and the 1990s," *American Quarterly* 57 (March 2005): 87–90.

7. Maria Ward, *Female Life Among the Mormons* (London, 1855), 38, 9, 230, quoted in Terryl L. Givens, *Viper on the Hearth: Mormons, Myths, and the Construction of Heresy* (New York: Oxford University Press, 1997), 139, 140.

8. "Scenes in an American Harem," *Harper's Illustrated Weekly,* Oct. 10, 1857, 648–50.

9. William P. MacKinnon, "Sex, Subalterns, and Steptoe: Army Behavior, Mormon Rage, and Utah War Anxieties," *Utah Historical Quarterly* 76 (Summer 2008): 227–46; Laurel Thatcher Ulrich, "Runaway Wives, 1830–1870," *Journal of Mormon History* 42 (April 2016): 1–26.

10. Paul H. Peterson, "The Mormon Reformation of 1856–1857: The Rhetoric and the Reality," *Journal of Mormon History* 15 (1989): 59–87; Ronald W. Walker, Richard E. Turley Jr., and Glen M. Leonard, *Massacre at Mountain Meadows* (New York: Oxford University Press, 2008), 20–32.

11. WW 5:53–54, 58, 61, 69, 78–80, 88–95 (May 29–31, June 14, 23, July 24, Aug. 15–16, Sept. 5–12, 1857); HS, 627, 628, 634, 635–38 (May 29, June 14, 23, July 24, Aug. 13–Sept. 26, 1857); Gary Vitale, "Abraham Lincoln and the Mormons: Another Legacy of Limited Freedom," *Journal of the Illinois State Historical Society* 101 (2008): 264–67; Richard D. Poll and William P. MacKinnon, "Causes of the Utah War Reconsidered," *Journal of Mormon History* 20 (1994): 16–44. General accounts of the Utah War include Norman F. Furniss, *The Mormon Conflict 1850–1859* (New Haven: Yale University Press, 1960); Kenneth M. Stampp, *America in 1857: A Nation on the Brink* (New York: Oxford University Press, 1990); William P. MacKinnon, ed., *At Sword's Point, Part I: A Documentary History of the Utah*

War to 1858 (Norman: University of Oklahoma Press, 2008); Matthew J. Grow, *"Liberty to the Downtrodden": Thomas L. Kane, Romantic Reformer* (New Haven: Yale University Press, 2009).

12. *Deseret News,* Oct. 7, 21, 1857.

13. Sandi Fox, *For Purpose and Pleasure: Quilting Together in Nineteenth-Century America* (Nashville: Rutledge Hill, 1995), 34–42 (chintz cutouts), 45–47, 86, 87, 134, 138 (geometric), 26–28, 50–67 (red and green), 148, 152 (mixed). See also the many examples of mixed motifs and techniques in *A Flowering of Quilts,* ed. Patricia Cox Crews (Lincoln: University of Nebraska Press, 2001), 32–39, 46–49. Three squares worked in worsted yarn by Sarah Foss and her daughters employ motifs similar to those appearing on all-wool coverlets from the same period. See Carleton L. Safford and Robert Bishop, *America's Quilts and Coverlets* (New York: E. P. Dutton, 1980), 64–72; Laurel Thatcher Ulrich, *The Age of Homespun: Objects and Stories in the Creation of an American Myth* (New York: Alfred A. Knopf, 2001), 323–39.

14. Susan Curtis, "Blessed Be God for Flowers: Nineteenth-Century Quilt Design," in *Flowering of Quilts,* ed. Crews, 11–23.

15. Richard H. Jackson, "The City of Zion Plat," in *Mapping Mormonism: An Atlas of Latter-day Saint History,* ed. Brandon S. Plewe (Provo: Brigham Young University Press, 2012), 44–45; C. Mark Hamilton, *Nineteenth-Century Mormon Architecture and City Planning* (New York: Oxford University Press, 1995), 14–19, 25–28.

16. *New York Herald,* June 1858, quoted in Hamilton, *Nineteenth-Century Mormon Architecture,* 40.

17. Carol Holindrake Nielson, *The Salt Lake City 14th Ward Album Quilt, 1857: Stories of the Relief Society Women and Their Quilt* (Salt Lake City: University of Utah Press, 2004), 93. Because Catherine Church's square is stained, the inscription on the pot is too faded to show up well in a photograph. The full verse is in Isaiah 35:1, KJV.

18. *Deseret News,* Feb. 25, 1857, 408. See *Utah Folk Art,* ed. Hal Cannon (Provo: Brigham Young University Press, 1980), 87; Tammy Horn, *Bees in America: How the Bee Shaped a Nation* (Lexington: University Press of Kentucky, 2005), 56–57.

19. For Church's biography, see Nielson, *Album Quilt,* 91–93. Her husband's second wife was a woman much older than she who had no children of her own but helped raise Sarah Ann's.

20. WW 4:436–37 (Aug. 14, 15, 1856); WW 5:29, 31, 32, 47, 67 (March 3, 9, 10, 11, 12, 14, April 14, July 7, 1857).

21. Mrs. J. Cain's square, in Nielson, *Album Quilt,* 85. In her diary for March 1, 1857, Zina D. H. Young mentions using a sewing machine in the Lion House. On the spread of machine sewing beginning in the 1860s, see Audrey M. Godfrey, " 'The Queen of Inventions': The Sewing Machine Comes to Utah," *Journal of Mormon History* 32 (Fall 2006): 82–103.

22. Dean May, "A Demographic Portrait of the Mormons, 1830–1980," in *The New Mormon History,* ed. D. Michael Quinn (Salt Lake City: Signature Books, 1992), 126. According to the 1860 census, 13.7 percent of the inhabitants of the United States in that year were foreign-born. The figure for Utah is 31.7 percent. (Campbell J. Gibson and Emily Lennon, "Historical Census Statistics on the Foreign-Born Population of the United States: 1850–1990," U.S. Bureau of the Census, Population Division Working Paper no. 29 (Feb. 1999), www.census.gov/population.

23. Nielson, *Album Quilt,* 156–58. The published edition of Pratt's biography acknowledges her presence on this mission but gives few details (*Autobiography of Parley P. Pratt,* ed. Parley P. Pratt Jr., 5th ed. [Salt Lake City: Deseret Book, 1961], 386–93).

24. Nielson, *Album Quilt,* 98–100.

25. Nielson, *Album Quilt,* 64–67; Ardis E. Parshall, "Josephine Marie Augustine de la Harpe Ludert Ursenbach," www.keeppitchinin.org.

26. Nielson, *Album Quilt,* 95, 153–54, 182–83.

27. "Nationality," ERS *Poetry,* 488–89.

28. William Bright, *Native American Place Names in the United States* (Norman: University of Oklahoma Press, 2004), 369, 370, 419, 507, 541, 549. For Wilford Woodruff's mastery of unfamiliar places on his journey south with Brigham Young, see WW 4:20–27, 318–28 (March 23–May 24, 1851; May 9–28, 1855).

29. LeRoy Hafen and Ann W. Hafen, *Handcarts to Zion: The Story of a Unique Western Migration, 1856–1860* (1960; Lincoln: University of Nebraska Press, 1992), 166–67; Robert F. Neslen Company, 1859, MOT; D. Clyde Lloyd, "You Are an Ancestor!," mimeographed booklet on the Henry Hugh Harries and Mary Rees family in my possession. Part of the company traveled the rest of the way by handcart. The Harrieses, who paid for their own ticket, were in a wagon train. Henry may have been chosen as an assistant to the company leader because he had been to Utah earlier. He was now returning from a mission to his native Wales.

30. Larry W. Draper, "A Demographic Examination of Household Heads in Salt Lake City, Utah, 1850–1870" (M.A. thesis, Department of History, Brigham Young University, 1988), 27–36.

31. Maureen Ursenbach Beecher, *Eliza and Her Sisters* (Salt Lake City: Aspen Books, 1991), 109–12, 116; Leonard Reed, "'As a Bird Sings': Hannah Tapfield King, Poetess and Pioneer," *BYU Studies* 51 (2012): 110.

32. *Deseret News,* Jan. 28, May 20, Aug. 5, 1857; Arrington, *Great Basin,* 109, and, on the collection and disbursement of the Perpetual Emigrating Fund, 97–108.

33. *Doctrine and Covenants,* 42: 30–36; Leonard Arrington, *Great Basin,* 7–9, 145–48; PS, 203, 229 (April 21, 1854; Feb. 25, 1856).

34. Book of Mormon, Ether 2:3; Ann Fairfax Withington, "Republican Bees: The Political Economy of the Beehive in Eighteenth-Century America," *Studies in Eighteenth-Century Culture* 18 (1988): 39–77; Jill Mulvay Derr, "'I have Eaten Nearly Everything Imaginable': Pioneer Diet," in *Nearly Everything Imaginable: The Everyday Life of Utah's Mormon Pioneers,* ed. Ronald W. Walker and Doris R. Dant (Provo, Utah: Brigham Young University Press, 1999), 230–32; Arrington, *Great Basin,* 116–20; Arrington, *BY,* 184–85; "A New Sugar Culture," *Deseret News,* Sept. 24, 1856, 3; "A New Plant," *Deseret News,* Feb. 4, 1857, 8; "Message from the Governor," *Deseret News,* Dec. 23, 1857; Rickey Lynn Hendricks, "Landmark Architecture for a Polygamous Family: The Brigham Young Domicile, Salt Lake City, Utah," *Public Historian* 11 (Winter 1989): 25–47; Colleen Whitley, *Brigham Young's Homes* (Logan: Utah State University Press, 2002), 100, 124; Judith M. Jacob, *The Washington Monument: A Technical History and Catalog of the Commemorative Stones* (Lowell, Mass.: National Park Service, U.S. Department of the Interior Northeast Region, 2005), 153–54. See also Hal Cannon, *The Grand Beehive* (Salt Lake City: University of Utah Press, 1980); Marilyn Conover Barker, *The Legacy of Mormon Furniture* (Salt Lake City: Gibbs Smith, 1995), 58, 59; Grow, *"Liberty to the Downtrodden,"* 68.

35. Joseph Cain, "The Bee," *Deseret News,* Jan. 25, 1851, 1; Michael Hicks, *Mormonism and Music: A History* (Urbana and Chicago: University of Illinois Press, 1989), 59–60, 65.

36. Born in Chestershire, England, in 1812, she was baptized by Parley P. Pratt in 1842, then married him shortly after arriving in Salt Lake City. The fabric she used, which came in different colorways, may have been manufactured in England for the American market. See Linda Eaton, *Quilts in a Material World: Selections from the Winterthur Collection* (New York: Harry N. Abrams, 2007), 160, 161; e-mail communication from Linda Eaton, July 23, 2009. On other uses of the American eagle, see Eaton, *Quilts,* 93, 109; on politics in quilts, Eaton, *Quilts,* chapter 6. For recent sales of artifacts made from the same fabric, see "Garth's Auction," www.prices4antiques.com/; "Auction Fall 2006" at www.cowanauctions.com, found on Google search, July 18, 2009.

37. Nielson, *Album Quilt,* 95–97. On eagle designs, see Celia Y. Oliver, *55 Famous Quilts from the Shelburne Museum* (New York: Dover, 1990), 46; Amelia Peck, *American Quilts & Coverlets in the Metropolitan Museum of Art* (New York: Dutton, 1990), 48–49; Pat Ferraro, Elaine Hedges, and Julie Silber, *Hearts and Hands: The Influence of Quilts in*

American Society (San Francisco: Quilt Digest Press, 1987), 20. See also variants in the eagle motif from the 1830s to the present by searching The Quilt Index, www.quiltindex.org.

38. ERS *Poetry*, 85; *Deseret News*, Aug. 3, 1850, 3, 5. Snow used the same image again in "The Fourth of July 1861" and "National Anthem, for the Opening of the Theater in Great Salt Lake City," ERS *Poetry*, 674, 631.

39. Bathsheba Smith to George Smith, March 18, 1854, BWS Letters.

40. Margaret Smoot to Abraham Smoot, May, June, Aug. 1856, MTS Letters.

41. Bathsheba Smith to George Smith, Jan. 6, 1856, BWS Letters. The words were not original. The entire song appears under the name G. Linnaus Banks in the *Millennial Star*, Dec. 3, 1853, 799. In *Broadside Ballads Online from the Bodleian Libraries*, ballads.boddleian .ox.ac.uk, the song appears without a composer's name or date.

42. Phebe Woodruff to Wilford Woodruff, Jan. 9, 1856, WW Corr.

43. Margaret Smoot to Abraham Smoot, May, June, Aug. 1856, MTS Letters.

44. Bathsheba Smith to George Smith, March 18, 1854, BWS Letters; WW 4:256 (March 14, 18, 1854).

45. Bathsheba Smith to George Smith, Dec. 26, 1855, BWS Letters.

46. WW 4:396 (Jan. 21, 1856).

47. Givens and Grow, 361–64, 366; Breck England, *The Life and Thought of Orson Pratt* (Salt Lake City: University of Utah Press, 1985), 195; HS, 576 (Dec. 25, 1855).

48. Bathsheba Smith to George A. Smith, Dec. 26, 1855, BWS Letters.

49. Phebe Woodruff to Wilford Woodruff, Jan. 2, 1856, WW Corr.

50. Phebe Woodruff to Wilford Woodruff, Jan. 2, 1856.

51. WW 4:333 (Aug. 1, 1855); Nielson, *Album Quilt*, 75–79; "Seth M. Blair," U.S. Attorney's Office, Utah District, www.justice.gov; Seth Millington Blair, FamilySearch .org; Harriet Ann Goodridge Hardy, findagrave.com.

52. Phebe Woodruff to Wilford Woodruff, Jan. 9, 1856, WW Corr.

53. Mary Richards to Samuel Richards, Dec. 26, 1855, MPR Letters.

54. Mary Richards to Samuel Richards, Dec. 31, 1855, MPR Letters.

55. MPR, 40, 41; SW 18, 21 (Aug. 20, 25, 1856). Wilford did not mention attending the Richards sealing.

56. WW 4:324, 366, 373, 305, 407 (May 21, Dec. 15, 18, Feb. 11, 1855; March 17, 18, 1857).

57. Susan and Beulah Woodruff to Wilford Woodruff, May 22, 1856, WW Corr; WW 5:21 (March 21, 1857).

58. In Jan. 1857, Brigham gave him permission to marry "Lydia Maxline." Perhaps the name was a pseudonym; no one has been able to find such a person in local records. See WW 5:11, 27, 70 (Jan. 23, Feb. 16, July 31, 1857).

59. Nielson, *Album Quilt*, 57; WW 5:22, 58 (Feb. 14, June 14, 1857); Alexander, *Woodruff*, 186.

60. WW 4:258 (April 4, 1854); WW 5:9, 104–5 (Jan. 18, Sept. 30–Oct. 4, 1857)

61. Preston Woolley Parkinson, *The Utah Woolley Family* (Salt Lake City: Privately published, 1967), 113, 116.

62. SW, 49 (Oct. 12, 1856).

63. SW, 78 (Dec 1, 1856).

64. SW, 20, 25, 27, 31, 43, 54, 55, 56 (Aug. 24, 31, Sept. 8, 14, 29, Oct 22, 23, 1856).

65. "History and Journal of Abraham Hoagland," 3, available as PDF file on George Q. Cannon Family website, www.georgeqcannon.com.

66. WW 5:11 (Jan. 22, 1857).

67. WW 5:41–43 (March 23, 1857).

68. Nielson, *Album Quilt*, 187–93; WW 3: 268 (Sept. 7, 1847); *The Pioneer Camp of the Saints: The 1846 and 1847 Mormon Trail Journals of Thomas Bullock*, ed. Will Bagley (Spokane, Wash.: Arthur H. Clark, 1997), 280, 282; Turner, *BY*, 241. See also "Abraham Lucas Hoagland 1," www.georgeqcannon.com/; Catherine Rich South Spencer, "Elizabeth Taylor Rich South," Nov. 1937, allenhackworth.com; Abraham Hoagland and Samuel Taylor Rich files, FamilySearch.org. The 1850 Salt Lake City census lists "Agnes Taylor" in the

Hoagland household along with children John (age ten), Elisabeth (age eight), Samuel (age seven), Abraham (age five), and Agnes (age one) (Ancestry.com). The first three are presumably her children by her first husband, John Rich.

69. WW 5:7 (Jan. 11, 1857).

70. WW 5:42, 43 (March 23, 1857).

71. Nielson, *Album Quilt*, 188. The other women were Ann Carrigan (Nielson, *Album Quilt*, 89), Mary Emma Hill (104–5), E. A. Hoagland (193), Elizabeth Horne (115), Matilda Rhoads (163), Josephine Richards (60), and Hannah Winder (143–44).

72. WW 5:61 (June 23, 1857); "Obituary," *New York Herald*, May 27, 1857, 4; "Another Startling Tragedy," *New York Herald*, May 28, 1857, 8. Reports of the story appeared in many newspapers, including the *Daily Chronicle & Sentinel* (Augusta, Ga.), May 29, 1857; *Frank Leslie's Illustrated Newspaper* (New York), June 6, 1857, 3; *Daily Evening Bulletin* (San Francisco), July 1, 1857. The most detailed secondary accounts are Steven Pratt, "Eleanor McLean and the Murder of Parley P. Pratt," *BYU Studies* 15 (1975): 1–27; Givens and Grow, 366–91.

73. *Daily Evening Bulletin,* July 1, 1857.

74. May 16, 1857, reprinted in *New York Herald,* May 28, 1857, 8.

75. *New York Herald*, June 9, 1857, 2.

76. Eleanor J. McComb [McLean Pratt], Account of the Death of Parley P. Pratt, ca. 1857, CHL, 7–9.

77. McComb, 12–15.

78. McComb, 17, 18.

79. This dating of the quilt is reinforced by the presence of a square by Sarah Delight Woodruff, who wasn't married until July 28 and therefore could not have signed as a "Woodruff" before then (WW 5:70 [July 28, 1857]).

80. *WW* 5:69, 74, 75–80; Harriet Ann Thatcher to William B. Preston, Aug. 5, 1857, William B. Preston Papers, Special Collections, Utah State University Library, Logan, Utah; Nielson, *Album Quilt*, 75, 128. When Brigham Young called on California Saints to return to the valley because of the impending war, Hezekiah Thatcher led a small company from northern California, merging with a group assembled by Perrigrine Sessions before crossing the mountains. Two of the Thatcher sons, Aaron and Moses, remained behind with Harriet's fiancé, William Preston, to serve missions before joining the others in Utah.

81. John Taylor, "The Rights of Mormonism . . . Delivered in the Bowery, Great Salt Lake City, August 30, 1857," *Journal of Discourses* 5 (1858): 182–92.

82. Nielson, *Album Quilt,* 33.

83. WW 5:104 (Sept. 30, 1857).

84. *Deseret News,* Oct. 21, 1857, 8.

85. WW 5:102–10 (Sept. 28–Oct. 18, 1857).

86. ERS *Poetry,* 556–57.

87. *The Genteel Gentile: Letters of Elizabeth Cumming, 1857–1858,* ed. Ray R. Canning and Beverly Beeton (Salt Lake City: University of Utah Library, 1977), 13–18, 20–23, 33–35; Grow, *"Liberty to the Downtrodden,"* 174–76.

88. WW 5:102–3 (Sept. 29, 1857). Major secondary works on the Mountain Meadows Massacre include Juanita Brooks, *The Mountain Meadow Massacre* (1950; Norman: University of Oklahoma Press, 1961); Will Bagley, *Blood of the Prophets: Brigham Young and the Massacre at Mountain Meadows* (Norman: University of Oklahoma Press, 2002); Ronald W. Walker, Richard E. Turley Jr., and Glen M. Leonard, *Massacre at Mountain Meadows* (New York: Oxford University Press, 2008). See also Turner, *BY,* 275–80.

89. Cedar City Ward, Parowan Stake, Relief Society Minute Book, 6, 8–11, CHL.

90. Walker, Turley, and Leonard, *Massacre,* 257, 258, 261, 199.

91. Cedar City Minute Book, 10, 11. Walker, Turley, and Leonard, *Massacre,* 134, 135, 217–19.

92. CBC, 490, 491, 492, 493 (Sept. 30, Oct. 6, 17, 1857); "Horrible Atrocities in India," *Los Angeles Star,* Oct. 10, 1857; "Public Meeting," *Los Angeles Star,* Oct. 17, 1857.

93. Walker, Turley, and Leonard, *Massacre*, 167, 263, 401 n59.

94. The Utah and East Indian massacres have also provoked similar floods of apologetics and interpretations. See, for example, Barbara English, "The Kanpeer Massacres in India in the Revolt of 1857," with a reply by Rudrangshu Mukherjee, *Past and Present* 142 (1994): 169–89.

95. CBC2, 699, 707, 710–14, 720, 723 (Jan. 8, 18–29, Feb. 22, 1858).

96. CBC2, 708–11 (Feb. 1–16, 1858).

97. CBC2, 733, 742 (March 7–8, April 3, 1858); Edward Leo Lyman, *The Overland Journey from Utah to California* (Reno: University of Nevada Press, 2004), 180–81; Walker, Turley, and Leonard, *Massacre,* 259. When Joel Johnson returned to Utah in 1860, he brought a new wife with him, a twenty-year-old Scandinavian woman he seems to have met on the trail. See Joel Hills Johnson, Susan Bryant Johnson, Margaret Threlkeld Johnson, findagrave.com; MOT.

98. CBC2, 760 (June 18, 1858); Walker, Turley, and Leonard, *Massacre,* 257.

99. Richard Poll, "The Move South," *BYU Studies* 29 (Fall 1989): 65–88.

100. Little by little, he managed to move his family to Salt Creek in Juab County, and then, in mid-July, began the arduous labor of bringing them back (HS, 656–61 [April 16–July 23, 1858]).

101. WW 5:179–81; 193–94 (March 30–April 8, May 28–June 1, 1858).

102. PS, 254–56 (April 5, May 9, 13, 17, 24, 26, 29, 1858). There is no entry in Patty's diary for May 29, 1853, but she must have attended Susanna's birthday party that day.

103. Poll, "Move South," 82.

104. MEK, July 22, 1858.

105. CBC2, 762 (July 1, 1858).

15. "The records of this House"

1. MTS, opening page; CBC, May 1, 1864; MEK, May 19, 1862.

2. PS, 343, 346–47 (March 14, 1855; Sept. 3, 1867; Jan. 13, 23, June 20, 22, 1868).

3. "Remarks by President Brigham Young, Made in the Old Tabernacle, G.S.L. City, Sunday December 8th, 1867," *Deseret News,* Dec. 14, 1867; "Female Relief Societies," *Deseret News,* Dec. 10, 1867; WW 6:309 (Dec. 26, 1866); SW, Dec. 5, 1867; Feb. 4, 11, 1868.

4. See Jill Mulvay Derr, Janath Russell Cannon, and Maureen Ursenbach Beecher, *Women of Covenant: The Story of Relief Society* (Salt Lake City: Deseret Book, 1992), 78–82. Arrington, *Woolley,* 337–38, 369, mentions the Relief Society among other things disrupted by the war, but also suggests there wasn't much interest in the Relief Society in the Thirteenth Ward in the 1850s. The most detailed discussion of the hiatus as an unsolved problem is in Richard Jensen, "Clothing the Indians and Strengthening the Saints: Organized Activity of Mormon Women During the 'Lapse' of the Relief Society, 1844–1867," *Task Papers in LDS History,* no. 27.

5. Arrington, *Great Basin,* 195.

6. "Dedication Hymn," ERS *Poetry,* 796.

7. Arrington, *Great Basin,* 196–99.

8. Lucy Smith to GA Smith, July 31, 1861; Feb. 30, 1862; Jan. 17, 186[3?], LMS Letters.

9. CBC2, 782, 821, 842, 876, 951, 963, 969 (Oct. 19, 1858; May 7, Sept. 14, 1859; Dec. 11, 13, 17, 1861; March 10, May 12, 13, 16, 17, 20, 21, 22, 23, 1862).

10. Arrington, *Great Basin,* 216–22; CBC2, 947–49, 965, 990, 992 (Nov. 10, 15, 20, 23, 24, April 3, May 27, 1862; March 9, 23, 26, 29, 31, April 1, 4, 1863; May 1, 1864).

11. PS, 269, 273–74, 275 (Sept. 5, 1859; Feb. 6, 11, 14, 22, 24, 25, 27, 28, March 2, 3, 15, 16, 17, May 5, 25, 1860). Spinning, weaving, dyeing, sewing, and knitting are ubiquitous in Patty's diary. Almost any page from 1859 to 1866 offers examples.

12. PS, 302, 303 (Oct. 17, Nov. 20, 21, Dec. 19, 1862; Sept. 10, 11, 12, 13, 17, 18, 1863).

13. Wilma Gooch Marriott, "Anna Serena Anderson Folkman," typescript, Interna-

tional Society, Daughters of the Utah Pioneers, Pioneer Memorial Museum, Salt Lake City. In 1861, Sorine or Serena became the third wife of Jeppe Folkman, a Danish immigrant who had already acquired a farm in Plain City.

14. MTS, April 19, May 13, Aug. 4–5, 11, Sept. 6, 11, 30, Oct. 1, Nov. 7, 1856.

15. In the spring of 1864, he took his daughter Susan and his Indian boy Saroquetes to Weber Canyon to shear 154 sheep, bringing the wool back to the city for the family to process. By the end of the decade, his wives were settled on different parts of his property, Sarah, the oldest, eventually moving to Bear Lake and then Cache Valley. See WW 5:336 (May 17–18, 1859); WW 6:49, 66, 167–68 (June 28, July 16, 1862; May 9–12, 1864; June 13, 27, Sept. 9, 1864; Aug. 29, 30, 1865; Sept. 17–23, 1866). See also Arrington, *Great Basin,* 205.

16. MEK, May 20, 1863.

17. WW 5:243–44, 341, 471, 493–94; WW 6:7, 9, 17, 95, 122, 135, 198, 266, 335–36, 416–17, 498, 518, 582–83.

18. Lowell C. Bennion and Thomas R. Carter, "Touring Polygamous Utah with Elizabeth W. Kane, Winter 1872–1873," in *Colonel Thomas L. Kane and the Mormons, 1846–1883,* ed. David J. Whittaker (Provo and Salt Lake City: BYU Studies and University of Utah Press, 2010), 179–80. See also Lowell C. Bennion, "Plural Marriage, 1841–1904," in *Mapping Mormonism: An Atlas of Latter-day Saint History,* ed. Brandon S. Plewe (Provo, Utah: Brigham Young University Press, 2012), 122.

19. ERS *Poetry,* 766–68. Eliza Snow composed poems for the July holidays in 1860, 1861, 1862, 1864, 1867, and 1868.

20. WW 5:609–11, 614 (Dec. 24, 1861).

21. WW 6:163 (April 3, 1864).

22. Carol Holindrake Nielson, *The Salt Lake City 14th Ward Album Quilt, 1857: Stories of the Relief Society Women and Their Quilt* (Salt Lake City: University of Utah Press, 2004), 7–9.

23. CBC2, 927, 928, 977, 978 (June 2, 3, 1861; Aug. 7, 10, 1862).

24. PS, 345 (Aug. 23, 1859; May 16, 1862); Arrington, *Great Basin,* 205–11; Melvin Bashore, "'Where the Prophets of God Live': A Brief Overview of the Mormon Trail Experience," BYU Digital Collections, overlandtrails.lib.byu.edu; Daniel Robison Company List, 1860, MOT; Turner, Charles, to J[ames] Cowper Wife & Family, July 1, 1861, in *Thomas Alfred and Elizabeth Cowper Jeffery Family History,* 874, MOT.

25. MTS, July 13, 1856.

26. PS, 337 (Dec. 8, 1866).

27. PS, 301, 309, 312 (Sept. 16, 1862; July 21, Nov. 28–Dec. 8, 1863).

28. PS, 302 (Oct. 18, 1862).

29. WW 5:392–94 (Oct. 20–Nov. 6, 1859).

30. WW 5:251–52 (Dec. 6–9, 1858).

31. WW 5:493–94 (Sept. 4–6, 1860).

32. CBC2, 855, 906, 907, 912 (Dec. 13, 1859; Jan. 6, 11, 16, Feb. 10, 1861). On Neyman's testimony about early baptisms for the dead, see Chapter 12. Her daughter Rachel, also a frequent visitor to the Crosby house, was a plural wife of Sidney Tanner, who had been one of their associates in San Bernardino.

33. MEK, March 1, 2, 1857. Linda Newell, in "Gifts of the Spirit: Women's Share," in *Sisters in Spirit: Mormon Women in Historical and Cultural Perspective,* ed. Maureen Ursenbach Beecher and Lavina Fielding Anderson (Urbana and Chicago: University of Illinois Press, 1987), 118–19, observed that Heber's assurance was the kind of argument that calmed women's apprehensions for decades.

34. Ronald W. Walker, *Wayward Saints: The Godbeites and Brigham Young* (Urbana and Chicago: University of Illinois Press, 1998), 118.

35. MEK, Oct. 5, Dec. 19, 1858; March 20, Sept. n.d., Oct. 27, 1859; July 1, 1861.

36. CBC2, 745 (April 18, 1858).

37. Z3, March 23, 1857.

38. MTS, June 16, Aug. 10, 16, 1856; July 9, 17, 18, 1857; Feb. 19, 20, 21, 23, March 25, 1859; April 14, 25, 1860.

39. James B. Allen, *Trials of Discipleship: The Story of William Clayton, a Mormon* (Urbana and Chicago: University of Illinois Press, 1987), 312, 313; WW 6:49, 53, 71 (June 1, 10, Aug. 23, 1862, and end-of-year summaries); WW 6:86, 144, 202, 268, 312, 384, 445, 514. Over this period, he administered endowments for almost five thousand persons. He spent ten days in the endowment house in 1860, forty-five in 1861, and sixty in 1862. Over the twelve-year period from 1857 to 1870, he averaged thirty-four days per year.

40. ERS3, 32; PS, 268, 269, 309 (Aug. 24, Sept. 14, 1859; Aug. 6, 1863); Z3, April 22, 1859. In a memoir, Lucy Meserve Smith listed "temple suits" among the textiles she manufactured during these years (Historical Record of Lucy M. Smith, Special Collections, University of Utah Library, Salt Lake City).

41. CBC2, 776, 848 (Sept. 10, 11, 1858; Oct. 13, 1859).

42. ERS3, 35.

43. Jill Mulvay Derr and Carol Cornwall Madsen, "Preserving the Record and Memory of the Female Relief Society of Nauvoo, 1842–92," *Journal of Mormon History* 35 (Summer 2009): 88–117; Fillmore Relief Society Minutes, June 16, 1868, 1, 1868–1877, CHL.

44. "Auto-biography," *Woman's Exponent* 12 (Sept. 1, 1883): 51.

45. Others had of course faced the problem of how to secure their eternal salvation while married to a man who was a non-Mormon, a disaffected Mormon, or a good man who seemed like the wrong eternal companion. Zina Huntington and her sister Presendia had faced this problem during Joseph's lifetime. Amanda Smith and Augusta Cobb dealt with it later, as did Hannah Tapfield King, the English poet who became Sarah's and Eliza's ally in rebuilding the Relief Society. See Leonard Reed, " 'As a Bird Sings': Hannah Tapfield King, Poetess and Pioneer," *BYU Studies* 51 (2012): 113–14, 118 n35, n36; Amanda Smith to Brigham Young, Brigham Young Office Files, 1234 1, box 66, folder 22, CHL; Hulda Cordelia Thurston Smith, "O My Children and Grandchildren,"*Nauvoo Journal* 4, no. 2 (Fall 1992): 5–8; Turner, *BY*, 238; Hales, *Polygamy*, 2:277 n22.

46. Sarah M. Kimball to Brigham Young, May 21, 1858, CR 1234 1, box 64, folder 6, CHL.

47. Sarah M. Kimball to Brigham Young, May 21, 1858.

48. WW 6:103 (March 1, 1863); "Horrible Explosion," *Deseret News,* May 6, 1863; "Auto-biography," *Woman's Exponent* 12 (Sept. 1, 1883): 51; Hiram S. Kimball, Reference: People, JSP.

49. Fifteenth Ward Relief Society Minutes, March 19, 1868, CHL.

50. Sarah M. Kimball and Eliza R. Snow, "Duty of Officers," Fifteenth Ward Relief Society Minutes, 1868–1869, CHL.

51. Carolyn Butler-Palmer, "Building Autonomy: A History of the Fifteenth Ward Hall of the Mormon Women's Relief Society," *Buildings and Landscapes* 29 (Spring 2013): 72–78.

52. "Address Delivered at the Laying of the Cornerstone of the Storehouse by President S. M. Kimball," Fifteenth Ward Relief Society Minutes, Nov. 12, 1868, CHL; "Auto-Biography," *Woman's Exponent* 12 (Sept. 1, 1883): 51, reprinted in Janelle M. Higbee, " 'President Mrs. Kimball': A Rhetoric of Words," M.A. thesis, English Department, Brigham Young University, 1998, 147, 154, and see 122–28; Jill Mulvay Derr, "The Liberal Shall Be Blessed: Sarah M. Kimball," *Utah Historical Quarterly* 44 (1976): 205–21, reprinted at signaturebookslibrary.org; Virginia M. Pearce, "In Blessing Others We Are Blessed," in *Women of Faith in the Latter Days*, ed. Richard E. Turley Jr. and Brittany A. Chapman (Salt Lake City: Deseret Book, 2011), vol. 1, 115–29.

53. "Address at Laying of Cornerstone by President Kimball."

54. Brigham Young, "An Address to the Female Relief Society," *Deseret News,* Feb. 24, 1869.

55. Brigham Young, "Address to the Female Relief Society."

56. "Secretary's Annual Report," Feb. 4, 1869, Fifteenth Ward Relief Society Minutes and Records, 1868–69, CHL; Fillmore Relief Society Minutes, June 16, 1868, 1, 1868–1877, CHL.

57. Roger D. Launius, *Joseph Smith III: Pragmatic Prophet* (Urbana and Chicago: University of Illinois Press), 90–92, 97–112, 200–209; Newell and Avery, *Mormon Enigma,* 271–74, 282–87; Ronald E. Romig, "Alexander H. Smith: Remembering a Son of Joseph and Emma Smith," *Journal of Mormon History* 37, no. 2 (Spring 2011): 13–16, 18–25; Steven L. Shields, "The Early Community of Christ Mission to 'Redeem' the Church in Utah," *Journal of Mormon History* 40 (2014): 158–61.

58. Quoted in Newell and Avery, *Mormon Enigma,* 284.

59. Affidavits CM. The box in which these affidavits are kept contained both bound volumes and loose sheets dated from 1869 to 1904. For more on the contents and origins of these documents, see Hales, *Polygamy,* 1:356–60, 2:343–45.

60. Affidavits CM, 1:25.

61. Not everyone gave a date. On discrepancies in people's recollections of these Nauvoo marriages, see Gary James Bergera, "Memory as Evidence: Dating Joseph Smith's Plural Marriages to Louisa Beaman, Zina Jacobs, and Presendia Buell," *Journal of Mormon History* 41, no. 4 (2015): 95–131.

62. WW 6:305, 439, 450, 456, 460, 470–71, 478, 501, 583 (April 29, Nov. 23, 1868; Jan. 15, Feb. 14, April 6, May 5, June 9, Oct. 28, 1869; Dec. 16, 1870); Jennifer Reeder, "'To Do Something Extraordinary': Mormon Women and the Creation of a Usable Past" (Ph.D. diss., George Mason University, 2013), 188.

63. WW 6:521–22 (Jan. 6, 13, 14, 15, 1870).

64. WW 6:517, 518–19 (Jan. 13, 1870).

65. Minutes of a Ladies Mass meeting, Jan. 6, 1870, in Relief Society Minutes and Records, vol. 1, 1868–1873, Fifteenth Ward, Salt Lake Stake, CHL.

66. WW 6:523–27 (Jan. 20, 24, 26, 28, 29, 30, Feb. 1, 2, 7, 1870).

67. Minutes of the 2nd Meeting of the Ladies Cooprative Retrenchment Society, Feb. 19, 1870, Relief Society Minutes and Records, 1868–1873, Fifteenth Ward, CHL.

68. Minutes of the 2nd Meeting of the Ladies Cooperative Retrenchment Society.

69. Minutes of the 2nd Meeting of the Ladies Cooperative Retrenchment Society.

70. "Indignation Meetings in the Settlements," *Deseret News,* Feb, 2, 1870, 1; "The Ladies Mass Meetings—Their True Significance," *Deseret News,* March 9, 1870.

71. The argument for polygamy as a solution to prostitution was presented, perhaps sardonically, in *Telyphthora, or, a treatise on female ruin, in its causes, effects, consequences, prevention, and remedy* (London: J. Dodsley, 1781), a work attributed to a Martin Madan, a Methodist minister who was trustee of a London hospital. In 1859, Samuel Richards presented Brigham Young with a copy of this book that he had apparently purchased while serving as mission president in England. The book with Richards's inscription and some other notes is at the CHL.

72. Walker, *Wayward Saints,* 136–38, 252, 325–30.

73. Walker, *Wayward Saints,* 52–58; Linda Wilcox DeSimone, ed., *Expose of Polygamy: A Lady's Life Among the Mormons* (Logan: Utah State University Press, 2008), 100–105, 134–35, 188–89 n1, nn4–6; 191 n4; Bradley and Woodward, 247–71.

74. On the complex relationship between New Movement women and their orthodox counterparts in Utah during this period, see Lola Van Wagenen, *Sister-Wives and Suffragists: Polygamy and the Politics of Woman Suffrage 1870–1896* (Provo, Utah: Joseph Fielding Smith Institute and BYU Studies, 2003); Beverly Beeton, "A Feminist Among the Mormons: Charlotte Ives Cobb Godbe Kirby," and Joan Iversen, "The Mormon-Suffrage Relationship: Personal and Political Quandaries," in *Battle for the Ballot: Essays on Woman Suffrage in Utah, 1870–1896,* ed. Carol Cornwall Madsen (Logan: Utah State University Press, 1997), 137–72; Walker, *Wayward Saints,* 136–38, 252, 325–30; Carol Cornwall Madsen, *An Advocate for Women: The Public Life of Emmeline B. Wells, 1870–1920* (Provo, Utah: Brigham Young University Press, 2006), 126–34.

75. Elizabeth Cady Stanton, "Overland Letters," *Revolution* 8 (July 13, 1871): 1, 2.

76. Walker, *Wayward Saints,* 274–79.

77. On the publication history of Stenhouse's memoir and a comparison between the 1872 and 1874 versions, see DeSimone, ed., *Expose of Polygamy,* 1–21, 168–78.

78. The *Exponent* assumed even greater potency in 1879, when its editor, Emmeline Wells, edged out Charlotte Godbe to became Utah's representative to the National Woman's Suffrage Association. Taking Zina Presendia with her to Washington, she had an audience with President Rutherford B. Hayes and presented his wife with a copy of *The Women of Mormondom,* a biographical compendium that practically deified Mormondom's female leaders. Although Lucy Hayes was cordial, she retained her anti-polygamy sentiments. Van Wagenen, *Sister-Wives and Suffragists,* 50–65; Madsen, *Advocate for Women,* 148–91. On the complex relationship between Charlotte Godbe and other women once affiliated with the dissenting movement, see Beeton, "Feminist Among the Mormons," and Iversen, "Mormon-Suffrage Relationship," 137–72; Walker, *Wayward Saints,* 136–38, 252, 325–30; Madsen, *Advocate for Women,* 126–34.

79. Bathsheba W. Smith to Editor, *Woman's Journal,* March 5, March 21, 1872, Church Historian's Office Letterpress Copybooks, 1854–1879, CHL; Van Wagenen, *Sister-Wives and Suffragists,* 32–35.

80. H.B.B., "Utah as a State," *Woman's Journal* 3 (May 4, 1872): 140. The *Woman's Journal* attempted to balance Mormon and non-Mormon accounts, as in "Practical Results of Woman Suffrage," *Woman's Journal* 2, no. 16 (1871): 125; "The 'Enslaved' Women of Utah," *Woman's Journal* 3, no. 32 (1872): 254–55; H.B.B, "Woman Suffrage in Utah," *Woman's Journal* 3, no. 27 (1872): 216. H.B.B. praised the establishment of the *Woman's Exponent.*

81. For the specific provisions, see Utah Commission: Agency History, #1249, Division of Archives & Records Services, archives.utah.gov. For an overview of attempts by Utah leaders to conciliate congressional concerns, see Howard R. Lamar, "Statehood for Utah: A Different Path," *Utah Historical Quarterly* 39 (Fall 1971): 307–27. Lamar notes on 317 that the Edmunds Act could not have been passed without lobbying by Protestant churches and the national religious press, concluding, "The coalition of churches and government to achieve separation of church and state in Utah again demonstrates what a limited and ambivalent meaning 'separation' had for most Americans."

82. "Preamble and Resolutions of the Women of Utah in Mass Meeting Assembled," 1886, in *First Fifty Years,* 520, 523, 524, 525.

83. WW 9:16, 112–16 (April 6–7, 1889; Sept. 25, 1890); Alexander, *Woodruff,* 250–59.

84. "States Grant Women the Right to Vote," National Constitution Center–Centuries of Citizenship, constitutioncenter.org; Jean Bickmore White, "Gentle Persuaders: Utah's First Women Legislators," in *Battle For the Ballot,* ed. Madsen, 291–307; Holly J. McCammon and Karen E. Campbell, "Winning the Vote in the West: The Political Successes of the Women's Suffrage Movement 1866–1919," *Gender and Society* 15 (2001): 60.

85. Madsen, *Advocate for Women,* 354. For brief biographies of other women involved in Relief Society and suffrage activism, see *First Fifty Years,* 626–93.

Index

Page numbers in *italics* refer to illustrations. Pages numbers beginning with 399 refer to endnotes.